Communications and Networking for the PC,
Fifth Edition

Larry Jordan
Bruce Churchill

NRP
NEW RIDERS
PUBLISHING

New Riders Publishing,
Indianapolis, Indiana

Communications and Networking for the PC

By Larry Jordan and Bruce Churchill

Published by:
New Riders Publishing
201 West 103rd Street
Indianapolis, IN 46290 USA

Printed in the United States of America 1 2 3 4 5 6 7 8 9 0

        CIP data available upon request

Warning and Disclaimer

This book is designed to provide information about the NetWare computer program. Every effort has been made to make this book as complete and as accurate as possible, but no warranty or fitness is implied.

The information is provided on an "as is" basis. The author and New Riders Publishing shall have neither liability nor responsibility to any person or entity with respect to any loss or damages arising from the information contained in this book or from the use of the disks or programs that may accompany it.

Publisher	Lloyd J. Short
Associate Publisher	Tim Huddleston
Product Development Manager	Rob Tidrow
Marketing Manager	Ray Robinson
Director of Special Projects	Cheri Robinson
Managing Editor	Matthew Morrill

About the Authors

Larry Jordan has a BS degree in Nuclear Engineering from North Carolina State University, and an MBA from The George Washington University. He has worked in engineering and computer science for 24 years, and has been involved with microcomputer systems since the purchase of his first PC in 1982. Jordan's areas of greatest interest include communications, networking, and PC systems integration. He has written many articles on these subjects for national magazines and users groups. He coauthored the first communications and networking book specifically written for the PC. Jordan has also developed system integration architectures, and managed development projects for point of sale, law firm automation, and public utility information management systems. He works for Integrated Systems Services Corportation (ISSC), a wholly owned IBM subsidiary, in the integration and marketing of micro-, mini-, and mainframe computer systems for electric power and gas utility companies.

Bruce Churchill has been a practitioner of the data communications art for 24 years, and has specialized in local area networks since 1982. He has taught data communications and LAN planning skills to MBA students at the postgraduate level and has implemented one of the Navy's first LANs in a shipboard environment. Since retiring from the Navy, Churchill has been active in designing local area, wide area, and wireless communications systems in the fields of transportation and law enforcement. Mr. Churchill is currently Director of Communications and Information Systems for RMSL Traffic Systems, Inc. in San Diego, CA.

Trademark Acknowledgments

All terms mentioned in this book that are known to be trademarks or service marks have been appropriately capitalized. New Riders Publishing cannot attest to the accuracy of this information. Use of a term in this book should not be regarded as affecting the validity of any trademark or service mark.

Acknowledgments

This book, like most other books, owes its existence to the efforts of many people. Our special thanks go to the staff at New Riders Publishing for their coordination and assistance during the production of this book.

Product Director
DREW HEYWOOD
Lead Editor
SUZANNE SNYDER
Editors
GENEIL BREEZE
LAURA FREY
SARAH KEARNS
ROB LAWSON
JOHN SLEEVA
Senior Acquisitions Editor
JAMES LEVALLEY
Acquisitions Coordinator
STACEY BEHELER
Editorial Assistant
KAREN OPAL
Publisher's Assistant
MELISSA LYNCH
Cover Designer
JEAN BISESI
Book Designer
ROGER S. MORGAN
Production Imprint Manager
JULI COOK
Production Imprint Team Leader
KATY BODENMILLER
Graphics Image Specialists
THERESA FORRESTER
CLINT LAHNEN
TIM MONTGOMERY
DENNIS SHEEHAN
SUSAN VANDEWALLE
Production Analysts
DENNIS CLAY HAGER
MARY BETH WAKEFIELD
Production Team
MONA BROWN
CHERYL CAMERON
TERI EDWARDS
KIM HANNEL
ANGELA P. JUDY
DEBORAH KINCAID
AYANNA LACEY
SHELLY PALMA
CASEY PRICE
CHAD POORE
RYAN RADER
MARC SHECTER
SCOTT TULLIS
DENNIS WESNER
Indexers
CHARLOTTE CLAPP
MICHAEL HUGHES

Contents at a Glance

Table of Contents

Introduction

Personal computer users have a need to connect their intelligent workstations to other computers for at least one of three reasons. First, the user may have a need to share peripherals such as printers with a user at another personal computer. Second, the user may have a need to access data or execute application software that resides on another computer. Third, the user may need special processing capabilities that are only available on another computer.

For those of you who have tried to connect your PC to another computer, you know how many pitfalls there are in such an endeavor. Using a personal computer in a stand-alone mode has one dimension—you interact with one computer despite the number of tasks or applications you run simultaneously in that computer. Sharing software applications or data with other computers through communications or networking connectivity has more than one dimension and therefore presents more complexity.

The task of connecting your PC to other computers often requires a thorough knowledge of connectivity hardware and software. When all your computer hardware and software are made by one vendor, this task may not be too complex. The vendor or a system integrator may even provide a "shrink-wrapped" solution to your connectivity needs. When you have computer equipment and software from a variety of vendors, connectivity becomes a more complex issue.

Who Should Read This Book

This book is for anyone involved in connecting an IBM Personal Computer or compatible to another computer. This book is designed to give you both the fundamental knowledge and the connectivity ideas that will help you succeed with your connectivity the first time you try.

This book provides more than theoretical information. It provides practical knowledge that will enable you to get a connectivity job done quickly and easily so you can get on with the applications and data-sharing work you need to do.

If this book were simple tabulations of technical facts, it would not serve you well in successfully completing a connectivity project. We provide both technical facts and information derived from personal experience that glues the facts together. We provide explanations of connectivity alternatives—how the alternatives operate and why you chose each.

We provide explanations the layman can understand. We provide enough details to enable you to design and install a system that works today and provides you with the foundation for future growth. Many figures and tables complement the text to make the task of PC and PS/2 connectivity as painless as possible.

How To Use This Book

This book is both a reading book and a reference book. You can approach the material in at least two ways. You may start at the beginning of Part I, Chapter 1, and read the book from cover to cover. You also may use the table of contents and the comprehensive index to skip around and read only those portions you need to complete a specific task. A connectivity novice probably will use the former technique, and the experienced person probably will use the latter.

To support the reader who wants to skip through the material and read only specific parts, we have repeated some information. Most people are interested in a specific connectivity configuration and will not find this repeated material inconvenient. If you have the need to use several connectivity techniques and must read several sections to get the information you need, you may want to skip the introductory material in some chapters. We minimized repetition where possible by referring you to other parts of the book for more details on certain subjects. We think you will like our tradeoff between repetition and forward/backward referrals.

How This Book Is Organized

This book is divided into three parts. Part I provides an introduction to connectivity fundamentals from the types and characteristics of communication channels to the media and topologies available from vendors. Part I also provides complete discussions of the layers of functionality that allow you to segregate and implement connectivity. This part takes you from internal PC data movement to high-speed data exchange with the outside world.

Part II of this book explores data communications. It starts with a complete exploration of the error correction that makes data communications reliable. Part II then reviews the controls and protocols that allow personal computers to communicate through telephone networks. Finally, this part provides the hardware and software information you will need to effectively and efficiently communicate between the IBM PC or compatible and one or more other computers.

Part III of this book explores the local area network (LAN) connectivity alternative. This networking section shows you how standards organizations have defined local area networks. Part III also explores the design and implementation aspects of LANs. Since 1983, someone has predicted every year that "this will be the year of the LAN." Industry surveys showed that in 1991 the number of LAN-connected PCs exceeded the number of stand-alone PCs for the first time. Part III of this book shows you how to get the most from this connectivity alternative.

Other Resources

One book cannot provide all the information you will need for computer connectivity. We have provided as much material in this book as practical, but there are limitations. We use the IBM PC and PS/2 as our focal point, and provide connectivity information from that vantage point. We provide enough information regarding other computers to get you started with the integration of these computers with the PC. We do not repeat technical information you will find in the installation and operation manuals that vendors provide with these computers.

Conventions Used in This Book

As you read through this book, you find that special formatting has been used throughout the text to help you get the most out of this book. To simplify the book's discussions when these special notes or special formatting are used, several conventions have been established.

Where appropriate, special typefaces are used as well. *Italics* are used to define terms introduced for the first time in a chapter, as well as to emphasize words.

Special Text Used in This Book

Communications and Networking for the PC features some special "sidebars," which are set apart from the normal text by icons.

Note. A note includes extra information that you should find useful, and complements the discussion at hand, instead of being a direct part of it. A note may describe special situations that can arise under certain circumstances.

New Riders Publishing

The staff of New Riders Publishing is committed to bringing you the very best in computer reference material. Each New Riders book is the result of months of work by authors and staff who research and refine the information contained within its covers.

As part of this commitment to you, the NRP reader, New Riders invites your input. Please let us know if you enjoy this book, if you have trouble with the information and examples presented, or if you have a suggestion for the next edition.

Please note, though: New Riders staff cannot serve as a technical resource for questions about software- or hardware-related problems. Please refer to the documentation that accompanies your hardware and software, or to the applications' Help systems.

If you have a question or comment about any New Riders book, there are several ways to contact New Riders Publishing. We will respond to as many readers as we can. Your name, address, or phone number will never become part of a mailing list or be used for any purpose other than to help us continue to bring you the best books possible. You can write us at the following address:

New Riders Publishing
Attn: Associate Publisher
201 W. 103rd Street
Indianapolis, IN 46290

If you prefer, you can fax New Riders Publishing at (317) 581-4670.

You can send electronic mail to New Riders from a variety of sources. NRP maintains several mailboxes organized by topic area. Mail in these mailboxes will be forwarded to the staff member who is best able to address your concerns. Substitute the appropriate mailbox name from the list below when addressing your e-mail. The mailboxes are as follows:

ADMIN	Comments and complaints for NRP's Publisher
APPS	Word, Excel, WordPerfect, other office applications
ACQ	Book proposals and inquiries by potential authors
CAD	AutoCAD, 3D Studio, AutoSketch and CAD products
DATABASE	Access, dBASE, Paradox and other database products
GRAPHICS	CorelDRAW!, Photoshop, and other graphics products
INTERNET	Internet
NETWORK	NetWare, LANtastic, and other network-related topics
OS	MS-DOS, OS/2, all OS except Unix and Windows
UNIX	Unix
WINDOWS	Microsoft Windows (all versions)
OTHER	Anything that doesn't fit the above categories

If you use an MHS e-mail system that routes through CompuServe, send your messages to:

mailbox @ NEWRIDER

To send NRP mail from CompuServe, use the following to address:

MHS: *mailbox* @ NEWRIDER

To send mail from the Internet, use the following address format:

mailbox@newrider.mhs.compuserve.com

NRP is an imprint of Macmillan Computer Publishing. To obtain a catalog or information, or to purchase any Macmillan Computer Publishing book, call (800) 428-5331.

Thank you for selecting *Communications and Networking for the PC, 5th Edition*!

Part I

Personal Computer Connectivity

Chapter Snapshot

Connectivity allows the PC user to reach out to other computers of all sizes and get information or share resources and data with others. Communications and networking provide the PC with this connectivity. The specific types of connectivity you need to access capabilities beyond your PC will depend on many complex elements. In this chapter, you learn the following:

✔ An overview of connectivity

✔ The different approaches to connectivity

✔ An overview of connectivity alternatives

✔ The future directions of connectivity

Connectivity provides the user the opportunity to quickly, and sometimes inexpensively, expand the computing power and resources of a PC by allowing the user to take advantage of capabilities beyond the confines of the local PC system unit. Use this chapter to get an overview of the flexibility and alternatives of PC connectivity.

CHAPTER

1

Introduction to Connectivity

T he process of designing a system that properly enables users to share entities between two or more intelligent processors starts with a discovery of the needs for sharing between computers. This process continues through several well-defined steps and, if successful, ultimately produces a system architecture of computers and peripherals that best meets these needs. This architecture defines the connectivity requirements necessary for the access and sharing of peripherals and remote processors.

This chapter and the ones that follow explore connectivity alternatives and how they fit into the overall architecture from the perspective of the PC.

Like a successful business partnership between people, successful connectivity requires compatibility and communications between computers at several levels. Also like a successful partnership, connectivity usually results in some compromises—all the users' needs are not equally met. The key to success is discovering the requirements that must be met and designing a system that meets these requirements, while providing as many "nice to have" features as possible within the project cost and time constraints.

Because of the complexity of systems today, organizations often use in-house *Management Information Services* (MISs) or outside firms that specialize in designing and implementing connectivity features to meet specific user needs. These organizations and the personnel that perform these services are called *systems integrators*. One of the skills an effective systems integrator provides is the study of user needs to differentiate "must have" from "nice to have" connectivity features and functions.

Because you bought this book, you likely provide connectivity or systems integration skills, or manage people who do so. This book provides both the overview and the details of connectivity so that you can determine user requirements. It also supplies the information you need in order to deliver the type of connectivity that best meets these requirements.

Understanding Connectivity From The Bottom Up

This book uses the term *connectivity* to mean the design and assembly of a system of computers that meets a specific set of user communication or networking needs. These needs usually include the sharing of data or resources between computers. In a client/server environment, these needs normally include distributed application functions and can include distributed data.

Connectivity between a personal computer and any other computer is implemented on two levels. First, you must select the appropriate *physical connections* that allow the computers to exchange compatible electrical signals. Second, you must select the appropriate combination of signaling schemes and protocols, called *logical connections*, that causes the electrical signals generated by one computer to result in the desired response at a second computer. Third, you must select connectivity software that supports the physical and logical connectivity features you need, as well as the application function you wish to execute.

Figure 1.1 shows how the physical and logical levels relate to each other and to connectivity software. This figure also illustrates the relationship between connectivity and the applications users employ. Often, the selection of physical and logical connections and the connectivity software that supports these elements is dictated by user application needs.

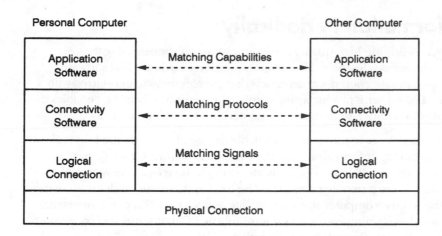

Figure 1.1
Connectivity
levels.

Different Approaches to Connectivity

Two schools of thought relate to connectivity. First, there is a school that believes you should design a system for every anticipatable form of communication or sharing between two or more computers. Second, there is a school that believes you should design a system to handle only the workload you expect for the first year and worry about the future when you get there. The first school assumes you will have the best connectivity between devices if you try to anticipate all needs up front. The second school assumes you will discover your real needs as you begin to use a system, thus allowing you to design the right system the second time around. Both techniques have merit.

It is almost impossible for you to anticipate all user needs during initial system design. Because of this limitation, many people begin the implementation of a new system with a *pilot*. A pilot can address many needs in a scaled-down version of the total system. By developing and operating this pilot, you can refine the requirements for a final production system. The pilot also allows you to fail and recover on a small scale. Such a recovery often results in a much better system than you could produce without this "real world" test of the design.

Regardless of the magnitude of a pilot, the single most important design consideration is the frequency of information or data movement between computers in a system. The actual use of the connectivity determines many final design alternatives. The spectrum of use extends from periodic to continuous data movement. The spectrum also extends from no sharing of devices to large-scale sharing of peripherals. The following sections explore these requirements in detail, and subsequent chapters also expand on these ideas.

Get Information Periodically

Many vendors provide high-quality communications hardware and software products with various features. Most communications hardware and software vendors also provide good documentation that enables users to get started with little pain. The software products also supply valuable online help that enables the communications novice to navigate this mysterious technology with ease.

The least expensive communications available for the PC provide the best tools for periodically moving information between computers. Figure 1.2 shows how a modem attached to a PC can communicate through the telephone system to a modem attached to a remote computer. The local and remote modems allow the PC and the remote computer to communicate as if they are directly connected. You can purchase communications software for the PC that sends and receives information through that modem connection.

Figure 1.2
Connectivity through the public telephone system.

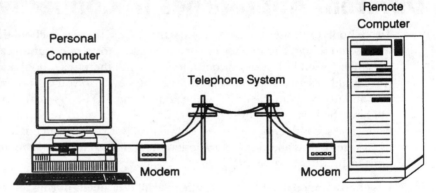

The most inexpensive combination of modem and software costs you less than $100. This combination lets you communicate, but does not offer fancy features and high speed. For a top-of-the-line combination that takes all the difficulty out of communication and provides the highest rate of data transfer, you will pay more than $100. The more expensive combination automates many functions and also provides special error-correction techniques that provide the highest possible quality of data transfer. The greater your need for error-free communications, the more attention you must pay to these error-correcting features.

The modem and communications software combination provides the least expensive alternative for periodic movement of data for two reasons. First, this combination works with most voice-grade telephone lines, enabling a PC and an attached modem to dial and communicate with a remote computer through the public telephone system. Second, you do not have to install a dedicated telephone line in

order to make periodic calls with the computer. You can make voice calls through the same line when you are not using it for communications between computers. For frequent computer communications, however, an alternative is required that does not inhibit voice communications.

Get Information Frequently

Users who need to move data and information between two or more computers frequently find it inconvenient to share the same telephone line between a telephone and a computer. Private telephone exchanges exist that let you communicate voice, computer data, and video concurrently through the same physical connection. Some businesses use these systems to communicate throughout a building or campus. The computer transmits signals through the same physical wire that the telephone uses. The communication system can keep the signals separated so you are not aware of the combined traffic traversing the lines. The communication system administrator is the only person who needs to be concerned with the hardware and software that perform this separation. The user simply operates a communications software package in the PC to connect and communicate with one or more remote computers.

If concurrent voice and data communications are not available through the same telephone exchange, other alternatives exist that let you communicate frequently between the PC and another computer. You can set up a dedicated telephone and modem that communicate continuously with the remote computer. With this arrangement, you can use a special data-grade telephone line and high-speed modem to move information and data quickly while retaining a large degree of reliability. You can connect the PC directly to another computer. The direct-connection techniques explored in later chapters are the RS-232C cable, coaxial cable, and *local area networks* (LANs). Figure 1.3 shows two direct-connection alternatives.

A direct connection between computers eliminates the need to dial the remote computer and also provides much higher data communication rates than those available with dial-up telephone communications. Direct connections can synchronize computers to ensure good reliability even at the high data rates mandatory for full-motion video and other image-intensive applications.

Communicate with Others

Many early users of the PC considered e-mail to be trivial. They saw no value in sending someone an electronic note when they could just as easily call on the telephone or walk by the person's office. PC users in large organizations have found greater use for e-mail, however, as PCs proliferate throughout business organizations.

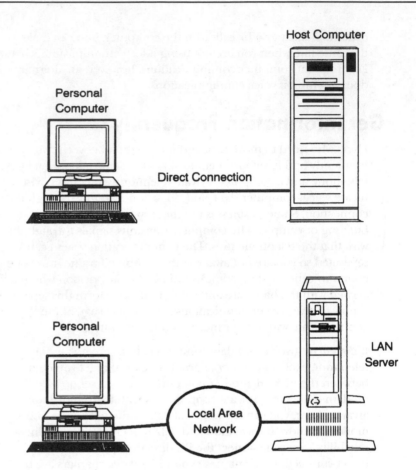

Figure 1.3
Direct
connectivity
alternatives.

E-mail has graduated from the simple exchange of notes to a complete set of applications that facilitates smooth office operations. Some software packages, such as Higgins and cc:MAIL, provide individual- and group-calendaring functions. These packages also provide services that help you manage the distribution of documents throughout an organization. This type of application is sometimes called *groupware.*

To be effective, groupware products require frequent communications between parties. When a person wants to arrange a meeting with a coworker or look at that person's calendar, the information has to be available. If the information is only available periodically or when the other person's PC is turned on, people will stop using a communications or information system.

Groupware applications often reside primarily in a local area network or on a host computer. The local area network, as discussed in detail in Part III, "Local Area Networking," provides information or data on one or more computers designated as servers. All PCs connected directly to the network can access shared data. A host, on the other hand, provides information or data on a single computer. All PCs connected directly to the host can access the shared data on that processor. Although most local area networks and host computers allow dial-up communications through the telephone system, many of them restrict communications to devices attached directly through more permanent connections.

Determining Connectivity Alternatives

Connectivity alternatives span the range from the stand-alone PC to the networked PC. You must determine the needs for data movement between applications used by all computers in a system before designing the system. The data- and application-sharing needs of a system determine both the hardware and software required.

Sharing needs fall into three main categories. First, a user might work in a stand-alone mode most of the time and only require periodic retrieval or delivery of data to another system. Second, a user might need to share the computing capabilities and the devices attached to a central *host computer* on a frequent basis, and thus share the logic of a host with other users. Third, a user might need to share the data, applications, and devices contained in or attached to a combination of other computers. This user, therefore, shares with others the resources of a *local area network* (LAN), a *wide area network* (WAN), or a combination of the two. The following paragraphs explore these connectivity alternatives.

Stand-Alone

Stand-alone operation, by its name, implies no support from other sources. As shown in figure 1.4, the applications and data reside inside the personal computer system unit or in devices directly attached to that unit. No other computer can access or share the applications and data without intervention from the operator. Such a PC may be equipped with communications or connectivity hardware and software that are used only occasionally.

Stand-alone operation of a personal computer does not preclude the sharing of data between this computer and another. It does, however, introduce a time delay in sharing. It also reduces the volume of information the personal computer can share with another system over a given period. These obstacles may be acceptable because of other considerations, such as connectivity cost or security required for the PC applications and data.

Figure 1.4
A stand-alone personal computer.

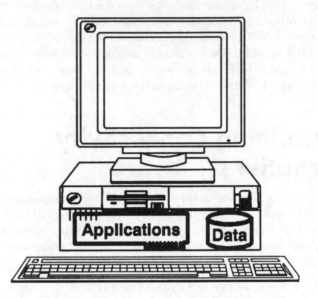

The operator of a stand-alone PC can move data to another system in one of four ways. First, the operator can copy data from one computer onto a physical medium such as a disk and load the data into the other computer from it. This is sometimes referred to as a "sneaker net" because of the walking required between computers. Second, the operator can start communications software in the PC and dial another computer through the telephone system to share data. Third, the operator can make a physical connection to another computer or system and start the software required to share data with the other computer or system. Finally, the operator can start connectivity software in a PC that is already physically connected to another computer. In this final case, the PC is physically connected to another computer all the time but logically isolated until software is activated to move data through the physical connection.

When stand-alone operation of a PC does not meet the connectivity requirements of its operator, you must consider permanently attaching the PC to another computer. First, you can set up the PC to share the logic of one or more hosts with several other users. Second, you can set up the PC to share resources with other personal computers. Additionally, you can set up the PC to do a combination of the two. Finally, you can establish a client/server environment that splits application functions between client processors (user devices) and server processors.

Shared Logic

Although the term *shared logic* traditionally means sharing the capabilities of a single processor with more than one user, this book expands the definition because of the evolution of computers. Before the arrival of the PC as a host terminal, users worked at simple, *dumb terminals* that were directly attached to the host through one of several types of cable. As shown in figure 1.5, the host contained all the intelligence. These *fixed-function* terminals provided display of host output and provided a keyboard for user interaction with the host. The host gave each terminal a slice of time to execute user commands. A single processor thus served several users by dividing its time among the users. The evolution of host computers and intelligent PC terminals has changed that concept.

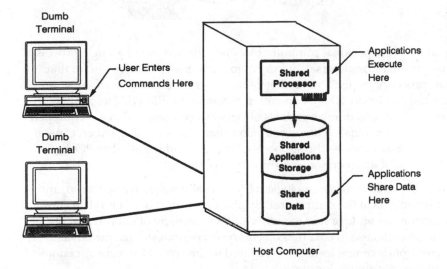

Figure 1.5
Shared logic connectivity.

Many large host computers today contain more than one processor. The largest IBM host computers contain several main and support processors. The main processors execute applications software and the environment these applications require in order to access and manipulate data. The support processors, such as the communications controller shown in figure 1.6, perform such functions as network management and peripheral control.

Support processors execute operations that off-load work from the main processors, thus enabling the main processors to perform operations specifically requested by users. The users, therefore, share the services of one or more main processors and several support processors.

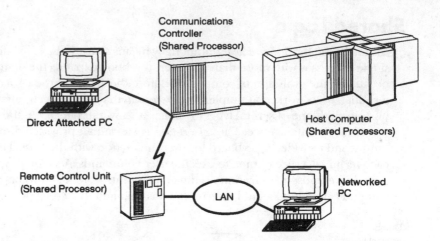

Figure 1.6
Shared
processors in a
connectivity
environment.

Communications Controller (Shared Processor)

Direct Attached PC

Host Computer (Shared Processors)

Remote Control Unit (Shared Processor)

LAN

Networked PC

On a smaller scale, a personal computer can share the services of a single processor with other personal computers. You can equip a powerful PC with software that enables its processor to perform local or remote user functions. For example, you can install the AIX or the XENIX operating system in an IBM PS/2 and support the operation of several dumb terminals or personal computers that are equipped to emulate dumb terminals. Thus, a computer that supports a single user, can—under some circumstances—also support other users working at other PCs by sharing the logic of its processor with the other computers.

The principal benefit from shared logic is the central storage, manipulation, and management of data at the central host. By placing the data in a central location, an organization can set up a staff to ensure proper handling of data. This staff can often perform such tasks as data backup and recovery from storage media failures at lower cost from a central location, compared to the cost of the same functions performed over distributed locations.

Shared logic does not always meet the needs of users who must share data and applications. Because of the application limitations of some host processors or because of the high entry-level costs, some organizations may prefer to share resources between personal computers. The following sections compare the shared resource system to the shared logic system.

Shared Resources

The term *shared resources* implies multiuser sharing of devices and data, as shown in figure 1.7. LANs today provide that feature and more. Early LAN implementations simply enabled more than one PC to access the same devices and data. These LANs did not ensure equitable sharing of devices. They also provided little protection to ensure the integrity of data.

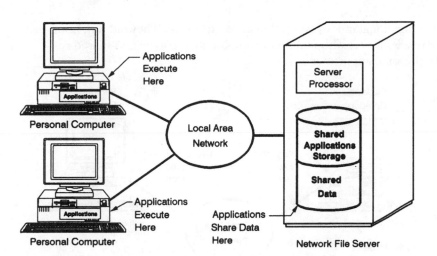

Figure 1.7
Shared resource connectivity.

LAN operating systems are now available from IBM, Microsoft, Novell, and other vendors, and provide good services at both the user and server end of the link. The communications industry coined the terms *client* and *server* to denote user and server nodes on a network. Vendors continue to work diligently to optimize the performance and functions for the client and the server.

IBM worked with Microsoft during the late 1980s to design and develop the LAN Server. The Microsoft version of this *network operating system* (NOS) was called the LAN Manager. IBM and Microsoft Corporation worked together to ensure the LAN Server and the LAN Manager provided the same *application programming interface* (API). With the introduction of Microsoft's Windows NT, this commonality ended. As discussed in Part III, "Local Area Networking," IBM, Microsoft, Novell, and other vendors are now competing head-to-head for this lucrative business and to create the de facto standards for NOS APIs.

Shared Logic and Resources

Connectivity in the 1990s is merging the features and functions of data communications and networking. Users in most organizations are finding the separation of shared logic and shared resources both inconvenient and unproductive. These users are demanding a complete integration of these two connectivity alternatives.

Many vendors began providing LAN solutions in the 1980s that enabled shared logic and shared resources to coexist on the same LAN wiring system. Figure 1.8 shows how many of these solutions worked. As you can see from this figure, a PC could execute application software that shared resources at a LAN *network file server*. A PC could also act as a terminal to access applications and data stored on a host.

These two operational modes satisfied many users' needs. They did not, however, satisfy the needs of users who wanted to combine shared logic and shared resources in the same applications.

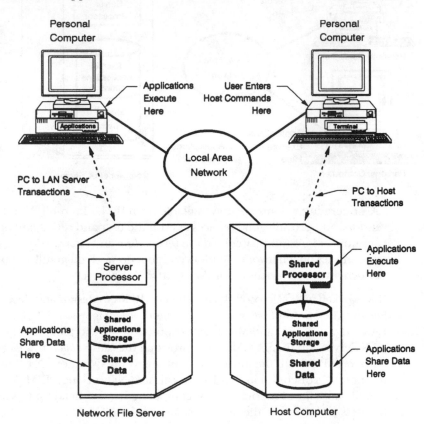

Figure 1.8
Combined shared logic and shared resource connectivity.

If you have ever tried to combine data communications and networking in a single workstation, as shown in figure 1.9, you know how frustrating that effort can be. If you are lucky, you find that they perform their intended functions when combined. If you are unlucky, you discover that the operation of one environment precludes the operation of the other. The answer to this problem is to start with a combination designed from the top down for *concurrent* operation in the same PC.

The greatest limitation in the integration of shared logic and resources is the DOS operating system. Microsoft designed the original *Disk Operating System* (DOS) as a single-tasking, single-user operating system. They also designed DOS with a memory limitation of 640 kilobytes (KB). These limitations carry over to become limitations in the integration of terminal communications and networking for the PC.

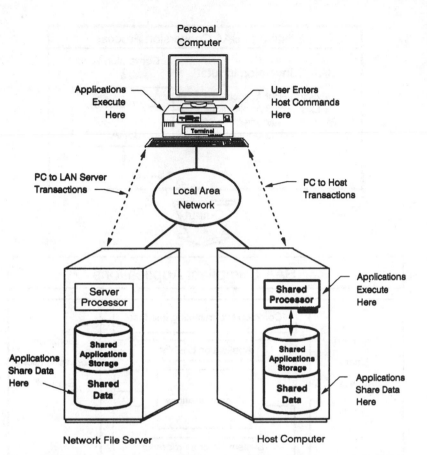

Figure 1.9
Concurrent shared logic and shared resource connectivity.

If you combine terminal communications and networking under DOS and find that they work together, you might find you have no memory left to perform other functions. You can communicate with a host and share network resources simultaneously, but you have so little free memory in the PC that you cannot execute applications to take advantage of these resources. Vendors are now solving this problem by integrating PC and network operating systems in order to combine shared logic and shared resource support.

Client/Server Computing

The ultimate integration of shared logic and shared resources is the application and data model called *client/server computing*. In the late 1980s, vendors began to introduce the operating system and hardware required to make this concept a reality in both a LAN environment and in a wider enterprise environment. Figure 1.10 illustrates the client/server model.

Figure 1.10
Client/server
physical and
logical views.

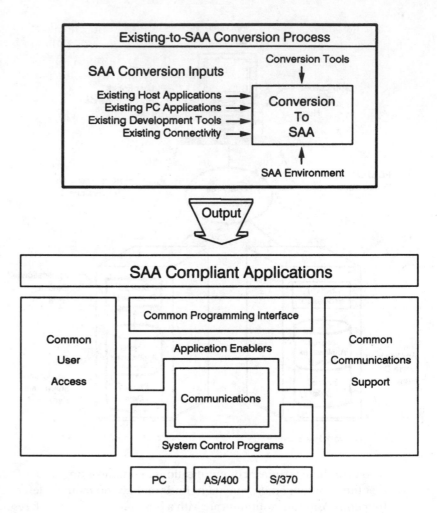

Recent advances in the application environment at the PC level have provided the greatest push for the evolution of the client/server model. The *graphical user interface* (GUI) of IBM's OS/2 and Microsoft's Windows operating systems provides application developers the tools necessary to build applications that take full advantage of the PC hardware to off-load application function from the traditional host processors. These operating systems combine the ease of use of the GUI with multitasking to provide an application environment that is the most productive in the history of computing.

As you can see in figure 1.10, the client/server model is basically an implementation of distributed or cooperative processing. At the heart of the model is the concept of splitting application functions between a client and a server processor.

The division of labor between the different processors enables the application designer to place an application function on the processor that is most appropriate for that function. This lets the software designer optimize the use of processors—providing the greatest possible return on investment for the hardware.

Client/server application design also lets the application provider mask the actual location of application function. The user often does not know where a specific operation is executing. The entire function may execute in either the PC or server, or the function may be split between them. This masking of application function locations enables system implementors to upgrade portions of a system over time with a minimum disruption of application operations, while protecting the investment in existing hardware and software.

Exploring Future Connectivity

Connectivity between computers in the past has produced a powerful synergy between the personal computer and other remote computers. Connectivity in the future will continue to evolve this power. Businesses will find connectivity—both internally and with external services—an absolute necessity to meet the demands of the user and to compete with other companies. Home owners will find connectivity opens whole new worlds of entertainment to them in addition to the educational and home management power it will provide.

The on-line services of today are an indication of the trend in future connectivity. In the early 1980s, services such as The SOURCE and CompuServe offered comprehensive messaging and conferencing facilities. The new breed of on-line systems provide these services and more. For example, Prodigy and CompuServe both offer full graphical user interfaces and a wide variety of information databases. Frequent travelers can log on with Prodigy, make flight reservations, and check the weather at their destination—all from the same set of graphical menus. America Online offers similar services and sports an easy-to-use graphical interface. Dow Jones News/Retrieval provides comprehensive, up-to-date business news, stock quotes, and trading trends.

Although current on-line services provide much needed information, they do not provide the open access and connectivity flexibility users will demand in the future. Existing services have proprietary protocols and user interfaces. Their databases are also private—you can get to data only through the access provided by the on-line service company. As personal computers continue to proliferate, the demand for standardized access and open access to information will continue to grow.

Internet is an open-access system that will be the model of future systems. Many users of the Net, as it is called, are "wired" and participate in "information surfing" through "cyberspace." This vast network was originally set up for government organizations, universities, and research institutions to facilitate the sharing of data among users. After two decades of growth, Internet now connects thousands of computers and provides communications services for over 10 million people.

Everything Will Contain a Computer

The next evolution of the client/server concept will place client computers in virtually every home in America. The impetus for this movement will be *interactive television.* For example, Microsoft and Tele-Communications, Inc. (TCI) are combining resources and skills to make this service a reality by placing a computer in a box on top of your TV set. Other cable TV and communications companies are combining resources to go after this same lucrative, future market. This movement will result in millions of powerful and easy-to-use client processors connected to hundreds of remote servers, the combination of which will provide hundreds of video channels, as well as the ability for users to interactively communicate with service providers.

A concept called the *smart house* will result in the implementation of PC-type processors throughout houses in the future and will drive connectivity alternatives. Electric utility companies and private industries are creating the capability to monitor and control these processor-driven electrical devices from remote locations. This capability will allow both the home owner and the energy provider to control and optimize the consumption of energy on a device-by-device basis. The remote controller will be able to "see" specific devices "through the wires" connected to the house and will be able to turn these devices on and off at different times during the day or night.

The need for full-motion video and videoconferencing will also create demand for connectivity between personal computers and service providers in the future. The movement creating this demand is the trend by American businesses to save money by reducing air travel. As Intel, IBM, Motorola, and other vendors continue to produce more powerful PC processors, the implementation of both full-motion video and videoconferencing becomes more viable.

Full-motion video and videoconferencing will not become widely used until the connectivity infrastructure is in place to support these communication techniques. The implementation of these technologies requires exceptionally high-speed communications between the PCs at each end of the conference connection. The link must be able to transport images at 15 to 30 frames a second to make videoconferencing acceptable to users. The principal bottleneck preventing the widespread use of full motion video and videoconferencing today is the lack of a de facto standard WAN system that can transport and manage the delivery of video frames at this speed. This limitation is likely to change over the next five years.

The Information Superhighway

Vice President Al Gore introduced legislation in December 1993 that is intended to facilitate the development and implementation of a national information superhighway. The primary goal of the legislation is to help fund the basic research and development of a connectivity system that will do for computers what the interstate highway system has done for vehicles. The difficulty of producing such a system, however, is the lack of a single, acceptable national standard for connectivity that supports all the types of connections and information traffic companies that institutions want today as well as the types required in the future. The Internet is a start, but it does not provide all the services users will demand later.

Designing and implementing a national interstate highway system for vehicles was easy compared to the task of doing the same for computer connectivity and data. Because of the physical limitations of vehicle design and speeds and the limitations of the human beings that have to steer and control these vehicles, the designers and builders of the highway system had a clear and concise set of functional requirements with which to work. They had to provide a system with controlled access that enabled vehicles to travel at speeds between 40 and 65 miles per hour (or whatever the local conditions called for). The design had to facilitate easy access and maximize the speed at which vehicles could safely travel. The system also had to be easy enough that anyone with a driver's license and a minimum of training could take advantage of it.

Although the interstate highway system has provided a much needed service over the years and continues to do so, it has several limitations that force travelers to sometimes select alternative systems to help them get from one place to another. Even though cars, trucks, and buses are safer to drive today than they were 50 years ago when the interstate highway idea first emerged, the maximum speed they are allowed to attain while traversing the system has not changed. Instead, other alternatives that allow higher speeds (i.e., high-speed trains and airplanes) now carry a higher proportion of travelers than they did 50 years ago. The interstate highway system also has fixed physical facilities that do not easily conform to the population's changing traveling patterns. Similar evolutionary considerations and limitations will likely demand future attention in the *National Information Infrastructure* (NII) the Clinton administration is proposing.

Over the past few years, several alternative information highways have emerged. Examples of these WANs include proprietary systems such as IBM's SNA and open systems such as X.25. Although these systems will continue to play a role in wide area networking and connectivity for many years, they will probably not become the National Information Infrastructure without additional changes and enhancements. For a WAN to become the de facto NII, it must have a low connection and usage cost while providing reliable support for the high-speed movement of data, voice, and video. The winner must also become the system of choice for a majority of vendors and users. Part II, Chapter 7 ("Data Communications: Wide Area Networks"), explores existing WANs and new alternatives that may evolve to become the electronic highway Al Gore envisions.

Chapter Snapshot

The communications channel is a key technical component in all forms of connectivity. A PC uses these channels for internal communications and for communications and networking with other, external computers. An understanding of the basics of communications channels helps both connectivity novices and experts take optimum advantage of PC connectivity. In this chapter, you learn the following:

✔ Communications channel terminology, types, and characteristics

✔ How electrical signals travel through communications channels

✔ How communications channels support data communications and networking

Without communications channels, PCs and PC connectivity would not exist. Use this chapter to understand the fundamentals of communications channels. This information will help you better understand the connectivity techniques discussed in later chapters.

CHAPTER 2

Communications Channels

Data and resource sharing, by its nature, requires connectivity between at least two computers. Most system integration projects often require the connection of many computers from PCs to large mainframes. To understand fully the best alternatives for connecting these computers into a system that ultimately meets user needs, you must understand some fundamentals of connectivity. This chapter begins by exploring the communications channel. The remaining chapters in Part I build on this information.

You can connect many computers and keep the entire system in the same room or same building. When you limit a system to a small area, you can limit the number of techniques required to connect all the components. Many systems begin this way, and then grow with time. You can start an implementation pilot in a limited geographical area and then expand the implementation after the pilot proves successful.

When a system has to go beyond a room or a single building, life gets more complicated. To move data between two computer systems over great distances, you have to use existing communications systems or install new ones specifically for your use. It is usually more economical to use communications systems already installed for general use. Installing a new system means running cables and wiring through areas already inhabited by humans. Such an undertaking makes sense if no other alternatives are available that meet your needs.

The Communications Channel

You do not have to be an expert in all aspects of hardware and software connectivity to do a good job. You do have to know enough technical details to meet the customers' needs. The information in the following paragraphs helps you decide whether existing communications systems can meet these needs. The information also helps you decide the best alternative if existing systems are not adequate.

A *communications channel* provides everything you need to get electronic information from one location to another. Communications channels come in a variety of forms, but they have one common element. A communications channel moves electromagnetic energy between a source and one or more destination points while retaining the information contained in the energy when it leaves the source. The channel can convert the energy from one form to another. It must, however, deliver the proper electromagnetic energy to a receiver such that the receiver understands the information sent by a transmitter.

The Ideal Channel

The ideal communications channel is a perfect vacuum. In a perfect vacuum no physical objects can reduce the level of energy sent out by a transmitter. In this environment, you could transmit a signal at one point and receive it at another point with no change in the signal. The signal would travel at the speed of light.

If you could construct a channel that contained a perfect vacuum, you could place devices anywhere along a channel without concern for loss of signal strength or errors introduced by outside elements. Unfortunately, no perfect vacuum is available for communications. Even the expanse of outer space contains stars, planets, and solar dust that can alter communications signals. The sun itself can alter electromagnetic communications because of its own electromagnetic emissions. Fortunately, some not-so-perfect materials make good communications channels.

Channel Types

Two basic types of channels are used in voice and data communications. The public telephone system or a commercial radio station best illustrates the first type. This channel type is *analog* and transmits signals such as those illustrated in figure 2.1. The cable that runs between a personal computer and a printer illustrates the second type. This channel type is *digital* and transmits square-wave signals such as those shown in figure 2.2. Both channel types have some common characteristics.

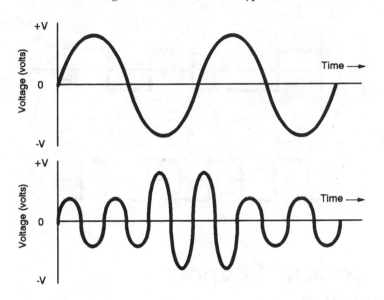

Figure 2.1
Analog electrical signals.

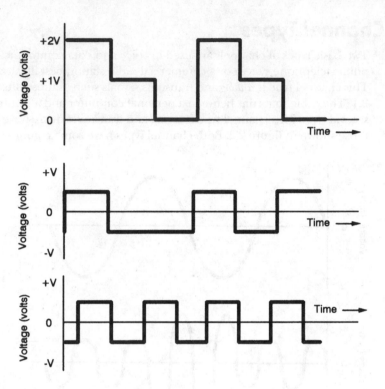

Figure 2.2
Digital electrical signals.

Communications Channel Characteristics

The physical capabilities of the communications media limit both analog and digital communications. Although research and development result in continuous improvements in these physical capabilities, no perfect channel exists. The best you can do is minimize the imperfections that reduce a channel's capability to convey information.

Signal Attenuation

Physical connectivity media alter electromagnetic signals by resisting their flow. Some metals such as copper are more efficient than other materials in conducting electrical energy between two points. Despite the quality of a conductor, it always contains impurities that resist the movement of the tiny sub-atomic electrons that make up the electrical current.

The *resistance* in a channel causes electrical energy to change to heat energy that transfers to the environment. This conversion takes place throughout the length of a wire conductor and results in a decrease in the electrical signal, a process called *attenuation*. At some point along the length of a channel, the strength of the signal decreases to a level not usable by a receiver.

Electronic Noise

Physical connectivity media alter electromagnetic signals by adding *noise* to the signals. The sub-atomic particles and molecules in a signal conductor vibrate. These vibrating elements emit electromagnetic signals that have no meaning. Physicists refer to this random generation of signals as *electronic noise*. When you are trying to achieve optimum connectivity between computers, this noise often results in the use of complex components designed to amplify an information signal to make it larger than the noise.

Because the strength of an electronic signal is large relative to the electronic noise, a communications channel can deliver electronic information to a receiver. As the signal travels through a conductor and decreases in strength, as described earlier, the strength of the signal can approach the strength of the electronic noise. When the signal strength is not significantly higher than the background noise, a receiver cannot separate the information signal from the noise.

Communications channels must keep the strength of a signal high enough for a receiver to understand its content without allowing electronic noise to reduce the quality of the communication. Vendors use three techniques to produce these results. First, a vendor can design and fabricate electronic *filters* that eliminate electronic noise without affecting an electronic signal. Second, a vendor can increase the strength of a signal; or third, a vendor can regenerate the signal as it moves along a communications channel. These *amplifiers* and *repeaters* must match the types of electronic signals the channel conveys or they cause more harm than good. An analog channel requires a different signal conditioner than a digital channel, as you see later in this chapter.

Analog Channel Capacity

Although all physical channels contain some attributes that limit their capability to convey information, they all convey information with characteristics specific to the type and design of the channel media. The limitations inherent in a channel determine the quantity of information the channel can convey over a given period. This attribute, called *channel capacity*, is the *bandwidth* of an analog channel.

Channel Bandwidth

A channel designed to convey analog signals has characteristics that limit how these signals can vary with time. An analog channel conveys a signal that has a voltage amplitude that increases and decreases over time according to a predetermined formula or algorithm. The rate of change of the signal is its *frequency* in *cycles per second* or *hertz* (Hz).

Figure 2.3 shows the elements that enable you to calculate the frequency of an analog electrical signal. The mathematical formula for frequency is as follows:

```
                    Velocity
    Frequency  =  ----------
                   Wavelength
```

In the preceding formula, velocity is the speed (meters per second) the signal is moving through the channel, and wavelength is the distance (meters) it takes for the signal to go through a full cycle.

Figure 2.3
Analog signal characteristics.

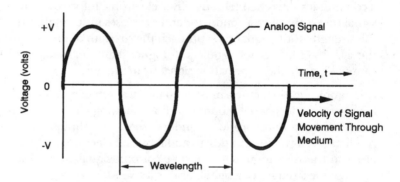

An analog signal can vary from a minimum to a maximum frequency. The physical medium and its electrical characteristics determine the optimal frequency range of the channel. The difference between the lowest and highest frequency of a single analog signal is the *bandwidth* of that signal. The difference between the lowest and highest frequency an analog channel can convey to a distant receiver that the receiver can understand is the bandwidth of the analog channel. The lowest and highest usable frequencies that bound the bandwidth are the half-power points of the channel. These frequency points are at the lowest power levels, measured in decibels (db), that the channel can convey.

An analog channel is a *broadband* channel when it can simultaneously convey multiple analog signals that span a broad band of individual frequencies. Such a channel can concurrently convey several analog signals through frequency separation techniques, discussed later in this chapter.

The range of frequencies a human can produce through voice and sound communications is a good example of bandwidth. Figure 2.4 shows the sound power a human vocal system can produce at various frequencies. As you can see from this figure, the power of human sounds at lower frequencies, or the base pitches, is much higher than the power at higher frequencies. Figure 2.4 also shows that the frequency range is from near zero to over 12,000 Hz, which translates into a bandwidth of over 12,000 Hz.

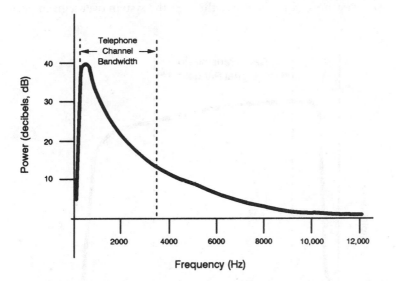

Figure 2.4
Bandwidth of the human voice.

If a communications channel is to convey the entire frequency range of human sounds, it must have a minimum frequency near zero and a bandwidth of over 12,000 Hz. Although modern, high-fidelity stereo equipment can reproduce most of this range, older voice communications systems do not have this bandwidth. Purchasers and users of sound entertainment systems often place great value on a system's capability to mimic the sounds of live events. They are willing to pay the price for a system that provides a high bandwidth. Unfortunately, users have much less control over the quality and communications capabilities of the public telephone system.

Telephone System Bandwidth

Because of technology limitations and cost tradeoffs made during the design of the public telephone system, this system can handle only a small part of the total bandwidth of the human voice. The system provides coverage for the portion of the voice bandwidth that can produce the greatest power. These are the sounds you most likely hear when you are talking directly with a person. Although this range is only from 300 to 3,300 Hz, the range is sufficient for you to convey messages to distant listeners.

Telephone system vendors would choose to transmit more frequencies today if they could start over. The public telephone system provides an adequate bandwidth for voice communications, but is a bottleneck for computer communications. Figure 2.5 shows the frequency range vendors use to convey data communications through the telephone system. If this bandwidth were wider, vendors could convey more computer data through the system over a given period.

Figure 2.5
Telephone signal amplitude versus frequency.

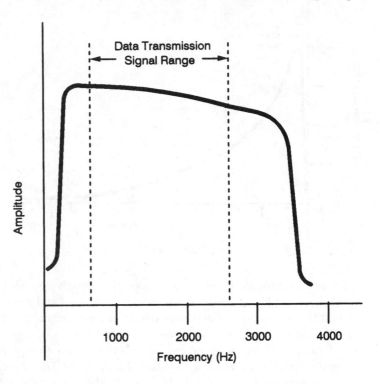

As you learn in later chapters, vendors of communications hardware have created ingenious methods of overcoming the bandwidth limitations of the telephone system. Connectivity often calls for the movement of data from a local area network with a high bandwidth through the public telephone system at a much lower bandwidth, and then on to another communications link with a much higher bandwidth. The matching of capacities of various channels is one of the greatest challenges in connectivity.

Digital Channel Capacity

A communications channel that conveys a digital signal has limitations that determine how often the signal can change states over a period. These limitations establish the maximum rate at which data can flow through the channel. This rate may change as technology improves, but at any given time the channel has a capacity to transmit a specific number of information bits between two devices in a specified period.

A digital system varies a signal between two or more discrete energy states as shown in figure 2.6. These energy states are discrete voltage levels. The voltage makes step changes distinct from the continuous voltage changes associated with the analog signals that flow through an analog channel. Devices transmit these digital signals through a channel without the use of an analog-based *carrier signal*. The digital channel conveys a signal at a discrete energy level at one frequency, or it transmits no signal—a design called *baseband*. The role of carrier signals is discussed later in this chapter.

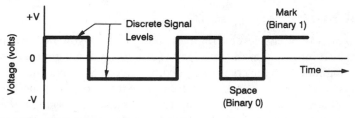

(a) Binary digital system signal.

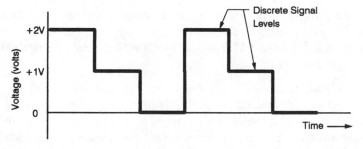

(b) Digital system signal.

Figure 2.6
Digital system electrical signals.

Computer and telephone system vendors use a variety of baseband signaling techniques to convey information or data. They may provide a *binary system* that uses only two energy states, as illustrated in figure 2.6. One state represents a binary zero and the other a binary one, collectively called *binary digits* or *bits*. Vendors use this type of binary signal scheme for the circuits that interconnect PC internal components. As you see in Chapters 3 and 4, binary circuits also provide the connectivity between the PC and external devices and peripherals.

Vendors sometimes design *digital systems* that use more than two energy states. Figure 2.6 illustrates such a system. The energy levels in a digital system are discrete and make step changes from one level to another. The difference between a digital system and a binary system is the number of discrete energy levels the system conveys. A binary system with its limit of two energy levels is a subset of a digital system and is a digital system as well.

Vendors often use the terms *mark* and *space* to designate the two logical binary values that the two line voltages represent in a binary channel. In one binary system, 5 volts (5V) can represent a logical 1, and 0 volts (0V) can represent a logical 0. In another system, +5V can represent a logical 1, and -5V can represent a logical 0. By always using *space* to indicate a binary 0 and *mark* to indicate a binary 1, you can describe a system without reference to the actual energy levels that make the system work.

Channel Bit Rate

Despite the number of energy levels a digital system provides, you measure its capacity to transmit information the same way. The *capacity* of a digital channel is the number of digital values the channel can convey in one second. The measurement is in *bits per second* (bps). Vendors quote this capacity as the *bit rate* of a channel. The channels available for communications and networking today have bit rate ranges from thousands of bps (*kilobits per second* or *Kbps*) to millions of bps (*megabits per second* or *Mbps*).

The duration of a bit signal directly determines bit rate—the shorter the duration of a bit signal, the greater the bps rating of the signal. Figure 2.7 shows the relationship between the duration of a bit signal in milliseconds (*ms*), the *bit time* of the signal, and the bps rating of the signal.

The bps rating of a digital channel is the theoretical rate at which it can convey digital bits. The actual data throughput of the channel, called the *channel data rate*, is usually less than the raw bit rate. The channel must provide *overhead* signals to synchronize communications between devices. This overhead is explored later in this chapter and in greater detail in later chapters.

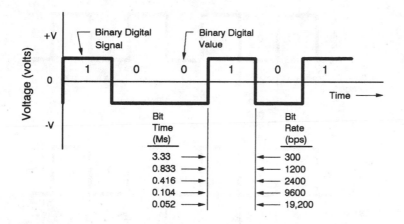

Figure 2.7
Binary digital communications signal characteristics.

Bit Rate versus Baud

Vendors often use the terms *bit rate* and *baud* without distinction, thereby adding some confusion to communications. Baud is a measure of the digital or analog signaling rate in a channel. Bit rate is a measure of the digital bit values the channel conveys with each baud.

Figure 2.8 illustrates the difference between baud and bit rate. As you can see in this figure, a channel can convey one or more bits during a single baud. For example, a modem can modulate a digital bit stream flowing at 2,400 bps by using a 600 baud signal rate. Each baud must convey 4 bits to achieve this 4-to-1 multiplication factor. As you see in Chapter 9, modem vendors use some ingenious techniques to get the most out of every baud they can convey through a telephone system.

Baseband versus Broadband Bit Rates

The distinction between the capacity of a baseband and a broadband system is sometimes confusing because vendors normally use a baseband data rate to describe either type of system. Although the bandwidth of a broadband system determines its capability to convey signals, the bit rate of a system can vary. As technology improves, vendors can squeeze more bits through existing broadband channels, thereby increasing their bit rates without changing their bandwidth.

The bit rate of a baseband channel, on the other hand, is fixed and does not change with technology improvements. The digital baseband signal uses the entire bandwidth of the channel to convey a signal. The only way to increase the digital bit rate is to decrease the bit time of the signal. The electrical characteristics of a channel often limit a vendor's capability to reduce this bit time, thereby fixing the maximum bit rate of the channel.

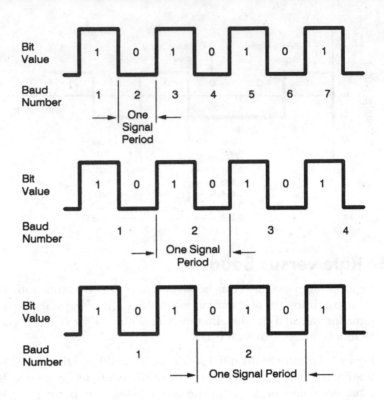

Figure 2.8
The relationship between bps and baud.

Vendors and computer manufacturers overcome the throughput limitation of baseband channels by using several such channels in parallel. These groups of channels are called a bus. As you see in the next chapter, many internal PC circuits use a minimum of eight parallel digital channels. These eight channels can increase the throughput of the system by a factor of eight. Instead of sending one binary value at a time in a serial channel, eight parallel channels can send eight binary values simultaneously. The most recent vintage PC system units contain buses of parallel digital channels that can simultaneously convey up to 32 bits from one internal device to another.

Before getting into the details of communications, you must understand the concept of data flow. Although a single electrical signal propagates in a given direction in a communications channel, two or more signals can flow in different directions simultaneously in a channel. Vendors can squeeze the last drop of capacity from a channel by optimizing the directional flow of signals.

Transmission Modes

Most internal PC data channels support simultaneous bidirectional flow of signals, but communications channels between the PC and the outside world are not always so robust. Figure 2.9 shows the three "plex" alternatives—simplex, half-duplex, and duplex—for communications channel design. These alternatives apply to both analog and digital channels.

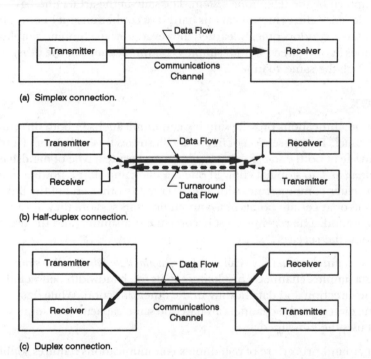

Figure 2.9
Direction of signal flow.

Simplex

The simplest signal flow technique is the *simplex* configuration. The 'a' section of figure 2.9 shows this design. A simplex channel allows data to flow in only one direction and is a *unidirectional channel*. This type of channel design is easy and inexpensive to set up. Vendors choose simplex signal flow when information does not need to flow back from a signal destination. A good example of this is public-broadcast television. The television station sends out electromagnetic signals that include the picture and sound you receive. The station does not expect and does not monitor for a return signal from your television set.

Although simplex has a place in communications, it has limited use in computer communications. Almost all connectivity projects require the flow of information in both directions between computers in a system. To achieve this bidirectional flow over short distances, vendors can use communications channels entirely within their control. This gives them great flexibility in system design.

To set up bidirectional data flow over long distances, vendors must live with the limitations imposed by the telephone system. The state-of-the-art technology limited early designs. The communications hardware could transmit in only one direction at a time. Vendors quickly learned, however, how to combine simplex communications in one direction with simplex communications in the other direction through the same channel.

Half-Duplex

Half-duplex communications provide simplex communications in both directions in a single channel. The 'b' section of figure 2.9 illustrates this technique. Hardware and software at both ends of the channel must execute a type of handshake, called *line turnaround*, to stop data flow in one direction and start it flowing in the other. A transmitter communicates with a receiver at the other end of the link. At certain intervals or at certain points in a communications session, they must turn the data flow around. The receiver must become the transmitter, and the transmitter must become the receiver.

A half-duplex channel, sometimes called a *bidirectional data bus*, has the same bandwidth as a simplex channel. The channel splits the bandwidth between data flowing in one direction and data flowing in the other direction. While data are flowing in one direction, the channel can have the same capacity as a simplex channel that uses the same media.

The line turnaround procedure of half-duplex communications requires sophisticated hardware and creates a time delay each time data flow changes direction. The hardware must detect the need for a turnaround and execute the procedure as quickly as possible. Despite the speed of these turnarounds, a pause in communications always occurs while the operation takes place. The total time consumed by turnaround pauses during a communications session effectively reduces the data throughput of a communications channel. The throughput in one direction plus the throughput in the other direction may be below the level that a vendor could obtain with simplex communications.

When vendors first implemented half-duplex communications through long-distance telephone systems, time delays associated with line turnaround were acceptable. Vendors were happy to get data moving in both directions. The turnaround delays were considered part of the price you paid for flexible communications. As the need for movement of large volumes of data grew,

however, users and vendors demanded a better alternative than half-duplex communications. The need for more efficient communications and improvements in hardware technology allowed vendors to design and implement bidirectional communications that do not require line turnaround.

Full-Duplex

Simultaneous bidirectional communications in a channel are called *duplex* or *full-duplex*. The 'c' section of figure 2.9 illustrates this channel design. As you can see from this figure, full-duplex is a dual-simplex configuration that requires full and independent transmit and receive capabilities at both ends of the communications channel. The transmitters and receivers at both ends of the link can exchange data or information simultaneously through the same physical channel.

By sharing the same channel and moving signals in both directions, a vendor can improve the throughput of a channel without increasing its bandwidth. This technique is particularly important in communications through channels outside the control of the vendor or user. Later in this chapter, the discussion of communications through the telephone system further explores full-duplex communications.

Before moving on to other capacity topics, one area of confusion requires clarification. Users often misunderstand the relationship between the number of wires in a communications channel and the channel's capacity to support duplex data flow. Half-duplex and full-duplex operations are independent of the number of wires in the communications line. You can perform both operations through *two-wire* and *four-wire* telephone systems. Public telephone vendors provide you with two wires between your location and a distant facility. Vendors of leased telephone lines usually provide four wires for data communications with distant equipment. Either communications system supports both half- and full-duplex.

Although some half-duplex systems are still in operation today, most of these systems are migrating to full duplex when it becomes economical to do so. A firm or organization normally keeps a system until it fulfills its original mission. The need that often drives an organization to move on to newer communications techniques is the requirement for greater data throughput.

Echo-plex

Vendors sometimes use the terms half- and full-duplex to describe the interaction between a terminal's keyboard and display when they should use the term *echo-plex*. Before the arrival of full-duplex channels, vendors designed terminals to echo a copy of each character to the local display as it sent the character to the host. This echo process provided the user with an immediate indication of each keystroke.

Without the local echo, the user would have to wait until the line turned around before the host could send a copy of the characters back for display at the terminal. It was more expeditious and less confusing to have the terminal echo characters to the screen.

With the arrival of full-duplex communications, it became possible to have the host echo each character it receives back to the sender through a process called *echo-plex*. When operating a terminal and host session in echo-plex mode through a full-duplex channel, the host can send a copy of each character back to the terminal for display at a rate not confusing to the user. If the character that comes back is the same as the one sent, the user can feel comfortable that the host received the character properly. If the character echoed back is not the same as the one sent, the difference indicates a problem with the communications link.

Signal Modulation

When moving a voice or data signal through a communications channel, the electrical energy in the channel must vary so that the information moves from one point in the medium to another. The process of varying the electrical energy is *modulation*. The high-amplitude, high-frequency, and fixed-frequency level of energy that flows through the channel is the *signal carrier*. An electronic device varies this carrier to reflect the information contained in a weaker voice or data signal.

Moving a signal from one end of a medium to another and retaining its original information value often means imposing one signal on another. Without help, original computer and telephone signals often lack the strength to go far enough to be useful. By *modulating* a *carrier signal* to reflect the information in the original signal, a *modulator* device can generate a combined signal strong enough to make it to its destination and retain its information imprint. For this process to work, another device called a *demodulator* has to separate the signal that arrives at its destination from the carrier that helped get it there. Figure 2.10 illustrates the modulation and demodulation process that takes place in a pair of modems that communicate through the telephone system.

The concept of modulation is important in connectivity because the different modulation techniques have inherent strengths and weaknesses that can affect the performance and reliability of a total system. By choosing the right components that provide matching modulation and demodulation, you can maximize the data handling capability of the system. Understanding the principles of signal modulation helps you provide a customer with a system that provides the most flexible growth path for the future.

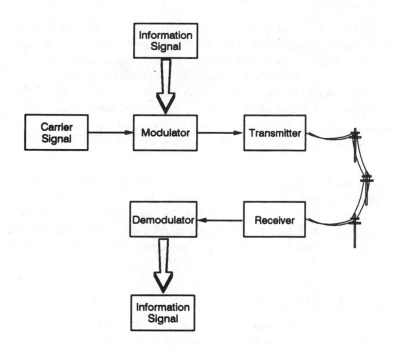

Figure 2.10
Carrier signal
modulation/
demodulation.

Modulation and Demodulation

The simplest form of modulation starts with a voltage signal that varies in level at a constant rate over time. If you plot the signal level versus time, the results are a sinusoidal wave as shown in figure 2.11. This sine wave has a constant maximum amplitude and a constant wave length. The constant wave length results in a constant frequency.

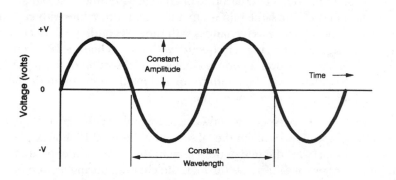

Figure 2.11
Sinusoidal signal
with constant
frequency and
amplitude.

An analog signal with constant values makes a good reference for other signals that do not have constant frequencies and amplitudes. By giving this constant signal a large amplitude, it makes a good *carrier signal* because it can retain its signal characteristics over great distances in a channel. A demodulator at the other end of the channel can lock in on this signal and separate it from other signals that are not so constant and lack the amplitude of the carrier. With appropriate filtering, the demodulator can extract the signal from the combined signal and noise even though the signal has decreased in amplitude because of energy losses in the channel.

Voice and data signals are imposed on a carrier from two perspectives. First, the information signal can vary with respect to time—called the *time domain* of a signal. Second, the information signal can vary with respect to frequency—called the *frequency domain* of a signal. To understand voice and data communications fully, you must understand these aspects of signal generation, propagation, and detection.

The Time Perspective

An electrical signal travels through a medium at a specific velocity. The physical attributes of the channel and the surrounding environmental conditions determine this velocity. The theoretical maximum speed of the signal is the speed of light. That speed is only possible for light itself. For a medium such as copper wire, a signal may travel at 50 to 85 percent of the speed of light, depending on the materials in the wire and its insulation. Even at that speed, it is possible to measure the strength of a signal versus time.

The time perspective of a signal shows how the signal is changing as a function of time. Figure 2.12 shows the time perspective of three signals. First, the 'a' section of figure 2.12 shows a signal with a constant rate of change with time. The signal strength oscillates between the same minimum and maximum values with each full cycle and follows a smooth curve as it changes with time. Second, the 'b' section of figure 2.12 shows a signal that changes frequency with time. The time between each full signal cycle changes over a period. Finally, the 'c' section of figure 2.12 shows a signal that oscillates between a minimum and maximum amplitude, but these values do not remain constant over time.

Figure 2.13 shows the time perspective of two digital signals. Both signals have the same square-wave shape. The signal in the 'a' section of figure 2.13, however, changes binary levels at twice the rate of the signal in the 'b' section of figure 2.13. Twice as many binary signal values pass through the channel during a given period for the first signal. These time perspectives are explored more after a discussion of the frequency perspectives of signals.

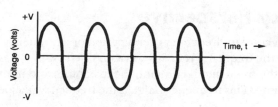

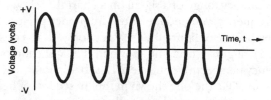

(a) Signal changes at constant rate with time.

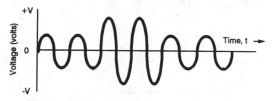

(b) Signal changes at a different rate with time.

(c) Signal amplitude changes with time.

Figure 2.12
Time perspective
of analog
signals.

Figure 2.13
Time perspective
of digital signals.

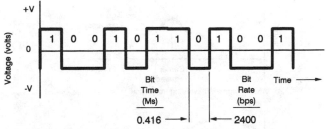

(a) Digital transmission at 2400 bps.

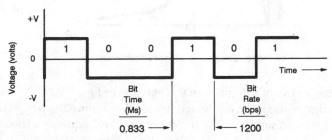

(b) Digital transmission at 1200 bps.

Personal Computer Connectivity

The Frequency Perspective

A signal has either a constant frequency over a period or a frequency that varies over time. Whether the frequency remains constant or changes, it has a maximum and a minimum. If the frequency is constant, the maximum and minimum frequency are the same. This frequency range is the frequency perspective of a signal.

When you plot the frequency range of a signal on a chart that shows the strength of a signal versus its frequency, you get one of two frequency perspectives. If you plot the frequency perspective of figure 2.12's 'a' section with its constant frequency, you get the straight vertical line shown in the 'a' section of figure 2.14. If you plot the frequency perspective of figure 2.12's 'b' section with its changing frequency, you get a curve like the one shown in the 'b' section of figure 2.14. If the frequency and amplitude of a signal vary with time, you can get the perspective shown in the 'c' section of figure 2.14.

Figure 2.14
Frequency perspective of analog signals.

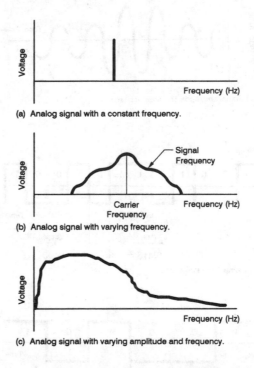

(a) Analog signal with a constant frequency.

(b) Analog signal with varying frequency.

(c) Analog signal with varying amplitude and frequency.

The frequency perspective of a digital signal is like that of figure 2.14's 'a' section. The amplitude range of the mark and space voltage determines the height of the vertical bar that signifies a single, constant frequency. This frequency allows a receiver to interpret each bit value at the other end of the channel.

Both analog and digital signals have frequency perspectives that act like finger-prints. You can distinguish a signal and separate it from other signals by knowing and looking for the frequency characteristics of that signal. This characteristic makes digital signals easy to separate from noise that contaminates a channel, as you see later.

Analog Signal Modulation

Several ways of modulating an analog carrier signal to convey information or data exist. Requirements such as the medium you use for connectivity or the through-put you must achieve usually dictate the modulation alternatives from which you can choose. Each technique varies a single characteristic of a signal, but you can combine some techniques to improve the amount of information transferred and thus the bit rate of a channel.

Electrical engineers developed many modulation techniques over the years by improving the hardware and media used in communications. The three primary analog techniques are *amplitude modulation, frequency modulation,* and *phase modula-tion.* The fourth technique applies to digital communications channels only and is called *digital modulation.* Each analog technique requires a carrier signal and results in a compound signal with unique characteristics.

Each modulation technique requires a matching demodulation technique on the receiving end of a link. Although the receiver must unravel a compound electrical signal, separating the carrier from the real signal, it may use somewhat different techniques to do so than the ones used to generate the signal. The key is to have a matched set—a pitcher and a catcher.

Amplitude Modulation

Amplitude modulation (AM) is the oldest form of signal modulation. Vendors first used this technique for radio broadcast. The modulation technique was easy to implement on the transmitting end, and the demodulation was easy and inexpen-sive on the receiving end.

An amplitude-modulated signal has a constant frequency but varies in amplitude over time to convey information. Figure 2.15 illustrates the AM technique. If you compare figure 2.15's 'a' section to the 'b' section, you can see that the carrier has a frequency much higher than the information signal it is to transport. After imposing the lower-frequency information signal on the carrier, the amplitude of the resulting compound signal varies within an envelope that matches the form of the information signal. Figure 2.15's 'c' section illustrates the resulting modulated signal.

Figure 2.15
Amplitude
modulation
signal
generation.

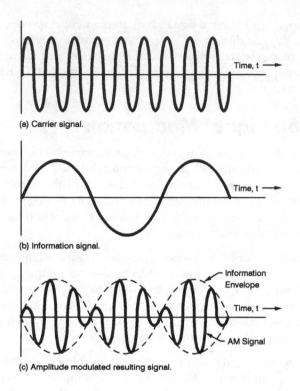

(a) Carrier signal.

(b) Information signal.

(c) Amplitude modulated resulting signal.

Although AM is easy to implement and has a long history in communications, it has several disadvantages that make it undesirable for situations that require reliable, low energy communications. Because the AM technique requires the modulation of signal strength over a predefined range, any noise that enters the channel from outside sources can adversely affect the demodulation of the AM signal. Electrical noise usually alters the amplitude of the signal and can result in the misinterpretation of the signal by the receiver. Thus, the use of AM requires substantial shielding of signal conductors to prevent noise contamination of the signal.

When communications require a long channel, amplitude modulation presents a problem. As the strength of a signal decreases in a channel with distance traveled, it reaches a minimum level unacceptable for adequate communications. Before the signal strength decreases to that level, the signal must be *reconditioned*. In analog communications, *amplifiers* receive the signal and increase its strength before sending it on down the channel.

The problem with amplifiers is that they amplify both the signal and the noise that has contaminated the signal up to that point. If a long channel requires several amplifiers, the amplified noise can prevent proper reception of the signal. AM signals are particularly susceptible to this problem because their amplitude variations convey their information—the signal characteristic most affected by noise. To reduce the amplification of noise in a channel, place amplifiers as close to the signal source as possible.

Frequency Modulation

Another modulation technique used extensively in radio communications is *frequency modulation* (FM). The FM technique requires more sophisticated hardware on the transmitting and receiving end of a link, but the results are often worth the extra complication. The introduction of FM to commercial radio broadcasts in the 1940s produced an industry that has yet to peak. No automobile would be complete today without FM reception.

A frequency-modulated signal has a constant amplitude but varies in frequency over time to convey information. Figure 2.16 illustrates this modulation technique. If you compare the 'a' section of figure 2.16 with the figure's 'b' section, you see that the carrier has a frequency much higher than the information signal it is to transport. After imposing the lower-frequency information signal on the carrier, the frequency of the resulting compound signal varies to match the form of the information signal. The 'c' section of figure 2.16 illustrates the resulting modulated signal.

The only significant disadvantage of frequency modulation is the bandwidth it takes to transmit a signal. As figure 2.17 shows, an FM signal has a wide spectrum of frequencies that span each side of the original carrier frequency. By requiring a wider bandwidth than an AM signal, the number of FM signals you can transmit through a medium with a fixed total bandwidth is smaller than the number of AM signals you can transmit through the same medium.

As you see and explore in greater detail in later chapters, the FM modulation technique plays a significant role in communications through the telephone system. Low-speed modems use FM techniques to convert digital signals into FM signals. This process of *frequency shift keying* (FSK) allows a modem to modulate and demodulate an FM signal between only two frequencies that represent the two binary digital values it receives from or transmits to a computer or terminal.

Figure 2.16
Frequency
modulation
signal
generation.

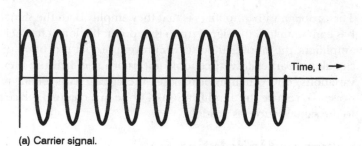

(a) Carrier signal.

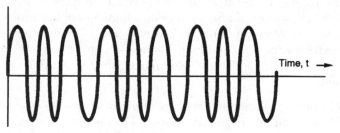

(b) Information signal.

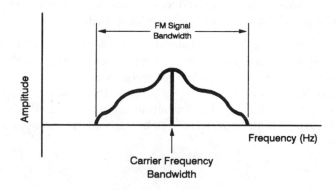

(c) Frequency modulated resulting signal.

Figure 2.17
FM signal
bandwidth.

Phase Modulation

The latest single-characteristic modulation technique employed in communications is *phase modulation* (PM). This technique does not apply widely to radio communications, but vendors use the technique to convey color information in color television broadcasts. Researchers developed PM as a better alternative to AM and FM techniques. Although PM is more difficult to understand than AM and FM, the concept is good to know. Phase modulation provides the signal modulation that allows computers to communicate at high data rates through the telephone system.

Phase modulation requires at least two analog signals. The first signal is the carrier; all other signals modify the carrier signal to convey information. A PM modulation device imposes information on the carrier by changing the shape of the carrier's signal curve at given points in time. Figure 2.18 shows the building blocks of PM. Both signals are sine waves that have the same fixed frequency and amplitude. They are, however, offset from each other. The two cross the amplitude reference line at different times and are, therefore, *different in phase.*

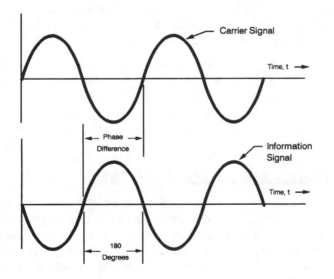

Figure 2.18
Carrier and information signals 180 degrees different in phase.

The difference in phase between two sine waves is a *phase angle.* The angle is a number of degrees from zero to 360. Two signals offset by one-half of a cycle are 180 degrees out of phase. Two signals offset by a full cycle are in phase—no phase difference exists between them. Figure 2.18 shows a carrier at zero degrees and an information signal 180 degrees out of phase with the carrier. Figure 2.19 shows the resulting compound, phase-modulated signal. From this figure, you can see how the amplitude of the signal follows a smooth curve until it reaches the phase shift.

At the phase shift point, the curve breaks its pattern and then resumes, but at a different point along the old pattern. The break point is the *phase change* that conveys the information for the compound signal.

Figure 2.19
Phase-
modulated
signal.

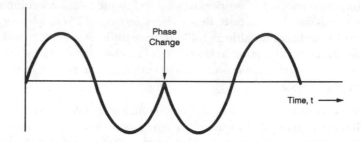

Because PM requires two signals with a phase difference between them, no single signal can create a phase modulation pattern. A reference pattern and a signal pattern are both required. The reference pattern allows designers to design and build PM circuits. With a fixed frequency carrier and a fixed frequency signal, you can easily design a circuit that locks onto the carrier's frequency and eliminates it to leave the information signal. Phase modulation also lends itself well to technology matching with digital communications systems.

Later chapters explore in greater detail how the PM modulation technique plays a significant role in communications through the telephone system. Medium-speed modems use PM techniques to convert digital signals into PM signals. This process of *phase shift keying* (PSK) allows a modem to modulate and demodulate a PM signal between phases that represent the digital signals it receives from or transmits to a computer or terminal.

Combined Phase-Amplitude Modulation

With many technologies, you often can combine more than one technique to produce another technique. Signal engineers did this by combining more than one of the three modulation techniques described earlier. The two most common combinations are AM with FM and AM with PM. By combining modulation techniques, designers can develop greater signal throughput in a given channel than its bandwidth allows for a single technique.

The most popular combination of modulation techniques is AM and PM. By altering the amplitude of a carrier and creating a phase difference between the carrier and the information signal, you get *quadrature amplitude modulation* (QAM). Vendors who make equipment that allows digital computers to communicate through analog telephone systems can obtain high data rates with QAM techniques. Figure 2.20 shows a simple QAM signal that has two amplitude states and

four phase shifts. The resulting signal can convey eight times more information during a given period than a signal that just uses one of these modulation techniques. Chapter 9 explores this technique more in its review of modem design.

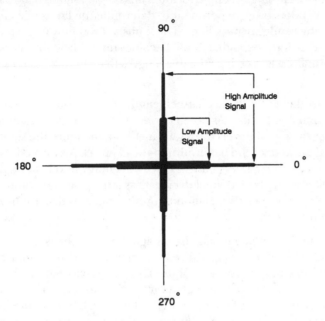

Figure 2.20
Quadrature amplitude modulated (QAM) signal.

Digital Signal Modulation

Analog modulation techniques do not apply to digital communications. Whereas an analog signal varies through a range of energy values with time, a digital signal makes step changes between two or more discrete energy states. Analog signal modulation also depends upon a carrier signal and an information signal that modulates the carrier. Digital modulation does not require the presence of an analog carrier.

The digital signal remains at a given voltage level for a specified period to signal a binary or digital value. The signal modulates from one discrete value to another only when the information changes value. A vendor also may use a digital carrier signal with a digital information signal to increase the amplitude of the information. By modulating a strong digital signal to match the bit pattern of a weaker information signal, the resulting high-amplitude digital signal has enough strength to go for a longer distance than the original information signal. The signal can travel farther than the original information signal because its strength is high relative to any noise it may accumulate as it propagates through a medium.

Bandwidth versus Channel Length

Several factors combine to limit the channel length a digital signal can traverse without revitalization. No single, simple formula links digital signal bandwidth and channel lengths. Vendors often experiment to determine the limits of a channel, and then publish the results as guidelines. The limits tell you how long you can extend the channel before the digital signal becomes unusable at the receiving end. Vendors normally select or specify cable lengths that fall well within such limits.

The three elements that limit digital channel length are electronic noise, signal attenuation, and signal reflection. As noted earlier, noise distorts an electrical signal. The farther the signal travels through a medium, the more the signal becomes distorted because of the bandwidth of the channel. Also noted earlier, the natural resistance in a channel changes electrical energy into heat or another form of energy. The strength of a signal decreases as it traverses a medium. A wire channel also requires a proper termination to prevent signal reflection from further distorting the signal.

Figure 2.21 illustrates the degradation a digital signal undergoes as it travels through a channel. The 'a' section of figure 2.21 shows an original digital signal a computer or telephone might produce. Figure 2.21's 'b' section shows that same signal after it has traveled 100 feet through a wire. The combination of noise and attenuation produces the kind of effect shown in the 'c' section of figure 2.21 after the signal has traveled another 400 feet. As you can see from this last figure, the digital signal can take on many characteristics of an analog signal as it degrades.

Figure 2.21
Digital signal distortion and attenuation with distance.

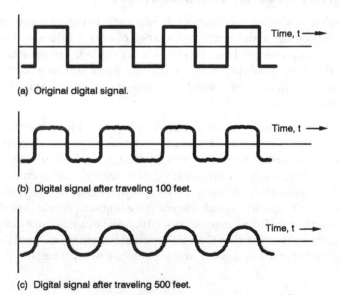

(a) Original digital signal.

(b) Digital signal after traveling 100 feet.

(c) Digital signal after traveling 500 feet.

Many channel types have well-known bandwidth versus length characteristics. Vendors use curves such as the one shown in figure 2.22 to determine the length of channel they want to use for specific applications. For a high-volume application that requires a high bandwidth such as a direct connection between two mainframe computers, a vendor can limit the length of the communications channel to a short distance. For a low-volume application such as the connection between a personal computer and a low speed printer, the vendor can specify a longer channel.

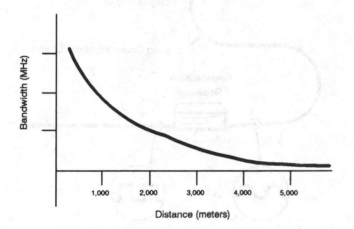

Figure 2.22
Medium bandwidth versus length.

Digital Signal Regeneration

In situations that require the movement of large volumes of information over long distances, vendors can provide devices that *regenerate* a digital signal. You can place these *repeaters* along the digital channel to receive the signal and rebuild it to its original strength and shape. The repeater catches the signal before it degrades to the point that it is unusable. After deciphering the digital signal from the degraded signal, the repeater reissues the signal into the communications channel as shown in figure 2.23. This regeneration process can take place as often as necessary between the source of a signal and its ultimate destination.

Digital signals cannot be amplified to increase their distance range in a channel. If you amplify a digital signal, you also amplify the noise that contaminates the signal. By amplifying the noise, you increase the risk that the receiver cannot properly identify the change in signal from one state to another. The amplified noise can become a substantial part of the signal. A repeater, on the other hand, removes the noise from a signal while it is regenerating the signal. To regenerate the signal, the repeater may have to regenerate the clock signal used to modulate the original digital signal and then regenerate the digital signal using this regenerated clock signal.

Figure 2.23
Digital signal
regeneration.

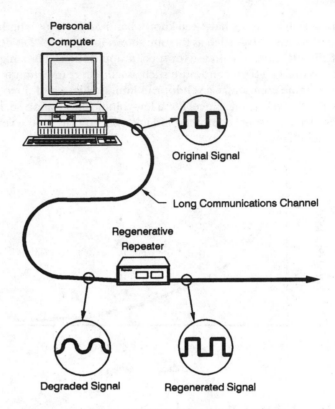

Personal
Computer

Original Signal

Long Communications Channel

Regenerative
Repeater

Degraded Signal

Regenerated Signal

Synchronization of Digital Modulation

Digital communications depend upon exact timing of signal generation and
reception to be successful. If the transmitter sends a signal and the receiver starts
to examine the signal at the wrong time, the receiver gets meaningless information. The receiver must look at the digital signal at the appropriate times to detect
the proper transition from one energy level to another, a process called *synchronization.*

Synchronization between a sending and receiving device requires an agreement on
bit time between the two devices. To determine bit time, the receiver must *regenerate
the clock signal* used by the sender to modulate the original signal. The receiver
must extract the clock signal from the total signal it receives. After the receiver
determines the bit time of the signal, it can then regenerate the digital signal as
long as the bit time of its clock remains synchronized with the bit time the sender
used to produce the signal.

Devices at each end of a digital channel can synchronize using one of two techniques. First, the transmitter and the receiver can work independently of each other and exchange a specified signal pattern at the start of each signal exchange, called *asynchronous communications*. Second, the transmitter and receiver can exchange initial synchronizing information, and then continuously exchange a digital signal stream that keeps them in lock step, called *synchronous communications*. Chapters 5 and 6 explore both techniques in detail. The following paragraphs discuss just the initial synchronization of transmission frames between a sender and receiver.

Asynchronous Signal Synchronization

Asynchronous communications require clock regeneration during the first bit period of each transmission frame. The technology that makes this clock regeneration possible is precise and high-frequency *signal sampling*. A receiver must monitor the communications channel and measure the voltage in that channel at a frequency that allows it to figure out the width of a bit period at the start of a transmission frame of data.

As shown in figure 2.24, electrical engineers found that the sampling rate of an asynchronous receiver had to be at least 16 times the bit rate of the digital signal coming through the channel. By reading the signal amplitude in the channel at a ratc 16 times the bit rate, the receiver can accurately locate the center of the first signal transition that occurs in a channel.

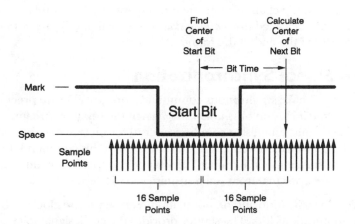

Figure 2.24
Digital signal sampling to determine bit time.

This *over-sample rate* allows the receiver to identify and measure the width of the digital signal that marks the start of an asynchronous frame. The *start bit*, shown in figure 2.25, must have a value of zero, sometimes called a *space*. Its width is in milliseconds and is the *bit time* of the digital signal. The receiver must set its signal sampling clock to match this bit time for the duration of the asynchronous transmission frame.

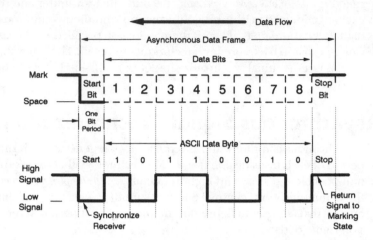

Figure 2.25
Asynchronous transmission frame of digital signals.

After successfully identifying and measuring the interval of an asynchronous start bit, an asynchronous receiver measures the voltage in the channel after each subsequent bit time. For eight-bit serial communications, the receiver does this sampling eight times and translates the signal strength it reads into a series of eight bit values it stores in a holding register. The receiver then does one final sampling of the signal strength in the channel after the ninth bit time. This sampling must result in a bit value of one called the *marking state* or *stop bit* that indicates synchronization is still correct at the end of the frame.

Synchronous Signal Synchronization

The technologies that make synchronous communications possible are precise *signal sampling* and the inclusion of *synchronizing data* in the serial bit stream. Synchronous devices must establish a common interval for bit signals—*bit time*—at the beginning of a transmission frame. They must maintain this common bit time throughout the transmission of the frame. Every bit period in a frame must result in the transfer of a binary signal from the transmitter to the receiver.

Synchronous signal modulation and demodulation require precise clocks at both ends of the communications link. The sender provides the clock signal to generate the transmission frames. The receiver provides a clock to decipher the transmission frame as it arrives. The first implementations of synchronous transmission required the clocking to come from a computer or special communications controllers. For most synchronous communications implemented

today through telephone systems, the transmitting modem that modulates the digital signal to analog provides the clock signal. The receiving modem derives the clock signal from the analog signal it receives and sends that clock signal to the computer.

The synchronization process between communicating devices is, nevertheless, the same regardless of the clock source. The sending and receiving clocks must be coordinated and precisely synchronized. A synchronous receiver must monitor the communications channel and measure the voltage in that channel at a frequency that allows it to synchronize quickly with the first bits it receives in a synchronous frame of data.

The sampling rate of a synchronous receiver must be higher than the bit rate of the digital signal coming through the channel. This *over-sample rate* allows the receiver to identify an initial series of synchronization bits and measure the width of the digital signals that convey these bits. The width of a synchronous bit signal (in milliseconds) is the *bit time* the receiver must use to sample the remainder of the transmission frame. The sending and receiving clocks synchronize and cause the voltage creation and voltage sampling to follow the same bit interval at each end.

Figure 2.26 shows two popular synchronous communications protocols. Although these two protocols use the synchronous technique of bit timing and transmission, they use different techniques to synchronize the sender and receiver at the beginning of each transmission frame. *Binary Synchronous Communication* (BSC) uses two eight-bit SYN characters. *Synchronous Data Link Control* (SDLC) uses one eight-bit flag field. The receiver has 16 bit times in which to synchronize with the sender in BSC. The receiver has eight bit times to do the same with SDLC.

As you see in later chapters, other synchronous implementations such as the ones used in local area networking provide similar bit time synchronization techniques.

Digital Signal Advantages

Because of the discrete nature of digital signals, it takes more *electrical noise* to corrupt the signal than it does to contaminate an analog signal of the same strength. If the voltage level that represents each digital value is far apart in magnitude, it takes a large amount of noise to get the signal to move from one digital value to another in error. Simple and inexpensive digital circuitry can separate a digital signal from the noise that contaminates the signal as it travels through a channel.

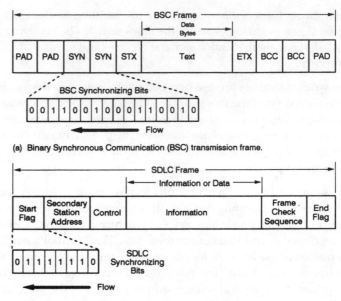

(a) Binary Synchronous Communication (BSC) transmission frame.

(b) Synchronous Data-Link Control (SDLC) transmission frame.

Most digital communications systems also send specific and separate data with the information they convey that allow the receiver to detect errors. The receiver can request a retransmission of the bad information. Analog communication does not lend itself to the detection and correction of errors. The analog error-detection data can become corrupted just as easily as the information itself.

Although digital communication offers many advantages over analog communication, some instances require the use of analog channels. Almost all older telephone system communications require analog modulation and demodulation. New telephone systems may offer all-digital communications or a combination of analog and digital communications. The following paragraphs explore the different modulation and demodulation techniques vendors use in telephone systems.

Telephone System Modulation Techniques

Long distance data communications have many features dictated by the design of the telephone system. The first computers could communicate only with local devices through parallel channels. As computers migrated across the country, users wanted to connect the computers to share information between them. The most obvious and economical communications channel available was the public telephone system. The telephone systems available today, however, impose many restrictions on data communications that will not go away for many years.

Because of the design of public telephone lines and equipment, computers must communicate through this system using *serial data communications* techniques. The system, originally designed for voice communications through a pair of wires, can support only serial communications. The simple analog signals used to transmit and receive voice signals do not require parallel signal paths. Now that telephone system vendors have large sums of money invested in voice communications equipment, it makes good sense to convert data communications into signals compatible with that equipment.

The future direction for voice communications networks is a gradual conversion to an all-digital system, but the conversion process will be slow. This *Integrated Services Digital Network* (ISDN) provides a minimum of two voice and one packet data circuits over lines previously used for only one voice circuit or one voice-grade data circuit. Until ISDN or a better alternative becomes available, you must live with the limitations of existing public and private telephone systems.

Analog Telephone Systems

The public telephone system most of us are familiar with has analog connections that come out to our house or business. Regardless of the vendor that provides your telephone service, the telephone lines and equipment these companies provide contain many common elements. The common elements do change, however, when the telephone lines connect with a business to support heavy voice and data communications traffic.

This discussion begins with an exploration of the analog lines telephone companies use to convey voice and light data communications traffic, and then progresses to the analog channels that can convey heavier voice and data traffic. Finally, the conversion from analog to digital channels is discussed.

Analog telephone systems provide either two or four wires that convey a *direct current* (DC) signal between your telephone handset and a local telephone company *central office* (CO). Most public telephone vendors provide direct dial service to households through two-wire systems. Vendors set up four-wire systems for high-speed data communications or to convey several voice signals through the same channel. In both cases, the signals that move through these lines have frequencies, voltages, and current levels designed for optimum voice transmission.

Figure 2.27 shows a simplified diagram of a two-wire telephone connection between two telephones connected to the same central office. As you can see from this figure, the telephone company powers the telephone wires with batteries. The voltage at the local CO is usually around 48 volts DC. The power source is available at all times, even when you lose power from the power utility. The connection to your telephone may also contain four wires. Only two of the wires conduct signals unless you pay for and use two telephone lines. Vendors call these wires *telephone twisted pairs* because of their continuous twist. The twist is a form of shielding to reduce noise interference on the lines.

Figure 2.27
Typical analog telephone connection.

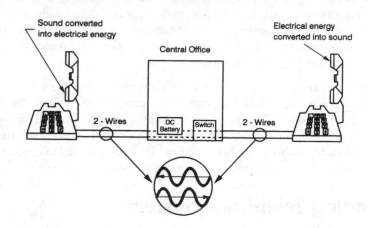

Analog Telephone Connections

Telephone lines that go through a central office switch can make two types of connections with other telephones. First, you can direct dial another telephone connected with the same CO.

Second, you can dial a telephone connected to another CO. In either case, the call requires the closure of electrical switches to make the connection—thus the name *circuit-switched connection.*

Local calls between two telephones connected to the same CO make the simplest type of analog telephone circuit. This type of call goes through a local loop, as shown in figure 2.28. After you dial the number you want, the CO makes the connection by closing the appropriate switches that create a continuous loop from your telephone to the other. If you make a call from one modem to another and the two modems connect to the same CO, the CO completes the same type of switched circuit for you. Figure 2.29 shows this loop.

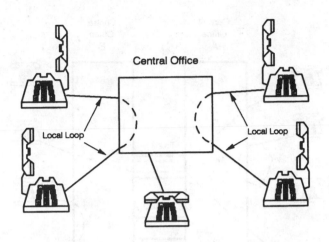

Figure 2.28
Local loop calls through a central office.

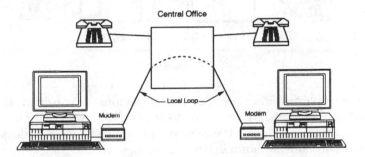

Figure 2.29
Local modem-to-modem analog telephone call.

Telephone calls between COs are more complex than local-loop calls. These calls go through *trunk lines*, as shown in figure 2.30. These trunk lines aggregate several telephone calls through either wire or fiber-optic cables. The COs at each end of the call must close the appropriate switches to make a complete circuit between the two telephones. After the COs complete the circuit, the call proceeds just like a local call. The aggregation performed by the telephone company between the two COs is not apparent to the caller—the process is transparent. The achievement of this transparent aggregation is the subject of our next discussion.

Multiplexing

The process of combining several signals and conveying them through the same channel simultaneously is *multiplexing*. The technique enables the telephone company to set up many telephone connections between telephones or computers through a few physical channels. This reduction in overhead enables the telephone provider to operate efficiently and keep operating costs down.

Figure 2.30
Local analog calls in the same city.

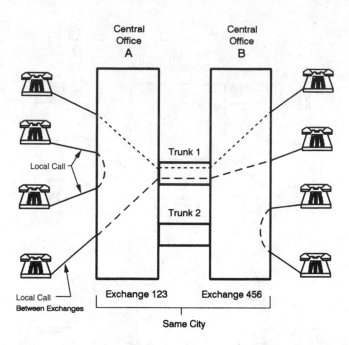

The need for multiplexing arises because of the limitations of the twisted pair that connects a telephone or other device to the local CO. These twisted-pair lines were originally designed to provide good voice service between a home or business and the CO. Their bandwidth, as shown in figure 2.31, supports one voice conversation at a time. The two wires enable your voice to go one direction through one wire, and the distant caller's voice to come your way through the other wire. The two voice signals take the entire bandwidth of the voice channel and move in both directions simultaneously. These *full-duplex* conversations leave no bandwidth for other calls or signals to move through the same wires.

Frequency Division Modulation

Telephone service providers overcome the limitations of the local loop by multiplexing several voice channels through a single trunk. The CO takes each voice channel and modulates the signal to a higher frequency, as shown in figure 2.32. Each voice channel gets a frequency slot in the trunk using *frequency division multiplexing* (FDM).

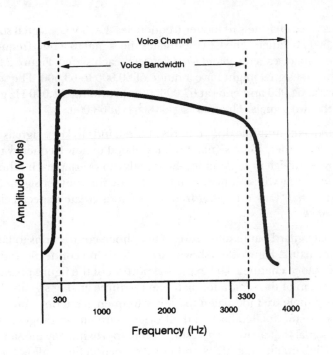

Figure 2.31
Voice channel and voice bandwidth.

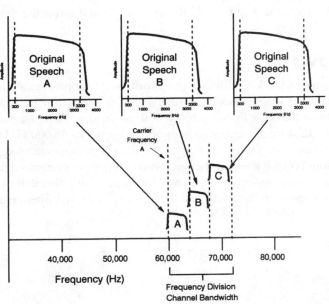

Figure 2.32
Frequency division multiplexing (FDM) of voice channels.

FDM modulates voice channels to higher frequencies. Each voice signal starts out in the 300 to 3,300 Hz range. The CO modulates the signal to a new frequency range with a clear space called a *guard band* between each signal. Figure 2.32 shows this process. The first signal might have a range of 60,000 to 63,000. The second signal then starts at 64,000 and ends at 67,000, thus providing a 1,000 Hz guard band between the two signals. The third signal starts at 68,000.

The FDM technique of multiplexing requires guard bands to keep signals from contaminating each other. If the signals are modulated to new frequency ranges that do not provide sufficient separation, the signals can overlap each other. Some of one signal can overlap the frequency range set aside for another signal. The extraneous signals that "walk on" other frequency bands create a special electronic noise called *crosstalk*.

FDM and adequate guard bands allow several telephone connections to take place through the same trunk. Figure 2.33 shows three telephone connections through the same long-distance channel. The exploded portion of the figure provides a simplified illustration of the separation between the three analog signals. The three telephone signals are modulated to higher frequencies at one end of the channel and then demodulated back to their original frequency ranges at the other end. The signal that arrives at a destination is approximately the same as the original signal. High quality amplifiers and noise reduction filters allow long distance service companies to provide signal quality that approaches that of a local loop.

FDM Groups

Companies that provide long-distance telephone service combine calls into groups. The providers of the long lines have standard combinations of voice channels. Figure 2.34 shows the basic building block of these groups. This *Channel Group* uses FDM to convey 12 voice channels through one trunk with a 48,000 Hz bandwidth. Each voice channel can convey voice signals or data communications signals. Data communications require a session between two compatible modems that use voice frequency tones to convey computer data. The signals going through the Channel Group are transparent to the trunk and to the companies that operate both the trunk and the CO switches at each end.

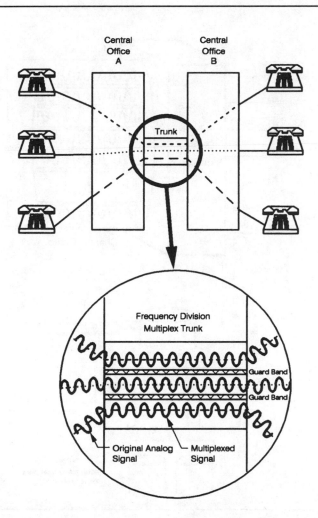

Figure 2.33
Frequency division multiplexing (FDM).

The long-line carriers aggregate Channel Groups into larger groups for longer distance communications. Figure 2.35 shows the aggregation hierarchy provided by AT&T. Although the number of voice channels and the frequency ranges for multiplexing are the same between North American companies, other countries do not provide the same levels above the *Supergroup*. North American trunks above the Supergroup must be demultiplexed to the Supergroup before they can convey signals through these systems. For example, AT&T would separate a *Mastergroup* into ten Supergroups, and then connect the Supergroups to comparable European Supergroups to convey trunk calls to European cities.

Figure 2.34
Analog
telephone
modulation
group structure.

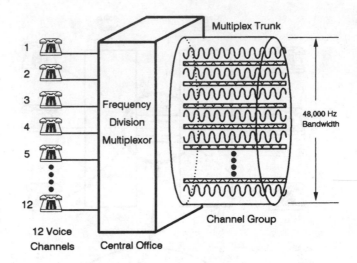

Figure 2.35
Hierarchy of
AT&T frequency
division
multiplexor
groups.

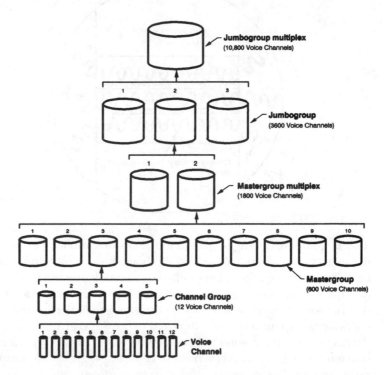

Many long-distance carriers are migrating to all-digital trunks to avoid some problems experienced with FDM modulation. AT&T started the conversion to digital trunks in 1963 and completed most of this conversion by the end of the 1960s. As the cost of conversion from analog signaling to digital decreases with time, the momentum to move to all-digital increases.

Digital Telephone Systems

Although some businesses have made the conversion to digital communications at the local-loop level, many subscribers are just making the decision to go in this direction, or they are in the process of converting. With the billions of dollars invested in analog communication equipment in homes and businesses, this conversion will take time. Until all local loop subscribers make the move to all-digital voice and computer communications, telephone companies must provide a window from the analog world to the digital world of communications.

Analog-to-Digital Conversion

To go from analog-based equipment to digital-based communications networks requires an *analog-to-digital conversion*. This is the reverse of the modulation/demodulation performed by modems to convey digital data through an analog telephone. Instead, a device called a *codec* (short for *coder/decoder*) translates analog voice signals into digital signals. The resulting digital signal can travel through all-digital communications equipment that provides more reliable and less costly service than equivalent analog equipment.

Signal Sampling

The codec process requires fast and precise signal sampling similar to the sampling performed in the asynchronous and synchronous communications described earlier. The 'b' section of figure 2.36 shows this sampling process. A sampling device converts the amplitude of an analog signal into discrete signals that have amplitudes that simulate the original analog signal. This conversion process is *pulse amplitude modulation* (PAM).

The PAM technique produces a stream of continuously varying digital signals. For effective analysis of the original analog signal, a PAM device must sample the signal voltage at a rate at least twice the frequency of the original signal. Thus, the minimum sampling rate for an analog voice signal with a channel bandwidth of 4,000 Hz is 8,000 samples per second. At least every 125 microseconds the PAM device must produce a signal with a discrete amplitude.

Figure 2.36
Pulse code
modulation
(PCM) and
pulse amplitude
modulation
(PAM).

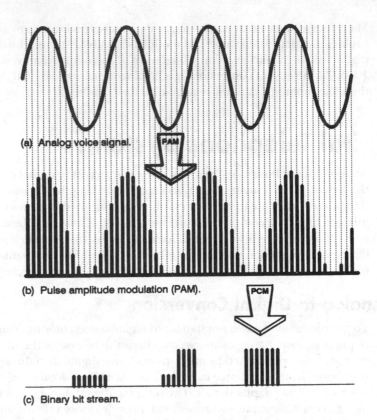

(a) Analog voice signal.

(b) Pulse amplitude modulation (PAM).

(c) Binary bit stream.

The discrete signals that result from this PAM analysis of an analog signal are no less prone to attenuation, distortion, and noise contamination than the original analog signals. If you convey the PAM signals through an analog communications channel and use signal amplifiers, the results are not usable. The decoder at the receiving end could not recreate the original voice frequencies that went into the coder at the source. Another modulation technique is required to make the final signal compatible with digital transmission and regeneration hardware.

Pulse Code Modulation

The final modulation required to make the analog signal compatible with digital circuits is *pulse code modulation* (PCM). PCM converts the stream of continuously varying PAM signals into a stream of binary digital signals as shown in the 'c' section of figure 2.36. This bit stream contains signals that have two discrete digital values. These binary signal levels have sufficient amplitude separation to make their transmission and regeneration simple and inexpensive for the telephone carrier.

The PAM sampling of an analog signal produces *quantizing levels*. The resulting signals it produces have many discrete pulse amplitudes proportional to the sampling rate. Telephone vendors discovered many years ago that systems that provide 128 discrete amplitudes provide the minimum signals required for voice regeneration at the receiving end of the link. With 128 quantizing levels, a digital system can segregate voice signals from noise just as well as older analog systems.

The sampling rate and the number of quantizing levels determine the bit rate of the digital communications channel. To convey 128 discrete volume levels requires seven binary data bits. The PCM component must generate all seven data bits each time the PAM component performs a sample of the analog signal. To operate the system, you need to sample at a rate of 8,000 samples per second and generate seven data bits each time. This produces 7 x 8,000 = 56,000 bps.

The digital communications channels in North America provide the capacity for digitized voice and controls. Besides the 56 Kbps of digitized voice, these systems provide an additional 8 Kbps for system control. The total bit rate is 64 Kbps. As you see in later chapters, this rate is the common denominator used in the design of many communications systems today. Although a channel capacity of 64 Kbps may sound high compared to the modem bit rates of 19,200 bps used today for asynchronous communications, it is not high enough for trunk communications between COs. The economies of scale for long-distance communications require vendors to combine several 64-Kbps channels into one channel of larger capacity.

Time Division Multiplexing

Vendors use a technique called *time division multiplexing* (TDM) to combine several digital voice channels into one channel. The technique interleaves more than one individual digital signal into another channel by giving each original signal time a slot in the multiplexed channel. Figure 2.37 illustrates this process.

TDM requires synchronization between the source and destination. Figure 2.37 shows three telephones communicating through a trunk that uses TDM. The exploded portion of the figure shows how each time slot for the three conversions has an identification. The CO at the transmitting end must provide the identification. The CO at the receiving end must recognize the identification of a set of binary signals and deliver them to the appropriate destination. AT&T standardized the protocols and TDM techniques used for digitized voice in North America. The lowest level is the T1 carrier.

Figure 2.37
Time division
multiplexing
(TDM).

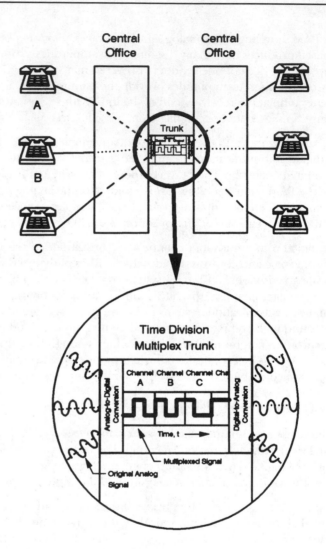

T1 Channel Banks

AT&T combines 24 digitized voice channels into one high-capacity channel called
the *T1 carrier*. These carriers provide digital repeaters every 6,000 feet and have a
total bit rate of 1.544 Mbps. Most installations limit the total length of these
channels to 50 miles, but millions of them are in operation in North America.
Figure 2.38 shows a typical T1 trunk that connects two COs.

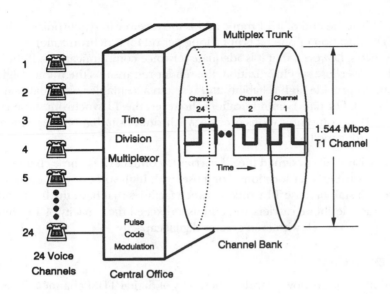

Figure 2.38
Time division
multiplexor and
T1 channel bank.

The time division of each voice channel in a T1 carrier follows a defined set of rules. These rules allow the CO at each end of a link to identify and separate each voice channel as it arrives. The CO converts each voice channel from analog signals to a 56-Kbps binary bit stream. It then combines up to 24 of these streams into a T1 channel and adds the necessary data to separate voice channels and control delivery of the signals. The T1 channel divides the bit stream into transmission frames.

T1 Transmission Frames

The AT&T T1 transmission frame is analogous to the synchronous transmission frames discussed earlier. Figure 2.39 shows this frame and its characteristics. The frame gives each voice channel eight bits as a time slot and adds a *framing bit* after each frame. The frame contains a total of 193 bits and travels through the carrier channel at a rate of 8,000 frames per second.

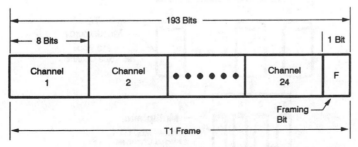

Figure 2.39
AT&T T1
transmission
frame.

The framing bit at the end of a T1 frame allows the receiver to synchronize with the frame. The duration of one bit is not a long period for synchronization. Experience shows, however, that it is adequate for voice communications. If the sender and receiver lose synchronization, the sender retransmits the frame. Digital communications provide high reliability and result in acceptable voice quality at the receiving end. For data communications, however, the T1 synchronization is not adequate. Data communications provide synchronization that is independent of the T1 synchronizing bit.

Although AT&T initially designed the T1 carrier to connect COs, these channels are now in use between user locations. For a user with high voice or data traffic, it makes sense to install or lease T1 trunks between facilities that have the high traffic loads. When the telephone carriers and end users exceed the capacity of T1, they must move up to channels with even greater digital capacity.

The Tx Hierarchy

Many telephone vendors now provide a hierarchy of digital TDM channels. These channels aggregate channels of lower capacity to channels of higher capacity in fixed increments as shown in figure 2.40. The range is from T1 to T4.

Figure 2.40
Hierarchy of digital time division multiplexors.

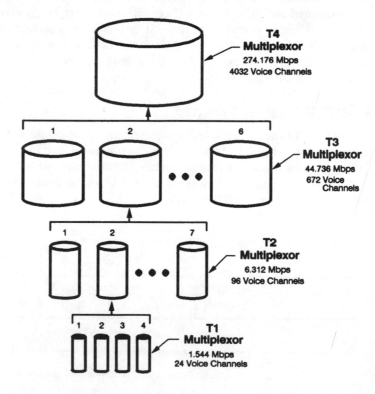

The data capacity required for a TDM channel determines the medium for the channel. The T1 and T2 rates are low enough that vendors can use twisted pairs of wires to convey the digital signals. Twisted-wire pairs cannot, however, carry the digital traffic that flows through the T3 and T4 carriers. The media often used in these service levels are coaxial and fiber-optic cables.

Unfortunately, the international community does not endorse the AT&T standards for T*x* circuits. International committees have endorsed digital communications that divide frames into 193 bits, but the synchronization bit is at the beginning of a frame rather than the end. These committees also support only two PCM transmission rates. One rate matches the 1.544 Mbps capacity of the AT&T T1 carrier, but the other rate is 2.048 Mbps, which does not match any of the AT&T rates. The differences between the PCM standards selected for international use and those developed by AT&T present inter-connectivity obstacles. Hopefully, these obstacles will diminish with the deployment of ISDN throughout the 1990s.

Summary

Communication channels provide the vehicles to get data from a source to a destination. Although physical channels contain common elements that hinder the flow of signals that convey voice and data signals, vendors use several techniques to overcome these limitations. As technology continues to improve with time, more alternatives become available.

The bandwidth and data rate of a communications channel are important connectivity characteristics. They often make the difference between a system that meets user needs and one that does not. A variety of analog and digital signal modulation techniques is available to improve the basic characteristics of a channel, but these techniques have limitations that must be understood. You can select the combination of channel characteristics and techniques that optimize system performance.

Historically, digital devices used asynchronous communications before synchronous became the norm. Because of the periodic nature of early communications and the low volume of data flow in early digital systems, asynchronous communications made sense. As data traffic grew with the increasing use of digital computers and as clocking techniques improved with time, it became more practical to use synchronous communications. You now have a variety of asynchronous and synchronous communications techniques to choose from to match end-user requirements.

Personal Computer Connectivity

Although digital communications offer many advantages over analog, you may have to deal with many analog components and systems in a total system design. Figure 2.41 shows how complicated a complete system can look from a signal perspective. A good understanding of the differences between these digital and analog signals and how to bring the two together is key to connectivity. The next chapter builds on the ideas presented in this chapter to show you how communications channels provide the link for data communications.

Figure 2.41
Signal modulation and demodulation combinations.

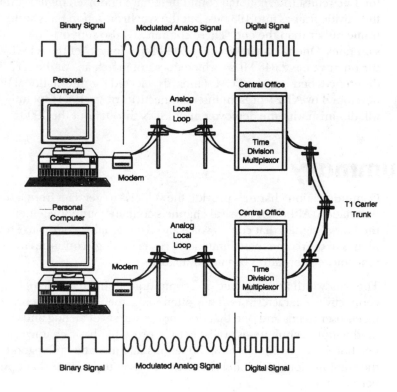

Chapter Snapshot

The development and implementation of communications and networking standards have been major factors in the evolution of connectivity both in the United States and around the world. The publication and general availability of these standards allows any connectivity vendor to develop products that conform with the specifications and requirements spelled out in these standards. Demanding conformance with published standards allows connectivity purchasers to select a variety of products from multiple vendors with some degree of assurance that these products will work together to meet the purchasers' needs. In this chapter, you will learn the following:

✔ The names and responsibilities of major connectivity standards organizations

✔ The layered design of connectivity hardware and software

✔ The Open Systems Interconnect (OSI) model

✔ Physical connectivity characteristics and functions

✔ An overview of distributed computing standards

Many organizations today plan to migrate from current vendor-proprietary connectivity systems to open connectivity systems which allow them to mix and match components from many vendors. Use this chapter to understand how standards will help these organizations and you achieve this open systems goal.

CHAPTER

Communications and Networking Functions and Standards

The connection of the PC into a system of other peripherals and computers often requires a variety of digital and analog communications. The variety of channel types is necessary because of the different types of hardware and the distances between this hardware in a system. System designers use digital channels to get data from one internal PC device to another. You also can use digital channels to move data between the PC system unit and other local computers or peripherals.

A system dispersed over a large geographic region requires communications through telephone systems. If you have a high volume of data traffic, you may want to connect with an all-digital communications system to achieve connectivity over a large area. If you do not have high enough data traffic to justify an all-digital communications system, you may have to use the public telephone system. The common carriers that provide these systems may use both older analog and newer digital communications channels to move your data across the country.

Aside from the multiplicity of channel types in a system, many complex systems also include hardware and components from many different vendors. Because of this variety of channels and vendors, it is important to have certain common denominators in a system design. You cannot provide this common foundation alone. Many national and international organizations can help to ensure interconnectivity and interoperability between disparate components and systems.

Data Communications Standards

Although the PC stores and communicates data as bits, the internal hardware must follow specific rules during the storage and transfer of the data. The *central processing unit* (CPU) and all its peripherals must "speak the same language," otherwise data transferred and stored will not be useful. Internal devices must follow certain rules and *conventions* to be compatible.

It may be reasonable for one vendor to standardize design and implementation of data transfer components within a limited environment. It is far more difficult for one vendor to police the actions of other vendors that participate in a much larger environment. To develop and publish universal rules and conventions, most countries have established standards organizations. Table 3.1 provides a list of some of the groups that influence and create standards to control the communications and networking connectivity between components and systems. Figure 3.1 shows their relationships. The recommendations and standards produced and distributed by these groups pervade connectivity, as you see throughout this book.

Table 3.1
Standards and Regulations Organizations

Organization	Description
IEEE	The *Institute of Electrical and Electronic Engineers* is an American professional group that, among its many functions, establishes electrical standards. The organization has a microprocessor standards committee that sets electrical and electronic standards for the design of microcomputer components and systems.
EIA	The *Electronics Industries Association* represents American manufacturers. The EIA publishes standards, such as EIA RS-232D and RS-449, that govern the electrical

Personal Computer Connectivity

Organization	Description
	characteristics of connections between the personal computer and external peripherals such as printers and modems.
CCITT	The *Consultative Committee in International Telegraph and Telephone* was an *International Telecommunications Union* (ITU) committee. Two study groups within the CCITT developed data communications standards. The standards produced by the CCITT study groups are international versions of the standards produced by the EIA.
ITU-T	The ITU changed the name of the CCITT to the *Telecommunication Standardization Section* (ITU-T) in 1993. The ITU-T now has the responsibility for the recommendations and standards originally developed and supported by the CCITT.
ISO	The *International Standards Organization* is a worldwide group composed of representatives from member nations. The *American National Standards Institute* (ANSI) represents the United States. The ISO develops international standards for data communications. It also developed a seven-layer reference model for *Open Systems Interconnection* (OSI) to define a universal architecture for interconnecting different types of computer systems.
ANSI	The American National Standards Institute is the ISO representative for the United States. ANSI develops and publishes standards for communications and networking. The most recent ANSI standard that affects connectivity is the *Fiber Distributed Data Interface* (FDDI) standard for networks.
NIST	The *National Institute of Standards and Technology* develops and publishes the *Federal Information Processing Standards* (FIPS) used in government procurement.

continues

Table 3.1, Continued
Standards and Regulations Organizations

Organization	Description
FCC	The *Federal Communications Commission* develops and publishes rules and regulations that govern communications equipment in the United States.
DOD	The *Department of Defense* of the United States develops and publishes Military Standards called MIL Specifications.
CBEMA	The *Computer Business Equipment Manufacturers Association* provides standards for the computer industry in the United States. CBEMA provides the technical committee for the FDDI work done by ANSI.
ECMA	The *European Computer Manufacturers Association* provides cooperative development of standards for European countries. ECMA provides the technical committee for the OSI model.

Rules and standards help to ensure upward compatibility and a growth path to new computers. Although newer computers generally have more processing power than their predecessors, these same computers must interface with many peripherals designed for less powerful computers. The recommendations and standards published by the groups shown in table 3.1 bring some sanity to the often chaotic world of connectivity.

Many older devices were designed to handle data in smaller groups of bits and at lower speeds than new PCs can manipulate and transmit. American and international standards ensure that internal computer data are properly divided into smaller groups of bits and delivered to these external devices. Control signals are delivered along with data to tell the receiving device how to handle the bits. Standards also provide the framework for speed matching and message exchange between the PC and other external devices.

Standards play a major role in the physical implementation of connectivity. Any time you work at the physical level of an electronic system, you must have a complete and unambiguous definition of the physical connectors and media that connect two devices. Rules of clarity apply to the electrical signals that enable devices to communicate. If two devices cannot make proper physical connections or exchange well-understood electrical signals, they cannot communicate effectively.

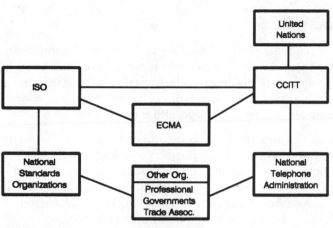

(a) International standards organizations.

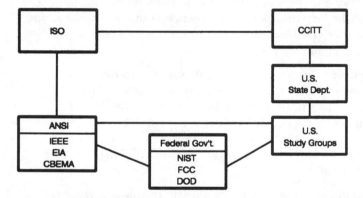

(b) United States standards organizations.

Figure 3.1
Relationships of standards organizations.

Many national and international standards apply to physical connectivity. An example is EIA RS-232D. As you see in detail in Chapter 8, "PC Communications Interfaces and Adapters," this standard covers all aspects of serial communications for a specific type of wiring configuration. The standard defines the physical requirements for the cable and the connectors at each end. The standard also defines the signal voltage required for each wire and the control associated with that signal.

Physical connectivity is only one of many areas you must work on when designing and building a complete system. Physical connectivity may even be the last element you define. It is, however, far from the least important aspect of connectivity. You must start with a firm physical foundation to ensure that all subsequent layers that build on this foundation perform as required.

Connectivity Layers

Over the past twenty years, vendors and international standards organizations have concluded it is best to describe and define connectivity in terms of layers. The classic analogy used to explain communications and networking layers is human dialog. During a conversation between two people three distinctive levels or layers make communication possible: cognitive, language, and transmission.

The *cognitive level* in a dialog requires that both parties understand the concept they are to discuss. Both parties do not have to have the same degree of understanding of the concept, but at least a fundamental understanding of the concept must exist at both ends of the conversation. For example, when a computer user calls a software hotline to solve a software-related problem, the help desk person should be an expert in the use of the software in question. The user making the call, on the other hand, is not expected to have the software knowledge that exists at the help desk. This user must be able to understand the software well enough to explain the problem to the help desk person. The expert at the help desk cannot, however, solve the end user's problem unless the user has some fundamental knowledge of the computer and software.

The *language level* of a dialog is concerned with the words that convey information—not the information itself. In the help desk example, both the help desk operator and the end user may possess the fundamental understanding of the computer and software that is not working properly, but unless both parties speak the same language, the problem cannot be solved. The solution to a problem spoken in German, regardless of how well explained, means nothing to an end user who only speaks English.

Finally, the *transmission level* of a dialog is concerned with the physical means of conveying information between two parties. At this level, the most appropriate physical technique is selected to effectively convey the information in a timely manner. In the help desk case, it makes sense to have end users communicate with the help desk operator by telephone if the help desk and the user are far apart. During the training of end users, on the other hand, the physical medium selected might be direct, face-to-face contact with the speaker combined with overhead projection of figures or text.

The last three paragraphs illustrate two fundamental concepts that make a conversation produce the desired results. First, each of the three layers is *independent* of the other. Each layer depends upon at least one of the other layers to be effective, but the contents of each layer are independent of the other. For a conversation to take place, a language must be spoken and the words must be conveyed between the parties, but the language chosen for the conversation does not affect the selection of the physical medium that transports the words. Second, both parties

must agree in advance as to the contents of each of the three layers. These agreements on the contents of each layer, with the underlying rules for the use of these contents, are referred to as *layer protocols*. These protocols are the interactions or *hand shaking* that takes place between layers. Layer protocols produce the "glue" that makes the entire process work to the satisfaction of both parties.

OSI Model

Just as conversations between two people require well-defined layers and protocols, computer networks must contain well-defined layers of functions and inter-layer protocols to control the interactions between computers. The connectivity model referenced most frequently by software vendors and used in network product design is the *Open Systems Interconnection* (OSI) model.

The ISO originally developed the OSI model to standardize the procedures for the exchange of information between processing systems. After six years of development activity, ISO working groups published the OSI reference model in 1983. The CCITT later adopted the model and gave it the designation *X.200*. The ITU-T now supports the OSI model.

The OSI model is gaining world-wide support. Organizations that struggled for years with inter-connectivity of systems from different vendors now have a standard to reference when procuring systems and connectivity solutions. Perhaps the greatest contribution to this momentum comes from United States federal government agencies. Compliance with the OSI model often appears in government requests for proposals for computer systems, as you will read later.

OSI Model Layers

The ISO working groups selected seven specific functional layers for the OSI model as shown in figure 3.2. These layers begin at the application layer, where end users interact with a system or where application software is executed. The layers progress down to the physical layer where logical information is converted into signals transported through physical media such as telephone wire.

Although the reference model defines the interconnection of open systems, the model assumes that these systems are composed of subsystems. As figure 3.3 shows, each layer in each system is contained in a subsystem. Each of these subsystems contains entities that provide services for a subsystem of higher rank in the model. All the network-support entities in a subsystem together form a layer in the model. *Peer-to-peer communications* between the entities in a given layer are done in accordance with specific rules defined by OSI protocols. Entities in one layer communicate with entities in another layer through well-defined *service access points* (SAPs) using specific *interface protocols*.

Figure 3.2
Reference model
for Open System
Interconnection
(OSI).

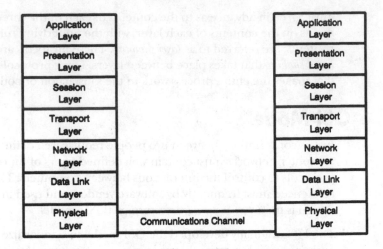

Figure 3.3
Open system
interconnection
layering.

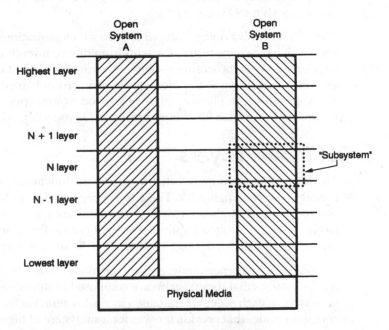

The reference model further defines the connections between layers and types of
data that pass through these connections. The entities in a layer have unique
addresses and communicate with entities in adjacent layers through service access
point connections. Normal and expedited data and network control information
are routed between entities through the service access points.

Expedited service data may be delivered across a connection before normal data sent earlier. The expedited data are never delivered later than normal data sent later than the expedited data. This interconnection of entities between layers and priority routing of data and control information form a complete network capable of tight control of information transfer using the layers described in the following paragraphs.

Physical Layer

The *physical layer* is the lowest reference model layer and the one that interfaces directly with the physical media. This layer supports *point-to-point connection* of two devices or *multipoint connection* of several devices, all of which can communicate with at least one of the devices attached to a multipoint line. The physical layer also supports both half- and full-duplex communication through either serial or parallel data paths.

The physical layer governs four basic areas of media connectivity. First, the mechanical characteristics of communication device interfaces are defined in this layer. Second, the physical layer governs the electrical signal design used to convey data. Third, the functional logic of electrical signals generated on certain wires in the physical media is specified in this layer. Finally, the physical layer defines the procedures or protocols that govern the sequence of events that must occur in order for the physical media to properly support the communications between two open systems.

ITU-T Recommendation X.21 is one important standard that defines physical layer requirements. The title of this standard is "General-purpose interface between DTE and DCE for synchronous operation on Public Data Networks" in which DTE is *Data Terminal Equipment,* and DCE is *Data Circuit-terminating Equipment.* This recommendation describes the interface required to operate a terminal or a microcomputer using the synchronous mode of communications to transmit or receive data through a public data network such as SprintNet or Tymnet.

The one aspect of X.21 that has not succeeded in the marketplace is its hardware interface requirements. X.21 calls for a nine-pin connection. Many implementations of X.21 use hardware that conforms with the EIA RS-232D standard instead. Later, this chapter examines the physical layer of connectivity in greater detail. Chapter 8, "PC Communications Interfaces and Adapters," looks at the specific hardware that implements this layer, including the EIA-232D interface.

Data Link Layer

The *data link layer* defines the protocol that detects and corrects errors that occur during data transfer through the physical media. The data link layer provides only error detection for asynchronous communications. Errors, therefore, must be corrected by higher-level hardware or software functions, often included in modem hardware or file transfer protocols. The data link layer in synchronous communications, on the other hand, provides complete error detection and correction.

The data link layer is responsible for dividing data traffic into *transmission packets* or *frames*. Data link functions provide the bits and bytes that separate and identify each field in a frame. This layer also ensures that data are made transparent to all communications devices such that all data pass through the network unaltered by the network and without producing side effects in the network.

Error correction and *frame sequencing* are important features of the data link layer. When errors are detected in received frames, this layer provides the request for retransmission of the bad frame. The data link layer also must ensure that data are delivered to the receiver in the same sequence in which they are transmitted. This layer also provides *flow control* to keep bottlenecks from developing and frames from accumulating in the open system.

The ISO standard *High-level Data Link Control* (HDLC) is the most important standard for the data link layer. The HDLC protocol is called *Link Access Protocol-Balanced* (LAPB) in the ITU-T X.25 recommendations for *packet-switched data networks* (PSDN). This *bit-oriented protocol* is replacing the less sophisticated byte-oriented protocols such as IBM's *Binary Synchronous Communications* (BSC) protocol. IBM's *Synchronous Data Link Control* (SDLC) is almost identical to HDLC, as you see in Chapter 6, "Synchronous Data Link Control."

Network Layer

The *network layer* handles the routing functions for data moving from one open system to another. This layer provides the addressing necessary to relay data through intermediate nodes or systems that provide the connectivity between nonadjacent open systems. The network layer ensures that data link layer frames are not lost when the frames traverse adjacent networks.

The network layer is the highest OSI level supported by some communication networks. As Chapter 7, "Wide Area Networks," discusses, the PSDNs based on *ITU-T Recommendation X.25* only support the first three OSI layers. Vendors and customers must provide the functions above the network layer.

Transport Layer

The *transport layer* of the reference model is responsible for maintaining a specific class of service for the user and for optimizing the resources that connect the two open systems. The transport layer establishes transport connections between session entities contained in two open systems. After a class of service such as batch

or interactive is selected, the transport layer establishes this service by setting up the necessary *transport connection*.

After the selected class of service is established, the transport layer is responsible for maintaining the service or notifying the session entities if sufficient resources are not available to maintain the class of service. The transport layer provides communications flow control beyond the frame-level control provided in the data link layer. To prevent congestion in a network, this layer segments *data* or *block data* to respectively form smaller or larger packets, thereby leveling the flow of data between session entities.

Session Layer

The *session layer* of the OSI reference model provides support for session connections between open systems. This layer manages the dialog between systems and is dependent upon the transport layer in the sense that each session connection is handled by one and only one *transport connection*. Several session connections can use one transport connection sequentially, but not simultaneously. The reference model does, however, enable the termination of one transport session and the initiation of another to overcome problems in a network—an action that might be required to maintain a specific class of service for a user. The session layer is designed to shield the higher layers from these changes in connection at lower layers.

The session layer manages the dialog between two open systems to ensure that data arrive at both ends of the link in a form meaningful to the applications operating at these ends. These services include controlling the two-way flow of data and synchronizing the data interchange between the open systems.

Beyond these services, the reference model enables the definition of further extensions to the session layer.

Presentation Layer

The *presentation layer* is responsible for controlling the syntax of data originated by two open systems and the transformation of data as they pass between these systems to ensure that the exchange of data is meaningful to both systems. This layer negotiates the data syntax between two systems at the start of a presentation connection and renegotiates a change in syntax if one is needed during the connection. For example, one system may use the ASCII character code and communicate with a system that uses the EBCDIC character code. The presentation layers of these systems must translate the characters as they pass between the systems. The presentation layers must provide ASCII-to-EBCDIC conversion in one direction and EBCDIC-to-ASCII conversion in the other direction.

The presentation layer is further responsible for *formatting data* to ensure proper output for specific devices. The presentation layer handles the mapping of screen display attributes from one system to another. For example, a host application written for IBM 3270 terminal display must have its output reformatted if the second open system used to access this application is not an IBM 3270 terminal. The reformatting of output for an IBM PC monitor when the PC is used to emulate a specific terminal type is another example of a presentation layer task.

Application Layer

The *application layer* is the highest OSI level. This layer contains *application entities* that control application processes through interactions called *application layer protocols*. The term *application* can be misleading, however, because this layer also controls operating system functions and the end-user interface with the system. Application layer protocols control the interaction between DOS and batch files. In an application such as a store point-of-sale system, the interaction between the sales and the inventory portions of the software also falls into this category.

The application layer protocols in this layer are normally classified in the following five categories or groups:

- ✔ Group 1—System management protocols
- ✔ Group 2—Application management protocols
- ✔ Group 3—System protocols
- ✔ Group 4—Industry-specific protocols
- ✔ Group 5—Enterprise-specific protocols

As these titles imply, the protocols range from horizontal significance, such as DOS and its internal and external features; to vertical significance, such as an accounting system and its combination of data and program files. The span is from national or international significance to industry significance and finally to individual store or company significance.

Reference Model Directions

Federal agencies were, at one time, leading the charge towards OSI conformance by enforcing the procurement of products that conform with the OSI model. The United States Government OSI Users' Committee developed the OSI procurement rules and published them in a document titled *Government Open Systems Interconnection Procurement* (GOSIP). The first draft of GOSIP was issued in 1986.

GOSIP began where OSI left off by defining the specific international standards that fall into each OSI layer. Figure 3.4 shows one draft of the GOSIP model. As you can see from this diagram, the federal government played a major role in the enforcement and refinement of OSI-specific protocols and compliant products. Recent revisions in the procurement practices of Federal agencies have removed the requirement for GOSIP conformance. Because of this change, information solution providers will have less incentive to conform with OSI protocols. Normal supply and demand in the marketplace will determine the industry endorsement and implementation of the OSI protocols.

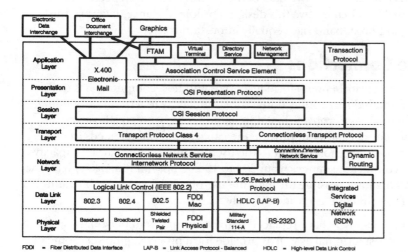

Figure 3.4
Government
Open System
Interconnection
Procurement.

FDDI = Fiber Distributed Data Interface   LAP-B = Link Access Protocol - Balanced   HDLC = High-level Data Link Control
FTAM = File Transfer and Access Method   MAC = Media Access Control

OSI and Data Transmission

This chapter explores the communications channel aspects of the OSI physical layer with an emphasis on PC connectivity. The following paragraphs build on information from Chapter 2, "Communication Channels," to show you how to create a system that includes both digital and analog channels. The basic concepts of digital and analog signal generation and modulation are expanded to explain the techniques vendors use to get data from a PC to local and remote computers and peripherals. This section is an illustration of the importance of standards in connectivity.

Physical Layer Functions

The physical layer of connectivity is responsible for the generation and delivery of signals that convey the information and data between two communicating devices.

The information and data originate as data bits, and the physical layer uses electrical signals to convey these bits. This layer is responsible for the delivery of bits from their source, through any number of communications channels, and finally to their destination.

Electrical Signaling Techniques

The physical layer may use several electrical techniques to transport data. For short-distance data transmission, *baseband* is often the technique of choice. Vendors build baseband channels that move data between devices at high speeds over short distances. Internal PC circuits have this design. For long-distance data transmission, baseband and broadband have equally important roles.

Direct Cable Connections

The physical connectivity between local terminals and host computers has traditionally been through direct connections. For connectivity in a room or building, vendors often use cables to convey digital signals directly between a host and a terminal. These special cables can provide the capacity a terminal needs to move user input to the host and host output to the user terminal. The channel capacity for these direct connections ranges from 300 to 19,200 bps. Bit rates as high as one million bps (1 Mbps) are possible through the use of special coaxial cables and matching synchronous communications hardware.

Over the past 13 years, users have replaced many terminals with personal computers that act like a host terminal as well as provide local processing power. Some of these same users have moved to configurations that require resource sharing between personal computers. These configuration changes brought changes in user requirements for channel capacity.

Local Area Network Connections

As user needs grew for high-volume data movement between a PC and a host, vendors began to realize the need for greater connectivity capacity. The connectivity method of choice is now the *local area network* (LAN). Although IBM developed and sold several connectivity systems in the 1970s that had LAN features and functions, Xerox Corporation produced the first system advertised as a local area network.

Xerox developed the signaling technique vendors now call Ethernet. IBM and others followed with other LAN implementations, but Ethernet still has a strong following in the marketplace. IEEE recognized the importance of Ethernet and published the 802.3 standard that defines the OSI levels 1 and 2 for this LAN. The standard calls for a maximum theoretical bit rate of 10 Mbps. Although actual 802.3 implementations often show an average channel capacity under 2 Mbps, this LAN design provides far greater signaling capacity than direct, digital cables.

IBM provided a strong contender for the 802.3 standard with the introduction of the IBM Token Ring network. The Token Ring, as specified in the IEEE 802.5 standard, uses the entire bandwidth of a cable to convey digital signals between network adapters. Through special synchronizing and regeneration techniques, IBM can provide either a 4 or 16 Mbps version of this LAN.

When communications needs go beyond the local area, direct-connection cables and LANs may not meet the distance requirements. Even with special cables and signal conditioners, these connectivity alternatives are limited to a radius of approximately six miles. When these limitations fall short of the distance requirements in a connectivity link, it is often necessary to communicate through a wide-area telephone connection.

Wide Area Network Connections

Many telephone systems existed before the advent of the computer and digital communications. These systems use analog electrical signals to convey the human voice across town or across the country. Newer telephone systems and the trunk lines that connect many telephone central offices are digital systems. The common carriers that provide telephone service to individual consumers also provide all-digital networks for subscribers with large data communications needs. All these telephone systems serve users over wide geographical areas—thus the name *wide area network* (WAN) is used.

Telephone systems that provide analog signaling at the user end require an analog connection. As you saw in Chapter 2, *circuit-switched* voice channels convey only analog signals that fall within a narrow bandwidth. A digital computer such as the PC must convert its internal digital signals into analog signals (tones that fall within the range the human voice can produce) that the telephone system can convey to the other end of the link.

The electrical interface at the user end of a circuit-switched analog connection (dial-up line) contains two wires that provide an electrical loop between the PC and the local central office. The PC must transmit and receive signals through this local loop. The maximum bit rate for this type of connection depends on the design of the modem that provides the conversion between the PC's internal digital signals and the external analog signals required for transmission through the telephone system.

The electrical interface of a leased-line analog connection contains two or four wires. These wires provide a direct connection between your computer and the one at the other end of the link. These lines are permanently pinned to create the circuit and are considered private lines. They often have special signal conditioning applied. The maximum bit rate of these leased analog lines is normally 56,000 bps.

A dial-up or leased-line WAN that starts out as analog at the user end may include digital circuits as a portion of the system. Telephone companies may convert these analog signals into digital signals to provide high throughput between central offices. The interface at the PC remains analog.

All-digital telephone systems require a digital connection at the user end. These systems may provide two or four signaling wires at the user's end and may be circuit-switched or leased lines. They enable the PC to convert its internal, unipolar digital signals into bipolar digital signals that can move through these wires and into the local central office. These all-digital WANs can support bit rates as high as 1.544 Mbps per user connection.

The digital data service provider may combine individual user circuits as it conveys them to a remote device or computer. PC equipment is responsible for meeting the data service provider's interface requirements. The service provider is responsible for maintaining the quality of the digital information and its delivery to a distant end. The oldest digital service in the United States is the *Dataphone Digital Service* (DDS) provided by AT&T. Other common carriers provide similar services.

The electrical signaling techniques two PCs use at two ends of a telephone system may be different. If a telephone system provides both analog and digital service, it may provide conversion between these two services. A PC at one end of the link can use analog signaling, and the PC at the other end can use digital signaling. Each PC must interface with and abide by the signal requirements at its end of the link.

Electrical Interface Controls

The physical layer of connectivity provides controls to ensure that data are properly conveyed and understood by a receiving device.

Electrical interface controls must travel through separate channels in parallel with data to coordinate functions between the sender and receiver. Later you see how communications adapters convert some of these electrical controls into elements of data transferred along with other data. The following paragraphs look at the two principal types of PC channels and the controls they provide.

Internal System Unit Bus

The PC system unit bus connects all the chips and components inside the system unit. The bus connects internal components to *input/output* (I/O) attachments that convert internal digital signals into signals conveyed to external devices such as printers and displays. Extensions to this bus connect to expansion slots that enable you to install adapters that can convey information from this bus to external devices.

The system unit bus actually consists of several communications channels. First, the data bus conveys data signals between components. Second, the address bus conveys data address information to the components that are to receive or send data. Finally, another series of channels convey command and control signals.

The original IBM PC contained a total of 62 printed circuit channels in its main I/O channel that included an eight-bit data bus. With the introduction of the IBM PC AT, IBM expanded the original PC bus. IBM added 18 new channels to handle additional data, address, and control lines in a configuration now called the *Industry Standard Architecture* (ISA). The ISA circuitry included a 16-bit data bus. The latest model IBM PS/2s have over 89 individual channels packaged together in a *Micro Channel Architecture* (MCA) bus. This bus contains 32 individual data channels and can convey either 16-bit or 32-bit data.

After IBM announced the proprietary Micro Channel Architecture, several vendors formed a consortium to develop a competing bus architecture to replace the aging ISA design. The result of their work is called the *Extended Industry Standard Architecture* (EISA). Many computer vendors now make personal computers that contain this bus. The EISA implementation enables you to retain older 16-bit ISA adapters when you migrate to the newer EISA-based computers that can support 32-bit adapters.

You must seriously consider the PC bus alternatives and available adapters when designing a total system. The selection of the bus design often dictates the design of the optional adapters. The different bus types have different physical expansion slots and different electrical signaling characteristics for these slots. You can install an old 8-bit IBM PC adapter in a PC that contains an ISA bus. You can also install an ISA adapter in a PC that contains an EISA bus. You cannot, however, install a Micro Channel adapter in an EISA-based computer or vice versa. Because of these compatibility issues, it is often necessary to decide on the design of the PC system unit before you begin the process of designing the remainder of a system.

Input/Output Attachments and Adapters

Connections between the PC and the outside world take place through built-in I/O attachments or through optional adapters. For the IBM line of personal computers, IBM designs the I/O attachments to match the system unit board and includes them as part of the board. IBM and others make optional adapters to extend these system unit capabilities. You must compare customer requirements to the capabilities that come with a system unit, and then decide what features to add.

To get from the internal bus to an external device, data must pass through an I/O attachment or adapter that works closely with the external device. This I/O control point conveys data to an external device through a set of connectors and a cable. It also provides signals that control the flow and use of data. The serial communications port in the PC is a good example of an I/O control point. Figure 3.5 shows the pin assignments for the EIA RS-232D connector that enables you to attach a device to this port. Each channel that goes between this port and an external cable carries a data or control signal.

Figure 3.5
EIA RS-232D
pin assignments.

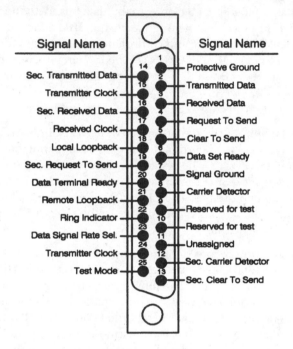

As you can see from figure 3.5, I/O attachments and adapters have a number of electrical interfaces. The device at the other end of the cable that connects with the port must understand and respond to the signals it receives. It must also provide its own set of signals to control the flow of data to and from the system unit. The signal assigned to each pin at the I/O control point must match the signal the device at the end of the link expects on that pin. Chapter 8 covers the details of the pin assignments of some popular connectors and cables.

Speed-Matching Functions

Another physical layer function is *speed matching* between different channels and is crucial for the interface between the PC system unit and I/O components. When it is not possible to make components and channels operate at matching speeds, signals must be stored someplace or periodically stopped. Without speed-matching capabilities, signals in one channel can overrun the capabilities of another channel resulting in lost or damaged data.

Vendors often include speed-matching features at levels above the physical layer. The protocols discussed in Chapters 5, "Communication Error Correction," and 6, "Synchronous Data Link Control," are examples of these high-level controls. Without some speed-matching support at the physical level, however, data could be lost before these high-level functions can react. As you see later in this chapter, most I/O attachments and adapters include registers and memory buffers that provide this minimum level of speed-matching.

Bit Stream Conversions

The physical layer performs the conversion of bits between parallel and serial communications channels. The PC uses either parallel or serial signals to communicate between components and devices. Most internal data and control movement is done through parallel channels. When it is necessary to move data or signals to devices and components outside the system unit, the communication channels can be parallel or serial.

Parallel connections with the computer's outside world may require little or no bit stream conversion. For the older 8-bit computers, such as the original IBM PC, no conversion was performed as data moved from the internal data bus to parallel channels that went to outside devices. The data moved from the internal bus, through the I/O adapter, and then on to the outside device. The I/O adapter handled all controls and signals, but did not have to funnel signals from one set of channels into a smaller number of channels. Parallel connections with more recent computers require bit stream conversions to match the large internal data bus with the smaller number of channels in external cables and devices. The physical layer functions in the parallel printer attachment must perform this conversion.

All serial connections with the outside world require *bit stream conversions* for all computers. The asynchronous data channels that connect the PC to a telephone system contain only one transmit and one receive channel. A serial I/O attachment or asynchronous communications adapter must convert data between the parallel data bus and the two data channels in the serial connection.

Bit Timing Functions

The physical layer plays a role in the determination and maintenance of the bit time that enables a receiver to segregate one bit from another. For both internal and external data transfer, the sending and receiving devices must agree on the duration of the signal that represents a binary digit. Chapter 2, "Communications Channels," reviews in detail the concept of *bit time* and its implications.

The physical layer functions achieve synchronized bit timing in one of two ways. First, two devices can be designed to operate at only one bit rate and form a matched set. The LAN adapters in two PCs connected to the same LAN are an example of this technique. The matched set simplifies the problem of synchronizing bit times between the devices. Second, devices may be designed to operate at a variety of bit rates. This design, typical of most data communications, requires more sophisticated bit time synchronization.

Transmission Framing

The physical layer provides the bits and data fields that enable the receiver to understand and use the information it receives. Aside from the data bits a sender transmits, it must also include flags and fields of data that enable the receiver to separate different kinds of information and deliver the information to the proper device or location. This *framing data* follows the signals that two devices exchange to synchronize bit times.

The physical layer can add framing information in three forms. First, it can add individual bits to delimit information. The asynchronous technique of serial communications calls for individual bits that separate bytes of data as they travel through a channel. Second, it can add characters that delimit specific kinds of information. The synchronous BSC protocol, for example, uses the STX character to signify the start of the information field in a BSC transmission frame. Finally, the physical layer can call for the addition of blocks of bits. The synchronous SDLC protocol uses eight-bit blocks to specify the address of a device and to provide control between devices.

Error-Checking Functions

The final physical layer function is *error checking*. The physical layer is responsible for the development and delivery of error-checking data. A receiver must check this error-checking data and report any errors to higher level layers for processing. Chapter 2, "Communications Channels," maintains that one of the advantages of digital communications systems is the end-to-end error checking and correction these systems can perform. The physical layer plays a major role in this important process, but complete error-correction functions are spread across several connectivity layers.

You can select an error-correction process by selecting a specific communications type. Because of the limited and controlled environment of the PC system unit, a simple form of error checking called *parity* is all that is needed to ensure proper operation. The channel lengths are short and the timing precise in the system unit. For communications with the outside world, error checking and correction is far more complex.

Error checking first became important during the development of asynchronous communications. During this period, it was necessary for a user to know that a communications link was not operating properly. The asynchronous communications type was not used for high-volume data traffic between computers. The parity error-checking technique was sufficient to support this type of operation. When data communications moved into high-volume data traffic during the 1960s, it became more important to detect and correct errors. Businesses could not afford to have mistakes in financial data or transactions that traveled through a data communications system. As you will read in Chapters 5 and 6, "Communication Error Correction" and "Synchronous Data Link Control," error detection and correction have made many advances during the last 30 years.

Physical Layer Summary

As you can see from the preceding paragraphs, the implementation of the physical layer of the OSI model requires rigorous adherence to standards. For computers to communicate properly, the physical hardware and electrical signals that tie them together must conform to well-defined rules and procedures. Any deviation from these standards can result in miscommunications and a failure of the connectivity between computers. Obviously, a failure at this level means a failure of the entire system.

Now that you understand the OSI model and its implementation in the physical layer, you can move on to higher levels of standards. Connectivity is necessary for computers to communicate and exchange data, but it is not sufficient to support the new trend in computing. The client/server movement demands an additional level of standards that, when complied with, ensures seamless, distributed computing in a system that consists of hardware and software from different vendors.

Distributed Computing Environment

As the day-to-day operations of most businesses and institutions depend to a large extent upon computers, users have become increasingly aware of the importance of open systems and interoperability between systems. Until the 1990s, large computer vendors were able to lock their customers into proprietary hardware and software systems. Although these systems created a standard that ensured a commonality between processors and peripherals, the standard forced the customer to stay within one vendor's set of products. The customer could sometimes choose a plug-compatible product or a clone of the vendor's product, but the customer was often responsible for ensuring that the product interoperated properly with other products.

Consumers in the 1990s are demanding open standards and the compliance of vendor products with these standards. Many organizations have established technical committees that define technical architectures for their organizations. These architectures define the rules, protocols, and standards with which computer and information systems must comply to meet the information exchange needs of the organization. The standards spelled out in these documents are often de facto industry standards or standards developed by national and international organizations.

The increasing popularity of distributed and cooperative processing, especially client/server implementations of these computing techniques, has resulted in the need for open systems standards for this area of computing. Two organizations that play a major role in promulgating such standards are the *Open Software Foundation* (OSF) and *UNIX International* (UI). Although both groups have a strong following, the OSF appears to be gaining the most momentum.

The OSF developed the *Distributed Computing Environment* (DCE) model for distributed computing, whereas UI developed the *Open Network Computing* (ONC) model. Minor differences exist between these models, but the DCE model has become more popular with vendors and application developers. Because of the popularity of this model, the following sections explore it and the *Distributed Management Environment* (DME) that builds on the DCE model.

DCE Elements

Rather than develop a set of open computing rules and guidelines in an ivory tower approach typical of many other standard-setting procedures, the OSF issued *Requests for Technology* (RFT) from computer vendors. From the responses, the OSF selected existing open and distributed computing system products as the basis for the DCE standards. With responses from over 50 vendors, the OSF had many alternatives for each area of the DCE. The participation of large vendors such as IBM, *Digital Equipment Corporation* (DEC), and Microsoft also helped ensure the acceptance of the standards that resulted from this solicitation.

DCE Architecture

DCE is a hierarchy of layers much like the OSI model, as shown in figure 3.6. Each layer builds on the functions in lower layers to provide the full support for distributed computing. The following paragraphs provide a brief explanation of some of these layers.

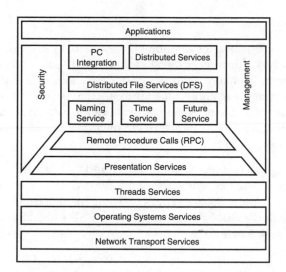

Figure 3.6
DCE
Architecture.

Threads Services

Distributed computing often requires the execution of parallel processes (*threads*) in the computers that share application functions. These processes execute concurrently to improve the performance and user acceptance of the application software. To facilitate this requirement, the OSF selected DEC's *Concert Multithread Architecture* (CMA) as the defining foundation for the *threads services* layer.

Remote Procedure Calls

OSF included *remote procedure calls* (RPC) as a layer in DCE to improve productivity in the development and deployment of distributed systems and to standardize the interface between client and server processors. The RPCs are written in a high-level language and execute in client processors to initiate standard application functions in server processors. These "macros" minimize data communications traffic in the network that connects clients with servers and provide an open access to multiple servers. The OSF chose Hewlett-Packard and Apollo's *Network Computing System* (NCS) 2.0 Remote Procedure Call as the basis for this layer.

The RPC is the glue that holds the DCE together. These scripts are easy to develop and provide a vendor-independent interface with servers—a critical aspect of open systems and distributed computing. They also support the execution of parallel threads as described earlier.

Naming Service

An important aspect of distributed computing is the capability to identify services available within a network. *Naming Service* calls for the list in a directory of anything a processor can access individually. Each service or device available to the network is considered an object, and each object has attributes that describe its features and functions. The data associated with each object is stored in a database called a *directory*. The DCE standards enable directories to include other directories in a hierarchical fashion.

To facilitate wide acceptance of the Naming Service and to ensure interoperability of processors world-wide, the OSF chose the OSI X.500 world-wide directory service as the basis for Naming Service. The X.500 implementation chosen for this basis was Siemens Nixdorf's DIR-X X.500 service. The OSF also added extensions from *DEC's Domain Name Service* (DECdns).

Time Service

Because of the physical and legal importance of time in a computer system, it is important to have the time synchronized between all computers that work in a cooperative processing architecture. With distributed processing taking place in many different time zones, synchronization is important to ensure the proper sequencing of timed events. The OSF selected *DEC's Distributed Time Synchronization Service* (DECdts) for this part of the DCE standards.

Distributed File Services

A key component in any distributed system is access to shared data. The OSF chose to add *Distributed File Services* (DFS) to the DCE to ensure open access (with appropriate security) to data. DFS simply enables a client processor to access and modify data stored in a file server processor. To minimize traffic in a DCE-compliant architecture, the OSF also calls for the caching of data in the client processor. When the client requests to modify data, a copy of the data is transported to the client processor in which it is cached during the read/modify operation. When the client processor completes the modification, the data is written back to the file server. A *token passing protocol* ensures the integrity of data in a multiuser environment—clients can modify data only when they have a *write token* from the file server.

PC Integration

PC Integration provides file access and print services for PCs operating under a variety of operating systems. The OSF selected Microsoft's LAN Manager/X for this portion of the DCE. Part III of this book provides a detailed description of this software.

Security

The integrity of distributed and cooperative processing systems and the security required to ensure this integrity are complex. The *security* function must identify system users and enable these users to perform only the operations they are authorized to perform. The OSF chose the Kerberos authentication system developed at MIT and enhanced by Hewlett-Packard. The Kerberos system is a security protocol that enables a client user to prove his or her identity to a server in a client/server environment. The client exchanges an encrypted Kerberos *ticket* with an authenication server. After the unique user ticket is authenticated, the user is given access to resources he or she is authorized to use.

Distributed Management Environment

Although management was a part of the original DCE model, the importance of this aspect of distributed computing has resulted in a new model that only deals with this aspect of system design. The OSF is currently developing a new set of management standards called the *Distributed Management Environment* (DME). To create this set of standards, the OSF issued RFTs just as it did for the DCE standards. The evolution and implementation of this set of standards will ensure the appropriate management and control of different types of systems that work together cooperatively to provide application functions in a multivendor environment.

Summary

You can see the importance of standards in the communications and networking industry from the information you read in this chapter. To provide connectivity between computers made by different vendors, you must depend upon these standards. The OSI reference model provides the overall guidance for standards and connectivity. You must, however, go beyond the global OSI model to achieve good connectivity between disparate computers.

The physical-layer functions reviewed in this chapter are only the beginning for connectivity. They provide an example of the importance of standards. To achieve meaningful communications and to support end-user applications, however, you must provide many more layers of connectivity functions. The client/server trend in computing, for example, demands an entirely new set of standards for distributed computing. As the power and pervasiveness of the PC continues to grow, the demands for standards to ensure connectivity between these and other computers also will grow.

The fundamentals explored in this chapter should provide you with a basic understanding of communications and networking. The remaining chapters of this book explore the techniques vendors use to implement the physical-layer functions. These chapters also explore the higher-layer functions that make connectivity meaningful for the end user.

Chapter Snapshot

The PC uses communications channels with the
characteristics described in Chapter 2 to send and
receive electrical signals both internally and externally
in order to move information and data between
devices. These signals and the physical devices which
convey them conform with hardware and software
standards that enable the PC to communicate with
other computers. In this chapter, you will learn the
following:

- ✔ The fundamentals of internal PC communications
- ✔ The fundamentals of PC communications with external devices
- ✔ An overview of data transmission techniques and protocols
- ✔ An overview of local area networking protocols

This chapter builds on information provided in earlier
chapters to show you more specific details of data
communications and networking. Use this chapter to
understand how all the physical and logical elements of
connectivity come together to enable the PC to interact
properly and effectively with other devices and computers.

CHAPTER

Data Transmission Fundamentals

The first three chapters provided a review of the fundamentals of signal generation and transmission. The role of standards in connectivity also was reviewed. Chapter 3, "Communications and Networking Functions and Standards," discussed the details of the physical layer of the *open systems interconnect* (OSI) model. You now are ready to apply this knowledge to data transmission between personal computers.

Data Transmission from Inside Out

Figure 4.1 shows the progression this chapter follows. The stand-alone PC's internal data bus is discussed first. You then explore the data input/output between the internal bus and directly attached peripherals. The differences between internal data movement and the movement of data to devices outside the PC system unit are presented next; and from communications with directly attached peripherals, you move on to communications and networking with other intelligent processors.

Figure 4.1
PC connectivity
alternatives.

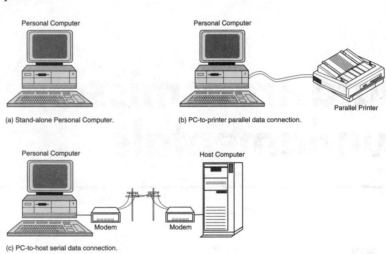

(a) Stand-alone Personal Computer. (b) PC-to-printer parallel data connection.

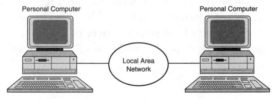

(c) PC-to-host serial data connection.

(d) PC-to-PC local area network connection.

Internal Computer Data Transfer

Although the PC has undergone many changes since IBM released the first model in August 1981, all PCs have one design aspect in common. Every PC has an internal set of channels that support high-speed data movement between chips and components inside the PC system unit. The channels that support this movement of parallel signals are collectively called the *I/O Channel* in the PC and the *Micro Channel* in the PS/2. The following paragraphs refer to both as a *system unit bus* or simply the *bus* unless there is a reason to distinguish between the two. Figure 4.2 shows a simplified diagram of the system unit bus contained in the PC.

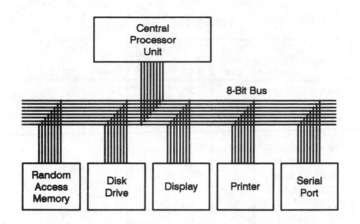

Figure 4.2
Simplified view
of a PC 8-bit
data bus.

The PC, like all other digital computers, stores and processes data as signals that represent logical 1s and 0s. Each of these 1s and 0s is a *BInary digiT* (*bit*) of information. When you combine eight bits into a group, the group is called a *byte* or an *octet*. The capability of a computer's CPU to manipulate bits determines its word size. If a CPU can store and manipulate eight bits at a time, it is a 16-bit CPU, and the computer built around this CPU is a 16-bit computer. In like manner, a CPU that can handle 32 bits internally is a 32-bit CPU, and the computer that uses the CPU is a 32-bit computer. Although these bit combinations are possible and PCs use these combinations, data movement between components in a system unit may not match the capability of the system unit processor.

As table 4.1 shows, the IBM PC's 8088 CPU could handle data in groups of 16 bits. These same data, however, moved through the system unit data bus eight bits at a time. The bus provided eight parallel data channels, a *byte-wide bus*, that could simultaneously convey eight individual electrical signals. The CPU reduced its internal storage from 16-bit words to eight-bit bytes before transmitting the data to other internal components—a multiplexing process called *gating*. Figure 4.3 shows a simplified diagram of this process.

After converting the 16 internal bits into two groups of eight bits, the PC's CPU sent the two bytes to other internal components. The eight bits traveled on data lines D0 through D7. The CPU began by placing the first bit, called the *least significant bit* (LSB), on line D0. It ended by placing the eighth bit, called the *most significant bit* (MSB), on line D7.

Table 4.1

System Unit	CPU Word Size	Data Bus		Micro Channel	
		8-bit	16-bit	8-bit	16-bit
IBM PC	16	X			
IBM PC XT	16	X			
IBM PC AT	16	X	X		
IBM PS/2 Model 30	16	X	X		
IBM PS/2 Model 50	16			X	
IBM PS/2 Model 60	16			X	
IBM PS/2 L40 SX	32		X		
IBM PS/2 Model 55	32			X	
IBM PS/2 Model 65	32			X	
IBM PS/2 Model 70	32			X	X
IBM PS/2 Model 80	32			X	X
IBM PS/2 Model 95	32				X

Figure 4.3
16-bit CPU gating 16 bits to an 8-bit data bus.

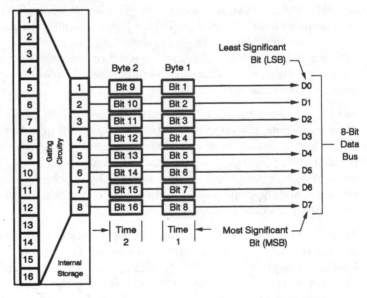

IBM designed later model PCs to both manipulate and move data in groups of at least 16 bits. Figure 4.4 shows this progression. As you can see from this figure, IBM PC ATs contained a 16-bit CPU and a 16-bit data bus. Early IBM PS/2 models contained a 16-bit CPU and a 16-bit Micro Channel bus. Later PS/2 models came equipped with a 32-bit processor and a 32-bit Micro Channel bus. The PS/2 Model 70 can communicate bits internally through either a 16-bit or a 32-bit channel, allowing vendors great flexibility in the design and manufacture of internal adapter boards. Other vendors provide similar support for both 16- and 32-bit buses.

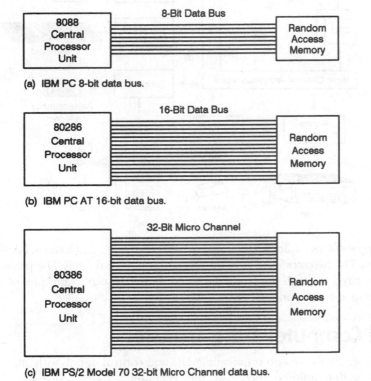

(a) IBM PC 8-bit data bus.

(b) IBM PC AT 16-bit data bus.

(c) IBM PS/2 Model 70 32-bit Micro Channel data bus.

Figure 4.4
IBM PC and PS/2 data bus progression.

Figure 4.5 shows a simplified diagram of a PS/2 system unit bus and the internal and external devices the bus can support. This bus can support other devices with the addition of optional adapters, as you see later in this chapter. The buses in other PCs provide similar support for internal and external devices. The adapters connect directly into the internal bus by plugging into expansion slots, sometimes called *I/O Channel Connectors*.

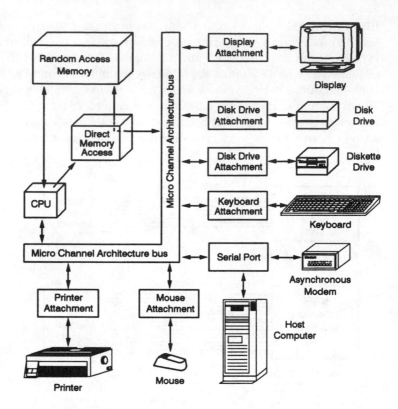

Figure 4.5
PS/2 Micro Channel Architecture bus and device support.

The following sections explore data transfer between the PC and external devices or processors. The two modes of data transfer are *parallel* and *serial*. The physical functions required for each mode are discussed, as are the two techniques of serial data transfer used in PC connectivity.

External Computer Data Transfer

The PC uses two modes of communicating data and control signals with an external device, depending on how close the computer is to the device. For distances less than ten feet, data are normally transferred using parallel communications. For distances between 10 and 50 feet, data can travel from the PC to another device through serial communications. Although both methods fall under the heading of input/output (I/O), many differences exist between these two types of communication. Serial communication is by far the most important type of connectivity that you encounter. The following paragraphs explore both modes of communication, but the emphasis is on serial data movement.

Parallel Data Streams

Parallel data channels can take several physical forms. Most of a PC's data buses are printed circuit boards. Other channels, such as the cable connecting the disk drive controller board to the disk drive in a PC, are flat ribbon cables.

Parallel data channels external to the PC system unit, such as the one shown in figure 4.6, are often shielded cables. This form of cable prevents extraneous electromagnetic signals from corrupting the parallel data signals as they move from source to destination. It also provides parallel paths that allow data and control signals to move simultaneously between the PC and the distant device.

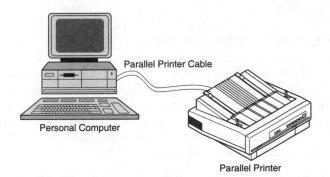

Figure 4.6
Parallel printer cable connection between a PC and a printer.

Parallel Printer Cable

Personal Computer

Parallel Printer

In parallel transmission, the number of bit values that transfer during one bit time depends upon the number of data lines conveying the data. For a system that contains eight data lines, eight bits transfer during one bit time. For a system with 32 data lines, 32 bits can transfer during one bit time. Obviously, the more data lines you can operate in parallel, the faster you can transfer data.

Serial Data Streams

The PC can communicate through one of two ways with a device located too far away for a parallel connection. First, you can install a direct serial cable between the PC and the device as shown in the 'a' section of figure 4.7. Second, you can install a local area network and connect the PC and the device to the network as shown in the 'b' section of figure 4.7. When the PC and the external device are too far apart for direct cable or LAN connections, you can install a modem to communicate with the device through the telephone system. Figure 4.7's 'c' section shows alternatives for this type of connection.

Figure 4.7
Serial
connections
between PCs
and other
devices.

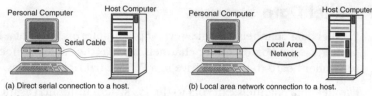

(a) Direct serial connection to a host.   (b) Local area network connection to a host.

(c) Serial cable connection between a PC and a modem.

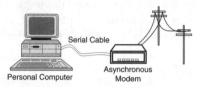

(c) Serial cable connection between a PC and a modem.

All serial connectivity has at least one common characteristic. In direct cable and network connections, data bits travel sequentially between a source and a destination. Although a cable or network can contain several physical channels, the data bits travel through a single channel. The connection can include two of these channels that allow data to travel in both directions simultaneously, but the data on one channel always travels in the same direction.

Serial data transfer requires conversion between the parallel data streams traveling through the PC's internal data bus and external serial bit streams. These parallel channels that convey from eight to 32 bits during a single bit time cannot convey these same data bits to and through a single channel using the same electrical techniques.

To fully appreciate data transfer alternatives, you must know some details of parallel and serial data transfer. The following paragraphs explore one parallel and one serial connection alternative to illustrate these data transfer modes. After this introduction, you explore the two techniques vendors use for serial data transfer.

Direct Parallel Connections

A CPU must transmit data bits to a parallel I/O attachment in groups that match the capability of the attachment's outgoing data bus. The CPU must break the parallel data stream into groups of parallel bits that match the number of data channels leading from the port to the external device. The number of data channels in the PC's parallel printer ports matches the design of the PC's internal character sets.

As discussed in detail in Appendix A, the PC uses the ASCII character set for internal character generation and storage. This character set requires a full eight data bits to represent all 256 characters the PC can display. When the PC communicates an ASCII character from one internal device to another or from the internal data bus to external parallel devices, it sends eight electrical signals to represent the character. Figure 4.8 illustrates this process. The PC's parallel printer port LPT1 is sending eight data signals that represent the ASCII character M through eight separate data lines to the printer.

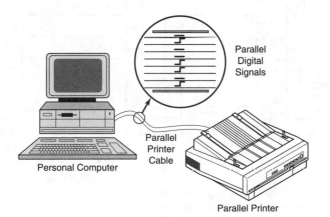

Parallel
Digital
Signals

Personal Computer

Parallel
Printer
Cable

Parallel Printer

Figure 4.8
Signal transmission through a parallel printer cable.

For simplicity, the original IBM PC with its eight-bit data bus is used to illustrate parallel data transfer. Figure 4.9 shows a simplified diagram of an eight-channel parallel cable connected to the parallel port of the PC. The PC's CPU in this figure contains the letter M. Assume that this CPU is executing software that is going to send the letter M to an external parallel printer. You can trace the movement of the digital signals that accomplish this task.

System Unit Data Bus

Figure 4.10 shows a snapshot of the electrical signals that convey the letter M from a PC's CPU through the system unit data bus to a parallel printer port. The CPU and its support chips place the signals for the letter M on the eight data lines simultaneously. The system unit clock acts as a strobe to tell the printer port when to read the signals on the data lines. The printer port samples all eight data lines and stores the logical binary values that match these signals.

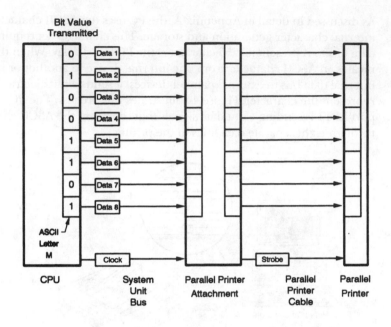

Figure 4.9
Parallel printer
connection
diagram.

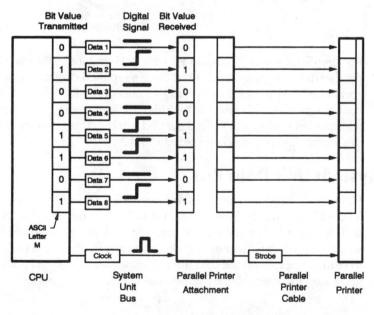

Figure 4.10
Parallel data
transfer from a
PC's CPU to its
parallel printer
port.

The parallel port stores the 1s and 0s in a temporary holding register while it prepares to send them to the printer. This register is part of the speed-matching functions of the port. It provides a one-byte buffer between the printer and the system unit bus. The CPU can start sending another character to the port without destroying the values sent for the previous character. This gives the port time to process the last character before it has to sample for the next one.

External Parallel Channel

The parallel printer port works through parallel control and data channels to coordinate and transmit data to an external device. After the printer port stores bit values for the letter M in the preceding example, it checks to make sure that the printer is ready to receive the character. The port reads the voltage signals on the control lines that return signals from the printer. If the printer is signaling an error, out of paper, or other fault condition, the parallel port must hold the letter M and notify the CPU of the problem.

The parallel printer port uses special interrupt signal lines to send alerts to the CPU. These interrupt lines are part of the PC system unit bus. The CPU handles interrupt signals on a prioritized basis. It responds to alerts from different devices in an order established by either the computer designer or the software the CPU is executing.

If the printer is available and ready to receive print data, the printer port creates the voltages that represent the M on the eight data lines that go to the printer. The parallel port then uses its own strobe signal as shown in figure 4.11 to tell the printer when to sample the signals on the data lines. After the printer receives the strobe, it reads the data lines and converts the voltage it reads into a series of logical 1s and 0s. The printer then goes to a local memory module, looks up the character that matches the series of bit values, and prints the character.

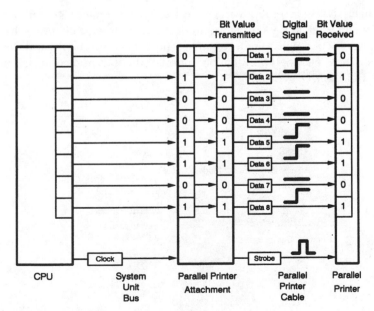

Figure 4.11

Parallel data transfer from printer port to printer.

Personal Computer Connectivity

The throughput of this type of parallel I/O is usually limited by the rate at which the destination device can handle data. The maximum data rate of the CPU, the system unit bus, and the parallel port normally exceeds the data rate of a parallel printer by a large margin. Other devices, such as an external disk drive, that require a parallel connection may be able to keep pace with the PC system unit. The software that controls the CPU must work closely with the parallel port that in turn works closely with the destination device to keep the rate of data flow within the range the device can handle.

Keeping parallel digital signals synchronized, as described in the preceding paragraphs, is not difficult because of the short distances the signals have to travel. Keeping parallel signals synchronized over long distances is more difficult. The electrical characteristics of no two wires are the same. Electrical signals do not travel at the same velocity through two different wires. When parallel channels are short, the mismatch in signal arrival times at a destination is small. The differences can be overcome with clock control signals.

When parallel channels are long, the mismatch in signal arrival times can be large. Control signals cannot overcome this large skewing of signal arrival times. The control and clock signals also are affected by this phenomena. Thus, for long-distance communications, it is often more practical and more economical to use serial communications equipment than to install parallel cables and the devices that enable them to function properly.

Direct Serial Connections

Serial data channels take several physical forms. Serial data channels external to the PC system unit, such as the one shown in figure 4.12, provide channels that allow control signals and data to move simultaneously between the PC and the distant device. These channels prevent corruption of the data and control signals as they move from source to destination.

Figure 4.12
Serial cable connection between a PC and a modem.

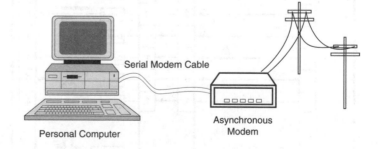

Serial Modem Cable

Personal Computer

Asynchronous Modem

The serial cable between the PC and the first external serial device normally contains only two data channels—one for sending and one for receiving data. This is in stark contrast to the parallel cable that contains eight parallel data channels. In parallel transmission, the number of bit values that transfers during one bit time depends upon how many data channels the parallel cable contains. In serial data communications, data bits move one at a time between the source and the destination. During one bit time, only one bit value moves from the sender to the receiver.

An important factor in serial data transfer is the timing of data transmission and the timing of data receipt. In parallel data transfer, data bits move simultaneously from source to destination, leaving no doubt about the association of bits with bytes. Serial data communication is not so simple.

Serial Communication Techniques

The techniques of serializing parallel data streams for transmission to the outside world are *asynchronous* and *synchronous*. As presented in Chapter 2, "Communications Channels," these techniques have many common characteristics. They also have a few significant differences. Figure 4.13 shows the primary functions of a serial communications adapter. This figure applies to both asynchronous and synchronous communications through serial cable connections.

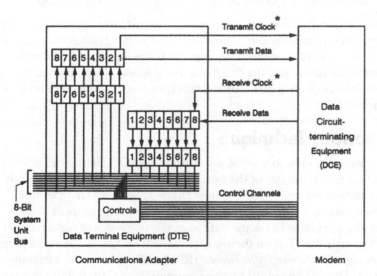

Figure 4.13
Overview of serial port principal operations.

For asynchronous transmission, the bit stream itself must contain its own synchronizing data for each byte of data. No separate clock signals are transmitted between an asynchronous port and the *data circuit-terminating equipment* (DCE) at the other end of the cable. The DCE gets its synchronization information from the beginning of the stream of binary data signals it receives from the port, or *data terminal equipment* (DTE).

Because of the higher speeds and the lower synchronization overhead normally associated with synchronous communications, the delivery of a synchronous data stream requires precise timing. Some synchronous DTEs send a *transmit clock* signal to a synchronous DCE through a clock channel that runs parallel with the data channel. Other synchronous DCEs separate the clock signal from the data stream they receive from a remote device and deliver that clock signal to the synchronous DTE along with the data. These clock signals enable the synchronous DCE and DTE to perform precise modulation of the data signals.

As you see in Chapter 8, "PC Communications Interfaces and Adapters," you can use the same *EIA RS-232D* cable between the two types of serial ports and a DCE. Some vendors also make DCEs that provide both asynchronous and synchronous modes of communication in the same unit. You can use one cable and one modem to communicate both asynchronous or synchronous data to remote devices. You just have to move the cable back and forth between the two types of serial ports or install a switch that enables you to match a port with a DCE operating mode.

Because of the common characteristics of serial communications techniques, you can learn many communications and networking fundamentals from the study of one technique. The asynchronous technique in the following paragraphs illustrates serial communications with the PC. At the completion of this discussion, you explore the details of both asynchronous and synchronous data transfer and how they work with the PC.

The Asynchronous Technique

A CPU must transmit data bits to a serial, asynchronous I/O attachment (*serial port*) in groups that match the size of the port's internal holding register just as it does in parallel communication. This *Transmit Holding Register* (THR) can hold eight bits at a time. When a CPU sends data to a serial port for transport to an external device, the port must break the data stream into groups of eight parallel bits that move through the THR on their way to the external device. A serial port also contains an eight-bit *Receive Buffer Register* (RBR) that captures the incoming serial data stream. The CPU can retrieve this incoming data eight full bits at a time.

These eight-bit transmit and receive registers match the asynchronous communications technique well. The maximum number of data bits an asynchronous port can transfer in a single transmission frame is eight bits. For synchronous protocols, the

transmit and receive buffers must be much larger. Instead of a single eight-bit register, most synchronous communications and networking adapters contain at least 8,000 bytes of memory dedicated to this buffering task.

To move data from the transmit register or buffer to a serial cable, a serial port must perform bit stream conversion. Figure 4.14 illustrates this process for the PC's serial port. The port receives data eight bits at a time through the PC data bus. The port hardware then performs a parallel-to-serial conversion for all eight bits. The port sends the data bits sequentially, one bit at a time, through the serial communications channel. PC serial port hardware must transform this serial bit stream back to a parallel bit stream at the receiving end.

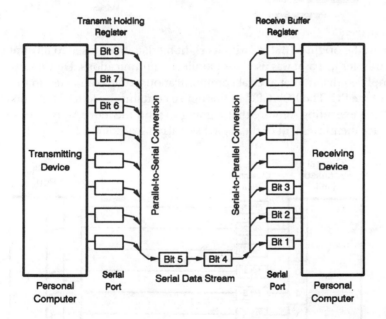

Figure 4.14
PC serial data channel.

Figure 4.15 shows a typical serial data communication channel for a PC. A serial communications cable connects the PC to a modem. As you can see from this figure, the serial data flows through the cable as a series of digital electrical signals. This kind of short-distance serial communication is relatively easy to implement because you can include wires to convey control and synchronization signals. For longer distance communications through the telephone system, it is not possible to send control and synchronization signals through separate channels. All signals travel through the same two wires.

Personal Computer Connectivity

Figure 4.15
Serial data flow
from a PC to a
modem.

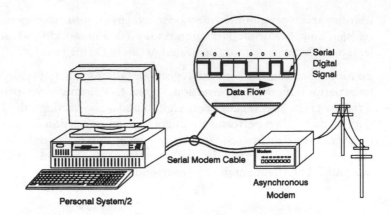

For simplicity, the original IBM PC with its eight-bit data bus is used to illustrate serial data transfer just as it was used for parallel communications. Figure 4.16 shows a simplified diagram of a serial communications cable connected to the serial port of the PC. The PC's CPU in this figure contains the letter M. Assume that the CPU is executing software that is going to send the letter M to an external modem. Trace the movement of the digital signals that accomplish this task.

Figure 4.16
Serial data
channel between
a PC and a
remote serial
device.

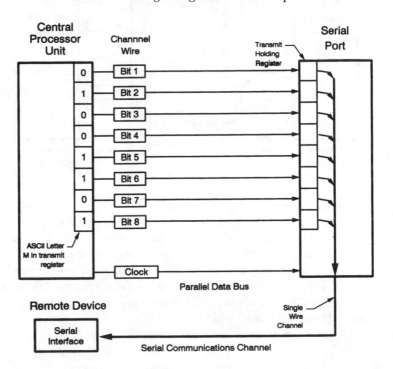

System Unit Data Bus

Serial I/O looks very much like parallel I/O for part of the data movement to the outside world. Figure 4.17 shows electrical signals that convey the letter M from a PC's CPU through the system unit data bus to a serial port. The CPU and its support chips place the voltage signals for the letter M on the eight data lines simultaneously. The system unit clock acts as a strobe to tell the port when to read the voltage on the data lines. The serial port samples all eight data lines and stores the logical binary values that match these voltage signals.

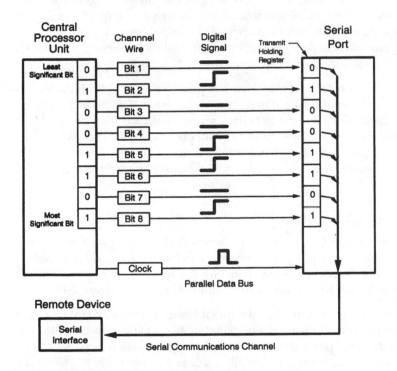

Figure 4.17
Parallel digital data stream for the letter M.

The serial port stores the 1s and 0s in a Transmit Holding Register while it prepares to send them to the modem. This register is part of the speed matching functions of the port. It provides a one-byte buffer between the port and the system unit bus. The CPU can start sending another character to the port without destroying the values sent for the previous character. This gives the port time to process the last character before it has to sample for the next one. Data communication software often provides additional buffering between the serial port and the software receiving or sending data through the port to improve system operations.

Controls and Interrupts

The serial port works through control channels to coordinate the transfer of data to an external device. After the port stores bit values for the letter M in the preceding example, it checks to make sure that the modem is ready to receive the character. The port reads the voltage signals on the control lines that return signals from the modem to the port. If the modem is not presenting a *Clear To Send* (CTS) signal, the port must hold the letter M until the modem is ready to receive it.

The serial port, just like the parallel port, uses special interrupt signal lines to send alerts and status to the CPU. These interrupt lines are part of the PC system unit bus. The CPU handles interrupt signals on a prioritized basis. It responds to interrupts from different devices in an order established by either the computer designer or the software the CPU is executing.

The operations of a serial port must have top priority for the CPU. If the CPU does not watch the status of the port, it may send a new byte of data to the port before the port has successfully sent the last character out to the external device. The receiving process requires the same level of attention. If the CPU does not remove a character from the port immediately after it arrives, the next character can overwrite the last one. Few other PC operations require this attention to detail and precise timing.

External Serial Channel

The serial port conveys bit signals to an external device through a transmit data channel. If the modem is ready to receive data, the serial port creates the voltages that represent the M on the transmit data line that leads to the modem. Each data bit moves sequentially from source to destination as shown in figure 4.18.

The serial port multiplexes the digital values it has in its Transmit Holding Register. The signal it produces is a series of digital signals separated in time intervals. At a minimum, the serial port must transmit eight digital signals to represent the letter M. As you see later, the port actually sends at least two more bits with each byte of data for synchronization and separation of the data bytes.

The serial port in figure 4.18 sends the letter M one bit at a time. The port starts with the least significant bit and ends with the most significant bit. The modem sees a series of voltage changes on its serial interface. The serial interface must interpret these voltage changes as data bits.

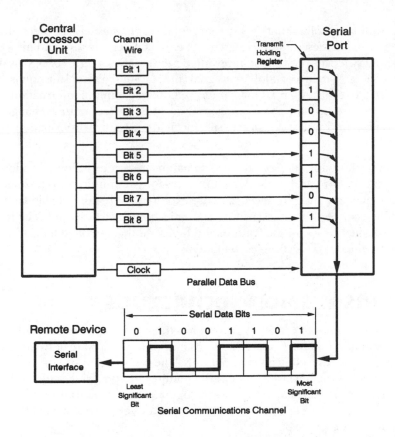

Figure 4.18
Serial digital data stream for the letter M.

Asynchronous and synchronous ports use different techniques to ensure the proper interpretation of data at the remote serial device. If the port is asynchronous, the modem must decipher the digital value of the signal on the transmit data line and modulate the value to a signal it can send on to the remote receiver. If the port is synchronous, it sends a clock strobe to tell the modem when to sample the signal on the transmit data line. When the modem receives the strobe, it reads the data line and converts the voltage it reads into a logical 1 or 0. The modem then modulates the digital signal to a signal it can convey through the telephone system.

The throughput of this type of serial I/O is usually limited by the maximum data rate of the serial port or the destination device. The maximum bit rate of the CPU and the system unit bus normally exceeds the bit rate of a serial communications port. Other serial connections, such as a local area network, may keep pace with a slow PC system unit. In any event, the software that controls the CPU must work closely with the serial port that in turn works closely with the destination device to keep the rate of data flow within the range the devices can handle.

Proper interpretation of a serial data stream requires *synchronization* between the data source and data destination to segregate bits, characters (bytes), and messages. Without synchronization, the receiving device receives a series of signals that have no meaning. Synchronization that signals the start of data transmission is necessary for the received signals to be interpreted as meaningful information. Beyond the synchronization phase, two communicating devices must exchange transmission bits or frames that contain specific fields of control, information, or data.

The following paragraphs explore the two data transmission techniques vendors use in communications and networking. Concepts for communications through the telephone system are introduced, and are explored in greater detail in later chapters. For example, Chapter 8, "PC Communications Interfaces and Adapters," contains a detailed review of the features and functions that enable the PC to communicate through direct cables to modems.

Data Transmission Techniques

Serial communications and networking requires the transmission of data link controls in addition to data. Communications hardware or software adds or deletes these OSI data link layer controls automatically. The information synchronizes the clocks contained in the hardware of both the sending and receiving stations. This ensures that the receiving station properly recognizes the signals transmitted by the sending station. The pattern of ones and zeros must not become distorted through the communications process.

The two serial communications techniques vendors use to synchronize and control data communications between computers are asynchronous (also called *start/stop*) and synchronous. The asynchronous technique is prevalent in several protocols. The PC's asynchronous communications port uses this protocol to transmit and receive a data stream compatible with the *teletypewriter* (TTY) terminals used in the 1950s and 1960s.

Optional adapters are available for the PC to implement the synchronous communications technique. The three most popular protocols that define the rules for message exchange through telephone systems are *Binary Synchronous Communications* (also called BSC or Bisync), *Synchronous Data-Link Control* (SDLC), and *High-level Data Link Control* (HDLC). If you connect a PC to a remote IBM host, you invariably use one of these protocols.

Optional adapters also are used to connect the PC to *local area networks* (LANs) that use synchronous communications. As you see later in this chapter, LAN communications provide rich connectivity between PCs located in a limited geographical area. Serial, synchronous communications techniques vary from one LAN vendor to another. All the techniques, however, include common denominators that make interoperability between networks possible.

Asynchronous Transmission

Historically, digital communications followed the capabilities and features of the devices used to convey information. The first devices to use digital communications on a large scale were printing telegraph systems. Although the first such systems simply automated the printing of messages sent in Morse code, subsequent systems quickly evolved to print both text and numbers.

In 1874, Jean Baudot, an officer in the French Telegraph Service, developed the first code of binary digits that devices could transmit long distance to remote printers. He designed this five-bit *Baudot code*, shown in Appendix D, to handle the physical characteristics of slow mechanical printers. The code contained only 32 characters, numbers, symbols, and controls that, by today's standards, was a small character code. The Baudot code revolutionized communications, nevertheless, because it could convey these elements of information in equal time intervals.

Baudot Communications

Baudot transmitters were somewhat cumbersome compared to today's intelligent terminals. An operator at one end of the link keyed in information at a terminal that produced a paper tape containing punched holes. The holes represented the text in equally spaced patterns. The operator then fed the tape into a Baudot transmitter. The transmitter converted the series of punched holes into a series of high and low voltage signals.

Because of the relatively constant speed of the paper tape feeder, the Baudot transmitter could produce a series of digital voltages a remote printer could easily decipher. As the transmitter encountered a series of punches that represented a character, it generated five equally long signals starting with the lowest order bit and ending with the fifth and highest order bit. Figure 4.19 shows the bit and voltage pattern the transmitter produced for the letter A. The voltage signals traveled across the country to a remote Baudot printer in the order shown in this figure.

A distant Baudot printer identified and printed text from the voltage signals it received. Early Baudot systems did not use a special signal to signify the start of a character. The printer had to assume that a character was inbound when the transmission line voltage went from an idle state to one of two binary signal states. After identifying the start of a character, the printer used its own built-in timing devices to decode the five voltage signals that represented each character. Later Baudot systems used a start and stop bit shown in figure 4.19 to signal the start and end of a character.

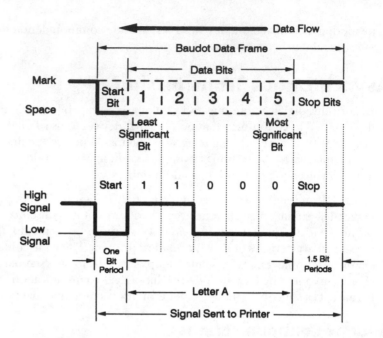

Figure 4.19

Baudot transmission of the letter A.

A lack of high-quality clocks and synchronizing signals limited these early digital communications. Devices had to use long digital voltage signals. The resulting transmission speeds were not much faster than a good typist can generate manually today. The Baudot operator could not directly transmit information from a keyboard, however, because the lack of precise clocks required the use of the paper tape as a synchronizing technique. Many features and characteristics of this early type of transmitter and receiver prevail today as you see throughout this book.

As commercial and military needs grew for faster and more powerful digital communications, scientists and engineers responded with improved signal synchronization and character sets. Innovations in technology during the 1920s and 1930s provided more precise electrical clocks and signal sampling techniques that supported faster data rates. American data processing experts contributed to this evolution by creating the seven-bit *American Standard Code for Information Interchange* (ASCII—pronounced "ask-he"). The original ASCII code contained 128 unique characters, numbers, symbols, and control signals still in use today as discussed in Appendixes A and B.

Asynchronous Start/Stop Communications

The combination of improved electrical timing and character codes lead to the serial signaling called asynchronous or start/stop communications. Serial ports or internal asynchronous modems that implement this technique, as shown in figure

4.20, divide text, data, or binary information into small groups of bits. For the PC, the asynchronous, serial port hardware breaks a data stream into groups that are 5, 6, 7, or 8 bits in length.

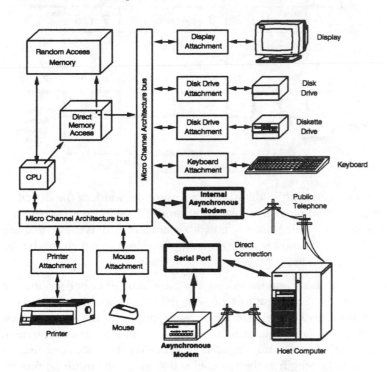

Figure 4.20
Asynchronous communications alternatives.

Asynchronous hardware gives to each group of bits it transmits a frame that delimits one transmitted group from another and provides synchronization between the transmitter and receiver. Figure 4.21 shows one of these asynchronous frames of digital signals. The following paragraphs provide a simplified overview of this *byte-by-byte synchronization*.

Asynchronous data, as their name implies, are not a continuous flow of synchronized bits. The communications hardware adds synchronizing information to every byte it transmits. As illustrated in figure 4.21, each asynchronous byte begins with a start bit that tells the receiving device to begin measuring the subsequent data for the presence of 1s and 0s. A high-voltage signal on the data line always precedes the start bit. This *marking line* or *marking state* provides a clear contrast for the start bit and allows the receiving device to detect the beginning of a new start bit.

Figure 4.21
Asynchronous transmission frame of digital signals.

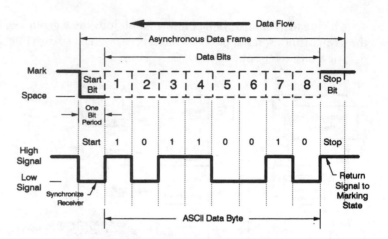

The asynchronous receiver must identify and measure the width of the digital signal that marks the start of an asynchronous frame. This start bit must have a value of zero, sometimes called a *space*. Its width in milliseconds is the *bit time* of the digital signal. The receiver must set its signal sampling clock to match this bit time for the duration of the asynchronous transmission frame.

After successfully identifying and measuring the interval of an asynchronous start bit, an asynchronous receiver measures the voltage in the channel at the end of each subsequent bit time. For eight-bit serial communications, the receiver does this sampling eight times and translates the signal strength it reads into a series of eight bit values it stores in a holding register. The receiver then does one final sampling of the signal strength in the channel at the end of the ninth bit time to verify the proper end of a transmission frame.

Asynchronous communications require that each transmitted frame ends with at least one stop bit. This last bit period must contain a value of one, sometimes called a *mark*. The mark originally provided the receiver time to process received data, and its duration had to be long enough for slow mechanical devices to finish their work. Current electronic devices require no more than one stop bit to accomplish their data processing tasks. This bit period returns the signal in the channel to the *marking state*, which allows the receiver to find the center of the next start bit.

The presence of a *stop bit* at the end of the asynchronous transmission frame enables the receiver to verify proper synchronization with the digital signal stream. If the ninth bit sample does not produce a value of one, the receiver assumes that a synchronization problem exists and discards the eight bits it collected earlier as data. If the ninth bit is a mark, the receiver assumes that synchronization is correct and processes the eight data bits. While processing the eight data bits, however, the

receiver must continue to monitor the channel for the arrival of the next asynchronous frame. The next frame may arrive any time after the preceding one. A new start bit may begin at the end of the stop bit from the previous frame.

The transmitter determines how close to its maximum capacity an asynchronous link operates. The asynchronous channel is operating at maximum efficiency when frames arrive contiguously at the receiver. The bits in each frame must be contiguous. The frames do not have to be contiguous. If the transmitter can operate fast enough to keep data flowing into the channel on a continuous basis, the only time lost during the transmission is the time required for all the start and stop bits to pass through the channel. No national or international standard exists for an asynchronous protocol that requires contiguous communications of asynchronous data frames. Standards do exist, however, that require contiguous transmission of frames in synchronous communications.

Synchronous Transmission

The move from asynchronous to synchronous communications followed many of the same technological innovations that allowed asynchronous communications to flourish. In the early 1960s, just as the asynchronous technique for connecting terminals to host computers was becoming popular, IBM decided it was not good enough for reliable, high-speed communications in an enterprise environment. IBM also concluded that the seven-bit ASCII character set did not provide enough symbols and controls to support networks of terminals and computers.

In the mid-1960s, IBM announced and began to ship products that implemented the synchronous flow of a new eight-bit character set, the *Extended Binary Coded Decimal Interchange Code* (EBCDIC—pronounced "ebb-see-dick"). The characters and the binary codes that represent these characters are shown in Appendix C. *Binary Synchronous Communication* (BSC) was the new data link protocol based on a synchronous-serial, digital communications technique. Figure 4.22 shows a simplified diagram of a BSC transmission frame.

As shown in figure 4.22, BSC supports the transmission of both transparent and non-transparent data and text—information that can contain strings of bits that match BSC control characters. The DLE STX control character sequence allows BSC to essentially turn off the search for and reaction to bit strings that look like protocol signals. The OLE ETX sequence of characters ends the transparent communication mode. When BSC is operating in the non-transparent mode, the devices that implement the protocol continuously look for protocol control characters and take appropriate action when they detect these characters.

Figure 4.22

Binary
Synchronous
Communication
(BSC)
transmission
frames.

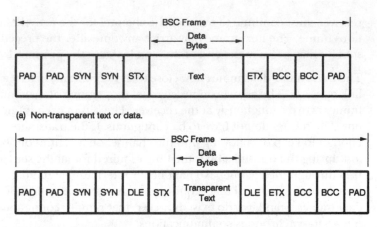

(a) Non-transparent text or data.

(b) Transparent text or data.

The combination of improved electrical timing that took place in the 1960s and the new EBCDIC character code allowed IBM to implement this popular communications protocol that is still in use today—over 30 years later. Hardware that implements BSC divides text, data, or binary information into groups of eight bits or bytes to match the number of bits in the EBCDIC character code. The hardware performs both physical and data link layer functions as you see in later chapters.

Binary Synchronous Communication

You can install an optional adapter in a PC expansion slot as shown in figure 4.23 to implement the BSC protocol. The hardware serializes the parallel bit stream from the PC data bus to match the requirements of a synchronous modem or communications channel. It also deserializes the bit stream from a DCE to match the requirements of the PC data bus. The adapter provides framing bytes and error-checking information to the bytes it transmits—data the receiver uses for synchronization and error detection. The adapter also interprets this same data it receives from other BSC systems. Finally, the BSC adapter participates in the determination and interpretation of the sampling rates required to support the synchronous serial flow of digital signals.

After successfully identifying and measuring the interval of a synchronous bit signal, a BSC receiver measures the voltage in the channel at the end of each bit time. The receiver does this sampling eight times and translates the signal strength it reads into a series of eight bit values it stores in a holding buffer. The receiver then checks the contents of the holding buffer to see if it contains control information or text.

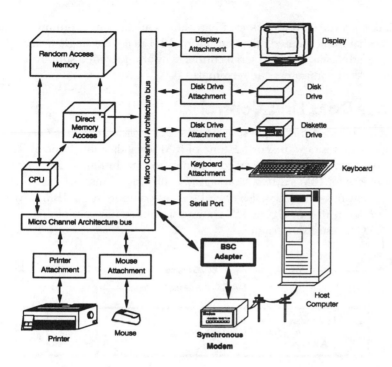

Figure 4.23
BSC optional
adapter data
flow path.

In contrast to the individually framed bytes transmitted in an asynchronous frame, BSC sends blocks of data framed by *control characters*. For example, the STX character signals the start of a string of text characters. The ETX signals the end of a string of text characters. A BSC receiver must monitor the communications link to identify these control characters. The BSC hardware keeps the text or data enclosed in the transmission frame and throws away the control characters. The end of the BSC frame contains two *Block Check Characters* (BCC) that allow the receiver to identify errors in the frame and request a retransmission of the frame, as discussed in Chapter 6, "Synchronous Data Link Control."

After implementing BSC in many hardware devices, IBM discovered the protocol did not adequately support one of the computer hardware configurations customers wanted by the mid-1960s. BSC performed well in direct, *point-to-point* connections between primary and secondary communications hardware. It also worked well in *multipoint* connections in which more than one device shared a single communications channel. BSC did not, however, perform well in a loop configuration in which each device had to receive the BSC frame and retransmit it to the next sequential device.

IBM also discovered that the character orientation and hardware-dependent implementations of BSC allowed too many limitations to creep into the connectivity between devices. The protocol allowed too many variations. The implementation of each variation produced unique sets of hardware that could not communicate with hardware that implemented other variations. IBM needed a single transmission architecture that standardized serial connectivity and provided support for complex networks of computers and terminals.

Synchronous Data Link Control

In 1969, IBM announced and began shipping the *Synchronous Data Link Control* (SDLC) protocol that is now the cornerstone of IBM serial data link control. This bit-oriented, synchronous-serial, digital communications technique is now one of the building blocks for IBM's *System Network Architecture* (SNA) discussed in Chapter 7, "Wide Area Networks." SDLC is also one of the key components in IBM's *Systems Application Architecture* (SAA). Figure 4.24 shows a simplified diagram of this ubiquitous SDLC transmission frame.

Figure 4.24
Synchronous
Data Link
Control (SDLC)
transmission
frame.

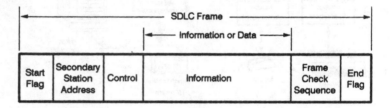

Although SDLC is an IBM invention, international communications groups adopted the technique with little change. The international implementation of SDLC is *High-level Data-Link Control* (HDLC) and is the basis for most digital synchronous systems that span different countries. Chapter 6, "Synchronous Data Link Control," covers the details of both SDLC and HDLC. For now, this chapter concentrates on the modulation and demodulation of the binary signals that make these synchronous-serial techniques possible.

You can install an optional adapter in a PC expansion slot to implement the SDLC physical and data link layer functions as shown in figure 4.25. The hardware serializes the parallel bit stream from the PC data bus to match the requirements for a digital data channel. It also deserializes the bit stream from the data channel to match the requirements of the PC data bus. The adapter provides framing bytes and error-checking information to the blocks of bits it transmits—data the receiver uses for synchronization and error detection. The adapter also interprets this same data it receives from other SDLC-based systems. Finally, the SDLC adapter participates in the determination and interpretation of the sampling rates required to support the synchronous-serial flow of digital signals.

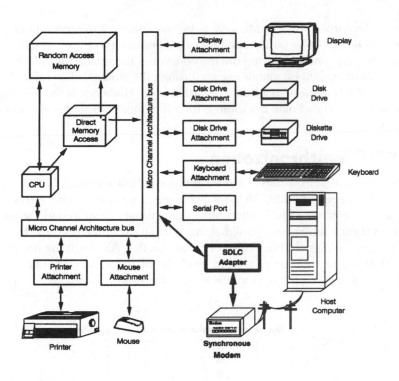

Figure 4.25
SDLC implementation with the PC.

SDLC is a *bit-oriented protocol* compared with the byte orientation of BSC. The SDLC protocol does not segregate information bits into characters. After the receiver decodes the Flag, Address, and Control fields, it receives and stores the bits in the Information field without concern for their content or meaning—a process called *transparent* communications.

An ending *flag* sequence of bits tells the SDLC adapter when it has reached the end of a frame. While reading this field, the adapter goes back and checks the previous 16 bits—the *Frame Check Sequence* (FCS)—to make sure that the frame contains no detectable errors. If the FCS does not match the information in the frame, the receiver requests a new copy of the frame from the transmitter. If the FCS and the information match, the SDLC adapter makes the information available for the PC to process.

Although a synchronous communications link can be more efficient than an asynchronous link, the implementation of the synchronous technique determines the ultimate efficiency of a link. The synchronous channel is operating at maximum efficiency when frames arrive contiguously at the receiver. The bits in each synchronous frame must be contiguous.

Information and control frames do not have to be contiguous. If the transmitter can operate fast enough to keep information or data flowing into the channel continuously, the only time lost during the transmission is the time required for synchronization and control bit signals to pass through the channel. The ratio of overhead to actual information in a frame determines the efficiency of the frame. SDLC requires less overhead than BSC, and is therefore more efficient under most circumstances.

BSC and SDLC Synchronization

BSC and SDLC use different strings of bits for frame synchronization. A BSC transmitter sends two eight-bit EBCDIC SYN characters. Two of these characters in contiguous sequence provide the 16 alternating signal voltages required to identify the boundaries of each subsequent bit signal. An SDLC transmitter, on the other hand, sends 16 zero bit signals followed by one eight-bit flag. Although the flag has the pattern 0110001, the transmitter actually sends the digital signal shown in figure 4.26. This technique of signal modification is *Non-Return to Zero Invert* (NRZI) on one.

Figure 4.26
Non-Return to Zero Invert (NRZI) on zero-bit insertion.

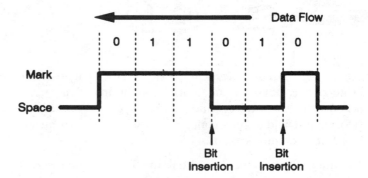

IBM originally implemented NRZI to overcome the problem of signal drift. Long strings of equal bit values kept the voltage at the same level in the channel for long periods. Without signal transitions during these long periods, the clocks of the transmitter and receiver could lose their synchronization. NRZI produced enough signal transitions to ensure synchronization between the clocks for the duration of a transmission frame.

The BSC link maintains synchronization after the initial SYN pair by using a steady flow of SYN characters in the text field. A BSC adapter inserts a SYN about once a second. The receiver uses the SYN bit sequence to verify or modify its bit time. The receiver throws away these SYN characters. The PAD character provides a known signal between BSC frames.

This sequence of bits allows BSC to continue communications when the transmitter has no data to send. It also provides a clear delimiter for the start of the next BSC frame.

The SDLC protocol depends upon the inclusion of a continuous flow of synchronizing information in the signal stream between the transmitter and receiver. The protocol uses zero bit insertion to provide this clock signal along with the other signals it sends and receives. The transmitter does the clock signal insertion. The receiver must separate the clock signal from the other signals and verify or correct its bit time. The clock signals add much less overhead to the bit stream than the SYN characters the BSC protocol uses.

Local Area Networks

The most recent implementation of synchronous connectivity is in LANs as shown in figure 4.27. Figure 4.28 shows the transmission frames for the three predominant types of LANs—Ethernet, Token Bus, and Token Ring. As you can see from this figure, all the transmission frames for these LANs differ somewhat, but they contain about the same information. This information flows as a continuous stream of bits using many of the same techniques the BSC and SDLC transmission frames use.

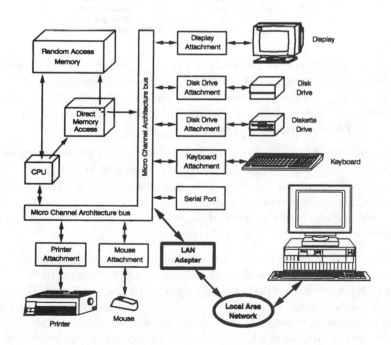

Figure 4.27
LAN-attached PC data flow paths.

Figure 4.28
Local area
network
transmission
frames.

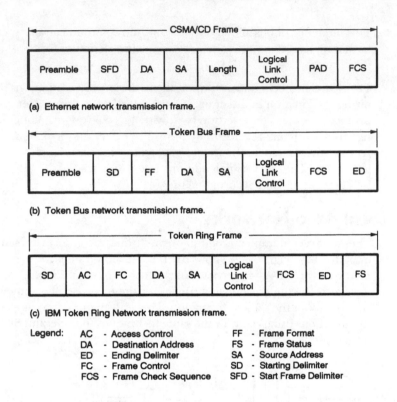

(a) Ethernet network transmission frame.

(b) Token Bus network transmission frame.

(c) IBM Token Ring Network transmission frame.

Legend:
AC	- Access Control	FF	- Frame Format
DA	- Destination Address	FS	- Frame Status
ED	- Ending Delimiter	SA	- Source Address
FC	- Frame Control	SD	- Starting Delimiter
FCS	- Frame Check Sequence	SFD	- Start Frame Delimiter

Local area networks use a series of binary signals at the beginning of each transmission to synchronize communications between LAN adapters. These strings of bits, called a *preamble* or flag, are the precursor for each packet of data that traverses the LAN. They contain enough signal transitions to enable the receiver to determine the bit time of the LAN transmission frame.

To further enhance the determination of bit time, most network implementations use the *Manchester Encoding* technique shown in figure 4.29. The Manchester technique was first used with the Ethernet LAN. It produces a signal transition with each bit time and allows each network adapter to recover the clock and remain synchronized with the clocks in the other adapters on the network. This technique requires a bandwidth double that of the data rate.

For the baseband, Token Ring network, one adapter on the network acts as an active monitor to make the bits flow through the network at a constant speed. Because this LAN is constantly processing transmission frames, a preamble is not needed. The network adapters must, however, derive the clock signal from the bit signals in the transmission frames. The encoding can be Manchester or the addition of bits that convey the clock. These techniques provide signal transitions when transmission frames contain long strings of 1s or 0s.

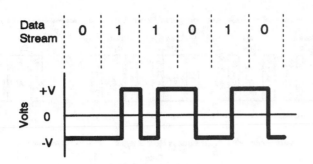

Figure 4.29
Manchester
encoding.

Synchronous Advantages

Synchronous communications and networking has several advantages when compared with asynchronous communications. One advantage is inherent in the technique of synchronizing the bit times between the sender and receiver. Other advantages came about because of the standardization of the higher levels of synchronous protocols as Chapter 6, "Synchronous Data Link Control," illustrates.

Asynchronous communications requires a high volume of synchronizing signals compared with synchronous communications. Each character or element of data that goes through the communications channel must have a flag to indicate the beginning and end of each byte of data or text. These flags have the equivalent length of one bit each. When you add these flags to the eight data bits required to transmit a byte of data, you add a 20 percent overhead to each byte you transmit, as shown in figure 4.30.

Synchronous data transfer, on the other hand, allows two devices to exchange synchronizing information once and then communicate for long periods with a minimum of resynchronization bits included in the data stream. The lower overhead of synchronous transmission makes a significant difference when two systems must exchange large volumes of data over a short period. Some vendors take advantage of this synchronous benefit by converting an asynchronous data stream into a synchronous data stream as they send the data stream through the telephone system to a distant device. A matching set of hardware at the receiving end demodulates the data stream back to an asynchronous stream of bits before they are delivered to the receiving device.

Another advantage of synchronous communications is that the data stream is a continuous flow of bit signals. If the receiver stops receiving the flow of signals, it immediately knows a problem exists. With the periodic flow of asynchronous signals, the receiver does not have an immediate indication when a communications link or transmitting device has failed. This and other features of synchronous transmission are discussed when later chapters explore the protocols in the layers above the physical layer.

Figure 4.30
Comparison of serial data transmission frames.

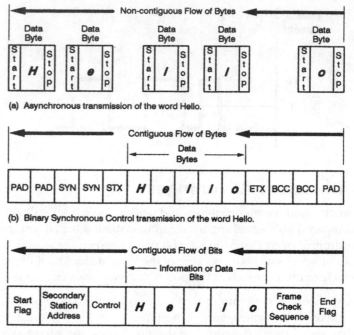

(a) Asynchronous transmission of the word Hello.

(b) Binary Synchronous Control transmission of the word Hello.

(c) Synchronous Data-Link Control transmission of Hello.

Summary

Data communication has come a long way since the era of teletypewriter terminals, but the legacy of early communication techniques stays with us today. The signaling techniques that became known as *asynchronous* provided a needed service for many years. Commercial and military organizations developed strategies and performed vital operations based on the communications that went through these links.

With the arrival of efficient synchronous data transmission, digital communications and networking have taken a permanent foothold in worldwide communications. Vendors and international organizations continue to up the ante every year for better and faster data transfer. Although this spiral requires improved technology, improvements in the data transfer methods and procedures also contribute to better and faster communications. New data transfer technologies enable vendors to do the same old tricks at a quicker pace. Better communications procedures often produce even more dramatic results.

The fundamentals explored in this chapter provide you with a basic understanding of data transfer. With this background, you now can explore the more complex and sophisticated aspects of connectivity that enable you to make the PC an integral part of a larger system of processors.

Part II

Data Communications

Chapter Snapshot

Data communications and networking would not be providing the services they provide today, nor would the growth of the information systems industry have been as great over the past 20 years, without communications error detection and correction. Businesses demand near perfection in data storage and manipulation. They demand no less as data moves between one computer and another. Errors caused by communications can be just as costly to a business as the errors created by application software. In this chapter, you learn the following:

✔ The basics of error detection and correction

✔ The hardware and software techniques of error detection and correction

✔ File transfer protocols

✔ Modem-to-modem error correction

Communications error detection and correction is currently available in a myriad of hardware and software products. Use this chapter to understand the strengths and weaknesses of the most popular techniques and protocols used to ensure the integrity of data as they move between computers.

CHAPTER

Communications Error Correction

Since the first implementation of a system designed to convey digital information, users and vendors of these systems have shared a concern for the detection of communications errors. When the telegraph system moved from a "nice to have" status in the early 1900s to a mission-critical system to support military and commercial users in the 1940s, error detection became a major concern. As data traffic grew following World War II, vendors took a serious look at detecting and correcting errors, and the control of data flow.

Chapter 2, "Communications Channels," reviewed the fundamentals of communications channels and explored both analog and digital signal modulation. Chapter 3, "Communications and Networking Functions and Standards," introduced the concept of layers and the OSI model. The lowest OSI level, the physical layer, used for serial communications and networking was also discussed. Chapter 4, "Data Transmission Fundamentals," covered the fundamentals of data transfer through external communications channels. This chapter goes one step farther and explores the error detection and correction functions of the OSI data link layer for asynchronous communications.

The techniques of data link control used in asynchronous communications are reviewed in chronological order, beginning with the causes and effects of data communications errors. Next, this chapter looks at the evolution of error control, data framing, and data routing. The following three chapters build on the information provided in this chapter. As you will see, the functions that fall within the data link layer of connectivity for asynchronous communications have much in common with the same functions in synchronous communications, local area networking, and wide area networking.

Communications Errors

Data communications errors can produce catastrophic results if not quickly detected and corrected. An error in the transmission of financial data can cause accounting books not to balance or the amount of a transaction to be recorded incorrectly. An error in the transfer of an executable software program can cause the software to malfunction or keep the software from operating at all. To prevent these types of problems, the system must detect and correct data communications errors before the transferred data are put in use on the receiving end of the communications link.

Data communications errors are undesirable changes in the bit patterns of data that occur after the data go from the internal PC bus en route to an external device or computer. The only acceptable changes that occur in data beyond that point are intentional changes created to alter data in a way that can be reversed on the receiving end. For example, hardware or software can compress data on the sending end to speed up communications; hardware or software must decompress that same data on the receiving end. Hardware or software also may encrypt data on the sending end and decipher the data on the receiving end to provide secure communications. This hardware or software must detect and eliminate unintentional data changes that occur in the communications link.

To understand the process of detecting and correcting errors, you must first understand the causes and effects of data communications errors. Errors can appear at any point along a communications link. When a personal computer sends data out the communications port, a bad set of hardware chips in the port can generate errors in the data stream. A poorly designed or manufactured modem can add errors to data as it modulates the data stream and sends it out through a telephone line. Faulty telephone company equipment also can generate errors. A bolt of lightning near a telephone line can create electrical noise and alter the signal patterns that represent data as shown in figure 5.1; a motor that starts near a telephone line can create noise also; or the modem or communications port on the receiving end of a link can generate errors.

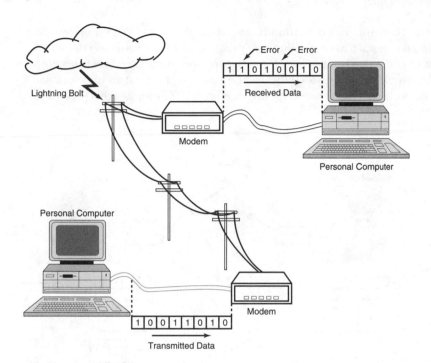

Figure 5.1
Communications
errors induced
by lightning.

Data communications systems must detect and correct damaged data communications signals. A system must detect interferences of short duration that only change one bit in a byte of data. The same system must detect interferences of long duration that create bursts of errors. All error-detection techniques are not, however, equally adept at handling both types of errors as you see later in this chapter.

Redundancy Error Detection Techniques

To detect and correct communications errors, a sender must provide a receiver with information that enables the receiver to verify proper receipt of information or data. The sender could simply send an entire set of information twice and let the receiver compare the two sets of information for error detection, but because of the time and computer resources it takes to perform this type of comparison, most people prefer other techniques. Vendors meet this demand with error detection methods based on mathematical calculations that hardware or software execute at high speeds.

The sender must use a mathematical technique to calculate error-checking data. The sender generates this *redundancy data* from the bit stream of information data it sends, and then appends the redundancy data to the end of the bit stream. The receiver must generate its own redundancy data from the information data it receives and compare the results with the redundancy data it receives from the sender. A favorable comparison indicates the absence of errors; an unfavorable comparison indicates the presence of errors. Figure 5.2 illustrates this process.

Figure 5.2
Creating and checking redundancy error-detection data.

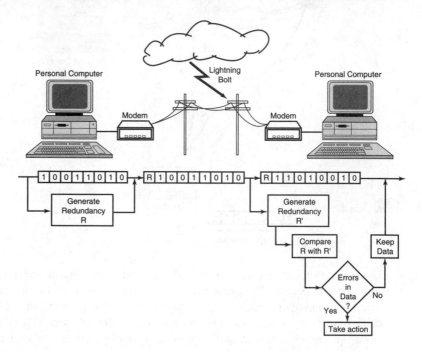

A sender and receiver must use identical techniques of generating redundancy information. The three error-checking techniques are: *vertical redundancy checking* (VRC), *longitudinal redundancy checking* (LRC), and *cyclic redundancy checking* (CRC). Sections 'a' and 'b' of figure 5.3 illustrate the respective VRC and LRC techniques of calculating error-detection data.

VRC requires the addition of a single bit to each byte of transmitted data to produce a specific parity for the entire byte. The sender and receiver can use either even or odd parity. Section 'a' of figure 5.3 shows the even parity algorithm, and section 'b' shows odd parity. If the sender is using even parity, it must ensure that each byte ends with a bit value that makes the entire byte contain an even number of 1 bits. If the sender is using odd parity, it must ensure that each byte ends with a bit value that makes the entire byte contain an odd number of 1 bits.

LRC requires the addition of a single byte (one character) after each string of transmitted bytes (characters). The LRC byte, as defined by ISO standard ISO-1155, must provide even parity for each longitudinal string of bit positions. The sender and receiver can use either even or odd parity as a VRC in combination with even parity for the LRC. Section 'a' of figure 5.3 shows the even parity VRC and even parity LRC; section 'b' shows the odd parity VRC and even parity LRC. This LRC character, sometimes called a *checksum*, checks the sum of the binary values for each bit position for all transmitted bytes.

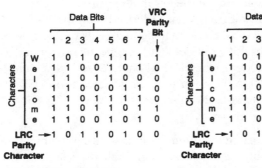

Figure 5.3
Vertical and longitudinal redundancy checking.

(a) Even VRC and Even LRC

(b) Odd VRC and Even LRC

The CRC can take several forms. Table 5.1 shows the four most popular polynomial equations used in CRC calculations. The selection of a specific communications protocol often dictates the use of a specific type of CRC. Vendors use the CRC-12 with older protocols when transmitting 6-bit character codes. For example, vendors use the CRC-12 with the *Binary Synchronous Communications* (BSC) protocol when transmitting the Six-Bit Transcode. More reliable communications protocols, on the other hand, use either the CRC-16 or the CRC-CCITT to calculate 16 bits of error detection data. The CRC-32 provides a full 32 bits of error detection data and is an option in many protocols. LAN protocols use the CRC-32 to ensure error-free data transfer.

Table 5.1
Mathematical Equations for Different Types of CRC

CRC Type	CRC Polynomial
CRC-12	$X^{12} + X^{11} + X^3 + X^2 + X + 1$
CRC-16	$X^{16} + X^{15} + X^2 + 1$
CRC-CCITT	$X^{16} + X^{12} + X^5 + 1$

continues

Data Communications

Table 5.1, Continued
Mathematical Equations for Different Types of CRC

CRC Type	CRC Polynomial
CRC-32	$X^{32} + X^{26} + X^{23} + X^{22} + X^{16} + X^{12} + X^{11} + X^{10} + X^8 + X^7 + X^5 + X^4 + X^2 + X + 1$

The error-checking data produced by a protocol is the remainder after the protocol divides its polynomial value into all the bits that require error checking. Protocols produce CRC data by dividing a constant (derived from the CRC polynomial) into the binary values of all bits contained in a block of data it transmits. The protocol discards the resulting quotient and retains the remainder. The protocol then appends this remainder to the block of bits as a *block check character* (BCC) or *frame check sequence* (FCS). A receiving station calculates its own CRC for the block of bits it receives and compares this remainder to the BCC/FCS it receives to determine the presence of errors.

Both the LRC and CRC error-detection techniques are more accurate than the VRC. The VRC is good for detecting single-bit errors in single bytes of data. The LRC is good for detecting single-bit and multiple-bit errors in individual bytes of data. The CRC-16 detects all single- and double-bit errors, all errors in bit streams with an odd number of bits in error, all error bursts shorter than 16 bits, and 99.9 percent of error bursts longer than 16 bits. The CRC-32 detects essentially all errors, which is the primary reason the IEEE selected this technique for all LAN standards.

Hardware or software can execute error detection either continuously for the duration of a communications session or for specific portions of a session. Asynchronous communications can use either of these techniques, whereas synchronous communications always use the continuous error-detection method. Asynchronous communications can execute error detection at the data byte level by examining the bit pattern in each byte of data or at the data packet level by examining the bit patterns of groups of bytes. Synchronous communications execute error detection at the packet level only. The following paragraphs examine both techniques.

Data Link Control

The layer of functions in a communications link that detect and correct errors is the data link layer. The first implementations of these functions were in the communications between teletypewriter terminals and provided little more than error detection. As communications became more sophisticated with the introduction of synchronous bit streams and complex data flow control, the data link layer of connectivity became a critical set of functions.

The following paragraphs review the data link functions vendors call *Data Link Control* (DLC), beginning with the rudimentary DLC functions in asynchronous communications and moving on to the more sophisticated procedures that make synchronous protocols the most powerful data movers of the 1990s.

Asynchronous Error Detection and Correction

Asynchronous communications hardware or software can perform three forms of error detection and correction. The simplest form of error detection is the *parity check* described earlier. The asynchronous communications adapter or the internal modem adapter executes this form of error detection for each byte of data transmitted if instructed to do so through software controls. Communications software operating in the PC on the receiving end of the link must monitor for these errors by reading certain hardware registers.

The next level of error detection for asynchronous communications is the *file transfer protocol*. Communications software normally executes these error-correcting file transfers. The highest level of error detection and correction is the continuous packet assembly and disassembly technique. Communications hardware or software can execute this procedure. The following sections provide detailed discussions of these three popular error-correcting techniques.

Parity Error Detection

Parity error detection has several limitations. Vendors have used parity error detection in data communications hardware and software since the 1960s, but this technique provides little value today. Most communications software available for the PC enables you to select even or odd VRC parity when transmitting with less than eight data bits. This selection enables you to communicate with older systems that still use parity error detection. The PC can monitor this parity, but typically ignores the results.

Parity error detection serves a useful purpose for communications between dumb terminals and large computers. The absence of parity errors indicates a good communications connection, whereas the presence of parity errors indicates a poor communications connection. The corporate communications manager can make reconfiguration decisions based on the level of parity errors on specific communications connections. With the introduction of the IBM PC with its eight-bit character set and high-speed communications capabilities, parity error detection became an antique. Because of its continuing presence in asynchronous hardware, however, the following paragraphs provide a brief explanation of this technique.

Input/Output Registers

Input/Output (I/O) registers in an asynchronous communications port or modem adapter activate, initialize, and monitor VRC parity error detection. Figure 5.4 provides a simplified diagram of the National 8250 *universal asynchronous receiver/transmitter* (UART) contained in most asynchronous communications hardware available for the PC. Figure 5.5 shows a list of the registers the two standard PC serial ports provide in their UARTs. The *Line Control* and *Line Status Registers* provide the initialization and monitoring windows into the communications hardware. The *Interrupt Enable Register* enables these registers to generate interrupt signals that tell the CPU to execute specific tasks.

Figure 5.4
Universal asynchronous receiver/transmitter (UART).

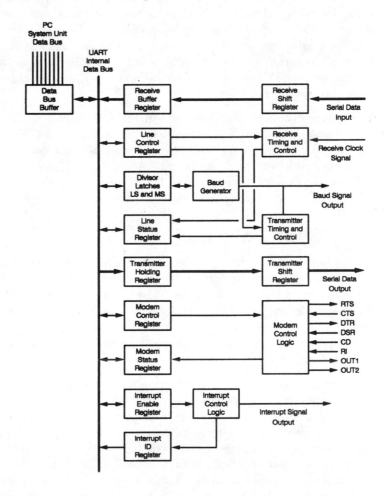

UART Register Address		
COM1 Adapter	**COM2 Adapter**	**Register**
3F8	2F8	Transmit Buffer
3F8	2F8	Receive Buffer
3F8	2F8	Divisor Latch LSB
3F9	2F9	Divisor Latch MSB
3F9	2F9	Interrupt Enable
3FA	2FA	Interrupt Identification
3FB	2FB	Line Control
3FC	2FC	Modem Control
3FD	2FD	Line Status
3FE	2FE	Modem Status

Figure 5.5
PC asynchronous port registers.

As shown in figure 5.6, the *Line Control Register* (LCR) selects and enables specific types of parity. LCR bit 3 turns parity error detection on and off. By setting bit 3 to a value of 1, you activate parity detection. By setting bit 3 to a value of 0, you deactivate parity detection. If you activate parity, LCR bits 4 and 5 enable you to specify the type of parity you want. If you deactivate parity, the values of LCR bits 4 and 5 have no meaning.

Line Control Register Bit Position							
7	6	5	4	3	2	1	0
Division Latch Access Bit	Set Break 0 = off 1 = on	Select Parity 000 = None 001 = Odd 011 = Even 111 = Space 101 = Mark			Stop Bits 0 = 1 1 = 2	Number of Data Bits 00 = 5 01 = 6 10 = 7 11 = 8	

Figure 5.6
Line Control Register (LCR).

LCR bit 4 selects even or odd parity. When you activate parity and set bit 4 to a value of 1, the port sends an even number of 1 bits in each byte and checks for an even number of 1 bits in each byte it receives. When you activate parity and set bit 4 to a value of 0, the port sends an odd number of 1 bits in each byte and checks for an odd number of 1 bits in each byte it receives.

LCR bit 5 selects mark or space parity. When you activate parity and set bit 5 to a value of 1, the port sets the parity bit to 0 for space parity for each byte it sends out. When you activate parity and set bit 5 to a value of 0, the port sets the parity bit to 1 for mark parity for each byte it sends out.

II

Data Communications

As figure 5.7 shows, the *Line Status Register* (LSR) monitors the data stream for parity errors. If the LSR detects a parity error, it places a value of 1 in bit 2. The only way the PC user can know about the error, however, is through communications software. If the communications software turns on the asynchronous port's interrupt logic, the detection of a parity error results in the generation of an interrupt signal for the PC's CPU. The communications software must respond to this interrupt and determine its cause at the *Interrupt Identification Register* (IIR) shown in figures 5.4 and 5.5.

Figure 5.7
Line Status
Register (LSR).

Line Status Register Bit Position							
7	6	5	4	3	2	1	0
Division Latch Access	Transmit Shift Register Empty	Transmit Holding Register Empty	Break Detect	Framing Error	Parity Error	Overrun Error	Data Ready

After the software identifies the interrupt as a signal pending at the LSR, it must check all the bit positions at the LSR to determine status. If LSR bit 2 contains a value of 1 when the CPU reads it, the LSR resets the bit position to 0 to enable the detection of future parity errors. After reading the LSR and detecting a parity error, the communications software must tell the user about the error.

Parity Limitations

The entire parity error-detection process is fast, but may be of limited value to users. The software informs the user of errors through screen messages, but provides no mechanism to correct the errors. If a parity error occurs during an interactive session with a host, the error may be an obvious alteration of a character or symbol. An error detected under these circumstances should not present an insurmountable problem for the user.

If a parity error occurs during the receipt of a file from a remote computer, the communications software may not inform the user, and may store the bad data in a disk file. The only way to correct these errors is to combine parity error detection with a higher level of error correction such as the file transfer protocol. File transfer protocols use special procedures to retransmit data when the receiver detects an error.

Asynchronous File Transfer

Transferring files between computers requires special communications techniques to detect and correct errors and to keep extraneous data or keystrokes from entering the files. PC users often have difficulty transferring files because of the jargon used to describe or control the process. Software vendors sometimes write file transfer procedures in generic terms that may not work with the user's communications software and hardware configuration. The following paragraphs discuss file transfer techniques and attempt to take some mystery out of this useful communications application.

A simple but time-consuming technique of transferring files between two computers to ensure file integrity is to transfer the entire file at least twice. You can send the file from one computer to another twice and store the file under two unique names during the process. You can then compare the transferred files to make sure that the contents of both are the same. If the sizes of the two files are the same and a file comparison indicates the files are identical, then you can assume with a high degree of certainty that neither of the files contains data communications-induced errors.

If you transfer a file twice and the two copies are not identical, you may have no way of knowing which file contains errors. If the files contain readable text, you can often use an editor to review the two files and correct errors. If the original file contains binary data or program object code, a visual comparison of the two files you received may not provide much insight into communications-induced errors. It might be impossible to determine which file is correct if they are different; both files can contain errors. The only way to make sure that you have successfully transmitted good data using this technique is to continue retransmitting the file until two received copies contain no differences—a process that can consume much time and resources when telephone lines are of low quality.

Data Packets and Protocols

To make the process of file transfer error detection and correction a manageable undertaking, vendors often provide communications hardware or software that divides a file into packets as it moves from one computer to another. These packets include error-detection information that enable the receiving computer to determine the presence of communications-induced errors. The hardware or software follows a procedure called a file transfer protocol to detect and correct errors.

Instead of transmitting a packet twice and comparing the first copy to the second, the sending computer derives information from the data it transmits and attaches the information to the packet. The file transfer protocol calculates a byte called a *checksum* or a pair of CRC bytes and attaches this information to the end of the packet. The receiving computer executes the same calculation and compares the results to the checksum or CRC it receives with the packet. If the checksum or CRC comparison is favorable, the data transmission continues with the next packet. If the checksum or CRC comparison is not favorable, the sender must retransmit the bad packet of data. The file transfer protocol must repeat this process, as illustrated in figure 5.8, until it transfers the entire file.

Figure 5.8
File transfer
protocol in
operation.

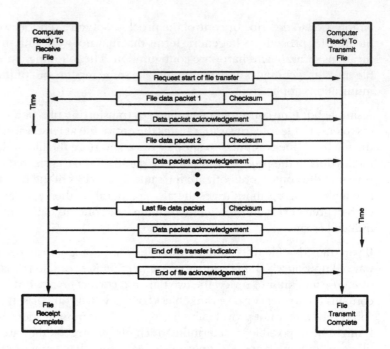

The checksum is an easy error-detection technique to implement, but its accuracy may not be sufficient for serious communications. Most PC communications software packages implement the checksum by adding the ASCII value of the bytes in a packet and then calculating an error-detection byte from the results. The software then transmits the error-detection value with the data packet as an additional data byte. Figure 5.9 illustrates this process with a segment of C source code.

Because it is easy to implement in most software languages, the software on both ends of the communications link can quickly calculate the checksum in a few short steps. This translates into a low overhead for a file transfer protocol. The protocol can spend most of its time sending or receiving data and little time calculating or sending the error-detection data.

Because of its simplicity, the checksum does not provide the high degree of error detection that you get in the more sophisticated CRC techniques. The sequential addition of ASCII values of data and the modulo arithmetic used in the calculation of a checksum give it a reliability of approximately 99.6 percent. Thus, if noise on the communications link results in errors in a data packet, the checksum provides a 99.6 probability of detecting the errors.

This probability may be misleading, however, if you do not consider the actual probability of an error occurring during a communications session. When you use

high-quality telephone lines where noise appears as bursts, which is the usual case with data communications through telephone lines, the probability of transmitting a file without errors with the checksum technique is greater than 99.9 percent. This level of error detection is sufficient for most hobbyists, but may not meet the stringent requirements of a business environment.

The CRC type of packet check is more reliable than the checksum and is gaining high acceptance in most asynchronous communications. Figure 5.10 shows a sample implementation of the CRC-CCITT. This type of error detection can ensure near error free data transfer even under the worst of conditions. Because of its reliability, business applications of file transfer protocols demand this technique.

```
/* makepack()
 *
 * Make the next Xmodem packet and
 * checksum error detection data
 *
 */
bool makepack(foo,blockcnt)
int foo;
unsigned char blockcnt;
{
    extern  unsigned char packet[134];
    extern  long fbytes;                        /* file bytes read so far */
    unsigned char sector[SECSIZE];
    int bytes;                                  /* bytes read this time */
    int index,checksum,eoxmfile,n;

    packet[0] = SOH;                            /* Start Of Header */
    packet[1] = blockcnt;                       /* packet block number */
    packet[2] = ~blockcnt;                      /* block number compliment */

    checksum = 0;
    bytes=read(foo,sector,128);                 /* get next 128 bytes */
    fbytes = fbytes + (long)bytes;              /* total file bytes */
    if (bytes == 0) return(bytes);              /* end of file, quit */
    if(bytes < 128)
        {
        for (index =  bytes; index < 128; index++)
            {
            sector[index] = NULL;               /* if not enough for 128 */
            }                                   /* bytes, pad with NULLs */
        }
    for (index = 0, n = 3; index < SECSIZE; index++, n++)
        {
        packet[n] = sector[index];              /* build packet */
        checksum += packet[n];                  /* calculate checksum */
        }

    checksum = checksum & 255;                  /* get rid of excess bits */
    packet[131] = checksum;                     /* put at end of packet */
    packet[132] = '\0';                         /* end of string marker */
}
```

Figure 5.9
Xmodem
checksum
calculation, C
source code.

Data Communications

Figure 5.10
Ymodem
protocol
CRC-CCITT
calculation, C
source code.

```
/* updcrc()
 *
 * Updates the CRC where x is the byte to be added to CRC
 *
 * CCITT polynomial used for CRC calculation.
 *
 * References globals: crc;
 * Modifies globals: crcaccum, checksum;
 *
 */
void updcrc(x)
unsigned char x;
{
        extern int crc;
        extern unsigned int crcaccum;
        extern int checksum;

        unsigned shifter, i, flag;

        for( shifter = 0x80 ; shifter ; shifter >>= 1 )
            {
            flag = (crcaccum & 0x8000);
            crcaccum <<= 1;
            crcaccum |= ((shifter & x) ? 1 : 0);
            if( flag )
                    crcaccum ^= 0x1021;
            }
}
```

Duplex Modes

Asynchronous protocols can be half- or full-duplex. Early protocols contained simple packet exchange procedures. Each device waits to send its next packet until it receives an acknowledgement or response for the last one it sent (see fig. 5.11). These half-duplex protocols enable transmission packets to flow in only one direction at a time. Because each device must wait for the device at the other end of the channel to formulate and send a response, users refer to these simple protocols as *stop and wait*. The response to each packet turns the line around in the same sense that half-duplex communications use *Request To Send* (RTS) and *Clear To Send* (CTS) electrical signals to turn a line around. The sender and receiver must agree on the direction in which the packets flow during a period and to change that direction when appropriate.

The latest asynchronous protocols provide some of the same high-performance features found in the most sophisticated synchronous protocols reviewed later in this chapter. These full-duplex protocols support the flow of packets in both directions simultaneously as shown in figure 5.12. Because each device can send many packets before it must receive acknowledgements for any of them, users refer to these complex protocols as *sliding windows*.

Sliding windows procedures enable a protocol to take full advantage of a communications link despite the time delays packets may experience in the link. The sender and receiver must agree on the direction certain types of packets can flow during a period and the number of unacknowledged packets they can tolerate

before waiting for the other device to respond. After the sender and receiver reach that agreement, the sender opens a window of packets and send them contiguously through the link. When a receiver gets a packet and formulates a response, it sends the response to the sender independent of the packets it may be receiving at the time.

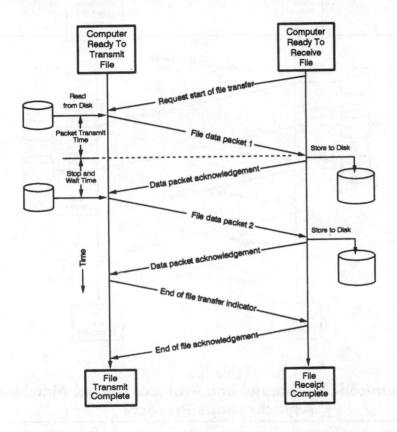

Figure 5.11
Half-duplex protocol in operation.

The term *sliding* comes from the movement of the window that transmits a given set of data or information. As a sender receives affirmative acknowledgements for packets sent earlier, it selects the next increment of packets to send—the sending window slides one increment. Until the receiver acknowledges all the packets in a given window, the sender cannot slide the window. The size of the window is the maximum number of packets a sender can transmit without receiving a single positive acknowledgement.

The duplex capability of these asynchronous protocols must match the capabilities of the communications channel that enables them to operate. Table 5.2 provides a matrix of communications channel and protocol support for half- and full-duplex. Older asynchronous protocols, such as Xmodem, that always operate in half-duplex may travel through half- or full-duplex channels. The newer full-duplex protocols such as MNP, on the other hand, require full-duplex communications. The reasons for these requirements are reviewed later.

Figure 5.12
Full-duplex, sliding window protocol in operation.

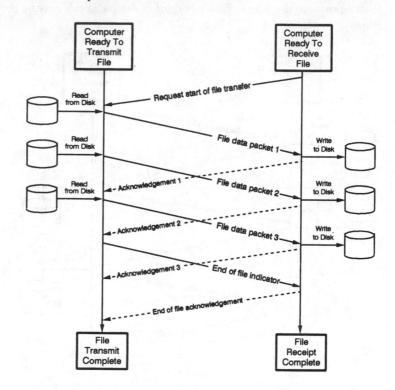

Table 5.2
Communications Channel and Protocol Duplex Matching
Asynchronous Protocol

Communications Channel	Half-Duplex	Full-Duplex
Half-Duplex	Supported	Not Supported
Full-Duplex	Supported	Supported

Asynchronous File Transfer Protocols

Asynchronous file transfer protocols have been evolving since 1977. The early ones such as the *MODEM protocol* had many limitations, but more recent vintages are powerful and reliable. Unfortunately, none of the asynchronous protocols have become national or international standards. Because of the powerful features and capabilities of these protocols, the following sections discuss some of the most popular, beginning with half-duplex protocols and progressing to full-duplex protocols. Software and hardware protocols also are reviewed.

Xmodem Protocol

Ward Christensen developed the MODEM file transfer protocol in 1977 to enable error-checked file transfers between microcomputers operating under the CP/M operating system. The MODEM protocol—designed and developed during a single weekend—provided a simple and easily implemented technique to ensure near error-free transfers of text and binary files. The enhancements added to MODEM to produce the *MODEM7, Xmodem, XmodemCRC,* and *Batch Xmodem* protocols extended the life of Christensen's original design. Because of the widespread use of the Xmodem version of the MODEM protocol, this version is discussed in detail in the following paragraphs.

Figures that depict its operation best describe Xmodem. Figure 5.13 shows the basic elements of the protocol, including the framing and error checking performed with each packet. Figure 5.14 shows a complete file transfer with an error occurring in the third packet. As you can see from this figure, Xmodem recovers from an error by retransmitting bad packets immediately after discovering an error. After receiving each packet, the receiver checks its contents to make sure that no errors exist. If the receiver finds no errors in the packet, it tells the transmitter to send the next packet. If the receiver finds an error, it tells the transmitter to resend the last packet. Xmodem can resend a single packet up to ten times before giving up and aborting the file transfer.

Xmodem uses the control characters described in Appendix B for protocol signaling. The protocol uses the NAK character to start a file transfer and to indicate an error in a data packet, and uses the ACK character to indicate receipt of a good packet and to acknowledge the completion of a file transfer. The Xmodem sender uses an EOT character to signal the proper completion of a file transfer, and a CAN to abnormally terminate or abort a file transfer. Xmodem considers more than ten attempts to resend the same data packet a fatal error and aborts the file transfer. The file transfer protocol usually displays a message to indicate receipt of each of these signals, so that the user is continuously aware of the transfer progress.

Xmodem is an excellent protocol for low-speed file transfers through high-quality telephone lines. The single-character signaling and 128-byte data packet translate into low overhead and efficient file transfers when good telephone connections are available. When telephone connections are low quality, Xmodem often fails to transfer files. Xmodem also requires a full eight data bits to send packet numbers to the receiver, which may be a problem for some host computers. Most personal computers, including the PC, can operate using eight data bits with no problems, but some larger computers only operate using seven data bits.

Figure 5.13
Xmodem file transfer packets.

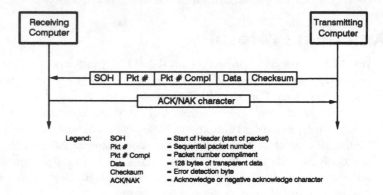

Legend:
SOH = Start of Header (start of packet)
Pkt # = Sequential packet number
Pkt # Compl = Packet number compliment
Data = 128 bytes of transparent data
Checksum = Error detection byte
ACK/NAK = Acknowledge or negative acknowledge character

Figure 5.14
Xmodem file transfer operation.

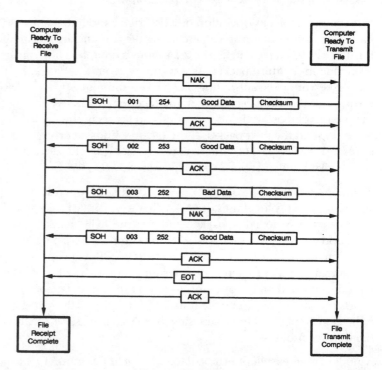

During the early days of file transfers between PCs, the predominant asynchronous modem speed was 300 bps. Typical PC communications equipment now includes a modem that operates at 2,400 bps or higher. One price users pay for faster modems is a higher communications error rate. Xmodem, designed for low error rates, typically fails at communications speeds above 2,400 bps unless assisted by an error-correction protocol built into the modem hardware.

The second change in communications that adversely affects Xmodem's performance is the arrival of low-cost, voice-communications services. Unfortunately, a hidden price users sometimes pay with these services is a higher communications noise level and data communications error rates. The higher noise levels may only be annoying during voice communications, but they are often devastating for Xmodem file transfers.

The high communications error rates that occur at high asynchronous communications speeds and on low-quality telephone lines are difficult for Xmodem to handle. For example, line noise often causes a series of data bit errors that can pass through Xmodem undetected. Xmodem uses a simple checksum that is the sum of the ASCII values of all 128 data bytes, *modulo 255*. Simply translated, multiple bit changes in a data packet caused by line noise can result in the same checksum as the original data. Thus, a packet error can occur without Xmodem detecting it and requesting a retransmission of the data.

Line noise can result in unnecessary Xmodem data transmission. The noise can alter the single ACK character that the receiving computer transmits to acknowledge proper data transfer. If the noise changes the ACK into any character except a NAK, the sending computer does not know to send the next sequential packet. If the noise changes the ACK into a NAK, the sending computer unnecessarily retransmits the last data packet.

Line noise also can alter the receiver's response causing an abnormal termination of a file transfer. An ACK or NAK character can become a Control-X character—the Xmodem CAN signal to *abort* the file transfer and terminate the transfer. This can happen at any point during a file transfer, and the user then must restart the file transfer from the beginning.

Users and vendors added many enhancements to Xmodem since 1977, but none of the changes overcame the following two major flaws in its design:

✔ Xmodem uses a single character ACK/NAK response to packet transfers. Without a packet and a packet number for all data transmissions, enhancements such as sliding windows cannot be added to Xmodem.

✔ Xmodem requires a full eight data bits for proper operation. This requirement precludes operation of Xmodem with some public data networks and mainframe computers.

Public data networks (PDNs) sometimes create time delays during data communications that can cause problems with file transfer protocols. These communications

II

Data Communications

services convert all data into packets and route the packets through ground and satellite equipment. The packet construction and routing can produce as much as a three second delay in the receipt of an acknowledge or negative acknowledge to a file transfer protocol's data packet transmission. For a 48 KB file this could add 19 minutes to a normal 6-minute file transfer when communicating at 1,200 bps— a 300-percent increase in file transfer time!

Some file transfer protocols such as *BLAST* and *Kermit* get around the PDN time-delay problem by providing a sliding window of packets. These protocols send data packets continuously without waiting for positive acknowledgements of each individual packet. At least one positive acknowledgement must come back from the receiver for a given number of packets. This technique requires a full-duplex communications link because data packets are sent out simultaneously with the receipt of ACK/NAK responses from the receiving computer. This technique also requires that the receiver's ACK/NAK response contain the packet number associated with the response. The sending computer must determine which previously transmitted packets it has to retransmit because of errors detected by the receiving computer.

Xmodem does not provide data packet numbers with its ACK/NAK responses, which limits it to half-duplex operations. The protocol sends a packet and then waits to receive a response from the receiver. An Xmodem transmitter can send the next packet only after the receiver responds to the last packet. Time delays caused by this half-duplex, stop-and-wait technique can cause protocol timeout problems that result in aborted file transfers.

Another characteristic of some PDNs that precludes the use of Xmodem is the parity bit. Some PDNs convert this data bit into a zero or one for network control and routing. Xmodem requires no parity and a full eight data bits for transmission of binary data, extended ASCII characters, and its own internally generated error-checking checksum. Because of Xmodem's eight data-bit requirement, it cannot be used with seven-bit PDNs.

The design of Xmodem also precludes its use with many mainframe computers. The front-end communications processors or TTY communications ports on some large computers only operate with seven data bits; Xmodem is incompatible with these machines. Other large computers have small communications buffers and cannot accommodate the receipt of a 128-byte Xmodem packet without losing characters.

In spite of its limitations, Xmodem will remain a popular file transfer protocol throughout the 1990s. Because of its inclusion in all popular PC communications packages, Xmodem provides at least one common protocol for data transfer between personal computers. As the need to communicate with larger computers or through PDNs becomes greater and the speed of modems continues to

increase, Xmodem's popularity may wane, giving way to the other protocols discussed in the following paragraphs.

Ymodem Protocol

The *Ymodem* protocol was first introduced in 1981 as a significant enhancement to the Xmodem protocol. Chuck Forsberg developed the protocol for the YAM communications program, originally written to run under the CP/M operating system. Forsberg released this program into public domain with the *sb* (*send batch*) and *rb* (*receive batch*) UNIX utilities that contained the same features.

Besides its robust features as a file transfer protocol, two additional attributes of Ymodem added significantly to its acceptance in the PC community:

- ✔ It was originally written in the portable C language

- ✔ It was released into the public domain with documentation showing implementation guidelines

No good PC communications software package is complete today without Ymodem.

Ymodem, which has less overhead than Xmodem, enables the transfer of 1,024-byte data blocks. This block length is almost ten times the length of Xmodem blocks, a feature which substantially reduces the protocol overhead, enabling Ymodem to outperform Xmodem under good line quality conditions. If the line quality is not good, Ymodem automatically decreases the data block length to 128 bytes to reduce the number of bytes that have to be retransmitted each time the protocol detects an error. Therefore, under the worst of conditions, Ymodem's performance equals that of the Xmodem protocol.

Ymodem is more reliable than Xmodem, which abnormally aborts a file transfer upon the receipt of a single Control-X bit pattern (ASCII value 024). Line noise can easily create this bit pattern and terminate a file transfer. Ymodem must receive two sequential Control-X or CAN characters before it abnormally terminates a file transfer. This redundancy reduces the probability that Ymodem abnormally terminates a file transfer in error.

Besides providing low protocol overhead and high reliability, Ymodem provides two other significant features for communications users. First, Ymodem uses the CRC error-detection technique to produce near error-free file transfers regardless of line quality. Second, Ymodem transmits file-related information to the receiving computer. Ymodem conveys a file's name, file time and date stamp, and size in the first block when it starts a file transfer. The receiving computer can use this information to display file transfer data and preserve a file's time and date stamp during a file transfer.

The final Ymodem advantage is its batch file transfer feature. Vendors added several batch modes to the MODEM and Xmodem protocol over the years—the most popular of which is in the *MODEM7* protocol—but none of these implementations survived in the PC community. The batch capability of Ymodem did survive and offers an advantage when several files must be transferred between two computers.

Unfortunately, Ymodem suffers from some of the same limitations associated with its parent protocol, Xmodem. Ymodem requires a full eight data bits as a communications parameter, which precludes its use with some computer systems. Ymodem also uses the stop and wait technique of sending a data packet and waiting for a positive acknowledgment before sending the next packet. This technique is not a problem for telephone communications because Ymodem uses low protocol overhead relative to the size of its data packets. For file transfers that go through satellite links or public data networks, however, the time delay required to receive each acknowledgement can increase the duration of file transfers.

Zmodem Protocol

Chuck Forsberg, dissatisfied with the limitations of Ymodem, went one step further in 1986 and developed the *Zmodem* protocol. The connection between Zmodem and any previous MODEM protocol is, however, hard to find. The features and functions of this protocol are so far superior to those in earlier Modem protocols it should have a different name to distinguish it from its predecessors.

Forsberg developed Zmodem to overcome some of the limitations of packet-switched networks. Telenet commissioned this to overcome limitations in their network and processors. Although many of Zmodem's features are similar to the ones included in Kermit, the Zmodem protocol is superior to Kermit for file transfers between PCs. Kermit provides better file transfer between PCs and hosts because of the number of versions available.

Besides batch file transfer, Zmodem can resume a file transfer at any point that a communications link fails. When the user restarts the file transfer, the protocol resumes the transfer at the exact byte in the file where the transfer terminated earlier. This feature is similar to the restart feature included in the proprietary BLAST protocol.

Zmodem also includes several file transfer features that two copies of the software negotiate at the start of each file transfer. Before a transfer starts, Zmodem checks to see if the file exists on the local disk. If the file exists and has the same contents, Zmodem does not perform the transfer, thus saving valuable time. The protocol also can negotiate the use of a CRC-32 to provide better error detection and correction than most other protocols. Finally, Zmodem can perform data compres-

sion during a file transfer to reduce the time required to move the file.

Zmodem has a flexible sliding windows technique. The protocol can transfer a file without waiting for positive acknowledgements of packets. It also can transfer up to 1,024 bytes in each packet. If the protocol starts with a packet size of 1,024 and the error rate on the line increases beyond a specific threshold, the protocol can reduce the packet size to improve data throughput. The protocol does support the XON/XOFF protocol used in some communications links for data flow control.

Although Zmodem provides many excellent file transfer features, it does have one limitation that precludes its use in some networks. The protocol requires a full eight data bits. It does provide an optional transparency mode that can disguise control characters; but unfortunately, this feature does not include the conversion of eight-bit data into seven-bit data (printable characters) to support the kind of communications the Kermit protocol performs best.

Kermit Protocol

In 1981, Columbia University had a variety of computers, including IBM mainframes, DEC minicomputers, and microcomputers made by several vendors. University personnel found they could not easily move files between machines. Improper translations of characters sometimes occurred with text files, and binary files either caused problems with the communications equipment or were not transferred because of communications equipment limitations. Necessity became the mother of invention.

University personnel and students, under the guidance of Frank da Cruz and Bill Catchings, set out to design and implement a file transfer protocol that enabled any type of computer to receive a file sent by another type of computer. The protocol they devised became known as *Kermit*, a name taken from Jim Henson's famous green frog. Universities and vendors added to Kermit's features over the years, and versions now are available for just about every computer make and model in operation. Columbia University maintains a library of tested and verified versions of the protocol.

The Kermit protocol is similar in many ways to the Xmodem protocol. The differences between Kermit and Xmodem, however, give Kermit more growth potential and allow more flexible implementations. Kermit also has capabilities that allow its use in situations that preclude the use of Xmodem.

Kermit is an excellent protocol for file transfers between dissimilar computers, high-speed file transfers, file transfers over long distances, and file group transfers. As figure 5.15 illustrates, Kermit has many optional features in addition to full packets with error checking for both data and ACK/NAK response data. Unfortunately, Kermit's features and flexibility add overhead to the protocol that may be undesirable under some circumstances.

Figure 5.15
Kermit file
transfer packets.

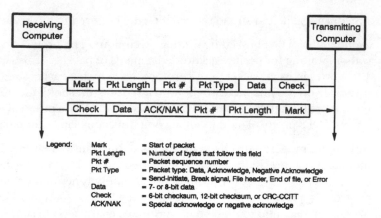

Legend:

Mark	= Start of packet
Pkt Length	= Number of bytes that follow this field
Pkt #	= Packet sequence number
Pkt Type	= Packet type: Data, Acknowledge, Negative Acknowledge
	= Send-initiate, Break signal, File header, End of file, or Error
Data	= 7- or 8-bit data
Check	= 6-bit checksum, 12-bit checksum, or CRC-CCITT
ACK/NAK	= Special acknowledge or negative acknowledge

For direct-dial communications at speeds under 2,400 bps between microcomputers made by the same vendor, Kermit's power goes to waste. A protocol such as Xmodem can be 10 to 40 percent more efficient under these circumstances. Kermit's power becomes important, however, in business, government, and educational institutions in which a variety of computers must communicate.

One capability that gives Kermit its power is the feature negotiation it performs each time it transfers a file. This *binding* process takes place through the exchange of *send-initiate* packets. As shown in the protocol diagram in figure 5.16, the sending computer transmits its send-initiate packet to the receiving computer. The receiver acknowledges proper receipt of the packet and sends its own send-initiate packet along with the acknowledgment.

During the send-initiate process, two Kermits compare features and select the ones both ends of the link can support. This send-initiate packet exchange enables any Kermit implementation to communicate with any other Kermit implementation. The transfer-by-transfer renegotiation also enables the computer operator on either end of the link to alter parameters such as packet size to optimize communications throughput based on the specific circumstances.

One feature two Kermits negotiate is the method of packet error checking. Kermit supports three techniques: a 6-bit checksum, a 12-bit checksum, and CRC-CCITT. The communications overhead of each of these techniques increases with its degree of error-detection capability. The 6-bit checksum adds one byte to each packet. Software calculates this checksum the same way that software calculates an Xmodem checksum. This technique is acceptable for good-quality telephone connections at speeds under 2,400 bps. The 12-bit checksum adds two bytes to each packet and is somewhat better than the single byte Xmodem checksum. This technique is better for low-quality telephone connections or high-speed communications.

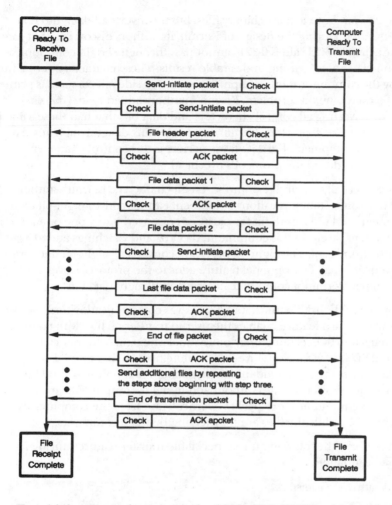

Figure 5.16
Kermit file
transfer protocol
in operation.

Kermit's best error detection is the 16-bit CRC-CCITT, which adds three bytes to each data packet. This error-detection technique is far superior to either the 6-bit or 12-bit checksum technique and is ideal for low-quality telephone connections or high-speed communications. The CRC provides almost 100-percent error detection and is good for financial data transactions.

Besides its error-detection power, Kermit provides three features that endear it to many users:

✔ It communicates through both seven-bit and eight-bit data ports, regardless of the communications hardware employed

✔ It moves groups of files without interruption

✔ It facilitates the addition of new capabilities as communications needs change

Kermit can transmit both text and binary files, but it converts all data into text during the transfer. During the design of Kermit, its authors discovered that some control characters (ASCII values 0-32) cannot pass through certain communications equipment without causing undesirable results. These characters were either modified by the communications equipment or caused side effects such as printer initiation. To overcome this problem, Kermit's authors added *control character conversion*. By converting all control characters and data bits that had these same bit patterns into printable characters, Kermit can convey any data through any data communications equipment. Kermit always performs this control character conversion, which adds to the protocol's overhead.

Kermit can convert all data and text into seven-bit characters. Kermit's authors discovered that some communications equipment cannot convey eight-bit data. This equipment used the eighth bit for parity or converted it to a one or a zero. To make all data transparent to this equipment, da Cruz and Catchings added *eight-bit prefixing* to their protocol. The eight-bit prefixing converts all eight-bit data bytes into two seven-bit bytes. This optional feature adds to the protocol's overhead only when two computers cannot communicate using a full eight data bits.

Kermit supports wild-card file transfers, which saves communication and user time. This optional wild-card feature enables the user to transfer all files with common file-name characters by executing one command. For example, a user can enter the command **SEND *.EXE** to archive on a remote host all files of the EXE type. This feature enables the same send-initiate negotiation to apply to several files, and enables Kermit to transfer the files without additional user input. File group transfer reduces communications packet overhead and frees the computer user to perform other tasks while the files are transferring between computers.

Kermit can perform the following three special file transfer features during its send-initiate negotiation:

- ✔ File attribute transfers
- ✔ Data compression
- ✔ Sliding windows

The file attribute capability enables Kermit to send up to 94 file characteristics along with the file, including file modification time/date and file size. The receiving Kermit can use these attributes to display file transfer progress or to preserve the file's time/date stamp during the transfer. The sliding windows capability enables Kermit to take advantage of full-duplex satellite and PDN communications links to hasten file transfers. The sliding windows along with Kermit's capability to perform repeat character data compression can result in substantial throughput improvements over half-duplex protocols such as Xmodem and Ymodem.

Kermit's developers added many options that enable the protocol to perform in spite of its environment. The user can select such items as communications flow control, timeout durations, a special eight-bit prefixing character, a packet termination character, and others. These features were added by Columbia University as well as other educational and business institutions. With each new release, Kermit comes closer to achieving its design objective of providing one low-cost protocol that facilitates file transfers between any two computers.

Protocol Comparison

Asynchronous, half-duplex, file transfer protocols provide a mix of powerful features. Vendors and hobbyists continue to improve upon these protocols. Every year another variation of one of these protocols appears in the public domain. The latest variation of the MODEM, Xmodem, and Ymodem series is the Zmodem protocol. This protocol combines many of the best features of its predecessors with a sliding windows capability that gives it the performance of the full-duplex protocols discussed later. Table 5.3 provides a comparison of three of these protocols.

Table 5.3
Asynchronous file transfer protocols

Attribute	Xmodem	Ymodem	Zmodem	Kermit
Types of File Transfer				
Single File	yes	yes	yes	yes
Batch of Files	no	yes	yes	yes
Text	yes	yes	yes	yes
Data	yes	yes	yes	yes
Binary	yes	yes	yes	yes
Required Data Bits	8	8	8	7 or 8
Error Checking				
Checksum	yes	yes	no	yes
CRC-CCITT	no	yes	yes	yes
CRC-32	no	no	yes	no
Error Checking Response				
Single Character	yes	yes	yes	no
Error-checked packet	no	no	no	yes
Data Packet Size (bytes)	128	1024	1024	0-94
Data Compression	no	no	no	yes
File Attribute Transfer				
File Size	no	yes	yes	yes
Time/Date Stamp	no	yes	yes	yes
Sliding Window Support				
Single Packet	yes	yes	yes	yes
Multiple Packets	no	no	yes	1-16
Negotiated Parameters				
Packet Size	no	yes	yes	yes
Packets in Window	no	no	yes	yes
Error-check type	no	yes	yes	yes
Data compression	no	no	yes	yes
Xon/Xoff Flow Control	no	no	yes	yes

Xmodem, Ymodem, Zmodem, and Kermit, despite their capabilities to ensure error-free file transfers, do nothing to improve the quality of normal interactive communications with remote computers. Many communications users discover that logging into and writing messages on a remote computer are sometimes difficult. Greek and math symbols—caused by communications noise—suddenly appear on-screen or get sent to the remote computer. The only way to eliminate this noise and its side effects with asynchronous communications is to use error-checking for all interactions between the two computers—not just during file transfers.

Continuous Asynchronous Protocols

As modem speeds continue to increase, the signals these modems use to transmit data become more sensitive to electronic noise in the telephone system. One way to ensure near error-free interactions between two computers at these high communications speeds is to use continuous error detection and correction between the modems that enable the computers to communicate through the telephone system. Currently, two alternative protocols enable you to accomplish this. Microcom Systems, a modem vendor, developed the *Microcom Networking Protocol* (MNP) that has become a de facto industry standard for error detection and correction between modems. A committee of the *International Telecommunication Union* (ITU), called the *ITU-T*, also developed an international standard called the *Link-Access Procedure for Modems* (LAPM) that can provide better error detection and correction than MNP. Both of these alternatives are discussed briefly in the following paragraphs and in detail in Chapter 9, "Telephone System Interfaces."

Microcom Networking Protocol

The protocol Microcom originally developed to ensure error-free communications between their own 1,200-bps modems has become widely accepted by other modem vendors. Although MNP can be included in either software or hardware, the protocol operates most efficiently when placed in a modem's *firmware* (hardware chips). When two modems use the MNP error-correcting capabilities, the resulting data stream and data link controls the modems exchange provide all the capabilities of a synchronous protocol and more.

The original version of MNP was a proprietary technique called the *Reliable Link Protocol* (RLP). A modem or software vendor could include the protocol in a product only after paying Microcom a $2,000 license fee. A few vendors paid the fee to study the protocol but few implemented it in products. The protocol did not gain popularity until Microcom released the lower three classes of MNP into public domain. Table 5.4 shows the classes of functions available in the MNP protocol today. Higher classes generally provide enhancements to the capabilities provided in lower classes.

Table 5.4
MNP Classes of Function

Class	Description
1	Asynchronous, half-duplex, byte-oriented, error correction
2	Asynchronous, full-duplex, byte-oriented, error correction
3	Synchronous, full-duplex, bit-oriented, error correction
4	Frame size optimized for error rate, reduced overhead
5	Data compression, throughput almost twice the connection speed
6	Universal Link Negotiation, automatic connection at the highest common speed and protocol
7	Enhanced Data Compression, throughput over twice the connection speed
9	Enhanced Universal Link Negotiation, sliding windows
10	Adverse Channel Enhancements, optimizes performance for poor connections, cellular telephone support

Note There is no MNP Class 8.

The increased error rate that vendors experienced when they began to develop V.22bis, 2,400 bps modems, described in Chapter 9 "Telephone System Interfaces," caused them to investigate different forms of continuous error detection and correction. Because MNP was originally designed for modem firmware, it was a natural for modems made by other vendors. As a result of the layered approach followed by Microcom in the design of MNP and its ease of implementation in firmware, many modem vendors now offer the MNP protocol as either a standard or an optional feature. Because of their popularity, the V.42 international standard for modem-to-modem error control now calls for MNP Classes 1-4 to function as fallback protocols in the event a V.42-compliant modem cannot agree to use LAPM with another modem.

If MNP is included in a modem at one end of the link but not in the modem at the other end, the modems communicate using standard asynchronous or synchronous techniques. If MNP is implemented in the modems at both ends of the link, the modems can perform a *switch to sync* and use an MNP protocol continuously throughout the session. This continuous error-correction approach enables many modem vendors to provide high throughput and near error-free communications at data rates far exceeding the 2,400 bps rate that provided the first incentive for them to incorporate the protocol.

Chapter 9, "Telephone System Interfaces," explores the different MNP protocol classes in detail. The MNP protocols that provide error correction are based on variations of the synchronous protocols described in the next chapter. Reading the description of the synchronous protocols provides you with a good background for the MNP details in Chapter 9.

Although MNP provides a robust set of link-access services, it is still a proprietary set of protocols above Class 4. Modem vendors can license the protocols from Microcom Systems to enhance their hardware offerings. Vendors also can include an international set of link protocols in lieu of or in addition to the MNP protocols. The following paragraphs examine this international standard.

Link-Access Procedure for Modems

The International Telecommunication Union, through its CCITT committee, published a recommendation for continuous modem-to-modem error detection and correction in 1988. The standard designation is *V.42,* and its title is *Error-Correcting Procedures for DCEs Using Asynchronous-to-Synchronous Conversion.* The International Telecommunication Union Telecommunication Standardization Sector (ITU-T)—the renamed CCITT—is now supporting the V.42 specifications. The primary error-checking protocol it calls for is *Link-Access Procedure for Modems* (LAPM).

Although increasing modem speeds and an associated increase in sensitivity to telephone line noise led the ITU to publish V.42, the recommendation applies to modems that operate at 1,200 bps and higher. Vendors currently provide V.42 error checking in modems that operate from 1,200 to 14,400 bps. As with MNP, LAPM works only between two modems that contain that capability and *negotiate* its use at the beginning of a connection.

The V.42 recommendation calls for a *primary* and a *fallback* link-access protocol. Modems built to this standard are supposed to try and use LAPM first when they make a connection. If the initial protocol negotiations fail, V.42 calls for a fallback to MNP Classes 1-4 operation. This selection of an error-checking protocol takes place within the first few seconds after the answering modem answers a call from a calling modem. If the modems cannot agree to support LAPM and negotiations for operation at one of the MNP levels fails, a V.42-compliant modem is supposed to fall back to normal asynchronous operation with no error checking.

As its title implies, the V.42 recommendation calls for a procedure that works with modems that convert asynchronous start-stop data streams into synchronous data streams or vice versa. The LAPM protocol strips the start-stop bits from each byte of data and places the remaining data bits into packets. The modem then transmits the packets through the telephone system to the modem at the other end of the link using the HDLC synchronous protocol described in Chapter 6, "Synchronous Data Link Control." The receiving modem must convert the synchronous data from packets into asynchronous start-stop bytes it then sends to the receiving computer. The principal objectives of the V.42 recommendation are as follows:

✔ Provide error correction for modems that perform asynchronous-to-synchronous conversion according to ITU-T Recommendation V.14

✔ Provide error detection in the form of 16-bit or 32-bit cyclic redundancy checks

✔ Provide automatic retransmission of data to correct detected errors

✔ Provide an initial start-stop, asynchronous handshake to negotiate the execution of the synchronous LAPM protocol

For modems that operate at 2,400 bps and higher, the inclusion of a continuous form of error detection and correction such as LAPM or MNP is a must to ensure near error-free communications. Because of its international backing, the V.42 recommendations and the LAPM protocol will play major roles in providing this service. The ubiquitous MNP protocols are also expected to provide a needed service for many years. Many older modems contain at least Class 3 of MNP and many new ones will contain Class 10 to ensure error correction in a cellular environment.

Summary

As you can see from the discussion of asynchronous error checking and file transfer, many alternatives are available to the PC user to ensure near error-free transfer of data. These techniques range from the simple parity error detection inherited from the old teletype terminals, to built-in error checking and correction at the modem hardware level. Even options for error detection and correction combined with multiple communications sessions with remote computers are available. With all these asynchronous techniques, however, large organizations still require some elements not provided in this technology.

Large organizations, with hundreds or thousands of terminals and PCs tied to host computers all over the world, need more than error detection and correction. They need powerful management and control of the networks that connect these devices. Synchronous data link control provides the building block for these networks as you see in the next chapter.

Chapter Snapshot

Synchronous data link control is the technology that enables large organizations to install and operate highly efficient wide area networks. This technology has evolved over the past 30 years to become the building block of large networks because of its reliability, flexibility, and efficiency. In this chapter, you learn the following:

✔ The basics of synchronous data link control

✔ Error control in network systems

✔ The specifics of Binary Synchronous Communications (BSC)

✔ The specifics of Synchronous Data Link Control (SDLC)

✔ The specifics of High-Level Data Link Control (HDLC)

Synchronous data link control enables communications and networking vendors to install computers and their peripherals in a distributed environment to meet user needs over a wide geographical area. Use this chapter to understand how this technology provides the building blocks for all major networks.

CHAPTER

6

Synchronous Data Link Control

Although asynchronous error detection provided a needed service during the early years of data communications, it proved inadequate for the high-volume, high-speed data communications needs that evolved in the 1960s. To meet these emerging needs, IBM developed the first communications protocol based on the synchronous technique of bit transfer. This protocol provided the first true data link control for a communications system. Other vendors later introduced competing synchronous protocols and data link controls.

Synchronous protocols evolved from half-duplex, character-oriented procedures in the 1960s to full-duplex, bit-oriented procedures in the 1970s and 1980s. Vendors developed the best protocols they could at each stage of the evolution. Improvements in communications hardware enabled vendors to improve protocols. Learning from the limitations experienced during the implementation of protocols also helped vendors improve their designs. Protocols such as the Asynchronous Transfer Method (ATM) developed in the 1990s have synchronous data link control as their basis.

Vendors implemented the first synchronous protocols in hardware. These vendors found that the technology available in the 1960s did not support protocol operation in software. By implementing the protocols in hardware, hardware developers could do error checking, transmission framing, and data routing fast enough to support communications at rates as high as 2,400 bps. Vendors also found that hardware implementations of protocols limited flexibility. Upgrading to a new version of a communications protocol required hardware changes—changes some customers could not or did not want to make. Changing hardware can be time consuming, costly, and disruptive.

As processor power increased during the 1960s and early 1970s, vendors found they could implement synchronous protocols in hardware or software. Some vendors, most notably IBM, chose to offload communications tasks to hardware platforms designed specifically to handle communications tasks. These *communications computers* now include communications controllers and control units dedicated to the execution of communications and networking tasks.

Common Synchronous Protocol Elements

Although synchronous protocols have improved over the years, many still contain common elements. The following sections review these common elements, and later in this chapter, you review the implementation of these same elements in three synchronous protocols. Figure 6.1 shows the relationship between these protocols and the OSI reference model discussed in earlier chapters.

Transmission Frames

One big difference between asynchronous and synchronous communications is the aggregation of data at the data link layer. As you saw earlier, the smallest unit of transmission in asynchronous communications is a byte of data. Asynchronous hardware transmits characters, data, or binary files as groups of bits with five to eight bits in each group. Asynchronous hardware converts bit streams from parallel to serial data and adds start and stop bits to each byte. These start/byte/stop transmission frames move individually from sender to receiver at a fixed bit rate but without mandatory aggregation into larger groups of bytes.

Synchronous protocols aggregate characters or strings of bits into groups to reduce communications overhead and to provide higher communications rates. Synchronous hardware encloses these data bits in packets that usually begin with a starting field and an address field. The packets always end in error-checking, redundancy

data and an ending field. Figure 6.2 is a diagram of two types of synchronous *transmission frames.*

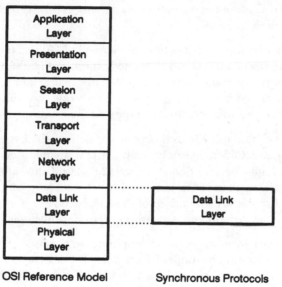

Figure 6.1
Synchronous protocols and the OSI reference model.

OSI Reference Model   Synchronous Protocols

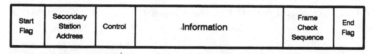

Start Flag	Secondary Station Address	Control	Information	Frame Check Sequence	End Flag

(a) Synchronous Data Link Control (SDLC) transmission frame.

PAD	PAD	SYN	SYN	STX	Text	ETX	BCC	BCC	PAD

(b) Binary Synchronous Communication (BSC) transmission frame.

Figure 6.2
Synchronous protocol transmission frames.

The bits in a synchronous transmission frame must be contiguous, and the bits in each field and the fields in each frame must follow one after the other with no time lapse between them. The transmission frames may or may not be contiguous, depending on the specific synchronous protocol you use. Each synchronous protocol defines the lapse allowed between transmission frames.

Communications Buffers

Synchronous communications require receive data buffers at each end of the link that match the size of transmission frames. As you saw in Chapter 5, asynchronous communications take place one byte at a time. Asynchronous devices can, therefore, operate with a hardware memory buffer as small as one byte. Synchronous protocols, on the other hand, transmit data as contiguous blocks of bits. Synchronous devices, therefore, often need larger memory buffers on the receiving end than asynchronous devices.

Receive buffers in synchronous devices that operate in half-duplex mode must store the entire contents of a transmission frame in memory. The storage enables the receiver to examine the frame for errors before discarding it or sending it to another device. The device needs storage space for only one transmission frame because it cannot receive another until it responds to the current frame.

The size of the receive buffer in a half-duplex device defines the largest transmission frame it can receive. Older devices typically contain small buffers because the cost of memory was high when vendors designed and manufactured these devices. Newer devices typically contain larger buffers. A synchronous protocol must divide data into frames within the size limitations of the data receive buffers of communicating devices or the devices will lose data during a communications session.

A receive buffer in a synchronous device that operates in the full-duplex mode must be larger than a comparable buffer in a half-duplex device. As you see later, full-duplex enables devices to communicate in both directions simultaneously and to send more than one transmission frame before receiving affirmative acknowledgement of previous frames. A full-duplex device, therefore, must be capable of storing the largest number of transmission frames it will receive in a sequence.

Synchronization

The synchronization between a sender and a receiver is significantly different for asynchronous and synchronous communications. As you saw in Chapters 4, "Data Transmission Fundamentals," and 5, "Communication Error Correction," asynchronous synchronization occurs at the beginning of each transmitted byte. The receiver must synchronize with the sender for each byte of data it receives, even if a high-level file transfer protocol is moving the data through the communications link.

Synchronous protocols require synchronization between the sender and the receiver for each transmission frame. The receiver synchronizes with the sender at the start of a transmission frame and maintains that synchronization for the duration of the frame. As you learn later, some synchronous protocols periodically exchange data to help keep the send and receive clocks synchronized.

Error Detection and Correction

The error correction support in synchronous protocols is generally superior to that in asynchronous communications. The only error detection defined by standards for asynchronous communications is the parity bit. This VRC works well for the byte-by-byte asynchronous technique, but is unacceptable for the longer groups of bits transmitted in synchronous frames. Older synchronous protocols use the VRC/LRC technique of detecting errors. Newer synchronous protocols rely on CRC-CCITT or CRC-16 procedures to identify and eliminate almost all communications errors.

Protocol Procedures

The power of synchronous protocols is in the standardized procedures they use to control data flow and operations for a communications link. No international standards exist for asynchronous data link control. IBM and others, on the other hand, developed several synchronous protocols that are now both industry and international standards.

Large networks of computer hardware require protocol procedures. These large networks perform more functions than just the transfer of data from one point to another. They require addressing schemes that enable one device to recognize another so that data and controls go to the proper destination. They also require the exchange of controls that pace the flow of data and identify connectivity problems. Without these procedures, vendors would be unable to design and implement the reliable networks required to support large enterprises.

Link Configurations

One requirement that encouraged IBM and others to develop synchronous protocols was the need for flexible link configurations. Vendors designed asynchronous communications to support point-to-point connectivity between devices as shown in figure 6.3. When vendors began to design larger networks of terminals and computers, they found asynchronous communications did not support these complex configurations well.

Some synchronous protocols support multipoint links. As figure 6.4 shows, these links have two or more communicating devices connected to the same cable or telephone link. A synchronous protocol provides the addressing scheme that regulates and controls the flow of data between devices that share a common channel. The procedure requires the recognition of one device as the *control station*, sometimes called a *primary link station* (PLS). All other devices on the same link are *tributary stations*, sometimes called *secondary link stations* (SLS). In a point-to-point configuration, the two devices at each end of the link are *link stations* (LS), which implies no hierarchical order.

Figure 6.3
Point-to-point
connectivity.

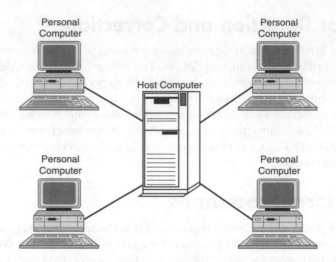

Figure 6.4
Multipoint
synchronous
connectivity
between
stations.

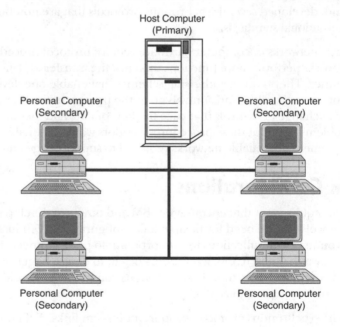

A control station enforces a message-exchange protocol that provides the following functions:

✔ Prevents congestion in the data link

✔ Ensures proper control of a multi-device installation

The two methods a control station uses to execute these functions are the *poll* and *select* techniques.

A PLS polls several SLSs simultaneously to determine which of them have data to send. Tributaries must accumulate data locally until they receive a poll from the control station. If a tributary has data to send when it receives a poll, the tributary must establish a dialog with the control station to send the data. This prevents multiple tributaries from attempting to transmit data simultaneously through the same link.

A control station selects a specific tributary if it has data for that device. By selecting a specific destination while all other tributaries are monitoring the line, the control station can establish a dialog and exchange data with that device without interference from the other devices. The other tributaries must remain passive until the control station completes the dialog with the selected station. Some synchronous protocols do provide a mechanism that enables one tributary to request service while the control station carries out a dialog with another device, as you see later.

One difference between synchronous protocols is the design of the address scheme they use in poll, select, and data exchange procedures. *Hierarchical protocols* enable only control stations to issue commands, whereas tributaries can only respond to commands received from control stations. This design enhances the security of a network by giving the PLS ultimate control over access to computer resources. *Peer-to-peer protocols*, on the other hand, enable both control and tributary stations to issue commands and answer with responses. This technique enhances the power and flexibility of networks and supports both distributed data and applications in client/server systems.

Some synchronous protocols include features that enable them to support *loop* configurations as shown in figure 6.5. Direct cable connections can provide the loop between devices located in a small geographical area. Telephone lines and modems can provide the loop between devices separated by large distances. The synchronous protocol that gathers data into frames for these loops must provide the addressing support needed for each device to receive a frame and send it on to the next node in the loop. All stations must be capable of receiving a transmission frame and forward that frame to the next station even if the next station is the one that originally generated the frame.

Duplex Modes

Synchronous protocols, like the asynchronous protocols described earlier, can be half- or full-duplex. Half-duplex protocols enable transmission frames to flow in one direction at a time. The sender and receiver must agree on the direction in which the frames will flow during a period and agree to change that direction when appropriate. Full-duplex protocols, on the other hand, support the flow of transmission frames in both directions simultaneously. The sender and receiver can transmit frames without first agreeing on the direction frames will flow.

The duplex capabilities of a communications channel and the duplex operation of a synchronous protocol must be compatible. Table 6.1 provides a matrix of communications channel and protocol support for half- and full-duplex. Older synchronous protocols that always operate in half-duplex can travel through half- or full-duplex channels. The newer full-duplex protocols, on the other hand, require a full-duplex communications channel.

Figure 6.5
Synchronous
loop
connectivity.

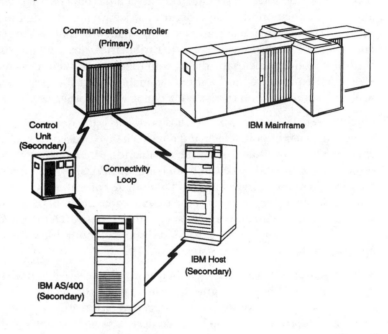

Table 6.1
Communications Channel and Protocol Duplex Matching Synchronous Protocol

Communications Channel	Half-Duplex	Full-Duplex
Half-Duplex	Supported	Not Supported
Full-Duplex	Supported	Supported

Data Transparency

The first synchronous protocols developed in the 1960s did not provide data transparency. The information field portion of their transmission frames had to contain printable text. Special communications control characters separated the fields in a transmission frame. Without data transparency, the transmission frame could not convey these special control characters as data. Including these characters in the text portion of a message could cause the protocol to fail.

Vendors added data transparency to these character-oriented protocols by including an additional control character to turn control on and off. By selecting one control character as a flag and placing it before the characters intended for control, vendors could send any type of data in the field originally intended for text only. The receiver did not react to a bit string that looked like a control character unless the special flag character preceded the string. This transparency flag was effective for making communications control characters visible to the receiver, yet it allowed bit streams that looked like control characters to pass through the link as data.

Data transparency in the early synchronous protocols consumed resources and was cumbersome. The transparency-flag character added overhead to the communications link. This overhead reduced the effective throughput of the link. Communications hardware had to "stuff" these flags into the bit stream at the sender's end. Hardware at the receiving end had to remove these special control characters. The process of making data transparent to the communications link was complex, which resulted in reduced reliability of the communications link.

The designers of later synchronous protocols built data transparency into the basic design of the protocols. These designers provided inherent data transparency by giving every type of transmission frame the same basic design. With inherent data transparency, communications devices can reliably send and receive any kind of data. The sender does not include special control characters in the transmission frame, and the receiver does not have to monitor for the presence of these control characters.

The following sections examine three popular synchronous protocols, beginning with the first synchronous protocol introduced by IBM and progressing to more recent vintages. Each protocol is examined in detail, and the section ends by discussing the synchronous protocol now accepted as an international standard.

Binary Synchronous Communications

IBM released the first products that included a synchronous protocol in the early 1960s. This *Binary Synchronous Communications* (BSC or *Bisync*) protocol became an enormous success for IBM. Other vendors subsequently adopted this protocol design for their products. Many BSC implementations are still in operation today. Table 6.2 provides a summary of the features IBM supports in the BSC protocol.

Table 6.2
BSC Features and Capabilities

Feature/Capability	Description
Half-Duplex Operation	The BSC protocol supports half-duplex operation and requires a line turn-around to change the direction of flow of transmission frames.
Character-Oriented Protocol	The information field of the BSC transmission frame conveys text, and control characters provide data link control. Transparent data communications require the DLE control character as a flag to identify subsequent control characters.
Message-Oriented Transmission Frames	BSC transmission frames exchange messages. The content of the frame determines its format.
Character Code Support	Vendors support BSC communications based on three character sets: seven-bit ASCII, Six-Bit Transcode, and eight-bit EBCDIC. The bit patterns of the control characters in each of these character sets are different.
Error Detection	The BSC protocol provides a *block check character(s)* (BCC) at the end of some frame types. The BCC length and format depends on the character code included in the information field.

Feature/Capability	Description
Synchronization	The start of each transmission frame includes two contiguous SYN characters that provide the signal transitions for synchronization between the sender and the receiver.

One feature that originally made BSC so popular is its support for multiple character sets. The three codes supported are the *Six-Bit Transcode* (SBT), the international version of the *American Standard Code for Information Interchange* (ASCII), and IBM's *Extended Binary Coded Decimal Interchange Code* (EBCDIC). Unfortunately, this flexible code support also makes BSC too complex. For example, the bit patterns for the control characters in each character set are different. As you see later, this multiplicity of code support translates into potential connectivity problems.

Link Control

The BSC protocol uses *link control characters* in transmission frames to synchronize and control the flow of data to one or more receivers. Table 6.3 shows a list of these control characters for the ASCII and EBCDIC character codes.

The following list provides a brief description of the results each of these characters produce for a communications link.

- ✔ **PAD.** *Packet Assembly/Disassembly* is a series of contiguous bits with the pattern 1111111, which assists older modems in performing bit synchronization. The PAD has a hexadecimal value of FF that is a blank character in ASCII; it has no character representation in EBCDIC.

- ✔ **SYN.** A pair of Synchronous Idle characters provides the signal transitions that enable two modems to agree on bit time at the start of each BSC transmission frame. The XSYN provides the synchronizing signal for transparent data. The X is part of a mnemonic indicating a two-byte sequence of which the first (or the only) byte is DLE (see table 6.3).

- ✔ **SOH.** *Start of Header* delineates the start of a block of control and routing data.

- ✔ **STX.** *Start of Text* character signifies the start of a block of text. The text that follows is user or application generated. The XSTX signifies the start of transparent text or data.

✔ **ITB.** *End of Intermediate Transmission Block* marks the end of an intermediate block of text when the sender transmits the text in multiple blocks. The last block of text ends with either an ETB or ETX. The XITB marks the end of transparent text or data.

✔ **ETB.** *End of Transmission Block* signifies the end of a message block when the transmission frame contains more than one message block. A block check character follows each ETB and provides error detection data for the block of text that precedes the ETB. This sequence demands a response for the receiver. The XETB signifies the end of a transparent message block.

✔ **ETX.** *End of Text* signifies the end of all messages and is followed by a BCC. This sequence demands a response from the receiver. The XETX signifies the end of all transparent messages or data.

✔ **EOT.** *End of Transmission* marks the end of all transmissions associated with a given message. The EOT places all receivers on the link in the reset mode and prepares them for the next series of transactions.

✔ **ENQ.** *Enquiry* requests a retransmission of a response to a message block. Devices use the ENQ to bid for a single, point-to-point communications link. The XENQ requests the retransmission of a response to a transparent block of text or data.

✔ **ACK0 or ACK1.** *Affirmative Acknowledgment* (ACKn) indicates proper receipt of the last transmission frame and a readiness to receive the next frame. The receiver alternates between the ACK0 and ACK1 to prevent line noise from erroneously creating what appears to be an acknowledgement.

✔ **WACK.** *Wait Before Transmit Affirmative Acknowledge* indicates proper receipt of the last frame but a temporary incapability to receive another frame.

✔ **NAK.** *Negative Acknowledge* indicates that the last frame contained errors and that the receiver is ready to receive another frame.

✔ **DLE.** *Data Link Escape* is a special control character that enables the sender and receiver to use transparent communications. The DLE precedes each character that should be treated as a control character by the receiver. The XDLE is a transparent DLE character.

✔ **RVI.** *Reverse Interrupt* requests an abnormal termination (abort) of a transmission. The RVI also can indicate an affirmative acknowledgement

of the last frame. A control station uses the RVI to select a tributary station for communications.

✔ **TTD.** *Temporary Text Delay* indicates that the station is not ready to transmit but expects to be soon. The TTD keeps the session between a control and tributary station active until the sender is ready to resume transmission. The XTTD indicates that the station is not ready to transmit the next block of transparent text or data.

✔ **DISC.** *Switched Line Disconnect* indicates that the sender is going to disconnect a switched telephone connection.

Table 6.3
BSC Protocol Control Characters

BSC Mnemonic	EBCDIC Character(s)	ASCII Character(s)
PAD	x'FF'	blank (x'FF')
SYN	SYN	SYN
SOH	SOH	SOH
STX	STX	STX
ITB	IUS	US
ETB	ETB	ETB
ETX	ETX	ETX
EOT	EOT	EOT
ENQ	ENQ	ENQ
NAK	NAK	NAK
DLE	DLE	DLE
ACK0	DEL x'70'	DLE 0
ACK1	DLE /	DLE 1
WACK	DLE ,	DLE ;
RVI	DLE @	DLE <
TTD	STX ENQ	STX ENQ
XSYN	DLE SYN	-
XSTX	DLE STX	-
XITB	DLE ITB	-
XETB	DLE ETB	-
XETX	DLE ETX	-
XENQ	DLE ENQ	-
XDLE	DLE	-
XTTD	DLE TTD	-

Link Control Sequences

A BSC transmission frame contains one of several possible link control sequences. Figure 6.6 shows some typical BSC frames. Because of the number of possible link control sequences and character codes, the sender and receiver must have matching capabilities. The two must be designed as a matched set or negotiate to a common set before transmission of messages begins.

Figure 6.6
Binary
Synchronous
Communications
transmission
frames.

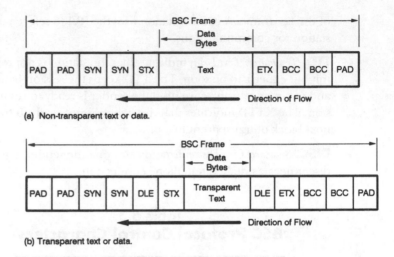

(a) Non-transparent text or data.

(b) Transparent text or data.

As Chapters 5 and 9 explain, MNP Class 1 and 2 byte-oriented, error-correcting protocols use packets that have a format similar to the BSC transparent frame shown in the 'b' section of figure 6.6. The ITU-T Recommendation V.42 calls for this same packet format in one of the alternative procedures modems can use when they cannot negotiate the use of the *Link-Access Procedure for Modems* (LAPM) protocol. The V.42 recommendation calls this protocol the start-stop, octet-oriented framing mode.

A simple exchange of text between a PC and a host computer illustrates the BSC protocol. Figure 6.7 shows the physical connection for this example and also shows the BSC sequence when a user sends a screen of text to a host. The sequence starts when the user presses Enter and ends when the host sends a response to the PC.

If two devices simultaneously bid for control of a point-to-point, half-duplex BSC link, a line contention develops. One device can actually start the ENQ bid after the other has started the bid because of the propagation delay of the transmission frame as it moves through the communications channel. In any event, both the devices must back off after they detect the contention and try an ENQ bid later. Each device waits a period (a *timeout*) based on a random number generated by the device. If the random number generated by each device is different (statistically, they almost have to be different), the device with the lowest number waits the shortest period and gains control of the line. Figure 6.8 illustrates the resolution of a BSC point-to-point contention.

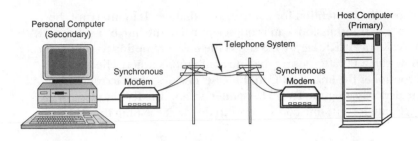

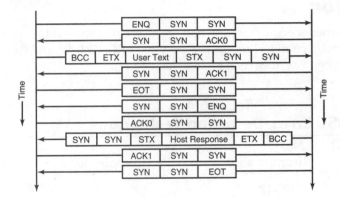

Figure 6.7
A PC with BSC sending a screen of data to a host.

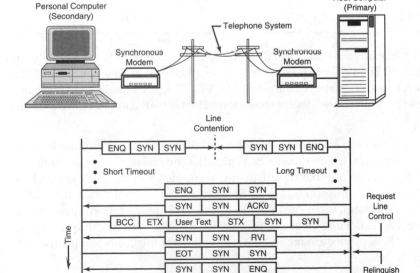

Figure 6.8
BSC line contention and control request.

A device that loses the contention for a line or one that needs to interrupt the current sequence of transmissions can request control of the line by issuing an RVI instead of an ACK0 or ACK1. Figure 6.8 shows the host attempting to gain control of the data flow with a PC after losing the line contention earlier. The device currently in control of the line, the PC in this case, decides when to relinquish control to the device issuing the RVI. The sender accepts the RVI in place of an ACK0 or ACK1 until it turns line control over to the device issuing the RVI.

Error Correction

BSC supports three types of error detection and one procedure for error correction. The three error-detection techniques are the VRC/LRC, CRC-12, and CRC-16. Table 6.4 shows when BSC uses each of these techniques.

Table 6.4
BSC Error-Detection Techniques

Code Set	No Transparency	Transparency
SBT	CRC-12	CRC-12
ASCII	VRC/LRC	CRC-16
EBCDIC	CRC-16	CRC-16

BSC uses odd parity for both the VRC and the LRC when the VRC/LRC technique is operational. The BSC sender appends the error detection data behind an ETB, ITB, or EXT as a block check character. The VRC/LRC is a single eight-bit byte. The CRC-12 consists of two six-bit characters. The CRC-16 consists of two eight-bit bytes.

The receiver must use a compatible mathematical technique to compute its own error-detection data. If the sender's BCC matches the receiver's calculated data, the receiver issues an alternating affirmative acknowledgement (ACK0 or ACK1) to ask for the next transmission frame. If the sender's BCC does not match the value the receiver calculates, the receiver issues a NAK to request a retransmission of the bad frame. Figure 6.9 illustrates this process. This ACKn/NAK technique is similar to the ACK/NAK procedure included in the asynchronous Xmodem protocol discussed earlier.

Multipoint Examples

To support multipoint connections between devices, BSC provides a device address along with other control data. When a control station wants to request data from any tributary that has data ready, it issues a *poll* message to all tributaries. When a control station wants to obtain data from a specific tributary, it includes the address of the tributary and a *select* message in the transmission frame. The only device that can respond to the select message is the tributary device with the designated address.

A tributary device can respond to a poll or select in one of the following three ways:

✔ An affirmative acknowledgement

✔ A negative acknowledgement, sent if it has no data to transmit when it receives a poll

✔ A message or data enclosed with the appropriate control characters

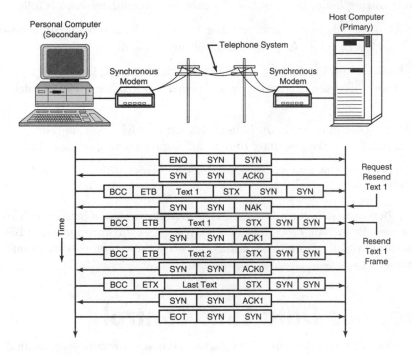

Figure 6.9
BSC error detection and correction.

Timeouts

The BSC protocol depends upon timeouts to maintain synchronization between communicating devices. After each one-second timeout, BSC requires the transmission of a SYN character. These characters provide the signal transitions that enable the devices at each end of the link to maintain an agreement on bit time.

The BSC protocol uses timeouts to ensure data flow control. BSC uses a two-second timeout before it sends a WACK or TTD. This enables a sender to keep control of the line and prevents a receiver from terminating an exchange. A BSC receiver gives a sender a three-second period to respond with the next transmission frame before starting an abort sequence.

BSC Summary

As you can see from the preceding paragraphs, BSC is a dramatic improvement over its asynchronous predecessors. The protocol enables vendors to install and control both point-to-point and multipoint connections. It also enabled vendors to improve the reliability, control, and throughput of communications links. BSC contains several limitations, however, that make more recent synchronous protocols more attractive.

The design and implementation of BSC contains four major handicaps as follows:

✔ It supports three character sets that require a selection of one set between two devices before they can communicate.

✔ It uses some characters from these three character sets for data link control. The use of control characters makes transparent data transfer cumbersome.

✔ It can communicate in the half-duplex mode only, which limits its capability to take advantage of new, full-duplex communications links.

✔ It does not check all transmission fields for errors, which limits its reliability.

IBM and others overcame these limitations through the design of better synchronous protocols. By the late 1960s, less than ten years after the introduction of BSC, these vendors introduced improved protocols. Two of these protocols are examined next.

Synchronous Data Link Control

While installing BSC-based systems, IBM discovered that many customers wanted to install devices in loop configurations. Cable loops were often less costly to install and maintain than other multipoint configurations. This presented many difficulties because BSC did not provide good support for loop configurations. Based on the customer requirements for loop installations, IBM redesigned the BSC protocol to give it more flexibility. The result of this work is the *Synchronous Data Link Control* (SDLC) IBM introduced in the early 1970s.

SDLC was so well designed that it has endured the test of time. Table 6.5 shows a summary of SDLC's characteristics. These characteristics have provided the

foundation for IBM's *System Network Architecture* (SNA) since its introduction in 1974. SDLC is also the data link control protocol that supports the Common Communications Support for IBM's *Systems Application Architecture* (SAA).

Table 6.5
SDLC Features and Capabilities

Feature/Capability	Description
Full-Duplex Protocol	SDLC supports simultaneous bi-directional flow of transmission frames through full-duplex communications channels.
Bit-Oriented Protocol	The entire SDLC transmission frame except the starting and ending Flag is transparent to SDLC communications hardware.
Transmission Frame Support	All SDLC transmission frames have the same format regardless of the data, information, or controls they convey.
Character Code Support	SDLC does not depend upon a character code for operation. No control characters are in the protocol except the starting and ending Flag fields.
Error Detection	The SDLC error-detection field always contains two bytes of CRC-CCITT data called a *frame check sequence* (FCS).
Synchronization	The starting Flag field provides the signal transitions that enable the receiver to synchronize with the sender. This flag marks the end of a transmission frame.

II

Data Communications

The two SDLC features that contribute the most to its success are the fixed format of its transmission frames and their inherent data transparency. Figure 6.10 shows the general SDLC transmission frame. As you can see, each field is one or more eight-bit bytes. A receiver knows where the transmission frame starts from the starting flag, and where it ends from the ending flag. The receiver can calculate the position of other fields from this information. The contents of a field can tell the receiver what subsequent fields contain, but the receiver does not have to decipher this information until it sees the ending flag. Information in the SDLC has position significance rather than content significance, which makes it transparent to the receiving hardware.

Figure 6.10
Synchronous
Data Link
Control (SDLC)
transmission
frame.

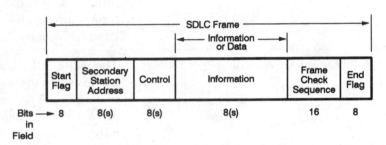

Although IBM uses EBCDIC as a character code for many SDLC implementations, the code does not affect the operation of the SDLC protocol. The information field of an SDLC transmission frame can contain any character code, or it can contain data as bit strings. The protocol has no concern with this data. The application that uses SDLC to move the data or information must interpret or use these bits. The operations of these applications are at a higher OSI level than the SDLC protocol.

Link Controls

The SDLC protocol has predefined fields in each frame that provide link control. The sender's hardware creates the header and trailer for each frame as shown in figure 6.11. These transmission frames contain three types of fields: framing data that indicate the start and end of each frame; control data that provide the data link control for the protocol; and optional information.

Although all SDLC frames have the same basic structure, the contents of each frame determines its type. Figure 6.12 shows the three types of SDLC frames: *information frames* (I-frames); *supervisory control sequences* (S-frames); and *unnumbered command/response frames* (U-frames). As you can see, all three types of frames contain the same header and trailer fields. The I-frame has one more transparent information field. The following paragraphs discuss these three frame types and all the SDLC fields.

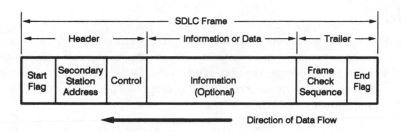

Figure 6.11
SDLC transmission frame header and trailer.

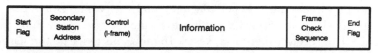

Figure 6.12
Synchronous Data Link Control (SDLC) transmission frames.

(a) Information Frame (I-frame).

(b) Supervisory Control Sequence Frame (S-frame).

(c) Unnumbered Command/Response Frame (U-frame).

I-Frames

The I-frame transfers user or application data. The Information field of the I-frame can be any length, but it must be a multiple of eight bits. The field can contain characters, data, or any other form of data. The Control field tells the receiver that the frame contains an Information field, as you see later.

S-Frames

The S-frame provides supervisory control for the communications link. S-frames, like the ACK0, ACK1, NAK, TTD, and WACK control codes in the BSC protocol, provide affirmative or negative acknowledgement to the other end of the link and request temporary pauses in the flow of transmission frames.

U-Frames

The U-frames do not have transmission sequence numbers like the other two frame types, which enables them to convey up to 32 commands and responses in the Control field. By including these commands and controls in an existing field, IBM reduces the SDLC overhead and keeps its design simple.

Flag Field

The SDLC Flag field provides the signal variations in the communications channel that enable a receiver to synchronize with the sender. The sender can transmit one or more of these fields as a preamble to the remainder of the transmission frame. The receiver determines the bit time of the frame from this field as discussed in Chapter 2, "Communications Channels."

The Flag field repeats at the end of the transmission frame as both a frame delimiter and a mark. The receiver monitors the bit patterns it receives in a frame, but takes no action until it sees the 01111110 flag bit pattern. Upon receipt of the ending flag, the receiver counts back eight bits to locate the end of the frame check sequence. The receiver then counts back 16 more bits to locate the start of the FCS. Likewise, the receiver can count forward from the beginning of the starting flag to locate the Address and Control fields. The contents of these two fields tell the receiver the total length of the SDLC header. By knowing the length of the header and trailer, the receiver can calculate the length of the Information field.

To maintain transparency of all fields bound by the starting and ending Flag fields, the SDLC hardware must ensure that no bit strings in the frame contain the Flag field pattern. If the SDLC hardware sees a bit string that has this pattern (six contiguous ones), it must do zero bit insertion to alter the pattern. When a sender does this bit stuffing, the receiver's hardware must remove and discard these inserted zeros.

The SDLC protocol supports an abnormal termination signal based on a continuous stream of one bits. If the receiver sees more than five contiguous one bits, it must decide whether the pattern is a flag, an abort command, or noise on the line. The receiver must then perform the proper SDLC sequence based on that pattern.

Address Field

The Address field provides either a destination address or a source address depending upon the status of the sender. If the sender is a primary link station, it places the destination address of the secondary link station in the Address field. If the sender is an SLS, it includes its own source address in the Address field.

A PLS can use the Address field to direct frames to more than one destination or to an unknown address. The PLS can send a frame to multiple addresses or to a group of addresses by adding multiple Address fields. If the last address bit is a zero, it tells the receiver that another Address Field is behind the first. If the last address bit is a one, it tells the receiver that no more Address fields exist. The PLS sends an FF hex address if it does not know the destination address for the frame.

Control Fields

The Control field determines the frame type and conveys data link controls. Figure 6.13 shows the Control field format for all three types of SDLC frames. Figure 6.13a shows the Control field encoding for modulo-8 operation (a sliding window that is eight frames wide); whereas, figure 6.13b shows the encoding for modulo-128 operation. A device transmits the *Least Significant Bit* (LSB) of the Control field first and the *Most Significant Bit* (MSB) last. For SDLC, the LSB is bit 7 and the MSB is bit 0. When the CCITT modified SDLC to create the High-level Data Link Control, they reversed the numbering of the bit positions, but not the contents of the fields. The SDLC numbering scheme describes this Control field.

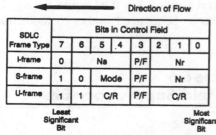

(a) SDLC Control Field for modulo-8 operation.

Figure 6.13
SDLC Control Field encoding.

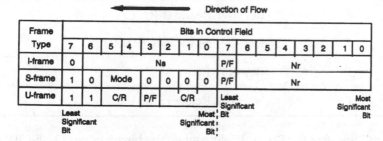

(b) SDLC Control Fields for modulo-128 operation.

As figure 6.13 illustrates, either the first one or the first two bits in the Control field determines the frame type. Bit position 7 alone can designate an I-frame; bit positions 7 and 6 specify a frame as an S-frame or a U-frame. The remaining bits convey the control information. For brevity, the modulo-8 field definitions are reviewed in the following paragraphs.

If bit position 7 of the Control field contains a zero, the SDLC frame conveys information and is an I-frame. Bits 6, 5, and 4 of an I-frame convey the *Send Sequence Number* (Ns) for the information. This number can range from 000 (zero) to 111 (eight). The Ns gives each frame an identifier that enables the receiver to request the retransmission of the frame by number if the receiver detects an error in the frame. I-frame bit position 3 indicates whether the frame is a *poll frame* (P) or the *final frame* (F) in a sequence. A primary link station sends a P value of 1 to signify a poll of a tributary. The tributary sends an F value of 1 to signify that it has no more information to send. I-frame bit positions 2, 1, and 0 convey the *Receive Sequence Number* (Nr). This number can range from 000 (zero) to 111 (eight). A receiver uses the Nr to indicate which transmission frame it wants to receive next.

If bit positions 6 and 7 of the Control field contain the binary values 10, the SDLC frame conveys supervisory control data and is an S-frame. Bit positions 5 and 4 indicate a device's mode or readiness to receive more frames. Table 6.6 shows the receiver mode that bit positions 5 and 4 indicate. S-frame bit position 3 provides the same poll/final (P/F) indication as bit position 3 in the I-frame. S-frame bit positions 2, 1, and 0 convey the same Receive Sequence Number Nr indication as bit positions 2, 1, and 0 of the I-frame.

Table 6.6
S-Frame Control Field Supervisory Bits

Bit	Position	
5	4	Receiver Mode
0	0	Receiver Ready (RR)
1	0	Receiver Not Ready (RNR)
0	1	Reject (REJ)
1	1	Selective Reject (SREJ)

If bit positions 7 and 6 of the Control field contain the binary values 11, the SDLC frame conveys unnumbered command/response data and is a U-frame. Bit positions 5, 4, 2, 1, and 0 contain the *Command/Response* (C/R) data link controls. Table 6.7 shows how to decode these bit positions. U-frame bit position 3 provides the same poll/final (P/F) indication as bit position 3 in the I- and S-frames.

Table 6.7
SDLC U-frame Command/Response Encoding

Command/Response Bit Position 54 210	Primary Link Station Command	Secondary Link Station Command
00 000	Unnumbered Information	Unnumbered Information
10 000	Set Initialization Mode	Request Initialization Mode
11 000	Set Alarm Mode	Disconnect Response Mode
00 100	Unnumbered Poll	Unnumbered Final
00 010	Disconnect	Request Disconnect
00 001	Set Normal Response Code	Reserved
00 111	Test	Test
00 110	Reserved	Unnumbered Acknowledge
10 001	Reserved	Frame Reject
11 101	eXchange Identification	eXchange Identification
10 011	Configure	Configure
11 011	Set Normal Extended	Reserved Mode Response

Information Field

The Information field is the only SDLC field that does not perform data link control functions. This field can contain any kind of text, data, or bit stream. The information does not have to be character-oriented text. This field does, however, have to contain multiples of eight bits. Because EBCDIC and eight-bit ASCII characters are eight bits in length, the Information field can contain text based on these character sets. To convey data streams that do not contain a multiple of eight bits, the sender must pad the end of the field with bits. The receiver must discard these pad bits.

Frame Check Sequence

The FCS is a two-byte field that contains CRC CCITT error-detection data. The receiver continuously calculates its own CRC throughout the receipt of a frame. When the receiver identifies the ending flag for the frame, it rolls back eight bits to the beginning of the flag, and then 16 more bits to the beginning of the FCS. The receiver then compares this FCS to the CRC it calculated during receipt of the frame. If the frame's FCS and the receiver's CRC are the same, the frame contains no detectable errors. If the FCS and the calculated CRC are different, the receiver assumes that the frame contains errors.

A set of devices uses the Control field Nr bits to correct frames that contain errors. The sender marks the Control field Nr bits of each numbered frame it sends to show the specific sequence number of that frame. The receiver updates its Nr counter each time it receives a good, numbered SDLC frame. If the receiver determines that a numbered frame contains errors, it must transmit an I- or S-frame to the sender and use the Nr bit positions in the Control field to request a retransmission of the bad frame.

Protocol Examples

To understand the power of the SDLC protocol, you have to see some examples of its data link control, provided in the following paragraphs. An illustration of the error-correction procedure discussed for the FCS field is presented first, followed by an example of data flow control based on the receiver ready bits in the Control field of an S-frame. This book does not try to illustrate all the potential SDLC procedures.

SDLC Error Correction

Figure 6.14 illustrates the SDLC error-correction procedure. The SLS transmits frames 0-2 to the PLS. The PLS finds an error in frame 1 and requests a retransmission of that frame. The request implicitly tells the SLS that frame 0 was good.

The SLS goes back to frame 1 and restarts the transmission. The sender includes a Final bit value of one for the third frame to indicate that it is the last frame in the sequence.

The procedure in figure 6.14 shows how SDLC retransmits bad data. When a device receives a retransmission request, it must go back to the frame that contains the bad data and resend that frame and all subsequent frames, even if the subsequent frames contain no errors. This is the same "go back n" procedure contained in the MNP protocol discussed earlier.

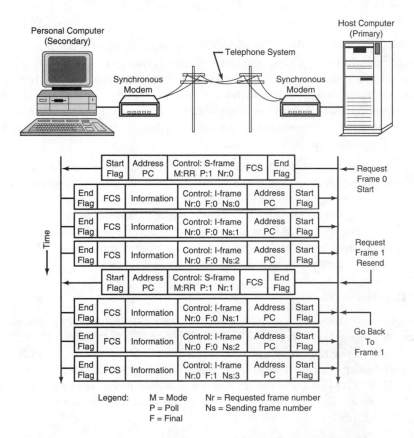

Figure 6.14
SDLC error detection and correction.

SDLC supports two sliding window alternatives—modulo-8 operating mode and modulo-128 mode. Modulo-8 operating mode enables SDLC to transmit up to eight frames without receiving an acknowledgement for any of the eight. Modulo-128 enables it to transmit up to 128 frames in a given sequence without receiving an acknowledgement for any of the 128. The modulo-8 alternative is good for communications through telephone lines that provide fast response time. The modulo-128 alternative is good for communications through satellite links and public data networks that either have built-in delays or slow response times under heavy traffic conditions.

The PLS specifies which of two window sizes it uses when it resets tributaries. The *Set Normal Response Mode* (SNRM) command specifies modulo 8 and causes the PLS and SLS to use the short form of the Control field shown in the 'a' section of figure 6.13. The *Set Normal Response Mode Extended* (SNRME) command specifies modulo 128 and causes the PLS and SLS to use the extended form of the Control field shown in the 'b' section of figure 6.13. These commands reset the Nr and Ns counters for the PLS and SLSs.

For modulo-8 operation, both the Ns and Nr fields contain three bit positions. These fields enable a sending device to number frames from 0 to 7 and a receiving device to request the retransmission of frames with a number from 0 to 7. Thus, a sending device must receive an affirmative acknowledgement of a frame number at least every eight frames or it does not know which Ns frame contains an error when it gets an Nr request for retransmission of a frame. These three-bit Ns and Nr fields result in a sliding window eight frames wide.

For modulo-128 operation, both the Ns and Nr fields contain seven bit positions. These fields enable a sending device to number frames from 0 to 127 and a receiving device to request the retransmission of frames with a number from 0 to 127. Thus, a sending device must receive an affirmative acknowledgement of a frame number at least every 128 frames, or it does not know which Ns frame contains an error when it gets an Nr request for retransmission of a frame. These seven-bit Ns and Nr fields result in a sliding window 128 frames wide.

SDLC Controls

The Control field of an S-frame enables a device to request a temporary pause in the receipt of transmission frames. Figure 6.15 shows an SLS that issues a *Receiver Not Ready* (RNR) in the middle of a file transfer from a PLS to an SLS. The PLS stops the transmission of information frames and starts to poll the SLS as soon as it receives the RNR. The PLS continues to poll the SLS until it receives a *Receiver Ready* (RR) response. The PLS resumes the transmission of the file with the next sequential Ns frame after it receives the RR.

A Control field of a U-frame enables a PLS to exert significant control over a tributary station. Figure 6.16 illustrates the use of several of the SDLC command/ response controls listed earlier in table 6.7. This figure shows the startup of a device that needs software from a host. The SLS issues a *Request for Initialization Mode* (RIM). The host responds with a Control field containing a *Set Initialization Mode* (SIM). The SLS responds with an *Unsequence Acknowledge* (UA). The host then sends the device the software it needs to operate and resets the SLS with another SNRM to prepare it for normal operation.

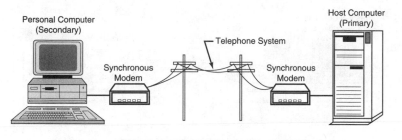

Figure 6.15
Temporary
pause in SDLC
data delivery to
PC.

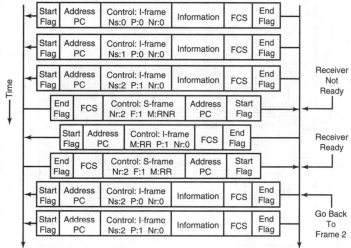

Configurations

As you can see from the preceding paragraphs, IBM developed a powerful and enduring protocol in SDLC. The fixed format of SDLC's transmission frame makes it easier to implement, and the definitions of the six fields in the transmission frame also make it possible to address and communicate with multiple secondary link stations simultaneously.

This book only reviews examples for point-to-point operation of SDLC, but SDLC does support multipoint and loop configurations as well. Figures 6.17 and 6.18 illustrate the basic SDLC link definition and the four major categories of connectivity that SDLC supports. As you can see from these figures, SDLC does address both switched-telephone links as well as leased-line configurations.

Figure 6.16
Primary and secondary exchange of commands/responses.

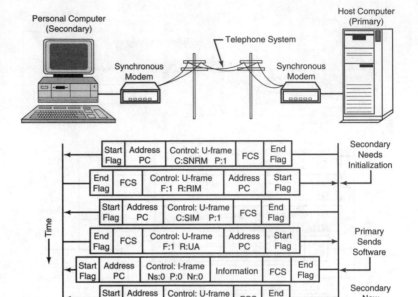

Figure 6.17
SNA data link components.

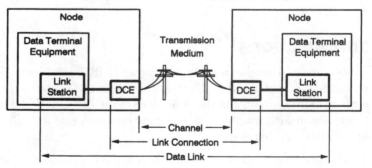

Derivative Protocols

The SDLC protocol enabled IBM to improve the reliability and performance of synchronous communications so well that others followed in their footsteps. SDLC contained so many good features that other vendors and international organizations adopted it with little or no modification. Table 6.8 shows a few of these derivative protocols.

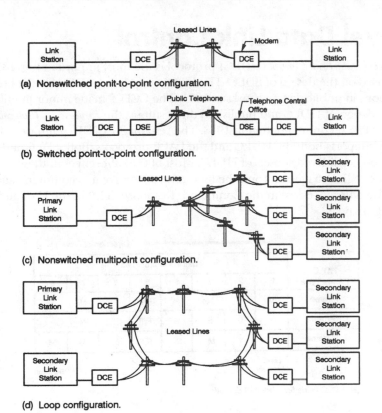

Figure 6.18
SDLC data link
configuration
alternatives.

(a) Nonswitched ponit-to-point configuration.

(b) Switched point-to-point configuration.

(c) Nonswitched multipoint configuration.

(d) Loop configuration.

Table 6.8
Protocols Derived from SDLC
Proprietary Protocols

Vendor	Protocol	Relationship to SDLC
Burroughs	BDLC	Same as SDLC
Univac	UDLC	Same as SDLC

International Protocols

Organization	Protocol	Relationship to SDLC
ISO	HDLC	Minor changes in SDLC
ITU-T	LAPB	Same as HDLC
ITU-T	LAPM	Same as HDLC
ANSI	ADCCP	Same as HDLC

High-Level Data Link Control

The *High-level Data Link Control* (HDLC) protocol is the most important non-IBM protocol based on the design of SDLC. The ISO first adopted HDLC for the link layer functions in public data networks in 1971. The CCITT made minor modifications in the design of HDLC and published the results as the *Link-Access Protocol, Balanced* (LAPB) recommendation in 1978. The renamed CCITT committee, the ITU-T, now supports both the HDLC and the LAPB protocols. Both SDLC and LAPB are now considered subsets of HDLC. Most of the differences in these subsets relate to link diagnostics and the hierarchy of control in a communications network. The differences are in the Command/Response fields of the U-frame shown in figure 6.19.

Figure 6.19
HDLC Control
Field encoding.

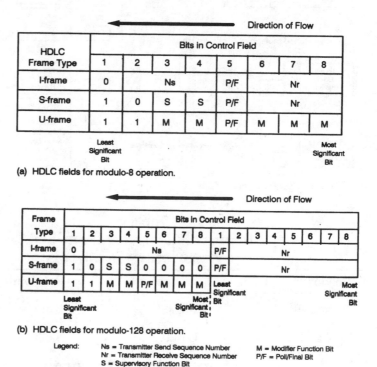

(a) HDLC fields for modulo-8 operation.

(b) HDLC fields for modulo-128 operation.

Legend: Ns = Transmitter Send Sequence Number   M = Modifier Function Bit
Nr = Transmitter Receive Sequence Number   P/F = Poll/Final Bit
S = Supervisory Function Bit

Three significant differences between SDLC and LAPB are as follows:

✔ SDLC has test and diagnostic commands not supported in LAPB.

✔ SDLC requires a hierarchical relationship between communicating stations, whereas LAPB requires a peer-to-peer relationship as shown in figure 6.20.

✔ SDLC supports both point-to-point and multipoint configurations, whereas, LAPB supports only point-to-point.

Fortunately, these differences are small enough that vendors can easily convert one protocol to the other for internetwork communications between the two.

Figure 6.20
SDLC and LAPB relationships between stations.

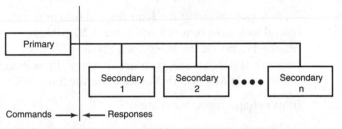

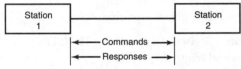

(a) SDLC hierarchical relationship between primary and secondary stations.

(b) LAPB peer-to-peer, point-to-point realtionship between stations

The ITU-T recommends the link-access protocol for two major wide area networks based on the design and operation of HDLC. First, it defines LAPB for use with networks that conform with the ITU-T Recommendation X.25 for *packet-switched networks* (PSN). As you see in later chapters, these X.25 networks provide a common denominator for the interconnection of hosts made by different vendors. Second, *Link-Access Protocol, D Channel* (LAPD) defines the requirements for the D control channel of the *Integrated Services Digital Network* (ISDN). The next chapter examines the features and functions of both these network architectures.

The ITU-T also defines a link-access protocol for asynchronous-to-synchronous conversion and error correction between modems used in general switched telephone networks. This LAPM protocol (*Link-Access Procedure for Modems*) uses the HDLC protocol and error control architecture to ensure near error-free communications outside of wide area network environments. Chapter 5, "Communication Error Correction," looked at this protocol briefly, and Chapter 9, "Telephone System Interfaces," examines it further.

Chapter Snapshot

This chapter explores the features and functions of several wide area network types: the X.25 packet-switched network, the Integrated Services Digital Network (ISDN), frame relay architecture, Broadband ISDN, and IBM's System Network Architecture (SNA).

In this chapter, you learn about:

✔ Function-layering in wide area networks

✔ X.25 levels

✔ Types of X.25 packets and channels

✔ Integrated Services Digital Network (ISDN) services and features

✔ Benefits of frame relay architecture

✔ Broadband ISDN (BISDN) features

✔ System Network Architecture (SNA) components and features

✔ SNA software modules

✔ SNA connectivity

CHAPTER

Wide Area Networks

E arlier chapters reviewed the techniques vendors use to detect and correct errors and the protocols vendors use to provide end-to-end control of a data link. This chapter continues this progression by showing you how vendors start with a specific form of data link control and add other layers of connectivity to provide *wide area networks* (WANs). Figure 7.1 shows the progression from synchronous protocols to two of the WANs reviewed in this chapter.

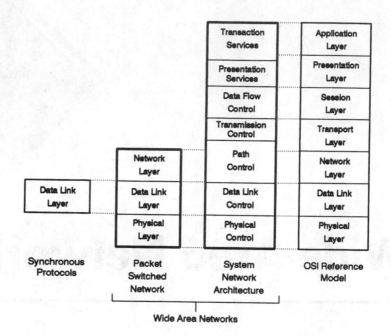

Figure 7.1
Progression from synchronous protocols to wide area networks.

The information in this chapter builds on information provided in preceding chapters. Some background material is repeated when necessary to clarify a point, but you should be familiar with the physical and data link control layers of connectivity to get the full benefit of this chapter.

Wide Area Network Perspectives

Wide area networks combine the continuous error-detection and correction techniques included in synchronous communications with robust network problem determination and data routing. These WANs are typically powerful backbones that ensure high-quality, reliable service for end users. They enable multiple users to access a variety of host computers simultaneously through the same physical medium. The network separates each user's session so that no user is aware of other users on the network. Portions of these WANs can be voice-grade telephone lines, and other portions can be digital data circuits. Some WANs are all-digital as you see later.

WAN Alternatives

Voice networks, such as the public telephone system, transmit and receive voice-frequency sounds as discussed in Chapter 2, "Communications Channels." You can

connect with these networks at data rates as high as 28,800 bps with current modem hardware without special amplifying and switching equipment. *Leased lines,* on the other hand, are telephone lines that include special conditioning or packet-switched systems. You can lease special data lines from several vendors (including AT&T) that support connection rates as high as 28,800 bps. Neither voice-grade nor leased telephone lines provide error detection and correction. Data communications hardware and software at each end of the link must provide this service.

All-digital data services provide both high-speed communications and error correction. Subscribers can start at rates as low as 9,600 bps and go as high as 56,000 bps. The T1 channel banks used in these systems communicate between switching centers at 1.544 Mbps. Users who need to communicate large volumes of data at high speed also can subscribe for this T1 service directly. These all-digital systems provide complete error detection and correction, as well as network control. Yet, the devices that communicate through these services must handle all data link controls to ensure proper delivery of data.

You also can subscribe to a *public data network* (PDN) to communicate with a remote computer or service company. These *packet-switched networks* (PSNs) provide special error detection and correction for digital data and are one variety of WAN. They take the data stream you want to send to a remote computer and divide it into small blocks. Each block contains a header to enable network nodes to deliver the block properly. Network-compatible hardware then wraps the block in a synchronous data link control transmission frame and routes the frame through the network. The frames travel through the network at high speed, normally reaching their destination in a fraction of a second. The last node in the network must ensure the proper sequencing of data blocks as it delivers the blocks to their destination.

Most PDNs conform with international connectivity standards. The most popular PDNs conform with the *ITU-T Recommendation X.25* interface specifications. These networks provide high-speed communications between computers made by most vendors today. Because of their international acceptance, they also provide data communications services between companies and organizations that span international boundaries. This type of WAN is examined later in this chapter.

The latest trend in WAN connectivity is the open systems, all-digital approach that also adheres to international standards. A world-wide effort to accomplish this objective is called the *Integrated Services Digital Network* (ISDN). ISDN has gained substantial momentum in Europe, but is just gaining widespread support in America. Several videoconferencing vendors now require ISDN connectivity because of its high data rates, and the fact that public telephone companies can provide the service. Both the original narrowband and the new broadband ISDN are discussed later in this chapter.

II

Data Communications

Another twist on the ISDN scheme is a WAN architecture called *frame relay,* which eliminates some of the bottlenecks in the X.25 recommendation to provide higher data rates and system throughput. Frame relay is a direct result of ISDN architecture work performed by ITU-T. This protocol, like its predecessor X.25, can be transported through an ISDN system. Many industry pundits now predict the frame relay and ISDN combination will soon replace aging X.25 systems because of the high-speed voice, data, and video transport capabilities of the combined architectures.

If you plan to purchase processors and connectivity hardware from a single vendor, you may be able to install a WAN made specifically for that vendor's equipment. Most large computer vendors supply the hardware and software that enable you to install and operate these WANs. The most popular vendor-specific WAN is IBM's *System Network Architecture* (SNA), discussed later in the chapter.

WAN Functional Layers

One feature common to all wide area networks is the layering of connectivity functions. As data move down through these layers, the network functions add specific information to the data. The information enables the receiving station to use the data after it arrives. Figure 7.2 illustrates this process for two stations that have connectivity that conform with the OSI model. Each layer adds header information to the packet or frame it receives from the next highest layer until the packet or frame ultimately reaches the data link layer.

The data link layer, typically either a *High-level Data Link Control* (HDLC) or *Synchronous Data Link Control* (SDLC) protocol, adds addressing, control, and error-detection headers and trailers. These support data transfer through the physical medium. The physical layer converts this final transmission package into electrical or light signals and conveys them through the communications channel.

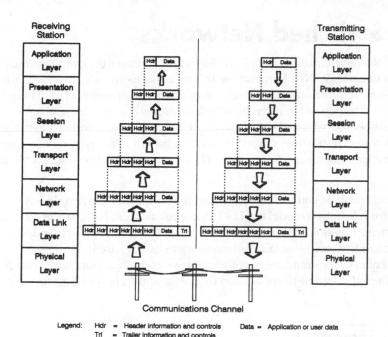

Figure 7.2
Data movement through OSI layers and between stations.

Legend: Hdr = Header information and controls   Data = Application or user data
Trl = Trailer information and controls

The station at the other end of the link must reverse this process. It receives the bit signals through the medium and converts them back into a transmission packet or frame of data and controls. The receiver then passes the packet or frame up through each OSI layer. As a layer receives the packet or frame, it reads the first header to figure out how to handle the bits that follow. After stripping off this header, the layer sends the package on to the next highest layer for further processing. This process continues until the user or application data reach their ultimate destination at the application layer.

All WANs use this layering technique, but vendors use different headers and trailers for different types of networks. Because of the similarities in the techniques, it is possible to interconnect different WANs and communicate between them. It is also possible to connect local area networks to WANs or to use WANs to bridge between LANs. These types of network interconnectivity are discussed in Part III, "Local Area Networking."

Packet-Switched Networks

The ITU-T Recommendation X.25 Level 3 is a protocol used in several popular *value added networks* (VANs). Vendors use this protocol to provide their users with near error-free communications between *data terminal equipment* (DTE). These computers and terminals are often hundreds or thousands of miles apart. Although most people refer to these VANs and PDNs as X.25 networks, the complete end-to-end connection between a terminal and a host or between two computers can involve capabilities from three other ITU-T Recommendations: X.3, X.28, and X.29.

X.25 networks provide connectivity functions that fall within the first three OSI layers. Figure 7.3 shows a model of ITU-T Recommendation X.25. If a need exists for connectivity functions above the network layer, the devices at each end of the link must provide them. Most PC implementations of X.25 are in modems or optional adapters. Communication software provides the functions above the X.25 level to deliver application-to-application or user-to-application dialogs through the network.

Figure 7.3
CCITT
Recommendation
X.25.

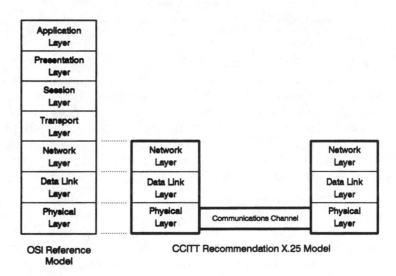

X.25 Levels

X.25 describes the following three levels of requirements for attaching a packet terminal to a PSN's *Data Circuit-terminating Equipment* (DCE), as shown in figure 7.4:

✔ *Physical level* describes the interface with the physical media. This layer corresponds to the OSI model's physical layer.

✔ *Link level* describes a subset of the High-level Data Link Control (HDLC) called the *Link Access Protocol-Balanced* (LAPB). This level corresponds to the OSI model's data link layer.

✔ *Packet level* describes the protocol for data transport through a PSN. This level corresponds to the OSI model's network layer.

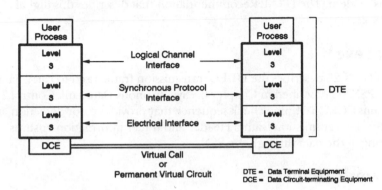

Figure 7.4
X.25 network levels and functions.

X.25 networks aggregate the connections from DCEs into high-speed trunk lines. A *Data Switching Exchange* (DSE) provides this aggregation, as shown in figure 7.5. A DSE takes three or more streams of data from DCEs and routes them to other DSEs. Connections between DSEs are typically 56 Kbps or higher, and each DSE node contains a switching computer that can simultaneously route data between many DCEs. The following paragraphs examine the X.25 layers of connectivity functions that support this data routing.

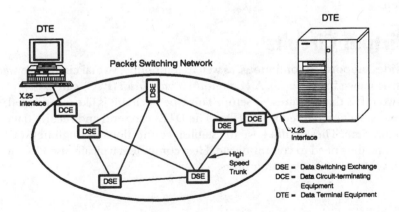

Figure 7.5
Packet-switched network components.

II

Data Communications

X.25 Physical Level

The physical level of X.25 describes the connectors and wires required for connecting to and sending data bits through a synchronous DCE that interfaces with the PSN. Its primary functions are to provide synchronization and pass data and control signals between a terminal or computer and the DCE, which is normally a synchronous modem. The ITU-T Recommendation that describes this digital interface is X.21.

X.25 Link Level

The link level of X.25 describes the HDLC transmission frame used to carry data through the PSN. As described in Chapter 6, "Synchronous Data Link Control," HDLC contains a CRC-16 frame check sequence that provides error detection and protection for the transmission frame. Header and trailer information ensures correct routing of the data through the PSN.

X.25 Network Level

The network level of X.25 describes the types and formats of packets used to set up X.25 connections (called *virtual calls*), send data over virtual circuits, control the flow of packets, and recover from failures. The first two X.25 levels were examined in the discussion of the physical and data link layer functions in earlier chapters. The following paragraphs concentrate on the details of level 3. As you see later in this chapter, this X.25 layer contains overhead functions required to ensure high-quality communications even with older error-prone networks. As networks continue to improve in quality and reliability, this overhead becomes an unnecessary burden.

X.25 Virtual Circuits

X.25 provides support for continuous, as well as temporary, virtual circuits between two DTEs, as shown in figure 7.6. A *Permanent Virtual Circuit* (PVC) can exist between two DTEs that requires no setup. This type of circuit is like a dedicated, leased-line connection between two DTEs. The DTEs can send and receive data packets at any time. They do not have to establish connections through network calls each time they need to communicate. Host computers typically use PVCs to move high volumes of data to other hosts.

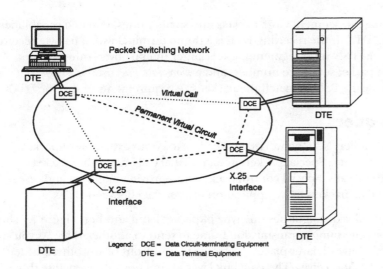

Figure 7.6
X.25 virtual
circuits.

II

Data Communications

Two DTE devices also can set up a *virtual call* (VC). This type of connection is temporary and requires a setup procedure for each connection and a special clearing procedure to ensure proper communications between the DTEs. A PC can set up one or more VCs for low-volume traffic, while maintaining a PVC with a host for high-volume traffic.

An optional X.25 feature enables a PSN to be set up to provide two classes of service: *high priority* and *normal priority*. A user's computer normally selects high priority for keyboard interaction with a remote host to get the best response time through the network. The network processes high-priority frames before processing normal-priority frames. A user's computer or terminal, on the other hand, selects normal-priority processing for batch operations that can be processed overnight or without user interaction. This dual class of service and its pricing structure enable the user to pay a premium for better response time and keep cost down for slower operations.

X.25 Packets and Frames

An X.25 network subdivides all data and information into discrete packets. Although X.25 recommends a maximum data field length of 128 bytes (the same as an asynchronous Xmodem data field length), options exist that allow sizes of 16, 32, 64, 256, 512, and 1,024 bytes. At subscription time, a user organization selects a specific packet size that the PSN uses for later calls.

A PSN may have to segment large packets into smaller ones to match capabilities of the receiving DTE. If the receiving DTE is a dumb terminal with a 64-byte receive buffer limit, the PSN must segment packets larger than 64 bytes into 64-byte packets. The packet sequence numbers and a *more-data flag*, used to show split packets, enable the PSN to match the packet-size requirements of specific DTEs.

Packet Headers

As described earlier, X.25 networks use headers to control the flow of packets through the network. Special packets initiate virtual calls, and other packets respond to these calls. Special control packets also provide interrupt and reset services, and data packets move application or user data between DTEs.

The packet header distinguishes one type of packet from another. Figure 7.7 shows an X.25 DTE generating a transmission frame to send to another DTE. As you can see, the DTE's network layer places its own header in front of any other headers that enclose data it receives. The data link layer of functions then enclose this X.25 packet in an HDLC transmission frame. Finally, the physical layer generates the bit signals required to convey the transmission frame through the X.25 medium.

Figure 7.7
X.25 packet and transmission frame.

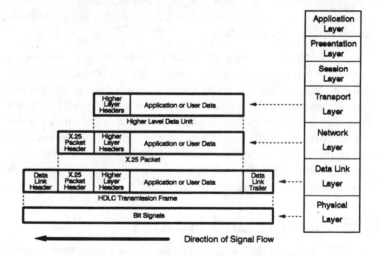

The HDLC transmission frame provides the fields required to make a point-to-point connection through the network, as discussed in Chapter 6; figure 7.8 shows these fields. The HDLC frame contains a Start flag that supports synchronization between sender and receiver. An Address field identifies the final destination of the frame, and the Control field supports all the LAPB commands and responses required to support peer-to-peer communications, as shown in figure 7.9. Error-detection data, included in the *Frame Check Sequence* (FCS), enables two DTEs or

two DSEs to eliminate almost all communication errors by resending packets that contain errors. The End flag tells the receiver where the frame ends.

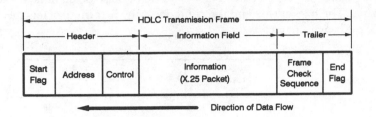

Figure 7.8
Packet-switched network HDLC transmission frame.

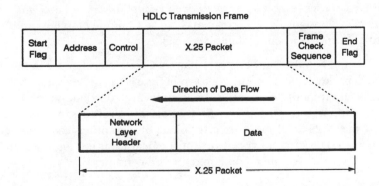

Figure 7.9
LAPB peer-to-peer, point-to-point relationship between stations.

The DTE places the X.25 packet in the Information field of the HDLC transmission frame. This packet contains the original user or application data and a network layer header, as shown in figure 7.10. The X.25 Packet flows as a synchronous data stream inside the synchronous HDLC frame. The receiver must first respond to the HDLC Address, Control, and FCS fields; then it can respond to the X.25 packet.

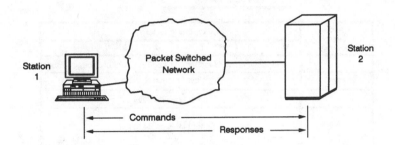

Figure 7.10
General format of an X.25 packet.

Data Communications

The network layer of X.25 can generate several types of X.25 packets. The network layer header specifies the format of the packet (see fig. 7.11). X.25 divides the header into eight-bit bytes called *octets*. The first three of these octets always follow the same format. The packet type and the contents of the first three octets specify the format of the remaining octets.

Figure 7.11
X.25 packet header general layout.

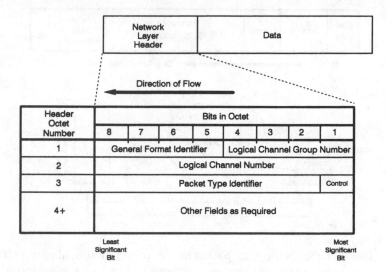

X.25 Channels and Groups

One of X.25's most powerful features is the capability to maintain multiple user sessions concurrently over a single physical connection to the network. The network assigns each user session a *Logical Channel Group Number* and a *Logical Channel Number*; X.25 assigns PVCs permanent Logical Channel Numbers and VCs Logical Channel Numbers when it establishes a call.

The Logical Channel Number and Logical Channel Group Number are in the first and second X.25 packet header octets, as shown in figure 7.11. The numbers enable network equipment to identify the source and destination of packets. Thus, more than one virtual circuit can exist over the same physical connection to the X.25 PSN. The user terminal or computer can separate sent and received HDLC frames based on the Logical Channel Number and Logical Channel Group Number contained in these frames.

X.25 Control Packets

A DTE can include X.25 controls in the packet header. The 'a' section of figure 7.12 shows the format of a control packet. The first four bits in the first octet and the last bit in the third octet of a control packet identify its control function. Table 7.1 shows some of these controls.

Header Octet Number	Bits in Octet							
	8	7	6	5	4	3	2	1
1	0	0	Modulo		Logical Channel Group Number			
2	Logical Channel Number							
3	Packet Type Identifier							1
4+	Additional Control Information							

(a) X.25 control packet header layout.

Figure 7.12
X.25 control and data packet headers.

Header Octet Number	Bits in Octet							
	8	7	6	5	4	3	2	1
1	Q	D	Modulo		Logical Channel Group Number			
2	Logical Channel Number							
3	P(R)			More	P(S)			0
4+	Data							

(b) X.25 data packet header layout.

Legend:
Q = Qualified data indicator
D = Packet receipt indicator
Modulo = 01 for modulo 8
10 for modulo 128
P(R) = Packet Receive Sequence Number
More = More data bit
P(S) = Packet Send Sequence Number

Table 7.1
Control Packet Types

Third Octet	Packet Type
00001011	Call request
00001111	Call accepted
00010011	Clear request
00010111	Clear confirmation

continues

Data Communications

Table 7.1, Continued
Control Packet Types

Third Octet	Packet Type
00100011	Interrupt
00100111	Interrupt confirmation
PPP00001	Receiver ready
PPP00101	Receiver not ready
PPP01001	Reject
00011011	Reset request
00011111	Reset confirmation
11111011	Restart request
11111111	Restart confirmation
11110001	Diagnostic

P = Receive Sequence Number, P(R)

Control packets can be three or more octets in length. Simple controls such as an Interrupt command or Call Accept response require only three octets; more complex packets, such as the Call Request, require at least five octets. The Call Request, for example, must provide the address of the caller and the address of the DTE it is calling. This request also can specify the facilities it wants to use at the remote DTE.

To enhance response to special user requests, X.25 provides an *interrupt packet.* When a user's DTE generates this packet type, the packet gets high-priority treatment throughout the network. Although an interrupt packet can carry data to a remote DTE, it normally conveys control information only. An example of an interrupt packet is the type of packet generated when a user wants to abnormally terminate host processing and presses the keyboard Break key. A user normally expects fast response to this action and a high-priority processing of the signal is appropriate.

An X.25 network also provides the following two mechanisms that support problem recovery:

✔ A reset capability enables a virtual circuit to be reinitialized without breaking the connection between the two communicating DTEs. This capability enables the network to recover from minor problems caused by host computer malfunctions or network errors.

✔ A restart capability enables the network to recover from major failures. A restart cancels all VCs from a DTE and resets all PVCs. To the DTEs connected to the network, a restart causes the association with the network to appear the same as it did when the X.25 service started.

X.25 Data Packets

X.25 provides a robust flow control technique similar to the scheme used in the MNP asynchronous protocol. Each X.25 data packet contains two sequence numbers in the third octet of its packet header (see the 'b' section of fig. 7.12). *Send Sequence Numbers,* P(S) and *Receive Sequence Numbers,* P(R) support data transfer, packet sequence verification, and packet flow control. A sliding window between the DTEs enables the sending of packets without immediate acknowledgment of proper receipt. The two modulo bits—8 or 128—specify the size of the window and support 8 or 128 outstanding, unacknowledged packets.

Packet sequence numbers provide the identification needed to operate the sliding window and ensure the proper sequencing of received packets. The receiver discards packets outside the window range. The receiving DTE requests retransmission of packets missing in the window sequence range and inhibiting the sliding of the window to a new range. This full-duplex flow control allows simultaneous, bidirectional flow of packets and prevents bottlenecks that can occur if the network loses or damages packets.

X.25 Packet Assembly/Disassembly

Terminals and personal computers often connect with a PSN through an X.25 *Packet Assembly/Disassembly* (PAD). ITU-T Recommendations X.3, X.28, and X.29 control the communications between a PAD and a DTE. Figure 7.13 shows a PAD implementation with a PC.

II

Data Communications

Figure 7.13
Packet-switched
network X-series
interfaces.

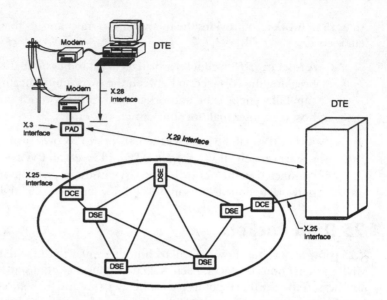

An X.25 PAD assumes that all connected terminals lack data-buffering capacity. Because a PAD has to communicate with terminals that range from old teletype devices to modern microcomputers, most PADs have default settings that enable them to support the limitations of a dumb terminal. To overcome this real or assumed set of limitations, X.25 provides buffering between the network and terminal devices. The PAD accumulates outgoing keystrokes until enough characters are available to fill a data packet or until the user presses the carriage return key.

A PAD constructs an X.25 packet with the appropriate header and trailer data, including the address of the recipient. When the data packet arrives at the other end of the link, a receiving PAD separates the X.25 header and trailer data from the packet. The PAD then sends the keyboard data to the appropriate host computer at a predetermined data rate. When a host transmits data to its PAD, the PAD executes the reverse of this procedure. The resulting host output arrives at the terminal at a rate that matches the terminal's capabilities.

Recommendation X.3

ITU-T Recommendation X.3 describes the functions of an X.25 PAD and the parameters used to control its operation. Because of differences between terminal types and the applications executed from various terminals, a PAD enables either a host or a terminal to set or alter up to 12 parameters. X.3 defines the parameters and the PAD's response to these parameters to provide user or host desired PAD performance.

Each terminal connected to a PAD gets a standard profile of parameters. Either the terminal or the host can modify this standard set of default parameters, as necessary. For example, a personal computer, when used as a dumb terminal, wants the PAD to create a packet for transmission each time the operator presses the Enter key or when a given amount of time elapses. This PC also wants the PAD to wait for a packet to fill during a file transfer operation.

Recommendation X.28

ITU-T Recommendation X.28 defines the interactions between a terminal and an X.25 PAD. X.28 specifies the use of an ASCII code variant consisting of seven data bits per character (eight bits when parity is included), as well as the control characters the PAD recognizes. X.28 also defines the operation of a *break signal*. A PC or terminal can send a break signal to a PAD to interrupt a process or application. This continuous, 150-millisecond binary signal (a space parity bit pattern) causes the PAD to send a reset packet to the host. Other terminal commands cause the PAD to set up or end a virtual call to a host and to read or alter the PAD control parameters. X.28 essentially provides each user with a customizable connection to an X.25 network.

Recommendation X.29

ITU-T Recommendation X.29 defines the interactions between a host and its associated PAD. Besides transmitting data through a PAD for delivery to a remote terminal or PC, X.29 defines control commands that enable the host to alter a PAD's operational characteristics. PAD parameters can be read or altered, or a virtual call with a remote terminal can be cleared (terminated).

Packet-Switched Network Summary

A PSN provides its users with many connectivity alternatives, despite their distance from application computers. When a user needs a low-volume data connection with a remote computer, a PSN connection may be less expensive than a private, leased line. A PSN also can support multiple host sessions from a single physical connection that may result in an economical connection for some users. A PSN also provides excellent data routing between DSE nodes to ensure that data arrives as fast as possible. Finally, a PSN provider takes away many connectivity concerns for a firm or organization.

Although an X.25 PSN provides flexible connectivity for user devices and host computers, this type of network does not always meet user needs. X.25 provides excellent support for data-only applications. This WAN protocol also provides good error detection and correction when older, error-prone network circuits are included in the WAN. The increasing demand for high data rates to support full-motion video, videoconferencing, and interactive television are making X.25 capabilities obsolete.

II

Data Communications

Integrated Services Digital Network

Historically, computers could communicate with each other in their native binary "language" only if they were close together or connected through a private, digital network. These direct connections and private networks contained special equipment that enabled computers to converse in high-speed streams of 1s and 0s. The increasing availability of low-cost, powerful, digital devices and systems, including personal computers, has created enough demand to change this situation. A worldwide effort is now under way to create standards for and implement a global digital communications system—the ISDN.

If it were not for the services it includes, the ISDN would be more properly called an integrated data network. As figure 7.14 shows, however, the ISDN combines a digital network with the communication methodologies and services discussed in earlier chapters. The main difference between this ISDN and the wide-area communications predominant today is that ISDN can provide an all-digital communications link between any two devices despite the distance or national boundaries separating them. Typical wide-area communications systems that exist today are either all-analog or a hybrid of analog and digital links.

ISDN completes the migration currently taking place from all-analog to all-digital communications. Figure 7.15 shows the progression from the all-analog communications systems that prevailed through the 1970s, to the analog and digital hybrid systems that exist today, and on to the final stage of this evolution—the all-digital system.

Most communications industry observers expect ISDN to be the next major step toward this all-digital worldwide communications system. These same observers predict that its success depends to a large degree upon its compatibility with and support for existing communications networks, which enable easy migration to this new technology. ISDN's evolution from its original narrowband support to its new direction in broadband support also enhances its opportunity to become the WAN technology of choice in the future for data, voice, and video applications.

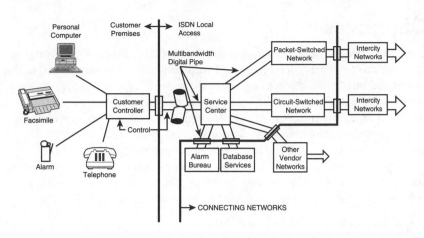

Figure 7.14
Conceptual view of ISDN.

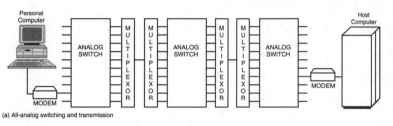

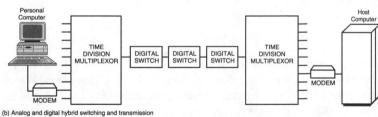

Figure 7.15
Transition from analog to digital communications.

(a) All-analog switching and transmission

(b) Analog and digital hybrid switching and transmission

(c) All-digital switching and transmission

II

Data Communications

ISDN Objectives

The original objective of ISDN (now called *narrowband ISDN* because of through-put limitations) was to develop a concept and sufficient rules that would lead to the development and implementation of a worldwide network of integrated communications and related services using a limited set of connection types and interfaces. That objective is rapidly coming to fruition through the successful efforts of many governments, agencies, standards organizations, companies, and individuals. To accomplish this formidable undertaking, these organizations and individuals developed a list of common sub-objectives—a list of needs they felt must be met to make a global network both feasible and desirable. The following key elements from the list of ISDN objectives are discussed in the ensuing paragraphs.

- ✔ Standardization of design and interfaces
- ✔ Transparency to network users
- ✔ Separation of competitive functions
- ✔ Support for existing communications systems
- ✔ Migration path from existing systems
- ✔ Support for multi-device sites
- ✔ Acceptable rate structure

Standards

ISDN's developers gave highest priority to the requirement of a single set of unambiguous standards to govern the development and implementation. Without a set of standards that all parties could agree upon, the success of ISDN could not be assured. With a complete set of standards in place early in the development of ISDN, compatibility between ISDN "products" could be maximized regardless of the origin of these entities, and also would provide the most cost-effective implementation.

No set of standards is ever perfect. Starting with a clear and concise set of rules does, however, reduce development costs and final product cost as competition develops. The development of narrowband ISDN standards that support data rates as high as 2 Mbps is now complete, thus providing a good launching pad for ISDN in the 1990s. The development of standards for broadband ISDN (BISDN) that support data rates as high as 622 Mbps is still in progress. This section looks at narrowband ISDN; BISDN is reviewed later in this chapter.

The worldwide nature of ISDN means it has to have its roots in and derive its momentum from worldwide participants with the authority to produce and

enforce standards. The *ITU Telecommunication Standardization Sector* (ITU-T) provides this level of participation. The ITU-T is a committee of the United Nations' *International Telecommunication Union* (ITU), and is the main controlling body for ISDN standards. The ITU is responsible for establishing effective and efficient telecommunications between member nations, and its current thrust in that endeavor is ISDN.

ITU-T has several study groups participating in the development of ISDN standards. These groups describe ISDN in terms of attributes. The following six attributes regulate ISDN's growth:

✔ The ISDN is to evolve from the existing telephone networks. These networks are already evolving from analog to digital.

✔ New services added to ISDN should be compatible with the basic 64 Kbps switched-digital channel.

✔ The ISDN probably will not be fully operational worldwide until the late 1990s.

✔ During the transition, the ISDN will rely on interconnections between national ISDNs and existing, non-ISDN public data networks.

✔ The ISDN will provide intelligence to perform service, maintenance, system control, and network management.

✔ The ISDN will use the layered protocols specified by the OSI reference model.

These attributes are coming to fruition in the form of published standards. Virtually all the key ISDN standards were promulgated by the ITU-T in November 1988. The remaining ISDN standards have rolled out rapidly since that meeting. Some of these standards allow enough divergence between nations to raise concern among industry observers that the implementation differences will impede worldwide compatibility of ISDN. Others feel the flexibility encourages ISDN implementations and that vendors will overcome differences without significantly altering the ISDN goals. Only time will tell.

Transparency

To enable maximum flexibility for both developers and users, ISDN must provide an independent layer of processes and functions that can be called upon to perform communications or network functions without the need to know how these functions are performed. This communications technique is called *transparency*. The objective of transparency is somewhat analogous to an objective of the postal systems that link most cities around the world.

The postal service is a network of people, vehicles, and transport techniques that convey a tremendous variety of letters and packages. The system moves information and products from one location to another without user concern for how the system operates. To use the postal system a person must deliver properly addressed packages to the system and retrieve packages from the system.

In a similar fashion, ISDN has to support a tremendous variety of data and information that must go from one location to another. A user must be able to take advantage of this service without concern for how the system operates. To use ISDN, the user's device must know where it wants to send data and how to exchange data with ISDN, despite the content of the data.

Separation of Functions

To ensure that ISDN provides a baseline set of capabilities and services across the entire network while providing maximum flexibility for optional services, ISDN must separate the network into clearly defined functions. This is necessary to enable countries to decide independently which functions to provide on a competitive basis and which functions to provide on a sole-source basis—to keep the economic systems of countries from impeding the acceptance and implementation of ISDN. Because of this feature, some countries have chosen to provide all functions from one source. Other countries, like the United States, are maximizing the competition for many functions.

Support for Existing Systems

To encourage the migration to ISDN, one of its objectives is to make its use and operation compatible with existing, leased-line and switched communications networks. With this compatibility available, organizations can go through ISDN and then through an older, point-to-point, leased-line to communicate with a distant computer. Organizations also can go through ISDN and then through a non-ISDN, switched telephone system to access a remote computer.

Migration Path

The introduction of new communications systems has proven most successful when a migration path from the old system to the new system exists. ISDN takes advantage of this technique by establishing an objective for phased implementation options. Most organizations like to retain the use of existing systems until it makes economic sense to replace them. By allowing a phased approach, the acceptance of ISDN should be greater. ISDN will coexist with these existing systems and provide the necessary interfaces and conversions of data to enable transparency of the resulting hybrid network.

Multi-Device Site Support

Besides supporting the connectivity of individual users, ISDN can support sites that have several communication devices aggregated through private telephone networks or local area networks. These sites require sophisticated interfaces to ISDN because they may have several devices that send and receive data using private, local addressing schemes. Because of the volume of data traffic associated with these sites, they also require special communications techniques that aggregate the data traffic from multiple devices into a single communications link to the outside world—a technique called *multiplexing*.

ISDN can provide a high-volume interface for sites that need multiplexed service to keep the interface from becoming a bottleneck. This speed-matching objective enables an organization's population of telephones or PCs to grow with full ISDN support. ISDN's capability for speed-matching also enables the organization to pay for communication services on an incremental basis that matches actual usage.

Rate Structure

In order to standardize pricing structures, one of ISDN's objectives is to make service price a function of the cost of providing the service and not a function of the type of data ISDN transports. This strategy forces services to compete independently by not enabling the charges for one service to subsidize the operation of another. Thus, by forcing each service to compete on its own merits, ISDN enables the marketplace to decide whether a service is earning the price it charges. Over-priced services can be displaced by more appropriately priced services, thus ensuring cost-efficient operation of the system.

Other Objectives

The move to ISDN, like the transition to many new technologies, is an evolutionary process. As the installed base increases, the objectives of the system change. The most obvious need for ISDN is the flexibility to support new technologies both internally and externally. Two current trends in computing are the migration from copper to fiber-optic conductors for all types of communications traffic; and the movement from single-tasking, single-processor workstations to multitasking, multiprocessor workstations that require the support normally associated with a multiworkstation site. An external trend is the increasing use of both image and video technology. These technologies produce volumes of communications traffic that are orders of magnitude greater than the volumes associated with the transmission of other types of text and data.

ISDN Services

ISDN begins by supporting all existing forms of voice and data communications and ends only where the human imagination ends, or where its capacity becomes saturated—whichever occurs first. The ISDN implementation trend depends to a large degree upon the economy, style, and alternative services available in the host country. As of this writing, users in some countries, including the United States, view ISDN as an alternative to existing central office telephone systems (Centrex) or the proprietary, multiplexing techniques used to connect multiple-Centrex sites. Users in other countries, particularly European users, have a broader perspective regarding the full exploitation of ISDN. The following list shows a sampling of the services these innovators now provide or plan to implement, and the following paragraphs discuss the most popular of the services.

- ✔ Local, national, and international telephone service

- ✔ Packet-switched data network connectivity

- ✔ Circuit-switched data network connectivity

- ✔ Electronic data interchange (EDI)

- ✔ Electronic Funds Transfer (EFT)

- ✔ Local, national, and international electronic mail

- ✔ Alarm monitoring and reporting

- ✔ Facsimile communications

- ✔ Teletext communications

- ✔ Videotex communications

- ✔ Videoconferencing

Old Dog—New Tricks

ISDN implementations usually begin by migrating to ISDN's all-digital voice and data services. Migration to ISDN for voice is a path known as *POTS-plus (plain old telephone service plus)* that includes a few new features unique to ISDN, such as calling party identification. Likewise, migration to ISDN for data is sometimes called *PODS-plus (plain old data service plus)* that includes data communications speeds that far exceed the limitations of traditional public telephone lines.

POTS/PODS services often provide enough economic incentive to get ISDN "in the door," but some vendors feel ISDN will penetrate much farther than this

unimaginative level. These forward-thinking firms are developing product lines to exploit many ISDN services. The following list shows a few of the voice-service features that will enhance future products. Although some of these services are available today from some telephone service vendors, ISDN will make them available to all subscribers on a worldwide basis.

- ✔ Incoming Call number identification
- ✔ On-line directory service and look-up
- ✔ Automatic speed calling of stored numbers
- ✔ Automatic redial of last number
- ✔ Automatic reverse charging
- ✔ Hot line set up by user
- ✔ Call waiting
- ✔ Automatic call forwarding
- ✔ Call transfer
- ✔ Call screening
- ✔ Prerecorded messages
- ✔ Conference calls
- ✔ Camp on busy number
- ✔ Automatic reminder calls
- ✔ Outgoing call screening
- ✔ Do not disturb
- ✔ Private network set up
- ✔ Special business group features

Facsimile

If the implementation of any technology can be described as rampant, *facsimile* (fax) fits this category. Although fax has been available for over thirty years, enabling users to transmit text and images between compatible units, the technology lay dormant for most of that time. A lack of standards between manufacturers and the limitations of data communications through the telephone system were the principal reasons for slow acceptance of fax during this period. Improvements in data communications hardware that allowed significant speed improvements

II

Data Communications

along with massive advertising of these units, however, turned this trend around in the last half of the 1980s. This momentum will continue with ISDN implementations.

New fax hardware, designated as Group 4 and designed specifically for ISDN, provides significant speed and quality improvements for the user. The Group 1 fax machines of the 1960s were cumbersome contraptions that provided a throughput of six minutes per page. The Group 2 hardware of the 1970s provided improved ease of use and cut transmission time to three minutes per page. The Group 3 machines in heavy use today are compact, microprocessor-driven devices that supply transmission speeds as low as 20 seconds per page.

Group 4 fax communicates through digital communications networks only, including ISDN. This technology enables the user to send text or graphics at a rate of three seconds per page or less. Besides speed improvements, Group 4 fax designers are taking advantage of the digital technology to improve the quality of transmissions as well.

Teletext and Videotex

Teletext and *videotex* may gain greater momentum with the introduction of ISDN. Both technologies have been hampered by limitations in communications technologies that will be mostly eliminated during the transition from analog to digital communications. Teletext uses television techniques to broadcast text and graphics to database subscribers, whereas videotex uses the public telephone system to communicate with its subscribers. Teletext has suffered from the one-way nature of its interaction with its customers—all customers can view a choice of video frames, but only customers with cable television can interact directly with the service. Videotex has suffered from the speed limitations of the public telephone system. Videotex displays and alters text quickly, and the display of full-screen graphics appears slow with the communications speeds available through analog telephone lines.

ISDN expands the horizons for teletext and videotex by providing improved two-way communications as well as the capability to transmit voice, data, and images simultaneously to each subscriber. Teletext subscribers could alter requests for services and provide direct feedback to the service vendor from the same ISDN-compatible terminal. Videotex subscribers could receive graphics and text at least six times as fast as they can receive them through the public telephone system today. These service improvements will increase the viability of both teletext and videotex, providing users with more alternative sources of information and entertainment as well as more methods of interacting with service vendors. For full-motion video and videoconferencing, however, broadband ISDN is the minimum required capability, as you see later.

ISDN Benefits

ISDN combines the benefits of digital communications with a multitude of services to provide the ISDN user with a greater variety of communications services than exist today. ISDN also can provide these services over a greater geographical area and at a lower cost than current services. The benefits of digital communications relate to the technology used to transport signals and the resulting communication quality and speeds. The economic benefits relate to the lower cost of constructing, operating, and maintaining digital networks as well as the throughput advantages of digital communications. The geographical benefits derive from the global nature of ISDN.

Digital communications over long distances are far superior to analog communications because of the techniques used to amplify the communications signals as they propagate across the country. With the analog switching and transmission systems typical of voice and data communications in the 1970s, the amplifiers used to keep signals at acceptable levels along a communications path also amplified background noise. The noise amplification was cumulative as the signal passed through each amplifying station.

With digital communications, on the other hand, repeater stations replace amplifying stations and completely regenerate the digital signals during the repeat process. Besides providing new, cleaned-up signals, the digital network also detects and corrects errors caused by severe noise. This ensures complete and accurate delivery of the signals to the receiver regardless of how many digital links or networks the signals have to traverse. These technical advantages enable digital networks to provide higher communication rates than analog networks, while maintaining higher quality transmissions at the same time.

Figure 7.16 shows a comparison of the typical digital and analog hybrid communications system used today compared to a similar ISDN system. This figure shows a limitation of 9,600 bps for a local analog line between the user and the central telephone office. This analog line acts as a bottleneck between high-speed user equipment and the high-speed digital trunk that typically exists between central telephone switches. Although these local loops can sometimes support data rates as high as 19,200 bps (without data compression), they cannot match the local-loop data rates provided by ISDN. As discussed later, the lowest level of ISDN service provides two 64 Kbps data channels and one 16 Kbps control channel—over six times the data rates provided by the best analog lines available today.

Figure 7.16
Current hybrid systems compared to ISDN.

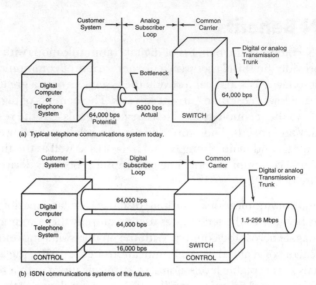

(a) Typical telephone communications system today.

(b) ISDN communications systems of the future.

The economic benefits of all-digital communications are a result of both technology and communications volume, as outlined in the following list:

✔ The technology required to switch and transmit digital signals is becoming less expensive than comparable analog equipment because of improvements in the *very large scale integration* (VLSI) technology used with digital signals.

✔ The economy of scale of combining voice, data, and other communications through the same network lowers the total cost of these services.

✔ Digital communications can operate over systems of somewhat lower quality than analog because of the signal regeneration and error correction employed.

✔ Digital communications provide more flexibility in the use of signal compression, thereby reducing the total traffic required to achieve the same communications.

✔ The volume of digital communications from computers and other devices is increasing at a much greater rate than voice communications. The elimination of devices such as modems required to connect these devices to analog communications networks increases the economic benefits of digital networks.

The geographical benefit of ISDN derives from the standardization of the network on a worldwide basis. Analog communications between computers were hampered for years because of the different standards and signaling techniques used in the design of the modems. Many computer users have found that compatibility between modems located in two different countries exists only at the lowest available modem speeds. Although these modems could communicate at speeds of 1,200 or 2,400 bps, users found that communications at the horse-and-buggy rate of 300 bps was the only way to ensure both compatible modem signaling and an acceptable error rate.

ISDN eliminates the analog hazard by providing built-in digital communications at a rate at least six times the fastest possible communications through the public telephone system and corrects errors as well as the best error-correcting modems on the market today. By adding an ISDN adapter to a PC and connecting the adapter to an ISDN wall outlet using the proper ISDN-compatible cable, a user can communicate with any other comparably equipped computer at a rate of at least 64,000 bps. This speed is a benefit you can easily measure.

ISDN Architecture

As discussed earlier, ISDN is far more than a digital communications network. ISDN is a defined set of services, interfaces, controls, and digital communications designed to serve a range of users from a single digital device such as a telephone to a firm with multiple digital devices located in several geographical areas. To provide these capabilities and to enable vendors to design devices, networks, and services to work with ISDN, the network must have a clearly defined architecture. The following paragraphs explore the design of narrowband ISDN that has evolved since its introduction in 1988.

ISDN Channels

ISDN communications take place through different types of channels, segregated according to their function as shown in table 7.2. Digital data flows through full-duplex B Channels that provide a throughput of 64,000 bits per second (64 Kbps). Signals, controls, and low-speed data, on the other hand, flow through D Channels. These full-duplex D Channels are typically packet-switched circuits and operate at 16 or 64 Kbps, depending upon the level of service installed. The D channel is used to set up all the calls on the B channels. This technique, called *common channel signaling*, enables the B channels to operate more efficiently because they do not carry signaling overhead.

ISDN H channels (H0, H11, and H12) provide higher data rates than the B channels. A user can subscribe to one of these channels for a single common communication trunk or subdivide the bandwidth using time-division multiplexing. These high-speed channels provide the data throughput required for slow-scan video and file transfers.

ISDN has defined only one analog channel. This A Channel is to have a bandwidth of 4 KHz and provides an interim step for voice-telephone communications during the transition from existing analog systems to ISDN. Other types of channels such as hybrid analog and digital access also are under consideration by international standards organizations and may emerge as standards.

ISDN is a simple, but elegant concept that combines channel types into two service levels. Users select these service levels, designated as Basic and Primary, to match the type of data to be communicated and the total data throughput expected for a site. The elegance in the design is that ISDN users get two or more 64 Kbps digital data channels that operate exactly the same way despite the traffic they carry. Users also can include one or more H channels for applications that require higher data rates.

Table 7.2
ISDN Channel Functions

B Channel	D Channel
Digital Voice	Signaling and Control
High bit-rate (64 Kbps)	Basic
Low bit-rate (32 Kbps)	Enhanced
Packet switched	
High-speed Data	Low-speed Data
Computer	Simple terminal
Circuit-switched	Videotex
Packet-switched	Teletext
Other	Telemetry
Facsimile	Facility security
Slow-scan video	Facility energy management

Basic Access Service

The *Basic Access Service* provides connectivity for users at sites that require relatively low data rates. As shown in the following list and figure 7.17, this access level provides a total data capacity of 144 Kbps and a total communications capacity of 192 Kbps by combining two B Channels and one D Channel. With Basic service, an end-user can simultaneously, and through one set of wires, place a voice telephone call, communicate between a personal computer and a remote computer, send a photograph to a relative by facsimile, and allow the electric utility to manage energy use in the home. Compare this with the functions you can simultaneously perform today through a single telephone line.

144 Kbps total data throughput

2 B Channels at 64 Kbps

1 D Channel at 16 Kbps

Although the name implies otherwise, Basic Access Service provides all the sophistication, features, and functions of the higher level of service. This level simply limits the total data throughput to match the needs of the user. Figure 7.18 shows typical Basic Access communication paths between two local users or a local and a remote user. In each case, the service level is the same. The differences are inside ISDN in the form of control, switch, and high-speed trunks not visible to the user. The next level of service expands this design by adding more B Channels and increasing the capacity of the D Channel.

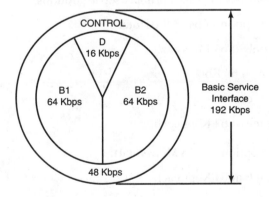

Figure 7.17
ISDN Basic
Service interface.

Figure 7.18
User connections
to an ISDN
system.

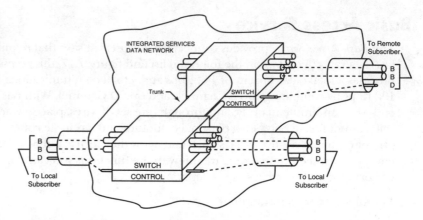

Primary Access Service

The *Primary Access Service* provides connectivity for sites that require relatively high data rates. As shown in the following list, this access level comes in one of two varieties. The 24-Channel option provides a total data capacity of 1.544 Mbps. Canada, Japan, and the United States use this option to match the 1.544 Mbps data rate of T1 transmission facilities provided by common carriers. The 31-Channel option, used in Europe, provides a total data rate of 2.048 Mbps. In either case, users can elect to take fewer B channels than the maximum, along with one D channel for common signaling.

The following list describes the ISDN primary service options.

✔ 24-Channel option (1.544 Mbps total):

23 B Channels at 64 Kbps each

1 D Channel at 64 Kbps

or

24 B Channels at 64 Kbps each

✔ 31-Channel option (2.048 Mbps total):

30 B Channels at 64 Kbps each

1 D Channel at 64 Kbps

or

31 B Channels at 64 Kbps each

At the primary level, all channels operate at 64 Kbps, including the D Channels. These channels combine to provide sufficient throughput to support a large business CBX/PBX or computer center. Two or more of the Primary Access interfaces can be combined, and all controls consolidated into one 64 Kbps D Channel. This combination can simultaneously support all data, voice, and other traffic going to and from a single location. When two or more Primary Access interfaces combine control into one D Channel, the second and subsequent Primary Access interfaces can consist of B Channels only. This maximizes the data-handling capacity of the interfaces.

✔ Primary-rate-interface H0 channel structure:

3 H0 Channels at 384 Kbps each

1 D Channel at 64 Kbps

or

4 H0 Channels at 384 Kbps each

✔ Primary-rate-interface H11 and H12 channel structure:

1 H11 Channel at 1,536 Kbps

or

1 H12 Channel at 1,929 Kbps

✔ Primary-rate-structure for mixtures of B and H0 channels:

3 H0 Channels at 384 Kbps each

5 B Channels at 64 Kbps each

1 D Channel at 64 Kbps

or

3 H0 Channels at 384 Kbps each

6 B Channels at 64 Kbps each

II

Data Communications

ISDN User Access

To fulfill the objective of uniform user access, ISDN provides a reference model and definitions for interface reference points and functional groupings of equipment. Figure 7.19 shows the four interface reference points and the six functional equipment groups and how they relate. The following section describes these elements.

Figure 7.19
ISDN reference
model.

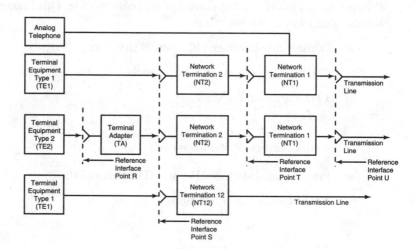

Figure 7.19
ISDN reference
model.

Functional Groups and Reference Points

The *Network Termination 1* (NT1) functional group provides the electrical and physical termination of the ISDN network and includes the features and functions that fall within the physical layer of the OSI reference model described in Chapter 3, "Communications and Networking Functions and Standards." NT1 provides the interface between customer equipment and the ISDN transmission system in the same sense that a telephone company's central office switch provides the interface between your telephone and the transmission system that connects central offices. These interface functions include line maintenance, performance monitoring, and data multiplexing from customer devices for transmission through trunk lines to other NT1s at other locations.

The *Network Termination 2* (NT2) functional group provides a single connection point to ISDN for several ISDN-compatible devices. The NT2 functions begin at Interface Point S, end at Interface Point T, and provide the features and functions that fall within the lower three layers of the OSI reference model: physical, data link, and network. This group of functions is normally contained in a customer-owned, *private branch exchange* (PBX) or a *local area network* (LAN) gateway.

The *Network Termination 1,2* (NT12) functional group combines the functions of NT1 and NT2 into a single group. This design will probably provide services in countries in which telecommunication administration and control are under the authority of organizations outside the customer's organization. Because of *Federal Communications Commission* (FCC) requirements, NT12 will probably not be used in the United States, but will be used in many European countries.

A *Terminal Equipment 1* (TE1) is any device that complies with ISDN interface specifications without assistance from external conversion devices, including digital telephones, Group 4 facsimile equipment, and terminals. These devices connect directly to an ISDN NT2 or NT12 using the physical interface defined by ISDN for Reference Interface Point S. A PC equipped with an internal ISDN adapter that complies with Interface Point S specifications is considered a TE1.

A *Terminal Equipment 2* (TE2) is a terminal or device that complies with ITU-T Recommendations but does not comply with ISDN interface requirements without external assistance. This group includes terminals designed to work with X-series public data networks, such as X.25, or with V-series modems, such as V.24. These devices include either an X.21 or an RS-232D interface to the outside world. Any PC with an asynchronous, serial port qualifies as a TE2.

A *Terminal Adapter* (TA) contains functions that enable a TE2 to connect with an NT2 or NT12. The TA converts the physical, electrical, and protocol characteristics of an X.21 or RS-232D interface at Reference Point R to those of a TE1 terminal at Reference Point S. This makes a TE2 look and act like any other TE1 at the point where the TA connects to either an NT2 or NT12. Thus, a PC containing only an asynchronous serial port can communicate with an NT2 PBX by communicating through a TA.

The interface points between functional groups are R, S, T, and U. These interface points represent the physical interface specifications defined by ISDN standards. Reference point U was required for compliance with FCC rules and only applies to ISDN implementations in the United States.

The analog telephone represents the analog channel required as a migration path from non-digital devices to the digital network of the future. The interface requirements and the breadth of analog device support is still under study by the ITU-T.

Terminal Configurations

ISDN simplifies the connections of terminals and computers by placing all such devices into only two categories, as shown in the following list. Devices without much native intelligence are simple or stimulus terminals, whereas devices that contain higher levels of intelligence and power are full-service or functional terminals. The terminal configuration category and type determine the message protocol used between the device and ISDN, as well as the total data communications capacity available at the terminal.

✔ Simple Terminal (Stimulus)

Digital telephone

Credit card terminal

Security device

✔ Full Service Terminal (Functional)

Intelligent terminals

Personal computers

Point of sale terminal

Word processor

Teletext terminal

Videotex terminal

Facsimile terminal

Host computer

Stimulus Terminal

The *stimulus terminal* encompasses digital telephones and other preprogrammed devices with low data traffic. These terminals have predefined functions encoded in *Read Only Memory* (ROM) and respond to simple keystrokes and incoming signals to execute these functions. Many of these devices contain a display capable of depicting outgoing and incoming information such as the telephone number dialed or the telephone number of an incoming call. The stimulus terminal typically connects to a single B Channel—a configuration called *Type 1*. For high-traffic implementation, a stimulus terminal is connected to two B Channels—called *Type 2 configuration*.

Functional Terminal

The *functional terminal* encompasses processor-driven devices that require a rich set of message signals and a high data rate. These terminals probably contain software that define their functions; their functions and thus their communications can be altered through programming changes. The functional terminal, equipped with a multitasking operating system and appropriate application software, can set up multiple sessions with remote computers or devices called *multiple call sequences*. These sessions can communicate through one or two B Channels simultaneously, as shown in figure 7.20. Each session appears as a separate TE1 to the network.

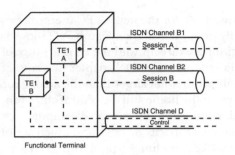

Figure 7.20
Multiple
functional
terminal call
sequences.

Personal Computer Support

The personal computer contains all the elements specified for a full-service, functional terminal and can be made completely compatible with ISDN. Firms with heavy communications traffic are typically the early adopters of ISDN. Figure 7.21 shows a configuration that might be typical of such a firm, including personal computer connectivity.

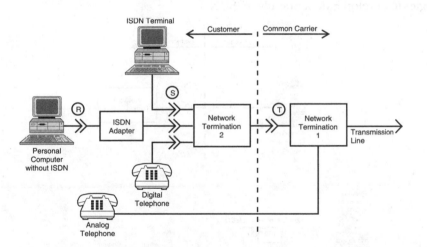

Figure 7.21
Initial ISDN
configurations.

Initial ISDN installations in firms replace or augment existing telephone communications and provide digital computer communications as a byproduct. To connect existing computers to these ISDN interfaces requires modification of their communications hardware or the installation of TA hardware. New ISDN interfaces should become available for most popular computers as native communications adapters and attachments. The decision to buy these internal devices versus external TA devices depends upon both the cost and features these devices provide. Hayes Microcomputer Products, a leading supplier of modems in the United States, is taking a leading role in the development of ISDN products for the PC.

As ISDN becomes available for the masses, PC users will be able to make ISDN connections directly from their homes. Figure 7.22 shows how a personal computer might communicate directly with the central office of a common carrier. In this example, the PC contains an ISDN adapter that connects directly with a wall outlet through a cable somewhat larger than the analog cables used today. The cabling system between the home and the central office provides the NT2-equivalent functions. With this connection, the personal computer has two B Channels available with a total data capacity of 128 Kbps, which is a marked improvement compared to the 9.6-19.2 Kbps limits typical with today's analog connections.

Ultimately, ISDN will produce all-native and all-digital connectivity between devices that communicate through the telephone system. As figure 7.23 illustrates, ISDN compatibility is expected to pervade computers of all types and sizes. Computers will communicate directly with NT2 devices. Other computers will communicate through gateways, controllers, and other computers that act as clustering devices. These clustering machines will provide one connection to ISDN and translate between the ISDN protocol and the protocol used on the other side. These devices reduce connectivity costs while enabling other communications and networking technologies to develop independently of ISDN.

Figure 7.22
Direct
connection
between a PC
and an ISDN.

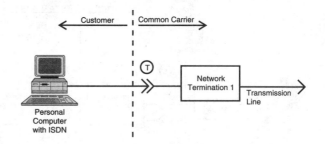

Figure 7.23
Typical ISDN
office of the
future.

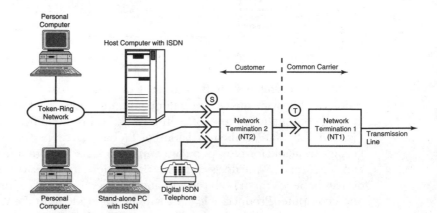

ISDN Implementations

ISDN is becoming real beyond the pieces of paper that define its standards. A new ISDN field trial or product announcement appears in the trade journals almost every month. Although more complex to implement than any communications standards preceding it, ISDN is beginning to have broad influence on technology and the marketplace.

ISDN in the United States

The *Regional Bell Operating Companies* (RBOC) have been a major driving force in ISDN trials that have taken place in the United States. These RBOCs encourage ISDN for the following principal reasons:

✔ ISDN enables the RBOCs to compete better with PBX and CBX vendors in providing end-users with voice and data services

✔ ISDN enables the RBOCs to counter the competition from other alternatives that enable customers to bypass them today.

✔ ISDN enables the RBOCs to lower the cost of their services because of the lower operating and maintenance cost of ISDN compared to analog equipment. Most RBOCs in the United States now sell some kind of ISDN service.

The vendors of central office switches are adding their fuel to the fire by announcing ISDN compatibility. The first four vendors to demonstrate ISDN capability are AT&T, Northern Telecom, Siemens, and NEC. With these four giants committed to ISDN, the remainder are probably not far behind.

The United States government also is expected to be a major factor in the adoption of ISDN. The *Government OSI Profile* (GOSIP) essentially mandates ISDN in all appropriate areas of government business. Federal request for proposals that include ISDN compatibility as a mandatory item will add substantially to the ISDN movement in the United States. The spinoff effects of federal mandatory requirements for UNIX and the TCP/IP protocol illustrate the impact these RFPs have in the marketplace—both UNIX and TCP/IP have received substantial benefits.

ISDN in Europe

ISDN is big news in Europe. Not only have some European countries embraced ISDN by offering it on a commercial basis, but also commercial companies have developed services that make it attractive to users. This enthusiasm for ISDN is expected to expand in Europe well beyond the 1990s.

II

Data Communications

France is not encumbered by an all-analog network and has made substantial progress in the move to ISDN. Almost all of France's communications networks are sufficiently compatible with ISDN that a software change is all that is needed to make the transition. Switching to ISDN also is more attractive because of products made available through collaborative partnerships.

France Telecom (FT) has offered commercial ISDN since 1987 and has actively pursued services to make the service attractive. FT formed basic partnerships with the following listed technology suppliers to determine user needs that can be satisfied by ISDN. FT works with these partners to develop applications to meet these needs. In some cases, the customers for solutions also become partners in the development and marketing of the solutions.

- ✔ Bull
- ✔ Digital Equipment Corporation (DEC)
- ✔ Electronic Data Systems (EDS)
- ✔ Telesystemes
- ✔ Apple Computer
- ✔ ICL

To further enhance the acceptance of ISDN, FT formed alliances with ISDN innovators to help make the applications they have developed emerge as products or services. The two common denominators in these applications are image transfer and incoming-call number identification. The common platform for most of the applications is the PC. Imaging supports teaching, real estate marketing, problem diagnostics, and geologic information display. Figure 7.24 shows a typical PC configuration that supports these applications.

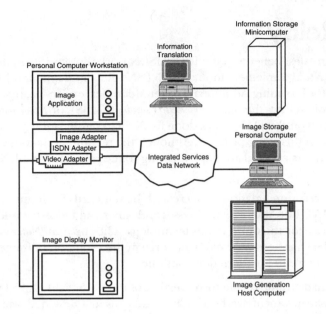

Figure 7.24
Typical image application with ISDN.

Data Communications

Future of ISDN

Because of the difficulty of designing and implementing a global communications and services network that is both effective and economical, ISDN will have many opportunities to fail over the next ten years. The increasing global nature of the world economy and of individual corporations, however, provides even more opportunities for the success of ISDN. A world filled with islands of information of great value to multi-national organizations creates a demand for connectivity. This demand will push the development and implementation of ISDN well beyond the 1990s.

ISDN may not be the final answer in communications technology, but it offers more pros and less cons than any other alternative as the year 2000 approaches. The increasing use of digital devices, particularly the personal computer, adds great pressure to the drive for digital communications between these devices. The quantum leaps in digital technology that are taking place will continue, and these advances will widen the gap between analog and digital switching and communications—making an all-digital network even more attractive.

The data throughput limitations of narrowband ISDN will eventually render its design obsolete. Its continuing evolution is discussed later in this chapter. For now, however, ISDN offers tremendous improvements over the public data networks based on older technologies. The work done by the ITU-T for ISDN also is having a major influence on these older technologies.

Frame Relay

One of the greatest benefits of the ITU-T ISDN work thus far is the effect it has had on the design and implementation of X.25 PSNs. Recommendation I.122 titled Framework for Providing Additional Packet Mode Bearer Service, first issued in 1988, has evolved into the *frame-mode bearer service* (FMBS), or *frame relay*. This WAN protocol builds on the ITU-T work done for X.25 to significantly improve the performance of this aging protocol. Although the recommendations were made for ISDN, vendors can and are implementing frame relay in non-ISDN environments.

The original recommendations that created the standards for frame relay came from the ITU-T, but American businesses and American industry standards are setting the pace for the world in this technology. The *American National Standards Institute* (ANSI) has become the driving force in the evolution of frame relay standards. This trend is expected to continue.

The ITU-T made frame relay a turbo version of the old reliable X.25 by eliminating unnecessary protocol overhead. When X.25 was first designed, wide area communication systems were not as reliable as they are today. To ensure error-free delivery of data packets in an error-prone environment, error checking, packet acknowledgments, and flow control were required between every node in the network. The error-free characteristics of modern, all-digital WAN circuits make this node-to-node "hand shake" unnecessary.

Frame relay expedites data frame delivery by requiring end-to-end error checking and acknowledgment. The probability of a data transmission error is so low today in all-digital systems, especially in fiber-optic networks, that node-to-node error checking and error correction does little—if anything—to improve the quality of data transmission. Frame relay removes this superfluous overhead, thereby increasing the data transfer capacity of WAN systems.

Frame relay further expedites the movement of data by eliminating call-management and flow control between the intermediate nodes in the system. X.25 requires state tables that must be maintained at each node for each virtual circuit to ensure proper management of the circuits and to minimize data flow bottlenecks. Frame relay enables system suppliers to provide this service, if it is needed, in a layer of function above the frame relay layer.

A combination of frame relay and the ISDN H channel that can transport its frames provides a throughput that will probably cause it to supplant X.25 networks. The combination can transport user data at a rate ten times that of X.25. For applications such as full-motion video and videoconferencing that require high data throughput and high-speed transmissions, frame relay and ISDN are a natural solution.

Frame Relay Architecture

The frame relay architecture is a simplified form of the X.25 architecture. Figure 7.25 shows a comparison of the two. As you can see, frame relay eliminates one entire layer of X.25 WAN functions.

Frame relay implements two layers of the ISO open systems interconnect model. The architecture has as its foundation the same physical layer used in the X.25 architecture. At the data link layer, frame relay and X.25 diverge. The Q.922 core functions ITU-T defines for this layer include an enhanced version of the *LAPD* protocol (*link-access protocol, D channel*) recommended for X.25 operation through an ISDN network. The principal difference between the LAPB and LAPD protocols used in X.25 and the Q.922 protocol used in frame relay is the contents and use of the address field.

The following list shows the ISDN Q.922 core functions. The WAN functions above the Q.922 core are the responsibility of software or hardware outside the scope of the frame relay network. Some of these potential functions are discussed later.

- ✔ Transmission frame layout and transparency

- ✔ Address field use in multiplexing logical connections

- ✔ Zero-bit insertion and extraction control

- ✔ Frame length control

- ✔ Transmission error detection control

- ✔ Congestion avoidance/recovery control

Frame relay streamlines the operation of the WAN and provides more flexibility and bandwidth for service providers. The architecture transports frames efficiently and effectively—building on the reliability of today's communications infrastructure. It also integrates well with other networking infrastructures to give vendors the best of all worlds when it comes to providing solutions to meet user needs.

II

Data Communications

Figure 7.25
Comparison of X.25 and frame relay protocols.

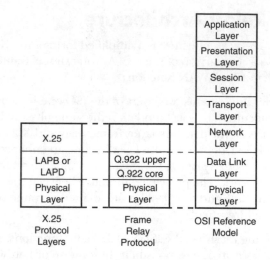

Call Control

Frame relay call control is handled by *frame-handler services,* but is more efficient than the packet handlers in X.25 networks.

The ISDN service subscriber connects with an access connection, which in turn provides access to the frame handler's capabilities. Because of the design of the frame relay transmission frames, each of the access connections can support multiple logical connections. The frame handler sorts out the frames from these multiplexed logical connections to deliver the frames to the appropriate destination.

Connection with an access connection is either semipermanent (*integrated access*) or on demand (*switched access*). Call control depends on the type of connection. Semipermanent connection does not require call control; on-demand connection does require call control. The actual frame relay connection takes place after the access connection is made, and it is either semipermanent or on demand as well.

The frame relay protocol calls for the exchange of messages during call establishment to determine the call control to apply to the connection. The contents of these messages must establish certain restraints such as bearer capability, but they also can enable other capabilities. The exchange of these messages enables the frame handler to set up and manage all logical frame relay connections.

Link-Layer Core Parameters

During call setup, link-layer core parameters are negotiated between each service user and the network through the exchange of a link-layer core parameters information element. The fields in this call setup element determine the characteristics of the data exchange through the frame relay connection. These characteristics include the following:

- ✔ **Maximize frame size.** This establishes the maximum frame size for both incoming and outgoing frames.

- ✔ **Registered/agreed throughput.** This establishes the average data throughput for the connection (frame relay information fields) in bits per second.

- ✔ **Minimum acceptable throughput.** This specifies the minimum throughput in bits per second the caller is willing to accept. During the call, this parameter enables the frame handler to determine the acceptability of the throughput. If the throughput is unacceptable, the frame handler clears (terminates) the call.

- ✔ **Burst size.** This parameter controls the burst potential of the call in both directions by establishing the maximum number of frames that can accumulate relative to the mean throughput of the call for both outgoing and incoming frames.

- ✔ **Maximum frame-rate value.** This parameter determines the maximum number of frames per second that can be sent in each direction measured at the user-network interface point.

Link-Layer-Protocol Parameters

A second type of call setup element called the *link-layer-protocol parameters information element* enables the end users of a frame relay call to negotiate protocol parameters. Each end of the link requests a specific set of parameters through the bit patterns in the element it transmits. These frames are exchanged between end users without network involvement. The fields in the frame contain the following requested parameters:

- ✔ **Window value.** This parameter specifies the maximum size of the sliding window in the flow control window for both outgoing and incoming frames. The size can be from 1 to 127.

- ✔ **Acknowledgment-timer value.** This parameter specifies the length of time in tenths of a second the sender waits for a positive acknowledgment of a frame before retransmitting the same frame.

- ✔ **Mode of operation.** This bit pattern specifies whether a three-bit or seven-bit frame sequence number will be used for the call.

User Data

Frame relay uses a modified X.25 LAPD packet to transfer user data. Figure 7.26 shows this type of frame. As you will recall from figure 7.8, the X.25 data packet contains a control field. The frame relay data frame does not require this field because only one type of data transfer frame exists. The other reason for this simplified data frame is the lack of necessity for flow control and error control signaling. All protocol signaling is done outside the data transfer connection.

Figure 7.26
Frame relay
frame format.

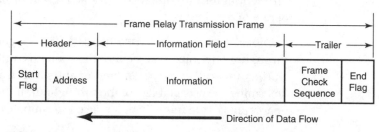

One important characteristic of the frame relay data frame is its capability to move through D channels of an ISDN network along with X.25 packets. Service providers can multiplex both protocols through the same channel because the network distinguishes the X.25 packet and the frame relay frame through the contents of the address fields of each. This provides the vehicle for upward migration from X.25 to frame relay in a phased approach.

Network Functions

Network functions for frame relay are handled by the frame handler. Each frame handler contains switching logic that enables it to route frames from the sender to the receiver. Address fields in the data transfer frame determine the routing of the frame. These address fields enable the switching logic to handle multiplexed logical connections through the same physical connection.

The error detection and correction for data frames is simple. The receiver and all intermediate nodes compare the data transfer frame's Frame Check Sequence against the FCS it calculates from the contents of the frame. If the calculated FCS does not match the one in the data transfer frame, the receiver or intermediate node discards the entire frame. A layer of protocol function above the Q.922 frame relay protocol must execute a procedure to correct the detected error.

Congestion Control

Frame relay congestion control is required to keep frame handlers from becoming overloaded under high-traffic conditions. Because of the streamlined design of frame relay "packets" and the desire to keep throughput as high as possible, the

ITU-T chose to use the Address fields of data frames to provide the signals that enable this protocol to ask end users for help in congestion avoidance and recovery.

Frame relay data frames contain two bit fields in each Address field that signals congestion. The frame handler in any intermediate node in the network can set these congestion notification bits when it detects congestion at its node. Downstream frame handlers, if any, pass the data frame on without modifying these bits. This procedure ensures the movement of the congestion signal from the network to the ultimate receiver of the data frame.

The responsibility of network frame handlers is to monitor receive and transmit queues (buffers) in the their network nodes to determine the need for congestion signaling. If these queues begin to fill up for any logical connection, the frame handler that controls the connection must determine the action to take to eliminate the congestion. The frame handler can set the congestion notification bits for one or many connections, as needed to assist in the elimination of the problem.

The frame relay users are ultimately responsible for the elimination of network congestion. They must respond to the congestion notification bits and reduce the number of frames per second they are sending through the network. Two techniques are used to perform this control: *backward explicit congestion notification* (BECN) tells the sender of data to slow down its transmission of frames; and *forward explicit congestion notification* (FECN) tells the receiver to slow down its transmission of frames in the "direction" it is receiving the current frame. Flow control functions above the frame relay layers must respond to the FECN signal to correct the problem.

Frame relay congestion recovery is required when a frame handler queue overflows, or a frame is discarded or lost. Frames dropped because of the overflow condition or frames a frame handler discards require action from the end users of the service. These user devices must execute recovery procedures. The logic that performs this recovery is above the frame relay protocol layer.

One recovery technique is to change the size of the flow-control window, which reduces the number of frames the user can transmit and have outstanding at any moment without matching receipt acknowledgments from the receiver. Reducing the window size slows down the rate of frame transmissions by reducing the sender's anticipation that transmitted frames will arrive at their destination error free. Reducing the window size also reduces the number of frames that frame handlers have to discard during a queue overflow condition. This reduction in discarded frames is important because the sender must retransmit the discarded frames, which can add to the congestion.

Following the successful execution of congestion recovery procedures, users can return to their maximum flow-control window size to resume normal communications.

II

Data Communications

This ensures recovery to the maximum data transfer rate between users. Under heavy loading conditions, frame relay network users may be required to frequently execute these recovery cycles. Automatic recovery functions in layers above the frame relay protocol expedite this process and smooth out the flow of frames.

The frame relay recommendations also contain procedures the network or users can use to help mitigate congestion. The network or a user device can use an address bit called *discard eligibility* (DE) to indicate frames that should be discarded first if a frame handler detects congestion. Users can set this bit when they temporarily transmit frames faster than the limit they established during call setup. Frame handlers also can set the bit when the transfer from a user exceeds its guaranteed transmission rate. The frame handler sets the bit for all frames from a user when the user exceeds its maximum rate established during the call setup. If congestion occurs at a node, the frame handler for that node can discard all frames contributing to the congestion that have the DE bit set. The users must then execute recovery procedures to retransmit the discarded frames.

Frame Relay Summary

As you can see from the preceding descriptions, frame relay provides a powerful tool in the connectivity toolbox. Vendors can implement this protocol in either ISDN or non-ISDN systems to significantly improve the performance of X.25 communications. Because of the higher quality of physical connectivity hardware compared to the era in which X.25 was first deployed, these vendors can implement frame relay without sacrificing any of the error correction and flow control provided in traditional X.25 PSNs.

As users continue to increase their demands for technologies that require high data throughput, such as full-motion video and videoconferencing, the demand for frame relay will increase. The deployment of ISDN systems by telephone and telecommunications companies across the country adds to the momentum for frame relay. All this bodes well for the enhancement of existing communications systems and the deployment of new systems. The momentum also will help bring to fruition the information superhighway.

Broadband ISDN

When the ITU-T first issued the recommendations for ISDN in 1988, telephone companies and network vendors were using copper wire in most of their networks. These networks could handle the 2 Mbps limits of ISDN without difficulty. Since that time, many telephone service providers and network vendors have installed

fiber-optic cables to replace copper networks. These new networks can transport digital data at rates far exceeding the rates available with copper systems.

To take advantage of the new fiber-optic networks and their bandwidth, the ITU-T introduced new recommendations in 1990 for *broadband ISDN* (BISDN). These recommendations protect vendor investments in narrowband ISDN facilities by requiring the new networks to support all the 64 Kbps circuit- and packet-switching supported in ISDN systems. The recommendations also enable vendors to transmit and control data, voice, images, and video at rates many orders of magnitude higher than its narrowband predecessor. Data throughput capacities of this magnitude enable vendors, for the first time, to provide videoconferencing at a full 30 frames a second—comparable to broadcast television.

BISDN can support single or multiple video transmissions through the same physical connection. Current recommendations enable data transfer at 155.52 Mbps per channel with a maximum subscriber rate of 622.08 Mbps. A full-duplex 155.52 Mbps service can transport several full-motion video signals simultaneously. A full-duplex 622.08 Mbps service can multiplex and transport multiple videoconferences simultaneously.

BISDN can transport video signals better than narrowband ISDN because of its transmission frame and switching architecture. The ITU-T recommends a fast switching technique called *cell relay* or *asynchronous transfer mode* (ATM) that can take full advantage of the high data rate of the fiber-optic cabling in such a network. Because of its flexibility and speed, ATM is expected to supplant its frame relay predecessor as new BISDN systems roll out across the country.

ATM enhances the high-speed transmission of voice, data, and video by building on X.25 and frame relay protocol techniques. ATM combines the best of these protocols and adds some new twists. Like frame relay, ATM assumes high-quality physical layer functions and eliminates the error correction and flow-control functions contained in the LAPD and LAPB protocols used with X.25. The protocol supports multiplexed logical connections through a single physical connection. ATM does borrow from X.25, however, by using packets rather than frames for data transmission.

ATM is a streamlined protocol compared with both X.25 and frame relay in the following two ways:

✔ Like frame relay, ATM eliminates the control field in data transmission packets; it does signaling and control through a separate, common signaling channel.

✔ ATM uses short, fixed-length packets called *cells,* which can be generated, transmitted, switched, and received faster than the variable length frames called for in frame relay.

II

Data Communications

All this streamlining enables ATM to take full advantage of the higher bandwidth of fiber-optic cable to move data from 5 to 300 times faster than frame relay can transport data in a copper system.

Another advantage of ATM is its dynamic selection of data rates. Traditional circuit-switching networks provide fixed data rates for each channel. Users must subscribe to one of these rates regardless of their changing data transport needs. ATM, on the other hand, supports virtual circuits whose data rates are dynamically selected when the circuit is set up. This provides users more flexibility and is a better match with new image and video technologies.

Broadband ISDN Summary

Although the narrowband version of ISDN is just beginning to take hold in the United States, plans are already in place to move up to the next level of transmission speed and services. Broadband ISDN takes the maximum data transfer rate up from 2 Mbps to 622.08 Mbps and also includes the ATM protocol along with small data packets called *cells* that combine to provide fast data movement and switching within BISDN networks.

BISDN no doubt will provide part of the backbone for the information superhighway communications pundits and politicians speak of so freely. With its high-data transport bandwidth and flexible connection support, vendors will be able to provide services never seen before. Companies and organizations will be able to further reduce their dependence on travel for meetings by installing powerful videoconferencing systems based on this technology. Homeowners will eventually be able to take advantage of such a system through interactive television.

ISDN, broadband ISDN, and spin-off technologies such as frame relay and asynchronous mode transfer are becoming common denominators for communications between computer equipment made by different vendors. Their origin as international standards also makes them good vehicles for communications between systems in different countries. Companies and organizations that have a large investment in existing computer hardware made by one vendor may not, however, find these open systems of connectivity a good investment to meet their user needs. A proprietary WAN such as IBM's SNA may be more appropriate.

System Network Architecture

System Network Architecture (SNA) is IBM's proprietary network architecture designed to ensure highly reliable and error-free connectivity between devices that support this architecture. IBM introduced SNA in September 1974 with the announcement of three products that contained SNA features and functionality.

At the time, SNA was little more than a statement of direction from IBM for future products. SNA has since evolved through new product releases to become a powerful "glue" in the connection of computers, terminals, and personal computers. Because of the pervasive nature of SNA, the following paragraphs review its features and functions.

SNA provides a layered architecture similar to that recommended by the ISO in the OSI reference model. IBM's architecture includes seven layers, as shown in figure 7.27. The major difference between the seven-layered OSI model and the seven-layered SNA design is that the OSI model standardizes protocols at each level to enable communications between different architectures. SNA, on the other hand, standardizes communications between nodes of a single architecture. The goal of SNA is to ensure end-to-end compatibility between IBM products that require or support communications.

Although the definition of the contents of each SNA layer may not be the same as the equivalent OSI layer, the total defined functionality is equivalent. Figure 7.28 shows a typical SNA implementation and the exchanges that take place between each layer. As you can see, SNA provides support for the layers above data link control. These layers build on the functions provided in the synchronous communications protocols and local area network protocols discussed in the preceding two chapters. Each of these layers and the protocol messages they exchange are examined later in this chapter.

Layer	Layer	Significant Functions
Application Layer	Transaction Services	Provides application services such as distributed data base access and document interchange.
Presentation Layer	Presentation Services	Formats data for different presentation media and coordinates the sharing of network resources.
Session Layer	Data Flow Control	Synchronizes data flow, correlates exchanges of data, and groups related data into units.
Transport Layer	Transmission Control	Paces data exchanges to match processing capacity and enciphers data if security is required.
Network Layer	Path Control	Routes data between source and destination and controls data traffic in the network.
Data Link Layer	Data Link Control	Transmits SDLC transmission frames between adjacent network nodes.
Physical Layer	Physical Control	Provides physical connectivity between adjacent network nodes.

OSI Reference Model

System Network Architecture

Figure 7.27
System Network Architecture layers and functions.

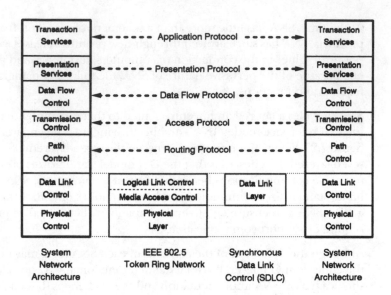

Figure 7.28
SNA layer-to-layer protocols.

SNA Features

IBM designed SNA to provide many features that enhance the efficiency, reliability, quality, and control of communications between SNA compatible products. The following sections discuss the most significant features of this architecture; the methods of SNA implementation are discussed later.

Upward Compatibility

Since its first introduction in 1974, SNA ensured upward compatibility of new products. As IBM released new products requiring more powerful or more robust communications capabilities, IBM added new SNA features. Each new release of SNA supported the functions provided in earlier releases. This upward compatibility enables companies to substitute one IBM product for another and to use old products in networks that contain new products. Companies can enhance their computing resources incrementally while protecting their investment in older hardware and software.

Resource Sharing

Because of its tight coupling between remote devices, SNA enables cost reductions through resource sharing. By using a common communications technique for all SNA compatible devices and processors, the same communications links can connect different types of equipment. By enabling terminals or personal computers to access a variety of host processors, the number of unique software packages and hardware devices can be kept to a minimum.

SNA capabilities, such as *Remote Operation* and *Advanced Program-To-Program Communications* (APPC), also enable resource reductions. Remote Operation enables operators in another location to operate a minicomputer to reduce operations personnel and training requirements. APPC enables more than one processor to share a common application so that the processing workload can be distributed to the most appropriate hardware. This client/server capability enables an organization to spread processing workloads to match end-user requirements.

New Technology Growth

Because of the common architecture provided by SNA, IBM and other vendors can introduce new technology products without requiring a large investment in communications support for these products. The segregation of SNA functions into different layers enables the replacement of older products with newer products that implement the same layer without adversely affecting the other SNA layers. For example, copper wiring can be replaced with fiber-optic cabling to reduce noise interference and increase data throughput without affecting the contents of data transmitted through the media. You also can add a new feature, such as digitized voice, in another layer without changing the cabling or methods of error detection and correction.

Network Dependability

SNA ensures high dependability and reliability—features mandatory for business networks. SNA can detect lost or damaged data and retransmit data to correct errors. Built-in SNA capabilities enable devices to collect and report error statistics that help remote network operators make sound decisions regarding network routing or the replacement of equipment. Problem alerts can be forwarded to operators that enable them to bypass problem areas permanently or temporarily while workers perform maintenance to correct the problem.

SNA provides network flow control to ensure proper delivery of data and the integrity of the network. Two classes of service enable end users to select data routing priority to ensure the proper response time for specific types of operations. The user can select high priority for keyboard work and low priority for batch remote job entry that does not require operator interaction. SNA also provides flow control pacing to prevent data overrun of devices or nodes in the network and to prevent congestion. SNA also enables you to specify alternate data routing and backup hosts to ensure high system reliability despite failures of a data path or processor.

Network Interconnection

SNA products provide the hardware and software required to exchange data between similar or dissimilar networks, including X.25 packet-switched networks.

Large companies often have different networks for different groups or divisions. SNA interconnection capabilities enable you to interconnect two SNA networks or interconnect an SNA network and a public-switched network without user knowledge of the interconnections. Users can execute applications at hosts in two different networks without being aware of the actual location or connection between these hosts and the user terminals. These interconnections enable organizations to set up separate administrative controls for different networks without reducing the sharing of resources connected to these networks.

Network Security

SNA provides high data and application access security. Login security prevents unauthorized access to applications or data. Data encryption capabilities also enable users to designate data streams as high security requiring automatic encryption. SNA encrypts data at one end of the link and deciphers the data at the other end to prevent unauthorized exposure of the data during transmission. The encryption/deciphering process is transparent to the users—they are unaware of the process. Data encryption is particularly important in military or high-technology applications in which security breaches can cost a country lives or cause a company financial hardship.

SNA Network Components

SNA provides networking functions in hardware and software components. Figure 7.29 shows the traditional SNA hierarchy of components. Figure 7.30 shows a more recent enhancement to SNA to support distributed processing. In these figures, the SNA hardware components are shown as three-dimensional boxes, and the SNA software components are shown as entities that reside inside the boxes. Each of these components is discussed in the following paragraphs.

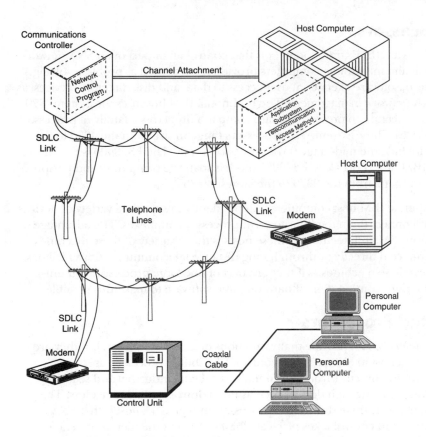

Figure 7.29
Traditional SNA hardware and software components.

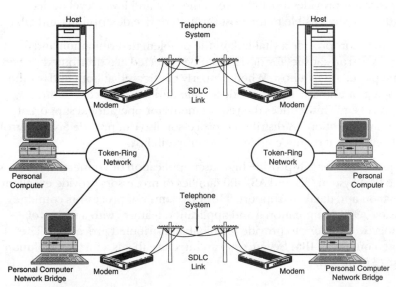

Figure 7.30
SNA distributed processing.

Host Processors

Host processors are IBM's traditional tools that control all or part of an SNA network. These mini- and mainframe computers provide services such as problem solving, computation, software execution, user access to data, and disk directory services, as well as SNA network management. The traditional IBM host uses the System/370 internal architecture to provide software compatibility across a family of processors of various sizes. These System/370 processors range in size from the 4300 to the 3090 and include the mid-range 9370 processor family. The ES/9000 is the latest family of IBM host processors. ES/9000 models span the computing and peripheral support range from the 9370 to the largest 3090.

You can operate IBM host computers independently to support a variety of devices, or you can connect them together to form processor complexes. The advantage of the common IBM architecture for these hosts is that a variety of these machines can be connected directly or through long-distance telecommunications facilities. Users access these machines as if they are part of one large processor. You must provide the right combination of hardware and software to make this possible.

Distributed Processors

Distributed processors can provide many functions of a host computer, but they are secondary to a host in SNA network control. Distributed-processor users can execute software directly through terminals or execute industrial and security software indirectly through devices such as flow controls or badge readers. The difference between these distributed processors and an SNA host is that SNA configuration and control takes place at a higher level in the hierarchy. The distributed processor provides a path between the host and lower-level devices. SNA makes these devices visible to the host through device descriptions and tables.

Distributed processors provide a vital link in the problem determination and control for SNA. Error statistics for devices can be collected at a distributed processor and passed on to a host. When properly configured at both ends of the link, a host operator also can activate or deactivate devices connected to the distributed processor. This reduces the requirements for operational support at remote computing locations. A distributed processor also can provide SNA control for attached devices that do not contain SNA compatibility.

Distributed processors usually provide high user application or connectivity features. The IBM System/3X and AS/400 families of processors provide excellent office automation and database support. The 9370 family of processors combine excellent System/370 computational and application features with a variety of internal connectivity options to provide formidable distributed processing. The ES/9000 hosts contain an IBM System/390 architecture that is a further evolution of the System/370 design.

Communications Controllers

The communications controller off-loads much of the lower level SNA work from a host. The IBM 3700 family of communication controllers manages the SNA network, controls communications links, and routes data. These front-end processors control the flow of data between hosts in a network, between different networks, and between devices attached to a network. These SNA workhorses also can accept data at different speeds and protocols and forward that data on to a host through high-speed, channel-attached pathways. Some controller models also accept direct connection of Token Ring networks to provide more connectivity alternatives.

Control Units

Control units act as concentrators as well as controllers to manage the data flow to and from downstream devices. These control units, sometimes called *cluster controllers*, normally communicate with remote communications controllers through leased telephone lines with a modem at each end of the line. Control units can be IBM 3274 or 3174 models. The 3174 Subsystem Control Unit is the most versatile of the IBM control units. It can provide connectivity from a communications controller to remote PCs or direct connectivity from an IBM host processor to local PCs. In both instances, the 3174 can be a Token Ring network gateway for LAN-attached PCs or a concentrator for several coax-connected PCs.

You also can set up a PC to emulate a control unit. The PC can act both as a controller and a terminal, or it can act as a gateway for a local area network. When the PC acts as a control unit for a network, the PCs connected to the LAN can emulate IBM terminals. The software in the gateway and the networked PCs must work together as a matched set. This combination uses network protocols to move data to and from a remote communications controller or host.

Workstations

SNA workstations provide end-user access to the resources shared through the SNA network. Workstations normally take the form of a terminal device, but can be any type of device that provides input/output for the network. The IBM 3270 and 5250 families of terminals were the standards for SNA terminals before the arrival of the PC. The 3278 terminal provided monochrome output, whereas the 3279 provided high-resolution color output. System/370 and System/390 processors normally support both of these terminals. The 5250 terminals normally connect to System/36, System/38, and AS/400 processors. Many companies are beginning to replace these terminals with the newer 3100 family of terminals or with PCs equipped with terminal emulation hardware and software.

Modems

SNA-compatible modems enable the connection of IBM SNA compatible devices to telephone lines. Besides converting digital data signals into analog signals compatible with the telephone system as described in Chapter 9, "Telephone System Interfaces," SNA-compatible modems actively participate in network problem determination. These microprocessor-driven modems enable multidropping of several terminal devices from one line and perform line problem determination to assist host-based problem determination software in isolating causes of failures or errors.

SNA Software

Many SNA features and capabilities are in software stored in SNA components or connections. The following paragraphs describe some of these SNA software modules.

SNA Access Methods

SNA access methods are included in software that resides in a network host. These access methods perform SNA network control by providing an interface between host applications and the network. They provide security to prevent unauthorized access to applications. They also provide network data flow control. The IBM *Advanced Communications Function/Virtual Telecommunications Access Method* (ACF/VTAM) is the most frequently used access method in SNA systems. ACF/VTAM monitors network performance and supports problem determination and analysis based on information provided by other SNA components in the network. VTAM also provides the support for interconnection of two or more SNA networks.

Network Management Programs

Network management programs are a family of host software packages that supports network monitoring and control. These programs detect and report errors to network operators. They also maintain network performance to enable the network operator to tune the network for optimum performance. Finally, network management programs assist the network operator in the day-to-day operation of the network. Examples of older IBM network management programs are as follows:

✔ *Network Problem Determination Application* (NPDA)

✔ *Network Communication Control Facility* (NCCF)

✔ *Network Performance Monitor* (NPM)

The latest network management software released by IBM is *SystemView*, which combines the best IBM network management capabilities into one, integrated, network management system.

Network Control Programs

Network control programs normally reside in the communications controller and manage the routing and flow of data between the controller and other network entities. Control programs, such as *Advanced Communications Function/Network Control Program* (ACF/NCP) control the configurations of lines to the controller and perform error recovery. An IBM communications controller equipped with ACF/NCP off-loads many SNA functions from a host, enabling the host to perform more appropriate applications-related tasks.

Application Subsystems

Application subsystems are the end-user windows into a host computer. These subsystems make it possible to interact with application programs by locating the programs for users, loading the programs, and transmitting data to and from the user. Application subsystems retrieve data from files, update data files, and provide the graphics and text output the user views on a monitor. These subsystems also support remote batch processing—programs that do not require user interaction.

The most frequently used SNA application subsystems are *Customer Information Control System* (CICS) and *Information Management System* (IMS). These subsystems provide terminal-oriented programming support and enable user access to databases. Other special purpose application subsystems, such as *Distributed Office Support System* (DISOS) and *Airline Control Program/Transaction Processing Facility* (ACP/TPF), provide document distribution and travel reservation services, respectively.

Application Programs

The final element in the host environment that interfaces with an SNA network is the application programs, which provide end-user services such as word processing, financial transactions, or scientific computation.

End-user organizations or outside vendors write application programs. Application programs can reside in a host, a cluster controller, or a workstation and can support a single user or multiple users simultaneously.

End Users

SNA defines the end user as both ends of an SNA connection. SNA end users include people who interact with network resources through workstations, as well as the application programs that provide processing services for the people using the workstations. SNA end users are both the sources and destinations of data and information that traverse the SNA network. When two processors share program execution during program-to-program interactions, the application software at each end of the link is an end user.

SNA Connectivity

SNA provides several means of connectivity between components that conform to the SNA specifications. Links communicate between nodes, and nodes combine into subareas to enhance control of a large network.

SNA Network Links

SNA networks use two types of links to connect communicating devices, depending upon the distance separating the devices. An SNA link includes the transmission media that connect two devices and a data link protocol that controls data movement through the link. As shown earlier in figures 7.29 and 7.30, the two most frequently used types of links are data channels and *Synchronous Data Link Control* (SDLC).

Channel Attachment

Data channels are high-speed connections between a host processor and another host or between a host and one of the main connectivity controllers in the 3270 Information Display System. These channel attachments enable data to pass between processors or between processors and controllers at data rates in the 100 Mbps range. These rates are significantly higher than the maximum data rates of telephone, coax cable, or Token Ring network connections. Parallel data paths in a data channel support the high data transfer rates.

Token Ring Network

The IBM Token Ring network provides SNA connectivity for devices and processors located in a small geographical area. Optional adapters are available for the PC that enable you to connect to an IBM 8228 *Multistation Access Unit* (MSAU) through either twisted-pair or coaxial cable. The MSAU is both a wiring concentrator and the network ring. Many ways to connect an IBM host to the MSAU are available. Small hosts such as the 9370 and AS/400 have internal adapters that provide Token Ring network connectivity. For large hosts, communications controllers and control units off-load network connectivity.

Bridge software is available that enables you to interconnect several Token Ring networks. These bridges can be local and require a PC with two network adapters. You also can bridge between two networks in different geographical areas. This technique requires a split-bridge that acts as a translator between a Token Ring network and an SDLC link.

Synchronous Data Link Control

SDLC provides SNA connectivity through the telephone system or through direct connections between devices and a host in special instances. An SDLC link can connect SNA devices to a host if the SNA access method provides support for that technique and the host has an *integrated communications adapter* (ICA) installed. In all other cases, SDLC provides the synchronous error correction and data routing through telephone connections using modems that support this connectivity option.

As discussed in detail in Chapter 6, "Synchronous Data Link Control," the SDLC link-level protocol is a subset of the HDLC protocol and provides robust error detection and correction. The CRC-16 provides a message frame check, and the sender retransmits bad messages until they are correct. Like HDLC, SDLC provides sliding window capability for message transmission to prevent network bottlenecks and improve communications response times. SDLC also handles data as a bit stream, thereby enabling any type of data to pass through SNA devices without undesirable side effects—a capability called *transparent data transfer.*

SDLC frames can be assembled and disassembled in hardware or software. Because of the processing required to perform this function, hardware normally generates the SDLC protocol. For example, the SDLC and multiprotocol adapters available for the PC perform these tasks to off-load the PC's CPU to perform other tasks.

Binary Synchronous Communications

For connectivity with older SNA hardware and packet-switched networks, SNA provides support for the Binary Synchronous Communications and X.25 protocols. IBM originally used BSC as the link-level protocol for SNA, but switched to SDLC. The character-oriented limitations of BSC caused customers to move to SDLC. X.25 interface support enables SNA networks to connect directly to PSNs and transmit data to remote SNA devices. X.25 capabilities also enable PSNs to connect two SNA networks. Both the BSC and X.25 give SNA upward compatibility for the migration from older to newer devices. This capability also enables X.25 networks to expand the SNA span of control.

II

Data Communications

SNA Nodes

SNA uses the concept of *node connectivity*. Hardware and software segregate into nodes based on the SNA functions they support and the SNA layers they implement. The three groupings are host, communications controller, and peripheral, as shown in figure 7.31. The SNA links described earlier connect these nodes.

Figure 7.31
SNA nodes.

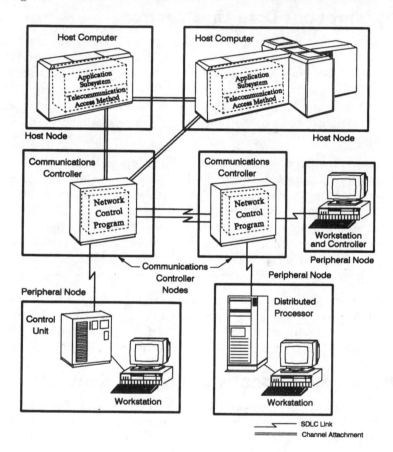

Host Nodes

Host nodes consist of host processors that supply the SNA access method and network control. Each host and its directly attached hardware is a node. Host nodes normally contain ACF/VTAM and are channel-attached to other SNA components.

Controller Nodes

Communications controller nodes consist of a communications controller and a network control program. These nodes provide the connectivity between host nodes and local or remote workstations. For example, an IBM 3725 and ACF/NCP software provide the SNA "glue" between a host and remote terminals.

Peripheral Nodes

Peripheral nodes consist of hardware and software that support end-user activity. Peripheral nodes normally fall into three categories: cluster controllers and downstream workstations; distributed processors and downstream workstations; and devices that communicate directly with communications controllers. A department, workgroup, or building that has its own 3174 Subsystem Control Unit or AS/400 processor is a typical implementation of a peripheral node.

Transmission Groups

SNA provides flexibility, reliability, and capacity control in the data communications across network links by supporting *transmission groups*. SNA *path control* combines one or more parallel links (data channels and SDLC links) and makes them appear to the network as a single link. As figure 7.32 illustrates, these transmission groups eliminate single points of failure between major SNA nodes.

When all transmission group links are operating properly, the group provides a large capacity for data traffic to prevent network bottlenecks. When a link fails or produces an unacceptable error rate, SNA can automatically route data through the remaining transmission group links. This built-in redundancy significantly reduces the probability of data loss or service disruption for end users.

II

Data Communications

Figure 7.32
SNA
transmission
groups.

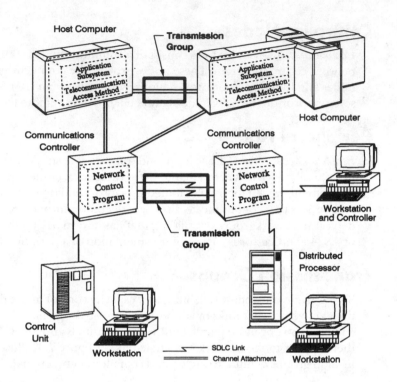

Subareas

SNA defines subareas to enhance configuration control of a network. As figure 7.33 shows, subareas consist of a host or communications controller node and its peripheral devices. These subareas facilitate the addressing of data messages to specific devices. Each subarea gets a unique number in the network, and within a subarea each device gets a unique element address. Message routing between subareas depends on subarea addressing only. After a message reaches the appropriate subarea, the element address specifies its destination.

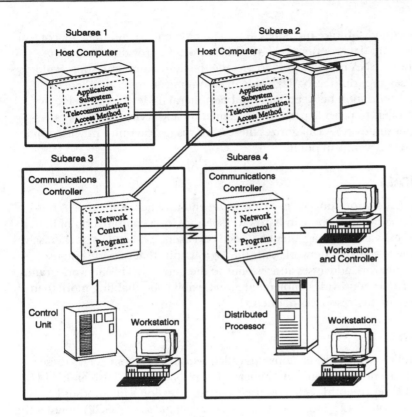

Figure 7.33
SNA subareas.

SNA Units

To enhance the functionality and control of an SNA network, different functions of the network are divided into groups called *units*. A host processor manages these units through a System Service Control Point.

Network Addressable Units

Two features make SNA node connectivity possible, one of which is *Network Addressable Units* (NAUs). To implement SNA in layers and separate functions into groups requires a technique of uniquely identifying network resources. NAUs provide this identification through network addressees. By routing SNA messages and control information along a path designated by these unique network unit addressees, data move to and from end users with reliability and control. A feature called the *Path Control Network* (PCN) implements the NAU addressees to ensure SNA route control and management.

SNA hardware and software include NAUs to provide end-to-end network control and point-to-point data routing. NAUs reside in hosts to provide connectivity support between SNA networks and to provide the destination and source addressees of end-user applications. NAUs reside in communications controllers to provide synchronization between hosts and peripheral nodes. NAUs reside in cluster controllers to provide peripheral destination and source addressees. As figure 7.34 illustrates, SNA categorizes these NAUs as logical units, physical units, and system services control points.

Logical Units

Logical units (LUs; pronounced "el-yu") provide end-user access to an SNA network. These logical units come in hardware, software, or a combination of both to provide data exchange management between end users. The end users themselves are not visible to the SNA network; only the logical units that provide end-user services have network addresses and visibility to the network. This network granularity to the LU level provides implementation flexibility by enabling more than one user to share the resources of one LU.

LU Sessions

LUs communicate through relationships called *sessions.* A PCN manages these sessions. Before end-users can communicate, the PCN must establish an LU-LU session. An LU representing one end user requests a session with another LU representing another LU end user. A *system services control point* (SSCP) handles the request and activates the LU-LU session. The Path Control Network routes control data that initiates and terminates the LU-LU session and the control data that manages the routing of messages between LUs. The Path Control Network also routes end-user application data between the two communicating LUs. The PCN handles the traffic between SNA physical units and SCCPs.

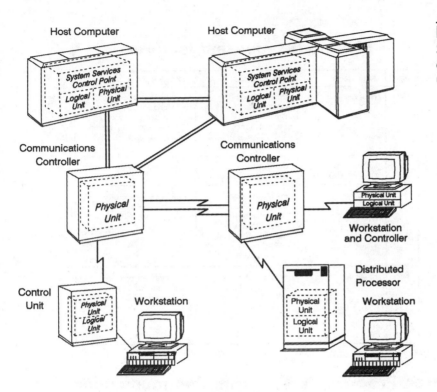

Figure 7.34
SNA network addressable units.

LU Types

Logical units are categorized into seven types based on features and capabilities. The support for these LU types depends upon the functions provided by a specific type of SNA node. Table 7.3 shows the relationship between SNA LU types and node types. Nodes that include LU types 2, 3, 4, and 7 support communications between software entities. In all cases, however, LUs can only establish sessions and communicate with the same type of LU in another part of the SNA network. Because of this requirement, a host subarea node normally provides multiple LU types to enable all end users to communicate.

Table 7.3
SNA node types and features.

Type	Node Name	Node Attributes	Node Functions

5	Host Subarea	Subarea node
		Contains an SSCP
		Contains a PU Type 5
		Supports LU types
		  1, 2, 3, 4, 6, 1,
		  6.2 and 7
			Controls network resources
			Supports application and
			  transaction programs
			Provides access to network
			Provides user services

4	Communications Controller Subarea	Subarea node Contains a PU Type 4	Routes and controls network data flow

2.1	Peripheral	Peripheral node
		Contains a PU Type 2.1
		Supports LU types
		  1, 2, 3, 6.2 and 7
		Supports Advanced
		  Program-to-Program
		  Communications
			Provides user access
			  to the network
			Provides user services

2.0	Peripheral	Peripheral node
		Contains a PU Type 2.0
		Supports LU types
		  2, 3, and 7
		Supports LU Type 1
		  for non-SNA
		  connections
			Provides user access
			  to the network
			Provides user services

Advanced Program-to-Program Communications

LU 6.2 is the latest IBM offering in support of end-user communications and a capability that is revolutionizing SNA communications. LU 6.2, also known as *Advanced Program-to- Program Communications* (APPC), enables peer-to-peer communications between any two computers connected to the SNA network. When LU 6.2 is available and software takes advantage of this capability at both ends of the link, program-to-program communications can take place without the need for a mainframe host to control the LU-LU sessions.

IBM first announced LU 6.2 in 1982. IBM and others use this capability to enhance distributed processing and to support client/server computing. For example, part of a database application can run on a host, while another part of the same database application runs on a PC. Vendors can allocate application function to a processor based on the location of the data to be manipulated or the CPU resources required to perform certain functions. LU 6.2 enables you to match computing workload and processor capability.

Another advantage of LU 6.2 is its network independence. You can implement LU 6.2 in an SNA, X.25, or other type of network. Network independence means that LU 6.2 could eventually provide a bridge between networks with dissimilar architectures.

The Extended Services for Operating System/2 (OS/2) provide complete support for LU 6.2. The Communications Manager included with this operating system extension provides LU 6.2 APPC functions. The APPC interface, along with the Presentation Manager interface included in the same package, provides software developers all the tools they need to create easy-to-use yet powerful distributed software implementation. The OS/2 Database Manager also supports the development of distributed database systems.

Physical Units

Although the name *physical units* (PU) implies a hardware component, this SNA entity is a combination of hardware and software. These elements implement several SNA functions. A physical unit represents and manages the resources of a physical entity such as a processor, controller, workstation, printer, or other end-user device.

The interaction of the PUs in a host and a communications controller during the activation of a host subarea node is a good example of the services provided by a PU. During this process, the host PU provides the address of a link that can be used for communications between the host and controller and establishes the link. After SNA establishes a link, the PUs in the host and controller negotiate to establish the optimum communications between the two devices based on the resources available at each end of the link. Before establishing or changing the communications between any two SNA nodes, the PUs of these nodes actively participate in creating and modifying links.

The PU of each node is a valuable SNA resource in maintaining high network reliability. The PU in a node can provide a trace path that enables the host to search for problem areas within the network. The PU also can monitor resource performance and report to the host SNA access method errors or failures associated with communications links or components. Network operators can use the information provided by PUs to correct problems and improve network performance and reliability.

System Services Control Points

System Services Control Points (SSCPs) reside in host processors to activate, control, and deactivate SNA network resources. The SNA access method such as VTAM implements the SSCP to control a portion of an SNA network called a *domain*. As shown in figure 7.35, two domains controlled by separate SSCPs can be connected to share resources and to provide backup capability between networks.

II

Data Communications

Figure 7.35
SNA domains.

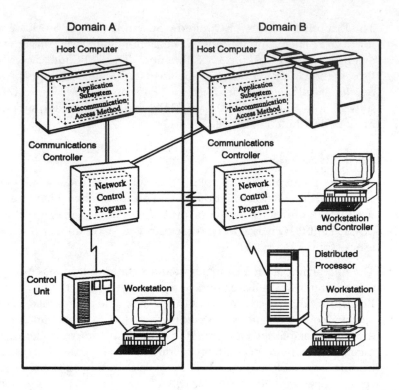

SSCP sessions enable the SSCP in one domain to communicate with the NAUs in the same domain or NAUs in another domain. An *SSCP-PU* session enables a host to control SNA nodes in the domain; network resources can be activated, monitored, or deactivated through these sessions. An SSCP-LU session enables a host to initiate and control LU-LU sessions that provide end-user access to the network.

An *SSCP-SSCP* session between two domains enables LU-LU sessions to be established across domains and supports resource sharing between these domains. SSCP-SSCP sessions also enable the SSCP in one network to act as a backup to an SSCP in another network; if one host fails, the SSCP in the other host can take over the control of network components in both networks. This last *cross-domain SSCP capability* enables a company to set up multiple-domain networks. This feature enables you to separate control and security by department or division while maintaining full resource sharing and high system reliability.

SNA Summary

SNA, with its proprietary, host-based origins, has emerged as a flexible method of providing connectivity and control between communicating devices. Since its introduction in 1974, IBM and other vendors have continued to develop and implement SNA in both hardware and software products. The architecture has evolved from a rigid host-to-terminal orientation to a more versatile processor-to-processor orientation to match the evolution of communications technology as well as workstation processing power.

The PC has been a major force in the evolution of SNA. A PC provides the ideal personal workstation that enables users to access and share resources managed by SNA networks. The introduction of LU 6.2 and Advanced Program-to-Program Communications provides the SNA enhancement needed to support distributed processing between several IBM processors, including the PC. Vendors also can use them to develop client/server applications.

II

Data Communications

Chapter Snapshot

This chapter introduces you to techniques and devices that you can use to move data from a PC to a remote device or computer. You will also review several PC communications interfaces and other equipment necessary in order to communicate with other devices. In this chapter, you will learn about:

✔ Types of communication adapters

✔ Serial communications interfaces

8

CHAPTER

PC Communications Interfaces and Adapters

Now that you understand the fundamentals of communications and networking, you can move on to the real world of hardware. This chapter builds on the ideas explored in earlier chapters. Although connectivity often requires combinations of communications and networking, this book separates these topics. Because networking hardware is intimately tied to the specific logical link and media access controls associated with the network design, networking hardware is covered in Part III, "Local Area Networking."

This chapter reviews the PC communications interfaces and adapters that enable you to communicate with other devices and computers. You also learn about the built-in ports, connectors, and external cables needed to set up the connectivity alternatives shown in figure 8.1. The chapter starts with the internal ports and adapters; moves on to external connectors and cables; and ends with a review of the special interfaces that enable you to directly connect computers using interfaces originally designed for other purposes.

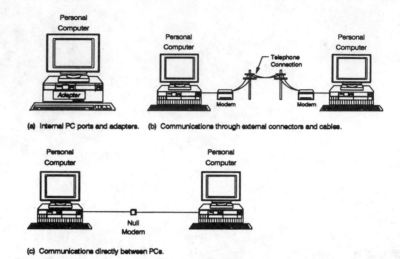

Figure 8.1
Communications
and networking
connectivity
alternatives.

(a) Internal PC ports and adapters.   (b) Communications through external connectors and cables.

(c) Communications directly between PCs.

To provide connectivity between a PC and other devices or computers, you need to become familiar with PC communications hardware. The serial communications protocol and the physical configuration you choose often dictate a specific set of communications hardware. The features and functions you want to include in your system also dictate specific hardware components. The information in this chapter helps you start this selection process. The information on telephone system interfaces in the next chapter builds on the information provided in this chapter.

Communications Adapters

To communicate with modems and other serial devices, electronic circuitry must convert the parallel bit stream used within the PC system unit into a serial bit stream that is compatible with these devices. As discussed in Chapter 2, "Communications Channels," several techniques are used in this conversion process. The following paragraphs explore several adapters that provide parallel-to-serial data conversion.

Asynchronous Communications Adapters

Vendors often use the term *asynchronous communications adapter* to describe the circuitry that enables a personal computer to communicate externally with serial devices; but this label is only one of many used to describe the adapter. Other names for this circuitry are *serial port, asynchronous communications interface,* and *Universal Asynchronous Receiver/Transmitter* (UART—pronounced "you-art"). These

names refer to a circuit board or a part of a circuit board designed to do parallel-to-serial or serial-to-parallel conversions of binary data and other serial communications functions.

As explained in Chapter 4, "Data Transmission Fundamentals," the PC communicates internally with a data bus composed of 8, 16, or 32 parallel wires. By using this technique, the PC can transfer an eight-bit character by sending all eight bits to a device simultaneously, resulting in rapid internal communications. When you must move data over longer distances, however, routing cables containing 8, 16, or 32 parallel data lines become costly.

Instead of dedicated computer cables, most computer communications arrangements use ordinary public telephone equipment. Because telephone systems provide either two or four wires for communications, the parallel bit streams that travel through a computer must funnel into a stream of sequential, serial bits that can travel through these telephone lines. The serial port performs the chore of an "electronic traffic cop." Figure 8.2 illustrates the process. At the receiving end, a serial port converts the serial flow of data bits back into a parallel flow of bits. The receiving computer then processes the information through its internal parallel bus.

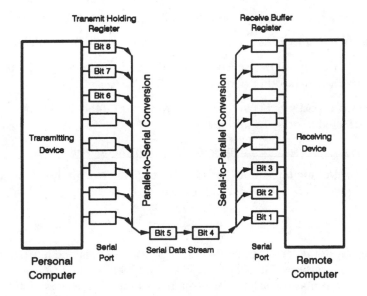

Figure 8.2
Serial data communications.

Because of the serial nature of telephone communications and the errors these systems can create, the serial port does more than just parallel-to-serial and serial-to-parallel conversions of bit streams. The following list shows other functions the asynchronous serial port can execute. To perform these diverse functions, the port includes an EIA RS-232D interface, a small microprocessor, a clock, and memory registers. The serial port is a self-contained microcomputer that can perform the functions described earlier without the need for user involvement.

- ✔ Monitors the communications link with a modem or other device to prepare the communications line for data transmission

- ✔ Enables software control of communications parameters

- ✔ Regulates data transmit and receive speeds to predetermined fixed rates from 50 to 19,200 bits per second

- ✔ Adds a start bit to each byte it transmits

- ✔ Adds error-checking parity bits to the end of transmitted characters if instructed to do so by the communications software

- ✔ Adds one or more stop bits to each byte it transmits

- ✔ Provides a single-byte buffer for data it is transmitting or receiving

- ✔ Detects and ignores false start bits it receives through the serial interface

- ✔ Deletes the start bit from each byte it receives through the serial interface from a modem or other device

- ✔ Checks for parity errors in bytes it receives from a modem or other device if instructed to do so by software

- ✔ Sends parity error indication to the communications software

- ✔ Deletes the stop bit(s) from each byte it receives through the serial interface from a modem or other device

Transmission Speed

One vital function of the serial port is data rate control. As explained in Chapter 2, data transmission is measured in *bits per second* (bps), which is called *bit rate* for asynchronous communications. Most PC serial ports support transmission bit rates from 50 to 9,600 bps; some later-model PCs support rates as high as 28,800 bps. Users select these bit rates through software control. The software can subsequently transmit and receive data through either modem or direct-connection interfaces with other peripherals or computers. As described in detail in Chapter 9,

"Telephone System Interfaces," modem hardware can provide data compression that enables the PC and its software to transmit data to the modem at twice the modem connection speed.

The important thing to remember regarding the selection of a bit rate is that the transmitting and receiving computers have to operate at the same rate. Otherwise, the received data appear to contain many transmission errors. Some auto-answer intelligent modems can detect and switch rates to match the rate of the incoming call. Some unattended communications software packages also can do this switching function. If neither the modem nor the communications software you use can automatically perform a switch to match the bit rate of a remote system, you must manually switch the communications bit rate with your communications software.

Data Framing

Because asynchronous communications is, by definition, not continuous, an asynchronous port receiving this type of data must know when data transmission is starting and stopping so that the receiving computer's timing device can synchronize with that of the transmitting device. The asynchronous hardware must re-synchronize for each data byte by using framing bits as signals. Contained between these framing signals are additional bits that convey data.

Asynchronous data framing begins with a start bit. The serial port adds a start bit to each string of data bits as the string passes through the serial port. The start bit tells the receiving computer to prepare itself for the receipt of data. The serial port on the receiving end, after synchronizing with the incoming signal, must strip the start bit from the data because it serves no further purpose.

The serial port also can add a parity bit to each byte of data it transmits. By adding the parity bit to each string of data bits, the serial port can make the total number of bits per character even or odd. The receiving computer's serial port can then check each set of data bits it receives to make sure that the set contains either an odd or even number of 1 bits. If the receiving serial port detects an error, it can tell the user about the error through communications software.

Following the transmission of a byte of data, the serial port must signal the end of the byte. The port does this by adding stop bits (equivalent to binary 1s) at the end of each byte of data it transmits. This "test period" tells the receiving serial port that it has received a complete byte of data. The port can then translate the serial data into parallel data and create an interrupt signal that tells the receiving PC's processor that data have arrived. The stop bit also enables accurate measurement of the start point for the next byte of data. Stop bits can be 1-, 1.5-, or 2-bit times in length. Normal use requires 2 with 110 bps, and 1 with 300 bps and higher.

Speed Matching

Communications software functions provide the speed-matching between two communicating PCs. The asynchronous adapter accepts data from the software and sends them to another computer. The adapter also receives data from another computer and makes them available for the communications software. Neither the PC system unit nor its operating system, however, provides adapter handlers or device drivers to support the movement of data between the adapter and the communications software.

Communications software or a library of device drivers must provide the data conduit between the asynchronous adapter and system unit memory. This software must provide interrupt service and temporary buffer storage to match the data transfer speed of the system unit and the data transfer speed of the asynchronous adapter. Chapter 10, "Communications Software," examines this concept more closely.

Some vendors combine serial ports with parallel printer circuitry and additional memory in a single adapter. Most of the vendors marketing these combination boards duplicate the functions of single-function boards so well that users cannot tell the difference. Vendors also make adapters that contain multiple serial ports to support simultaneous communications with several modems or remote devices.

Synchronous Communications Adapters

The second type of communications adapter used with the PC is the *synchronous adapter*. This device does parallel-to-serial and serial-to-parallel conversions of bit streams like the conversions performed by the asynchronous adapter. There is one significant difference, however—the synchronous adapter divides a data stream into blocks of bits, whereas an asynchronous adapter divides a data stream into bytes.

Synchronous adapters implement specific synchronous data link control protocols. Two popular protocols are *Binary Synchronous Communication* (BSC) and *Synchronous Data Link Control* (SDLC). Although the IBM *System Network Architecture* (SNA) supports both protocols, the SDLC protocol is by far the most powerful. Chapter 6, "Synchronous Data Link Control," describes both BSC and SDLC. Other chapters describe the implementation and support of BSC and SDLC in network configurations.

Multiprotocol Adapters

A multiprotocol communications capability provides many advantages to business environments that require communications between the PC and other devices, or host computers, using a variety of protocols. To conserve the use of system unit expansion slots and to provide programming flexibility, IBM and other vendors offer multiprotocol adapters that provide asynchronous, BSC, and SDLC communications in one device. With the arrival of modems that provide both asynchronous and synchronous capability in the same unit, this multiprotocol capability enables communications among a large variety of devices from the same hardware configuration.

Terminal Emulation Adapters

Emulation is a technique used with the PC to make it behave almost exactly like a specific type of mainframe or minicomputer terminal. The implementation of this technique often requires both hardware and software components. Most vendors consider these hardware/software combinations proprietary because they enable you to connect with a host that has unpublished interface specifications.

Terminal emulation enables you to take advantage of the capabilities of the PC and a host from a single interface. You can execute any PC software you want that fits within the memory constraints imposed by the terminal emulation package. You also can switch to a session with the host and execute software that resides in that machine.

Hardware terminal emulators normally fit in a PC expansion slot. These emulators can make the PC act almost exactly like a standard mainframe terminal. Most emulators of this type reproduce the characteristics of the IBM 3270 or 5250 families of synchronous terminals. With the proper hardware and a matching software package, the PC can be connected to a control unit and participate as a mainframe workstation. Some 3278/79 terminal emulation software packages work with Token Ring network adapters to provide 3270 connectivity through a Token Ring attached to an IBM 3270 Information Display System.

Software terminal emulators often operate alone to make a PC appear like a standard ASCII terminal to a minicomputer or a mainframe. Terminals most often emulated are the IBM 3101, DEC VT 100, DEC VT 52, and ADDS Viewpoint. If a large computer expects one of these terminal types, it is easier and less expensive to make the PC look like one of these terminals than to add software to the large computer to accommodate the personal computer.

The differences between terminal types are the escape codes that produce specific screen display functions and the keystrokes that produce specific host operations. If you do not use the same codes with your PC that the large computer expects, you may get screens full of garbage rather than legible text. If your keyboard does not produce the functions the host expects, you may get unpredictable results from interactions with the host.

Serial Communications Interfaces

To get from the serial communications port or adapter to another device requires the use of specific connectors and cables. Without standards for these interfaces, the communications business would not be the thriving industry it is today. This section explores the serial interfaces you are likely to use to connect the PC to a system of other computers or devices.

The EIA RS-232C Standard

When shopping for data communications equipment, you may see the phrases "standard RS-232C" and "RS-232C-compatible." These statements usually mean that the device or cable uses a DB-25 connector; they do not guarantee that the device supports all the signals defined by the EIA RS-232C standard. This can be confusing for a new communications user. Many users have purchased RS-232C cables to connect modems and serial printers to PCs and found that some of their modem or printer features do not work because the cable does not convey all the necessary signals. Because of a lack of uniformity in the implementation of the RS-232C standard, some serial printers do not work at all without special cables.

The *Electronic Industries Association* (EIA) published the RS-232C standard in 1969. RS is an acronym for Recommended Standard, and 232 is the identification number for that particular standard. The letter C shows this is the third revision of the RS-232 standard. The purpose of this standard is to define the electrical characteristics for the interfacing of *data terminal equipment* (DTE) and *data circuit-terminating equipment* (DCE). For the PC user, these terms refer to the PC and a modem, respectively.

Although the EIA published interface standards such as RS-449 after 1969 that provide more flexibility and features than RS-232C, none displaced RS-232C in the marketplace. Because of the popularity of this interface and the need for some clarifications, the EIA published a new RS-232 revision in 1987. The new standard is EIA RS-232D.

The ITU-T published its own serial interface recommendation based on the EIA RS-232C standard. This V.24 recommendation is almost identical to RS-232C, as discussed later. The ITU-T has yet to publish a recommendation based on RS-232D.

The EIA RS-232D Standard

The RS-232D standard defines a range of bit rates, a range of cable lengths, and the physical requirements for a serial interface. The standard calls for data transfer rates from 0 to 20,000 bps through serial cables up to 50 feet in length. EIA RS-232D also eliminates some confusion associated with RS-232C by calling for a specific set of DB-25 physical connectors.

As you see in Chapter 9, vendors do not always stay within the RS-232D specifications. Although they stay within the physical connector requirements, some vendors push data rates as high as 115,000 bps through standard serial ports and cables. They accomplish this by limiting the cable lengths to less than six feet.

Figure 8.3 is a diagram of the application of the RS-232D interfacing cable with the PC. From this figure, you can see that the RS-232D interface plays a critical role in PC communications. Cables and connectors that conform with EIA RS-232D provide the connectivity between the PC and the modems that enable PCs to communicate through the telephone system. Other devices, such as serial printers, can be configured as DCE or DTE devices, depending on the manufacturer. You also can use these cables and connectors to communicate directly between a PC and another computer that contains a DCE interface.

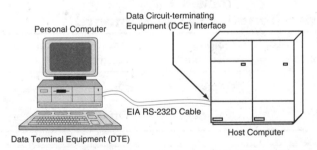

Figure 8.3
EIA RS-232D interface applications.

(a) EIA RS-232D cable connection between a PC and a host computer.

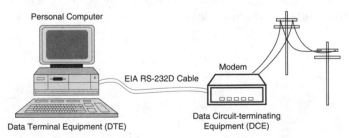

(b) EIA RS-232D cable connection between a PC and a modem.

RS-232D Signal Characteristics

To ensure that binary data transmits properly and that communications equipment controls perform properly, it is necessary to agree on data and control signals. The RS-232D standard provides voltage ranges for data and control signals to satisfy these requirements. Table 8.1 and figure 8.4 show these ranges.

Figure 8.4
EIA RS-232D
signal levels.

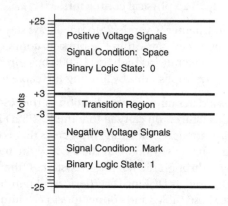

Table 8.1
Interchange Voltage Standard

Interchange Voltage	Binary Logic State	Signal Condition	Interface Control Function
Positive	0	Space	On
Negative	1	Mark	Off

The PC user is not normally concerned with the voltage ranges and signals associated with those ranges as they pertain to communications. These signals are of concern to hardware vendors and provide the basis for the design of serial ports and modems. When properly implemented, the operation of these signals is not visible to a user.

RS-232D Pin Assignments

Figure 8.5 shows the physical implementation of the RS-232D standard. This figure illustrates the pin assignments most vendors use in RS-232D connectors. Although these pin assignments are in EIA RS-232C, the International Standards Organization document IS0 2113 controlled the design of the physical connector. Both the pin assignments and the physical layout of the DB-25 connector are now mandatory in EIA RS-232D. RS-232D calls for a female connector at the DCE, and a male connector at the DTE.

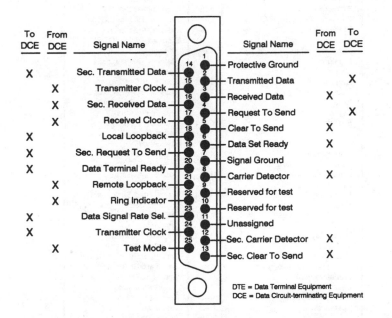

Figure 8.5
EIA RS-232D pin layout and assignments.

Although RS-232C specifies 25 signals for a serial interface, it does not define all the signals. RS-232D goes beyond RS-232C by defining additional signals that support the testing of communications hardware. Table 8.2 shows the circuit assignments for EIA RS-232C, EIA RS-232D, and ITU-T V.24. This table illustrates the functions added in RS-232D. These added features, with the clarification of the physical connector, breathed new life into the RS-232 interface. It will likely remain a viable connector for both asynchronous and communications until all-digital telephone systems become widely available.

Table 8.2
EIA RS232-C/D and CCITT V.24 circuits.

RS-232C/D		CCITT V.24	
AB	Signal ground	102	Signal ground
		102a	DTE common
		102b	DTE common
CE	Ring indication	125	Calling indication
CD	Data Terminal Ready	108/2	Data Terminal Ready
CC	Data Set Ready	107	Data Set Ready
BA	Transmitted Data	103	Transmitted Data
BB	Received Data	104	Received Data
DA	Transmitted Signal Element Timing (DTE Source)	113	Transmitted Signal Element Timing (DTE)
DB	Transmitted Signal Element Timing (DCE Source)	114	Transmitted Signal Element Timing (DCE)
DD	Receive Signal Element Timing	114	Receive Signal Element Timing (DCE)
CA	Request to Send	105	Request to Send
CB	Clear To Send	108	Ready for Sending
CF	Receive Line Signal Detector	109	Data Channel Received Line Signal Detector
CG	Signal Quality Detector	110	Data Signal Quality Detector
		128	Select Transmit Frequency
CH	Data Signal Rate Selector (DTE source)	111	Data Signal Rate Selector (DTE source)
CI	Data Signal Rate Selector (DCE source)	112	Data Signal Rate Selector (DCE source)
SBA	Secondary Transmitted Data	118	Transmitted Backward Channel Data
SBB	Secondary Received Send	119	Received Backward Channel Data
SGA	Secondary Request To Send	120	Transmit Backward Channel Line Signal
SCB	Secondary Clear To Send	121	Backward Channel Ready
SCF	Secondary Received Line Signal Detector	122	Backward Channel Received Line Signal Detector
(LL)	Local Loopback	141	Local Loopback
(RL)	Remote Loopback	140	Remote Loopback
(TM)	Test Mode	142	Test Indicator
		118	Select Standby
		117	Standby Indicator

Note: Parantheses indicate RS-232D requirements not in RS-232C.

To help you understand the RS-232D serial interface, the following paragraphs discuss some of its pin assignments. The RS-232D pin labels assigned by EIA are from the perspective of the DTE (PC, in this case). Figure 8.5 shows the direction each signal flows.

Transmit Data (TD, Pin 2)

The signals on this pin transmit from the PC to a modem or printer. The serial port maintains this circuit in the marking condition (logic condition 1, equivalent to a stop bit) when no data are available.

Receive Data (RD, Pin 3)

The signals on this pin transmit from a modem or printer to the PC's serial port. This circuit remains in a marking condition when no data are available.

Request To Send (RTS, Pin 4)

This circuit sends a signal to a modem or printer to request a clearance to send data on pin 2. This signal and the Clear to Send circuit work together to control the flow of data from the PC to a modem or to a serial printer. Synchronous communications use this signal to control the flow of data between modems.

Clear To Send (CTS, Pin 5)

A modem or serial printer sends this signal to tell the PC that it is ready to receive data. When this circuit is OFF (negative voltage or logic 1 state), the receiving device is telling the PC that it is not ready to receive data. Synchronous communications use this signal to control the flow of data between modems.

Signal Ground (SG, Pin 7)

This circuit serves as a signal reference for all other circuits used in communications. This signal is at zero voltage relative to all other signals.

Carrier Detect (CD, Pin 8)

A modem sends the PC an ON signal on this circuit when it receives a carrier signal from a remote modem. The CD (carrier detect) indicator on the front of a modem indicates the presence of this signal.

Data Set Ready (DSR, Pin 10)

A modem turns this circuit ON (logic 0) to tell the PC that it is properly connected to the telephone line and in the data transmission mode. Auto-dial modems send this signal to the PC after successfully dialing a host computer.

Local Loopback (LL, Pin 18)

The PC sends this signal to the modem to start a local loopback test. The modem goes into a test mode when it receives this signal.

Data Terminal Ready (DTR, Pin 20)

The PC turns this circuit ON when it is ready to communicate with a modem. Some modems cannot signal the PC that a proper telephone connection exists until the PC turns this circuit ON. If the PC turns this signal OFF during communications with a host system, this type of modem drops the telephone connection.

II

Data Communications

Modems such as the Hayes Smartmodem provide a switch that enables you to override the DTR logic. This switch, when properly positioned, causes the modem to ignore the status of the DTR circuit and maintain the communications connection even when the PC turns off the DTR signal (this enables bit rate and parity changes while on line with a host). Figure 8.6 shows the function of the DTR signal and its relationship with the CTS, DSR, and RTS signals. Figure 8.7 shows the typical signal combination used for most PC communications.

Figure 8.6
Typical modem
signal logic.

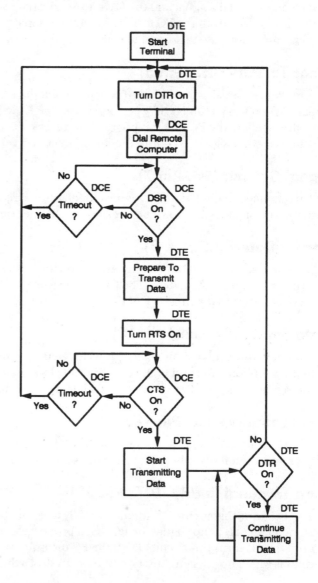

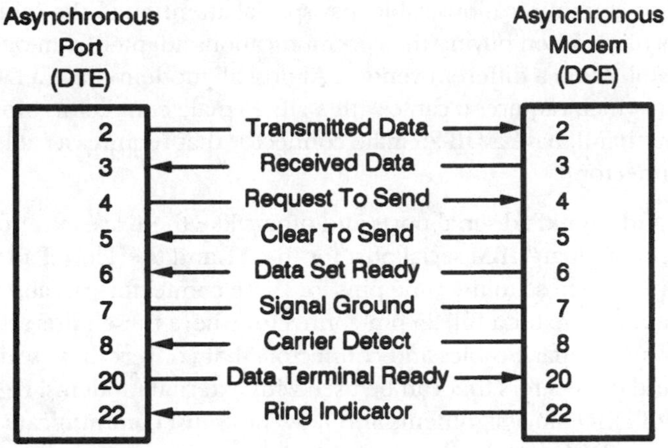

Asynchronous Port (DTE)		Asynchronous Modem (DCE)
2	Transmitted Data →	2
3	← Received Data	3
4	Request To Send →	4
5	← Clear To Send	5
6	← Data Set Ready	6
7	Signal Ground	7
8	← Carrier Detect	8
20	Data Terminal Ready →	20
22	← Ring Indicator	22

Figure 8.7
Typical signals used in asynchronous communications.

II

Data Communications

Remote Loopback (RL, Pin 21)

This circuit enables the modem to test the communications channel that connects with the PC.

Ring Indicate (RI, Pin 22)

An auto-answer modem uses this signal to indicate a telephone ring signal. The modem turns this circuit ON during each ring and OFF between rings.

Test Mode (TM, Pin 25)

The modem sends this signal to tell the PC when a local loopback (LL, Pin 18) or remote loopback (RL, Pin 21) test is in progress.

A personal computer serial port may not provide all the signals discussed in the preceding paragraphs. Still, understanding each signal may help when interfacing serial devices with PC serial ports. The following section discusses the details of cable and connector selection.

EIA RS-232D Cables

A communications cable transmits the RS-232D signals to and from a serial port. The cable can be round or flat; the cable's shape makes no difference in its capability to support communications. The types of connectors provided on each end of the cable or the number of wires connected to the pins in the connectors can, however, make a difference.

When purchasing a communications cable, pay special attention to the cable's connectors, particularly when buying the communications adapter from one vendor and the cable from a different vendor. Almost all modems have a DB-25 female connector, which requires a cable with a DB-25 male connector. Most serial ports, on the other hand, have a DB-25 male connector that requires a cable with a DB-25 female connector.

The IBM PC AT and ThinkPad serial ports and others like them are exceptions to the DB-25 rule. The standard IBM serial port for the AT and the ThinkPad is a DB-9 male connector. IBM chose to use nine pins for these connectors because not enough space was available for a full 25-pin connector where these ports are located. Several vendors make cables and connectors that convert these serial ports to DB-25 cables and connectors that can be used with external modems. Figure 8.8 shows a diagram of DB-9 pin assignments and how they must communicate with a DB-25 connector at a DCE (modem).

Figure 8.8
IBM PC serial port pin assignments.

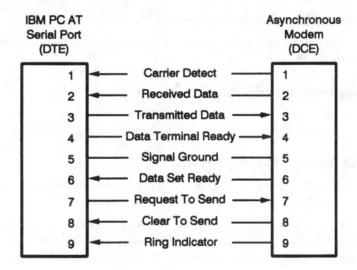

Communications cables do not always provide full support for all RS-232D signals. The so-called "Basic 8" pins are 1 through 7 and 20, and many communications cables contain only these pins. Many microcomputers can communicate properly with such a cable. PC serial ports are an exception; they require pin 8 to provide full communications support. Some communications software packages also require pin 22 (ring indicate) to provide auto-answer for incoming calls.

You may want to buy the parts at a local electronics parts supply store and make your own communications cable to extend the RS-232D adapter. You can buy a flat 40-wire ribbon cable; strip off all but 25 wires; and then attach compression-type connectors on each end. The advantage in making your cable is that you know that all 25 pins exist in the cable, although you may use only nine of the pins.

Null Modems

If you are the proud owner of a new PC, but you have several hundred programs that you developed on an older machine, you may want to transfer some software to your new machine. To do that, you may want to connect the two computers using a device called a *null modem* or *modem eliminator* A null modem, which is not a modem at all, is a cable or a set of connectors designed to eliminate the need for a modem. The null modem makes each computer operate as if it were communicating with a modem.

Figure 8.9 illustrates the problems two PCs can have when trying to communicate directly. In section 'a' of figure 8.9, a PC's asynchronous port is communicating with an asynchronous modem. The two devices have compatible transmit and receive signals. In section 'b' of figure 8.9, on the other hand, two PC asynchronous ports are both expecting to receive and send data on the same lines. Without the addition of a null modem, the PCs in section 'b' cannot communicate directly.

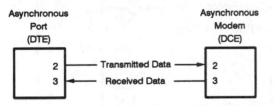

(a) Computer to modem EIA RS-232D communications interface.

Figure 8.9
Computer and modem interfaces.

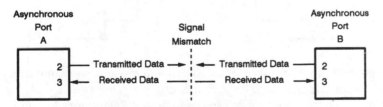

(b) Computer to computer EIA RS-232D interface mismatch.

Figure 8.10 shows the null modem solution to the incompatibility of direct PC-to-PC communications. By crossing the Receive Data and Transmit Data lines, the asynchronous port in PC A receives signals through the line that PC B's asynchronous port uses for transmission and vice versa. This sleight of hand with cable wires enables the two ports to communicate directly because each port can treat the other as a DCE even though it is a DTE.

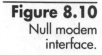

Figure 8.10
Null modem
interface.

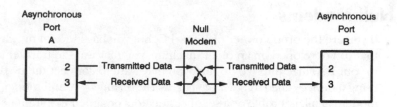

You can purchase null modems from a variety of computer electronics stores. Make such a purchase with care, however, because several ways are available to connect the cable pins to get two PCs to talk with each other. The connections shown in figure 8.11 should work between the PC and most other microcomputers.

Figure 8.11
Null modem
diagram.

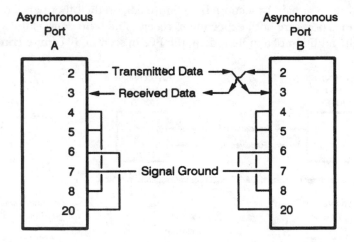

By making a direct PC-to-PC connection through a null modem, you can quickly transfer data between the PCs without the limitations of modems and telephone connections. A serial port supports data rates as high as 9,600 bps for older PCs and 28,800 bps for newer models. Modem data rates cover this same range, but require matching capabilities at each end of the link. Direct connections not only enable rapid data transfer (as high as 115,000 bps with data compression and short serial cables), they also eliminate line noise and other types of errors associated with data transfers through modems and telephone lines.

Summary

As you can see from this chapter, many techniques and devices are available that you can use to move data from a PC to a remote device or computer. The variety grows every year. Before the 1980s, the only way to move data at high speeds with reliable delivery was through synchronous adapters and modems. Vendors now use sophisticated technology that enables them to get the same results for both asynchronous and synchronous communications. The price difference between these techniques decreases every year.

You must determine the need for a specific type of communications hardware based on total user needs. For situations that require periodic connections to remote devices, dial-up facilities may meet all communications needs. For situations that require continuous connections, leased lines may be required. The selection of either asynchronous or synchronous communications is often dictated by the system the user must access. Many non-IBM hosts still use asynchronous communications. IBM hosts provide asynchronous communications through code and protocol converters.

When reliability and availability are critical success factors, the communications technique of choice is usually synchronous. To take full advantage of a system from a remote location, the user must provide a synchronous connection between the PC and the remote system. As you see in the next chapter, many telephone system interfaces support this communications technique.

II

Data Communications

Chapter Snapshot

There are many techniques and devices that provide synchronous and asynchronous connections between PCs and remote devices or computers. In this chapter, you will learn about:

✔ Modems as analog network interfaces

✔ Differences between asynchronous and synchronous modems

✔ Modem speeds, capabilities, and features

✔ Modem protocols

9

CHAPTER

Telephone System Interfaces

N ow that you understand PC adapters and ports, it is time to explore the devices that let you communicate with other computers through tele phone systems. Figure 9.1 shows the progression of this chapter, which begins with a discussion of the hardware that enables you to communicate between a PC and a remote computer through the telephone system, and ends by exploring the hardware that enables you to communicate through an all-digital data service.

Figure 9.1
Analog and
digital telephone
system
communications.

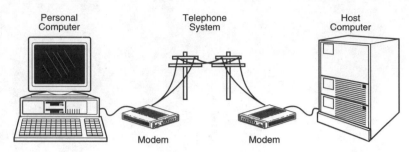

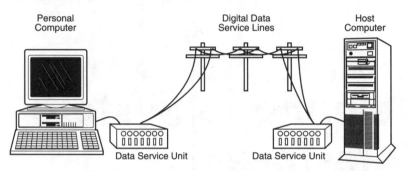

(a) Digital signal transmission through the telephone system.

(b) Digital signal transmission through a digital telephone system.

To connect the PC with other devices or computers, you need to become familiar with hardware that enables you to communicate through analog and digital telephone systems. The selection of that equipment depends on the serial communications protocol and the physical configuration you choose. The selection also depends upon the features and functions you want to include in your system and the budget you establish for this endeavor. The following section reviews these aspects.

Modems—Analog Network Interfaces

When a communications link must be established between a PC and another computer more than 50 feet away, the most economical method of doing so is usually through the public telephone system, sometimes call a *general-switched telephone network* (GSTN). To do this, a device called a *modem* must be installed between the PC's system board and the telephone system. This device is the final link between a digital-based PC and analog-based telephone systems.

Without the modem, data communications would not be the booming industry it is today. PC owners would also lack a powerful personal computer application. Modem speeds and capabilities are increasing and their costs are decreasing, making the process of selecting and purchasing a modem a complicated matter. Fortunately, many vendors of new modems are now complying with international standards published by the *International Telecommunications Union Telecommunication Standardization Sector* (ITU-T), formerly the CCITT. The following paragraphs provide a review of modem technology and these standards to make the selection process less painful for you.

How Modems Work

In the simplest terms, a modem converts the binary electrical signals it receives into analog signals the telephone system can transmit. Modems also convert analog signals they receive from the telephone system into digital signals a PC can receive. These modems modulate digital signals (square wave electrical signals) into analog signals (oscillating electrical signals) and demodulate analog signals into digital signals (see fig. 9.2). The name modem comes from the MOdulate-DEModulate functions the device provides.

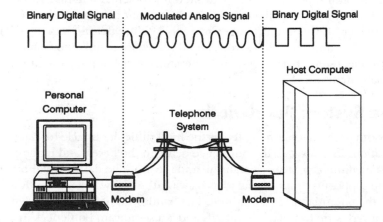

Figure 9.2
Digital signal modulation and demodulation.

The nature of the signal conversion process depends upon the source and destination of the signal the modem receives. As shown in figure 9.3, the modem receives the binary signals from a terminal or computer and converts them into *voice-frequency signals* (tones). The modem then transmits these sounds through the public telephone system. On the receiving end, another compatible modem converts these sounds back into binary electrical signals and sends these binary signals to a terminal or computer. In special cases, a modem also can receive signals that it converts and sends to a serial printer.

Figure 9.3
Digital-to-analog signal modulation.

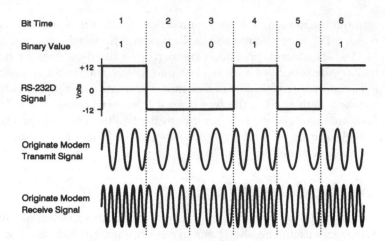

Digital signals must be converted into analog signals for transmission over telephone lines because of the equipment used in the telephone system. Many pieces of public telephone equipment provide amplifying and filtering functions that alter square wave signals into unrecognizable garbage by the time they reach the other end of a communications link. To avoid this problem, modems convert digital signals into analog signals compatible with telephone equipment as discussed in Chapter 2, "Communications Channels." Before delving into the details of modem features and capabilities, you should review some limitations imposed by the telephone system that affect modem design. The following paragraphs discuss these limitations.

Telephone System Bandwidth

The bandwidth of the telephone system is the most difficult obstacle for data communications. *Bandwidth* is the difference between the lowest and highest frequency a medium can properly transmit and receive. The data throughput a medium can support is proportional to its bandwidth—the wider the bandwidth, the greater the potential data throughput. The bandwidth of the public telephone system is not very wide by today's standards and is a significant bottleneck in data communications.

The public telephone system provides a bandwidth that covers the range of sounds produced by the human voice. That range restricts data communications. Human speech ranges between 20 and 18,000 *Hz* (cycles per second), with most voice sounds in the 100 to 3,500 Hz range. The original designers of the public telephone system chose a bandwidth of 300 to 3,300 Hz, as shown in figure 9.4. This range is a little smaller than the full range of the human voice and is a compromise between cost and full frequency support.

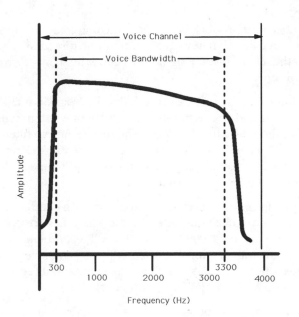

Figure 9.4
Bandwidth of public, circuit-switched telephone lines.

The bandwidth of the telephone system is adequate for voice communications, but severely limits data communications between devices that can achieve far greater frequency ranges. To overcome this small frequency range and produce maximum data communications throughput, modem vendors developed a sophisticated signaling technology.

Early modem products designed to provide communications speeds greater than 1,200 bps (*bits per second*) operate in a half-duplex mode. These modems use the same frequency range for both transmitting and receiving data. The transmit and receive modes consume the entire bandwidth. Two protocols, *Request to Send* (RTS) and *Clear to Send* (CTS), control the direction of data flow for these modems. To overcome the time delays required for these protocols, vendors installed four-wire, leased telephone lines in place of the less-expensive, public telephone lines. The four-wire lines provide double the bandwidth of two-wire public telephone lines, enabling simultaneous transmission and receiving of data, or full-duplex operation. Newer technology enables modem vendors to overcome this half-duplex limit of two-wire systems at speeds above 1,200 bps. Modem vendors now make modems that can operate at connection speeds of 28,000 bps using standard two-wire telephone connections.

Echo Suppression

Another limitation for data communications through the public telephone system is *echo suppression*. The public telephone system uses echo cancelers to reduce low-power signal reflections produced by signal-switching stations. These devices eliminate echoes by enabling signals to move in only one direction at a time. When a person talks into the telephone, the signals that carry the speaker's voice propagate to the distant listener.

Electronic filters eliminate return signals received while a person is talking. When the speaker stops talking and begins to listen, the telephone system senses the change and switches the echo filter direction. The turnaround in filter direction is approximately 300 milliseconds and is not normally noticeable during voice communications. The directional filtering and turnaround time delay is, however, a significant impediment to data communications.

Directional filters provide good, clean connections for voice communications, but limit data communications to half-duplex operation when they are operating. At a data communications speed of 28,000 bps, the 300-millisecond line turnaround delay is equivalent to the transfer time for at least 864 text characters. For long communications sessions that include the flow of data in both directions, this turnaround delay can produce a significant bottleneck.

To improve the data throughput of modems, vendors devised a way to electronically disable directional filters. These vendors designed modems that transmit an echo-canceling tone—a 2,225 Hz tone for Bell systems or 2,100 Hz for systems compliant with ITU-T standards—through the telephone line at specific intervals to turn off the echo suppression. By eliminating this suppression and the line turnaround protocol required to make it work, modem vendors can significantly increase the data rate through the telephone line.

Unfortunately, echo cancelers installed in the 1960s are not as sophisticated as later models and do not always obey the disabling tone signal. These older echo cancelers are a formidable problem for modems that operate at speeds above 1,200 bps. When the disabling signal does work properly, the modem must take over the echo cancellation process. Taking over that process is easy at low communications speeds, but becomes more difficult as the speed of the modem increases.

Background Noise

Background noise is the final limitation on data communications imposed by the public telephone system. Modems convert digital signals into tones of approximately -10 *dBm* (dBm is a relative measure of signal strength equivalent to 1 milliwatt into a 600 ohm load). The magnitude of these modem signals, however, drops to the -30 to -40 dBm range by the time they reach a remote modem. A background noise of approximately -50 dBm also exists on the line. As the ratio of signal strength to background noise decreases, it becomes more difficult for the modem to separate the received signal from the normal line noise.

Vendors found that increasing the complexity of modems to increase their data throughput increases the signal and noise separation problem as well. Signal and noise separation limitations prevented modem vendors from producing modems that operated above 4,800 bps over public telephone lines for many years. The development and perfection of *automatic signal equalization,* which culminated in real hardware in 1984, enables modem vendors to more easily separate noise from data. Hardware vendors were finally able to design reasonably priced 4,800 and 9,600 bps modems for use with public telephone lines. Since that time, vendors have taken advantage of this technology to increase modem connection speeds to 28,800.

Leased Telephone Circuits

One way to eliminate many limitations associated with the public telephone system is to lease telephone lines from a common carrier. Carriers can provide two kinds of conditioning equipment that enable modems to communicate at higher data rates. These carriers use two types of equalizers to improve the characteristics of the analog signals that propagate through the lines. Without increasing the usable bandwidth of the telephone lines, the conditioners enable modems to demodulate analog signals with greater reliability at higher speeds than they can achieve with public telephone lines.

One type of line conditioning provides attenuation equalizers, which keep the signal strength of transmitted frequencies at approximately the same level throughout the length of a communication link. Without these attenuation equalizers, higher-frequency signals decrease in strength (*attenuate*) more in a given length of telephone circuit than lower-frequency signals. By equalizing the strength of each frequency, a receiving modem can decipher phase shifts and amplitude changes of signals with greater reliability at higher rates.

The second type of conditioning provides delay equalizers, which offer different delays for different signal frequencies. The delays ensure that all frequencies arrive at the other end of a channel at approximately the same time. Without delay equalizers, signals with higher frequencies arrive before signals with lower frequencies even though they leave the signal source simultaneously. The delay equalizers make it easier for a modem to identify and demodulate a signal that contains several frequencies or one that rapidly changes phase. This conditioning enables the modem to operate more reliably and at a higher speed than it can with public telephone lines.

Modem Speeds and Protocols

The jargon associated with modem speeds creates confusion when it comes time to select a particular make and model. Most of this confusion comes from the misuse of the terms *baud* and *bits per second* (bps). The following paragraphs eliminate some of this confusion by defining these terms and translating them into rates and measures you can better recognize.

Baud

Baud is the number of signal events transmitted per second; users frequently confuse baud with bits per second. Signal events are changes in the frequency, phase angle, or voltage transmitted between two or more communications devices. One baud equals one such signal event per second, but the event can communicate more than one bit to the receiver.

For communications below 600 bps, the baud rate and bps transmitted between devices is the same. In other words, a 300 baud modem is the same as a 300 bps modem. The rates differ at 600 bps and higher because vendors combine several analog transmission techniques so that each signal event carries two or more binary bit values.

Bits per Second

Vendors rate modems based on the number of *bits per second* they can convey to a distant modem with compatible functions. The maximum rate at which a modem can transmit or receive these data determines its maximum throughput. Bits per second are the number of binary digits transferred per second, sometimes called *bit rate*. Table 9.1 shows the relationship between baud and bps for typical modems manufacturers in the United States today.

As you can see from this table, modem manufacturers improved the speeds of modems dramatically over the years and increased modem throughput by a factor of 32 while increasing modem signal rates by only a factor of 8. This feat of imposing multiple-bit indications upon each individual signal change enables these manufacturers to work within the limited signaling capabilities of the public telephone system. Vendors use this technique to provide faster modems at reasonable costs to meet the needs for faster data traffic.

Table 9.1
Modem Speeds and Signal Encoding

Modem Speed (bps)	Modem Signal Rate (baud)	Speed/Signal Ratio (bits/baud)
300	300	1
1,200	600	2
2,400	600	4
9,600	2,400	4

Bit Time Synchronization

A modem and a communications port or adapter must use the same technique of synchronizing the transmission of bits. If the adapter is asynchronous, the modem must communicate with the adapter using asynchronous signaling conventions. If the adapter is synchronous, the modem must communicate with the adapter using synchronous signaling conventions.

Generally, a modem must also communicate with another remote modem using signaling conventions that match the communications port or adapter it supports. In the 1960s, 1970s, and early 1980s, devices that contained asynchronous communications ports required asynchronous communications between the modems that connected them to the telephone system. New modulation techniques and protocols such as MNP and LAPM discussed in Chapter 5, "Communications Error Correction," add some confusion to this picture. Two PCs can communicate asynchronously with the modems at each end of a link, yet the modems attached to these PCs can communicate with each other using synchronous techniques, as you will see later in this chapter.

The most significant difference between asynchronous and synchronous modems is the way they decipher and maintain the bit time of the signals they receive from a distant modem. As discussed in earlier chapters, an asynchronous modem must re-determine bit time for each byte of data it receives. Synchronous modems determine and maintain bit time for larger blocks of data bits.

II

Data Communications

Modems can be categorized in several ways, including signaling technique, speed, protocols, features, intelligence, and physical housing. Figure 9.5 shows typical methods used to categorize modems. Table 9.2 shows the speed classifications used in the discussion of both asynchronous and synchronous modems. The other characteristics of modems are discussed later.

Figure 9.5
Modem classification categories.

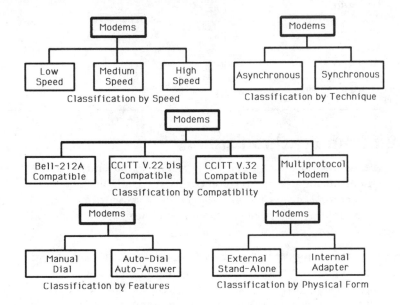

Table 9.2
Modem Speed Classifications

Modem Class	Bits Per Second
Low speed	Under 1,200
Medium speed	1,200-4,800
High speed	Over 4,800

Modem Types

During the 1960s and 1970s, before the arrival of very large-scale integration of computer chips, asynchronous communications were not adequate for reliable business communications. Hardware limitations made it impractical to send and receive data at asynchronous rates above 1,200 bps. The single start bit used for sender/receiver synchronization was too short for high-speed communications. Vendors developed synchronous modems and communications protocols to overcome this limitation.

Asynchronous and synchronous modems differ in the way the sender transmits its clock signal to the receiver. Asynchronous modems send a single start bit with each byte of data as a clock indicator. As discussed in Chapter 2, "Communications Channels," the receiving modem must sample the arriving analog signal at 16 times the incoming baud to correctly identify the middle of this single start bit. Synchronous modems, on the other hand, send at least eight contiguous bits at the start of each transmission frame, giving the receiver ample time to measure the bit time of the frame. This longer stream of synchronizing bit signals enabled synchronous modems to operate at faster data rates than asynchronous modems for many years.

Asynchronous and synchronous modems also differ in the length of time they remain synchronized during communications. Asynchronous modems synchronize at the start of each byte of data and remain synchronized for the duration of the byte. Synchronous modems, on the other hand, must synchronize at the start of a transmission frame and remain synchronized for the duration of the frame. Synchronous modems provide a continuous clock signal at the sending end of a link and a continuous clock regeneration at the receiving end. This continuous clocking eliminates the problem of drift between the clocks at each end and provides more reliable demodulation of the incoming signal than you can get with asynchronous techniques.

Older synchronous modems required more sophisticated and complex hardware than asynchronous modems of the same vintage that operated at the same data rate. Extracting the clock signal from the incoming analog signal was difficult for the designers of the first 2,400 bps synchronous modems. Technology limitations also made it impossible to design and implement asynchronous modems that could deliver data as fast as the fastest synchronous modems.

Improvements in technology now enable modem vendors to provide both asynchronous and synchronous modems that can operate at the same data rates. As you saw earlier, most asynchronous modems operate between 300 and 1,200 bps. For asynchronous communications above 1,200 bps, most modem vendors use synchronous communications techniques between modems to help in the reduction of communications errors. Synchronous modems, on the other hand, operate in the 1,200 to 28,800 bps range using standard synchronous data link protocols that have been around since the early 1970s.

The following paragraphs provide more details of the specific signaling techniques and characteristics of modems. Asynchronous modems must connect with an asynchronous serial port or adapter in the PC, and some asynchronous modems have the form factor of an adapter and include serial port components, as you see later. Synchronous modems must connect with a synchronous adapter (SDLC or BSC) in the PC. Table 9.3 shows a list of the modems available. Many of these modems are examined in the following paragraphs.

Table 9.3
Modem Speeds and Capabilities

Modem Type	Data Rate (BPS)	Signal Technique	Asynch/ Synch	Duplex Mode	Telephone Line
Bell 103	300	FSK	Asynch	Full	Switched
Bell 212A	1,200	PSK	Asynch	Full	Switched
CCITT V.22	1,200	PSK	Asynch	Full	S or L
CCITT V.23	1,200	PSK	A or S	H or F	S or L
WE 201A	2,400	PSK	Synch	Half	Switched
WE 201B	2,400	PSK	Synch	Full	Leased
WE 201C	2,400	PSK	Synch	Full	Switched
CCITT V.26	2,400	PSK	Synch	Full	Leased
CCITT V.26bis	2,400	PSK	Synch	Half	Switched
CCITT V.26ter	2,400	PSK	Synch	Full	Switched
CCITT V.22bis	2,400	QAM	A or S	Full	S or L

Modem Type	Data Rate (BPS)	Signal Technique	Asynch/ Synch	Duplex Mode	Telephone Line
CCITT V.27	4,800	PSK	Synch	Full	Leased
CCITT V.27bis	4,800	PSK	Synch	Half	Switched
CCITT V.27ter	4,800	PSK	Synch	Full	Switched
Bell 208A	4,800	QAM	Synch	H or F	Leased
Bell 208B	4,800	QAM	Synch	Half	Switched
Bell 209A	9,600	QAM	Synch	Full	Leased
CCITT V.29	9,600	QAM	Synch	Half	Switched
CCITT V.32	9,600	QAM	A or S	Full	Switched
CCITT V.32bis	14,400	QAM	A or S	Full	Switched
CCITT V.33	14,400	QAM	Synch	Full	Leased
CCITT V.34	28,800	QAM	A or S	Full	Switched

Low-Speed Asynchronous Modems

Although popular with personal computers through 1982, low-speed asynchronous modems have taken a back seat to their faster brothers. Almost all modem manufacturers, however, continue to produce these Bell-103 modems because certain situations require low-speed communications. Generally, the price of these modems reflects the features and functions they contain. For example, less expensive models may not support auto-dial and auto-answer and may not be capable of storing telephone numbers. Expensive models, on the other hand, may provide auto-dial of telephone numbers stored in disk files or in the modem's own memory.

The distinguishing characteristic of the Bell-103 modem is the way it handles data. These modems use specific audio-frequency ranges to differentiate between transmitted and received data. Figure 9.6 shows these ranges and the frequencies that transmit space and mark signals. Table 9.4 shows the Bell-103 originate-mode frequencies for transmitted and received data and the binary logic associated with these frequencies.

Figure 9.6
Bell-103 modem transmit and receive frequencies.

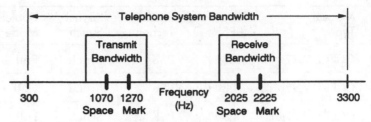

(a) Bell-103 modem originate-mode signal frequencies.

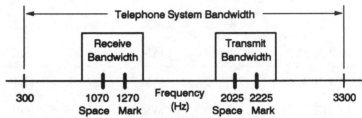

(b) Bell-103 modem answer-mode signal frequencies.

Table 9.4
Bell-103 Originate-mode Frequencies.

Direction	Signal Logic	Name	Frequency (Hz)
Transmit	0	Space	1,070
Transmit	1	Mark	1,270
Receive	0	Space	2,025
Receive	1	Mark	2,225

Frequency shift keying (FSK) provides the originate and answer modes for Bell-103 modems. The modem that initiates a communications link is in the *originate mode,* and the remote modem that responds to the initiation and completes the communications link is in the *answer mode.* The receive frequencies for the answer mode

are the same as the transmit frequencies for the originate mode. Similarly, the receive frequencies for the originate mode are the same as the transmit frequencies for the answer mode. Figure 9.6 shows the relationship between these frequencies.

Bell-103 modems require matching modes for proper communications. Because of the difference in transmit and receive frequencies, one modem must operate in the answer mode. The other modem must be in the originate mode. If the modes do not match, both modems will try to transmit and receive using the same frequencies and no data can move between them.

The important thing to know about originate/answer modes is that Bell-103 modems can provide one or the other, or both. If you never plan to have your modem answer an incoming call from another computer or terminal, you do not need the answer-mode capability. Originate-only modems are generally less expensive than modems that support both modes, but most modems available today provide both modes.

Low-speed modems are good for applications that require communications in the conversation mode or the transfer of small files. The maximum continuous transfer rate at 300 bps is 30 *characters per second* (cps), which translates into about 300 *words per minute* (wpm), as shown in table 9.5. An outstanding typist would have difficulty taxing such a configuration. Another advantage of 300-bps communications is that many people can comfortably read text at that speed. Listing a file on your monitor can be done if you want to read the information, but have no need to store it for later use.

Table 9.5
Data Transfer Rates of Asynchronous Modems

Modem Speed	Characters per Second	Average Words per Minute	Average Pages per Minute *
300	30	300	0.9
1,200	120	1,200	3.6
2,400	240	2,400	7.2

continues

Data Communications

Table 9.5 Continued
Data Transfer Rates of Asynchronous Modems

Modem Speed	Characters per Second	Average Words per Minute	Average Pages per Minute *
9,600	960	9,600	28.8
14,400	1,440	14,400	43.2
28,800	2,880	28,800	86.4

*Assuming 2,000 characters per page and no data compression.

For applications that involve the frequent transfer of large files or the clustering of input from several terminals, low-speed modems are not a good choice. It takes about one minute to transfer 2,000 bytes of text at 300 bps. This translates into approximately 30 minutes of connect time to transfer a 60 KB file. To transfer several 60 KB files means that you must dedicate the computer to communications for a significant period. You must provide operator support for the entire session if your communications software does not provide the option to transfer multiple files. For applications of that type, most businesses and hobbyists choose at least medium-speed modems.

Medium-Speed Modems

Medium-speed modems operate from 1,200 to 4,800 bps and achieve a higher data throughput than low-speed modems by using more sophisticated signaling techniques. Instead of shifting frequencies to signal a change from a one bit to a zero bit, these modems use phase and amplitude modulation to create more bit patterns on the telephone line at a faster rate than low-speed modems. Figure 9.7 illustrates these techniques.

The following paragraphs discuss asynchronous and synchronous modems, beginning with modems that operate at 1,200 bps through dial-up, switched, telephone circuits. Next, some early models of synchronous modems that operate at 2,400 bps and one modem standard that supports both asynchronous and synchronous communications at 2,400 bps are discussed. Finally, you learn about a synchronous modem that can provide 4,800 bps communications through leased or switched lines.

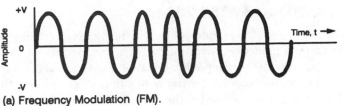

(a) Frequency Modulation (FM).

Figure 9.7
Time perspective of analog signal modulation.

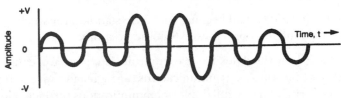

(b) Amplitude Modulation (AM).

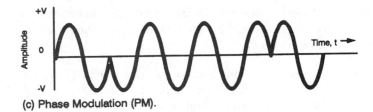

(c) Phase Modulation (PM).

1,200 bps Asynchronous Modems

At the low end of the medium-speed spectrum, *Phase Shift Keying* (PSK) provides 1,200-bps communications. These modems use phase shifts to convey two bits (*dibits*) for each baud. Unfortunately, modem vendors can implement three different PSK techniques in modems. In the United States, the two prevalent techniques are *Bell 212A* and *Racal-Vadic*. All the most popular personal computer modems provide support for Bell 212A communications. For international communications, the most popular 1,200-bps signaling scheme conforms with ITU-T Recommendation V.22. For proper 1,200-bps communications, the modems at both ends of the communications link must use one of these signaling schemes.

Compatibility of 1,200-bps modems is often an issue with PC owners because compatibility varies with the make and model of the modem at each end of a communications link. Some 1,200-bps modems operate in half-duplex only. Other modems offer compatibility with either Bell-212A or Racal-Vadic systems. More expensive medium-speed modems are usually compatible with both Bell-212A and Racal-Vadic. Some so-called *triple modems* go the extra mile and support Bell-103, Bell-212A, and Racal-Vadic protocols in one unit.

Western Electric 201 and AT&T 2024A

The *Western Electric 201* (WE 201) modem is one of the oldest pieces of synchronous hardware that still influences communications today. Because of its popularity in the 1960s and early 1970s, many WE 201s are still around. AT&T now provides the 2024A that uses modern hardware to emulate operation of the WE 201. Although the WE 201 is discussed in the following paragraphs, the information applies to the 2024A signaling techniques as well.

By the late 1960s, the WE 201 had become a de facto standard for synchronous communications around the world for the following reasons:

✔ The WE 201 provided flexible telephone line support. You could use the WE 201 for half-duplex communications through a two-wire public telephone circuit or for full-duplex communications through a four-wire, leased, telephone circuit.

✔ The WE 201 used a phase shift keying technique that enabled easy extraction of the clock signal at the receiving end. The AT&T 2024A now provides this capability.

The 2024A conveys two bits each time it executes a phase shift. The modem uses an 1,800 Hz carrier and conveys signal changes at 1,200 baud. For each baud, it transmits a phase shift that represents a dibit, as shown in table 9.6.

Table 9.6
AT&T 2024A Dibit Encoding

Phase Shift (Degrees)	Dibit Encoding
45	00
135	10
225	11
315	01

The low signaling rate and simple PSK technique used in 2024A modems enable a pair of these modems to communicate data with few errors at 2,400 bps. A 2024A modem's internal clock can phase lock with the incoming analog carrier signal to eliminate all but single-bit errors under most conditions. The single-bit errors that do slip by are easily detected and corrected by the synchronous data link protocol that controls the flow of bits through these modems.

Although Bell 212A asynchronous modems use essentially the same PSK signaling technique as 2024A modems, they do not detect and correct communications errors. A file transfer protocol such as Xmodem can, however, provide error detection and correction during the transfer of a file to overcome this limitation. During interactive communications between a user and a remote computer, another technique is required to ensure error-free communications. Some vendors provide synchronous protocols such as LAPM and MNP in the modem hardware to detect and correct errors throughout a communications session.

ITU-T V.26 Modems

Because of the popularity of the WE 201 modem, the ITU-T published Recommendation V.26 that defines a 2,400 bps modem with almost the same features and functions contained in a WE 201. The differences in the two modems are their support for switched telephone lines and their reliability. Although the WE 201 operates with switched or leased lines, the first V.26 modem specification called for leased-line support only. Later V.26bis and V.26ter (Latin for second and third) recommendations call for support of both types of circuits.

The WE 201 and its new brother, the 2024A, generally provide greater reliability and easier configuration than V.26 modems. While the WE 201 and 2024A provide only one dibit encoding scheme, V.26 modems provide Alternative A and B dibit encoding schemes. Table 9.7 shows Alternative A, and Alternative B is the same as the dibit encoding shown for the AT&T 2024A in table 9.6. Besides the confusion alternative encoding schemes can cause, Alternative A does not provide a phase shift for bits with a binary value of zero. Long strings of zero bits can cause the sending and receiving modems to lose synchronization in the middle of a transmission frame, resulting in a reduction in data throughput as the synchronous data link protocol corrects the errors.

Table 9.7
V.26 Alternative A Dibit Encoding

Phase Shift (Degrees)	Dibit Encoding
0	00
90	01
180	11
270	10

ITU-T V.22bis Modems

The ITU-T revised an earlier V.22 recommendation that applied to 600-baud, 1,200-bps modems to produce Recommendation V.22bis for 600-baud, 2,400-bps modems. Fortunately for all parties involved in medium-speed communications, manufacturers of 2,400-bps modems followed this ITU-T recommendation rather than create a new twist. The V.22bis specification calls for a combination of phase shift keying and amplitude modulation called *quadrature amplitude modulation* (QAM) (see fig. 9.8).

Figure 9.8
Quadrature
amplitude
modulation
(QAM).

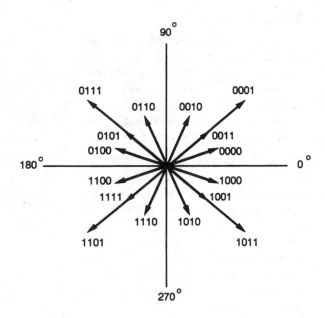

The V.22bis QAM combines 12 phase shifts with two amplitudes, which produces a 16-point signal structure that provides 16 possible carrier states. The four phases that have modulated amplitudes have two possible amplitude levels and provide two possible bit patterns per point. Many people call this QAM signal the "star" or "constellation" because of its shape.

The V.22bis specification contains a 600-baud line-signaling rate. During each signal period (baud), the modem conveys four data bits (*quad bits*). This combination of 600 baud and four bits per baud produces 2,400 bps. This signaling technique is also simple enough to support full-duplex operation through both leased and switched telephone lines. The technique further supports both asynchronous and synchronous communications through leased and switched telephone circuits.

The V.22bis recommendation calls for a fall back to 1,200 bps when excessive telephone line noise causes problems at 2,400 bps. Unfortunately, vendors

implement the fallback in different ways. Some use the V.22 recommendation and fall back to either 1,200 or 600 bps; others use the Bell 212A technique and fall back to either 1,200 or 300 bps. You must ensure compatible fallback rates and signaling techniques at both ends of a communications link.

ITU-T V.27 Modems

The ITU-T published Recommendation V.27 in 1972, approximately four years after the WE 201 modem became an industry standard. This recommendation increases the number of bits per signal change to three. During each baud, a V.27 modem uses phase shifts to convey three bits (*tribits*) by using the data encoding scheme shown in table 9.8. Recommendation V.27 calls for a signal rate of 1,600 baud that results in a data rate of 4,800 bps.

Table 9.8
V.27 Tribit Encoding

Phase Shift (Degrees)	Tribit Encoding
0	001
45	000
90	010
135	011
180	111
225	110
270	100
315	101

Although the first implementations of V.27 doubled the number of phase shifts available to carry bit signals, these modems lacked the sophistication now available as standard modem circuitry. The first V.27 implementations had manual controls that required operator attention to adjust the modem to match the conditions on the telephone line. Later V.27bis and V.27ter recommendations removed the requirement for manual adjustment based on the availability of modem hardware that could do signal equalization automatically.

II

Data Communications

Western Electric 208 Modems

One popular synchronous modem is the Western Electric 208 (WE 208). Because of the monopoly AT&T had on the modem market for many years, they had a ready market for this modem. As a result, many WE 208 modems are still in operation today.

The following differences exist between WE 208 and ITU-T V.27 modems:

✔ The WE 208 uses different phase shifts to convey tribits as shown in table 9.9. Special circuitry enables the WE 208 to detect errors more easily than the V.27. The difference in phase shifts in the WE 208 also supports the operation of error-detection devices in the modem.

✔ The WE 208 can use feedback from its error-detection hardware to cause automatic resynchronization with a remote modem if the error rate gets too large. If the WE 208 cannot properly extract a 1,600 baud clock signal from the analog signal it receives, the modem will retrain with the remote modem.

Table 9.9
WE 208 Tribit Encoding

Phase Shift (Degrees)	Tribit Encoding
22.5	001
67.5	000
112.5	010
157.5	011
202.5	111
247.5	110
292.5	100
337.5	101

A WE 208 modem conveys tribits with each baud at a signal rate of 1,600 baud to produce 4,800 bps. Older 208A modems supported half- or full-duplex operation over leased lines. The newer AT&T 2048A and 2048C modems have the same signaling and operation capabilities as the 208A with the 2048C providing faster startup than the 2048A. The WE 208B modems provide half-duplex, 4,800-bps operation over switched lines.

High-Speed Modems

Vendors had to wait for technology improvements before they could design and manufacture affordable modems that operate above 4,800 bps. When the technology became available, vendors increased the signal rate of modems from 1,200 baud to 2,400 baud—the theoretical limit of telephone circuits. Vendors also increased the number of bits per baud to increase the total throughput of modems. Several high-speed modems are discussed in the following paragraphs.

ITU-T V.29 Modems

The ITU-T recommended the first implementation of the QAM signaling technique in its V.29 recommendation for synchronous modems. This recommendation followed the implementation of a similar QAM technique in Bell 209 modems. Both the V.29 and the Bell 209 operate at 2,400 baud and convey four bits (quad bits) with each baud. Although the results are a data rate of 9,600 bps for both the 209 and the V.29 modem, they use different phase shifts and amplitudes to convey bits and are therefore incompatible.

The V.29 modem uses four signal amplitudes distributed across eight phase shifts to achieve 9,600 bps. Figure 9.9 and tables 9.10 and 9.11 show these amplitudes and phase shifts that provide quad bit communications. The V.29 modem uses a variation of 9,600-bps QAM when the telephone line noise is too high to support 9,600-bps operation. At the first noise threshold, the modems at each end of the link stop using the amplitude modulation and start sending tribits. This drops the data rate to 7,200 bps and improves the receiving modem's capability to separate the analog signal from line noise. At the next noise threshold, the modems drop back to four phase shifts and a single amplitude to send dibits. This drops the data rate to 4,800 bps and improves the receiving modem's demodulation again.

Table 9.10
V.29 Data Bit Q1 Encoding

Signal Amplitude	Absolute Signal Phase (Degrees)	Data Bit Q1 Value
3	0, 90, 180, 270	0
5	0, 90, 180, 270	1

continues

Table 9.10 Continued
V.29 Data Bit Q1 Encoding

Signal Amplitude	Absolute Signal Phase (Degrees)	Data Bit Q1 Value
1.41	45, 135, 225, 315	0
4.24	45, 135, 225, 315	1

Figure 9.9
CCITT V.29 QAM signal pattern.

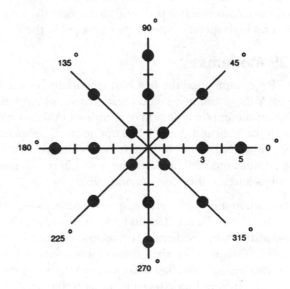

Table 9.11
V.29 Data Bits Q2, Q3, and Q4 Encoding

Phase Shift (Degrees)	Data Bit Q2 Value	Data Bit Q3 Value	Data Bit Q4 Value
0	0	0	1
45	0	0	0
90	0	1	0
135	0	1	1
180	1	1	1

Phase Shift (Degrees)	Data Bit Q2 Value	Data Bit Q3 Value	Data Bit Q4 Value
225	1	1	0
270	1	0	0
315	1	0	1

One common feature between Bell 209 and V.29 modems is support for synchronous multiplexing of the data streams from more than one device. Figure 9.10 shows such an implementation. The V.29 fan out capability enables it to concurrently support from one to four synchronous devices with combined data rates up to 9,600 bps. This multiplexor option at one end of the link requires a matching multiplexor option at the other end to separate multiplexed signals into separate digital signals.

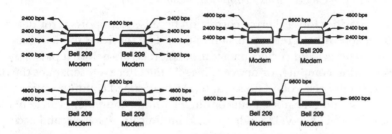

Figure 9.10
Bell 209 synchronous modems with multiplexors.

ITU-T V.32 Modems

The ITU-T Recommendation V.32 defines a family of two-wire, full-duplex modems that can communicate through switched or leased telephone lines. These modems can operate in the asynchronous or synchronous mode. The following list shows the principal characteristics of this family of modems. Vendors began to release modems in this class for the first time in 1986. These modems raised the 4,800-bps limit of communications through voice-grade telephone lines by a factor of two by using new, sophisticated hardware to execute forward error correction and echo cancellation.

✔ Full duplex operation on general, switched telephone lines and two-wire point-to-point leased lines

✔ Channel separation by echo cancellation

✔ Quadrature amplitude modulation for each channel with synchronous transmission at 2,400 baud

✔ Any combination of the following data signal rates: 9,600 bps, 4,800 bps, or 2,400 bps

✔ At 9,600 bps two modulation schemes, one using 16 carrier states and one using extended coding with 32 carrier states

✔ Support for the following modes of operation:
mode 1–9,600 bps synchronous
mode 2–9,600 bps asynchronous
mode 3–4,800 bps synchronous
mode 4–4,800 bps asynchronous

The ITU-T V.32 recommendation incorporates an advanced version of the QAM technique used in the V.22bis and V.29 modems discussed earlier. V.32 requires the transmission of five data bits with each baud signal change and a signaling rate of 2,400 bps. The total bit throughput is 12,000 bps, but the effective data bit throughput is 9,600 bps. One out of five of the transferred bits provides an error-correction technique called *Trellis Coded Modulation* (TCM).

Trellis coding provides forward error correction because it supports error detection and correction without retransmission of data. The receiving modem uses *Viterbi decoding* to detect and correct data transmission errors before it passes the data to the receiving computer or device. This scheme effectively separates the data signal from the high background noise caused by high-speed communications, and also eliminates the sporadic noise faulty or old telephone equipment can generate. This technique enables two V.32 modems to communicate effectively and accurately even across noisy telephone connections.

Another unique feature of the V.32 standard is the technique it recommends for the separation of transmitted and received signals. Instead of consuming a wide bandwidth by using separate frequencies for sending and receiving data, a V.32 modem uses a special echo canceling process to calculate the received signal. It subtracts the transmitted signal and echoes from the total line signal. Frequency-division signal separation limits full-duplex modem speeds to 2,400 bps, but this special echo canceling enables full-duplex, 9,600-bps operation on public telephone lines.

Because of the difficulties of implementing the V.32 specification, some modem vendors developed special techniques for dial-up communications at speeds of 9,600 bps and higher. Some of these vendors chose to use variations of the techniques prescribed in the V.32 recommendations, and others chose to use completely proprietary techniques. For example, Hayes Microcomputer Products used V.32 techniques in its first Smartmodem 9600, whereas the Telebit Corporation used proprietary technology in its Trailblazer modem.

Ping-Pong Protocol Modems

Hayes developed a special synchronizing technique that enables fast line turn-around that makes a half-duplex modem simulate the operation of a full-duplex modem. This *ping-pong protocol* uses ITU-T V.32 signal modulation techniques with special flow control procedures to make data appear to flow in both directions concurrently. The special flow control procedure makes this protocol incompatible with the international standard V.32-compliant modems.

The Hayes ping-pong protocol automatically switches the direction of data flow based on the volumes going in each direction. This technique optimizes the total throughput of the communications connection. The modem provides this rapid-fire technique of switching the direction of flow at the 9,600-bps data rate. It also provides the same technique at the 4,800 bps fall-back rate the modem uses when the error rate is too high for 9,600-bps communications.

The Hayes V-Series 9600 modems that contain the Hayes ping-pong protocol can operate at 9,600 bps only when communicating with another Hayes V-Series 9600 modem. These modems can communicate with non-Hayes modems at lower speeds if they contain matching protocols. The best approach to achieve full-duplex communications at 9,600 bps is to purchase a modem that conforms with the ITU-T V.32 recommendations.

Packetized Ensemble Protocol Modems

The Trailblazer modem developed by Telebit Corporation provided the first implementation of a technique called the *Packetized Ensemble Protocol Modem* (PEPM). These modems have the following two unique design features that enable them to achieve high communications speeds while retaining near error-free data transfers.

✔ Uses synchronous communications techniques to communicate faster over dial-up connections than V.32 modems.

✔ Uses an error detection and correction technique similar to the MNP and LAPM protocols, which eliminates the bad side effects of high-speed data communications and corrects errors detected during communications.

A PEPM uses a unique method of overcoming the bandwidth limitations of the telephone line. Instead of using one or two carrier signals, the Trailblazer uses 512 frequency-divided carriers. By dividing the telephone bandwidth into many carrier signals, this modem can achieve high data throughput over good telephone lines. The modem reduces throughput in 100-bps decrements when line conditions degrade. When two PEPM modems begin communications, the receiving modem determines which of the 512 frequency bands are usable. The receiving modem tells the originating modem which frequencies it can use. The originating modem then selects a technique of sending bits in parallel through the good bands. The originating modem must also send CRC error-detection data to the receiver, and the receiver has to request the retransmission of groups of bits that contain errors. This error-detection technique also enables the two modems to automatically fall back to fewer frequency bands if the errors and retransmissions are too high in some bands.

The PEPM fallback is automatic and is less of a penalty for poor line conditions than the factor of two fallback contained in the V.32 modem specification. Figure 9.11 shows this incremental fallback. Actual tests of the Trailblazer show a throughput in the 10,000-to-12,000-bps range for long distance data communications. This is a better rate than the V.32 modem can achieve under the best conditions. As with other proprietary products, however, the modems at both ends of the link must be Trailblazer- or PEPM-compatible before you can achieve these data rates.

Figure 9.11
Modem transmission rate reduction with line noise.

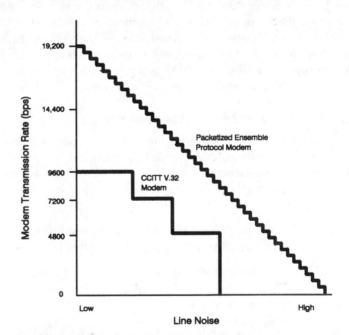

ITU-T V.32bis Modems

In February 1991, the ITU-T ratified the V.32bis standard to establish a new data rate limit for dial-up modems. This standard built on and superseded the existing V.32 standard to increase the maximum data rate from 9,600 to 14,400 bps. V.32bis also added many network management options.

V.32bis calls for the same echo cancellation and Trellis coding techniques required in V.32 to optimize the use of the telephone bandwidth. Because of the sensitivity of high-speed modems to electronic noise, V.32bis also enables the modem to fall back in data throughput above certain noise thresholds. The fallback speeds are 12,000 and 7,200 bps. Special rate sequences enable V.32bis modems to both downshift or upshift their operating speeds quickly as line conditions change during a connection.

Besides a high data rate, the V.32bis offers many network management advantages over earlier generations of modems, as outlined in the following list:

✔ Enables vendors to add an optional password protection to enhance system security

✔ Supports dial back that many networks use to ensure proper access to information systems

✔ Enables vendors to add remote modem management that can both reduce the manpower required to operate a network and make it faster to reconfigure the network

V.32bis offers two other features that endear it to network and systems managers. The standard enables you to implement the ITU-T V.42bis data compression standard in the same modem, as discussed later in this chapter. This compression technique can increase the effective V.32bis throughput by a factor of four to 57,000 bps. V.32bis further supports both data and FAX transmissions, which provides great flexibility in the design and implementation of a modern communications network.

ITU-T V.33 Modems

The ITU-T Recommendation V.33 defines the highest modem speed recognized by the international community for leased telephone circuits. V.33 calls for both QAM and TCM modulation techniques and a signal rate of 2,400 baud. A combination of 32 individual signal states enable these modems to convey data at a rate of 14,400 bps through leased lines.

The actual data throughput of a V.33 modem may be much less than 14,400 bps. These modems sometimes have difficulty separating signals from noise with a signal density four times that of a V.32 modem. Hardware is available that can separate an analog signal from line noise at 9,600 bps and produce few misinterpretations of the signal. Separating noise from a signal at 14,400 bps, however, is far more complex. The contrast between signal phases and amplitudes for 14,400 bps is much smaller than the same elements for 9,600 bps. Therefore, it takes less line noise to cause the receiver to misinterpret a 14,400 bps signal.

When a V.33 modem misinterprets noise as a signal, the synchronous protocol that moves data through the modem must correct the mistakes. As discussed in Chapter 6, "Synchronous Data Link Control," the BSC and SDLC protocols can detect and correct almost all errors caused by the misinterpretation of signals. To correct these errors, however, the protocols must retransmit large blocks of data. When frequent retransmissions occur, the effective data throughput of the link decreases. For modem-to-modem communications at 14,400 bps through a noisy line, the effective throughput of the link can drop below the level that two 9,600-bps modems can achieve using simpler signaling techniques.

ITU-T V.34 (V.fast) Modems

The latest standard for modem communications through general-switched telephone networks is currently designated V.fast, sometimes abbreviated V.FC. Although several vendors are already shipping modems and claim full compatibility with this future ITU-T V.34 recommendation, the publication of the final standard is not expected before the end of 1994. Some vendors are shipping V.fast modems that can be field upgraded with new ROM chips or upgraded through communications techniques to comply with the final ITU-T V.34 standard.

The ITU-T is developing the V.34 standard to enable modem vendors to take advantage of new, more capable telephone systems. The modulation enhancements the standard recommends enable modems to operate better over noisy telephone connections and better maintain proper connections under adverse line conditions. The greatest advantage offered in this recommendation, however, is the opportunity to double data communications rates when upgrading from a V.32bis modem.

V.fast recommends a maximum data rate of 28,800 bps for full-duplex, asynchronous, or synchronous communications through high-quality lines. Table 9.12 shows the full spectrum of fallback data rates for a V.fast modem. As you can see, V.fast starts at the highest V.32bis data rate of 14,400 bps. This speed is used only under adverse line conditions.

Table 9.12
V.fast Connection Speeds

Connection Rate	Line Condition
14,400 bps	Worst
16,800 bps	
19,200 bps	

Connection Rate	Line Condition
21,600 bps	
24,000 bps	
26,400 bps	
28,800 bps	Best

Vendors such as Microcom Systems are delivering early versions of V.fast-compliant modems (designed based on draft recommendations from the ITU-T) that can transfer PC data at rates of 115,200 bps and higher. The Microcom DeskPorte FAST Modem can combine V.42bis data compression with the modem's 28,800 bps connection speed to reach this rate while still working with a PC serial port. To achieve throughput above 115,200 bps requires the use of a parallel cable between the modem and the PC's parallel port. Special device-driver software also is required to redirect data to the parallel port; this enables you to use, without modification, existing software designed to communicate through the serial port.

Cellular Modems

Because of the increasing popularity of cellular telephones in densely populated areas, the demand is increasing for modems capable of communicating through these devices. Several vendors are now making modems that can connect directly to a cellular telephone and support data communications between a PC or laptop computer and a remote system. These modems require special capabilities to overcome the limitations of cellular networks.

If you have used a cellular telephone for voice communications, you probably know what it is like to carry on a conversation with someone while one of you is traveling in a vehicle. As the traveler moves from one geographic cell to another or goes under obstacles, the cellular connection can become noisy or temporarily break. These conditions can create difficulty for modem communications.

Special capabilities are required to enable a modem to make a call and maintain communications through a cellular telephone or device. The mobile modem called the *cell-side* or *remote* must retain its connection with the conventional, *land-side* modem by providing special modulation and negotiation techniques. Because of inconsistent line conditions when the call is placed and while the call is under-way, cell-side and land-side modems must make a connection at a low speed, say 1,200 bps, and then upshift the connection speed until it reaches an optimum operating level. To get optimum performance during a connection, these modems must also dynamically upshift or downshift the data rate in response to changing line conditions. MNP Class 10, discussed later in this chapter, provides the protocol that enables two modems to execute this dynamic shifting.

Cellular telephone equipment often requires power levels at the modem-to-telephone interface different from land-side modem-to-telephone interfaces. A cellular-telephone modem must alter its signaling power level to match the requirements of the telephone system. The range of power levels is usually -10 dBm to -35 dBm, with a typical requirement of -18 dBm. The specifications for the cellular telephone equipment should indicate this required power level.

The ultimate cellular modem provides data and fax transmission from the same laptop computer that enables you to make voice calls to land-side sites. Several vendors, including IBM, are expected to deliver these multipurpose modules for laptops in 1994 and beyond. With such a device, the laptop user has no need for an office with a telephone and a fax machine. These telephone-modem combinations give the user the freedom to work from any location that provides cellular telephone service, which includes most densely populated areas in the United States.

Cable TV Modems

Because of the popularity of cable television and the bandwidth of the cables that deliver the video services to customers, several modem vendors are investigating the development of modems to communicate through this media. The coaxial copper cable used in most cable television networks could communicate data at rates far in excess of the public telephone systems while concurrently delivering the television channels. Modems would still be required to modulate the digital PC signals to and from analog signals compatible with the cable system.

If cable service providers replace copper systems with fiber-optical cabling, the delivery bandwidth will increase significantly. Because fiber conveys digital signals, these new systems would not require modems to support communications between PCs. The PCs would need a digital adapter capable of transmitting and receiving optical signals concurrently with the delivery of television channels.

Modem Features

With this background of modem speeds and protocols, you can move on to the features that make one modem more appropriate in a given situation than another. Conformance with a specific modem standard or design specification is only the beginning. Vendors provide a variety of modem features that distinguish their products. The following section examines many of these features.

Table 9.13 shows a list of features available in modems. Most hobbyists find that a modem offering only a few of these features meets their needs. Some business

applications, on the other hand, require a full-featured modem that supports most of the listed features. Note, however, that the term "full-featured" differs from one modem manufacturer to another. If you need several capabilities in a single modem, investigate the actual features provided by available models before purchasing one. The following paragraphs describe the most important features and functions to look for in a modem.

Table 9.13
Intelligent Modem Features

Help command	Command modes
Command recognition	Command abort
Quit command	Manual dial
Dialing directory	Dial tones
Name selection dialing	Last number redial
Repeat dialing	Number linking
Directory modification	Auto-answer
Busy mode	Protocol switch
Error control	Data compression
Flow control	Break handling
Set answerback string	Set backspace character
Set attention character	Set disconnect character
Modem register contents	Modem switches
Built-in self-test	Line monitor
Screen display	FAX communications

Command Modes

Because of the early dominance of the Hayes Smartmodem in the PC community, most modem vendors today include a Hayes-compatible command mode in their products. This AT command mode enables you to use software designed specifically for the Hayes command set. Modems also can include support for ITU-T Recommendation V.25bis commands. Besides the Hayes and V.25bis modes, some modems also have a mode specifically designed by the modem manufacturer. The manufacturer's own mode often duplicates the Hayes mode, and can provide additional capabilities beyond those found in the Hayes mode. You issue a short command sequence to the modem to switch modes. The Hayes mode provides an "OK" response to commands (when the verbal or verbose response mode is in effect). Another character prompt, such as a "$" or a ">" symbol, indicates the vendor-specific mode. The Hayes mode requires a carriage return at the end of a command to initiate execution of the command. Some vendor-specific command-mode commands begin execution after you type the first letter of the command word.

Some modems require specific communications software speed and parity settings before they can recognize commands, whereas others accept commands despite the communications parameters used. Some experimentation may be required to determine the parameters that work. Modems that require a specific set of communications parameters often have to be reset through software commands. Some also have to go into a dormant mode before they can accept a new set of parameters, and others provide an external reset button or an off/on switch that resets most or all the modem's parameters. Stand-alone modems can be easily switched off and back on, but internal modems require that you turn the computer off for a power-off reset. For that reason, some internal modems can be reset through software controls.

Hayes and Hayes-compatible modems automatically switch parameters to match the received parity and data bits. When one of these modems receives the *attention code* (AT), it determines the transmission data rate (bits per second) of the PC serial port from the "A" and the number of data bits and parity from the "T". The modem switches parameters to match the incoming command string and retains these parameters until it receives another command string preceded by the AT attention code. The modem must be in the command mode to change parameters.

Dial Tones

Modem dialing commands usually include a selection of *pulse* or *touch-tone dialing*. The dialing signals the modem transmits to the telephone system are the type specified by a dialing prefix command. Some modems enable the dial type to change during the dialing sequence to match in-house telephone equipment. This feature also can include a secondary dial-tone wait command. Dial-tone wait commands cause the dialing sequence to pause until the modem detects a secondary dial tone. This feature is better than a simple time delay in a dialing sequence because the time delay may not be long enough to accomplish the objective.

A good intelligent modem not only waits for a secondary dial tone during a dialing sequence, it also senses and switches between touch-tone and pulse dialing. This type of modem usually provides a *blind dialing mode* also. Blind dialing enables the modem to dial even when it does not detect a dial tone. Some PBX telephone systems use nonstandard tones, and a regular tone-sensing modem may not be able to detect them. This type of telephone system can result in a "dead line" appearance to a modem, and blind dialing is the only way to avoid the problem.

Hayes and Hayes-compatible modems support both touch and pulse dialing. The vendors for these modems use the "AT" command followed by a "T" for touch tone and a "P" for pulse dialing. These modems also enable the insertion of a comma that causes a pause in the dialing sequence. Programmable registers specify the length of the pause.

Line Monitor

Another characteristic of modems is the method they use to communicate dialing information to the PC user. Some modems use a speaker to help the user understand the dialing process. After initiating a call, the user can hear the dialing sounds and the results of the call—or a busy signal. Other modems use screen messages to tell the caller the results of a call. After you initiate a call, the message may read Call in progress... and a busy signal may result in a message that reads Line busy. Both methods work, but the sounds of a telephone dialing and modems synchronizing are somehow more comforting and natural.

Auto-Answer

Many intelligent modems not only operate in an automatic answer mode, but also enable you to specify how many rings should occur before the modem answers the telephone. For example, the command ATS0=5 causes a Hayes-compatible modem to answer a call on the fifth ring. You also can force the modem to answer the telephone, which is necessary when you directly connect two computers with modems without going through the telephone system. You can place a short length of telephone cable between two Smartmodems and execute a force-to-answer ATA command on one modem and a force-to-dial ATD command on the other modem to establish a link between the two modems. The force-to-answer feature also enables you to use the same telephone line for voice and data communications.

Busy Mode

Some modems include a busy command that enables a user to make the telephone line look "off hook" to an incoming call. This command is useful for bulletin-board operators who want to use the system temporarily for other applications, but want

II

Data Communications

the system to appear busy to callers. You can use the busy command on a voice line to keep calls from coming in. Through software control, the modem can create a busy signal for specific hours of the day every day of the week.

Protocol Detect and Switch

The auto-answer mode of some modems automatically detects and matches the signaling technique of an incoming modem call. Signal detection includes such things as modulation frequency and phase angle determination. Almost all modems can detect and match the signals from Bell-103, Bell-113, and Bell-212A modems. Some modems also include Racal-Vadic signal matching. The switch between Bell-103/113 and Bell-212A or Racal-Vadic also is a switch between 300 bps and 1,200 bps. Most of the V.22bis-compatible modems automatically detect and match signals that move data at 300 to 2,400 bps. V.32bis modems often include detect and switch capabilities for the full range from 300 to 14,400 bps signaling protocols. If a modem does not provide this signal-matching capability, you can usually execute a detect and match procedure through software controls.

Error Control

Some modem vendors implement protocols in hardware to detect and correct errors that occur during data communications. The MNP protocols discussed in Chapter 5 are popular, but the LAPM protocol recommended by the *International Telecommunication Union* (ITU) is gaining momentum. Vendors now choose from the following protocols when they design and build modems.

✔ Microcom Networking Protocol (MNP) Classes

✔ Link-Access Procedure for Modems (LAPM)

Modems equipped with error-control protocols also must contain standard techniques to negotiate the use of these protocols with other modems. When one modem dials another modem through the telephone system, the two modems must exchange a series of signals or handshakes. The first handshake enables them to select a common, electrical-signaling technique. The next handshake enables them to select a common form of error control that prevails throughout that specific communications session. Because of changes in the noise level in the telephone network, two modems can elect to use a different signaling protocol and a different error-control protocol each time they connect.

When two modems connect, they can select a common error-control protocol or agree to use no error control if no common protocol exists between them. These error-control negotiations take place automatically and often without the user's knowledge. Because of the transparent nature of these negotiations and the possibility that two modems can decide to use no protocol, many users execute one

of the file transfer protocols described in Chapter 5 when transferring blocks of text or data. If two modems do elect to use an error-control protocol and the PC user also elects to use a file transfer protocol to transfer a file during the connection, the resulting error-correcting overhead in the data stream between the modems could be double the level required to ensure near error-free communications. This double overhead slows down the file transfer without adding much in the way of error control.

When two modems negotiate error control, they do so through a two-step bidding process. The two modems first exchange a rapid sequence of signals to verify that both modems support feature negotiations. If this bidding is successful, the two modems compare features and select the most advanced error control common to both modems. For example, two V.42 modems can choose to use the LAPM protocol. A V.42 modem can, however, choose to use an MNP Class 1–4 protocol when it is communicating with a modem that contains only that protocol. If the V.42 modem dials into an older modem that contains no error-control protocol, the two modems can communicate without error detection and correction.

Because of the popularity of the MNP and LAPM protocols, the following paragraphs examine these error-control techniques in detail. The information in these paragraphs builds on information in Chapters 5 and 6. You may want to read the MNP and LAPM descriptions in Chapter 5 and the descriptions of the synchronous protocols in Chapter 6.

Microcom Networking Protocol

As discussed in Chapter 5, the MNP protocols are available in multiple classes. Modem vendors can choose to implement any or all of the 9 classes. (The classes are 1–7, 9, and 10; no layer 8 exists.) The most popular classes are 2, 3, 4, 5, and 10; these and the other MNP classes are discussed in the following paragraphs:

✔ **MNP Class 1.** This class provides the least robust capabilities of all the MNP protocols and adds the greatest amount of overhead. Two modems equipped with Class 3 can detect and correct errors in a half-duplex asynchronous data stream. In addition to the normal start/stop overhead associated with asynchronous communications, Class 3 converts the data stream into packets, which adds overhead to the original data stream it receives from the PC. Although the overhead enables two MNP Class 1 modems to provide continuous, near error-free communications, the protocol slows down data throughput between the modems (adds to the total number of bits received from the sending PC) by approximately 30 percent. The data packets Class 1 uses are similar to the BSC transparent frames described in Chapter 6.

✔ **MNP Class 2.** Two modems equipped with MNP Class 2 can detect and correct errors for full-duplex, asynchronous data streams. Because full-duplex operation enables two modems to send and receive data simultaneously through a telephone network, the error-checking overhead does not reduce throughput as much as Class 1 operation. The throughput reduction is approximately 26 percent when compared with a normal asynchronous data stream. The data packets Class 2 uses are similar to the BSC transparent frames described in Chapter 6.

✔ **MNP Class 3.** In addition to error detection and correction, MNP Class 3 provides an improvement in data throughput by turning an asynchronous data stream into the equivalent of a synchronous data stream. The protocol strips off asynchronous start and stop bits it receives from a PC and forms packets of continuous data bits similar to the packets used in the SDLC and HDLC protocols described in Chapter 6. By eliminating the start-stop bits, MNP reduces the overhead and increases the throughput of the link. For every eight data bits, asynchronous communications add one start bit and at least one stop bit. These synchronizing bits add a 20 percent overhead to the communications link. MNP eliminates the entire 20 percent, but adds some overhead when creating the packets.

This class adds overhead to a data stream to provide data link controls. The protocol adds 11 percent as synchronizing, header, and error-checking bits for a net decrease of nine percent compared to the original asynchronous data stream. Besides bits that provide a synchronizing clock signal and header information in front of data, MNP adds a CRC-16 frame check sequence behind the data to support error detection on the receiving end. The receiving modem disassembles the data packets, checks for errors, and transmits good data on to the receiving computer. If the modem detects an error in a packet, it requests a retransmission of that packet.

✔ **MNP Class 4.** In addition to the synchronous framing technique provided in Class 3, MNP Class 4 provides the capability to adjust packet size to improve throughput. The *Adaptive Packet Assembly* and *Optimized Data Phase* features enable two Class 4 modems to dynamically adjust packet size to optimize performance. These protocols monitor the telephone line condition (based on the frequency of bad packets that must be retransmitted) and adjust the amount of data included in packets.

MNP Class 4 data packets dynamically grow when communications line quality improves. As the line condition improves, the protocol increases

the amount of data in each packet up to a fixed limit. This reduces the amount of overhead required to acknowledge the receipt of error-free packets. If the line condition degrades, the protocol reduces the amount of data that goes into each packet, which reduces the size of packets that must be retransmitted when an error is detected on the receiving end of the link. Two modems equipped with this class of service can increase or decrease the size of data packets many times during a single communications session.

MNP Class 4 normally enables two modems to reduce the total number of bits that must move through the telephone line when two PCs are communicating. In addition to the dynamic adjustment of packet sizes, Class 4 streamlines packet headers. These combined features enable two modems equipped with MNP Class 4 to increase data throughput by approximately 22 percent compared with the data stream they receive from and deliver to the PCs at each end of the link.

✔ **MNP Class 5.** This class adds capabilities to Class 4 that enable two modems to dramatically reduce the number of bits required to enable two PCs to communicate. By compressing the data stream on the sending end and decompressing the data stream on the receiving end, MNP Class 5 can almost double the throughput of a communications link. This data compression technique replaces repeating or redundant bit patterns with encoded data. The protocol places the encoded data stream in the packets it transmits to the receiving modem.

✔ **MNP Class 6.** This class enables two modems to provide near error-free asynchronous communications in half-duplex mode at speeds between 4,800 and 9,600 bps. *Universal Link Negotiation* enables two modems equipped with this class of service to automatically connect at the highest common data rate and MNP protocol level. Microcom developed this class of protocol to support the V.32 standard discussed in this chapter. The effective throughput for two modems can be as high as 19,200 bps when they operate at a connection speed of 9,600 bps and agree to use this MNP class.

✔ **MNP Class 7.** This class provides *Enhanced Data Compression,* which works with the capabilities in Class 4 to provide data throughput of over twice the modem connection speed. This technique dynamically adjusts to the type of data being transmitted and uses a method called *probability of character frequency* to provide better compression than that provided at the Class 5 level.

✔ **MNP Class 9.** This class adds an enhanced *Universal Link Negotiation* and full-duplex, *sliding-windows* capabilities. MNP Class 9 offers a *go back n* method of error correction that enhances its sliding windows method of transmitting packets. When the receiver detects an error in a packet, say packet number $n+1$, a message is returned to the sender indicating that an error occurred in that packet. When the error message is received, the sender goes back to packet n and starts resending data with the next packet beyond n. This go back n technique sometimes requires the retransmission of more packets to correct an error than the selectively-repeat type of packet retransmission used in the Kermit sliding windows protocol discussed in Chapter 5, but the technique is easier to implement in firmware.

✔ **MNP Class 10.** This class improves modem operation over poor telephone connections. *Adverse Channel Enhancements* (ACE) optimize the modem's performance when it is communicating through a poor connection. When operating in the auto-reliable mode, the modem makes multiple negotiation attempts when it connects with another modem that has MNP Class 10 capability. Class 10 also supports cellular telephone communications. *Dynamic Transmit Level Adjustment* automatically calculates the optimum data transmission rate for a cellular connection. This feature also enables two modems to dynamically increase or decrease the data rate to compensate for changes in the quality of the cellular connection.

Link-Access Procedure for Modems

Since 1988, modem vendors have been able to incorporate an internationally accepted error-correction protocol in their modem products. The International Telecommunication Union through its CCITT committee first published a standard for continuous modem-to-modem error detection and correction in 1988. The standard designation is *V.42*. The *International Telecommunication Union Telecommunication Standardization Sector* (ITU-T), the renamed CCITT, now supports the latest release of the V.42 specifications. The primary error-checking protocol it calls for is *Link-Access Procedure for Modems* (LAPM).

The V.42 recommendation contains specifications that standardize the processes modems must perform to provide the highest possible quality of data transfer regardless of their operating speed. The specifications define two types of functions. First, they define the control functions a modem must provide to negotiate and execute the operation of error-correcting procedures after the physical connection is established. Second, they define the error-control functions the modem must continue to provide after the initial negotiations are completed.

A V.42-compliant modem can negotiate the execution of several error-correcting protocols with another modem. If the modems at both ends of the connection contain V.42-compliant protocols, they are supposed to select the LAPM protocol over alternative protocols based on the design of MNP Classes 1-4. If the calling modem is V.42-compliant and the answering modem is not but does contain one of the MNP classes, the two can negotiate the execution of the highest common MNP protocol.

The LAPM protocol has the following advantages over the MNP protocols:

✔ LAPM always transfers data in a bit-oriented, transparent mode using the HDLC protocol discussed in Chapter 6. MNP Classes 1-2 use a byte-oriented, transparent mode based on the BSC transparent technique discussed in Chapter 6; MNP Classes 3 and 4 use a bit-oriented mode similar to the HDLC technique LAPM uses.

✔ LAPM can use either a 16-bit or a 32-bit frame check sequence (FCS) to detect errors. MNP Classes 1-4 always use a 16-bit FCS regardless of the importance of error detection.

✔ LAPM uses a robust sliding-windows technique to expedite communications. The lower MNP classes do not provide this performance enhancement.

✔ LAPM can work with the ITU-T V.42bis data-compression technique to quadruple data throughput (the data transfer rate will be four times the modem connection speed). MNP Classes 1-4 do not provide data compression.

Keep in mind, however, that vendors do not always follow the V.42 standard when they build modems advertised as V.42-compliant. Some vendors prefer MNP Class 10 over LAPM and build their modems to follow that priority when they negotiate protocols. Vendors also can provide a software-driven override that causes the calling modem to terminate the call if it cannot negotiate the preferred protocol. The documentation that comes with a modem normally spells out these options for the user.

Data Flow Control

Modems that provide error control often provide data flow control also. This method of speed-matching, described in Chapters 5 and 6, ensures that data are not lost during the retransmission process that corrects blocks of bad data. The retransmission process takes time, and communications between the modem and PC must be temporarily halted during the retransmission time delay. Without data flow control, the PC could send more data to the modem than the modem could store during the retransmission period, and the data overrun would be lost.

Modems with data flow control often include more than one technique that can do this task. These modems also require communications software that supports these techniques to ensure proper data flow control. The two flow control methods recommended in ITU-T V.42 and most often used by modem vendors are the RTS/CTS and the XON/XOFF protocols. The RTS/CTS requires the PC to send an electrical Request to Send signal to the modem when it wants to transmit data. The PC cannot send data until it receives an electrical Clear to Send response from the modem. The XON/XOFF requires the modem to send the PC an XOFF character to stop the transmission of data and an XON character to resume the transmission of data. Both techniques accomplish the same objective and are local handshaking between the modem and the PC.

Data Compression

Another feature vendors often provide with modems that requires modem-to-modem negotiations is data compression. Vendors use this feature to reduce the total data throughput required to transfer information or data. Data compression uses encoding to eliminate redundant bit patterns on the transmitting end and requires a matching decompression decoding technique on the receiving end. The receiver must reconstitute the data to their original form.

To provide data compression and decompression with normal analog signaling, two modems must use matching capabilities. Many different data compression algorithms exist. Vendors often provide proprietary techniques, or they use the MNP methods described earlier. The ITU-T V.42bis data compression standard is the only internationally recognized data compression alternative. To take advantage of data compression, the modems at each end of a link must be set up in advance to use the same compression and decompression techniques, or they must negotiate the use of the same techniques after they make a connection.

Hayes Microcomputer Products provides a proprietary adaptive compression feature in its V-series modems. This feature automatically begins when two Hayes V-series modems agree to operate in one of their error-control modes. Hayes went one step beyond data compression with its adaptive design. Their compression algorithm adapts to the type of data flowing between the modems to provide the greatest throughput for that specific type of data.

Data compression enables two modems to move data two to four times faster than the data signaling rate they are using to communicate. For example, PCs connected to V.42 modems can communicate with their modems at 19,200 while the modems communicate with each other at 9,600 bps. Modems with MNP Level 5 or higher also can do this two-to-one data reduction as they modulate and demodulate digital signals. Modems that include the V.42bis compression technique can do a four-to-one data reduction for some types of data. By reducing the total

quantity of data before sending them out, these modems overcome many data throughput limitations of the telephone system. Figure 9.12 illustrates this technique; the two PCs are communicating at 28,800 bps through a telephone system that can handle signaling at 14,400 bps or less.

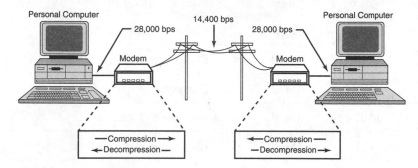

Figure 9.12
Compression/
decompression
data rates.

Break Handling

Modems must properly transmit break signals generated when a user presses specific PC keys to interrupt a host process. When no error-control protocol is in use, modems have no problem transmitting this signal because software controls generate and transmit the signal. When an error-control protocol is in operation at the modem hardware level, the protocol can damage the interrupt signal by making it shorter or longer than the signal generated by the communications software. The modem must recognize a break signal received from the PC and preserve the duration of this signal across the communications link. If the break signal is not properly maintained, it does not have the desired effect on the host process.

Modem Registers

Communications software often must query the contents of a modem's internal registers. Vendors use this technique to automatically detect and modify the contents of register or to detect register content changes. A modem should provide commands that enable a software package to both query and modify the contents of its registers. The list of Hayes Smartmodem 1200 registers and the parameters they control, shown in table 9.14, illustrate the functions registers provide. Most Hayes-compatible modems implement these registers in the same sequence and use the same command syntax to change register contents. Incompatibility between communications software and a Hayes-compatible modem is often traced to incomplete or incorrect implementation of these registers.

Table 9.14
Sample of Hayes Smartmodem S Registers

Register	Range	Units	Function
S0	0-255	rings	Ring to answer on
S1	0-255	rings	Count number of rings
S2	0-127	ASCII	Escape code character
S3	0-127	ASCII	Carriage return character
S4	0-127	ASCII	Line feed character
S5	0-32, 127	ASCII	Backspace character
S6	2-255	seconds	Wait time for dial tone
S7	1-255	seconds	Wait time for carrier
S8	0-255	seconds	Pause time for comma
S9	1-255	1/10 sec	Carrier detect response time
S10	1-255	1/10 sec	Delay time between loss of carrier and hangup
S11	50-255	millisec	Duration and spacing of touch tones
S12	20-255	1/50 sec	Escape code guard time

Modem Switches

Some communications software packages require special signals that must either be present or absent between the computer and a modem for the software to function properly. For example, some communications software packages require modems to ignore the *Data Terminal Ready* (DTR) signal or the software cannot change communication parameters while on line with a host system. Otherwise, the modem loses the carrier during the parameter change and loses the connection with the remote computer. Modems normally enable you to set these signals either through software controls or manual switches. The ideal design enables both manual and software changes in these signal switches.

The location of a modem's switches is an important consideration if the position of the switches requires frequent changes. The switches for some modems are behind the front cover and changing switch positions can be difficult for a hardware novice. The switches for some modems, on the other hand, are on the back of the unit and are easily accessible for switch position changes.

Modem Self Tests

The built-in self-test features in a modem are pattern generator and error-checking circuitry. These features enable the modem to be tested as a stand-alone device or with a similarly equipped remote modem. The tests verify the modem's capability to accurately send and receive data. The three types of test modes are: the analog loop-back self-test, the digital loop-back self-test, and the remote digital loop self-test.

The *analog loop-back self-test* verifies the operation of a local modem as a stand-alone unit. The self-test circuitry sends data through the modem's transmitter. The test loop routes the transmitter output back into the modem's receiver, which routes the data to the self-test circuit. The self-test circuitry compares transmitted patterns to received patterns and notifies the user if it detects errors.

The *digital loop-back self-test* verifies the operation of a remote modem. The local modem sends data to the remote modem's receiver. The remote modem loops the data through its transmitter and returns the data to the local modem. The local modem compares these data to the data pattern it originally transmitted. If the local modem detects errors in the returned data, the modem notifies the local user. The remote digital loop self-test is identical to the digital loop-back self-test except it requires no remote operator assistance.

Modem Indicator Lights

Most stand-alone modems have indicators on the front panel that show action and status. These indicators are often cryptic symbols that have little meaning for the communications novice. Different vendors also use different symbols, which leads to further confusion when a person uses more than one modem. The following definitions help to clear up some indicator confusion.

- ✔ **Auto-Answer.** Indicates the auto-answer status of the modem. When this indicator is on, the receiving modem automatically answers the calling modem.

- ✔ **Carrier Detect.** Indicates whether the modem has detected a carrier signal from a remote modem. This indicator has to be on for the modem to transmit data.

✔ **Data Terminal Ready.** Indicates whether the terminal is ready to receive and send data. This indicator must be on for the modem to maintain the connection with a remote modem.

✔ **High Speed.** Indicates the modem operating speed. When the indicator is on, the modem is operating at its maximum rated speed (for example, 2,400 bps for a 2,400 bps modem). When the indicator is off, the modem is operating at a rate less than its maximum rated speed.

✔ **Modem Check.** Has an assigned special meaning for modem testing. The modem manual specifies the exact meaning of this indicator.

✔ **Modem Ready.** Indicates the operating status of the modem. When this indicator is on, the modem is ready to receive and send data.

✔ **Off Hook.** Indicates the status of the data line connected to the modem. When the modem is using the telephone line, the indicator is on. This indicator is also on when a modem is making the telephone line appear to be busy.

✔ **Receive Data.** Indicates the receipt of data from a remote modem. When this indicator is on, data are coming in from the remote modem.

✔ **Send Data.** Indicates the sending of data to a remote modem. When this indicator is on, the modem is sending data to the remote modem.

✔ **Test Mode.** Indicates the modem is in a test mode.

Modem Screen Displays

Some vendors now make modems that contain screen displays in addition to indicator lights. An LCD screen can display useful information that indicator lights could never convey, particularly for modems that can operate at multiple speeds and with multiple error-correcting protocols. Other examples of information displayed by LCD screens include indications of asynchronous or synchronous operation and whether data compression is on or off. For modems that support data and FAX communications, the display can tell you which mode the modem is using.

Screen displays are useful for modems that can alter their data transfer rate after a connection is made. As a modem changes its modulation technique to optimize operations with changing telephone line quality, the user can monitor the changes at the display. A vendor also can display error-detection and recovery statistics on a modem's screen.

FAX Capabilities

A modem that enables you to send and receive both data and fax transmissions can reduce total hardware cost in an office environment. Many modems today provide ITU-T Group III fax compatibility. They also comply with the EIA-578 standard, which defines the interface requirements between a computer and fax hardware and software.

Fax-compatible modems can work with an EIA Class 1 fax software package executing in the PC to send text or graphics directly from the PC disk drive to a remote fax device. Two fax-modem-equipped PCs also can exchange fax transmissions from disk to disk without ever scanning or printing the transmitted information.

Fax modems should negotiate the highest common speed with the remote fax device or modem. The selected speed should also be the highest rate that can be maintained under the existing telephone line conditions. Typical fax transmission speeds are 2,400, 4,800, 7,200, 9,600, 12,000, and 14,400 bps.

Stand-alone Versus Board-mounted

Although they execute the same functions, *stand-alone* modems and modems mounted on *adapters* have advantages and disadvantages particular to their design. The type you choose likely depends on your specific communications application and the advantages provided by one modem type.

Tables 9.15 and 9.16 show the general pros and cons of the stand-alone and board-mounted modems. In almost every case, an advantage for one type is a disadvantage for the other type. From this list, you can see that a board-mounted modem is a logical choice for the owner of a portable or laptop computer who plans to travel with the computer and wants to minimize the number of gadgets that have to be carried separate from the computer system unit. People who want a complete communications hardware package that does not require external cables, boxes, and power supplies might also want a board-mounted, internally installed modem.

Table 9.15
Stand-alone Modems

Pros:
Can be used with any computer or terminal
Has indicator lights that show action and status
Can have a display to show additional status

continues

Table 9.15, Continued
Stand-alone Modems

Pros:
Heat load is external to computer system unit
Can be removed from serial port so that port can be used for other applications
Has power on/off switch for last-resort modem reset
Can have external switches that you can set

Cons:
Requires space adjacent to computer
Must be transported when computer is taken on trip
Requires a power supply connection
Requires an RS-232D cable
Requires a serial port connection

Table 9.16
Internal Expansion-board Modems

Pros:
Requires no space outside computer system unit
Requires no serial port connection
Requires no RS-232D cable
Requires no external power supply
Software can control switch settings
Is transported inside the computer system unit

Cons:
Consumes one expansion slot inside system unit
Cannot be used with incompatible computer
Provides no indicator lights to show action and status
Provides no hardware reset switch
Requires installation inside system unit

A stand-alone modem is a good choice for people who use several different computers and terminals that require a modem for communicating with other devices. This type is easily moved from one device to another. A stand-alone modem also is a good choice for communications software developers and bulletin board operators. The indicator lights and displays on a stand-alone modem serve as helpful diagnostic tools and busy-signal indicators. Just by watching the data send and receive, auto-answer, and bps rate indicator lights, a software developer can eliminate many hours of debugging time. An external modem's indicator lights and display also provide problem and activity indicators for auto-answer software operators. A host or bulletin board system operator can determine the system's status at a glance by observing the modem lights.

Modem Interfaces

Most asynchronous and synchronous modems use the same interfaces, but not the same control signals. The connector that enables you to attach a cable between an asynchronous or a synchronous (SDLC or BSC) port and a modem must conform with either EIA RS-232D or ITU-T V.24 specifications. The design of the modem determines how it uses the 25 signals supported by these interfaces.

Synchronous modems generally use more signal lines than asynchronous modems. Synchronous modems that provide a backward channel need the secondary RS-232D signal lines reviewed in Chapter 8, "PC Communications Interfaces and Adapters." Synchronous modems that require external clocking from the terminal or PC also must use the receive clock signal. Synchronous modems further provide, through the transmit clock signal line, the clock signal it extracts from the incoming analog telephone signal.

Asynchronous and synchronous modems can use different interfaces with the telephone system. Synchronous modems may not require the *Data Terminal Ready* (DTR) signal provided in a serial interface. A modem requires the DTR only when it provides communications through dial-up switched circuits. The modem uses the DTR to break a connection with a remote modem.

Although most asynchronous modems include auto-dial features, most synchronous modems do not support direct dialing of remote modems. Early synchronous modems provided auto-answer, but did not initiate calls. Another device called an *auto call unit* (ACU) worked with a communications controller to place calls. The controller sends special dialing instructions to the ACU that makes the call. When the remote modem answers the call, the ACU turns the line over to the synchronous modem to synchronize and communicate with the remote modem.

Many new synchronous modems still depend on non-synchronous circuitry to make calls. Some modems have a second EIA RS-232D connection that enables you to use an ACU to place calls. Other modems that contain both asynchronous and synchronous hardware use the asynchronous side to place calls and then switch to synchronous communications when the remote modem answers. This later technique enables you to use the asynchronous, Hayes AT command set to make calls using communications software.

Another difference between asynchronous and synchronous modems is their support for multiple terminals or PCs. Asynchronous modems support a single device or terminal. Because of the inherent multipoint support in synchronous protocols, on the other hand, vendors often provide models of synchronous modems that support more than one device or terminal. They take advantage of the multipoint synchronous capability to optimize the use of a single, leased telephone connection.

Multipoint synchronous modems provide two or more synchronous ports that can simultaneously support more than one piece of *data terminal equipment* (DTE). Implementation of fan out can reduce the total cost per port for the DTEs compared to the cost of a configuration that provides a separate modem for each DTE. Some synchronous modems include multiplexors that provide you with more connectivity options. A multiplexor-modem contains circuitry enabling a modem to be an intermediate node in a network. This type of modem must extract the clock signal from the incoming line and pass this signal to all downstream modems. The multiplexor-modem and all downstream modems use the same clock signal to demodulate the analog signals they receive.

Modem Summary

With this exposure to some characteristics and capabilities of modems, you can better select the type you need. Table 9.17 shows a sample modem-evaluation matrix. You may want to use a similar matrix when selecting one for your use.

Table 9.17
Sample Modem Evaluation Matrix

Modem Feature	Modem #1	Modem #2	Modem #3
Modem Type:			
Stand-alone			
Expansion board			
Transmission Protocols:			
Bell 103			
Bell 212A			
Racal-Vadic			
V.22			
V.22bis			
V.32			
V.32bis			
V.33			
Error Controls:			
MNP Class 4			
LAPM			
Data Compression:			
MNP Class 5			
V.42bis			
BPS Rate Capability:			
300			
1,200			

continues

Table 9.17, Continued
Sample Modem Evaluation Matrix

Modem Feature	Modem #1	Modem #2	Modem #3
2,400			
9,600			
14,400			
Duplex Modes:			
Half			
Full			
Switch Position Control:			
Manual switch only			
Software switch only			
Both			
Built-in Test Modes:			
Self test			
Analog loop-back			
Remote digital			
Line quality			
Communication Modes:			
Asynchronous			
Synchronous			
Modem Operating States:			
Off-line command			
On-line communication			
Quit (dormant)			

Modem Feature	Modem #1	Modem #2	Modem #3
Command Help File:			
Available on-line			
Available off-line			
Command Compatibility:			
Vendor-unique mode			
Hayes-compatible mode			
Parameter Change Recognition:			
From dormant state			
From command state			
Both			
Dial Types Available:			
Pulse (rotary)			
Touch tone			
Detect and switch			
Call/Answer Modes:			
Manual originate			
Manual answer			
Auto-answer			
Dialing Modes:			
Keyboard input			
Software disk directory			
Modem-stored directory			
Automatic Dial Design:			

II

Data Communications

continues

Table 9.17, Continued
Sample Modem Evaluation Matrix

Modem Feature	Modem #1	Modem #2	Modem #3
Dial from menu			
Dial by host name			
Redial busy number			
Redial x times			
Repeat dial last number			
Link alternative number			
Tone Recognition:			
First dial tone			
Secondary dial tone			
Busy signal			
Dead line			
Blind dial			
Commands Available:			
Set disconnect code			
Set answer-back code			
Set backspace code			
Set attention code			
Wait delay during dial			
Make line busy			

When serial communications through analog telephone circuits do not meet your needs for the movement of high volumes of data between locations, consider an all-digital communications link. Chapter 2, "Communications Channels," describes the signaling techniques vendors use for these networks. The following section examines the devices that enable you to transmit digital data through all-digital networks.

Digital Network Interfaces

The binary digital signals that travel through the internal PC data bus must undergo a conversion before they can travel long distance through a digital network. Vendors can convey digital signals over short distances using several signaling techniques. The digital signals that travel over long distances, on the other hand, must follow certain rules to ensure reliable communications.

The transmission of digital signals over long distances requires signaling techniques that eliminate the buildup of direct current. Unless the signals make approximately equal transitions from negative to positive voltage over specific periods, direct current builds up and interferes with the demodulation of the signal at the receiving end of a link. Figure 9.13 shows the contrast between typical unipolar digital signals that travel inside the PC and the polar and bipolar signals vendors transmit through digital cables and networks.

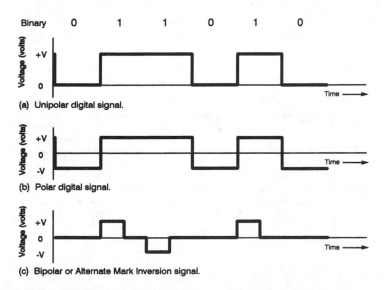

Figure 9.13
Digital electrical signals.

A PC data bus is typically a collection of unipolar circuits. Two voltage states convey binary digital values, but the voltage does not change polarity. These circuits use a positive voltage such as +5V for the duration of a bit time to signify a logical one. These same circuits return the voltage to zero for the duration of a bit time to signify a logical zero. To convey these unipolar signals over long distances, a hardware device must convert them into either polar or bipolar signals.

A polar circuit uses two voltage states to convey digital signals. The voltage must be within a positive range to convey one binary value and within a negative range to convey the other binary value. An EIA RS-232D interface is a good example of a polar circuit. The voltage must be in the +3V to +15V range to signify a logical zero and in the -3V to -15V range to signify a logical one. These circuits are *non-return to zero* (NRZ) because the signal never returns to or stays at zero voltage while conveying data. If the total number of ones and zeros is approximately equal over time, the polarity changes will sum to zero voltage to eliminate direct current problems.

A bipolar circuit uses three voltage states to convey digital signals. The simplest bipolar circuits use zero voltage to signify a logical zero and an alternating positive and negative voltage to signify a logical one. These bipolar channels are return to zero circuits, and the signals they convey are *alternate mark inversion* (AMI) signals. The alternation between positive and negative voltage must sum to zero over given periods to eliminate direct current problems.

The vendors that supply digital networks provide additional signals to maintain synchronization between network components and to control network operations. The additional bits violate the normal bipolar switches in polarity and the channel becomes a violated bipolar circuit. Figure 9.14 shows this type of signaling scheme.

Figure 9.14
Normal and violated bipolar signals.

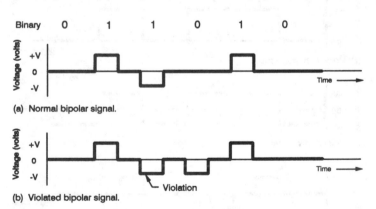

(a) Normal bipolar signal.

(b) Violated bipolar signal.

Network vendors provide bipolar violations called *zero suppression* that ensure synchronization between the network and the components that convey the digital signals. The zero suppression code provides signal transitions that enable devices to recover and regenerate the network clock signal. Zero suppression circuits insert logical ones when long strings of zeros pass through the network. The additional ones provide the signal transitions that enable regenerative repeaters

and receiving devices to determine and maintain bit time. The receiving devices must segregate and discard the zero suppression code.

Digital networks require precise timing throughout to remain synchronized with attached devices. The Bell System's *Dataphone Digital Service* (DDS), for example, uses a single nuclear clock located in Phoenix, Arizona as a master network clock. Most facilities can maintain synchronization with the network for up to two weeks after losing the link to the master clock. Eventually, however, these facilities lose synchronization and fail to operate properly.

Network Service Units

To communicate through a digital network, a PC must use a network service unit. The two types of service units are the *Data Service Unit* (DSU) and the *Channel Service Unit* (CSU). The DSU provides a direct network interface for processors that do not contain sophisticated digital interfaces. The CSU provides a simpler interface for facilities that provide powerful, digital communications functions. Figure 9.15 shows typical DSU and CSU implementations.

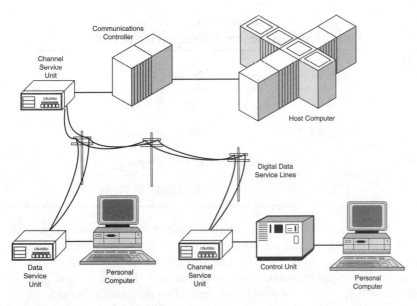

Figure 9.15
Data Service Units and Channel Service Units.

Data Service Unit

A DSU provides all the intelligence required to support a direct interface with a digital network. The DSU can detect and discard the bipolar violations provided for network synchronization and control. It also can recover the network clock signal and regenerate a unipolar signal compatible with the internal bus of a computer. Finally, a DSU can understand and generate network control codes to assist in network operations.

You can connect a DSU to a PC and communicate through a digital network without concern for network operations. The DSU makes the digital network transparent to the user just as a modem makes an analog telephone network transparent. The differences between these combinations are reliability and data throughput. The DSU and the digital network can easily detect and correct errors before they get to the PC. This digital communications technique also enables the PC to communicate with a remote device at a much higher data rate.

The physical interface between a DSU and a PC depends upon the data rate of the connection. Table 9.20 shows the data rates and interface requirements for Bell DSUs. As you can see from this table, you can use the same EIA RS-232D interface between a DSU and a synchronous port that you use with a modem for data rates from 2,400 to 9,600 bps. For a 56 Kbps Bell DSU, you must use a special 34-pin ITU-T V.35 interface. Comparable interfaces from other vendors may provide more flexibility.

Table 9.20
Bell DSU Interface Requirements

Data Rate (bps)	Required Interface	Physical Connector
2,400	EIA RS-232D	DB-25, 25-pin
4,800	EIA RS-232D	DB-25, 25-pin
9,600	EIA RS-232D	DB-25, 25-pin
56,000	ITU-T V.35	Winchester, 34-pin

A PC located outside a city serviced by a digital network can communicate with a remote DSU through an analog telephone circuit. You can communicate through a set of modems as shown in figure 9.16. After the PC makes the connection through the modems, the PC can communicate through the remote DSU just as it does with a local DSU. The limitation of this type of connection is the data rate between the two modems, which is typically less than 29,000 bps.

Channel Service Unit

A digital network vendor provides the user with a CSU when the user's facility provides all the network intelligence. The CSU contains no digital network

intelligence; it simply provides a bipolar transmit and receive port between the user's equipment and the network. The customer's equipment must eliminate network bipolar violations and recover network timing to regenerate unipolar computer signals. This equipment must also interpret and generate network control codes.

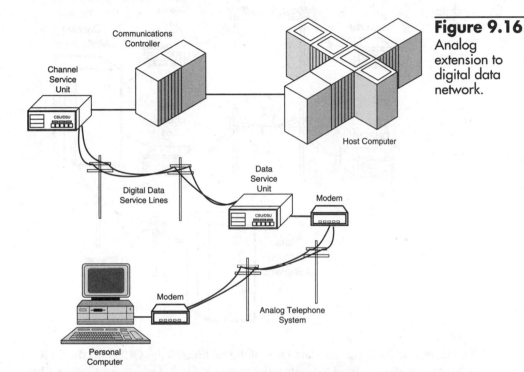

Figure 9.16
Analog extension to digital data network.

A CSU normally connects directly to a communications controller or a host computer designed to provide a direct interface to a digital network. Bell CSUs require the same interfaces as Bell DSUs that operate at comparable speeds. Other vendors may provide different configurations, but the signals that pass between the CSU and the customer's equipment are the same. These signals must meet the specifications of an *Office Channel Unit* (OCU) provided by the digital network vendor.

Office Channel Unit

The *OCU* is the digital equivalent of a central office switch for an analog telephone circuit. It can receive data rates of 9,600 bps or 56 Kbps from remote DSUs or CSUs and aggregate these signals using the *time division multiplexing* (TDM) techniques described in Chapter 2. The vendor then aggregates these 64 Kbps trunks into T1 channel banks, as shown in figure 9.17. The T1 channel banks can convey both digitized voice and data between destinations.

Figure 9.17
Digital data service time division multiplexing.

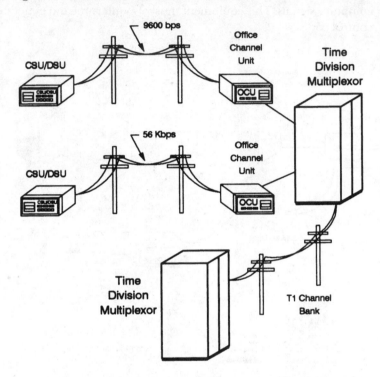

The difference between the data rates of digital links to the OCU and the 64 Kbps trunks is the bits required to control the network. One of every eight bits (8 Kbps for a 64 Kbps line) conveys control information for circuits called *unclear channels*. Some channels, such as microwave links, do not require this control information; they can provide a full 64 Kbps for digitized voice or digital data in a clear channel. The terms *unclear* and *clear* refer to the need for control information—both provide the same digital communications capabilities.

Summary

As you can see from this chapter, you can use many techniques and devices to communicate data from a PC to a remote device or computer. The variety grows every year. At one time, the only way to move data at high speeds with reliable delivery was to use synchronous adapters and modems. Vendors now use sophisticated technology that enables them to achieve the same results for both

asynchronous and synchronous communications. The price difference between these techniques decreases every year.

You must determine the need for a specific type of communications hardware based on total user needs. For situations that require periodic connections to remote devices, dial-up facilities may meet all communications needs. Situations that require continuous connections may need leased lines. The selection between asynchronous and synchronous communications is often dictated by the system the user must access. Many non-IBM hosts still use asynchronous communications. IBM hosts provide asynchronous communications through code and protocol converters.

When reliability and availability are critical success factors, the communications technique of choice is usually synchronous. To take full advantage of an IBM SNA system from a remote location, for example, the user must provide a synchronous communications channel between the PC and the SNA network. Although the PC can often use the same modem for both asynchronous and synchronous communications, the serial port that drives the modem in synchronous mode must provide the synchronous bit stream and a matching link level protocol such as BSC or SDLC as discussed in Chapter 6, "Synchronous Data Link Control."

II

Data Communications

Chapter Snapshot

This chapter examines different types of communications software, and discusses the relationship between PC software and hardware. In this chapter, you will learn about:

✔ Software layers

✔ The function of the communications software package

✔ Communications software design concepts

✔ How to evaluate communications software

✔ Unattended asynchronous communications software

Communications
Software

After assembling the pieces of hardware described in Chapter 9, "Telephone System Interfaces," you need communications software before the PC can communicate with other computer systems. Before delving into the subject of communications software, however, the following paragraphs review the relationship between PC software and hardware.

Software Layers

As figure 10.1 shows, the *central processing unit* (CPU) is the piece of hardware that directs the flow of communications within the PC. Three kinds of software control this processor. The first layer of control comes from instructions stored in memory chips called *read-only memory* (ROM). An operating system provides the second layer of instructions and control. Communications software provides the final layer of control. This software draws upon the capabilities of the ROM and the operating system to execute user-directed data communications functions. Figure 10.2 shows the logical relationship between these three layers of software and the hardware that supports data communications.

Figure 10.1
PC asynchronous communications hardware and software.

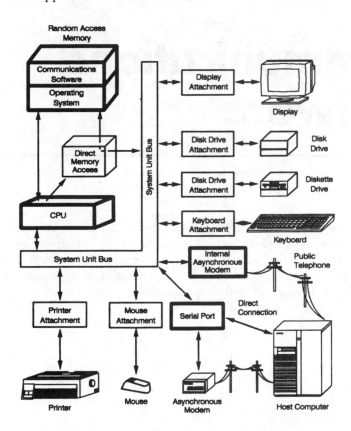

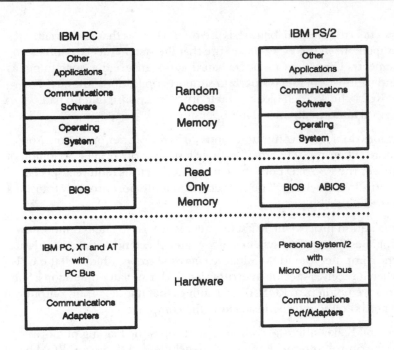

Figure 10.2
IBM PC and PS/2 communications elements.

ROM BIOS Software

When the computer first starts up, it must have software built into the hardware to ensure proper start up. This software must also support more powerful software that loads from disk after start up. ROM software, stored in a variety of hardware chips in the PC, executes this function. The ROM software is permanently embedded in the hardware so that it cannot be erased or changed for the lifetime of the computer. Each time the computer begins operation, this software executes an identical set of start-up operations. It then stands by with an identical set of *basic input/output system* (BIOS) functions to support system operations.

Although important to proper system start-up and reliability, the initial start-up ROM does not play a role in later operation of communications software. This portion of ROM performs several tasks, as shown in the following list. The ensuing paragraphs describe these tasks and the roles they play in support of data communications.

✔ Executes initial system error and reliability tests

✔ Performs initial system chip and equipment set up

✔ Performs initial optional equipment tests

✔ Sets up initial interrupt-handling vectors

✔ Loads operating system from disk

The initial system error and reliability tests are brief routines that test certain hardware components in the PC to make sure that the system meets a minimum set of requirements. These tests are not exhaustive, but ensure that such things as disk drives and memory operate properly to support applications software. For example, the ROM checks each block of memory to make sure that no bad memory chips will abnormally affect later operations.

ROM instructions do not test communications ports for proper operation. You must run a more exhaustive set of maintenance tests to verify proper operation of this hardware. For the RS-232D port, these maintenance tests require a special cable to support a loop-back test. The test verifies that the port properly transmits and receives predefined bit patterns.

The next initialization process the ROM executes is crucial to later communications operation. Besides reading system switches and checking optional hardware installed in the computer, the ROM initializes *interrupt vectors,* which tell the CPU what to do when it receives specific interrupt signals during later operations. Some of these vectors are pointers to ROM BIOS routines that handle input/output with the RS-232D port(s) or adapter(s) installed in the computer.

The final step ROM takes after the computer starts up is the loading of more powerful system control software. For a PC that includes a disk drive, a ROM-based *bootstrap loader* starts the operation of the disk drive and also loads a more powerful operating system into the PC's memory. This operating system, sometimes called the *disk operating system,* assumes control of the PC after it loads into memory and begins to execute.

Operating System

PC users have many *operating system* (OS) alternatives from which to choose. The first OS available for the PC was MS- or PC-DOS (often called DOS) jointly developed by Microsoft and IBM. This is still the most popular OS with communications users even though it has many more limitations than more recent OS alternatives. Microsoft offers Microsoft Windows as an enhancement to DOS. IBM also provides an alternative in *Operating System/2* (OS/2). Finally, several vendors offer UNIX and its derivatives. All PC operating systems provide a base level of common hardware control functions, and give you the necessary commands to control all the peripherals shown in figure 10.1. They also control the transfer of programs and data between disk files and RAM memory, as well as many design characteristics of the software that can be loaded and run in the PC. Figure 10.3 shows a technical diagram of the various layers of software required to support communications.

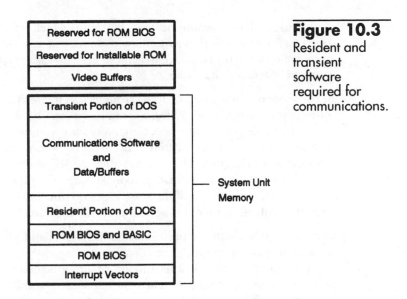

Figure 10.3
Resident and transient software required for communications.

The operating system contains several software programs that direct the operation of internal PC components. Without the existence of the operating system, the power and flexibility expected from microprocessor-controlled personal computers would be sorely lacking. All PC operations and applications build upon this foundation of software layers.

Communications Software

The next layer of software required for communications is either a *language interpreter* or a *communications software* package. This layer includes a high-level language interpreter such as BASIC if the communications application operates in an interpretive mode. Interpretive BASIC software does not require an assembly or compilation process before it executes. Instead, a software developer writes the BASIC software with an editor and stores it as ASCII text or as a meta-language. When you run the software, an interpreter reads, interprets, and executes the software one line at a time. These interpreter applications normally have file names that have extensions other than EXE or COM. For example, interpretive BASIC programs have a BAS file name extension.

Compiled or assembled communications applications load and execute without the support of a language interpreter. These directly executable applications programs have file names that end with EXE or COM, and, when loaded into PC memory, have the relationship with ROM BIOS and DOS shown in figure 10.3. These machine-code programs usually operate faster than interpretive programs because they do not interpret source code one line at a time. They also can have direct links with the communications hardware, which improves their execution speed. Software developers write these communications software packages in the C language or assembly language to achieve high execution speed and obtain direct access to system unit hardware.

In the sequence of software loading from disk to memory, the communications software is the last to load. When a communications application loads, it sets aside a certain amount of random access memory for communications buffers. For communications software written in BASIC, a section of memory is used for software house cleaning. This space enables BASIC to reorganize data. Software developers monitor memory usage to make sure enough free space is available for this house cleaning. Users of these packages do not concern themselves with this level of detail unless they choose to modify the software.

Communications software performs both high-level and low-level operations. This software must interact with a user or a set of user-written procedures at one end and translate these interactions into information the communications hardware understands at the other end. The communications software must also monitor the communications hardware and execute operations dictated by signals generated by this hardware.

Software-Hardware Compatibility

A key factor in the proper operation of communications software is compatibility between the BIOS and operating system that controls the CPU and the communications software. The communications software must be designed to operate with the specific operating system the user has chosen for the PC. Software interrupts and system calls issued by the communications software must be understood and properly executed by BIOS and the operating system. If not, communications may fail. For example, a communications package written for execution under the PC-DOS or MS-DOS operating system may not operate properly under OS/2.

The introduction of the PS/2 has added to potential software-hardware incompatibilities. The PS/2 has two more communications-related functions in its *Advanced Basic/Input Output System* (ABIOS) than the IBM PC, XT, and AT have in their BIOS. This makes it possible to write software that will work perfectly well with the PS/2 but fails in an older PC. A good software developer provides techniques to ensure that the communications software matches the hardware if there are subtle differences such as this BIOS extension. For example, the developer can provide an operational profile that is modified during installation to tell the communications software whether to use special or hardware-dependent extensions.

Software Design Concepts

Communications software, like most other types of software, can be designed in several ways and still accomplish the same objectives. The software design can affect the performance of the package or only the user interface. The following sections discuss the four major design models vendors use for communications software.

Data-Handling Techniques

Besides communicating properly with an operating system, the software must provide a mechanism for transferring data from one device to another. The operating system can control each of the PC's peripherals, but the software must decide the device destination for data. After selecting the device to receive certain data, the software must handle the process of moving the data from one device to another. The software must also tell the user when a communications error occurs and provide the user with a method to terminate operations when errors are excessive. Software designers use either polling or interrupt-driven techniques for these data-transfer and error-handling operations.

Although both polling and interrupt-driven communications software accomplish the same objectives, they differ significantly in the methods they use to accomplish these tasks. Both accept input from the keyboard and transfer data to and from the communications link. They also display user input and data received from a distant computer. The major difference between the polling and interrupt-driven techniques is the method designers use to determine the need for action and the time it takes the PC to execute the action.

Polling Software

The polling technique can result in slow reactions to changes. This method typically forces the CPU to continually check the keyboard and the serial port buffers to see which of these devices have data available. A software developer can combine this continuous polling technique with a method of handling the data that it finds in a device's buffer. For instance, a developer can require the CPU to process all data it finds in a given buffer before continuing the polling process. A developer also can write the software to handle only part of the data it finds in a buffer and then continue with its polling process.

Regardless of the polling design, the communications software may respond too slowly to user commands or incoming data. If the user wants to terminate an operation in progress, the CPU may be emptying a communications buffer when the user executes the termination command. In this case, several characters appear on the display between the user action and the termination completion. If data are coming into the serial port at a rapid rate and the user decides to send a file to the remote computer simultaneously, incoming data may be lost while the CPU is busy sending out data.

Interrupt-Driven Software

The interrupt-driven input/output control technique, on the other hand, causes a program to react quickly to changes under most circumstances. The interrupt technique enables the CPU to continue executing a designated task until it needs to perform a different task. The process does not waste time polling devices that have no data. When a device has data available, it sends the CPU an *interrupt request,* as shown in figure 10.4, indicating the need for service.

Figure 10.4
Hardware interrupt logic of the IBM PC.

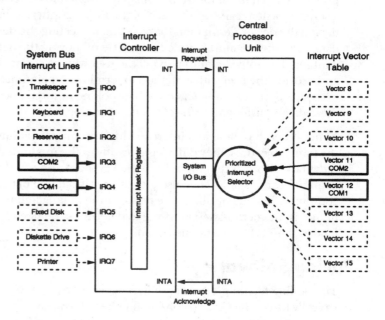

Whether the CPU stops an activity to service a device depends on the interrupt priority given to that device by the operating system and the communications software. The software can turn off or mask minor interrupts to keep them from interfering with other important tasks. The software also can give interrupts different levels of priority that determine their order of execution when more than one interrupt requires simultaneous service. For example, a software author can program the ESC key to transfer the user from the conversation mode to the command mode instantaneously, regardless of other operations under way when the user presses the ESC key. A software designer also can make a software package react quickly to specific characters or signals that arrive at the serial port. Because of the rapid response of interrupt-driven techniques, software that uses these

techniques can keep better pace with remote systems, resulting in a lower probability of data loss.

The disadvantage of interrupt-driven software is the complex design required to assign proper interrupt priorities. In the polling design, the CPU always knows where data are coming from and handles devices one at a time, based on the polling sequence. With interrupt-driven design, however, an interrupt can occur at any time during a program execution. The software has to recognize the origin of the interrupt and determine what action to take, based on preselected priorities. The software also has to preserve the status of the operation in progress when the interrupt occurs and then return to that same point when the interrupt service is complete.

Software developers often use packages of interrupt-driven routines or libraries when they develop communications applications. By using a package of these routines, a developer can quickly design and write a communications application. The library vendor is responsible for developing, testing, and maintaining the interrupt library. The communications application vendor is responsible for developing, testing, and maintaining the application. With this division of responsibility, each vendor can concentrate his efforts on one level of software development, thereby providing end users with more powerful software.

IBM provides a special library of communications functions to complement OS/2. The OS/2 Extended Services Communications Manager module includes these functions as *Dynamic Linking Routines* (DLRs) in *Dynamic Linking Libraries* (DLLs). The *Asynchronous Communications Device Interface* (ACDI) is the DLR that provides multitasking, interrupt-driven support for PC serial ports. Vendors can write communications applications that call these standard routines through *application programming interfaces* (APIs). The DLRs can be linked directly to applications or loaded when the application executes. These DLRs interface with lower-level device drivers to provide control over communications and networking hardware and to control data flow to and from the hardware.

The techniques vendors use to transfer data to and from serial ports are normally transparent to users. If the techniques work, the user is not aware of their presence. If they do not work, the user is aware that functions in the software are not performing as required. A feature users are always aware of, however, is the interface the vendor provides for control of the communications software.

Predominant User Interface

Software vendors design communications software as either *conversation-mode* or *command-mode* predominant. When the user starts a communications software package, the software goes directly into either the conversation mode or the command mode. The user must instruct the software to make a switch to get to the other mode. The active mode determines what actions the user can perform.

II

Data Communications

The command mode provides off-line communications between the PC keyboard and the communications software. This mode enables the user to perform functions that do not involve the computer at the other end of the communications link. For example, the user can store a telephone number in a dialing directory or change the software's operating profile, neither of which requires interaction with the remote computer. When the user finishes off-line command-mode functions, however, he or she can return to the on-line conversation mode to resume interactive communications with the remote computer.

Conversation Mode

Conversation-mode-predominant software assumes that the user will normally be in the conversation or terminal mode when communicating. This design is excellent for interactive communications with bulletin boards and older information systems and is the design many vendors choose for their software. With this type of software, a user goes into the command or off-line mode only when he or she needs to change a communications parameter, select a telephone number, or execute another non-conversation action. No data move between the PC and the remote computer while the software is in this command mode. When the user completes off-line action, the software immediately returns to the conversation mode.

Command Mode

Command-mode-predominant software, on the other hand, assumes that the user often wants to be in the off-line mode when communicating. Businesses that frequently execute batch-mode file transfers often prefer this type of software. Command-mode software is also easier for communications novices to use. The command menus prompt users for input.

With command-mode software, the user remains in the command mode until he or she requests a switch to the conversation mode. After switching to the conversation mode, the user can return to the command mode at any time during a communications session by striking the required conversation-mode escape key. This option enables the user to execute several off-line operations without returning to the conversation mode. The user can list files, delete files, or change communications parameters without switching back and forth between off-line and on-line modes.

Command-mode software also helps to eliminate the confusion some users experience when switching between the off-line and on-line modes. Conversation-predominant software does not always provide a clear indication when it changes from on line to off line or vice versa. Command-mode software provides a better indication because menus appear on-screen when the user is in the off-line mode.

Off-Line Command Mode

The off-line mode of communications software is either menu or command driven. Menu-driven software always provides the user with a list of options to choose from in the off-line mode. Command-driven software, on the other hand, requires the user to execute commands without a list of available options. Both types of software often provide help files to explain command functions, but the command-driven type can provide two levels of help. The first level only lists the available commands, whereas the second level provides more specific details about each command.

Menu-Driven Software

Menu-driven communications software is generally easier for communications novices to learn and use. The command prompts lead novices through a sequence of easy-to-follow choices. The selection of a choice at one menu often leads to another list of alternatives. The menus provide a decision tree with two or more branches at the end of each branch.

Although easy to learn and use, menu-driven communications software packages often become inconvenient and frustrating as the novice becomes familiar with data communications. Going from one menu level to another can become an annoying chore. Users of packages that contain several levels of menus often develop "menu disgust."

Command-Driven Software

Command-driven communications software is a good choice for the experienced communications user. The user can go from conversation mode to command mode and execute several commands in quick succession, without going through a series of time-consuming menu prompts. The user can always ask for help when commands fail to produce desired results. This type of software is sometimes intimidating for the novice and often requires more frequent use of the software documentation or on-line help. Because of this intimidation factor, the user might overlook features and not take full advantage of the package.

The ideal communications software package offers the best of both worlds. The novice can start using the package in a menu-driven mode and then switch to a command-driven mode after achieving proficiency. This type of software also might offer a configuration feature that enables different users to default to one or the other of these modes automatically when the software begins operation.

II

Data Communications

Software Screen Displays

With the introduction of Microsoft Windows and the OS/2 Presentation Manager, yet another method of categorizing communications software has emerged—character-based and graphics-based software. A *character-based* design uses the original character-based DOS command screen, whereas *graphics-based* software uses one of two panel techniques. Both provide display and user input control, but the graphics technique can provide a more consistent user interface.

Character-Based Display

Character-based software provides its own vendor-specific screen layout, menus, and user input techniques. This type of software also may use graphical panels for output display. The problem with these panel techniques is that vendors of different packages often use different techniques to display information and obtain user input. Vendors who develop graphics-based software from either a Microsoft Windows or a Presentation Manager toolkit, on the other hand, provide user interfaces consistent with all other applications developed for these environments.

Graphics-Based Display

Graphics-based communications software, by its nature, provides a menu-driven user interface. This does not, however, dictate either a command or conversation predominant design. The software can be in either the command or conversation mode when it first begins operation, and requires user input to change to the other mode.

With the *graphical user interfaces* (GUI) available in Microsoft Windows or OS/2 Presentation Manager, vendors can combine command and conversation modes of operation. One panel can execute command mode operations while one or more other panels provide on-line communications with a remote computer, as well as other application functions. Scroll bars enable the user to scroll back through information received while the user executes functions in other panels. A developer's imagination is the only limit with this powerful and rich operating environment.

Information service providers are now taking advantage of GUI techniques to provide easy-to-use interfaces for their customers. Both Prodigy and CompuServe provide full-fledged graphical road maps of their services before and after the PC and modem dial into the network. Some users of these services may not even know when their PCs make the connection with the remote service computers because of the masking the interface provides for the complexity that goes on behind the scenes.

Software Intelligence

The number of features included in a communications package determines its level of intelligence. Software packages range from dumb to smart. Software vendors design dumb terminal packages to provide only the basics, whereas smart terminal software provides many automated functions. The prices of these packages usually reflect their level of intelligence.

Dumb-Terminal Software

Dumb-terminal software enables the PC to emulate an asynchronous terminal that has no disk drives or other data-storage devices attached. This type of software often supports data entry and display. Such a package cannot store and retrieve information to eliminate the complexities or tedium of logging onto remote computers. Dumb-terminal software also provides no file transfer capability.

Smart-Terminal Software

Smart-terminal software refers to packages that give the PC real communications power. Besides data entry and display, these systems enable the user to store and retrieve host telephone numbers, automatically dial telephone numbers, and transfer disk files. Smart-terminal software usually provides many built-in features that make the task of data communications easier. This type of software often includes features that enable the user to customize features and functions to give the package a personal touch.

Some smart-terminal packages are available in the *public domain,* and others are commercial packages. The commercial status of a package, however, does not always reflect its level of performance or quality of documentation. Some of the best smart-terminal software also is available as *shareware* or *freeware.* If you continue to use these packages after an initial trial run, you are expected to make a contribution to the software vendor.

Qmodem and ProComm are two examples of high-quality, communications software that have versions available as shareware. Other communications packages are only available as commercial products, and many of these packages have loyal fans who will not use another package even if it is free. Long-time owners of the Crosstalk and Relay packages, for example, often feel lost with any other communications package.

Because of the variety of options available in smart-terminal communication packages, the selection and purchase of a commercial package can be time-consuming. One element that makes the selection of a package difficult is the jargon vendors use to describe software capabilities. Software publishers use terms such as *download* and *break signal* without prior definition. They also use different terms to describe the same process or capability, thus adding to the confusion. To eliminate some of this confusion and to make the selection and use of a communications package easier, the following paragraphs provide a detailed explanation of most of the terms used to describe asynchronous communications software capabilities.

Smart-Terminal Software Capabilities

Smart-terminal communications software is like any other applications software. No single package is likely to satisfy all wants and needs. The best you can hope to achieve is to obtain a package that provides most essential features and some nonessential but desirable features. Table 10.1 provides an overview of the features included in many smart-terminal packages.

Table 10.1
Communications Characteristics and Capabilities

Installation and Setup:	
Operating system required	Manual and autodial modems
Modem speed flexibility	Documentation manual
User help files	User support
Error handling	Display width selection
Parameter selection	Duplex mode selection
Command files	Batch mode
Prestored strings	Password storage security
Modem Controls:	
Originate/answer mode switch	Dialing directory
Disk directory listing	Auto-redial
Clock-controlled operation	Telephone hang up
Data Redirection and Flow Control:	
Data capture to printer	XON/XOFF protocol

Installation and Setup:	
Data capture	Data upload
Upload throttle	Upload/download local echo
Binary data transfer	Protocol file transfer

Data Manipulation:	
Line feed control	Blank line expansion
Character filter	Translation table
Terminal emulation	Case conversion
Tab-to-space conversion	

Special Features:	
Split screen	Elapsed time of call
Break signal	Remote takeover
External file manipulation	Return to operating system

Although many features are common to both business and personal communications software, vendors often implement these features in different ways to match the needs of a target market. The following paragraphs briefly discuss communications software features and emphasize some of the differences between business and personal applications.

Installation and Setup Features

Vendors use a variety of features in the initial installation and setup of their packages. These features are described in the following paragraphs.

Operating System Required

Because of the availability of communication packages that operate under the DOS, Windows, OS/2, or AIX operating systems, you must decide which system you use before you select your communications package. Although some packages operate under only one of these systems, others are available for more than one system. Care must also be taken because of the different file formats used by different operating systems. Files downloaded using an AIX communications package, for example, cannot be accessed later under PC- or MS-DOS because the disk formats are different.

Manual and Auto-Dial Modem Support

A user may have only a manual-dial modem, but when selecting a software package it is a good idea to get a package that supports both manual and auto-dial modems. Having a communications package that supports only manual-dial modems or only auto-dial modems limits flexibility in hardware configurations. With the rapid increase in the capabilities of modems and the rapid drop in their prices, a new auto-dial modem may become a necessity long before expected. An auto-dial modem might also have to be relinquished for repairs for a period of time, resulting in the need to use a spare manual-dial modem.

Modem Speed Flexibility

A communications package should be able to support communications speeds from 300 bps to as high as 28,800 bps. The user should be able to upgrade from a 2,400-bps modem to a 9,600-bps or 28,800-bps modem without having to buy a new communications package; this helps to minimize the costs associated with changing software and retraining personnel. Nearly all communications packages use different commands to perform the same function, so going to a new package means users have to learn new commands.

Documentation Manual

A communications package is incomplete without a good documentation manual. A package that contains many special features is of little use without a manual that tells how to use the features. A documentation manual does not have to contain the background information on communications provided in this book, but it must fully explain every package feature.

User Help

User help is important for communications packages not used frequently. This feature also is helpful for the user not accustomed to that particular package. On-line help is not a replacement for a good documentation manual, but provides a quick reference for the key strokes and commands required to perform certain functions. Help should be readily accessible (single key stroke or mouse click) and written in clear, concise English. Context-sensitive help that provides information relative to the position of the cursor or mouse pointer can provide excellent assistance when the user is performing complex procedures.

User Support

When all else fails, a user must be able to get support from the software publisher. Good user support means that a technical person is available, when required, to help solve application problems. No communications software package is perfect, particularly new ones coming out on the market, and most of the problems encountered cannot be solved by a software salesperson. Before purchasing a software package, check with local PC users' groups and other people who own and use the package to make sure it is well supported.

Error Handling

A software package's capability to handle errors is vital. A good package should either warn the user before an error occurs so that preventive action can be taken or provide a clear, understandable error message when an error does occur. The package should also enable the user to continue with communications if a minor error occurs. Operations that can result in significant errors should also be designed to give the software user the opportunity to abort a command before the error is made. For example, a user should be told that captured data will be lost if an attempt is made to return to the operating system before the data are saved. The user should be given the opportunity to go back and save the data before finally returning to the operating system.

Parameter Selection

To properly communicate with a remote computer, a communications user must be able to select the appropriate communications parameters required by the remote system. These parameters include bps rate, number of data bits, type of parity error-checking, and number of stop bits. The software package may provide default values for these parameters, but it must also provide the option of modifying the default values both before and after a connection is made with a remote system.

A good communications package also enables the user to modify the standard (sometimes called *global*) default values. A new set of default values replaces the original set. These new default values are normally stored in a disk file for later use. Some software packages also enable the user to store specified sets of parameters for each host or service system. A user loads a parameter command file or selects a remote system from a displayed directory to put the specific parameters into effect.

Several communications packages are designed to work with direct-connect auto-dial modems, and the communications parameters associated with each telephone number are stored in a file with the number. When the software is instructed to dial a number, the associated communications parameters are automatically put into effect before the number is dialed. These parameters remain in effect until modified by the user.

In each of the preceding cases, the default or selected parameters are communicated to the PC's internal modem or serial port to set the stage for communications under a specific protocol. The software must initialize the serial communications hardware automatically, or it must be instructed to initialize the hardware before communications with a remote system is established. If any of the parameters are modified during a communications session, the software must reinitialize the communications hardware to put the new parameters into effect.

The option of listing selected parameters is another good feature. If difficulty is encountered during a communications session and the selected parameters cannot be listed, troubleshooting the problem becomes difficult. Establishing proper communications parameters to use with a new system may require some experimentation with different parameters. That trial-and-error process is difficult to perform without the capability to list the communications parameters.

Duplex-Mode Selection

A communications package should enable a user to switch between half-duplex and full-duplex modes, because business and personal communications applications often require connection to both half-duplex and full-duplex remote systems. Most information services and bulletin board systems operate in the full-duplex (host-echo) mode, but other microcomputer and mainframe systems may operate in either the full- or half-duplex mode.

To properly communicate with a variety of systems, a user must be able to switch between the full- and half-duplex modes both before and after a communications link is established. Some bulletin board and remote systems may require a user to switch duplex modes after establishing a communications link. If a *remote system operator* (SYSOP) answers a page or interrupts your communications session to deliver a message (switches from automatic operation to the conversation mode), the remote computer's software also may switch from full duplex to half duplex. When this happens, characters are no longer echoed back to the user's terminal. To see the characters typed locally, the user has to make a modem switch to half-duplex or a software switch to local echo. A software package that offers a single-keystroke toggle switch between full-duplex (remote echo) and half-duplex (local echo) is useful under these circumstances.

Some software packages enable the duplex mode or host-echo mode to be changed through a menu selection. This method is acceptable if switching to the menu does not disconnect the telephone connection. Modems that monitor the Data Terminal Ready signal generated by the serial port will drop the telephone connection when the user enters the menu mode to change parameters. An external Hayes Smartmodem has a switch that enables the user to override monitoring of the DTR signal, but some modems do not have this override option.

Command Files

Command or *script files* enable a user to store several parameters in a disk file for repeated use. These files can contain many or all the software package commands that can be entered from the keyboard. Communication parameters, such as parity and number of data bits, may be modified, and a telephone number can be automatically dialed by a command file.

Command files offer several advantages for business applications, including the following:

✔ They save users from repetitive typing of commands.

✔ Different user disks can be set up, containing passwords and system log-in information specific to certain individuals.

✔ They can contain telephone numbers and passwords, eliminating the necessity for separate lists that have to be kept to call and log in with remote systems.

Batch Mode

Batch-mode operation is similar to command-file loading and execution, but it supports several commands not supported by command files. A command file can modify communications parameters and dial a telephone number when used with an auto-dial modem, but a communications operator must take over to continue the session after the communications link is established. A batch file can modify communications parameters and dial a telephone number, but it also can continue the communications session after the connection is established with a remote system. Login messages can be sent and files transferred between the PC and any other system without operator assistance.

Users can use batch files to delay execution until a specified period of time has elapsed. Unattended file transfers can execute late at night when telephone rates are lowest. This capability could be a valuable asset for a business with branch offices in different time zones.

Clock-Controlled Operation

Clock-controlled operation allows the internal PC clock to control the automated capabilities of command, batch, or script files. The user can design these files to execute specific operations at certain times of day or night. For instance, he or she can set up the software to dial a remote system at 3:00 a.m.; perform all log-in functions; upload a text, data, or program file; log off the remote system; then return the PC to the operating system—all without the attendance of a local or remote system operator. A user can execute clock-controlled operation to take advantage of low, late-night telephone rates and to transfer files, freeing the machine for other tasks during business hours.

Clock-controlled operation is sensitive to proper communications when it is used for unattended operation. The software must be capable of performing rudimentary artificial intelligence. After a command string is transmitted to a host, the software must check to see that the remote response indicates proper receipt of the command and repeat the command if the response is not correct. This eliminates the problems encountered with noise-generated command transmission errors.

Predefined Strings

Frequent communications with systems that require log-in commands can result in repetitive typing. In such cases, *predefined strings* that can be uploaded to a system can be a useful feature for both business and personal applications. Many PC communications software packages enable predefined strings to be uploaded with either a one-keystroke or a two-keystroke combination, which makes this feature even more convenient. When predefined strings are provided by a package, the user must be able to easily and quickly list the strings while logged in with another system; it is easy to forget which string goes with each key and a quick reminder is sometimes necessary.

Password Storage Security

For software packages that enable the user to store and retrieve character strings, security for stored passwords should be considered. The listing of stored character strings on the monitor should enable the user to omit stored password strings. This keeps onlookers from stealing passwords to time-sharing or information services.

Modem Control Features

Good smart-terminal software packages are designed to take full advantage of the features included in popular, intelligent modems. The features discussed in the following paragraphs are associated with the use of auto-dial, auto-answer, intelligent modems.

Originate/Answer Mode Switch

It is necessary to switch a modem from the originate-mode to the answer-mode when receiving a call from a remote terminal or another microcomputer. Manual-dial modems provide a switch that activates the mode change, but intelligent modems may be switched manually or through software control. Communications packages often enable the user to switch from one of these modes to the other by

pressing either one or two PC keys. Menu-controlled originate/answer mode switches can be more cumbersome to use than single-key toggle switches unless the package contains only one command menu.

Dialing Directory

When a software package enables the user to store telephone numbers that can be used with auto-dial modems to access remote systems, the package should also enable the user to list the dialing directory of stored telephone numbers. Numbers buried in command or batch files are inconvenient to locate when the number has to be dialed without use of the command or batch file. A brief summary listing of the major communications parameters that will be automatically invoked when a number is dialed from the directory is also a good feature.

Auto-Redial

Some information and support services run on microcomputers and enable only one user at a time to access the system, whereas others have a limited number of incoming connections. The telephone numbers of these services are frequently busy. Instead of manually redialing a number from the keyboard, an auto-dial modem can be software-controlled to redial a telephone number until a connection is made. Software packages that offer this capability also provide an alarm signal that gets the user's attention when the carrier of a remote system is finally detected. It is often necessary to use an auto-redial to get through to a bulletin board system on weekends or holidays.

Telephone Hang-Up

Some business communications involve systems that do not automatically break the telephone connection when a user logs off. To break a connection with one of these systems, the user should be able to execute a software command that "drops the line" when an auto-dial/auto-answer modem is being used. Without this option, the modem might have to be turned off to break the connection, and frequent off/on cycling of a modem could shorten its life.

Software packages that offer the telephone hangup feature generally require that the modem respond properly to the serial port's DTR signal or to an attention code sent to it through the serial port. The modem should be set up to drop the carrier signal and the telephone connection when the DTR signal is turned off by the software or when it receives an attention code followed by a hangup command sequence. If the modem is not properly configured, a telephone-hangup command does not work properly, which requires the DTR-signal technique.

II

Data Communications

Data Control Features

Smart-terminal software enables the user to redirect the flow of data to different devices and to transfer data to and from the PC. The following paragraphs describe features associated with these capabilities.

Data Capture to Printer

A communications package should enable the user to send data to a printer at the same time the data are being displayed on a monitor. Sometimes it is necessary to log a conversation with another person or print a download menu contained on a bulletin board to eliminate repeat listings of the menu during selection of a download file. A user may also want to log sessions with time-sharing systems to refer to later; this is particularly useful when transactions result in the transfer of funds. Logging conversation-mode transactions also is a good way to develop training material for later time-sharing or information service system classes.

The simultaneous communications and printing capability offered by most software packages is usable only in the conversation mode. A dot-matrix printer can keep pace with conversation-mode data transfer rates, but may not be capable of keeping pace with file transfer rates. A general rule is to print only the data being continuously transmitted at a rate less than the speed of your printer. A 300 character-per-second printer can keep pace with a 2,400-bps (240-character-per-second) modem, but the same printer cannot keep pace with a 9,600-bps (960-character-per-second) modem. A difference in communications speed and printer speed may not be a problem for some software packages because of the way they buffer incoming data, but some experimentation may be required to ensure a proper match.

Spooler software can be used with the printer option to facilitate simultaneous printing and downloading of data when using a slow-speed printer. A user can scan the messages on a bulletin board, mark messages of interest, and then go back and list those messages while simultaneously printing them. After listing these messages, the user can go on to other bulletin board functions or download a file while the print spooler continues to send the messages to a printer. A print spooler also can be used to handle print-screens without interrupting data transfer. By pressing the shift and PrtSc keys simultaneously, a user can send screen contents to the printer as communications continue.

Multitasking operating systems such as OS/2 and AIX also support internal spooling of data to printers. Communications software written for these environments can take advantage of this capability to provide speed matching between the serial port and the printer. These operating systems can use random access memory or disk space to buffer incoming data until such data can be directed to the printer.

A single-key toggle or mouse-click command that enables the user to turn the print function on and off without interrupting the transfer of data is also a desirable feature. This option enables the user to selectively send text to a printer by pressing one or two keyboard keys. Software that requires the user to go into the command mode to turn the print function on is cumbersome and requires either data receipt interruption or a pause in data transfer before printing can be initiated. This frequently results in desired data scrolling off the screen.

Exercise caution when using the simultaneous print option with certain printers. Some non-IBM printers go off-line when they receive XOFF characters, which can cause the PC keyboard to lock up (not respond to key strokes) until the printer is manually returned to on-line status. Printers also can respond to format effector characters, such as form feeds, transmitted for monitor control and waste paper.

XON/XOFF Protocol

File-transfer applications that involve data-transmission rates greater than 1,200 bps may require XON/XOFF communications speed-matching protocol. This protocol enables the software designer to use less memory for a communications receive buffer because communications speed-matching does not have to be handled solely by the buffer. Most mainframe computers use the XON/XOFF protocol, so that business applications that involve file transfers with mainframe computers can make good use of this capability.

File transfer protocols that provide XON/XOFF support are required for communications with some remote computers, particularly older IBM mainframes. Two protocols that support XON/XOFF for the PC are Kermit and Zmodem. Without this support, a file transfer can exceed the buffering capability of the receiving computer, resulting in data loss or abnormal termination of the file transfer.

Data Capture

Data capture, also called *downloading*, is the process of storing received data in memory or in a disk file. Most communications applications require this capability. Some packages enable data capture directly to a disk file, whereas others only enable data capture to random access memory for later storage in a disk file. Some packages provide both options. Most personal-communications applications require direct-to-disk capture capability, but many business applications require the memory-capture option because the captured data must be modified before they are sent to a disk file or because the file-transfer rate is too great for capturing data on a diskette.

Data capture to memory can provide communications speed-matching at high connection speeds. The capture buffer is a portion of unused RAM set aside to temporarily store received data. Most software designers provide at least 20 KB of capture buffer. To keep the receive buffer from overflowing and to enable operation with small receive buffers, some communications packages also can be set up to automatically dump the capture buffer contents to a disk file when the buffer becomes full. For the transfer of large files, a large capture buffer and automatic buffer dump are recommended.

Data capture to a memory buffer has several advantages over data capture directly to disk, including the following:

✔ It is at least two times faster than data captured directly to disk.

✔ It can usually be toggled on and off by pressing a single key or clicking the mouse pointer on a symbol. The toggle enables a user to capture segments of received data instead of capturing and storing all incoming data.

✔ It can be easily and quickly erased if the user decides not to save the data to disk. Hand in hand with that advantage, however, is the disadvantage that data captured to memory can be easily lost because of power surges or errors that require the system to be reset as part of the recovery process.

Despite these advantages, data capture to a hard disk is the best option for the following reasons:

✔ A hard disk enables data transfer from memory to a file at high speed.

✔ Data stored on disk is nonvolatile and is not lost in the event of a power failure during the file download.

This option is more expensive than data capture to memory or disk because of the cost of the disk, but the data integrity and transfer speed can easily justify the extra cost.

In addition to the selection of where to capture data, some communications packages enable the user to select the type of data to be captured. The user can elect to capture only incoming data transmitted from a remote system, only data entered from the local PC keyboard, or both incoming and outgoing data. This option is good for business applications, but most personal applications do not require it. If only local keyboard input is being captured, a file can be opened and a series of batch-mode commands entered into the file. Then the file can be closed and immediately put into operation. Frequent use of this option can improve the efficiency of data communications and reduce communications cost for a business.

Data Upload

The term *upload* describes the process of transferring a local disk file to a remote host system. Both business and personal communications applications make use of this capability to transfer files containing memos, reports, data, or software to remote computer systems. File transfer protocols are normally used to ensure error-free data transfer, as discussed in Chapter 5, "Communications Error Correction."

Some communications software enables data to be transferred directly from memory to the communications port. This option requires the user to transfer the file to a memory work area, and then send the file out through the communications link. Such a capability reduces the workload placed on a disk drive when frequent file transfers are performed.

Upload Throttle

When files are being uploaded to a mainframe system, it may be necessary to match the file transfer rate with the response of the mainframe. Some large host systems do not enable you to send a line of data until you are prompted to do so. The prompt can be a letter, character, number, or combination of all three, and it is a signal indicating that the mainframe is prepared to receive more data. Data sent before the prompt is received are usually lost. Uploading a file to such a system without providing a mechanism to wait for prompts results in the truncation of each line; a later listing of the file shows the beginning of each line missing. To match the upload speed of the PC with the system response of a mainframe, it is sometimes necessary to throttle the upload.

Communications software packages provide several types of upload throttles. The three major types are time delays, character-receipt delays, and character prompt delays. A *time-delay throttle* enables the user to select the length of time delay between the upload of each line of data. A *character-receipt delay throttle* enables the user to specify the number of characters that must be received from the mainframe before a new line of data is uploaded. A *character-prompt delay* enables the user to specify the exact character string that must be received from the mainframe before a new line of data is sent.

Of the three types of upload throttles, the time-delay throttle is the least effective because it requires the user to specify the longest expected mainframe response; selecting a long time delay to reduce the probability of losing transmitted data can result in long and costly data transfers. The character-receipt delay is effective if the mainframe continues to properly receive data. If an error occurs and the mainframe begins to reject data, the PC continues to transmit data if the proper number of characters (error messages in this case) keep coming in over the data line. The character-prompt delay is the most effective because it ensures that data are transmitted only when the proper signal is received from the mainframe.

Upload Local Echo

For file transfers performed without a file transfer protocol, such as the upload of a text file to a host text editor, a software package can include a provision for displaying the data as they are transferred. A communications novice may need this type of feature to prevent improper file transfers. If a user selects the wrong file to upload to a host or bulletin board system, the user may have no way of discovering the error. With local echo of the file during transmission, operator errors can be noted and file transmission aborted, saving the user time. The same is true for downloading text files. While viewing a file being downloaded, a user can elect to abort the download process if the file turns out to be the wrong one or contains unexpected data.

The disadvantage of local echo during a file transfer is that the screen scrolling slows down the movement of data on the receiving end. This is normally not a problem when the PC system unit operates fast enough to keep pace with the incoming data. Screen display can be a problem for slow system units.

Binary Data Transfer

A business communications package must enable the transfer of non-ASCII files. It is often necessary to transfer machine-code files to protect the source code from being stolen or modified by users. Users also may need to transfer binary data such as spreadsheets and word processing text files. Some communications software cannot send or receive machine code because some of the binary strings contained in the files appear as end-of-file markers causing the transmit or receive mode to terminate abnormally. Communications software can be designed to overcome this problem and is usually required for business applications.

File Transfer Protocols

The term *file transfer protocol* refers to special error-checking techniques used during file transfers. Several of these techniques are used in communications software, but they generally do the same thing. The protocol signals (sometimes called *handshaking*) used by these packages enable them to transfer text, data, and machine-code files, and to perform sophisticated error-checking to make sure that files are transferred properly. The handicap in using these protocol file-transfer techniques is that the computers on both ends of the communications link must be using compatible software; no standard exists that controls these protocols, and no two are exactly alike. This means that a business must standardize its communications software to take advantage of protocol transfers.

Besides enabling the user to transfer machine-code files, the protocol technique offers the following advantages:

✔ Some protocols enable transfer of multiple files by enabling the user to invoke "wild card" commands in much the same way as multiple files can be copied to a printer from a PC. All files with a particular extension or with a specific string as part of their file name can be transferred by entering one file transfer command.

✔ Data are transferred in blocks and some packages enable the user to select the block size. Each block is checked for transmission errors and blocks containing errors are retransmitted.

✔ The error checks performed under protocol file transfer are usually of the *cyclic redundancy check* (CRC) type described in Chapter 5. The CRC is a mathematically computed checksum, and its value is uniquely calculated for each block of data. Chapter 5 describes the features and functions provided by the most popular PC file transfer protocols including Xmodem, Ymodem, Zmodem, and Kermit.

Data Manipulation Features

Smart-terminal software enables the user to select certain options that pertain to received or transmitted data manipulation. The following paragraphs describe some of these features.

Line Feed Control

Not all communications software packages add line feeds after each carriage return received or transmitted. Business communications software should enable the user to decide whether line feeds should be sent following each carriage return or added after each received carriage return. Without this capability, transferred files may have to be edited to remove or add line feeds, and conversation-mode communications may be difficult to perform.

The need for line-feed control depends upon the operation in progress. If a line feed is being added to each transmitted line by a remote system and another one is being added by the PC's communications package, the received data will have a blank line between each line of data. If line feeds are not being added to the end of each transmitted line by the host, and the PC's communications package is not adding one, the data received by the PC cannot be listed and edited until line feeds are added. If data are being received in the conversation mode and neither the PC software nor the remote station software is adding line feeds at the ends of data lines, each line will overprint the previous line on the PC monitor, making it difficult for the user to read the data.

Blank Line Expansion

Some host-computer software packages change modes of operation in response to blank lines; this requires the use of communications software that eliminates undesired mode changes. The message-receive functions of many e-mail systems change from the message input mode to the message edit mode when a blank line is received. The file-creation mode of some mainframe editors also changes from the input mode to the edit mode when a blank line is received. A line containing only a carriage return means "end of text" to these systems. To avoid mode changes when the user wants to upload text containing blank lines to such a system, a communications package must convert lines containing only a carriage return into a space followed by a carriage return—a technique called *blank line expansion.*

Character Filter

Some mainframe and microcomputer communications software transmit control characters. These characters do not print on most computer terminals, but the characters are printed on a PC monitor. To eliminate these annoying and some-times confusing characters, it is necessary for software to filter them out of the incoming stream of data. Some PC software packages enable the user to turn the filter on or off by executing a command string. Business applications that require remote demonstrations of software running on a computer that transmits control characters would benefit from the filter option.

Translation Table

Translation tables enable the user to redefine incoming or outgoing character codes. Any of 256 ASCII character codes can be redefined so that a different character is passed back to the PC than the one represented by received data, or a character is sent out of the communications port different from the one entered at the keyboard. ASCII code can be converted into EBCDIC code or vice versa. Certain characters can be redefined as nulls or spaces or can be left out of the translation table entirely to filter out incoming or outgoing data.

Terminal Emulation

Another form of the translation table is called *terminal emulation.* Terminal emula-tion in a communications hardware package enables a user to communicate with a host system set up to communicate only with a specific type of terminal. Terminal emulation causes the PC to act almost exactly as the type of terminal the host is programmed to expect. Terminals often emulated include the Digital Equipment Corporation VT 52 and VT 100 and the IBM 3101 because of their popularity in business computing. Because some communications packages are dedicated to

terminal emulation, this capability is explored at greater length later in this chapter.

Data Compression

Some smart-terminal software packages support data compression to improve the throughput of data between two computers. Data compression is the conversion of repeated bit patterns to coded bit patterns that reduce the total number of bits transferred during a communications session. The receiving computer must perform data expansion to reconstruct the original bit patterns compressed by the sending computer. To work properly, the communications software on both ends of the communications link must use matching data compression and data expansion techniques. This technique is used in the BLAST communications software, the MNP protocol, and the Kermit file transfer protocol to reduce file transfer time by as much as 50 percent for text, data, and binary files.

Care must be taken in the use of data compression. Many modems today provide data compression that conforms with the ITU-T V.42bis standard. If two modems negotiate the use of this technique at the start of a communications session, data compression provided in the communications software would be redundant with that provided in the modem hardware. This redundancy could actually result in a slower transfer of data during the session than could be achieved with modem-hardware compression alone.

Data Encryption

Some smart-terminal software packages support data encryption to provide communication security between two computers. Data encryption normally uses a cryptography key to encipher transmitted bit patterns and decipher received bit patterns continuously during a communications session. To work properly, the communications software on both ends of the communications link must use matching enciphering and deciphering techniques. Because of the computing overhead required to encipher and decipher data, this feature often is provided with an option to turn the data encryption on and off. Such an option is often used in terminal-emulation software that provides IBM SNA compatibility.

Case Conversion

Many older computer systems do not recognize lowercase letters. Some of these systems automatically convert lowercase to uppercase, but many systems do not perform that function. To overcome this problem, a PC software package must perform the conversion from lowercase letters to uppercase letters before the characters are transmitted.

Tab-to-Space Conversion

Some PC text processors, such as the IBM Personal Editor, use tab (Control+I) characters to represent spaces in stored files. These tab characters save valuable disk space by representing up to eight spaces each. Other systems, however, do not always follow the same convention. To keep files that contain tab characters intact, it may be necessary to convert tab characters into spaces. Several PC communications packages enable the user to turn this automatic conversion on and off by executing a command from the keyboard.

Special Features

Smart-terminal software packages often provide other features that do not fall into any well-defined category. The following sections describe these special features.

Split Screen

When communicating with another person or a group of people through a data communications link, it is less confusing to have a split-screen communications option. When the communications package splits the screen horizontally, displaying received characters in one window and transmitted characters in another window, the PC can both transmit and receive text without confusing the user. Without a split screen, simultaneously transmitted and received text cannot be distinguished. The split screen is especially useful for on-line conferencing. The Microsoft Windows and OS/2 Presentation Manager graphical user interfaces provide excellent tools to provide this split-screen technique.

Elapsed Time of Call

It is convenient to have an *elapsed-time-of-call indicator* when communicating with a time-sharing information service. Information services generally charge a rate based on connect time, so the elapsed-time indicator can help a user save connect-time costs. This feature also can serve as a reminder of costs when calling a long-distance number to get in contact with a remote computer system.

Break Signal

Many mainframe and some information services require a *break signal* to interrupt program execution. A communications package should be able to send a 200-to-600 millisecond sustained high signal (equivalent to a logical 0) with either a single or a dual key stroke. This signal can interrupt program execution or get the immediate attention of an information-service system. Most software packages fix the duration of the break signal, but some enable the user to specify the signal length.

Note that the break signal is not the same as the PC Ctrl+Break key combination. The Ctrl+Break is actually a Ctrl+C and is used in some software applications to terminate the execution of the software. The communications break signal is a sustained voltage signal (not a control character) and does not interrupt the operation of the user's software.

Remote Takeover

Some PC communications packages enable remote users to call in and take over the operation of a personal computer. To perform this function, both the remote and local PC systems normally have to be equipped with communications software from the same vendor. Businesses can use this capability to transfer files without having to provide computer operators at both ends of the communications link. A branch office can send a file to a branch office in another time zone either before or after the normal working hours of the receiving office. This capability also is used to provide help desk support for remote users; the help desk calls in and executes software on your PC while you watch or participate in the operation.

Disk Directory Listing

The capability to list the disk directories of all disk drives is another good communications software feature. When uploading files, this function enables the user to select files for transfer. When downloading files, this function enables the user to select file names not currently in use. If the package stores communications parameters in disk files, the disk directory listing provides the user with a menu of parameter files. For packages that support batch file operation, this option enables the user to view the menu of available batch files.

External File Manipulation

Users often need to delete old files as new ones are being created during a communications session. Users also may need to rename files created by a communications software package (for example, a command file) or files improperly named during file downloading. Users may further need to run an external program or execute an operating system program (for example, FORMAT or CHKDSK) during a communications session. These operations can be done more quickly and easily if the user can perform them without exiting the software package. The PC communications packages that provide these options can save time and money when file transfers are frequently performed.

Return to Operating System

The capability of a communications package to return the user to the operating system is often overlooked when a package is being evaluated. A user should not have to reboot the system unit each time a communications session is completed. A user should be able to terminate communications and return to the operating system to perform other computer operations by entering a simple command. Many packages program a function key or the Alt key combined with another key to provide a shortcut back to the operating system. Other packages require that the user go through a series of menus before returning to the operating system. Either option is acceptable, but the single- or dual-key shortcut is faster to execute and easier to remember.

Some packages enable the user to return to the operating system without breaking the telephone connection with a remote system. This feature enables the testing of a downloaded program to make sure that it was properly received before terminating the connection to the remote system. It also enables the user to view a downloaded file, and then return to finish the communications session.

Background Operation

Several communications packages support a background mode during certain operations. They provide background operation of time-consuming tasks such as file transfers. Software packages that enable file transfers in a background mode also enable the user to perform other foreground tasks while the file transfer is executing. Other packages enable the communications software to reside in RAM but remain in the background until needed. The user can press a hot key to bring the software operation to the foreground.

Some communications packages offer compatibility with multitasking operating environments such as DESQview, Microsoft Windows, and Operating System/2 (OS/2). These environments enable the user to switch from one active or foreground task to another. This feature provides the user more flexibility in communications and often reduces the time required to switch between communications and another task.

Background communications software has several limitations that must be understood in order to prevent communications failures. These limitations are as follows:

✔ Loading more than one software package into a background "stay resident" mode can cause interrupt conflicts such that the operation of one package interferes with the operation of another.

✔ Communications software has to be tightly coupled to the PC hardware to respond quickly enough to support high data throughput rates; this tight coupling prevents communications software from being swapped to disk in a multitasking environment.

✔ Background operations, such as file transfers, must adhere to a strict set of rules to prevent file creation and expansion damage to other files being simultaneously created or changed by a foreground task.

Good background operation software takes care of these limitations for the user and explains the limitations in the accompanying documentation. OS/2 provides excellent support for both foreground and background communications in a multitasking environment.

Evaluating Communications Software

The evaluation and selection of a communications package may not be an easy task. Changing needs and capabilities in a business environment and changing budgets in a personal situation contribute to the complexity; but as happens with other software packages, decisions have to be based on the best information available at the time.

The initial approach to selecting a software package is first to assess communications needs. A list of essential features should be developed, followed by a list of nonessential, but desirable, features. Only then should you consider available communications software packages.

To place communications packages in proper perspective, it is a good practice to produce an evaluation matrix similar to the one shown in table 10.2. Information can be recorded on such a matrix by reviewing the manuals provided with software packages. Newsletters and magazines also publish software reviews containing data that can be used in completing the matrix. Local PC users' groups often have a *special-interest group* (SIG) dedicated to communications. Information can be obtained through conversations with the members of such a group. You also can solicit software vendors for information; many of them have toll-free telephone numbers.

Table 10.2
Smart Terminal Communications Software Matrix

Software Feature	Package #1	Package #2
Operating system required		
Manual and auto-dial modem support		
Modem speed flexibility		

continues

Table 10.2, Continued
Smart Terminal Communications Software Matrix

Software Feature	Package #1	Package #2
Documentation manual		
User help		
User support		
Error handling		
Parameter selection		
Duplex-mode selection		
Command files		
Batch mode		
Clock-controlled operation		
Predefined strings		
Password storage security		
Originate/answer mode switch		
Dialing directory		
Auto-redial		
Telephone hang-up		
Data capture to printer		
XON/XOFF protocol		
Capture to memory		
Capture to disk		
Data capture selection		
Data upload		
Upload throttle		

Software Feature	Package #1	Package #2
Upload local echo		
Binary data transfer		
File transfer protocols		
Line feed control		
Blank line expansion		
Character filter		
Translation table		
Terminal emulation		
Data compression		
Data encryption		
Case conversion		
Tab-to-space conversion		
Split Screen		
Elapsed time of call		
Break signal handling		
Remote takeover		
Disk directory listing		
External file manipulation		
Return to operating system		
Background operation		

II

Data Communications

Experience using a package is a valuable part of determining your communications needs. Public-domain and inexpensive BASIC programs are excellent learning tools. A user can experiment with these programs and learn a great deal about communications through trial and error. Many bulletin board and public host systems operating in major metropolitan areas can be used as guinea pigs during this learning process.

Terminal-Emulation Software

Terminal emulation, according to the strict data communications definition, comes in the form of hardware only. Emulation done in software is *terminal simulation.* Most software vendors use the term *emulation* to describe the terminal simulation their software performs, and that definition is used here.

Terminal emulation enables a user to communicate with a host system that expects a specific type of terminal; it causes the PC to act almost exactly as the type of terminal the host expects. Many vendors provide emulation of the Digital Equipment Corporation VT and the IBM 3101 asynchronous terminals because of their popularity in business computing. Many vendors also provide emulation of the IBM 3270 series of synchronous terminals.

Terminal emulation usually pertains to keyboard key assignments and screen displays. Terminal-emulation software translates certain PC key combinations to character strings normally produced by the keys of the emulated terminal. Terminal-emulation software also translates received character strings to strings that cause the PC screen display to perform like the emulated terminal. These screen control characters are escape codes. They clear the screen, locate the cursor in a specific row and column, and control screen attributes such as reverse video and blinking characters. The following list shows additional terminal-emulation features found in several commercial products.

- ✔ Supports graphics displays

- ✔ Provides user-programmable keys

- ✔ Enables multiple configurations to match several hosts

- ✔ Provides command or hot key switch to/from PC-DOS

- ✔ Provides smooth scrolling of screen text

- ✔ Enables the user to select color combinations

- ✔ Provides true underlining of text

- ✔ Provides or simulates boldface characters

- ✔ Displays double-high, double-wide characters

- ✔ Provides on-line help

When the PC includes terminal emulation, the user can access and use a remote host system without keyboard and screen display incompatibilities. The other two alternatives to terminal emulation are emulation on the host end of the communications link and emulation between the PC and the host. The host can be programmed to respond to PC keyboard input and to transmit screen controls the PC understands. This emulation enables the host and the PC to work efficiently and effectively as a team.

You also can combine terminal emulation with code and protocol translators to set up communications with a host computer. These translators normally connect asynchronous devices to a synchronous network that uses BSC and SDLC protocols. An example of such a device is the IBM 7171. This protocol converter enables IBM 3101 terminal or PCs with 3101 terminal emulation software to access a host that works with 3278 or 3279 synchronous terminals. Translators and converters eliminate the compatibility problems associated with vendor-specific protocols typical of host computers and older model word processors.

You can combine terminal emulation and local area networks to simulate the operation of terminals connected to a cluster controller or control unit. When a PC contains terminal-emulation software and connects to the network, the user can access a remote mainframe computer and execute programs or edit files. If the host does not support direct connection to the network, a gateway on the network acts as a traffic cop to direct the flow of data to and from the host. A single Token Ring network allows up to 260 microcomputers to access an IBM host with this technique. Using the PC as a mainframe terminal can be cost effective because the cost of a personal computer is sometimes less than the cost of a stand-alone mainframe terminal. A PC equipped with terminal-emulation hardware and software also eliminates the need for both a personal computer and a host-specific terminal.

Unattended Asynchronous Communications Software

Although considered by many as a hobbyist application, unattended communications systems have become popular in business and personal data communications applications. During the past ten years, unattended communications systems have gone from home-grown bulletin boards to powerful business support systems. This type of software provides many communications novices with their first taste of communications between personal computers. After this experience, many PC users are ready to move on to more powerful applications of unattended host, bulletin board, and e-mail systems run by the country's largest information suppliers.

Many software vendors have released powerful and useful unattended communications systems for the PC. The Close-Up and Carbon Copy packages are excellent examples of *remote takeover systems* (RTSs). The Major BBS and the PC Board are examples of *bulletin board systems* (BBSs) that provide e-mail, file transfers, and the execution of external programs. These commercial packages, usually written in the C programming language, provide high performance and rich functionality. A few unattended communications packages still around today are written in interpreter or compiled BASIC, but many packages that started this way have subsequently been translated to C.

Several unattended communications systems are available that provide an introduction to this type of software at low cost. The *Remote Bulletin Board System for the PC* (RBBS-PC) is a good example of this type of software. Originally ported from the CP/M operating system to run on the IBM PC in 1982, this software has become a favorite for weekend software hackers and hobbyists. Members of the Capital PC Users Group in Washington, D.C., have been instrumental in the enhancement and distribution of this software since its original port to the PC.

Remote Software in Perspective

Users often categorize remote communications systems as remote takeover, bulletin board, or e-mail systems, but systems are available that provide all three capabilities in one package. Figure 10.5 illustrates the difference between remote takeover and bulletin board systems. As you can see from this figure, an RTS-equipped personal computer primarily provides remote program operation, whereas a BBS-equipped personal computer primarily provides message exchange.

Figure 10.5
Remote takeover and bulletin board systems.

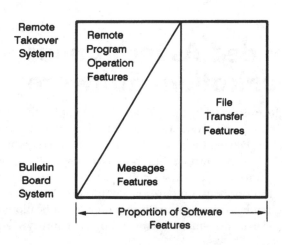

A remote takeover system can accept calls from remote terminals and execute commands received through the serial port in the same way that it executes local keyboard commands. A bulletin board system, on the other hand, can store messages received from a remote computer and transmit messages to that same remote computer. Some special-purpose bulletin board systems can automatically transmit and receive messages; these systems are e-mail systems.

Normally, both RTS and BBS software can receive and transmit files. Some e-mail systems also enable you to transmit files as attachments to messages or mail. These systems enable users to transfer ASCII text files and binary program and data files between a local microcomputer and a remote, unattended PC. Special error-checking protocols transfer the files and correct errors caused by the telephone system.

Remote Software Capabilities

Unattended communications software can be used as both a personal and business productivity tool. Besides eliminating the need for an operator at one end of the communications link, these packages offer strong support for specific types of information exchange. The following paragraphs explore the practical uses of this software. Later sections of this chapter explore the capabilities associated with specific types of unattended systems.

Practical Applications

Bulletin board software can serve as a tool for enhancing productivity and scheduling. How many times have you wanted to get information to members of a group quickly and had to resort to letters or post cards because of the lead time required for normal group newsletters? Have you ever had a need to collect written text or data from several sources on a tight schedule but had to wait for several days for the information to arrive by mail? Unattended remote communications software can solve these problems for you while providing other data-transfer power.

Availability Mismatches

Unattended communications software eliminates the need to have two communicating parties available simultaneously to transfer files or data. With unattended software operating on a 24-hour-a-day basis, other parties can call in and leave or retrieve messages or transfer data at any time, day or night, without disturbing the system operator. An author can work halfway through the night and still meet a 9:00 a.m. deadline halfway across the continent by transmitting the work to a remote, unattended PC when he or she finishes the work. Many newsletter and magazine editors who use unattended communications software to collect articles appreciate the lack of operator attention required with these systems. They go to bed the night before an article deadline date and awake the next morning to find a disk full of valuable information.

Availability mismatches also occur between company offices located in different time zones. Remote takeover and bulletin board software provides an extra three-hour communications period in the mornings and evenings for offices located on opposite United States coasts. Reports, data, or messages can be transferred while the recipient is still at home asleep or watching the evening news.

Order Taking

Bulletin board systems often serve as electronic order-taking devices. The system presents callers with bulletins on the latest merchandise available and enables them to order from a menu by selecting a number associated with an item of interest. The software also may take charge card information and validate the identity of callers based on data stored in an on-line database. This application of bulletin board software enables a retailer to get notices of product and price changes to potential customers quickly. It also speeds up the ordering process by eliminating mailing delays.

Tool for the Handicapped

Bulletin board software is a useful communications tool for the hearing and speech impaired. Information on upcoming social or educational group events can be posted on an electronic bulletin board to eliminate or augment the need for telephone answering machines or operators. Information left on a telephone answering machine is of no use to the deaf and people with certain hearing impairments. Bulletin board software not only provides these people with information, it enables them to interact with the system to select specific information of interest. The BBS also enables the users to exchange messages with others who have similar impairments.

Transport Elimination

Unattended communications software can eliminate the shipping or mailing of information or software. Some situations make the transport of information (both printed matter and electronically stored data) impractical, and thus can make good use of remote, unattended communications software. Some hospitals eliminate the need to decontaminate notes and records made in infectious disease wards by entering the information into a terminal located in the contaminated area. The information transfers electronically to a remote bulletin board system in a "clean" area of the hospital. This electronic transfer of information saves the hospital time and money by eliminating complex physical decontamination procedures.

True RTS "host" software gives a PC owner the power of his or her computer from any location equipped with a terminal, modem, and public telephone. An unattended host software system enables a remote caller to take over the PC and

operate it through a telephone link almost as if the caller is sitting at the PC's keyboard. A person can take a laptop or portable computer on a trip and use any remote telephone connection to tap into his or her PC at home if it includes an RTS software package. A writer can create a news article during an airline flight to a distant location and then transmit the article back to a PC at home from his or her hotel room. The only limitation to host software application is the user's imagination.

Software Support

Many software vendors have found remote takeover systems invaluable in the support of their software packages. A software vendor can dial into a remote computer equipped with both an RTS and the vendor's software. The RTS enables the vendor to execute the software on the PC to diagnose a problem or to help the user understand how to use the vendor's software. The user can watch the operation to learn more about the vendor's software package or participate in the execution of the vendor's software as part of a training exercise. This type of remote operation can save a vendor many hours during problem diagnosis. It also can save a user the same number of hours in learning to use a new package.

Group E-mail

A PC equipped with an unattended e-mail system can eliminate travel and enhance communications between the members of a working group. Two or more of these systems can exchange messages and mail between group members at specific times of day or on a 24-hour-a-day basis. Users can submit mail for delivery to a remote system by simply designating the name of the recipient. The e-mail system stores the mail and then calls the remote system to deliver the mail. These PC-based systems can act on a stand-alone basis or with a local area network.

Remote Takeover Software

Remote takeover software, as its name implies, enables callers to dial in and take over the operation of a remote PC. Figure 10.6 shows the logical connection between the local and remote PC. This type of communications requires a matching set of software on the local and remote PCs. The PC that supports remote takeover is an *asynchronous remote takeover server* (ARTS). The ARTS software normally runs in a hidden, background mode on the remote PC and supports asynchronous communications with, and complete takeover of operation from, a remote PC. The PC that performs the remote takeover must execute an *asynchronous remote takeover terminal* (ARTT) version of the same software in a foreground mode. The ARTS and ARTT software work together to ensure synchronization of operation between the local and remote computer.

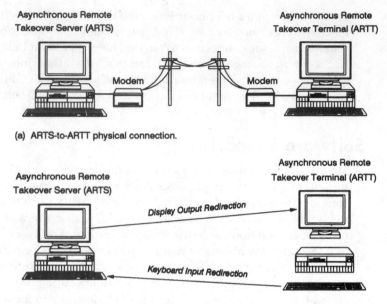

Figure 10.6
Remote takeover
software logical
connection.

(a) ARTS-to-ARTT physical connection.

(b) ARTS-to-ARTT logical connection.

After a successful security screening, the keyboard and the screen of the local
ARTT PC and the remote ARTS PC act as one. A copy of all screen output on the
remote PC is trapped by the ARTS software running in the background on that
computer and sent out by the communications port. The local ARTT-equipped PC
receives that output and produces the same display results that appear on the
ARTS-equipped computer. Similarly, the ARTT and ARTS software work together
to make keyboard input from either the local or remote computer perform the
same functions at the ARTS-equipped computer.

The ARTS software can operate in a stand-alone or LAN-attached personal
computer. First, it can run in the background while a work station user executes
either stand-alone or LAN-based application software in the foreground on the
same PC. Second, it can operate in a LAN-attached PC set up solely for remote
access to the LAN. In the first mode, the ARTS enables either the local or remote
user to initiate a call to link the ARTS and ARTT computers. In the second mode,
a distant ARTT computer can dial into a modem connected to the LAN-attached
ARTS computer and execute LAN-based software. The ARTS and ARTT software
packages must work together and work with the LAN operating system to provide
proper support for remote takeover of the ARTS workstation/server.

Although the ARTS/ARTT combination provides only a one-on-one relationship
between the ARTS server and the remote ARTT terminal, this type of software is
invaluable for remote support of software applications. This software pair enables

the ARTT user to execute software on the ARTS computer while enabling users at both ends of the link to observe the screen output from the software. Both the local and remote user can interact simultaneously with application software executing in the foreground mode on the ARTS-equipped PC. This software combination also enables an ARTT user to dial into the ARTS computer and run any stand-alone or LAN-based software at full ARTS-computer execution speed.

RTS software can provide great productivity enhancements for remote execution of applications or for problem diagnosis. Although many features contained in different commercial RTS packages are similar, some subtle differences may determine the success or failure of an implementation in a specific situation. Because of the uniqueness of some user needs, it is important to understand the characteristics and capabilities available in RTS software before purchasing a package. The following list contains typical RTS software features.

- ✔ Configuration control
- ✔ System security
- ✔ Remote dial-in
- ✔ Software execution
- ✔ Error correction
- ✔ File transfers
- ✔ User-to-user chat
- ✔ Screen capture
- ✔ Remote printer support
- ✔ System logs

As you can see from the features normally contained in RTS software, this type of software can provide powerful communications services. Companies use RTS software to perform remote tests of systems and to update software contained on these remote systems. Companies also use RTS packages in training programs that educate remote users on the features and functions of application packages. Specific employees also can use RTS to perform work from home. These users dial into their ART-equipped PCs at work to perform application operations from home. Although RTS software packages provide a robust set of communications features and functions, they may not meet certain communications requirements. Organizations that need systems that support groups in the transfer of information, files, and messages will find the unattended software described in the following section more appropriate than RTS. Bulletin board systems are discussed next, followed by a discussion of e-mail systems.

Bulletin Board Systems

Bulletin board systems are by far the most popular unattended communications software. These systems provide access to wide varieties of information, from serious business ventures to home-computer games. From a grass roots beginning, the BBS developed into a powerful business tool along with the PC. The original BBS software came from the homes of personal computer hobbyists. This software was in interpreter BASIC and widely distributed without charge to anyone interested. More recent implementations, written in either the C language or assembler, are full commercial packages.

The wide distribution of BBS software is good for the PC owner because these packages provide a good place for you to get started with PC communications with a small investment. You need a PC, modem, and smart-terminal communications package to dial into one of these systems and browse to your heart's content. Most BBS packages work in the TTY output mode, which means you do not have to run in any specific terminal emulation mode for proper screen and keyboard operations. The simplest and least expensive terminal communications configuration works with these systems.

Although the operation of a BBS is transparent to most callers, the details of its operation are important to someone interested in setting up and operating one for the first time. Tables 10.3 and 10.4 provide lists of typical BBS features.

Table 10.3
Bulletin Board System Features

Configuration Control:	
Remote access code	Expert mode
Ring-back control	Disk drive assignments
System file designation	Prompt sounds
Maximum time on system	Maximum number of messages
User inactivity limit	Number of system bulletins
User activity display	Communication port
Modem sound control	Operator availability
Caller options	Local display
Help files	Communication parameters

File Transfer:	
File directories	Error-checking protocol
XON/XOFF protocol	File statistics

Chat Mode:	
Available hours	Operator paging

System Options:	
Case conversion	Line feeds
Nulls	Prompt sounds
Screen size	Expert mode
Terminal emulation	

Message Subsystem:	
Message privacy	SYSOP comments
Message scan	Message word processor

System Logs:	
Caller log	User database
Database maintenance	

Remote Takeover:	
Remote execution	File protection

Reliability:	
Normal operation	Abnormal operation

Table 10.4
Bulletin Board System Operator Controls

Necessary Controls:

System bulletin, menu, and file revisions

Message entry and deletion

User database listing and modification

Selective user lockout

Disk file directory listing

Disk file viewing

File directory modifications

Listing of caller comments file

Deletion of caller comments file

Modification of caller time limit

Modification of system default parameters

Desirable Controls:

Caller log statistical analysis

Caller log deletion

User database statistical analysis

Disk and file directory mismatch analysis

Password-protected remote takeover

As you can see from the remote takeover and bulletin board characteristics and capabilities just described, this type of software can provide the PC with significant unattended communications power. Another type of special-purpose unattended communications software, however, also is popular with PC owners. E-mail software enables the PC to send and receive messages between one or more users. This software, described in the following paragraphs, does not require an active user at either end.

E-Mail Software

E-mail software and the bulletin board software just described have many things in common, but e-mail software usually provides more powerful message delivery capabilities. Bulletin boards enable the system operator or callers to leave messages for other callers, but callers do not receive the messages unless they call the bulletin board.

Commercial store-and-forward systems, such as the e-mail subsystems in Prodigy and CompuServe, provide more sophisticated versions of this passive *computer-based mail system* (CBMS) design. The power of these CBMS systems, however, can be tapped only if message recipients actively participate in the process. The user must periodically call into the CBMS to retrieve messages.

A CBMS is a good choice of message system if message recipients have access to only dumb terminals. These store-and-forward facilities enable several widely dispersed users to exchange mail. The advantage of CBMS systems is that users do not have to purchase computers and e-mail software; they just call the store-and-forward service and send or retrieve their mail as required. The trade-off is network-service subscription and connection costs for a commercially operated facility versus long distance telephone rates and a dedicated microcomputer required to operate a private e-mail system.

PC owners have another alternative. If the PC owner is willing to leave the computer unattended and dedicated to communications, e-mail software can be used to send and receive messages, reports, and files. A PC can be set up in a business office as an electronic intraoffice memo system to eliminate "telephone tag" and to reduce the frequency of face-to-face meetings.

The increase in office productivity produced by an e-mail system can easily justify the cost of the computers and the dedicated telephone lines needed to establish the "PC network." You can set up such a system just for local calls. The exchange of messages outside the local area takes place through commercial CBMS facilities or public data networks to reduce long-distance telephone costs.

The major advantage of unattended e-mail systems is the control they provide the local operator. An e-mail system operating on a PC can provide all the capabilities of commercial CBMS software in addition to control over the delivery and delivery timing of information. You can tell the system when to deliver certain messages and files, and the system automatically calls other systems to deliver the specified information at the specified times.

Table 10.5 lists the features included in some PC-based e-mail packages. PC-based e-mail systems usually work with standard PC hardware containing limited disk space. The system features assume that a single individual or small group will use the e-mail system, and that each user will have system operator privileges. There are no callers in the same sense as bulletin board operation because the software and hardware do the calling without operator attendance.

Table 10.6
E-mail Software Features

System Customization:	
System configuration	
Correspondence Addressing:	
Assign mailboxes	Group addressing
Hidden distribution	Address maintenance
Send Mail:	
Send to mailbox	Send to list
Send to phone number	Blind copy
Reply requested	Express delivery
Registered mail	Delayed delivery
Outgoing mail	Automatic retry
Protocol transfer	
Receive Mail:	
Mail scan	Mail search
Display mail	Print mail
Forward mail	Reply to mail
Delete log entry	Save mail file
Delete mail file	
File Maintenance:	
File editing	Choice of editor
File merge	

Miscellaneous:	
On-line help	Input prompting
Single-level password	Multilevel password
Calendar	Correspondence template
Data base update	Gateways

E-mail Gateways

E-mail systems can sometimes be used as gateways to other types of electronic communication services. They can be used to send messages to an unattended TELEX machine. Gateways also can send and receive messages from e-mail systems made by other vendors. For example, a local system may be set up to send messages from local users to remote users through the e-mail capabilities of service providers. Many e-mail systems also provide routing through MCI Mail so that hard copies of messages are delivered to users who do not have data communications. These are valuable connections for local in-house systems that must communicate with other offices.

The international X.400 e-mail standard will provide the common denominator for message exchange between dissimilar e-mail systems in the future. This Open System Interconnect protocol ensures compatibility between the source and destination information contained in e-mail messages to ensure proper delivery of the messages despite the number of systems they pass through. The ITU-T X.500 recommendations define the directory services that X.400-compliant systems must use to determine the proper destination address of the intended recipient of a message. This recommendation defines a database for mail recipients equivalent to the telephone White and Yellow pages.

As e-mail becomes more widespread and sophisticated, an increasing number of features will become available. Integration of unattended e-mail systems into other applications is an area of continued growth. Examples of these combinations are the merging of voice, data, and image into electronic form. The systems store this data on a hard disk or optical disk for delivery to other users. E-mail systems are also moving into the financial world through *Electronic Data Interchange* (EDI). These systems enable corporations and government agencies to exchange electronic documents and make financial transactions without the need for paper or human interactions. Most of these electronic interchange systems are in their infancy. As their level of sophistication increases, users and consumers will have additional options for service transactions not available today.

Evaluating Unattended Communications Software

Because of the number of aspects a PC owner must consider when selecting an unattended communications package, the task of making a single choice can be overwhelming. To make the task easier, you should take a structured approach, similar to the approach shown for terminal communications software.

The first task in selecting a package is to assess unattended communications needs. Develop a list of essential features and a list of nonessential, but desirable, features. Only then should you consider available unattended communications software packages.

To place packages in proper perspective, it is good practice to produce an evaluation matrix similar to the ones shown in tables 10.7, 10.8, and 10.9. After a matrix is completed showing the strengths and weaknesses of packages in a given category, it becomes easier to select the appropriate package.

Table 10.7
Remote Takeover System Evaluation Matrix

Software Features	Pkg #1	Pkg #2	Pkg #3
Configuration Control:			
Select modem type			
Touch tone dialing			
Rotary dialing			
Reboot on hangup			
Select screen type			
Screen update speed			
Action key definition			
Protocol selection			
Printer operation			
Store passwords			

Software Features	Pkg #1	Pkg #2	Pkg #3
System Security:			
Password encryption			
Dial back			
Remote Dial-in:			
Dialing directory			
Password protection			
Software Execution:			
Well behaved			
Other			
Error Correction:			
Stop-and-wait			
Non-stop			
File Transfers:			
Natural commands			
Xmodem protocol			
Ymodem protocol			
Zmodem protocol			
User-to-user Chat:			
Chat window			
Movable window			
Screen Capture:			
Snapshot			

continues

II

Data Communications

Table 10.7, Continued
Remote Takeover System Evaluation Matrix

Software Features	Pkg #1	Pkg #2	Pkg #3
Continuous			
Playback			
Remote Printer Support:			
Remote print			
Local print			
Disable print			
System Logs			

Legend: E = Excellent, G = Good, F = Fair, - = Not supported

Table 10.8
Bulletin Board Software Evaluation Matrix

Software Features	Pkg #1	Pkg #2	Pkg #3
System configuration			
Parameter detect/switch			
File protection			
ASCII file transfer			
Xmodem protocol			
Ymodem protocol			
Zmodem protocol			
XON/XOFF flow control			
File size indicator			
Operator chat mode			
Operator page hours			

Software Features	Pkg #1	Pkg #2	Pkg #3
Case conversion			
Help files			
Message storage			
Message retrieval			
Message maintenance			
Message scan			
Message protection			
Message word processor			
Local snoop toggle			
Log-on bulletin design			
File directory listing			
Directory maintenance			
Callers data log			
Users database			
Users log maintenance			
SYSOP special controls			
Caller defaults recall			
Terminal emulation			
Expert/novice menus			
Remote operation			
Disk area restriction			
Unattended reliability			
Unattended security			

Legend: E = Excellent, G = Good, F = Fair, - = Not supported

II

Data Communications

Table 10.9
E-mail Software Evaluation Matrix

Software Features	Pkg #1	Pkg #2	Pkg #3
System configuration			
Assign mailboxes			
Group addressing			
Hidden distribution			
Address maintenance			
Send to mailbox			
Send to list			
Send to phone number			
Blind copy			
Reply requested			
Express delivery			
Registered mail			
Delayed delivery			
Outgoing mail			
Automatic retry			
Protocol file transfer			
Mail scan			
Mail search			
Display mail			
Print mail			
Forward mail			

Software Features	Pkg #1	Pkg #2	Pkg #3
Reply to mail			
Delete log entry			
Save mail file			
Delete mail file			
File editing			
Choice of editor			
File merge			
On-line help			
Input prompting			
Single-level password			
Multilevel password			
Calendar			
Correspondence template			
Database update			
Gateways			

Legend: E = Excellent, G = Good, F = Fair, - = Not supported

As you can see from tables 10.7, 10.8, and 10.9, significant differences exist between the capabilities and features of the different types of unattended communications packages. Remote takeover software packages provide the greatest level of support for the execution of native software stored on the remote PC. Bulletin board software packages, on the other hand, provide the greatest level of support for information and data exchange among the members of a specific group of callers. Finally, e-mail software provides the greatest level of support for the exchange of mail among the members of a specific group of users. Although all three types of software provide unattended operation and have some overlapping features, they are different in concept and implementation.

II

Data Communications

Because of the differences in packages, it is a good idea to experiment before making a significant commitment to one type of software. Experience using a bulletin board package is a valuable part of determining your communication needs. Public-domain and inexpensive programs such as RBBS-PC are excellent learning tools. A user can experiment with these programs and, through trial and error, discover the power and limitations of unattended software. The RBBS-PC source code, system files, and documentation can be obtained by downloading the files from many public bulletin board systems.

Summary

As you can see from the number of characteristics and considerations described in this chapter, unattended communications software is somewhat complex, but can offer some users great communications power. Unattended communications software provides the PC owner with a communications tool that can both receive and deliver messages to callers. It can also provide callers with software. Unattended communications software also can provide an excellent vehicle for experimentation with the types of smart-terminal software.

Part III

Local Area Networking

Chapter Snapshot

Local area networks have become a key enabling technology for a fundamental shift in the way businesses operate and communicate, both internally and externally. The key to understanding how LANs facilitate group interaction is comprehending the relationship among applications, operating systems, networks, and the specialized software that supports the client-server paradigm. In this chapter, you learn about:

✔ LAN software technology

✔ The LAN software required to support basic file and print services, including redirector-server protocols such as NetWare Core Protocol and Server Message Block

✔ Client-server architecture and its role in groupware applications development

✔ Emerging groupware categories

✔ Major operating systems MS-DOS, OS/2, and Windows NT, and their characteristics that relate to LAN support

✔ Network operating system characteristics and features, including shared resource support, mass storage devices, fault-tolerance, security, and administration

✔ LAN transport protocols used within single networks

CHAPTER 11

Local Area Networks: From the Top Down

In many organizations, a generic class of software known as groupware has begun to affect the way business is conducted. *Groupware* can be loosely defined as software designed to run on a multi-user system and to enable workgroup members to cooperate on closely linked activities. A prime example of groupware is Lotus Notes, which enables a collaborative workgroup to create and share various types of data in a Notes "database." These data types might be relational databases, word processing documents, spreadsheets, or e-mail. Lotus Notes is designed not only to run in a LAN environment, but also in a wide area network (WAN). Individual clients running Notes can dial into centralized bulletin board systems that run server versions of Notes to share information. An excellent example of this is the Virtual College program run by New York University's School of Continuing Education. You can read more about the Virtual College in Chapter 13, "Internetworking and Interoperability."

The capability of certain software packages to run in a network environment does not happen by accident. Like most MS-DOS, Windows NT, or OS/2-based applications, groupware relies upon the PC's host operating system for resource support, including file management, printing, and the user interface. In a LAN environment, the PC operating system must be extended to support the sharing of data between applications running in different physical computers. Likewise, resource management must be extended to cover peripheral devices not connected to the application's host computer. This extension is provided in the form of a network operating system. Finally, software is required that establishes a reliable and accurate connection between the user's application and a particular network service required by the application. This network service may be basic file service, a client-server application, printing, or communications support. This communication must be established and maintained regardless of the relative locations of the two computers running the application. As discussed later, the current trend is to merge the functions of the host operating system and the basic network operating system. Windows NT and OS/2 are examples of this trend.

The purpose of this chapter is to explore LANs from the top down in the context of the OSI model. This chapter focuses on the software that supports the interaction between high-level user applications in the network environment. The issues of how data move from place to place within a local network and between networks are discussed in Chapters 12, "Local Area Networks: The Communications Perspective," and 13, "Internetworking and Interoperability," respectively. This high-level software is given the generic name of *applications support software,* and includes the following components:

- ✔ The PC operating system—MS-DOS, OS/2, or Windows NT

- ✔ The Network operating system—Novell's NetWare, IBM's OS/2 LAN Server, Windows NT Advanced Server, or Banyan's VINES

- ✔ The presentation layer software needed to establish communications across a LAN between a server and its clients—*NetWare Core Protocol* (NCP) and *Server Message Blocks* (SMB)

- ✔ The software components needed to connect applications running on two or more computers on one network—IBM's *Network Basic Input/ Output System* (NetBIOS), *NetBIOS Extended User Interface* (NetBEUI), *Network Dynamic Data Exchange* (NetDDE) used by Windows For Workgroups and Windows NT, and OS/2's Named Pipes.

This chapter focuses on *intra-network* communications; Chapter 13 addresses *inter-network* communications.

Figure 11.1 shows a simplified view of the above listed components and their relative dependency. The figure also shows how applications software running on workstations and servers relies on the underlying support software. This chapter does not address the lower-layer details of LAN physical connectivity as represented by the Token Ring in figure 11.1.

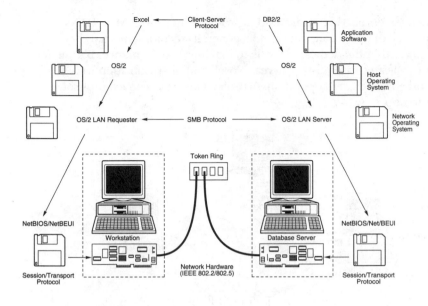

Figure 11.1
Local area network system software architecture.

Terminology

The local area network in figure 11.2 is used to illustrate some basic terminology appropriate to applications support software components. Other terminology is defined throughout the chapter.

The term *server* refers to a software application that offers a well-defined service to network users. Servers can be software components running in ordinary PCs, or special purpose hardware and software designed to optimize a particular function. The most common types of servers are *file servers, print servers, communications servers, database servers,* and *mail servers.* Multiple services are often found at a single network location. The server depicted in figure 11.2 is a dual-purpose file and print server. The five PCs attached to the LAN in figure 11.2 are commonly called *workstations,* or *clients,* and are typically used for host terminal applications (discussed in Part I), graphics design, word processing, database applications, software development, project management, and a variety of other uses. Special purpose workstations, usually higher in cost and more powerful in performance, can be attached to the LAN for computationally intensive tasks such as simulation, *computer-aided design* (CAD), or multimedia applications development.

On LANs, servers can be dedicated, or non-dedicated. A *dedicated* server is set up for the sole purpose of providing one or more services to users on the network. A *non-dedicated* server can function as a workstation while sharing one or more attached resources such as directories and printers. LANs supporting non-dedicated servers also are referred to as *peer-to-peer* networks. Most LANs enable either type of operation, but vendors generally recommend that their servers be operated in the dedicated mode to maximize performance. Banyan and IBM support dedicated operation, whereas Novell and Microsoft support both dedicated and non-dedicated operation. Artisoft's Lantastic is an example of a purely peer-to-peer network.

Figure 11.2
Basic local area network components.

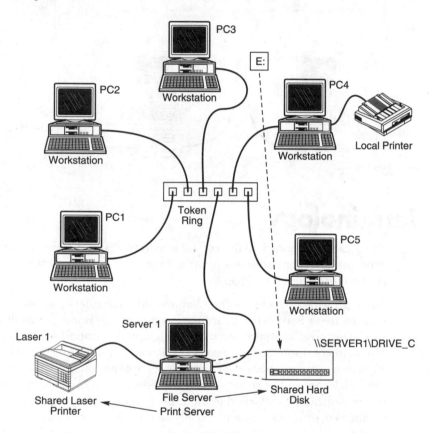

The body of rules that enables the orderly, reliable transfer of data among the stations on the network in figure 11.2 is collectively known by the term *protocol.* In the context of the International Standards Organization seven-layer model discussed in Chapter 8, "PC Communications Interfaces and Adapters," protocol refers to the rules associated with how a layer in one machine communicates with the same layer in another machine. Examples of protocols include the previously mentioned NetWare Core Protocol and Server Message Block working at the presentation layer. The protocols in any layer include *interface standards* for requesting service from the layer below and providing service to the layer above.

Examples of interface standards are NetBIOS (interface to layer 5) and Microsoft's *Transport Data Interface* (TDI—interface to layer 4).

The original IBM NetBIOS protocol was defined in terms of layers 5 through 1. A widely accepted protocol such as NetBIOS may become a *standard*. Standards are *de jure*, meaning that they are legislated by recognized national and international bodies, or *de facto*, meaning standards set by a vendor's influence in the marketplace. De facto standards often become de jure standards as they gain national and/or international acceptance. NetBIOS is a de facto standard. Ethernet began as a de facto standard but has been adapted to the ANSI/OIEEE 802.3 Local Area Network standard in the United States and the ISO International Standard 8802/3. The LAN in figure 11.1 uses several standard protocols including Server Message Block, NetBIOS, and the IBM Token Ring (IEEE 802.5), of which only the latter is a formal standard.

The terms *virtual* and *transparent* are often used in discussions on local area networks and other data processing subjects. A process is virtual if it does not exist but appears to; a process is transparent if it exists but does not appear to. In figure 11.2, a *virtual drive* process links the MS-DOS logical drive "E:" on the workstation PC3 to a subdirectory on the file server's shared hard disk. In this case, the file server's subdirectory appears to be a local disk drive to an applications program running on PC3, but obviously does not physically exist on that workstation.

The separation of physical aspects of a LAN (adapter cards and connecting cables) and the applications that run on it is a good example of transparency. The underlying physical communications protocol of a LAN (for example, Token Ring, Ethernet, or ARCnet) is transparent to the user's application. In other words, a database software package does not operate any differently on an Ethernet, ARCnet, or an IBM Token Ring LAN. Closely related terms are *physical* and *logical*. A physical entity can be seen and touched; a logical entity exists as a process or an activity, but in general cannot be seen or touched. A floppy disk is physical, whereas software on the floppy disk is logical.

In the context of local area networks, the term *host* can have several meanings. It refers to the microcomputer in which a workstation or server application runs on the network. It also can refer to the native operating system on a workstation or server. Thus Windows NT and OS/2 are host operating systems, and a PC can be host to a server or a workstation application. The more traditional data processing context of host refers to a mainframe or minicomputer providing centralized applications support. The use of the term *host* in Part III, "Local Area Networking," encompasses any or all of these meanings.

An Overview of Applications Support Software

Applications support software is first invoked when an application requests resources from a source remote from its host. Depending on the application, different means of invoking the support software are used. *Redirector* software is responsible for determining whether the requested resource is local or remote. The requirement may be to open a file, print a file, or execute a client-server function. In the standard file server or print server cases, the redirector determines that the resource (directory or printer) is not local and requests NetBIOS. The redirector and NetBIOS both belong to the network operating system. The redirector and the server hosting the desired directory or printer communicate through a peer-to-peer protocol called *Server Message Block* (SMB) or *NetWare Core Protocol* (NCP). In a client-server application, the client operating system uses a remote inter-process communications service such as *Named Pipes, Remote Procedure Calls* (RPC), or *Mail Slots*. Both OS/2 and Windows NT support these services.

SMB uses the NetBIOS interface and its underlying protocol, such as NetBEUI, to accomplish workstation-to-server communications. NCP uses a direct interface to IPX, Novell's layer 3 network protocol, to accomplish the workstation-server exchange. Interprocess communications typically use the Transport Data Interface to move data around the network.

Figure 11.3 shows the allocation of major software components to the seven-layer model. Note that parts of this allocation are considered to be somewhat imprecise. In figure 11.3, three points are particularly significant—these are shown by numbered arrows. Arrow 1 represents the manner in which applications programs request services from the host and network operating systems. Arrow 2 represents the manner in which network operating systems request logical connectivity between stations (and applications) on the network. Arrow 3 represents a standard interface to multiple standards for reliably transporting and routing data. Arrow 4 represents a standard interface through which the transport software providing logical connectivity requests physical conveyance of the data between network stations.

The following sections describe the manner in which end-user applications interact with applications support software and the more significant features of applications support software components. The discussion emphasizes MS-DOS, OS/2, and Windows NT host operating systems, the major network operating systems, and alternative protocol stacks to link client and server applications across single and multiple LANs.

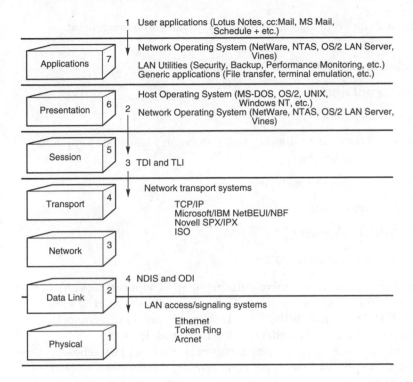

Figure 11.3
Application support software and the OSI model.

High-Level Applications Software

As this book goes to press, the software category of groupware is beginning a major push into the corporate desktop marketplace. Perhaps the best known, but by no means in sole possession of the category, is Lotus Notes. Notes is really part of several groupware categories, each of which is accumulating more entries by the month. The better-known groupware categories are presented in the following list. These are only the beginning—more are sure to follow as Novell/WordPerfect, Lotus, IBM, and Microsoft, among others, introduce group-enabled versions of their well-established application bases. Groupware categories include the following:

✔ E-mail

✔ Desktop videoconferencing

✔ Group scheduling

✔ Electronic meeting support (agenda formulation, idea processing, meeting reports, action items)

- ✔ Electronic conferencing (administration, discussion management, interface to e-mail software)

- ✔ Workflow automation

- ✔ Bulletin board systems

- ✔ Image management

- ✔ Whiteboard (interactive drawing and annotation to illustrate key points in documents or graphics)

- ✔ Database management and query tools

- ✔ Software development

- ✔ Multimedia development

- ✔ Major document production

A casual inspection of these categories reveals that network support plays an essential role in the success of each of them. Some categories will severely strain current LAN technology, especially those in which images are a main component such as image management, multimedia development, and desktop videoconferencing; or where graphics play a major role such as in whiteboard, electronic meeting support and electronic conferencing. Applications support software is improving rapidly with each new generation of operating system as network support becomes increasingly seamless. This trend will facilitate the continued growth in both breadth and depth of groupware applications. To support this trend, applications support software requires the following characteristics:

- ✔ Tight integration with off-the-shelf standard applications

- ✔ High degree of interoperability among operating systems

- ✔ Comprehensive addressing and naming architectures

- ✔ Seamless integration across e-mail systems

- ✔ High bandwidth transport protocol

Host Operating Systems

Host operating systems provide basic resource management and a user interface for a single microcomputer and its attached input/output devices. Operating systems are classified by the number of users and by the number of simultaneous tasks they are designed to support. *Single-user* systems generally have limited, or no support for file sharing or access security, two features inherent in *multiuser* systems. *Single-tasking* systems are designed to support only one program running at a time in the host computer. *Multitasking* systems are designed to enable execution of multiple programs nearly simultaneously on a single processor. *Multiprocessing* systems support the use of multiple processors to execute simultaneous tasks; moreover, multiprocessing systems can be either *symmetric* or *asymmetric.* Symmetric multiprocessing systems enable any task to be assigned to any processor. Asymmetric multiprocessing systems assign one processor to the operating system and other processors to one or more applications.

Operating systems range from the simplest single-user, single-tasking systems such as MS-DOS to multiuser, multitasking systems such as UNIX, OS/2, and Windows NT. Windows NT and Banyan's VINES SMP (based on UNIX) support symmetric multiprocessing.

MS-DOS

Today's LANs designed for the MS-DOS environment are built on a foundation of services first introduced by MS-DOS version 3.1 and continued through its succeeding versions. This version of DOS was the first to incorporate specific functions for the sharing of devices and files. Clearly, MS-DOS 3.1 was destined to be the forerunner of newer and more powerful operating systems that encompass the full capabilities of the 80386 and 80X86 microprocessor architectures. The multitasking counterpart to these MS-DOS versions, OS/2, is in its second major release as this book goes to press and has become a significant element of IBM's strategy for its Systems Application Architecture. Likewise, Windows NT represents Microsoft's multitasking strategy for networking its core office applications. It is important to understand the basic structure of the MS-DOS series, as well as its capabilities and limitations in the network environment. Many proprietary and "generic" network operating systems rely in varying degrees on the services and standardization provided by MS-DOS.

MS-DOS provides the three basic components for control and management of peripherals and the user interface as follows:

✔ COMMAND.COM command processor program

✔ MSDOS.SYS file (IBM version: IBMDOS.SYS), which is the heart of the operating system

✔ IO.SYS file (IBM version: IBMBIO.SYS), which provides lower-level support for the hardware functions of certain peripherals

In addition to these software files, PCs have an installed *Read-Only-Memory* (ROM) chip set that has firmware for the lowest-level hardware control of the more standard I/O devices, including the keyboard, certain video displays, floppy disk drives, serial ports, and parallel ports. This firmware is called the *Basic Input/Output System* (BIOS). IO.SYS and BIOS are hardware-dependent elements of the operating system. The sequence of operations to load and execute a program from floppy disk illustrates the relationship between these DOS elements and is shown in figure 11.4. It is important to keep this basic structure in mind as you investigate network operating system architectures.

Figure 11.4
MS-DOS file loading sequence.

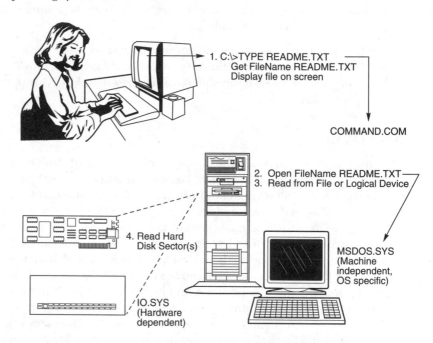

1. C:\>TYPE README.TXT
   Get FileName README.TXT
   Display file on screen

COMMAND.COM

2. Open FileName README.TXT
3. Read from File or Logical Device

4. Read Hard Disk Sector(s)

MSDOS.SYS (Machine independent, OS specific)

IO.SYS (Hardware dependent)

The real value of MS-DOS version 3.1 and its successors is the standard, albeit limited, support they provide for network software developers. Prior to version 3.1, many LAN vendors had developed proprietary methods to handle the protection of files and records in a multiuser environment. This protection depends on techniques such as *file access control, file locking,* and *byte-range locking.* Applications developers could not rely on any one scheme to be dominant to achieve the critical mass of software development for LANs. MS-DOS provides the basic structure for LAN development through a series of network-oriented function calls. Many of these require additional network operating system software to function properly, but at least the applications developer can rely upon a standard way of linking applications programs to a shared network environment. Some typical MS-DOS network-related function calls are summarized in table 11.1, which also indicates whether additional network redirector software is required to execute the call.

Table 11.1
MS-DOS LAN Support (Partial)

Software Interrupt 21H (MS-DOS Service)

Function	Meaning	LAN Software Required
3DH	Open File	No
44H	Device Driver Control	No
5BH	Create New File	No (Semaphore usage*)
5CH	Control Record Access	No
5EH(00)**	Get Machine Name	Redirector***
5EH(02)	Set Printer Setup	Redirector
5EH(03)	Get Printer Setup	Redirector
5FH(02)	Get Redirection List	Redirector
5FH(03)	Redirect Device	Redirector
5FH(04)	Cancel Redirection	Redirector

*See the discussion under Multiuser File Management

**( ) indicates subfunction number

***Redirector indicates that Redirector (NET.EXE) or compatible software be installed

OS/2

OS/2 is the PC-based, multitasking operating system jointly developed by IBM and Microsoft and currently being marketed and maintained by IBM. OS/2 provides significant enhancements to the management of PC resources compared to MS-DOS, but its importance to local area networking relies on the following five major features:

✔ *Application Program Interface* (API)

✔ Multitasking design, which provides a vehicle for more efficient and standardized server software

✔ Support for interprocess communications among workstations and servers in a network environment

✔ New high-performance file system to replace or supplement the current *File Allocation Table* (FAT) system

✔ Extended Services, including the Communications Manager and the Database Manager and its related IBM SAA *Distributed Database Connection Services/2* (DDCS/2)

Chapter 14, "Network Operating System Implementation," discusses OS/2 LAN server, the IBM server extension of OS/2.

Application Program Interface

Whereas MS-DOS uses the method of software interrupts (as shown earlier in table 11.1) to provide DOS services to applications, OS/2 uses *Applications Program Interfaces(APIs)*, which act like subprograms to a process (application) currently running in the host computer. APIs bring an entirely new perspective to the development of sophisticated systems software and applications in a network environment, and are in turn made flexible and extensible by other architectural features inherent in OS/2 design.

LAN Manager, Microsoft's original LAN extension to OS/2, uses over 120 APIs for various network support services. A major benefit of OS/2 is and will continue to be increased standardization of LAN functions. It is interesting to note that these same LAN Manager APIs have now been incorporated into Windows NT Advanced Server, a competing product to IBM's OS/2-based LAN Server. This provides a high degree of interoperability between LAN Manager and NT Advanced Server.

Multitasking

To provide its multitasking features, OS/2 supports multiple sessions, processes and threads. A *session* is simply a virtual computer from the user's perspective. A session supports all or a portion of the screen and attached input devices, such as the keyboard or a mouse. This level of multitasking also is supported by MS-DOS extensions, such as DESQview and Microsoft Windows. A *process* is a program in its execution mode, such as when a financial program calculates and prints a loan amortization schedule. If provided with appropriate resources, such as a screen window and the keyboard, the process becomes a session. A session provides the user with a visual, manageable window into the executing process. A *thread* can be likened to a function or subprogram running within a process. A routine to calculate periodic interest payments in the previously mentioned loan amortization program is an example of a thread.

The key point to remember about sessions, processes, and threads in OS/2 is that they can run virtually simultaneously in a single microprocessor. That is, they appear to be simultaneous, but in fact each is assigned a discrete time slice for execution—hence, the utility of OS/2 in a network server environment. By their very nature, servers are multitasking network resources. They must manage simultaneous requests for hard disk access, perform print management services, and perhaps control one or more communications resources. OS/2 provides a stable, standard development platform on which to build multitasking server applications. Some of the more common applications will be services for file, printer, security, and remote access management.

Interprocess Communications

Interprocess Communications (IPCs) are part of the OS/2 design to support multitasking. IPCs enable two processes or threads within the *same* computer to exchange data through a variety of mechanisms supplied by OS/2, including *Shared Memory, Semaphores, Queues, Signals,* and *Named Pipes.* For LAN applications, IPC enables two processes on *different* computers to communicate as if they were in the same computer. The Named Pipe mechanism accomplishes this task. Beginning with OS/2 version 1.1, Named Pipes and Mail Slots were implemented in the host operating system. Named Pipes are created by a process running on an OS/2 server node and are used by client processes running on OS/2 or MS-DOS workstations. Named Pipes are two-way virtual circuits for more complex data exchange.

As PC-based LANs continue to mature, network operating systems such as OS/2 LAN Server and Windows NT are capable of supporting both the existing *file server models* and the emerging *client-server models* for distributed processing. The major difference between the two models (compared in fig. 11.5) lies in the nature of the data requests passed from workstations to servers and the location of the primary application program. In the file server model, these requests consist of commands to open and close data files on the file server and the movement of data files between the file server and workstation. The data files in turn are used by the application program running on the individual workstation. File service is required for basic network operating system housekeeping functions.

In the client-server model of distributed processing, the total application can consist of a file server process communicating with a workstation process using the Named Pipes API. The server runs the back-end (computational) application process while the client workstation runs the front-end (user management) application process. The client front-end provides the user a window into, and control of, the application running on the server. A current, well-known example of this is Microsoft's SQL Server, a database engine that executes on a server. Workstations on the network can run any compatible front-end query program from either an MS-DOS or OS/2 host operating system. The traffic between the client and the server consists of high-level data queries and the information provided by the server in response to those queries. The data passed is in the standard SQL query language format.

Figure 11.5
File server and client-server models compared.

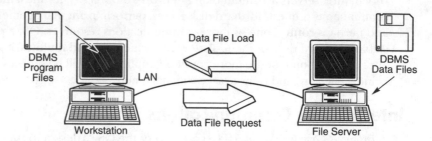

File Server Model

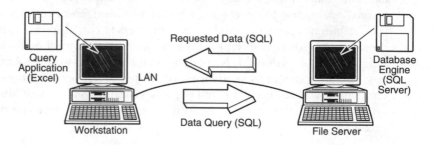

Client-Server Model

High Performance File System (HPFS)

OS/2 version 1.2 introduced the *High Performance File System* (HPFS) as the long-awaited replacement to the MS-DOS *FAT file system*. The need for HPFS has been intensified by the increasing size of hard disks, particularly in the network environment. HPFS has three distinct parts: a new means of organizing data on the hard disk, conversion of applications program file requests into hard disk device driver commands, and implementation of *installable file systems*. Table 11.2 highlights some differences between the FAT system and HPFS.

Table 11.2
FAT and HPFS Differences

Feature	FAT File System	HPFS
Max file name length (chars)	8 basic.3 extended	254
No. of delimiters	1	Many
Max path length (chars)	64	260
File attributes	Bit flag	Bit flag + 64 KB of ASCII or binary data
Directory structure	Unsorted linear list	Sorted B-Tree
Directory location	Root directory on Track 0	Near seek center of volume
File allocation information	FAT on Track 0	Located near each file in its Fnode
Free disk space information	FAT on Track 0	Located near free space in bitmaps
Minimum allocation unit	Cluster (4 KB or more)	Sector (512 bytes)
Maximum volume size	32 MB (DOS)	2,199 GB

The HPFS introduces some incompatibilities to existing applications software. The length of file name and existence of multiple (.) delimiters are two of the more obvious differences. Others include the use of *Extended Attributes* (EAs) and *Access Control Lists* (ACLs). Up to 64 KB of EAs can be associated with a file, each in the following highly generic form:

```
name = value,
```

in which *value* can be an ASCIIZ string or a binary value. OS/2 APIs for querying and setting file information have been appropriately expanded to handle EAs.

Support for the existing attributes of Read-only, Hidden, System, and Archive will be continued to maintain backward compatibility. ACLs are supported by the current versions of LAN Server and LAN Manager. As the name suggests, ACLs are used to store items such as access rights and passwords for users accessing that file in a network environment.

Because HPFS is a radical departure from the FAT file system, IBM has defined a new partition type for HPFS (Type 7). HPFS volumes can exist on the same disk as other types, including FAT, UNIX, NetWare, and others. Existing MS-DOS and OS/2 applications can exploit the enhanced performance features of HPFS by using the 8.3 file name format. Because this format is a subset of an allowable HPFS file name, backward compatibility is ensured.

OS/2 Extended Services

The two major components of Extended Services are *Communications Manager/2* (CM/2) and *Database Manager OS/2* (DB2/2). CM/2 provides a family of communications protocols enabling access to IBM's full range of local and wide area networking architectures. DB2/2 is a 32-bit database manager and the OS/2 component of the IBM *Distributed Relational Database Architecture* (DRDA).

Communications Manager/2 (CM/2)

CM/2 provides a complete array of protocols for communicating in the local area and wide area network environments. The intent is to have a unified set of APIs to call virtually any protocol needed to communicate with any level of platform, from mainframes thousands of miles distant to PCs connected on the same network. By having these APIs under one umbrella, overall management is simplified and mutual interference between protocols is minimized. The major functions that CM/2 supports include the following:

✔ Access to SNA networks, both the older hierarchical type and the newer *Advanced Peer-to-Peer Network* (APPN) using *Advanced Program-to-Program Communications* (APPC) and *Common Programming Interface-Communications* (CPI-C) APIs

✔ SNA Gateway service for up to 256 clients

✔ Mainframe terminal emulation using Asynchronous and 3270 protocols through the *Server-Requester Programming Interface* (SRPI), *Asynchronous Communications Device Interface* (ACDI), and *Emulator High Level Language API* (EHLLAPI)

✔ Access to X.25 packet-switched wide area networks through the X.25 API

✔ Access to ISDN networks through the ISDN Connection Manager Interface

✔ Network management using IBM's Netview through an API call for messages to Netview and through the *Service Point Applications Router* (SPAR) and *Remote Operations Service* (ROP) for messages from Netview

✔ Common services such as ASCII-to-EBCDIC conversion, error tracing and logging

CM/2 supports virtually all types of physical connectivity, including dial-up and leased phone lines, IEEE LAN standards, X.25, and direct connections to local mainframes.

Database Manager OS/2 (DB2/2)

DRDA, IBM's architecture for multiple platform, distributed database connectivity, includes five major database management systems as follows:

✔ DB2/2 operating on OS/2 platforms

✔ DB2/6000 operating on AIX (IBM's UNIX implementation) platforms

✔ SQL/400 DB2 operating on AS/400 minicomputer platforms

✔ SQL/DS DB2 operating on S/370 VM mainframe platforms

✔ DB2 operating on S/370 MVS mainframe platforms

OS/2 and DB2/2 are considered by IBM to be a strategic PC-based client or server platform for accessing any or all the above databases in client-server architectures. In the full implementation of the DRDA strategy, database accesses can be made from a client machine to any DRDA database server without requiring knowledge of where, or on what type of machine the desired database engine resides. Full database security, including multiuser access and transaction integrity, is maintained across local area and wide area networks. DB2/2 consists of the following three parts:

✔ Database Services

✔ Database Tools

✔ Remote Data Services

Database Services, the *Structured Query Language* (SQL) engine for DB2/2, can be configured as a stand-alone database or as a networked database server. Database Tools consist of a number of database utilities including Query Manager and a variety of configuration and indexing capabilities. Remote Data Services include transparent SQL access, *remote procedure calls* (RPCs), transaction rollback across the network, and network directory maintenance.

The software that enables remote access for DB2/2 to other DRDA databases is *Distributed Database Connection Services/2* (DDCS/2). In brief, DDCS/2 enables any DRDA database to become a server for the OS/2 DB2/2 and for other MS-DOS and Windows clients. A fully operational client-server application using an AS/400 server requires SQL/400 on the AS/400; DB2/2 on the OS/2 client; DDCS/2 on the OS/2 client; and appropriate communications connectivity (LAN or WAN) between the two sites.

Windows NT

Windows NT is the newest entry into the PC operating system sweepstakes and represents Microsoft's challenge to OS/2 and UNIX as the preeminent multitasking operating system. From a networking perspective, Windows NT offers all the features of OS/2, including API calls, multitasking, interprocess communications and improved file systems. Additional network-relevant features such as advanced security, the Windows NT Registry, peer-to-peer networking, and support for symmetric multiprocessing are provided by Windows NT. Chapter 14, "Network Operating System Implementation," discusses Windows NT Advanced Server—the LAN server extension of Windows NT.

Interprocess Communications

In addition to the IPCs supported by OS/2, NT adds support for remote procedure calls. RPCs enable a client program or process to call supporting processes on remote (that is, networked) computers. NT's version of RPC is compatible, but not compliant with the *Open Software Foundation's* (OSF) *Data Communications Exchange* (DCE). Although not compliant, NT's RPC facility is interoperable with other DCE-based RPC systems. In this case, interoperability is more important than compliance. A unique feature of NT's RPC is that it uses other IPCs to transmit data to and from remote computers—these are Named Pipes, Windows Sockets, and NetBIOS.

File System Support

Windows NT adds a new file system called the *NT File System* (NTFS), while supporting the FAT and HPFS file systems. HPFS implementation in Windows NT differs somewhat from that in OS/2. For example, the Access Control List and hot-fixing features of OS/2's HPFS are not supported in Windows NT. However, these features are included in the NTFS system. NTFS, HPFS, and FAT are file systems for reading and writing from hard disk devices. Windows NT supports other operating system components implemented as file systems, including the Redirector and Server, the Mail Slot File System, the Named Pipe File System, and the CD-ROM file system.

Table 11.3 compares the NTFS and HPFS file systems. As you can see from this comparison, NTFS is a more robust file system than HPFS. The transition from

FAT through HPFS and NTFS reflects the concurrent transition from 8086, eight-bit CPU architectures to current Pentium and PowerPC processors with the capability of supporting multiple, very high-capacity disk drives. As disk drives become larger and faster, a greater need for fault tolerance in mass storage systems exists. NTFS addresses this need and others. Increased use of networking makes file security more critical than before—again, NTFS meets this need.

A key feature of NTFS is the concept of multiple data streams. *Streams* are multiple instances of the same file, with each instance determined by a change in attributes. Because file data is considered an attribute in NTFS, multiple streams can represent related changes in file data. An example of this might be different versions of the same word processing document. In NTFS format, the file names would be as follows:

```
business_plan:version_1
            :version_2
            :version_3
```

This characteristic of NTFS provides basic compatibility with the Macintosh file system. The Services For Macintosh feature of Windows NT Advanced Server relies upon the existence of an NTFS volume to provide a Macintosh/FAT or Macintosh/NTFS file transfer capability.

Table 11.3
NTFS and HPFS Differences

Feature	NT File System	HPFS
Max filename length (chars)	255	254
Filename case sensitive	Yes (POSIX-compliant)	No
No. of delimiters	Many	Many
Convert to DOS 8.3 file name	Yes	No
Max path length (chars)	No limit	No limit
File attributes	Bit flag + everything, including data	Bit flag + 64 KB of ASCII or binary data
Directory structure	Sorted B-Tree	Sorted B-Tree

continues

III

Local Area Networking

Table 11.3, Continued
NTFS and HPFS Differences

Feature	NT File System	HPFS
Directory location	Master File Table	Near seek center of volume
File allocation information	Master File Table	Located near each file in its Fnode
Free disk space information	Volume Cluster Bitmap	Located near free space in bitmaps
Minimum allocation unit	Cluster (512, 1,024, 2,048, or 4,096 bytes)	Sector (512 bytes)
Max volume size	264 Bytes	2,199 GB
POSIX-compliant	Yes (IEEE 1003.1)	No
Recoverable File System	Yes	No

Windows NT Registry

The Windows NT Registry is a master configuration database for the operating system. The Registry handles such functions as storing configuration data for hardware and software installations, keeping track of device drivers, and user management of the system configuration. The Registry extends the functionality of the .INI files in Windows and the CONFIG.SYS and AUTOEXEC.BAT files in MS-DOS. These extensions include preference files for multiple users of the same machine and the capability to place executable code in the Registry file. Examples of network-specific data maintained in the registry include adapter card data, user profiles, security authorizations, printer connections, NTAS services, and bindings between adapter cards and transport protocol such as NT's native NBF (equivalent to IBM's NetBEUI).

Security Architecture

Windows NT offers a sophisticated security system, providing the capability of meeting United States government standards for C-2 Level, the security requirements of which include the following components:

✔ Owners of resources control access to their resources

✔ Persistence of object protection by the operating system regardless of the status of a process using that object

✔ User authentication by user name and password during login

✔ Protected access to audit records of security-related events

✔ Protection from external tampering

Entities in the security subsystem include users; groups (of users); objects (files, directories, print queues, processes, and so on); permissions (read, delete, write, take ownership, and so on); Access Control Lists; security access tokens; and subjects. A *subject* is a combination of a user's access token and a program or process running in response to a user action. When a user is given certain access rights to an object (a file, for example), any program the user runs must honor the same access rights. NT employs discretionary access control, which means that the owner of a resource determines who has access to the resource and what rights the user has while accessing the resource.

Peer-to-Peer Networking

Windows NT provides peer-to-peer networking equivalent to Windows for Workgroups as it comes out of the box with the added advantage of many new operating system features, including those discussed earlier. File sharing and print sharing operate the same as in Windows for Workgroups, but security features are enhanced, reflecting the more robust security architecture in Windows NT. Performance in a peer-to-peer environment is enhanced due to the multitasking architecture of NT. OS/2 does not support peer-to-peer networking in its basic form.

Symmetric Multiprocessing

The multitasking architecture of Windows NT is similar to that of OS/2 except that NT enables concurrent execution of multiple threads on different processors. Applications can be written to execute threads on all processors equally or to limit execution to a subset of available processors. Recall from the OS/2 discussion that threads are individual pieces of code scheduled within a process; in the case of multiprocessing, threads are the smallest executable code elements that can run on an individual processor. Another twist on multiprocessor use is that multiple threads of a server process can service multiple clients simultaneously on different processors.

III

Local Area Networking

Network Operating Systems

In PC-based LANs, network operating systems function at the following two levels:

✔ They provide resource management for services on server machines

✔ They provide the user and applications software a "window" to the LAN environment at each workstation machine

The file server and workstation components of the network operating system work together to provide an integrated system control capability to users and network managers on the LAN. The manner in which these two components interact is a major factor in LAN operating system design and network performance. You should realize that an OS/2-based file server does not imply the necessity for an OS/2-based workstation. A typical OS/2 LAN environment can consist of one or more OS/2-based LAN servers and a mixture of OS/2, MS-DOS, or Windows-based workstations. Under specified conditions, this environment also can support a mixture of Windows NT, UNIX, NetWare, and OS/2-based servers.

LAN operating systems are arguably the major determinant of overall network performance as indicated by metrics such as throughput and response times under a load of multiple users. Network server software is particularly important because server multitasking requirements can be very demanding. Workstation network software such as IBM's OS/2 Requester has less effect on network performance, but determines the major user management capability of the network. LAN utilities, which are merely specialized forms of applications software, have the least impact on network performance. Utilities provide the tools for users to more effectively manage the network and its resources. LAN utilities are most often extensions to the basic capabilities of network operating systems. These utilities can run on file servers, workstations, or both. Many value-added utilities are currently offered by third-party vendors for most of the major network operating systems.

Every LAN requires a control mechanism to manage shared resources, just as stand-alone microcomputers require operating systems to control their locally attached resources. Operating systems also have the responsibility to provide an orderly method for users to interact with the resources under their control. A LAN provides added value to a set of independent microcomputers by connecting them and facilitating resource and information sharing. This added value can best be managed by an operating system specifically designed for the LAN environment. Like a microcomputer operating system, a *network operating system* (NOS) has features that must be evaluated to determine the best match for a particular combination of applications, hardware, and budget.

Table 11.4 provides an overview of key features that prospective network purchasers and managers should look for in a network operating system:

Table 11.4
Key Network Operating System Features

Feature	Feature Description
Hardware independence	The capability of a NOS to operate in more than one vendor's network hardware environment
Bridging	The capability of a NOS to support the connection of two or more dissimilar hardware LANs under a common network operating system
Multiple server support	The capability to support more than one server and to transparently manage communications between servers
Multiprocessor server	The capability to operate support reliably on a symmetric or asymmetric multiprocessor server host
Multiuser support (Synchronization)	The capability to provide adequate and *standardized* protection for applications programs and their data files in a multiuser environment
Network management	The degree to which the NOS supports network utility and management functions such as system backup, security management, fault tolerance, performance monitoring, and so on
Security and access control	The capability of a NOS to provide a high degree of network security through the control of users and resources
User interface	The degree of human engineering reflected in menus, screens, commands, and user control over network resources

Figure 11.6 illustrates the relationship between applications software, host operating system, network operating system, and lower-level network communications functions in an MS-DOS environment. This figure is shown from the perspective of

III

a workstation on the network. The user's view of the network is transparent through an applications program, or explicit through menus and command lines that provide control of network functions. Many network functions are themselves special-purpose applications programs. When an application program is running in a workstation, a *redirector* or *shell* program continuously screens requests for files or devices. The redirector knows what devices and drives are remote because it is given this information by the user mapping local device names to network resources.

Figure 11.6
Workstation system software architecture (MS-DOS environment).

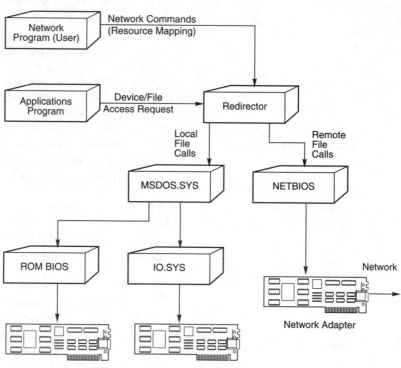

File requests such as opening a word processor data file on a subdirectory on a local drive are passed to a normal MS-DOS or OS/2 file handling routine for input and output processing. File requests to a subdirectory on a network drive located on the file server are passed to network device drivers. These device drivers provide the necessary network processing such as redirector-server dialog, transport protocol handling, and proper routing. The network adapter card works just like any other adapter card in the workstation—it provides the basic hardware and firmware support for an input/output device, in this case a local area network communications system. In this illustration, the components of the workstation

part of the network operating system are the network management program and its user interface, and the redirector, or shell, which is transparent to the user. The network management program and other network utilities are usually considered applications programs.

Figure 11.7 illustrates the relationships described earlier as they appear on the network file server. This figure assumes that a Novell file server is dedicated to running network services. The file server can run either a proprietary operating system such as NetWare, or a more standard multitasking host operating system such as OS/2, Windows NT, or UNIX. The peripherals attached to the file server, such as hard disk drives, tape backup units and printers, are supported by the file server operating system just as workstation local I/O devices are supported by their host operating systems. Current file servers run a markedly unstandardized collection of system software. Examples are UNIX System V on Banyan's file servers; NetWare 4.*x* on Novell's file servers; OS/2 on IBM's file servers; and Windows NT on the Windows NT Advanced Server. Figure 11.8 depicts how a file server multitasking operating system is structured. This particular view shows the NetWare operating system, but the principle is similar on other multitasking systems.

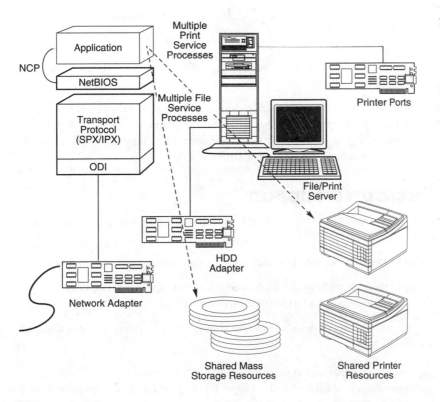

Figure 11.7
File server software layers (NetWare environment).

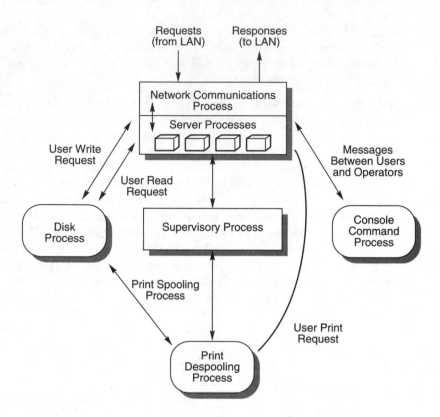

Figure 11.8
Multitasking server operating system (NetWare example).

The various parts of a network operating system combine to perform a variety of tasks to support network activities. These tasks consist of shared resource support, file management, and general management functions such as system backup, fault tolerance, security management, and performance monitoring.

Shared Resource Support

In general, shared resources supported by network operating systems include the following:

- ✔ Mass storage devices such as hard disks, tape drives, and optical disks

- ✔ Output devices such as dot matrix and letter quality printers, laser printers, plotters, and large screen video displays

- ✔ Communications devices such as modems, bridges, routers, gateways, and facsimile

Mass storage server processes, also known as *file servers*, manage the attached physical storage media and offer the sharing of the logical file directory structure

contained on the media. Output server processes typically use the storage facilities of the file server to queue output requests and manage user access to the devices. Further discussion on communications servers occurs in Chapter 13, "Internetworking and Interoperability," which deals with connecting multiple LANs with, and through, wide area networks.

File management is the foundation of any multiuser data processing system, and LANs are no exception. In the early days of PC LANs, multiuser file management was largely done within applications software by proprietary methods—the result was almost total lack of standardization and the paucity of network-capable software. Current and evolving host and network operating systems are rightfully assuming this responsibility. This can be seen, for example in the API calls within OS/2 and Windows NT that support various multiuser file management functions.

Today's LANs provide varying selections of network management functions for users and network Administrators. These functions can be built-in to the network operating system or can be stand-alone applications programs. Table 11.5 lists some OS/2 LAN Server APIs that provide network Administrator support. A growing number of third-party network utility programs are available for the major network operating systems. The extensibility of OS/2 contributes to continued growth of this third-party industry.

Table 11.5
OS/2 LAN Server APIs for Network Administrators

Statistics	Access to Resources
Auditing	User Management
Group Management	Network Configuration
Remote Utilities	Network Messages
Print Queues	Print Jobs
Network Profile	Alerts
Error Logging	File Sharing Management
Remote Execution	Character Device Management

Sharing expensive resources was the original impetus behind the growth and acceptance of local area networks for PCs. In this context, resources included peripherals (devices) and file directories. The rationale for LANs is now more related to workgroup efficiency than to the sharing of resources. Specialized

III

Local Area Networking

devices still exist that dictate sharing from an economic sense. The concept has not changed—only the complexity and sophistication of the devices themselves. Current generation LANs have increased functionality to support laser printers of all sizes and varieties, optical disk units and CD-ROMs, backup tape units, modems, and, of course, the ubiquitous hard disk drives on file servers.

Regardless of the resource involved, sharing requires a concept known as *redirection*. Redirection takes place on the workstation and enables logical resource names (for example, drive designations) within the host operating system to be assigned to remote shared resources. For example, the logical printer device in MS-DOS, LPT1: can be redirected to a network printer attached to the file server. Likewise, COM1: can be redirected to a shared modem on the network; drive F: to a subdirectory on the file server; and so on.

Inherent to the sharing process is the use of a workstation-server protocol. The more common of these are Microsoft's Server Message Block and Novell's NetWare Core Protocol . Communications between the workstation's redirector or shell and the server are accomplished using this protocol. SMB and NCP are discussed further in the topic area of intra-LAN protocols.

Mass Storage Resources

Mass storage resources and their management play a major role in effective LAN operations and in the design of network operating systems. Mass storage media are the "main battery" of the file server. An understanding of the physical and logical elements of mass storage is necessary to properly evaluate alternative LAN products. The following discussion should be viewed from the perspective of the file server.

Figure 11.9 summarizes the relationship between mass storage elements. The largest entity of mass storage on a network is the *physical drive*. Several drives can be attached to a single file server as illustrated in figure 11.10. This is a common configuration when using hard disk drives with the *Small Computer Systems Interface* (SCSI), which allows chaining of I/O devices, including hard disk drives, tape drives, and CD-ROM drives, among others. Most LANs allow more than one file server, thereby providing potential for gigabyte-range data storage capabilities. The LAN operating system should be checked for its capability to logically support the maximum physical storage capacity of all installed file servers. Physical drives consist of one or more rotating magnetic surfaces, or *platters*, mounted on a common spindle. Each physical drive is connected directly or through another drive to a *disk controller card* in the server.

The largest logical entity on a hard disk drive is the *partition*. A partition is mapped to a physical segment of the disk reserved for all volumes and directories under a single Disk or Network Operating System. Partitions are created by the host

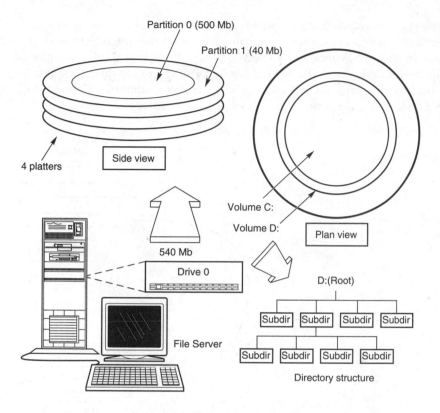

Figure 11.9
Mass storage device organization.

operating system. For example, MS-DOS- and OS/2-compatible hard disks can be divided into a maximum of four partitions. One common partitioning scheme is to put a LAN operating system, such as Novell's NetWare, on one partition and use a second partition for MS-DOS if the file server is non-dedicated (used as a concurrent workstation). Other partitions can be used for other operating systems as required by network or stand-alone applications. Typically, a dedicated file server's hard disk is set up for a single partition for the network operating system. Partitions are physically composed of contiguous *tracks* on the disk surface. Tracks also are referred to as *cylinders* in those drives with multiple platters (the rule in current generation drives).

When a partition is created, it is formatted by the appropriate host operating system or network operating system. The process of formatting each partition divides the partition logically into one or more *volumes*. Partitions are generally formatted to contain only one volume unless the partition size is larger than the maximum supported by the host operating system. In this case, the partition is divided into a primary partition and a secondary partition. The primary partition contains a single volume; the secondary partition can contain multiple volumes.

III

Local Area Networking

Volumes are contiguous physical areas within a partition and are also recognized as logical entities by the operating system. A volume is sometimes referred to as a *logical drive*. In MS-DOS, Windows NT, NetWare, and OS/2, logical drives are given alphabetic device designators (Drive A:, Drive C:, Drive D:, and so on). A volume can be either fixed or removable. Examples of removable volumes are floppy disks, removable hard disk drives, optical cartridges, and tape cartridges.

Figure 11.10
File server drive chaining (SCSI configuration).

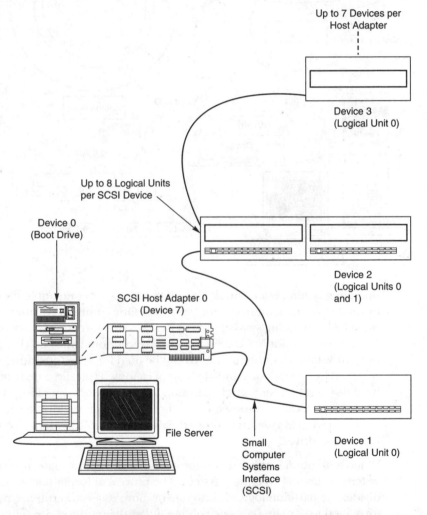

Tape mass storage devices also use the volume terminology, with a volume generally corresponding to an entire tape cassette, or to a single track on a cassette. However, the primary unit of physical division on a tape volume is the *block*, and the primary logical entity is the file. Blocks and files on tape volumes are physically contiguous. The tape drive is a *sequential access* device, whereas the hard disk is a

random access device. Sequential access devices store and retrieve data in contiguous blocks during I/O operations, whereas random access devices can store or retrieve data anywhere on the media surface on successive I/O operations.

Hard disk formatting is a two-part process. *Low-level formatting* of a partition creates physical tracks and sectors. These are then used by low-level device drivers for basic data storage and retrieval. *High-level formatting* establishes the root directory and file allocation tables and copies DOS system files onto the hard disk. These elements are the key to operating system file management. The operating system understands file structure and the device driver understands physical location on the disk. The file system device drivers support the file management requirements of the operating system.

When volumes are created, a *directory* structure is established. Almost all LAN operating systems use some form of *hierarchical* directory structure similar to MS-DOS, which in turn is based upon long-time UNIX operating system file conventions. The hierarchical file structure consists of a *root directory* and one or more *first-level subdirectories*. Each of the subdirectories can consist of one or more *second-level subdirectories*, and so on. This is shown in figure 11.9. Each volume on the hard disk has a corresponding root directory. Novell's NetWare uses a proprietary directory system on its servers. This system is different from MS-DOS and is optimized for high-performance network file operations—hence the need to create a separate partition for NetWare.

In practice, workstation logical drive designators (D:, E:, F:, and so on) are linked to specific subdirectories on the file server. This concept is generically known as redirection and is illustrated in figure 11.11. Any logical drive designator not assigned to a local device by the host operating system can be linked to a file server subdirectory by the network operating system. All network operating systems work in this general manner, although the command syntax details may differ.

Redirection is supported by an extension of the normal DOS path name to indicate the machine name where the resource is located. For example, a subdirectory named *word5* under the subdirectory *apps* under the root directory *system* on the server named *SERVER_01* is to be referred to as the following in the notation used by Microsoft and IBM in their network operating systems:

```
\\server_01\system\apps\winword6
```

Similar notation is used in Novell's NetWare. Because these path names can get tedious to work with, *aliases*, commonly called *sharenames*, are assigned to the path to simplify reference to and use by workstations. The path, or sharename, then becomes a shared resource and can be linked to any number of connected workstations. For example the preceding path name can be assigned the sharename *wordpro*, as in the following:

```
wordpro=\\server1\system\apps\winword6
```

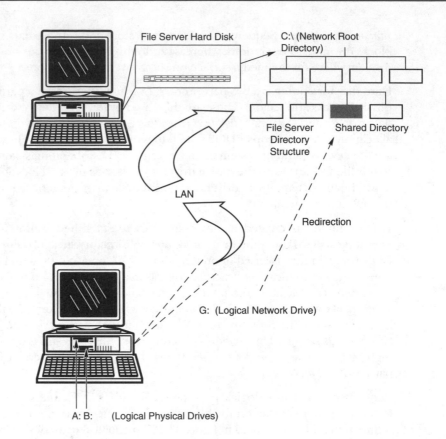

Figure 11.11
Linking directories on the file server.

Subdirectories contain files, the basic logical elements of any operating system, including those that control networks. Unlike volumes, files are not necessarily physically contiguous on a hard disk device. In the MS-DOS world, this leads to the requirement for a *File Allocation Table* (FAT), to provide a road map for the operating system to locate segments of files scattered around the disk. The FAT works in conjunction with the directory for each volume to provide file identification and location services for the host operating system. In OS/2, a new file structure called the *high-performance file system* is supported. Many of the long-standing performance limitations of the MS-DOS file system are significantly improved by HPFS. Windows NT introduces the NT File System, which improves upon the HPFS file system. Each operating system is backward-compatible to all previous file systems—for example, Windows NT supports the FAT and HPFS systems, and OS/2 supports the FAT system.

Because of the need to operate dissimilar workstations and a growing array of sophisticated data storage devices on networks, interoperating with different file structures is a requirement. These file structures include the Macintosh, UNIX,

DEC's VAX/VMS, HPFS, MS-DOS FAT system, Windows NT File System, CD-ROM, Write Once Read Many (WORM) drives, and others. Developments such as the *Installable File System* (IFS) feature of HPFS and Novell's extended file system in NetWare 3.*x* and 4.*x* are beginning to meet this need.

Output Resources

Network operating systems manage output resources through the use of print servers. *Print servers* consist of software that places redirected print jobs into one or more queues (waiting lines), manages the queues, and routes jobs to the appropriate output device. Print servers also manage shared device configuration.

In many networks, print servers are located with file servers. Specialized print server nodes independent of a host workstation are increasingly available. The print server must have either of the following:

✔ The required local I/O ports to attach supported printers up to a specified maximum number of serial and parallel devices

✔ Knowledge of where else on the network to send the print job

Print services must contend for the resources provided by a typical file server, including processor time and mass storage access.

Workstation applications access a print server by *spooling* a print job from the workstation to a temporary file on the file server. The print server process *despools* the print job from its temporary file to the destination printer. Think of spooling as copying a file from the workstation to the server, and despooling as copying a file from the server to the printer. The application has no knowledge of where the output is actually taking place, but only knows to send the job to a previously redirected logical output port.

An important consideration for network planning is whether the network operating system supports printers attached anywhere on the network or only those attached to the file server. Obviously, the former arrangement provides the greatest flexibility. In any case, print jobs can only be sent to printers identified as shareable by the network operating system. A printer not shared to the network is a local resource for its host computer only.

Performance considerations dictate that any workstation running print server software should have light-to-moderate local processing loads. One alternative is to dedicate multiple network stations as print servers, a luxury affordable only in larger organizations. A perhaps more flexible alternative is to use a dedicated print server device such as Intel's NetPort that does not require connection to a workstation. A NetPort device connects directly to a network cable on one side, and to one or more printers on the other side.

As with mass storage resources, output resources are managed by redirection from workstations. In this case, the local devices are parallel and serial communications ports, LPT1:, LPT2:, COM1:, and so on. In configuring the print server, an attached printer is connected to a server physical port, say LPT1:. On one workstation, the application is configured to the MS-DOS logical port LPT2:. On another workstation, the application is configured to the OS/2 logical port LPT3:. The applications may be different, yet both workstations can be redirected to the physical printer on the print server's LPT1: port. Figure 11.12 illustrates printer port redirection.

Figure 11.12
Network printer redirection.

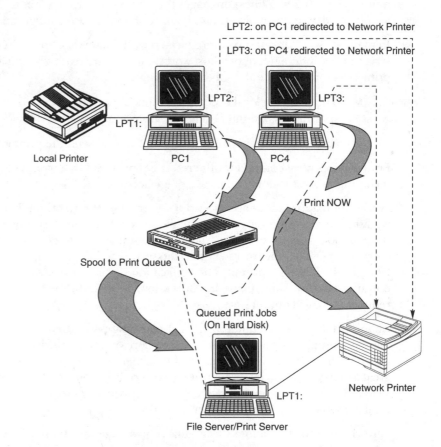

The print server must accommodate multiple requests for print jobs—often arriving faster than the printer can print. The overload is handled through a queuing mechanism that generally works on a *first-in, first-out* (FIFO) basis. Most network operating systems provide print queue management functions that enable workstation users or a network manager to designate certain jobs as high priority or to cancel jobs in the queue. The more sophisticated queue managers, such as those in NetWare 3.*x*/4.*x*, Windows NT, and OS/2 LAN Server provide time-

scheduled printing, full remote queue management, and user notification when jobs are complete or an error occurs on the output device. Figure 11.13 shows the queue management process in a typical LAN configuration.

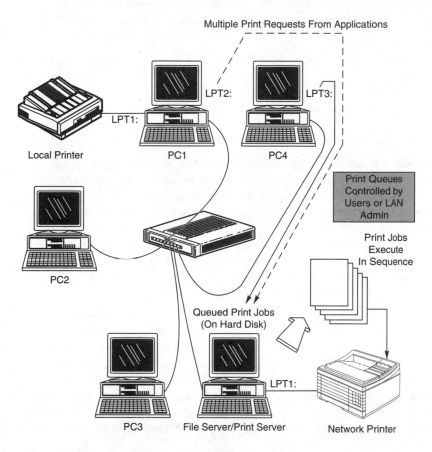

Figure 11.13
Network printer queue management.

Multiuser File Management

The unique concept of a network directory is its capability to be shared among several users. This sharing assumes that the users accessing the directory file(s) have passed network level security to get there in the first place. The tools that enable sharing are *file access* and *file sharing attributes, locks,* and *semaphores.* By MS-DOS and OS/2 convention, a file can be initially opened, or accessed for the following:

✔ Read only

✔ Write only

✔ Read and Write

These are termed *access attributes*. An access attribute is assigned by the application that opens the file—for example, if a data base management system executes a command requiring file modification, the file is opened for Read/Write access. File sharing attributes come into play only if a second or subsequent attempt is made to open the file. File sharing attributes are defined by MS-DOS and OS/2 as follows:

✔ Exclusive (non-shareable)

✔ Write access denied (shareable read-only)

✔ Read access denied (shareable write-only)

✔ Deny None access (shareable read-write)

These attributes are assigned implicitly by applications programs or explicitly by users. The file's assigned sharing attribute determines the action to be taken on the second or subsequent attempt to open the file by other users. This is illustrated by the sequences shown in figure 11.14. A network operating system can use these features to give users control over file sharing on the network. For example, this is done by the NET SHARE command in Windows NT or by the FLAG command in NetWare. Both MS-DOS and OS/2 enable the user to set the file attribute of Read-only at the operating system level through the ATTRIB command. This setting generally overrides access settings made through the NOS.

If a file is opened (initially accessed) for Read/Write with a Deny None sharing attribute, there must be an additional means to control updating of the file by more than one user. The term commonly used to describe this process is *synchronization*. Synchronization of file updates can be accomplished by the use of *file locks* and *byte-range locks* or by the use of *semaphores*. File locking protects the entire file from multiple user updates—byte-range locking protects a specified range of byte offsets within a file. Locking an entire file against multiuser updates within the MS-DOS or OS/2 environments is done by assigning the sharing attributes of Exclusive or Write Access Denied.

Record locking is more complex, but absolutely essential in most multiuser applications, especially database applications. The concept of record locking is an applications-oriented term because the operating system knows nothing about records. The application context converts a record into a byte-range offset within a file. Record locking can be done through *physical locks*, which are used by MS-DOS and OS/2 and work by protecting a specified range of byte offsets within a file. The operating system ensures that another application (or process in OS/2) cannot write to, read from, or lock the protected byte range. Locks are also classified as *wait locks* or *no-wait locks*. Wait locks delay and retry if the requested byte range is already locked. No-wait locks inform the requesting application or process that the requested byte range is already locked.

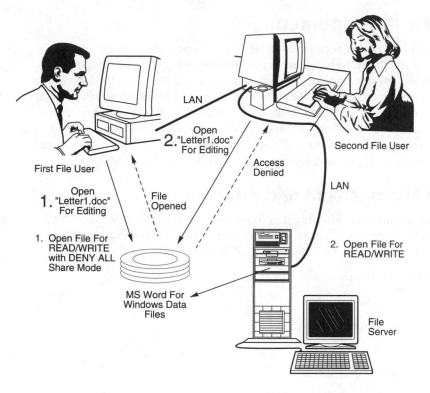

Figure 11.14
File sharing
operation in
MS-DOS.

LAN

Open
2. "Letter1.doc"
For Editing

Second File User

First File User

Access
Denied

Open
1. "Letter1.doc"
For Editing

File
Opened

LAN

1. Open File For
READ/WRITE
with DENY ALL
Share Mode

2. Open File For
READ/WRITE

MS Word For
Windows Data
Files

File
Server

Because of the intricate coordination required between processes within a multitasking environment such as OS/2, the use of byte-range locking within a file and invoking the lock interval for a minimum essential time are good network programming practices. OS/2's DosFileLocks API allows one byte range to be unlocked in the same call as another range is locked. Some systems, such as NetWare, permit multiple ranges of bytes to be locked on one call. This capability is useful in a transaction-oriented applications in which several records can be updated in one logical operation.

Semaphores are also not directly supported by MS-DOS, but they are provided as extended functions by various MS-DOS network operating systems. OS/2 fully supports semaphores. A *semaphore* is simply an addressable entity stored on disk or in memory that can be named, set, tested, changed, and cleared. Semaphores can be applied to files, a specified range of byte offsets within a file, or any shareable network device, such as a printer or modem. A semaphore is a logical control mechanism, whereas a lock is an access denial mechanism. A semaphore, which is more general than a lock, can be set up to have any meaning, including access denial, as long as all using processes understand and adhere to the defined meaning.

Network Management

The final topic of this generic overview of network operating systems deals with network management. Network management software is almost always bundled with the basic network operating system and provides a wide variety of services to both users and managers. Management functions can be built-in to basic network software running in both the workstation and file server, or they can be executed as stand-alone programs. Networks require a basic set of utilities to provide a workable management capability. These include security (access control) management including auditing, fault tolerance, backup, and performance monitoring.

Security Management and Auditing

The most basic management function that a network must provide is security management. In general, security management can be divided into the following four parts, not all of which are implemented in some networks:

- ✔ Network access
- ✔ User-level security
- ✔ Resource-level security
- ✔ File access
- ✔ Auditing

Figure 11.15 depicts a general security architecture for PC-based LANs, showing the relationship between the preceding parts.

Network Access

Network access is controlled by a *network login process*. The login process works in conjunction with user-level security, typically incorporating a *user account* containing a *user name* and an associated *password*. The login process runs on one or more network servers and provides the initial security check because each user must log in to at least one server to share resources on a network. The server(s) maintaining the network log in process run a validation check on the user name and associated password. Failure to pass the validation check causes the login attempt to fail. In some systems, the account that is the target of one or more invalid login attempts is locked from further login attempts until cleared by a supervisor. Network access security is only effective if the passwords assigned to users are properly protected and managed. Network access security should be mandatory for all users and uniformly administered for best results.

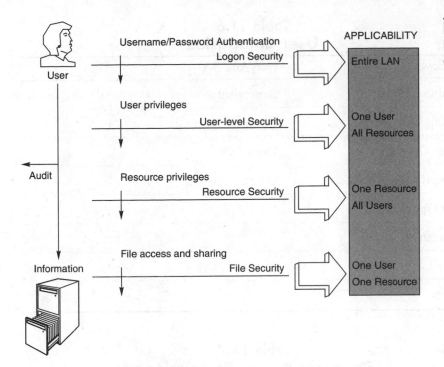

Figure 11.15
Network security concepts.

User-Level Security

User-level security is designed to assign privileges to individual users according to their functions and need to access specific network resources. User-level security works by assigning basic user categories (network privilege classes) and resource access privileges to user accounts. A *user profile* consists of a user category and a set of resource privileges assigned to a designated user. Table 11.6 provides examples of specific user categories by comparing Windows NT and NetWare network implementation. Resources include file server directories, printers, and external communications devices. For each registered network user, a set of privileges, permissions, or rights (terminology varies among network operating systems) relative to that user on one or more assigned resources is granted. Depending on the network operating system, user resource privileges can apply to some or all resources. Table 11.7 compares resource privileges granted to users by Windows NT and NetWare operating systems.

III

Local Area Networking

Table 11.6
User Categories

Windows NT	NetWare 3.x
Administrators	Supervisors
Backup Operators	Network operators
Server Operators	Users
Account Operators	Guests
Print Operators	
Replicators	
Users	
Guests	

Table 11.7
Resource Access Permissions

Windows NT*	NetWare 3.x**
Read	Read
Write	Write
Delete	Create
Execute	Delete
Take Ownership	Search
Change Permissions	Open
No Access	Parental
	Modify

*Applies only to designated resources

**Applies to all directory resources

All the network operating systems discussed in Part III implement the user group concept, although specific features relative to group management may differ. A *user group* is a class of users that shares a common function or needs to access common information sources on the network. In some networks, individual users may be assigned privileges equivalent to those of an existing group, thus simplifying network administration. Group assignments (more than one group can be assigned to a single user) are usually part of the user profile.

Resource-Level Security

Resource-level security is designed to protect individual resources on the network, independent of specific user privileges. Because network resources give access to specific classes or forms of information, resource security protects information. On mass storage devices, resource security levels can apply to just a specific directory or to a directory and its child subdirectories. The latter case is generally referred to as *inherited privileges*. In some systems, such as Banyan's VINES, no independent resource security exists—all access control is done through access control lists that specify authorized users for that resource.

In the case of NetWare 3.*x*, users and resources are assigned privileges (also known as *rights*) independently. If a user attempts to access a certain directory, the *effective access rights* are determined by comparing the user rights with the directory rights. The effective rights are simply the most restrictive rights of those the user carries and those held by the directory. Directory rights apply only to a specific directory level, whereas user rights apply to the entire directory structure on the user's logged-in file server. Figure 11.16 illustrates these concepts.

File Level Security

File level security generally affects whether a specific file is modifiable or shareable. File modification is controlled by the Read-only attribute. File sharing is controlled by the Shareable attribute.

Auditing

The basic function of an auditing capability is to determine who performed certain defined events considered critical to the maintenance of adequate network security. For example, in Windows NT file auditing can reflect which user performed a particular file event such as Read, Write, Execute, or Change Permissions, and whether the event succeeded or failed. Access to auditing records can itself be controlled through Access Control Lists.

Fault Tolerance

Fault tolerance is the combination of hardware and software techniques that ensures a degree of network operation and file integrity under various failure conditions.

The more common failures are loss of electrical power and hard disk failure. Total file server failures are possible, but more rarely encountered. The most obvious fault tolerant technique is to employ an *Uninterrupted Power Supply* (UPS) at least for each server, and preferably for all critical workstations. Appropriate UPS equipment can be connected to a file server's serial port for automatic shutdown service. The serial port monitors whether the UPS is operating from normal AC power—when the UPS detects a switch to battery-powered operation the server receives a signal from the UPS and starts an automatic shutdown process on the network.

Figure 11.16

Comparing resource and user access rights to obtain effective rights.

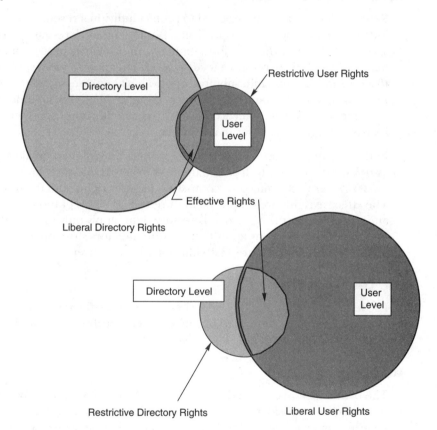

Novell's NetWare has been a leader in defining fault tolerant features for PC-based local area networks. The *System Fault Tolerance* (SFT) feature for NetWare was originally defined for the following three levels of protection:

✔ Level I—Surface defects and disk mirroring

✔ Level II—Disk duplexing

✔ Level III—Duplexed servers with hot standby

Windows NT Advanced Server, OS/2 LAN Server, and VINES also implement the equivalent of Levels I and II in their operating systems. Of the major network operating systems, only NetWare implements Level III as of this writing.

Disk mirroring uses a single disk controller card and two hard disk drives. Disk duplexing uses dual disk controllers and a hard disk drive on each controller. In each case, all disk operations on the primary drive are duplicated on the backup drive. Figures 11.17 and 11.18, respectively, illustrate the differences in system configuration between the two methods. The most recent form of disk protection is the *Redundant Array of Inexpensive Disks* (RAID) concept. RAID is defined in six levels: level 0 through level 5. The hardware used to implement RAID is most often the Small Computer System Interface because the RAID concept uses multiple drives and SCSI is a multiple drive peripheral interface standard. RAID is not only a fault tolerant system, but a throughput improvement system as well. In fact, some levels of RAID only provide throughput improvement and not fault tolerance. RAID can be implemented at the bit/byte level or at the disk sector level. Figure 11.19 illustrates the four RAID levels that implement mirroring.

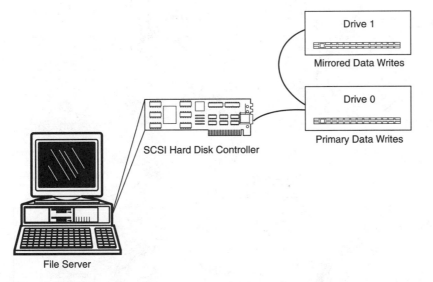

Drive 1

Mirrored Data Writes

Drive 0

Primary Data Writes

SCSI Hard Disk Controller

File Server

Figure 11.17
Fault tolerance with mirrored disk drives.

III

Local Area Networking

Figure 11.18
Fault tolerance
with duplexed
disk drives.

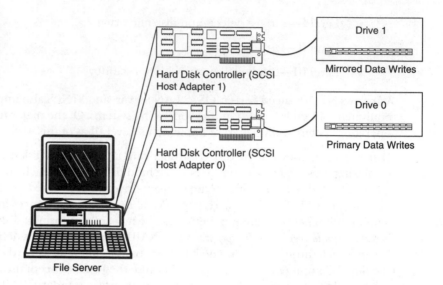

Figure 11.19
Redundant array
of inexpensive
disks (RAID)
levels (sector
writes only).

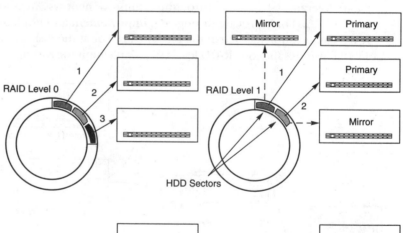

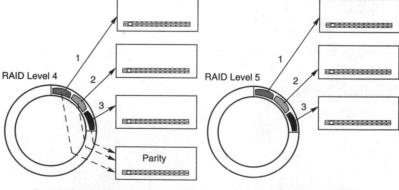

A *transaction tracking system* (TTS) capability protects critical files against file server or hard disk failures. TTS works on a *transaction*, or group of related file activities. A typical transaction applies to database operations and can encompass a series of related file updates resulting from a single user activity. Transaction operations are very typical for accounting applications in which a single General Ledger posting can cause updates to accounts payable, accounts receivable, and inventory files. Transactions have *boundaries*, which define where the transaction starts and where it ends. TTS works by ensuring that all activity within a transaction boundary completes successfully or not at all. In other words, if a hard disk or file server failure occurs within the time period of a transaction boundary, the entire transaction is *rolled back* to its pre-start state. All file updates as of the moment of failure are backed out, and the entire transaction must be repeated when normal operation is restored. Figure 11.20 illustrates this process.

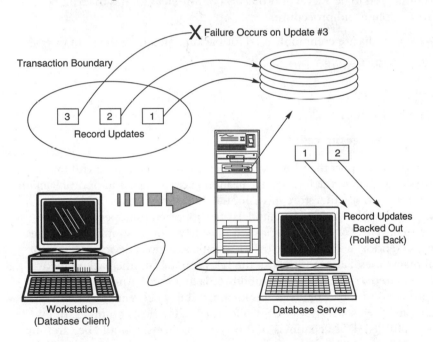

Figure 11.20
Transaction rollback recovery operation.

TTS support can be transparent to the using application if the application uses the appropriate APIs. For example, an application written using Btrieve Record Manager, NetWare's support for database-oriented *NetWare Loadable Modules* (NLMs) can be programmed to indicate starting and stopping of logical transactions. If TTS is active, the application has access to transaction concurrency control, and this access is transparent to the application user. Similar capabilities are available in the Database Manager module of IBM's OS/2 Extended Services. Transaction integrity support is inherent in the NT File System under Windows NT.

Because of the extra processing required to implement fault-tolerant features, certain performance penalties are inevitable. The proper balance between the extra reliability provided by fault-tolerant processing and maximum response time or throughput performance is a tradeoff. The user organization must determine the tradeoff and what, if any, fault-tolerant processing will be bypassed.

Archiving and Backup

Another critical utility in multiuser environments is the capability to safely back up data files. Backup can always be accomplished by procedure and discipline, but some network systems provide additional features to make the job easier and more bullet-proof. Strictly speaking, backup systems are not fault-tolerant systems, although they may be referred to as such in vendor literature. Fault tolerance is generally considered to be a level of protection beyond techniques that can be imposed by discipline and procedure.

Several types of media are commonly used for backup, including the following:

✔ Removable hard disk cartridges

✔ Tape cassettes

✔ Floppy diskettes

✔ Optical storage devices

Some systems even support the 11-track tape reels used in mainframe and mini-computer systems. In general, less standardization exists in tape and optical backup media than in hard disks, therefore it is essential that a prospective LAN buyer determine precisely what brands and models are supported by a specific LAN operating system. The LAN operating system must have (or be supplied from the backup media vendor) an I/O device driver specific to a given device or family of devices. In many cases, liaisons with both the LAN vendor and the backup media vendor are required to ascertain compatibility or lack thereof. Another source of potential problems with backup devices is incompatibility between the network adapter card and the backup device controller card in the host computer. Interrupt channels (IRQs), DMA channels, and I/O port addresses should be carefully inventoried at all potential host computers to prevent hardware conflicts.

A variety of features are found in backup systems. A backup drive (tape drive, for example) may be attached to the file server or to a workstation. In some networks, the network must be shut down to do backups—referred to as *off-line backups*. In others, backups can be done concurrently with network operations and are, therefore, *on-line backups*. Network backup can be centralized or distributed. *Centralized backup* puts one or more devices at a single location and enables only the network administrator to control backups from a single location, thus preserving a

higher degree of data integrity and security. *Distributed backup* uses one or more backup device locations and enables anyone on the network to back up to this device(s). A distributed backup system is also referred to as a *backup server*, because it serves any authorized user on the network. Figures 11.21 and 11.22 illustrate the difference in the two modes of operation.

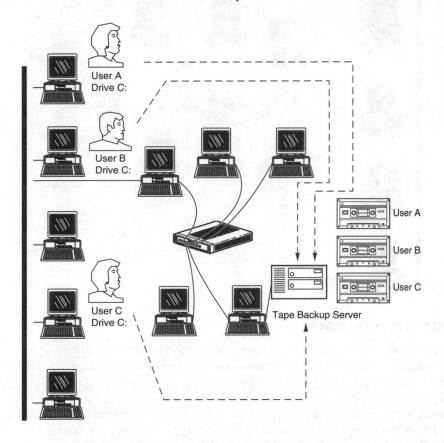

Figure 11.21
Decentralized tape backup—user controlled.

Backup systems commonly provide a scheduling feature that usually offers the option of backing up at designated clock times or at specified intervals (or both). If a particular network operating system does not support on-line backups from the file server, workaround options are available. If a tape drive is attached in a stand-alone mode to a workstation, that workstation can download file server directories or files and back them up locally. This system requires adherence to a more rigid discipline to compensate for lack of centralized network control over the operation. Finally, mature backup systems offer an archiving library feature. This feature typically enables the user (in a distributed system) to specify a file, and the software indicates a specific tape cartridge on which that file can be found. In a large system, time savings can be substantial.

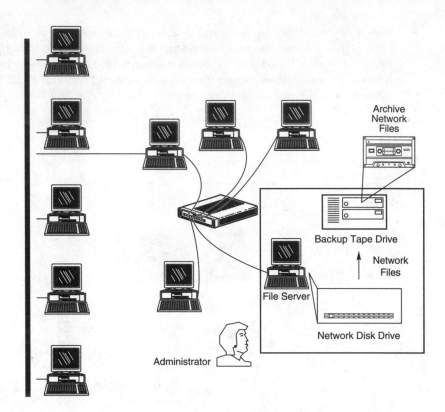

Figure 11.22
Centralized tape backup— administrator controlled.

Archive Network Files

Backup Tape Drive

Network Files

File Server

Network Disk Drive

Administrator

Performance Monitoring

Performance monitoring is a management function provided by both third-party vendors and network operating system vendors. Performance monitoring is important because it provides tools for the network administrator to improve network performance. Performance monitoring yields statistics on network throughput, server performance, hard disk performance, and network interface card operation. Performance Monitor in Windows NT; Server Manager, Monitor, PERFORM3, and LANalyzer For Windows in NetWare; *Simple Network Management Protocol* (SNMP) in TCP/IP for OS/2; and MNET on VINES are examples of performance monitoring software available in the major network operating systems.

Linking Applications Across Single Networks

An application running in a LAN environment must ultimately communicate with compatible applications in other workstations and/or servers on the same LAN or on other LANs or host systems that may or may not be directly connected. For this to happen successfully, the application must follow a prescribed set of rules on how it establishes a link and exchanges data with the corresponding remote application. Keep in mind that "remote" in this context means any network resource not connected to the workstation running the application. The remote application can be in the same room, in a different building, or across the continent. For purposes of the following discussions, remote connectivity is considered to be at the single LAN level—multiple LAN internetworking considerations are discussed in Chapter 13, "Internetworking and Interoperability."

Not every network operating system supports every transport service. The trend with VINES, OS/2, Windows NT, and NetWare network operating systems, however, is to develop a comprehensive strategy to provide parallel support for all the major services. To view this strategy in its proper perspective, look at the layer 5 and layer 3 interfaces. Ideally, a particular transport service should remain transparent to the underlying hardware implementations covered in Chapter 12, "Local Area Networks: The Communications Perspective." Similarly, the transport services should remain transparent to network applications. As if these requirements were not stringent enough, you also want multiple transport services to be resident and available on demand by multiple applications.

This chapter discusses what transport services, or sets of prescribed protocols, are commonly available to support distributed applications and their significance in the larger context of standardization efforts. Among the more commonly used are redirector-server protocols, Named Pipes and Mail Slots, NetBIOS, NetBEUI, APPC/PC, TCP/IP, XNS, and OSI. More detailed protocol descriptions of APPC/PC, TCP/IP, XNS, and OSI are discussed in greater detail in Chapter 13.

Redirector-Server Protocol

The primary redirector-server protocols in use in today's LANs are the Server Message Block in IBM and Microsoft networks and the NetWare Core Protocol (NCP) in NetWare networks. The basic purpose of both protocols is to control remote file and print services over a network. The SMB protocol has four types of server message blocks, as follows:

- ✔ Session control
- ✔ File management
- ✔ Print queue management
- ✔ Message management

Session control establishes the dialog between the workstation and server. File management blocks extend normal DOS file commands across the network. Print queue management provides control and status of print server queues. Message management SMBs control the sending and receipt of user-to-user messages on the network. Each SMB is a formatted packet with specific data meanings defined within the packet.

NCP is somewhat more robust than SMB because it provides considerably more functions and implements the Burst mode for large file transfers. Burst mode is an efficient means with which to transfer large files because up to 64 KB of data can be transferred without any further NCP protocol exchange. Novell has determined that Burst mode provides an approximate four-fold gain in throughput over non-Burst mode redirector-server exchanges. Table 11.8 provides a comparison of SMB and NCP protocol, showing the major functional classifications for each protocol and how they map to each other.

Table 11.8
NCP and SMB Protocol Compared

NetWare Core Protocol	Server Message Block
Accounting services	
Bindery services	
Connection services	Session control commands
Directory services	File access commands
File services	File access commands
File server environment	
Message services	Message commands
Print services	Print commands
Queue services	
Synchronization services	File access commands
TTS services	

Named Pipes and Mail Slots

The Named Pipes and Mail Slots protocols were mentioned earlier as major interprocess communications features of OS/2 and Windows NT. For applications connectivity on a contiguous network, Named Pipes is more efficient than

NetBIOS, and in all likelihood will become a dominant *intra-LAN* client-server standard. Because it is a part of the OS/2 and Windows NT operating systems and indirectly supported by MS-DOS (by virtue of recognizing Named Pipe file names), Named Pipes will have a catalytic effect on the standardization of groupware and other client-server applications development. Technically, Named Pipes is an applications-level interface to OS/2. The Windows NT version has its own file system, called *Named Pipes File System*. In certain applications, Named Pipes can work in concert with Redirector-Server protocol depending on the function to be executed on the remote server. Named Pipes is very efficient for transaction-based communications, whereas redirector-server protocols is more suitable for file and print services.

Mail Slots are similar to Named Pipes except that opening and closing calls are not required. Mail Slots can be implemented as First Class—acknowledged datagrams, or Second Class, unacknowledged datagrams. Windows NT implements Second Class Mail Slots only; OS/2 implements both classes. Mail Slots are most suitable for broadcasting service availability or system messages.

Network Basic Input/Output System (NetBIOS)

The capability of applications to link up depends directly on the communications services provided to them by the network operating system. The most common example is the communications service referred to as NetBIOS, designed to enable communications between applications on a single logical LAN.

NetBIOS has been adopted as a de facto LAN-to-applications program interface standard by the LAN industry. It is important to differentiate between the NetBIOS interface and the NetBIOS protocol implementations. The application calls the NetBIOS interface and receives responses from that interface—the details of what happens within a particular NetBIOS protocol stack are unknown to the application.

One of the more confusing aspects of NetBIOS is its relationship to applications level software in non-IBM networks. Many networks now offer "NetBIOS compatibility." What does this mean, and how does it affect network performance? Is it really necessary? The answers to these questions are important to the network manager who has the task of choosing the "right" network software. To answer these questions, you must understand what is included within the "black box" behind a NetBIOS software interrupt or API.

Although "NetBIOS compatible" software may accept the standard NetBIOS calls and return the same results, the "black box" underneath NetBIOS may be significantly different. Most vendors implement an emulation of the layer 5 protocol, but use different transport and network layer protocols, including TCP/IP and Novell's SPX/IPX.

The most common user interface to NetBIOS consists of executing certain commands supported by compatible LAN operating systems. These LAN systems support calls from an application or from the Redirector through the software interrupt 2A. Third-party applications programs can directly access the services supported by NetBIOS through software interrupt 5C. This interrupt invokes a NetBIOS emulation program, as discussed earlier. If an applications program is written to use interrupt 2A or 5C, the emulation program ensures a standard processing sequence. The application program provides certain required data elements, which are put into a format called a *Network Control Block* (NCB). The call to interrupt 2A or 5C is then made, and the emulator handles the required LAN processing (see fig. 11.23). The advantage of this sequence is that applications programmers can use the standard NCB format to set up the LAN as an I/O device. This effort at standardization had a profound effect on the overall acceptance of LANs, both for software developers and for the ultimate benefactor—the user.

Figure 11.23
NetBIOS
interface to
applications and
transport
protocol stack.

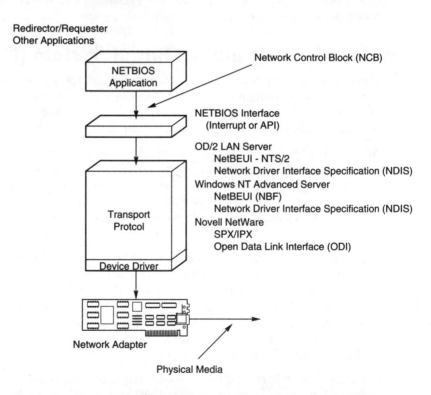

For applications not requiring specific session-level compatibility, a NetBIOS interface is not required. Session-level compatibility is required if the IBM PC Network-compatible *Name Management Protocol* (NMP) is used by a specific application software package. The naming service supported by NetBIOS recognizes human-readable names linked to a specific workstation or file server on the network. This name is logically assigned to one of several possible objects active in the network node. For example, shared directories have names; attached printers have names; and names are maintained for several possible message recipients using that node. The disadvantage of this naming convention is that no central "telephone book" is maintained on the network. Each workstation or file server keeps only its own name directory. NetBIOS-compatible network adapter cards support up to 17 names per device, one of which is reserved for the permanent name of the device itself. The NetBEUI protocol extends this name capacity to 254 names. The naming convention is shown in figure 11.24. Figure 11.25 summarizes the view of NetBIOS from the different perspectives of IBM and non-IBM LANs.

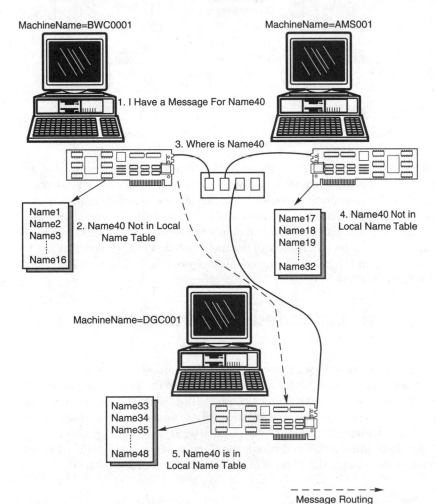

Figure 11.24
NetBIOS naming convention and operation.

MachineName=BWC0001

MachineName=AMS001

1. I Have a Message For Name40

3. Where is Name40

Name1
Name2
Name3
⋮
Name16

2. Name40 Not in Local Name Table

Name17
Name18
Name19
⋮
Name32

4. Name40 Not in Local Name Table

MachineName=DGC001

Name33
Name34
Name35
⋮
Name48

5. Name40 is in Local Name Table

- - - - - →
Message Routing

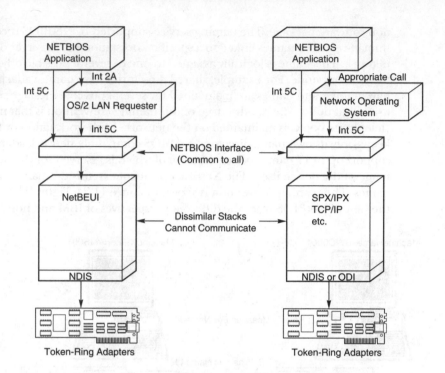

Figure 11.25
IBM and non-IBM NetBIOS implementations compared.

When an application wants to cooperate with its counterpart on a remote LAN, a service other than NetBIOS is more appropriate. The NetBIOS protocol was not designed for remote communications and operates somewhat inefficiently for this purpose. Lack of support for a more robust and centrally-managed resource naming system is a particularly critical omission from NetBIOS. NetBIOS naming conventions should not be confused with the more robust VINES StreetTalk or *NetWare Directory Services* (NDS) name protocols designed for internetworking use. Chapter 13 discusses these in detail.

Network Basic Extended User Interface (NetBEUI)

NetBEUI was developed by IBM for use on Token Ring networks. It has the same basic applications interface as NetBIOS, but does not use the proprietary lower-level protocol developed by Sytek under license to IBM. NetBEUI is currently used by Windows NT in its peer-to-peer networking and Advanced Server architectures. The Windows implementation is known as the *NetBIOS Frame* (NBF) protocol. NetBEUI interfaces with NetBIOS through the *Transport Data Interface* (TDI) and with LAN adapters through the *Network Driver Interface Specification* (NDIS).

Advanced Program-to-Program Communications/PC (APPC/PC)

Whereas NetBIOS was designed as a mechanism to connect applications in the pure LAN environment, APPC/PC was developed to support IBM's vision of linking applications across an entire continuum of computing machinery, from mainframes to minis to PCs. Moreover, these applications would have peer-to-peer status rather than the older SNA hierarchical arrangement in which the mainframe host controlled the entire network.

APPC/PC is the APPC interface defined for PCs connected to LANs. The protocols supporting APPC/PC parallel the NetBIOS protocol. APPC/PC's protocol is the *Logical Unit Type 6.2* (LU 6.2) and consists of session, transport, and network layer services. PCs using APPC/PC are identified to an SNA network as *Physical Unit Type 2.1* or *2.0* (PU 2.1 or PU 2.0). A PU 2.1 is a peer-to-peer type station, whereas a PU 2.0 is a terminal controller type station. SNA gateway stations emulate a PU 2.0 station, because they provide the same functionality to a LAN as terminal controllers do to attached terminals. Peer-to-peer stations are capable of transferring data with each other; a PU 2.0 station expects to be connected to a host front-end processor, or in IBM's terminology a communications controller running a version of the Network Control Program. Connected PU 2.1 stations can use either LAN physical connections or an SDLC link.

TCP/IP

Transmission Control Protocol/Internet Protocol (TCP/IP) originated within the *Department of Defense's* (DOD) long-standing *Arpanet* wide area network. Arpanet has been subsumed as one component of the *Defense Data Network* (DDN), but has always been one of the most sophisticated wide area networks in the world. The current incarnation of Arpanet is known simply as the Internet. The capability of the Internet to interconnect a large variety of dissimilar host computers worldwide is made possible in part by the TCP/IP protocol. Only in the late 1980s has TCP/IP transitioned from relative obscurity in the commercial world to become a major force in standardizing the interconnection of commercial networks, both LANs and WANs.

Today, TCP/IP has become the protocol of choice to connect such diverse systems as UNIX, Macintosh, OS/2, Windows NT, and various mainframe and minicomputer operating systems and their dissimilar file structures. Proprietary operating systems such as NetWare, VINES, and Windows NT now support the TCP/IP protocol with a variety of implementation schemes. A standard is being developed to combine the NetBIOS interface with TCP/IP protocol. This standard is defined in two documents: *Request For Comments* (RFC) 1001 and RFC 1002. This means that users of otherwise incompatible operating systems can now accomplish basic file transfers across a wide variety of networks, regardless of the details of physical connection. As with other sets of transport services, however, not all TCP/IP implementations are alike, therefore the end-user must shoulder the burden of compatibility and interoperability.

TCP/IP includes the following three generic application protocols:

- ✔ File Transfer Protocol (FTP)
- ✔ Simple Mail Transfer Protocol (SMTP)
- ✔ *Telnet*—a terminal emulation program

Underlying these applications are two lower layers of protocol, the *Transport Control Protocol* (TCP) and the *Internet Protocol* (IP). TCP is a reliable, connection-oriented protocol. *Reliable* means that the transport-level protocol guarantees that data packets arrive in sequence and error-free, with no missing data. *Connection-oriented* means that the protocol establishes a session between two remote stations or processes and maintains that session during the entire interval required to transfer data packets. TCP/IP also supports a *User Datagram Protocol* (UDP) designed for rapid, one-way delivery of relatively short messages. This concept is termed a connectionless service. UDP is not reliable, depending instead on the reliability inherent in lower level protocols such as the IEEE 802.X series. Figure 11.26 illustrates the conceptual differences between TCP and UDP services.

TCP/IP can run on any combination of layers 1 and 2 as long as the appropriate drivers (interface software between layers 2 and 3) are available. This linking of TCP/IP and lower level protocols is done through a process called *binding*. In the binding process, the layer 3 and 4 protocol stack is made to communicate with the appropriate LAN communications protocol, such as Ethernet, Token Ring, or ARCnet. Although TCP/IP is most commonly found on Ethernets, it can now be bound to a wide variety of LAN hardware implementations. Because of TCP/IP's importance to internetworking, from whence it was derived, Chapter 13 presents a discussion on protocol details.

One product developed to work on top of TCP/IP is worthy of discussion in its own right. The product is the *Network File System* (NFS) from Sun Microcomputers. NFS is a generic capability supported by TCP/IP, but not a TCP/IP protocol per se. Figure 11.27 shows the NFS protocol hierarchy. NFS is compatible with file systems on over 100 computers, from mainframes to PCs. NFS consists of two additional protocols: *Remote Procedure Call* (RPC) at the session layer and *Extended Data Representation* (XDR) at the presentation layer.

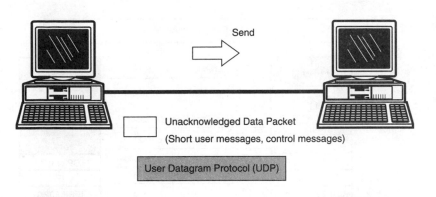

Figure 11.26
Datagram and transmission control protocols compared for TCPP/IP.

Send

Unacknowledged Data Packet

(Short user messages, control messages)

User Datagram Protocol (UDP)

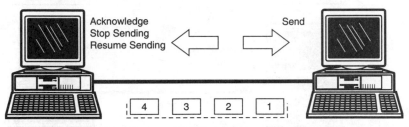

Acknowledge
Stop Sending
Resume Sending

Send

| 4 | 3 | 2 | 1 |

Sequenced Data Packets with Acknowledgement and Flow Control

(File transfer, EMail)

Transmission Control Protocol (TCP)

III

Local Area Networking

RPC is a machine and operating system independent protocol designed to execute commands on a remote node of the network. NFS commands are file-oriented and pass parameters such as directory, file name, and file attributes. NFS commands are set up like subprograms or procedures in a software program, hence the name Remote Procedure Call. XDR is a way of normalizing data representation among a large number of otherwise incompatible operating systems. The normalization process involves byte-ordering (which byte in a data word is the high-order or most significant byte); word length (how many bytes in different types of data); and how numbers are represented (floating point usage). The NFS protocol works with all popular operating system file formats, including the Macintosh Hierarchical File System, DEC's VAX/VMS, MS-DOS FAT, and all versions of UNIX among others. An important criteria in evaluating TCP/IP implementations is whether NFS is supported. For example, TCP/IP services for Windows NT (version 3.1) does not support the NFS standard, whereas OS/2, NetWare, and VINES do. The Windows NT version of RPC is not compatible with the NFS version.

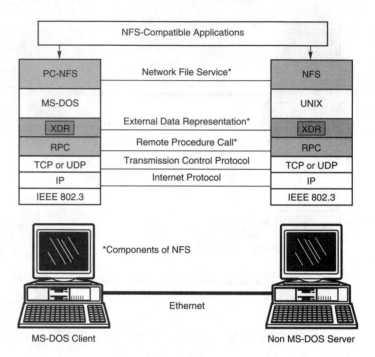

Figure 11.27
Network File
System (NFS)
architecture.

Xerox Network Services (XNS) Including Novell's SPX/IPX

XNS has been the transport protocol of choice for many network operating systems. XNS has an Ethernet heritage and along with TCP/IP was one of the earlier practical internetworking protocols. NetWare's *Sequenced Packet Exchange* (SPX) is based on the XNS *Sequenced Packet Protocol* (SPP), and *Internet Packet Exchange* (IPX) is based on the XNS *Internet Datagram Protocol* (IDP). XNS spans the session layer through the network layer and, like TCP/IP, can work with several physical network implementations such as Ethernet, ARCnet, and Token Ring. Windows NT implements certain features from the general XNS protocol set— among them are the *Courier Protocol* (layer 5), Sequenced Packet Protocol (layer 4), *Packet Exchange Protocol* (PEP) (layer 4), and the Internet Datagram Protocol (layer 3). To implement its StreetTalk naming service, Banyan uses a variation of the Xerox Clearinghouse Protocol.

OSI

The ultimate dream of networking professionals is to have a single consistent set of protocols that can be used worldwide as a basis for interoperable communications

between dissimilar computer systems and networks. This dream may never come to pass in reality, but if it does, it will be through the efforts of the *International Standards Organization* (ISO) and its model for *Open Systems Interconnection* (OSI). OSI is the basis for the seven-layer protocol model discussed throughout this book and for continuing efforts to find long range solutions to the problems of standardization. The problem thus far with the implementation of the OSI protocol is the multiplicity of options developed at each layer; this inevitably leads to diverse implementation schemes and a commensurate breakdown of standardization.

The ISO protocol stack that will be supported by major LAN software vendors is the *ISO TP4*, or *Transport Class 4*. This is a connection-oriented protocol, which as discussed earlier means that a virtual circuit is established between the two entities communicating with this protocol. ISO TP4 is the highest grade of service available among the ISO transport protocol and assumes that the underlying network is unreliable. In other words, TP4 does its own error checking.

A general protocol such as the ISO stack must encompass so many contingencies that it becomes burdensome for certain LAN implementations. Most LANs can count on a reliable low-level link and therefore need streamlined protocol stacks for optimum performance.

Multiple Protocol Selection

Microsoft and Novell have developed different versions of a multiprotocol management scheme. Standard interfaces to network adapter cards include Microsoft's *Network Driver Interface Specification* (NDIS) and Novell's *Open Data Link Interface* (ODI). OS/2 implements NDIS as the native multiprotocol interface as a component of *Network Transport Services/2* (NTS/2). Through Novell, translation from NDIS to ODI is accomplished in the NetWare Requester For OS/2 package. This package enables an OS/2 workstation to access a NetWare Server. IBM provides two conversions from ODI to NDIS: one for NetWare Requester for OS/2 and one that runs under NTS/2. Higher-level (session layer to transport layer) multiple stack interfaces include the Transport Data Interface implemented by Microsoft and the AT&T Streams and *Transport Layer Interfaces* (TLI) implemented by Novell. The goal of a multiple protocol interface is to address arrows 3 and 4 in figure 11.3—the interface between the network operating system and the transport protocol stack, and between the transport stack and the underlying physical network implementation. Ideally the operating system should have access to a selection of popular protocol stacks; likewise the protocol stacks should be independent of the choice of Ethernet, ARCnet, or Token Ring physical networks. Multiple protocol selection design is migrating towards a capability to load a number of supported protocol sets dynamically as needed.

Summary

In this chapter, LANs were discussed from the applications support software perspective. The relationship between host MS-DOS, Windows NT, and OS/2 operating systems; network operating systems; and the software required to link applications was highlighted. These concepts and relationships are crucial to an understanding of not only how networks operate, but to making informed decisions on the specific network software architecture to meet an organization's business needs. In support of an application, the network operating system eventually calls on the services provided by the underlying network hardware implementation. The details of the physical aspect of moving information on the LAN and its significance are covered next.

Chapter Snapshot

From the preceding chapter, we learned that LANs are a sophisticated form of distributed processing that enable a variety of shared applications and resources. In this chapter, we step back and look at LANs as a fundamental means of communicating data in a relatively small area and at relatively high speeds. Lower level communications considerations can sometimes have a financial impact out of proportion to their effect on applications development. In this chapter you will learn about:

✔ LAN hardware and communications terminology

✔ Basic LAN adapter card design elements

✔ The differences between media, including physical characteristics and costs

✔ Topology types, including the rules for Ethernet, Arcnet, Token-Ring and FDDI layouts, and their significance in LAN planning

✔ The characteristics of baseband and broadband signaling

✔ Physical and Data Link protocol descriptions, and their relationship to higher layers in the OSI model

✔ Practical considerations in LAN performance assessment

CHAPTER

12

Local Area Networks: the Communications Perspective

This chapter focuses on basic terminology and concepts associated
with the underlying communications technology of local area
networks (LANs). Although LAN technology provides the means to move
data between stations on the network and to manage access to the stations' data
path, certain LAN industry standards such as Ethernet, ARCnet, and IBM Token
Ring relate more to communications than to data processing and are, therefore,
discussed in that context. The remainder of the chapter describes the physical
components of LANs: the network adapter card, wiring types and layouts, the
representation of data, and the basics of physical and data link layer protocols for
the most common LAN types. The chapter also covers the impact of physical
factors on LAN selection and performance, and how the shared applications and
LAN systems software discussed in the preceding chapter rely on the physical
connectivity provided by a LAN. Another chapter objective is to make common
networking terms such as *star, ring, bus, broadband,* and *baseband* meaningful to the
potential network student, buyer, and manager.

Network Adapter Cards: Getting the Data In and Out

Figure 12.1 illustrates the basic concepts of a simplified LAN. Hardware components consist of four PCs, a printer, and an internal hard disk attached to the PC called SERVER1. In each PC, an adapter card is required in one of the expansion slots; this card is commonly referred to as a *network adapter card* (NAC) or *network interface card* (NIC). Increasingly, peripheral devices such as printers have imbedded LAN adapters or interface devices that connect directly to the network. Designed for LAN communications functions, the adapter card fulfills the same purpose as the RS-232-C asynchronous communications card does in a modem/telephone network—to provide the required functions for data to move from the PC or peripheral to the network, and from the network to the PC or peripheral. Each station on the LAN containing a network adapter card is referred to as a *network node.*

Figure 12.1
Basic LAN hardware components.

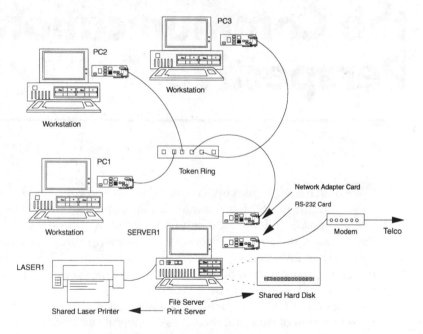

The network adapter card plays a major role in determining local area network performance. It is also the physical and logical link between the microcomputer or peripheral hosting the NAC and the network to which it is attached. On one side, the adapter card must exchange data with the host computer's microprocessor and internal RAM through the computer's *internal bus*; on the other side it must

transmit and receive data at the speed and in the format required by the network physical data path, or *media.* Figure 12.2 shows various means of connecting NACs to the media.

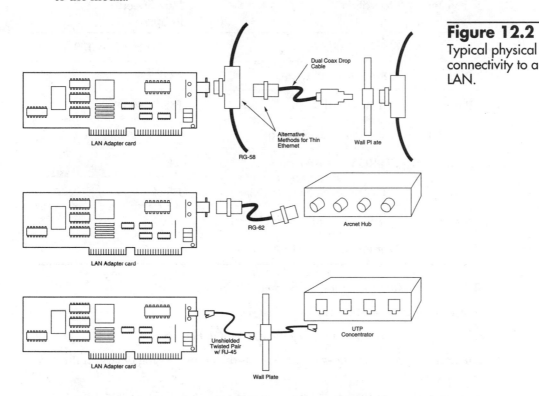

Figure 12.2
Typical physical connectivity to a LAN.

A major factor that characterizes a LAN is the speed at which data move on the network. Table 12.1 contrasts the speeds of 100, 16, 10, and 2.5 Mbps LANs such as FDDI, Token Ring, Ethernet, and ARCnet, with other forms of data movement to and from, or within a PC. The table points out that network data rates can vary widely from internal computer and typical wide area network data rates. The table also shows the large disparity between asynchronous link and LAN data rates.

Local area network data transfers are done in a serial mode—bit by bit. A mismatch in data rates between the network and its host processor requires *buffering,* or temporary data storage, to prevent the loss of data as it goes into the host computer. The network adapter card's job is to manage data rate mismatches, which usually occur because the network adapter card processes data packets slower than the network carries them and slower than the host computer is capable of moving data to and from the card. In other words, the network adapter card becomes a bottleneck between the network media and its host computer.

Table 12.1
Data Transfer Rate Comparison

Transfer Type	Operation	Max Speed (Mbps)
Serial	Network data rate	$100.0/16.0/10.0/2.5^1$
Parallel	EISA Bus read/write	$33.0^{2,4}$
Parallel	PCI Bus read/write	$132.0/264.0^{3,4}$
Parallel	Hard disk transfer rate	13.8^5
Parallel	CD-ROM transfer rate	$3.6^{5,6}$
Serial	T-1 Wide Area Network	1.544
Serial	High-speed data leased line	.056
Serial	Modem at 14,400 bps	0.0144^7

[1]FDDI/Token-Ring (16 Mbps)/Ethernet/ARCnet data rate

[2]Figures shown are for burst mode, 32-bit data path

[3]Figures shown are for burst mode, 32-bit/64-bit data path

[4]The network sees much slower node speeds due to processing delays on the adapter card

[5]IBM 400 MB SCSI HDD. Hard disk/CD-ROM times do not include average physical media access time

[6]Triple-speed drives

[7]Analog data rate at modem RJ-11

The adapter card can contain significant amounts of *firmware*, or software in one or more *Read-Only Memory* (ROM) chips. This software is primarily designed to implement communications protocols. Firmware can include protocols up to and including any layer of the OSI model. Most commonly the cards have firmware for layers 1 and 2 of the OSI model.

Adapter cards are designed to communicate with the host computer through *Direct Memory Access* (DMA) channels, *Shared Memory, Interrupt Request Channels* (IRQ) channels, and/or Input/Output ports. Figure 12.3 illustrates the basic functions of a network adapter card, including basic data conversions (for example, parallel to serial), packet assembly and disassembly, network access control, data buffering, and network signaling.

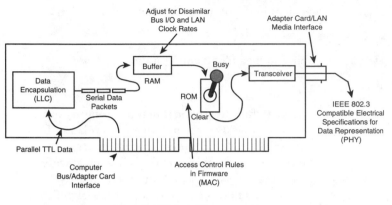

Figure 12.3
Basic LAN adapter card functions.

Of significance to LAN Administrators is the potential for conflict between LAN adapter cards and other expansion cards in the PC that use the same channel or port. In some designs, the adapter card uses a portion of the PC's extended RAM (addressable memory between 640 KB and 1 MB), which may conflict with devices such as VGA video adapters. Channel conflicts prevent both the LAN and the interfering card's device from working properly, or at all. A well-designed adapter card lets you change the various interface channels by means of dip switches or jumper blocks.

LAN adapters that provide various installation aids, including automatic configuration, are becoming more and more common. A well-planned network installation should include a thorough inventory of all I/O channels in use on each workstation and server. With the growing use of laptop and notebook computers, portable LAN adapters that attach to the laptop's parallel port or that can be inserted into a *Personal Computer Memory Card International Association* (PCMCIA) slot are becoming increasingly available. These adapters can be obtained for Ethernet, ARCnet, and Token Ring networks with a choice of LAN media connectors.

Local Area Network Classification

From pure communications and physical perspectives, the type of network selected by an organization has a significant bearing on several factors of importance to network management, including the following:

✔ Hardware and installation capital costs

✔ Ease of installation

✔ Ease of maintenance including fault tolerance and fault isolation

✔ Ease of expansion

✔ Physical design flexibility and ease of reconfiguration

✔ Performance

Thus, the prospective user should carefully weigh the inherent strengths and weaknesses of a particular network's physical configuration and its relationship to the first two layers of the OSI model. In evaluating these characteristics, some thought should be given to the vendor's strategic direction as new product lines evolve. Although the most significant LAN strategies are oriented towards the higher OSI layer functions and potential network applications, some significant directions can be seen in hardware evolution. The increasing penetration of twisted-pair Ethernet and Token Ring systems is a current hardware trend. Other trends include the continued movement towards higher data rates in both copper and fiber-optic media and greater recognition of the importance of wireless media. In many LAN installations, hardware costs associated with the first two OSI layers can become a significant economic consideration.

Four ways of classifying networks as data communications systems are as follows:

✔ Type of data path

✔ Means used to represent data on the media

✔ Physical network layout

✔ Media sharing

The commonly used terms for these concepts are *media, signaling, topology,* and *access protocol,* respectively. Layer 1 protocol incorporates the first three of these classifications, whereas layer 2 protocol addresses access and media sharing.

Media

Media is the general term used to describe the data path that forms the physical channel between local area network devices, or nodes. Media can be twisted-pair wire, such as that used for telephone installations, coaxial cable of various sizes and electrical characteristics, fiber optics, and wireless, supporting either light waves or radio waves. Wire or fiber-optic media are referred to as *bounded media.* Wireless media are sometimes referred to as *unbounded media.* Media differ in their capability to support high data rates and long distances. The reasons for this are based in physics and electrical engineering and include the concepts of noise absorption, radiation, attenuation, and bandwidth.

Noise absorption is the susceptibility of the media to external electrical noise that can cause distortion of the data signal and thus data errors. *Radiation* is the leakage of signal from the media caused by undesirable electrical characteristics of the media. As discussed later in this chapter, radiation phenomena is now being converted from a liability to an asset in new wireless in-building networking concepts. Radiation and the physical characteristics of the media contribute to *attenuation,* or the reduction in signal strength as the signal travels down the wire or through free space. Attenuation limits the usable distance that data can travel on the media. *Bandwidth* is similar to the concept of frequency response in a stereo amplifier—the greater the frequency response, the higher the bandwidth. According to a fundamental principal of information theory, higher bandwidth communications channels support higher data rates. In this context, the medium is configured to represent one or more communications channels.

Twisted-Pair Wire

Twisted-pair wire traditionally has been the most limited form of data path, both in speed and distance. In many cases, twisted-pair media require an unpleasant choice between acceptable data rates at short distances, or lower data rates at acceptable distances. It has always been the cheapest form of wiring to install, primarily because of the low cost of the media itself. Twisted-pair cable typically costs five to ten cents per lineal foot for unshielded wire, and about 25 cents per foot for shielded wire. Shielded wire typically is used in an electrically noisy environment to limit the effects of noise absorption. Unshielded twisted pair, commonly referred to as UTP, is by far the more common of the two configurations. Continuing developments in LAN technology have made twisted-pair wiring more commonly used for LAN media. Advanced circuitry now enables the optional use of twisted-pair wiring on traditional coaxial networks, such as Ethernet and ARCnet. The *Institute of Electrical and Electronic Engineers* (IEEE) has designated the twisted pair version of Ethernet as 10BASE-T, in which the 10 refers to the Ethernet clock rate of 10 Mbps. Twisted pair versions of the high-bandwidth *Fiber Distributed Data Interface* (FDDI) are available. The *American National Standards Institute* (ANSI) has drafted a standard called TP-PMD or *Copper Distributed Data Interface* (CDDI) for high-speed twisted-pair wiring.

Twisted-pair cable is the most common communications wiring installed in offices today, and can take on an entirely different personality depending on the type of signaling employed. The gamut runs from RS-232, which nominally supports 19,200 bps up to 50 feet; to Ethernet 10BASE-T, which supports 10 Mbps up to 328 feet. Four categories of data-grade UTP (categories 2, 3, 4, and 5) have been defined by *Electronics Industry Association and Telecommunications Industry Association* (EIA/TIA) Technical Systems Bulletins 36 and 40. Category 2 wiring is rated for 4 Mbps; Category 3 wiring is rated for UTP Ethernet; Category 4 is rated for 16 Mbps

Token Ring; and Category 5 is rated for 100 Mbps CDDI. Category 1 wiring has been defined for voice telephony use. These categories form part of the Commercial Building Telecommunications Wiring Standard, EIA/TIA 568. This standard covers building wiring plans for UTP up to 100 Mbps data rates.

AT&T's *Premises Distribution System* (PDS), the IBM Cabling Plan, and the EIA/TIA 568 standard describe cable and wiring specifications for voice and data. AT&T and EIA/TIA specify UTP only, whereas IBM only deals with shielded twisted-pair cabling. The EIA/TIA standard (renamed SP 2840) encompasses both horizontal wiring and backbone wiring. *Horizontal wiring* usually refers to wiring confined to one floor of a building. *Backbone wiring* is typically used to connect different floors and runs in vertical risers within a building. Backbone wiring also connects different buildings. The objective of EIA/TIA 568 is to provide a standard wiring environment that can accommodate LAN equipment from any vendor. Equipment contained in rooms or areas generically referred to as *wiring closets* can consist of distribution frames, patch panels, and LAN-related hubs, modems, and servers. The following five commercial building wiring elements are defined by EIA/TIA 568:

✔ **Work Area (WA).** Communications outlets (CO) and end user equipment. Communications outlets accommodate voice telephony, UTP, coaxial cable, and fiber-optic wiring in various configurations.

✔ **Telecommunications Closet (TC).** Collection point for horizontal wiring from communications outlets

Horizontal wiring is wiring from the CO to the nearest TC on the same floor. Maximum distance from CO to TC is 295 feet (90 meters). Permissible wiring includes 100-ohm UTP, 150-ohm shielded twisted pair (STP), 50-ohm coaxial and 62.5 micron core fiber optic.

✔ **Intermediate Cross-connect (IC).** Collection point for vertical backbone wiring from telecommunications closets in a single building and cross-connect point to campus backbone wiring.

✔ **Main Cross-connect (MC).** Collection point for all backbone wiring on the campus

Backbone wiring is wiring from MC to building ICs on campus, and from building ICs to TCs within same building. Maximum distance from MC to IC varies from 984 feet (300 meters) for UTP to 4,920 feet (1,500 meters) for fiber-optic cable. Maximum distance from IC to TC is 1,640 feet (500 meters). Permissible wiring is the same as for horizontal wiring, although inter-building wiring would virtually always be fiber optic.

✔ **Administration System.** Cross-connects, inter-connects, and documentation required to support and manage the cabling system.

Figure 12.4 summarizes the commercial building wiring standard. *Entrance facilities* are also defined by the EIA/TIA 568 standard as the point at which the *local exchange carrier's* (LEC's) wiring enters the building. EFs also are referred to as the demarcation point, or *demarc*, between the LEC and the premises.

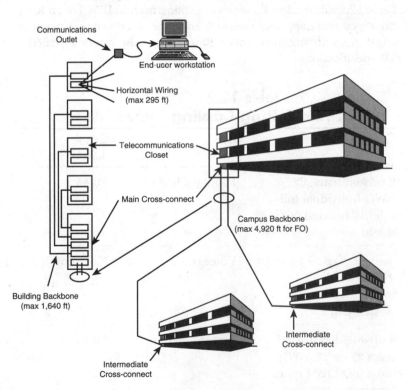

Figure 12.4
EIA-TIA 568 (SP 2840) commercial building wiring standard.

Communications Outlet

End-user workstation

Horizontal Wiring (max 295 ft)

Telecommunications Closet

Main Cross-connect

Campus Backbone (max 4,920 ft for FO)

Building Backbone (max 1,640 ft)

Intermediate Cross-connect

Intermediate Cross-connect

III

Local Area Networking

In the preceding terminology, EIA/TIA 568 enables freedom of interpretation depending on physical characteristics of the building or building complex. A building complex is referred to as a *campus*. For example, in the event that no campus exists, the IC is the MC. One or several TCs can be on a single floor. The Entrance Facility can be located in the MC building or in multiple buildings in a campus configuration. Wiring planners also must take into account the difference between the topology limitations for each type of LAN, as discussed later in this chapter, and the building wiring standard;the LAN topology restrictions always take priority in the event of a conflict.

Token Ring networks use a robust form of *shielded twisted-pair* (STP) wiring that includes multiple twisted pairs and individual-pair, metallic-foil shielding, all encased in a metallic braid and outer sheathing similar to coaxial cabling. Some Token Ring cabling includes extra twisted pairs for simultaneous data and voice conveyance. This type of cable is an excellent choice for building-wide wiring systems, particularly if the communications capability is planned prior to building construction. Table 12.2 summarizes the types of cabling used in IBM Token Ring LANs. Listed cabling costs are approximate, with evidence of a downward trend as more Token Ring systems are installed. Token Ring systems also can be installed according to PDS specifications.

Table 12.2
IBM Token Ring Cabling Types

Cable Type	Composition	Use	Cost/ 1,000 Ft.
1	2 twisted pairs, 22 AWG Individual foil shields, braided outer shield	High-grade data	$0.43
2	Same as Type 1 except 4 additional unshielded twisted pairs	Voice/data	Not avail
3	4 unshielded twisted pairs 22 or 24 AWG; must meet IBM specs for attenuation and impedance	Low-grade data	$0.16

Cable Type	Composition	Use	Cost/ 1,000 Ft.
5	2 fiber-optic cables	Dual fiber rings	$1.32
6	2 twisted pairs, 26 AWG single inner foil shield, braided outer shield	Patch panels	$0.38
8	4 flat parallel wires 26 AWG individual copper shields and outer braid	Under carpet	Not avail
9	Same as Type 1 except 26 AWG wire vice 22 AWG	Medium-grade data	Not avail

Although telephone wiring is common in most offices, its use in LANs requires careful planning and survey. Most telephone outlets have two pairs of wires; one pair is used as the telephone "tip" and "ring" (voice) channel, and the other pair is available for other uses. At a minimum, the unused pair must be checked for continuity throughout the area in which the LAN will be installed. Planning for new office spaces should include a detailed assessment of this potential wiring source. In many cases, these spare pairs may not meet LAN electrical specifications and should be thoroughly performance-tested before a commitment is made to use them throughout the organization. At the very least, the use of standard twisted pair usually results in restrictions in the size of the LAN and the number of stations that can be connected to the media. A more conservative approach is to have a telephone installer remove all existing wire and to install all new LAN wiring separately marked from any telephone wiring. This greatly facilitates later troubleshooting and precludes old wire bundles from cluttering the interior of building walls and false overheads in ceilings.

Coaxial Cable

The next most common form of media is *coaxial cable*. This cable has been used for years in the communications and data processing industries. Amateur radio, Cable TV, CB radio, cellular radio telephones, and various mainframe data terminals all use some form of coaxial cable. Many of today's LAN systems use coaxial cable; table 12.3 depicts the more common of these. IEEE uses the 10BASE5 designation for thick Ethernet coaxial cable and 10BASE2 for the thin Ethernet coaxial cable.

The impedance values are shown because of the importance of not mixing components of dissimilar impedances on the same network segment. These components include the cable proper and various pieces of hardware used to construct coaxial networks, such as T-connectors, barrel-connectors, and segment terminators. Figure 12.5 illustrates these components.

Figure 12.5
Coaxial media
components.

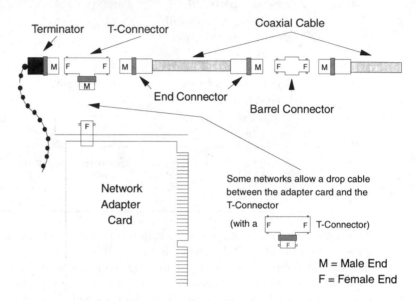

The cost of coaxial cable, even the higher grade low-loss and double-shielded varieties, has decreased drastically in recent years due to its greatly increased use in computer installations. Coaxial cable can support data rates of up to several tens of Mbps at distances up to several thousand feet. Certain types of signaling enable high data rates over distances of several miles.

Table 12.3
Common Coaxial Cable Types

Network Type	Cable Type	Cost/Ft($)[1]	Impedance (Ohms)	
Ethernet (Standard)	Type N		50	1.01
Ethernet Transceiver[2]	Multi-wire		50	0.92
Ethernet (Thin)	RG-58		50	0.29

Network Type	Cable Type	Cost/Ft($)[1]	Impedance (Ohms)	
ARCnet	RG-62		93	0.19
Broadband (Drop)	RG-59		75	0.19
Broadband (Trunk/Feeder)	RG-11		75	0.25

[1]Costs are in order of magnitude only per 1000 Ft

[2]Required with N-type Ethernet installations

Coaxial cable is difficult to connect to network devices and generally requires more planning than twisted-pair systems. Many coaxial systems require the connector on the main cable to be attached directly to the adapter on the PC; a situation that reduces flexibility in locating workstations and servers. A better arrangement is the use of a drop cable, as shown in figure 12.5. This enables the use of wall jacks and a neater installation. Network administrators should determine the permissibility of drop cables within the LAN topology rules before committing to final wiring and location plans. In general, a drop cable can be used as long as the wiring allows an unbroken bus path through the network node's adapter card. If a drop cable is used, its length must be doubled and added to the total accumulated bus length to stay within topology rules as discussed in the next section.

Additional flexibility for planning coaxial networks is provided by hardware that enables mixing of different coaxial cable types. For example, 3Com provides a multiport repeater that allows connection of Type N Ethernet through an *Attachment Unit Interface* (AUI) cable port and multiple RG-58 Thin Ethernet ports. Other hardware, such as 3Com's CableTamer balun, enables the mixing of two dissimilar impedance cables, in this case RG-59 (75 Ohm) and RG-58 (50 Ohm), or RG-62 (93 Ohm) and RG-58 (50 Ohm). Figure 12.6 illustrates the configuration possibilities with this type of hardware.

As mentioned earlier, the radiation from coaxial cables can be converted from a liability to an asset through the use of "leaky coax." At least one vendor provides the configuration illustrated in figure 12.7 that enables the use of portable radio frequency devices in large buildings that might not otherwise have RF coverage. Typical locations are underground garages, convention centers, hotels, and industrial buildings with high RF shielding. Portable devices that can be utilized might include various cellular data or voice equipment or *personal digital assistants* (PDAs) with radio modems incorporated. The cables used are particular types of coax known as *HELIAX* (antenna to second bi-directional amplifier) and *RADIAX* (radiating element). HELIAX is a low-loss cable, often used in outdoor UHF and microwave antenna installations. RADIAX is a specially fabricated HELIAX cable that allows the leakage of RF energy. You can expect good coverage to extend a 30-foot radius from the RADIAX cable, with fringe coverage possible out to 60 feet.

Figure 12.6
Dissimilar media mixing on LANs.

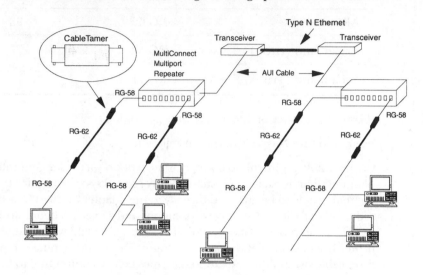

Figure 12.7
Leaky coax architecture (typical 2-floor configuration).

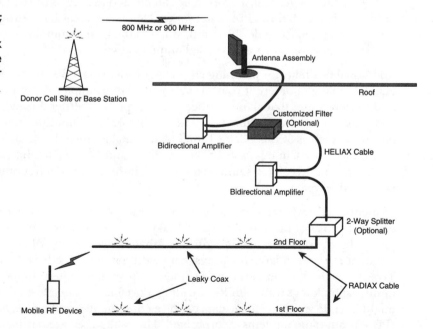

Fiber Optics

The newest form of bounded media is fiber optics, which has superior data handling and security characteristics. Fiber-optic cables cannot be easily tapped and can support data rates of several hundred Mbps. Connection costs for fiber-optic networks are currently high, but are expected to decrease significantly in the next few years. Several vendors are capable of supplying fiber-optic versions of Ethernet and Token Ring networks. Fiber-optic cable costs range from $1.20 to $1.70 per lineal foot plus approximately $100 to $125 per cable for termination hardware and labor. Ethernet-compatible fiber-optic transceivers range from $350 to $600 per PC connection.

A fiber-optic cable is physically small, but its inner core, acting as the signal path for a light source, is capable of exceptionally high bandwidths, up into the gigabit range. Two sources of light can be used as transmitters: *Light Emitting Diodes* (LEDs) or *Light Amplification by Stimulated Emission Radiation* (Lasers). The type of transmitter has a major bearing on maximum range; LED fiber-optic systems are capable of ranges up to 3,000 meters, whereas laser fiber-optic systems can transmit up to 30 kilometers. Fiber-optic cables are impervious to any type of *electromagnetic interference* (EMI), including the more severe *Electromagnetic Pulse* (EMP) interference generated by a nuclear blast. Furthermore, fiber-optic cables do not radiate and therefore are not a cause of interference, nor can they be monitored through radiation intercept.

Fiber-optic media are not without limitations, however. Bend radius is a critical parameter in installations, making physical layout more challenging than with twisted-pair or coaxial media. A bend radius that is too tight causes distortion and attenuation of the light signal due to changes in the electrical and physical characteristics of the inner core. The installation of fiber-optic connectors and line splicing is still a fine art because of the criticality of proper inner core alignment at fiber junction points. This requirement adversely affects installation costs compared to those of copper-based media. Fiber-optic channels are half-duplex, meaning that light signals can only move in one direction at a time. A full-duplex circuit would cause light wave interference without special electronics and is generally not economically viable. As in the case of most electronic limitations, it is reasonable to expect that full-duplex fiber-optic networks may someday become as common as full-duplex copper circuits.

Fiber-optic media can support high bandwidth applications including videoconferencing to the desktop, digital voice/image/graphics networking in the local area network environment, and long-haul transmission of digital voice and data in the wide area network arena. Fiber is particularly appropriate for campus and multi-building backbones and for high-security applications such as financial transactions, military operations, and public safety. Fiber-optic media are the basis for several high bandwidth networking standards such as Fiber Distributed Data Interface (FDDI) and *Synchronous Optical Network* (SONET).

III

Local Area Networking

Wireless

Wireless systems have become the high-profile segment of personal communications connectivity because of their capability to free the user of the many restrictions inherent in being tied to a wired network. The capability to connect through a growing variety of providers to a complete array of services including voice, circuit- and packet-switched data, position determination, paging, and one-way messaging is finding a wide appeal among businesses of all types. Chapter 15, "Wireless Networking," explores the characteristics and applications of wireless networking in greater detail.

Topology

Topology is the technical term for a simple concept—the way networks are physically connected together. To the LAN end user, topology is not significant; but to the LAN manager or to an organization's microcomputer support department, topology influences certain factors important to network selection and management, including the following:

✔ Complexity and cost of network cable installation. Cable installation often can be a major cost factor for an entire network system.

✔ Redundant or fail-safe design.

✔ Fault isolation.

✔ Strategy for physically expanding and reconfiguring the network.

Current literature most commonly classifies a topology as belonging to one of three types: *star, ring,* or *bus.* In terms of currently available products, a more practical classification would include *distributed star, bus,* and *branching tree.* A distributed star network has hubs that can be interconnected and that support a varying number of network stations. Some hubs are internally wired as rings; others are wired as buses. Ring networks are inherently unterminated. Bus networks consist of a single, terminated cable to which network stations connect. A *terminated cable* has terminator hardware at both ends that have the same impedance as the cable itself. Branching tree networks are associated with a particular type of LAN closely related to cable TV distribution systems. Distributed star, bus, and branching tree topologies have variations as shown in figures 12.8 through 12.10. Although many distributed star networks appear physically similar, the electrical functioning of the star's hub can be radically different.

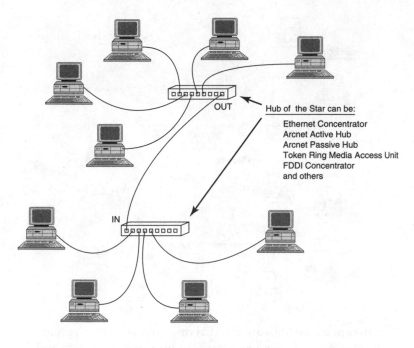

Figure 12.8
Distributed star topology options.

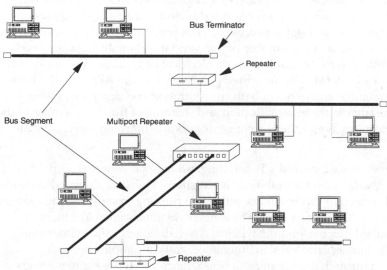

Figure 12.9
Bus topology options.

III

Local Area Networking

Figure 12.10
Branching tree
topology.

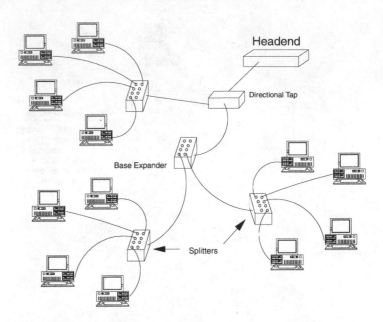

In coaxial ARCnet networks, the hubs are wired as rings and are either *passive repeaters* or *active repeaters*. Active repeaters are responsible for amplification and retiming of data packets enroute to connected stations. Passive repeaters re-route the data with no additional signal processing. The practical difference between the two types of repeaters is in the number of ports and the allowable distances each can support. IBM Token Ring hubs contain electrical ring circuits and are referred to as *Media Access Units* (MAUs). In twisted-pair Ethernets and ARCnets, the hubs are *wiring concentrators* and perform both concentration and signal processing functions. The latter include amplification and retiming of the signal similar to the ARCnet repeater function. Ethernet concentrators are internally wired as linear buses.

Star-wired networks such as IBM's Token-Ring, twisted-pair Ethernet, and ARCnet are particularly well-suited for multifloor installations. Hubs on star-wired networks are frequently placed in wiring closets, with cable running from the wiring closet to wall outlets in selected office spaces. These networks are installed in a manner similar to standard office telephone systems. A well-designed wiring closet aids considerably in fault-isolation and maintenance, and can simplify network reconfiguration through the use of *patch panels*. Patch panel use enables servers and other special purpose devices, such as gateways and bridges, to be easily moved to different network segments. Figure 12.11 illustrates such a system.

An example of inherent redundancy in a PC LAN topology is the IBM Token Ring. Media Access Units provide redundancy through the use of a backup wire path as shown in figure 12.12. The figure shows ring reconfiguration resulting from a media failure. The MAU also has built-in hardware features to isolate failed station loops from the active ring.

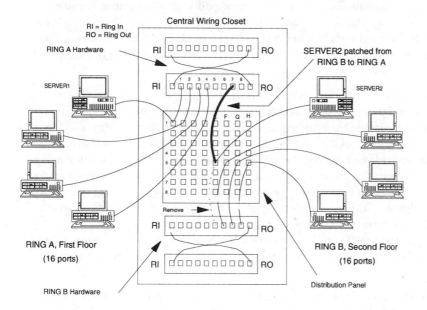

Figure 12.11
A typical wiring closet cable plan.

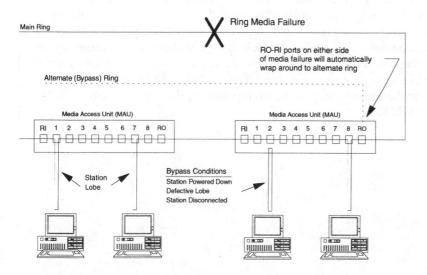

Figure 12.12
Media failure recovery on Token Ring LAN.

III

Local Area Networking

Star-wired networks are the superior choice for fault detection and isolation. The latter function is considerably aided if the star hub has LED indicators for connected segments or intelligent network fault isolation and management as discussed in the preceding paragraphs. When network workstations contain adapter cards incorporating net management features, fault isolation can be accomplished on all network segments. Bus networks are more difficult to diagnose because no built-in means are available to isolate faulty cable segments. *Time-Domain Reflectometers* (TDR) can be used on a bus network to locate cable faults by measuring the elapsed time from transmission of a probe signal to receipt of the reflected signal from the location of the fault.

Intelligent hubs provide a variety of connection options, including coaxial, fiber optic, and twisted pair. These hubs can have extended interconnection features that make them suitable for building and wide area internetworks, discussed in Chapter 13, "Internetworking and Interoperability." Intelligent hubs also can incorporate network management capabilities that enable remote monitoring and network reconfiguration. The logical extension of this concept is the development of even higher levels of functionality within intelligent hubs: including the incorporation of bridging, routing, gateways to WANs, transparent multimedia support, and hierarchical network management functions. Active repeaters, MAUs, wiring concentrators, and intelligent hubs can be connected together in a variety of ways to extend LAN coverage and to permit the incorporation of dissimilar network topologies.

Distributed star networks are expanded by connecting additional hubs, as shown back in figure 12.8. A typical installation can consist of several intelligent hubs wired into a ring configuration with a fiber-optic backbone. Each hub can host some combination of coaxial and twisted pair connected workstations. Although bus networks are not as well suited for multi-floor installations, they are well-suited to linear expansion. This expansion can be accomplished by cutting into a stretch of cable or by moving the terminator, as shown in figure 12.13. Bus networks, moreover, can be reconfigured into a *tree* topology by the use of repeaters as shown back in figure 12.9.

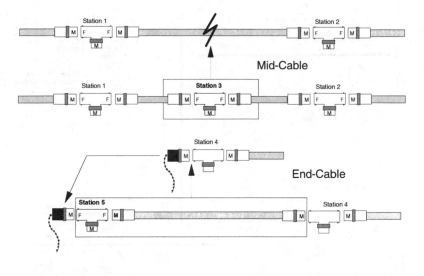

Figure 12.13
Coaxial LAN expansion techniques.

Each of the several LAN protocol types have topology rules that must be followed to maintain specified performance. These rules are a consequence of the electrical signaling used by the LAN; the relationship between the signaling used and the LAN's access protocol; and the presence of varying types of hubs. Signaling and access are discussed later in this chapter. Topology rules generally describe the following elements:

✔ Maximum segment length (terminator-to-terminator on bus networks or hub-to-station distance on star-wired networks)

✔ Maximum number of stations allowable per segment

✔ Maximum number of segments

✔ Maximum total electrical length of a single logical LAN

✔ Maximum number of repeaters allowed

✔ Hub configurations

✔ Type of connections allowed including placement of terminators and loops

Figures 12.14 through 12.18 summarize these rules for coaxial Ethernet, UTP Ethernet, ARCnet, Token Ring, and FDDI. In addition to topology rules, different network types have optional combinations of media types and topology, which are summarized for currently known systems in table 12.4.

III

Local Area Networking

Figure 12.14
Ethernet coaxial
LAN design
considerations.

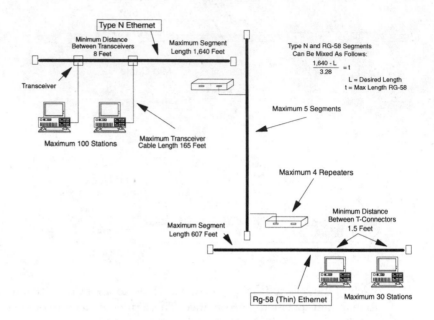

Figure 12.15
Ethernet twisted
pair LAN design
considerations.

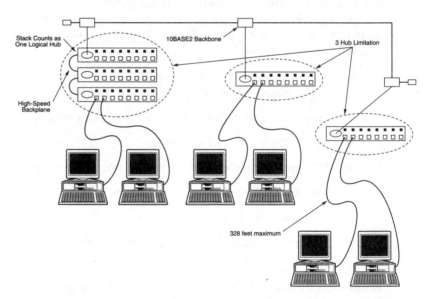

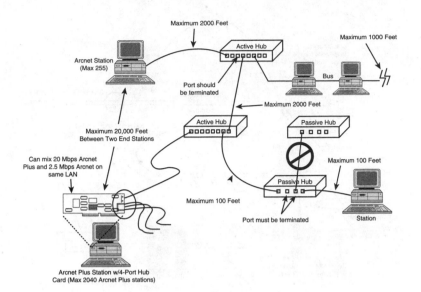

Figure 12.16
Arcnet/Arcnet Plus LAN design considerations.

Maximum 2000 Feet

Active Hub

Maximum 1000 Feet

Arcnet Station (Max 255)

Bus

Port should be terminated

Maximum 2000 Feet

Maximum 20,000 Feet Between Two End Stations

Active Hub

Passive Hub

Can mix 20 Mbps Arcnet Plus and 2.5 Mbps Arcnet on same LAN

Maximum 100 Feet

Passive Hub

Maximum 100 Feet

Station

Port must be terminated

Arcnet Plus Station w/4-Port Hub Card (Max 2040 Arcnet Plus stations)

Figure 12.17
Token Ring LAN design considerations.

III

Local Area Networking

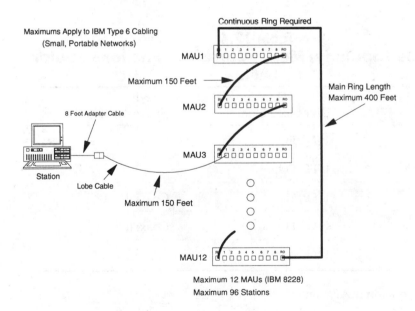

Continuous Ring Required

Maximums Apply to IBM Type 6 Cabling (Small, Portable Networks)

MAU1

Maximum 150 Feet

MAU2

Main Ring Length Maximum 400 Feet

8 Foot Adapter Cable

MAU3

Station

Lobe Cable

Maximum 150 Feet

MAU12

Maximum 12 MAUs (IBM 8228)
Maximum 96 Stations

Figure 12.18
FDDI LAN design
considerations.

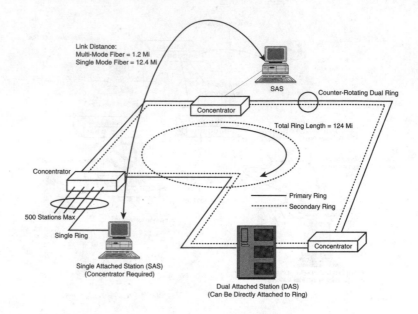

Table 12.4
Allowable Topology/Media Combinations for Popular LANs

Network Type	Topology/Media Allowed	
	Distributed Star	Linear Bus (BNC)
Ethernet	UTP, FO	Coaxial
Token Ring	UTP, FO	
ARCnet	UTP, FO	Coaxial
ARCnet Plus[1]	UTP, FO	Coaxial
FDDI	UTP (CDDI), FO	

[1]New 20 Mbps version of ARCnet

Wireless networks typically consist of a control hub connected to a wire-based LAN. The control hub then communicates with user modules that in turn connect one or more workstations. This configuration is discussed in Chapter 15, "Wireless Networking."

Signaling

Signaling is the method by which a network represents data as a serial stream of 1s and 0s on the media during its movement between the output of the source network adapter card and the input of the destination network card. It also refers to the manner in which digital 1s and 0s familiar to a computer are transmitted on the network data path. Signaling is generally the responsibility of the network adapter card. In some networks, such as certain forms of Ethernet, signaling is accomplished in a separate transceiver attached directly to the network media and connected to a network node by a transceiver cable, or *Attachment Unit Interface* (AUI). Figure 12.14 showed this arrangement, which is a significantly more costly configuration than the more popular direct connection in figure 12.13 that uses thin Ethernet cable. In most current networks, transceivers are built into the network adapter card. The two basic categories of LAN signaling are *baseband* and *broadband*. The term "broadband" can be somewhat misleading, because it not only refers to a type of LAN signaling, but also to any type of LAN or WAN with high bandwidths, such as fiber optic-based systems. In the context of this discussion, broadband means a particular method of signaling.

Before discussing baseband and broadband networks, the terms *bandwidth* and *Frequency Division Multiplexing* (FDM) require definition. Radio frequency bandwidth was earlier defined as the amount of frequency spectrum that a communications system needs to modulate a signal. A very common example is the AM broadcast band, which extends from 540 Kilohertz (KHz) to 1,600 KHz. The total spectrum allocation for the AM broadcasting service is 1,060 KHz (1,600 - 540 = 1,060). This service supports 106 channels in the United States because the FCC has allocated 10 KHz of bandwidth to a single AM channel. Each AM broadcast channel carries (is modulated with) a certain type of information, such as voice and music entertainment.

Another well-known example is cable TV (CATV). For the television broadcasting service, the FCC has defined a TV channel as 6 Megahertz (MHz) wide. The information in a single TV channel is more extensive than AM broadcasting and consists of video frames, color coding, and audio (voice and music). The required bandwidth for TV channels is commensurately higher than for either AM or FM broadcasting. Standard CATV, therefore, has a bandwidth of 300 MHz to support the transmission and distribution of fifty 6-MHz-wide TV channels throughout a specified subscriber community.

In a data transmission system, a specific relationship exists between the measures of bandwidth (measured in Hz) supporting the system and the resulting data rate (measured in bps). This relationship depends on the *signaling efficiency*—the number of bits that can be represented by one signaling unit (bits/Hz). Signaling efficiency depends on the modulation scheme used in a data transmission system.

Remember that LAN data rate is a measure of the amount of serial data that can be transmitted in a unit of time. Given a certain modulation type, the higher the bandwidth, the greater the data rate that can be supported. The exact nature of this relationship is beyond the scope of this book, but suffice it to say that an information channel with a 6-MHz-wide bandwidth could support a 12-Mbps data rate LAN with a signaling efficiency of 2 bits/Hz. You can see other examples of this phenomena with modems that support data rates up to 28,800 bps on a 4 KHz standard telephone bandwidth. This efficiency is achieved through advanced modulation and data compression techniques.

You might wonder why information is divided into discrete channels across the available bandwidth in some communications systems, such as in the AM and TV examples described earlier. The process of creating these channels divides the available frequency spectrum for a particular service into well-defined segments. This process is known as *Frequency Division Multiplexing* (FDM). The FDM process creates a series of fixed bandwidth channels, each with its lower and upper limit frequency. Stating the earlier discussion in another way, broadcasters and the FCC have multiplexed 106 AM radio channels into a single 1,060-KHz-wide band by dividing that band into 106 equal parts, or 10-KHz-wide channels. You encounter this concept again in the description of broadband networks.

In the *baseband* system, shown in figure 12.19, a digital data stream is sent in its basic form to the network media. This data stream is transmitted at a rate that consumes the entire bandwidth available on the media. A serial stream of bits is packed into formatted data packets by the network adapter card and converted to an electrical format suitable for transmission on the data path. The serial data packets are sent and received at a specific design data rate—typically 1-100 Mbps. In a baseband network system, no signal conversion device is required between the network node and the data path. In other words, data is sent in its basic digital form, hence the term baseband. With simpler electronics, baseband LANs are generally cheaper and simpler to acquire and install than broadband systems.

A broadband LAN can make efficient use of high capacity Cable TV distribution media. As previously discussed, this type of cable supports a minimum bandwidth of 300 MHz. By using state-of-the-art electronic components, bandwidth can be increased to 500 MHz and beyond. This high capacity can be fully exploited in broadband local area networks. Through the FDM process, broadband LANs partition the available bandwidth into individual channels, each of which is designed for a specific service or function.

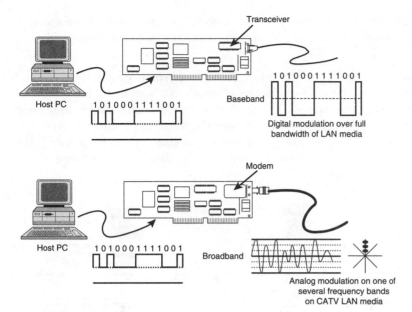

Figure 12.19
Comparison of baseband and broadband signaling.

Using the TV broadcast analogy, each TV channel is fixed in bandwidth and designed for a specific function—the transmission of standard TV video and audio signals. In a broadband LAN, the channel widths remain fixed at 6 MHz but the use of a channel varies according to the desired data rates and connectivity requirements for various services. Some examples of channel usage for broadband network services include the following:

✔ 48 dedicated point-to-point circuits, designed to allow any two stations to exchange data at a rate of up to 9600 bps. Each circuit is functionally equivalent to a leased line typically used between a terminal controller and a host computer communications controller.

✔ 128 switched point-to-point circuits, designed to connect any two stations at data rates of up to 9,600 bps. This service is functionally equivalent to a small *Private Branch Exchange* (PBX) used for data communications.

✔ A 10-Mbps Ethernet

✔ A closed-circuit video system

In a broadband LAN, data are represented as analog signals similar to the transmission methodology employed on radio frequency networks. This requires modems to convert the computer's digital signals into analog signals in the radio frequency range for transmission, as shown in figure 12.19. The modem must have a data rate capability equal to the desired data rate on the broadband channel. A high-speed data channel (such as a 10 Mbps LAN) requires a commensurately high-speed modem.

Broadband modems can be either fixed-frequency or frequency-agile. *Fixed frequency* modems are designed for a specific channel on a broadband LAN and cannot be tuned to other channels. Standard telephone modems used in wide area networks are fixed frequency units—in this case, the frequency is an audio frequency compatible with the telephone network rather than a radio frequency. *Frequency-agile* modems can be tuned to different channels on the broadband network, as shown in Figure 12.20.

Figure 12.20
Broadband LAN
multi-channel
design.

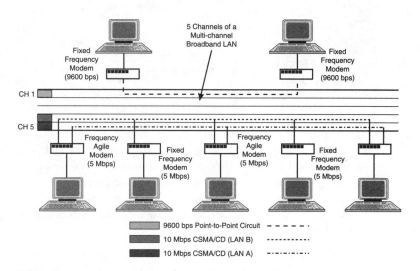

Broadband networks are classified as either dual cable or single cable. *Single-cable* systems are more practical for ordinary use because they use fewer components and are, therefore, more reliable and cheaper to install. The broadband IBM PC Network is an example of a single-cable system. In both systems, a device known as a *headend*, or *cable retransmission facility* (CRF) is located at the base of the branching tree topology. In a single cable network, the total available bandwidth is divided into three bands of frequencies used for forward transmission, reverse transmission, and a guard band in between. *Forward transmission* is from the headend to LAN stations; *reverse transmission* is from LAN stations to the headend. The bandwidth allocated to reverse transmission determines how many 6-MHz channels can be established on the LAN.

The headend of the IBM PC Network is called a *frequency translator.* The frequency translator is located on the network so that it can translate a frequency in the reverse direction to a frequency in the forward direction. Figure 12.21 illustrates

this scheme in the context of the broadband IBM PC Network. Three standards are used to determine bandwidths of the forward and reverse transmission paths: *sub-split, mid-split,* and *high-split.* These standards support 4, 17, and 30 6-MHz channels respectively in the reverse band. The IBM PC Network is a mid-split system, using a reverse frequency channel of 47.75 MHz to 53.75 MHz and a forward channel of 216 MHz to 222 MHz. Dual cable systems allocate one cable for forward transmission and one cable for reverse transmission; thus, the entire bandwidth is available for channel assignment.

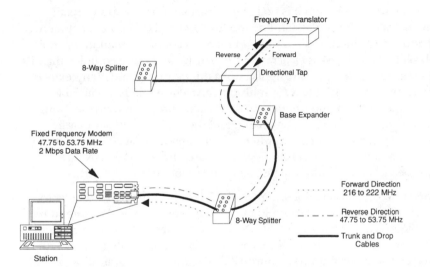

Figure 12.21
IBM PC Network (broadband) signaling architecture.

As more diverse services are added to a broadband LAN, additional special hardware is required. Frequency translators become more elaborate. Special modems must be provided for video and digital voice services. A variety of RF modems may be required depending on the specific services required. Data-switching devices are required for PBX-type services.

The added capacity and service flexibility provided by broadband LANs comes at a substantial price. The tradeoff for this highly capable type of LAN is an increase in cost and complexity. The requirement for relatively expensive variable frequency and high-speed modems is a major cost factor, as is the increased complexity of the network adapter cards. Installation of broadband LANs is difficult because of the criticality of component placement and the radio frequency characteristics of the broadband media. For these reasons, and the lack of easily available and low-cost modem technology for key applications, it is not likely that broadband technology will ever find the widespread acceptance enjoyed by baseband personal computer LANs.

Another reason for the lack of widespread acceptance of RF broadband technology is the emergence of high bandwidth baseband networks such as FDDI, FDDI-II, SONET, and ATM and the availability of efficient methodology to digitize speech and video. With an all-digital environment, the need for expensive RF components to convert digital data to analog signals on broadband network channels is no longer compelling.

Examples of baseband systems include the various versions of Ethernet, IBM's Token Ring, and ARCnet systems. IBM's PC Network is the best-known example of a broadband network, although it is no longer distributed by computer retail stores. The motivation for understanding the fundamental differences between baseband and broadband LANs lies more in market economics than in technology. The broadband network is clearly more expensive and more complex than its baseband counterpart, but in some applications this extra cost and complexity is justified by an organization's need for multiple services on one physical cable. Because it is inherently a radio frequency (RF) system, broadband provides much greater geographic coverage than baseband, and therefore is very popular in educational and research institutions where widely separated facilities need to be connected. Even in these scenarios however, RF-based broadband LANs are increasingly being replaced with high-data-rate fiber and wireless systems.

In many practical LAN installations, high and low bandwidth baseband networks have been effectively combined to exploit the advantages of each. A common use of this technique is to use a fiber-optic LAN such as FDDI to connect several lower bandwidth baseband LANs, such as Ethernet. In this case, the fiber-optic system is referred to as a backbone network. Figure 12.22 illustrates this application of high bandwidth LANs.

One of the most common signaling techniques in wireless networks is *spread spectrum*. Wireless signaling of the spread spectrum type can be accomplished by frequency hopping or direct sequence coding. *Frequency hopping* is accomplished by transmitter frequency changes over a defined bandwidth every few milliseconds. The receiver must be capable of precisely tracking each frequency hop as it occurs. Different network stations use different hop patterns. *Direct sequence coding* works by dividing each transmitted bit into a number of "*chips*" (for example, 5-10), combining these chips with a pseudo-random noise signal at a higher signaling rate, and then transmitting the resultant chips across the defined bandwidth in a known pattern that can be reassembled at the receiver. Chapter 15 discusses spread spectrum in greater detail.

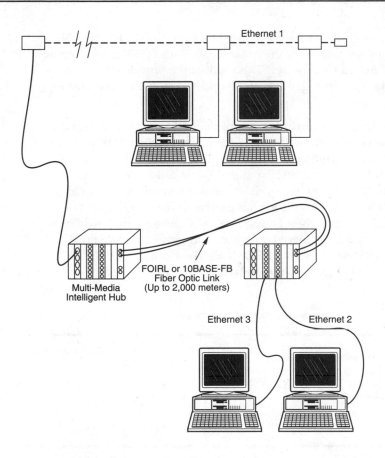

Figure 12.22
Fiber optic interrepeater link (FOIRL) used as a multi-LAN backbone.

Protocol

A *protocol* was previously defined as the set of rules by which data communications are conducted. The preceding chapter applied this definition to LAN protocols designed to connect distributed applications software. In the context of the OSI model, these protocols were in layers 5 and above. The significance of a layered communications model is ultimately economic—without a strategy to standardize protocols within well-defined layers, achieving communications compatibility would be very difficult and costly. The layered design of the OSI model enables the step-by-step achievement of standardization.

For example, physical and data link layer protocols can be developed independently of the higher layers. This is precisely what the IEEE has been doing with its 802-series local area network standards. For purposes of this chapter, protocol discussion focuses on the two lowest layers of the OSI model (Layers 1 and 2) that correspond to the IEEE 802 standards. These form the foundation for all other LAN standardization efforts and are the most advanced in implementation.

Although the OSI model specifies a single data link layer, the IEEE 802 LAN standards provide for two sub-layers: the *Media Access Control* (MAC) sub-layer and the *Logical Link Control* (LLC) sub-layer. This partitioning provides the same interface to the network layer regardless of the underlying media access technology.

Figure 12.23 shows the architecture of currently defined LAN physical and data link protocols in the context of the IEEE 802 standards. Ethernet has made the transition from a de facto protocol, supported by DEC, Intel, and Xerox, to the full-fledged ANSI/IEEE Standard 802.3, entitled *Carrier Sense Multiple Access with Collision Detection* (CSMA/CD). This standard also is approved international standard ISO 8802/3. IBM's Token Ring has prompted the development of ANSI/IEEE Standard 802.5, entitled *Token Passing Ring*. ARCnet does not have a recognized IEEE standard, but has achieved widespread acceptance as a de facto standard. In 1992, ANSI developed an ARCnet standard known as ATA/ANSI 878.1. The newer ARCnet Plus does not yet have a recognized standard.

Figure 12.23
OSI Layers 1 and 2 as implemented on LANs.

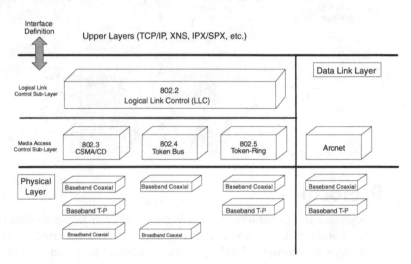

By definition, activity within the lowest two layers of the OSI model, as reflected in Ethernet, ARCnet, IBM's Token Ring, and FDDI, is independent of activity within the higher layers. However, a layer 3 protocol must make requests to, and receive responses from a layer 2 protocol for a LAN to work properly. This request for service and subsequent response(s) is known as an *interface definition*. In theory, layer 2 provides a standard set of services for layers 3 and higher. An example of this concept is the network layer requesting the data link layer to transmit a data packet to a specific destination on the LAN. The network layer is not concerned with how the data gets to a specific destination node—that is the job of the data

link layer. Figure 12.24 illustrates this concept. The idea of an interface definition applies between any two layers in the OSI model. Moreover, it applies in both directions, up and down through the model layers. A request from layer 3 to layer 2 causes an eventual response back from layer 2 to layer 3, and so on.

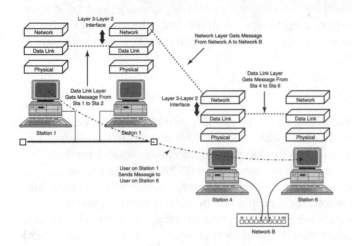

Figure 12.24

Comparative roles of data link and network layers in OSI model.

If you refer back to Chapter 11's figure 11.3 (*Application support software and the OSI Model*), arrow #3 depicts the logical transport and physical network boundary in an overall LAN architecture. This particular interface is significant because it represents the capability of dissimilar physical networks to interface to a variety of transport protocols. Thus a TCP/IP transport system can overlay an Ethernet or a Token Ring, providing the proper driver software is available.

As an example of the importance of standard protocol, consider the case of a business that purchases a low-cost Ethernet LAN from Vendor A. This LAN is advertised as "IEEE 802.3 compatible," which means that the protocol for layers 1 and 2 follow the ANSI/IEEE specification. If in the future this business wants to equip newly acquired workstations with more robust IEEE 802.3 adapter cards supplied by Vendor B, network compatibility can be maintained in the upgraded LAN. In this case, the network side of the adapter card maintains IEEE 802.3 standards, whereas the host computer side and/or adapter on-board processing can be upgraded to enhance performance.

Alternatively, consider the same business with on-site LAN adapters from Vendors A and B that now decides to expand its operation into another city. The physical characteristics of the LAN in the new city are not required to conform to the Ethernet-compatible standard. This business can use a different LAN physical and data link standard such as ARCnet in the new city. However, all the intervening higher layers must be equivalent if linking applications between the LANs in the two cities is a requirement. This application linkage might take the form of electronic mail or a form of groupware as discussed in Chapter 11. The general rule is that networks not physically joined do not have to be equivalent at layers 1 and 2. Unless higher layers are protocol-equivalent, however meaningful communications between individual users on the separated LANs are not possible. Proper selection and configuration of network operating systems is necessary to ensure that equivalent protocol stacks are available at sites that must communicate with one another.

Physical Layer

The two most stable protocol layers for LANs are predictably at the lowest levels of the seven-layer model. Physical protocols deal with how signals are transmitted to the data path, the electrical representation of data, allowable network media, network cable pin definitions (such as found in the RS-232-C standard), and design data rates. The physical layer also provides certain services for the data link layer. In the Ethernet protocol, for example, the physical layer indicates the presence or absence of a data signal on the network media. The physical layer also detects collisions and signal errors. Physical layer compatibility enables the network adapter card from one manufacturer to communicate at the most basic level with cards from other manufacturers on the same network.

Data Packets

The network shown earlier in figure 12.1 must distribute processing and data storage tasks among a number of users who may require near simultaneous access to the server PC. Basic network control requires placing a structure on the data flow in a well-defined manner. Basic control implies the following elements:

✔ An orderly means of enabling each device to access the network (link establishment)

✔ Delivery of the data to the correct recipient (addressing)

✔ Assurance that transmission errors have been minimized (error detection and correction)

A prerequisite to basic network control is the placement of serial data streams into formatted packets, or *frames*, by the data link protocol. These frames are then transmitted according to the physical layer protocol. Figure 12.25 shows an example of a formatted data frame and its relationship to the physical network for the commonly found Ethernet.

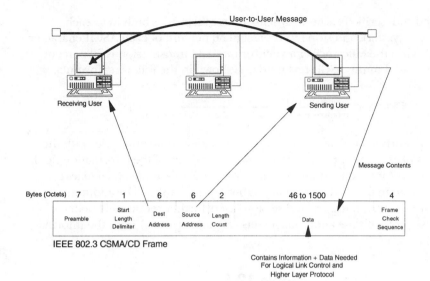

Figure 12.25
IEEE 802.3
(Ethernet) frame
format.

Figure 12.22 IEEE 802.3 (Ethernet) frame format.

Data frames are characterized by a well-defined format consisting of a number of fields as indicated by the example in figure 12.25. At the minimum, LAN data frames contain header, or control field(s), a source address field, a destination address field, the information field, and a means to detect and correct errors (frame check field). The information field of a frame has many uses. Any control data required for the processing of OSI layers above the data link layer is imbedded in the information field. Such data includes the source and destination network numbers used by the network layer. These numbers are required to route frames between widely separated networks. Other parts of the information field can be used to support processing requirements for the transport and session layers. The application being supported by the network protocol takes the balance of the information field for usable information.

LAN data are packaged differently from data transmitted by asynchronous modems (described earlier in the book). Asynchronous data are transmitted one character at a time, with certain characters in the ASCII set controlling the data link. LAN data travel as relatively large blocks with each bit having significance, and

are packaged as described earlier. Asynchronous overhead is built in to each character—parity, start, and stop bits represent 30 percent of each ASCII character transmitted. Thus the efficiency of asynchronous data transmission is 70 percent when parity is used in the ASCII text mode, as shown in the following formula:

$$\text{Efficiency} = \frac{\text{Information}}{\text{Information} + \text{Overhead}} = \frac{7 \text{ bits}}{7 \text{ bits} + 3 \text{ bits}}$$

LAN framing overhead is determined by the frame definition and varies with the type of protocol employed. Efficiency depends on the size of the information field. Table 12.5 shows some comparative efficiencies. For LANs, these efficiencies are the maximum attainable and assume no higher-layer protocol. The addition of protocols for network, transport, and session layers further reduces efficiencies because these protocols use additional octets (eight-bit groups) from the information field of a frame.

Table 12.5
Data Transmission Efficiencies

Data Transfer Protocol	Efficiency
Asynchronous w/o parity	80%
Asynchronous w/ parity	70%
Ethernet[1]	64-98%
Token Ring[2]	0-99.95%
ARCnet[3]	9.1-70.5%

[1]Efficiency is dependent on frame size (ranges from 72 to 1,526 octets)

[2]Maximum frame size dependent on Token Holding Time (maximum time station can transmit data before relinquishing the token). In the information context, a token transmission has an efficiency of 0%.

[3]Efficiency depends on frame size (ranges from 8 to 260 11-bit units). The 11-bit unit introduces an additional 27% loss of efficiency.

Media Access Control (MAC) Sub-Layer

The Media Access Control Sub-Layer protocol combines with the physical layer protocol to determine how a local network station gains access to the data path. As an analogy, think about how on-ramp traffic lights meter cars onto a busy freeway.

The cycle-time of the ramp meter light is automatically controlled by the flow of traffic sensed upstream of the ramp according to a predetermined algorithm. Media access protocol also determines the format of the data packets transmitted over the network.

Media access rules for networks fall into two basic categories: contention and non-contention.

Contention protocol is designed to handle the case of two or more stations unpredictably accessing the network simultaneously—that is, they are contending for access to the network. If more than one station has data on the network at the same time, a *data collision* occurs. The rules for this case must take into account the presence of signals already on the network (*carrier sense*), and the detection and prevention of collisions (*collision detection* and *collision avoidance*). Thus contention rules are often categorized as *Carrier Sense Multiple Access, with Collision Detection* (and/or *Collision Avoidance*), CSMA/CD(/CA). Ethernet is the most common of the contention-based networks and uses the CSMA/CD protocol. This protocol operates by the following rules:

✔ The physical layer senses the presence of a *carrier* on the network, indicating that data is present on the network.

✔ If data is already present on the network, the physical layer signals the data link layer not to pass data for transmission.

✔ If no data is detected, the physical layer signals the data link layer to begin passing data for transmission.

✔ If the physical layer detects a collision on the network by recognition of an increase in signal level beyond a certain threshold, it transmits a collision signal to the rest of the network.

✔ The remainder of the network stations revert to a receive mode when they hear the collision signal.

✔ The transmitting station waits a randomly determined interval before rescheduling the transmission. This random back-off time makes the Ethernet protocol statistical in nature, which means that performance under loaded traffic conditions cannot be predicted with certainty.

Collision detection and subsequent actions are shown in figure 12.26.

Non-contention protocols are characterized by a predictable order of accessing the network. Polling schemes fall into this category, as do token-passing networks. A historical example of a polling network scheme is Novell's original S-Net system. The file server software at the hub of this star-wired network sequentially polled each attached workstation looking for data transfer requests.

III

Local Area Networking

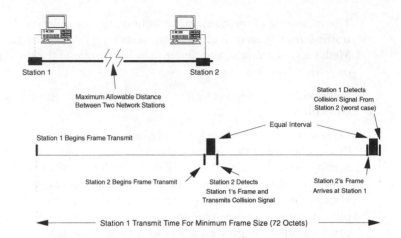

Figure 12.26
Ethernet collision detection for minimum frame size.

Token-passing networks are dominant in non-contention protocol systems and include ARCnet, ARCnet Plus, IBM's Token Ring, and the Fiber Data Distributed Interface. In the IEEE LAN standards scheme, token-passing networks can have a Bus topology (IEEE 802.4), or a Ring topology (IEEE 802.5). ARCnet is described by the ATA/ANSI 878.1 standard. ARCnet Plus is a 20 Mbps upgrade of ARCnet but is not yet described by any standard. FDDI is actually a series of standards of the American National Standards Institute X3T9 Committee. These standards describe the following FDDI components (abbreviation and standard designation in parenthesis):

✔ *Physical Layer Medium Dependent* (PMD) (ANSI X3.166)

✔ *Single-Mode Fiber PMD* (SMF-PMD) (ANSI X3.184)

✔ *Physical Layer* (PHY) (ANSI X3.148)

✔ *Media Access Control* (MAC) (ANSI X3.139)

✔ *Station Management* (SMT) (ANSI X3T9.5)

✔ *Logical Link Control* (LLC) (IEEE 802.2)

The ANSI X.3T9 committee is developing new standards for low-cost fiber and twisted pair (both STP and UTP) that will be abbreviated LCF-PMD and TP-PMD, respectively.

Because token passing is inherently predictable, tokens can be monitored to determine network performance. Token Ring uses a *Net Management* (NMT) protocol, which is a part of IEEE 802.5. FDDI uses *Station Management* protocol, ANSI X.3T9.5. NMT and SMT perform network management functions by exchanging certain management frames between stations on the networks.

Token-passing networks have a common characteristic of controlling access to the media by passing a special control frame, or *token*, around the network in a predetermined order. Beyond this common feature, IBM's Token Ring, FDDI, and ARCnet networks differ in protocol implementation. In Token Ring and FDDI, the passing order around the physical ring is sequential. Network stations with data to send "capture" the token and append their data by adding more frames to the token. The data packets are then "dropped off" at the destination node. FDDI incorporates an "auction" process to determine which station on the ring initiates the free token. In ARCnet, the order of token movement is determined by the network address rather than physical placement. The token is passed from lower to higher sequential network addresses. Network stations with data to send transmit a Free Buffer Inquiry frame to the destination station. The destination station responds with an ACK or a NAK frame. Receipt of an ACK frame causes the sending station to begin transmitting data to its destination.

Token Ring protocol uses a free token and a busy token concept and only transmits one frame per token capture in the 4-Mbps version. The 16-Mbps version uses a Token Hold Timer similar to FDDI to enable stations to send multiple frames of data until the timer expires. If a 4-Mbps Token Ring station has data to send, it changes the token status to busy and combines the token with one data frame. The busy token is split—part goes in front of the data frame, and part goes behind the data. The 802.5 protocol also provides a priority mechanism in the token structure. The token contains a priority (P) field and a reservation (R) field. Token Ring also uses one station designated the *Active Monitor* (AM) to control ring operation. In the case of priority conflicts, the station with the highest priority number captures the token. Other stations insert their priority numbers into the token's R field. The Active Monitor then stores the lowest reserved priority to ensure that lower priority stations receive an adequate amount of bandwidth. The Active Monitor is determined through a bidding process that gives monitor status to the highest detected address on the ring.

FDDI protocol can be broken into general phases: the claim process, token generation, data transmission, and error recovery. The claim process acts like an auction in which each station transmits a value for a timer called the *Target Token Rotation Timer* (TTRT). A station receiving a claim either inserts its own claim if its TTRT is less, or passes the claim on if not. Eventually, the station with the lowest TTRT is determined and that station releases the free token. The free token passes around the ring until a station has data to send. At this point, the station with data removes (captures) the free token and sends data frames until there is no more data to send or until another timer, called the *Token Holding Timer* (THT) expires. At the end of its data transmission, the station transmits another free token. Each station in the ring repeats data frames and extracts those addressed to it. Error recovery is invoked by use of yet another timer, called the *Valid Transmission Timer*

(VTT). If the interval between a valid frame or token exceeds VTT, an error condition exists, most likely caused by a break in the ring. In this case, the detecting station reinitiates the claim phase—if no free token is received, that station initiates a beacon signal. The beacon is designed to begin isolation of the location of the error in ring operation.

Logical Link Control (LLC) Sub-Layer

The LLC sub-layer is the direct interface between the network layer and the data link layer of a local area network. Regardless of the underlying media access sub-layer implementation (IEEE 802.3, 802.4, 802.5, FDDI), the network layer sees a common set of services. LLC establishes a hierarchical set of addresses known as *Link Service Access Points* (LSAPs). The sending LSAP is called the *Source Service Access Point* (SSAP), and the receiving LSAP is called the *Destination Service Access Point* (DSAP). Multiple LSAPs are possible within one network station. The purpose of an LSAP is to enable the establishment of multiple data link connections in support of higher layers in a single network station. The complete address for a single connection on a specific station includes the MAC address concatenated with the LLC LSAP address. Figure 12.27 illustrates this concept.

Figure 12.27
Operation of the
IEE 802.3
Logical Link
Control protocol
with Ethernet.

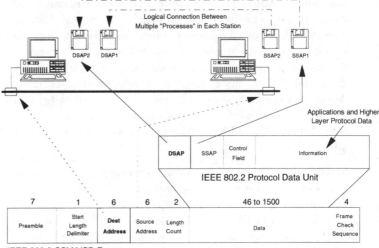

Protocol Summary

You might ask why knowledge of network protocols is important. The major significance lies more in standardization and economics than in technology differences. Ultimately, standardization translates to economy of scale and reduction in capital investment costs to acquire communications capability. All three lower-level protocols discussed in this chapter have benefited from standardization efforts.

Ethernet adapter cards have been reduced in size by half their original dimensions for the IBM PC. Reduced chip counts were made possible by the development of specialized chips, such as the Intel 82586 Ethernet Controller. These chips have in turn been cost-effective to produce because the Ethernet protocol has achieved a high degree of stability. Texas Instruments has produced the Token Ring chip used on network adapter cards of several LAN vendors, including Thomas-Conrad and SMC. Likewise, the ARCnet controller chip is manufactured in large enough quantities to make ARCnet adapter cards commodity items in the LAN marketplace.

Engineers have computed and debated the relative merits of token-passing versus contention-access schemes in various LAN configurations. It is generally recognized that Token Ring networks perform better in high traffic load situations than Ethernet LANs. Conversely, the Ethernet protocol supports lighter traffic loads more efficiently than the Token Ring. To the average user, however, performance differences in LANs are less dependent on lower level protocols than on file server and hard disk performance and network software design. A specific set of lower level standards, such as ARCnet or Ethernet, only guarantees the most basic compatibility within the OSI communications model.

For example, look at Ethernet in the context of its layer 1 and 2 protocols. Two dissimilar networks, LAN A and LAN B implement 802.3 standard protocol. LAN A uses Novell's *Internetwork Packet Exchange* (IPX) layer 3 protocol, and LAN B uses DOD's *Internetwork Protocol* (TCP/IP) for layer 3. Because both LANs use Ethernet, they can be connected through a repeater or a bridge. However, applications software on LAN A workstations that use layer 3 protocol for communications (like e-mail) cannot share this application with workstations on LAN B (see fig. 12.28).

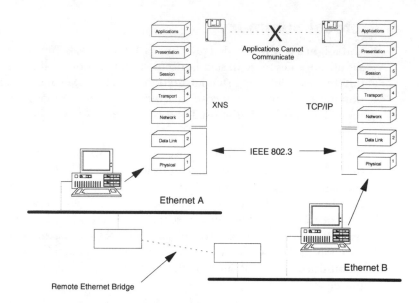

Figure 12.28
Transport stack incompatibility with common IEEE 802 implementation.

Practical Considerations in LAN Communications

The term *throughput* is a measure that describes the total amount of data that can be handled per unit of time in a practical network configuration. Such a configuration includes the media, network adapter cards, host computer's processor and RAM configuration, mass storage device on which shared data is typically stored, and packet structure used by the network. In contrast to this is the network data rate, which is a measure of how much data can be handled per unit of time between two adapter cards on a network. Throughput is a function of packet structure, network adapter card design, media access methodology, hard disk performance, and host processor speed. Data rate is a function of the physical layer implementation on the network adapter card and the electrical characteristics of the media.

Throughput can be thought of as data rate minus the sum of packet overhead and the processing bottlenecks inherent in a local area network. If throughput is measured at the application level (the only practical point at which to do so), packet overhead is the ratio between information bytes actually used by the application and the total number of bytes in a packet. Processing bottlenecks include network adapter cards, internal data movement within workstations and servers, and mechanical access to shared hard disk tracks (or cylinders) for data reads and writes. Throughput depends not only on data rate and design bottle-

necks, but also on the manner in which the network is being used. Clearly, file transfers put a higher processing load on the overall network than occasional record updates in a database management system. Typically, word processing has an even lighter traffic load.

Processing bottlenecks are also dependent upon the role of the network station. Servers are more prone to bottlenecks because they are by definition designed to handle multiple network service requests. As a general rule, servers should have the fastest hard disks, the biggest disk cache memories, the fastest processors, and the most robust network adapter cards. As servers become more powerful in their capability to handle multitasking, workstations must commensurately increase their capability to avoid becoming the weakest link in the chain. An inherent hierarchy exists in the throughput chain: workstation, server, and network communications capacity.

Data rate is a useful measure because it provides an upper limit on network communications capacity. Unfortunately, vendor literature tends to emphasize data rate rather than throughput, because data rate is easier to measure and is a constant number. In the higher performance networks such as Ethernet or the IBM 16 Mbps Token Ring, current network station processing limitations mask the total capacity of the network media access and physical protocol. These limitations affect both workstations and servers. As network station hardware improves with the introduction of 32-bit network adapter cards, faster hard disks and internal processing, network media access, and physical protocols might become the throughput bottleneck. The introduction of fiber optic networks, however, with data rates of 100 Mbps and higher will again focus the performance spotlight on network station considerations.

Response time is the interval from the time a request is entered at a workstation until the associated response is received back at that workstation. Response time is a two-way travel measure, and differs from throughput because a user can directly observe and measure response time. A slow response time on a network causes users to lose confidence in the benefits of distributed processing. Figure 12.29 illustrates how network components affect both throughput and response time.

Figure 12.29
Throughput and
response time
derivation.

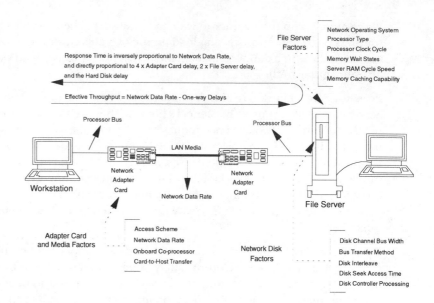

Response Time is inversely proportional to Network Data Rate,
and directly proportional to 4 x Adapter Card delay, 2 x File Server delay,
and the Hard Disk delay

Effective Throughput = Network Data Rate - One-way Delays

Processor Bus

Processor Bus

LAN Media

Network
Adapter
Card

Workstation

Network Data Rate

Network
Adapter
Card

File Server

File Server
Factors

Network Operating System
Processor Type
Processor Clock Cycle
Memory Wait States
Server RAM Cycle Speed
Memory Caching Capability

Adapter Card
and Media Factors

Access Scheme
Network Data Rate
Onboard Co-processor
Card-to-Host Transfer

Network Disk
Factors

Disk Channel Bus Width
Bus Transfer Method
Disk Interleave
Disk Seek Access Time
Disk Controller Processing

Summary

The network characteristics discussed in this chapter specifically describe the communications performance of LANs. This chapter extended the discussion in Chapter 11 on LANs as multiuser distributed processing systems down to the data link and physical layers. This sequence of coverage should provide you with a solid understanding of the importance of the OSI model in understanding LAN technology, applications, and trends. A basic knowledge and awareness of communications principles as they apply to LANs is primarily useful in assisting potential managers to understand inherent limitations in a LAN architecture. This knowledge also provides additional insight into the economics of competing products.

Other major LAN performance and selection factors are tied to non-communications characteristics such as the design of microcomputers used as server nodes, network adapter cards, hard disk performance, and network operating systems. These types of real-world system considerations virtually always decrease LAN throughput well below the maximum limit supported by particular communications technologies. For example, consider the 10-Mbps Ethernet. The current generation of PC LAN products reduces effective throughput to a fraction of the nominal 10-Mbps data rate. Many of these products, such as hard disks and network operating systems, are not directly related to Ethernet technology.

A variety of developments are in progress that will significantly increase the capability of local area networks to handle high data rate applications such as real-time video, digital voice, imagery, and multimedia. New technologies such as high-speed Ethernet, Asynchronous Transfer Mode LANs, and FDDI will bring a whole

new perspective to what can be accomplished at the individual workstation. The challenge, of course, is to develop the software and applications that can exploit these high bandwidth communications channels, as well as make fundamental changes in organizations to accommodate the proliferation of electronic and multimedia interaction possibilities. LAN managers are also becoming more challenged to devise enterprise networks that are not "box canyon" designs—in other words, to build multivendor interoperable networks that can be easily extended to accommodate the ever-increasing introduction of new technology.

III

Local Area Networking

Chapter Snapshot

Traditionally, about 70 percent of all intra-company communications have been local in nature. However, the meteoric rise in popularity of the Internet, Lotus Notes, e-mail, and embedded fax modems indicates that the corporate network planner must become more familiar with the details of interoperability between LANs and a growing selection of WAN hardware, software, and protocols. In this chapter, you will learn about:

✔ The impact of *Xerox Network Services* (XNS) on LAN transport protocol

✔ TCP/IP protocol from the wide area network perspective and its impact on interoperability between dissimilar network systems

✔ IBM's peer-to-peer internetwork protocol—APPC/PC

✔ The ISO protocol for OSI Layer 3

✔ Internetworking naming service overview

✔ Types of internetworking communications devices

✔ Electronic mail systems and APIs

✔ The distributed architecture and internetworking features of Lotus Notes

Internetworking and Interoperability

Connecting local area networks to each other and to wide area networks is receiving major consideration in many medium- and large-sized organizations. A major factor contributing to this is the value of accessing and exchanging information. LANs add value to an organization's use of PCs through resource and information sharing.

Interoperability is the ability of users on dissimilar networks to easily exchange information, regardless of distance or differences in hardware, software, or protocols. This means that no matter how complex or geographically dispersed a network is, all users can effectively share information. Typically such a combination of LANs and WANs is referred to as an *internetwork*.

Internetworking goes beyond the bounds of a single LAN by providing access to e-mail and public and private information. An accompanying interoperability strategy can add even more value to an investment in LAN-distributed processing. By connecting dissimilar networks, interoperability makes an internetwork seem transparent to its diverse users. Internetworking technology provides the tools to build *enterprise networks*—the integrated connectivity needed by multi-site organizations.

Multi-site organizations need to move information for e-mail and document transfer, as well as for the support of virtual conferencing. In the early years of PC LAN availability, individual users could access wide area networks in a stand-alone mode by connecting a modem and a telephone line to their workstation. Today's products enable the shared usage of concentrated and specialized resources from any location on the LAN; hardware and software can provide individual workstations access to a wide variety of commercial and private network systems. These systems span the entire fabric of business, government, and educational endeavor. Moreover, individuals can now typically dial in to a LAN with a laptop or remote PC and be a full participant on the network.

Ideally, you would build an internetwork from a single vendor's products, which would provide all the hardware, software, and protocols needed to assure connectivity and transparency between users. Because of today's multi-vendor communications environment, however, such a utopia rarely exists, and an interoperability strategy is required to assure successful implementation of an internetwork system.

This chapter explores the significance of internetworking as a tool, and the significance of interoperability as a strategy to achieve an enterprise networking solution. You learn about the technology and interoperability factors that make internetworking an essential part of the business process and about many of the connectivity options available to current LAN users. Examples are provided of how internetworking is implemented by current LAN products and what services can be linked to LANs. You will discover that a well-defined interoperability strategy allows internetworking to provide an increased return on significant investments in PC and LAN technology.

Internetworking, Interoperability, and the OSI Model

Chapter 11, "Local Area Networks: From the Top Down," briefly discusses transport protocols and their connection to LAN systems software, specifically their interface to network operating systems. Three of these protocols—*Xerox Network Services* (XNS), Transport Control Protocol/Internet Protocol (TCP/IP) and Advanced Program-to-Program Communications, PC version (APPC/PC) OSI transport—are significant because the manner in which they are implemented determines the degree of interoperability achievable in these internetworks.

Xerox Network Service (XNS)

XNS provides several classes of service for LANs that span a rough equivalence to OSI layers 3–7 (excluding layer 5). These service protocols are shown in figure 13.1. This section discusses the class of service equivalent to ISO Layer 3. In XNS terminology, this is referred to as the *Internet Datagram Protocol* (IDP). Datagram service routes packets as independent units without any effort to assure delivery or to guarantee that packets arrive in the correct sequence. XNS uses datagram service for IDP since Layer 4 *Sequenced Packet Protocol* (SPP) provides end-to-end error recovery and sequencing service to IDP. This protocol is supported by 3COM's series of gateway products. Novell uses a variation of IDP in its IPX protocol. This protocol functions as follows:

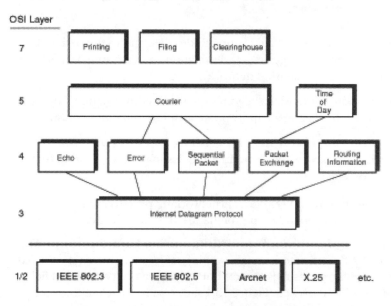

Figure 13.1
XNS protocol and the OSI Seven-layer Model.

✔ User interaction with applications software determines the destination of the message or file. This is normally done through a distributed naming service such as StreetTalk in the Vines network operating system.

✔ The applications program passes the data and a request for routing service through the protocol stack to XNS IDP software.

✔ XNS uses a portion of the packet data field to insert routing information to get the data to the destination. This portion is in the header of the internetwork packet as shown in figure 13.2.

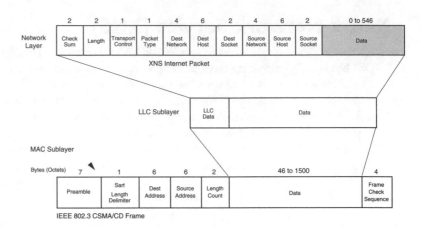

Figure 13.2
XNS internetwork packet format.

IEEE 802.3 CSMA/CD Frame

✔ XNS software in intermediate routing nodes determines the path to be taken by the packet as it goes to its destination (on the same network, or on a geographically dispersed network).

✔ The destination workstation separates the routing information from the data and puts the data in an appropriate location in memory or on a mass storage device.

✔ The destination XNS software notifies the destination application that data has been received.

This generalized description of the XNS internetworking process is illustrated in figure 13.3. The details are dependent on the nature of the application program.

IDP supports the *Routing Information Protocol* (RIP), another Layer 3 protocol. This protocol is used by XNS routers to maintain routing tables in an internetwork. RIP packets have the same header as IDP packets but also implement additional fields in the data segments of IDP packets. Figure 13.4 shows an RIP packet. In typical network implementations, RIP drivers are used in both workstations and servers to transmit requests for routing information to a directly connected router (a specially-configured network station). The router indicates available routes to send data to a remote network.

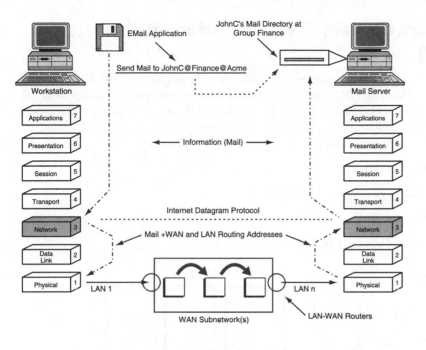

Figure 13.3
Basic XNS processing example.

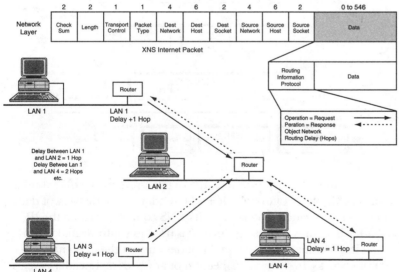

Figure 13.4
XNS Routing Information Protocol.

Transport Control Protocol/Internet Protocol (TCP/IP)

Figure 13.5 illustrates the various protocols available within the TCP/IP standards. You can see that TCP/IP Layers 3 and 4 can overlay several popular lower level network implementations such as Ethernet, Token Ring and Public Data Networks. In turn these two layers support a variety of services provided by TCP/IP systems. This chapter focuses on the following protocols available in Layer 3:

✔ *Internet Protocol* (IP)

✔ *Address Resolution Protocol* (ARP)

✔ Reverse ARP

✔ *Internet Control Message Protocol* (ICMP)

Figure 13.5
TCP/IP protocol and the OSI Model.

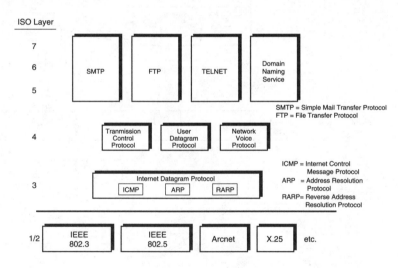

Functionally similar to the XNS IDP protocol, IP is a datagram protocol that relies on an upper layer (TCP) protocol to provide end-to-end, reliable delivery of data. The IP protocol is somewhat more robust than its XNS counterpart (see the IP header in fig. 13.6). This is not surprising since IP is used in sophisticated world-wide networks and in its formative stage could not depend on the existence of highly reliable subnetworks. In general, inspection of any protocol header reveals the features provided by that protocol. Features implemented by the IP protocol include the following:

✔ **Type of Service field.** Provides handling instructions for the packet as it traverses other subnetworks.

✔ **Data fragmentation.** Allows for maximum packet sizes in different networks (such as ARPANET, Ethernet, X.25).

✔ **Time-To-Live field.** Ensures the packet is purged from the internet if it becomes "lost."

✔ **Upper layer protocol designation field.** Allows the IP packet to interface to different Layer 4 protocols (such as TCP, XNS, ISO Transport Protocol Class 4).

✔ **Options field.** Allows certain extensions to the protocol that are not normally used but may be needed for special applications.

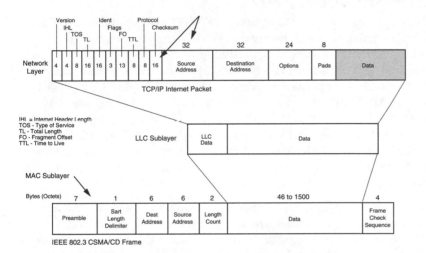

Figure 13.6
TCP/IP internet packet format.

The *Address Resolution Protocol* (ARP) is used to map the 32-bit IP address to an Ethernet 48-bit address. The ARP is necessary because there is no pre-established relationship between IP and Ethernet addresses.

The *Reverse Address Resolution Protocol* (RARP) is essentially a "who am I" broadcast that is transmitted by a new station entering the network. The broadcast is responded to by a RARP server that maps the requester's Ethernet address to an IP address appropriate to the internetwork configuration.

The *Internet Control Message Protocol* (ICMP) is a special purpose set of messages that are used between internetwork nodes to resolve problems in packet processing. These messages include:

✔ **ECHO REQUEST.** Determines whether a destination will respond; determines path timing.

✔ **SOURCE QUENCH.** Reduces transmission rate for a fixed period of time.

✔ **ROUTING CHANGE REQUEST.** Redirects packets (due to expiration of Time-To-Live parameter).

✔ **TIME STAMP REQUEST/REPLY.** Estimates average delay on the network (affects transmission rate on the network).

Advanced Program-to-Program Communications (APPC)

APPC, or more appropriately the PC version, APPC/PC, works somewhat differently than the preceding protocol, because APPC/PC's role is not general internetworking. APPC/PC is designed specifically to allow peer-to-peer communications in the IBM SNA environment. APPC/PC's session layer interface differs from NetBIOS and implements a set of protocols known as Logical Unit 6.2 or LU 6.2. PCs running APPC/PC services are identified to the SNA hierarchy as either a Physical Unit 2.0 or 2.1 (PU 2.0 or PU 2.1). A *Physical Unit* is a classification of a type of SNA network node—each PU has certain defined capabilities, including what other PUs it can communicate with. A PU 2.1, for example, can only communicate with another PU 2.1 (peer-to-peer) whereas a PU 2.0 can communicate with a PU 4 (front-end processor, or communications controller).

LU 6.2 protocols cover the functions normally associated with Session, Transport, and Network Layers. LU 6.2 is implemented through conversation verbs and control verbs. *Conversation verbs* regulate the flow of data between two applications programs; *control verbs* establish and manage the APPC/PC link. ATTACH_LU, a particularly important control verb, defines which LUs will be communicating and where they are located by network and node addresses. Another important control verb, ATTACH_PU, defines how the invoking PC will be connected to other SNA nodes. Some legal connections are shown in figure 13.7.

As previously mentioned, APPC/PC has a different session level interface to a network operating system or applications program than does NetBIOS. Whereas NetBIOS is designed for local area network connectivity, APPC/PC is designed for connectivity between PCs and designated IBM host systems. APPC/PC is the architecture upon which a user can build an integrated network of IBM PCs, minicomputers and mainframes and thus has a fundamentally different purpose than NetBIOS.

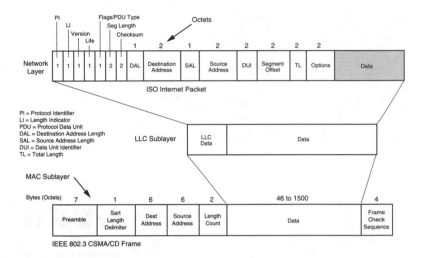

Figure 13.7
ISO internetwork packet format.

PI = Protocol Identifier
LI = Length Indicator
PDU = Protocol Data Unit
DAL = Destination Address Length
SAL = Source Address Length
DUI = Data Unit Identifier
TL = Total Length

ISO Layer 3 Protocol

As with the previously discussed protocols, ISO Layer 3 provides network level services that include:

- ✔ Addressing

- ✔ Routing

- ✔ Packet fragmentation

- ✔ Packet life (datagram service)

- ✔ Class of service provided

These services are accommodated by the packet format shown in figure 13.8. Note the similarity to the packet format and services provided by the TCP/IP Layer 3 protocol. ISO Layer 3's distinguishing characteristic is that it is defined abstractly to provide the greatest possible flexibility in implementation. Unfortunately, flexible protocols are an anathema to interoperability and achieving such a condition on an ISO internetwork will be a major technical challenge.

III

Local Area Networking

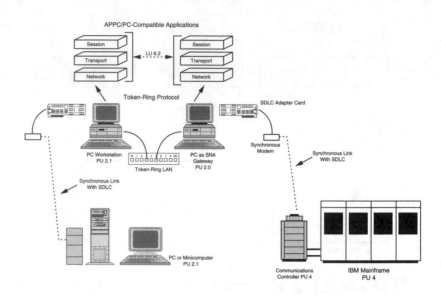

Figure 13.8
APPC/PC connectivity examples.

Transport Protocol Interoperability

The key to internetwork effectiveness is whether any combination of the preceding protocols can coexist on the internetwork, or whether two different implementations of the same protocol can interoperate. In a pure LAN context, evolving network operating systems handle the first problem by implementing parallel protocol stacks. Microsoft calls this the Transport Data Interface—Novell calls it Transport Layer Interface. Parallel protocol stacks are only part of the solution, however, because they do not in themselves guarantee equivalent implementation across different vendors' product lines.

Keep in mind that the more complex the protocol (indicated by the number of different fields in the header), the more difficult it is to attain interoperability between systems. The syntax (format) and semantics (meaning) of each field must be implemented exactly alike or problems will occur in internetwork protocol execution. In most cases, interoperability can only be assured by compliance testing using all possible combinations of software and hardware in the connectivity loop. A protocol analyzer is an important compliance-testing tool. The Sniffer from Network General, for example, can be configured to run on IBM's Token Ring, Ethernet, ARCnet, and other physical network implementations. Protocol suites supported include all the following major stacks:

- ✔ NetWare Core Protocol/SPX/IPX
- ✔ Server Message Block (SMB)/XNS
- ✔ SMB/NetBIOS/TCP/IP

✔ SMB/ISO

✔ SNA/SMB/NetBIOS

Before testing with a tool such as The Sniffer you need to determine a specific test configuration as well as comprehensive test plan. The test plan should indicate what actions will stimulate the test network and should indicate the expected responses from the appropriate protocol stacks. Data collection and analysis is handled by the protocol analyzer. Typical problems that might be discovered include errors in field coding (syntax errors), incorrect query/reply sequences (timing errors), and interpretation of field data (semantic errors). The consequences of lack of interoperability range from non-communication to reductions in network performance. Non-interoperability has institutional ramifications as well—lack of user confidence can lead to non-use of e-mail and other network features with a consequent loss of productivity.

Name Services

Although not strictly required for internetworking, name services contribute to the utility of widely distributed networks by providing transparent addressing and location services. You could, for instance, send a message to the following address:

    John_Jones@Marketing_Group@Acme_HQ

This address is easier to use than looking up John Jones' user name on his LAN and the LAN's phone number. A *name service* automatically links users to a variety of resources, among them telephone numbers, directories on file servers, mailing lists, and shared printers. Subsequent access to these resources is accomplished simply by specifying the name.

General Characteristics

Network software, supported by a name service, handles the details of finding the destination and delivering the data. To be most effective, name services should have two main properties:

✔ Persistence

✔ Centralized control

In a persistent name service, such as Banyan's StreetTalk Service and NetWare 4.*x* Network Directory Service, assigned names remain in effect until removed or changed. Non-persistent name services, such as NetBIOS in OS/2 and Windows NT, remove the network name when the host workstation is powered down.

III

Local Area Networking

In any given network, a form of centralized control over names is desirable. Some implementations allow only one name catalog per logical network, regardless of the number of servers installed; other systems assign one catalog per file server. Catalogs serve the same function as the telephone book in a city. A distributed network's set of network catalogs is analogous to a stack of telephone books from different cities. In a centralized system, communications between servers containing catalogs is crucial to keeping location data accurate for system-wide resources.

Xerox Clearinghouse, an example of a generic naming service that has both persistence and centralized control, uses a hierarchical naming system. Its syntax is as follows:

```
Item (or name)@Group@Domain
```

In practice, *item* or *name* represents a single user, file server, printer, directory or list of names associated with a particular physical network. *Group* typically represents a workgroup or department, and is equivalent to a specific logical network. The name service is responsible for linking the *Group* name to a logical network number. *Domain* represents the entire organization and may be used to link the organization to a larger multi-organizational network such as a commercial e-mail service. Figure 13.9 illustrates this hierarchical naming system. A variation of this protocol is used by Banyan's VINES network operating system StreetTalk Service.

Figure 13.9
Hierarchical network naming concept.

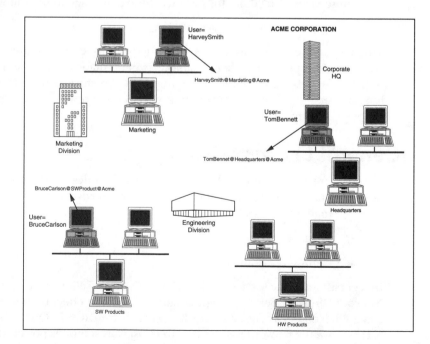

NetBIOS-based networks use the *Name Management Protocol* (NMP), originally provided as part of the Localnet/PC protocol under license from Sytek. NMP is neither persistent nor centralized. Names are assigned to network resources only while those resources are powered up and active on the network. Because control is not centralized, NMP is not well-suited for internetworking. NMP requires that each node on the network maintain its own list of names—if a node cannot find a name in its list, a broadcast is made to the network to locate the unknown name. Broadcasts such as these would be highly inefficient in a WAN environment.

Novell has added an interim naming service to NetWare 2.*x* and 3.*x* called the NetWare Name Service. However, this naming service does not implement a hierarchical scheme. NetWare Name Service creates server domains and profiles. *Domains* are groupings of servers that share the same lists of login user names, groups, and print queues. When new users, groups, or print queues are added to the network, the lists are replicated throughout the domain. *Profiles*—subsets of domains—are groupings of users and the servers to which they connect. Profiles are limited to eight servers because NetWare limits users to a maximum of eight server attachments. Domain structures are also implemented in OS/2 LAN Server and Windows NT Advanced Server.

In a persistent naming service, user logins are mapped to a particular user profile. That profile is in turn mapped to a server, which identifies the user's location on the network for individual routing. Any workstation or server on a single LAN has a unique *node address*—its network adapter card serial number. This naming device assures universal uniqueness. Packet routing on a single LAN requires only source and destination node addresses. Ethernet or Token Ring packets use an 8-byte field for source and destination addresses. If a user on a LAN is not physically connected to the source LAN, a *network address* is needed. Network addresses are interpreted at the network layer of the source LAN for routing outgoing packets to destination LANs. One or more subnetworks may be traversed during the routing process. Once this packet gets to the destination LAN, the node address is mapped, or associated, to a specific user on that LAN. The Data Link Layer knows nothing about the network address and the Network Layer knows nothing about the node address.

X.500 Directory Services

X.500 is an international naming service recommended standard defined by CCITT and adopted by ISO. The motivation for such an international standard is clear: with the proliferation of e-mail systems, the number of incompatible addressing schemes is growing. One of the major impediments to the widespread use of e-mail is the inability to find a particular user's address based on a standard search criteria regardless of the e-mail system used. X.500 provides the tools to implement a distributed addressing database common to all major e-mail systems. *NetWare*

III

Local Area Networking

Directory Services (NDS) found in NetWare 4.*x* is one of the first major systems to implement an X.500-compatible distributed directory system. NDS specifics are found in Chapter 14, "Network Operating System Implementation," in the discussion about NetWare 4.*x.* NDS departs from strict X.500 standards in the areas of security and directory rights.

The major elements of the X.500 standard are users (people or software processes), directories (local and remote), and objects (entries in the directory). A software process, for example, would be a directory replication operation between remote directories. Network users can directly access directory services through *Directory User Agents* (DUA) and *Directory Service Agents* (DSA). DUA and DSA communicate through a *Directory Access Protocol* (DAP). Directories communicate with each other through *Directory Service Protocol* (DSP). Software processes can use DAP or DSP. Directories themselves consist of a *Directory Information Base* (DIB), a hierarchical database containing information concerning objects contained within the directory. An *object* is a record in the DIB.

Partitioning makes user access to remote directories more efficient in software implementation. In a large organization, it is not feasible to maintain the entire organization's directory at all locations. Partitioning divides the database into segments needed at each location. Each node in the organization's hierarchical tree contains DIB objects for itself and subordinate nodes. A Master DIB knows which partition contains a particular object and the location of that partition. A directory object search uses the following sequence:

1. Search local DIB

2. If not found then go on to next step

3. Query Master DIB using appropriate remote link(s)

DIB has endless uses because objects can be defined as virtually any entity having to do with communications. The X.500 standard already provides for object attributes including country, location, organization, organizational unit, and common names; postal addresses, functional titles, telephone numbers, facsimile numbers, ISDN numbers, and Telex numbers. The DIB is extensible; new objects and object attributes can be defined in addition to the standard definitions. The increased use of X.500 is virtually assured given the current emphasis on enterprise networking and global connectivity.

Internetworking Devices

The nature of internetworking requires devices that have specialized functions beyond the movement of data within a single network. These devices may link LAN-to-LAN, LAN-to-WAN, or both according to the needs of the internetwork applications. These devices may serve to regulate the access to limited wireline facilities, such as cluster controllers, concentrators, and multiplexers; to provide translation of protocol, such as gateways and front-end processors; or to facilitate various types of packet routing, such as routers and bridges. Basic knowledge of how these devices work and fit into the overall internetworking architecture is important for network planning and design efforts.

Individual LANs or WANs forming the elements of an internetwork are known as *subnetworks*. These relationships are illustrated in figure 13.10.

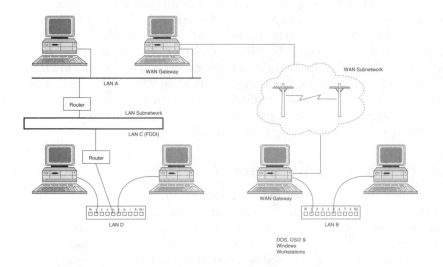

Figure 13.10
General internetworking architecture.

Wide Area Networks (WANs)

WANs are extensively discussed in Chapter 7, "Wide Area Networks," specifically the X.25 packet-switched network protocol and IBM's proprietary *System Network Architecture* (SNA). This chapter's main concern is connecting LANs to certain types of WANs for host connectivity, interconnecting remote LANs using WANs as subnetworks, and accessing LANs from remote workstations through WANs. Other WANs commonly used to connect LANs are T-1 links, *Switched Multi-megabit Data Service* (SMDS), Frame Relay, *Synchronous Optical Network* (SONET), and *Asynchronous Transfer Mode* (ATM).

Proprietary networks are designed and marketed by a single computer vendor. Two of the most prominent proprietary networks include IBM's *System Network Architecture* (SNA) and DEC's *Digital Network Architecture* (DNA). SNA is discussed in detail in Chapter 7. From the perspective of a LAN user, connection to such networks is through gateways—SNA and DNA interconnects that allow LAN workstations to participate as members of the appropriate proprietary network.

These types of gateways can be connected to host communications controllers either directly or by means of dedicated lines using synchronous line protocols. Products are available that allow MS-DOS and OS/2 applications to logically connect to mainframe or minicomputer applications using SNA and DNA as routing and transport systems. Software also is available that allows selected mainframe and mini hosts to function as servers for connected LANs.

Packet-switching is an efficient method of transmitting large volumes of data between widely-separated processing sites. X.25 is an international standard of the CCITT for the interconnection of *Data Terminal Equipment* (DTE) devices to a packet-switching network. LANs can connect to *packet-switched networks* (PSN)—or *Public Data Network* (PDN)—through an X.25 gateway. In this case, the X.25 gateway, or server, emulates a *Packet Assembler-Dissambler* (PAD) which is the *Data Communications Equipment* (DCE) device on a PDN. LANs can also connect to PDNs through standard telephone lines. The telephone number dialed is the number of a local PDN node (PAD) which is in turn directly connected to the network. When you connect to CompuServe, for example, the PDN connection is indirectly completed through an asynchronous gateway on the LAN.

WAN Data Communications Devices

Internetworks that include wide area networks and mainframe host connectivity use communications components that are not typically seen in workgroup LAN and asynchronous environments. The most common of these items include synchronous modems, cluster controllers, multiplexers, front-end processors, and concentrators. These devices are located between the appropriate gateway device and the wide area transport system, usually a telephone or data network. Front-end processors are connected to mainframe computers and act as a communications routing and processing device for the main CPU. Basic functions and configurations of these devices are illustrated in Figures 13.11 through 13.15.

Gateways

A *gateway* is one of several types of communications servers. The function of a gateway is to allow two or more dissimilar networks to communicate as a single logical entity. In the context of the LAN system software discussed in Chapter 9, "Telephone System Interfaces," *dissimilar* means that the transport protocols are different, and that the underlying physical networks are different. Host and LAN operating systems may also be dissimilar. Among the more common types of gateways are those that connect LANs to proprietary mainframe architectures such as IBM's SNA and DEC's DECnet. Other common forms of gateways connect LANs to a variety of wide area network protocols such as asynchronous and synchronous on the public telephone network, T-1 multiplexed data on private networks, X.25 on public data networks, ISDN, international Telex and facsimile.

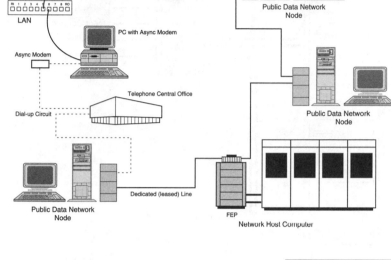

Figure 13.11
Direct-and-dial-up telephone connections to a Public data network (PDN).

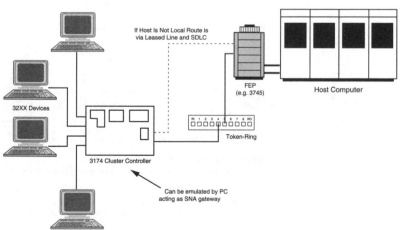

Figure 13.12
Functional concept of a cluster controller.

Figure 13.13
Functional concept of a front-end processor (FEP).

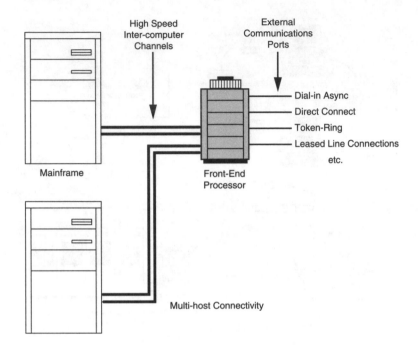

Figure 13.14
Functional concept of STDM and T-1 multiplexers.

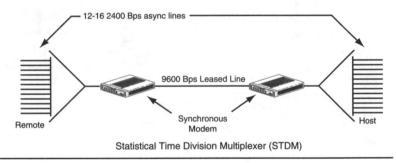

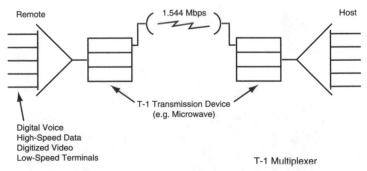

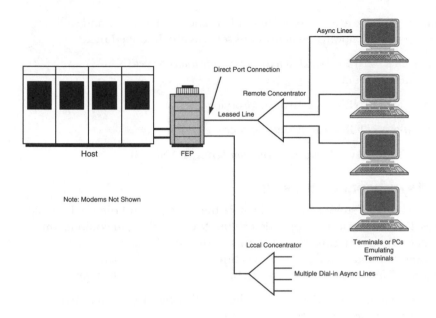

Figure 13.15
Functional concept of local and remote concentrators.

Asynchronous Gateways

Asynchronous gateways convert data on a LAN to a form suitable for transmission and reception by modems. (V.32/V.42 and V.FAST modems are asynchronous devices.) Asynchronous gateways include modem servers (allow authorized LAN users access to modems attached to the server) and remote access servers (allow remote users to dial in to the local LAN). Modem servers communicate with client workstations to determine the client's desired destination service. A network user, for instance, may want to connect to Dow Jones News Retrieval whereas another user may want to connect to a remote LAN for e-mail. The server determines the appropriate telephone number to dial (for public-switched telephone networks) and the asynchronous communications parameters needed to connect to the desired service. These numbers and parameters are established during server installation and configuration. Remote access servers enable authorized remote users to dial in to the LAN and have similar network services as any local user. Modem servers exchange client-server protocols over the LAN; remote access servers exchange client-server protocols over the wide area connection.

Asynchronous gateways are implemented in a variety of ways. Generally, a software interface at the workstation allows either a third-party communications software package or some other applications program to request access to one or more dial-up modems attached to the server. This interface may take the form of a software interrupt such as IBM's INT 14 or Novell's INT 06B or a procedure call such as IBM's *Asynchronous Communications Device Interface* (ACDI).

III

Local Area Networking

Asynchronous gateways are implemented with a variety of hardware and software design features. The following asynchronous services are described next:

✔ Novell's *NetWare Asynchronous Communications Server* (NACS) and related products

✔ Banyan's VINES Asynchronous Service

✔ Windows NT Remote Access Service

✔ IBM's *LAN Asynchronous Connection Server* (LANACS)

NetWare Asynchronous Servers

Novell's asynchronous support services include both dial-out and remote PC dial-in capabilities. Dial-out services are provided by the NACS working in conjunction with workstation-hosted terminal emulation software. Workstation terminal software is logically connected to the NACS through the *NetWare Asynchronous Services Interface* (NASI). Dial-in services can be provided in one of two ways:

✔ Connecting to the LAN through the NACS using supported remote access software packages.

✔ Connecting to the LAN through an 80386-based server called the NetWare Access Server.

All asynchronous support services use *Wide Area Network Interface Modules* (WNIMs) at either the NACS or the NetWare Access Server. *WNIMs* are multi-line asynchronous adapter cards, capable of supporting up to four modems each. As many as four WNIMs may be located in an asynchronous communications server or access server. A single network can have more than one NACS or NetWare Access Server. Software implementation requires the following features:

✔ A WNIM control program on the server.

✔ NASI for dial-out connections. This interface at the workstation allows terminal emulation software packages to connect with asynchronous ports on the NACS server. NASI supports Crosstalk MK 4, ProComm, and other popular asynchronous terminal emulation software.

✔ NASI-supported asynchronous communications software for dial-out connections. Supported software runs on up to 4 workstations simultaneously (per licensed copy) through the NACS asynchronous ports.

✔ Supported remote access software for dial-in connections through the NACS. This software allows a remote PC to dial in to the LAN and operate as a remote workstation. Up to four workstations on the LAN can serve as hosts (per licensed copy of remote access software). Remote access software is designed for relatively light use.

✔ NetWare Access Server for dial-in connections. This server functions like a NACS for remote access except that it is designed for heavy-duty use. The NetWare Access Server requires a minimum 80386 platform and supports up to 16 individual dial-in sessions. One session is reserved for remote network supervisors. Each remote session uses a virtual 386 machine with 640 KB of RAM.

Figure 13.16 illustrates some typical network configurations that use the preceding list of features. The NACS/NASI hardware/software combination provides the following dial-out asynchronous terminal support functions through the use of ASCOM IV:

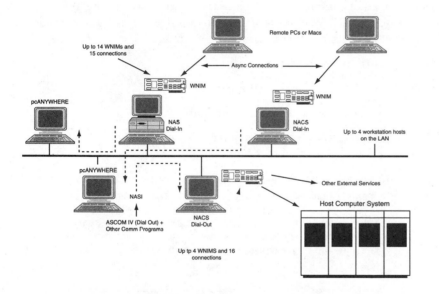

Figure 13.16
Novell NetWare asynchronous server architecture.

✔ Up to 16 shared asynchronous communications lines (hardware feature through use of WNIMs)

✔ Communications speeds up to 19,200 bits/sec per line (WNIM hardware feature)

✔ Multiple file transfer protocols, including ASCOM IV, XMODEM, Kermit, BLOCK, and BLOCK V

✔ Support for several common asynchronous terminal emulations

✔ User-defined modem support to accommodate non-Hayes protocols

✔ ASCII-to-EBCDIC conversions

✔ Administrator-controlled security for limited access by LAN users

✔ Script files allowing fully automated terminal operations

✔ Dial directory for automatic dialing

Banyan VINES Asynchronous Support

The VINES asynchronous communications service enables users to connect to WANs, host computer systems (mainframes or minicomputer installations), or on-line database and e-mail services. Banyan file servers can be set up with direct line connections or any of a variety of modem communications systems. Like other Banyan services, asynchronous service uses the StreetTalk naming convention. The term *connection name* refers to a specific host computer or on-line service, regardless of the number or type of communications paths that exist between the Banyan server and the host system. This concept is illustrated in figure 13.17. A server has the following asynchronous service features:

✔ One asynchronous service

✔ Up to 30 connection names for the service

✔ Unlimited dial-out lines per connection name

✔ Number of direct lines per connection name equal to the number of direct line connections to the server

✔ Maximum number of asynchronous hardware connections to the server depends on the specific server model used (up to 30 on the CNS)

Figure 13.17
VINES
Asynchronous
Terminal Service.

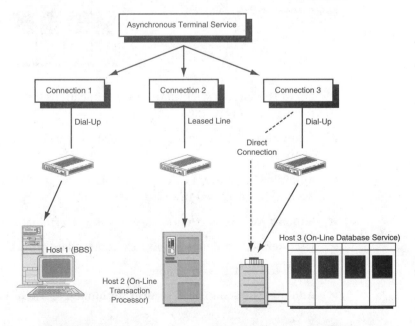

For each connection name, certain parameters must be specified, such as line speed, number of data bits, parity, number of stop bits, and terminal emulation type. This process is typical of most PC communications software. Users log in to the network with asynchronous connection names provided in their user profiles. The user profiles also contain directory search paths to locate the corresponding *connection files* (files that contain communications parameters for a connection name). This process is shown for a typical installation in figure 13.18.

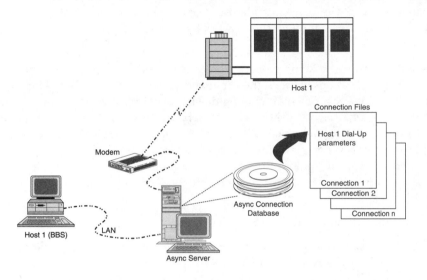

Figure 13.18
VINES connection files.

VINES provides both dial-out terminal emulation and remote PC dial-in for asynchronous communications support. All asynchronous services use the *Intelligent Communications Adapter* (ICA), a six-port adapter card. From one to five of these cards can be located in VINES servers, providing up to 30 asynchronous ports per server attached to the LAN. ICAs support a variety of line protocols including asynchronous, SDLC, HDLC, and X.25. Asynchronous connections are supported up to 19,200 bps.

The terminal emulation services are integrated with the VINES StreetTalk naming service to allow customized emulation for individuals and groups. The terminal service is essentially a special-purpose asynchronous communications program, not unlike Crosstalk Mark 4 or ASCOM IV. It provides the following standard features:

- ✔ Common DEC, IBM and TTY terminal emulation
- ✔ Autodial directory support
- ✔ ASCII file transfer
- ✔ Kermit protocol for binary file transfer
- ✔ Multiple server dial-out access for any user

Windows NT Advanced Server Remote Access Service

Windows NTAS *Remote Access Service* (RAS) provides access to a Windows NT-based LAN through the use of asynchronous communications lines. As with all LAN services, RAS is a resource manager. RAS resources are communications ports and remote users or networks. Each supported communications port (a standard COM port) has an associated modem and, because modem parameters are configurable, a wide variety of modems can be supported. RAS also uses standard Windows NT network management services such as audit trails, error logs, and alerts. RAS can be managed from any workstation on the network by anyone with proper access privileges.

RAS consists of two parts: the Remote Access Server and the Remote Access Client workstation. Communications between the client and server are accomplished by means of a variety of WAN protocols including dial-up asynchronous, X.25, and *Integrated Services Digital Network* (ISDN). The RAS Server manages communications port drivers and network routing details as well as RAS security. The RAS Server also uses the Windows NT alert service to generate messages based on pre-designated events (error thresholds or certain audit conditions). This alert facility works with the Windows NT Event Viewer to provide the RAS Administrator with audit-monitoring capability.

Basic features of the Windows NTAS RAS Service include:

✔ Client access to applications servers on the LAN such as Lotus Notes, SQL Server, and SNA Server For Windows NT

✔ Support for high-performance multiport asynchronous, X.25 and ISDN adapters, and WAN protocols

✔ Gateway service to other servers on the LAN through equivalent NetBIOS-compatible protocol stacks running on RAS Server and other servers

✔ Point-to-point connectivity between client and server while restricting access to remainder of the LAN

✔ Four-point security protection with user account database, login authentication, pre-set call-back, and optional security hosts

✔ Support for up to 64 simultaneous remote connections

✔ Support for Named Pipes, Remote RPC, and LAN Manager API

ISDN service consists of one 16 Kbps D channel and two 64 Kbps B channels. The D (Data) channel is a low-speed data channel for signaling functions. The B (Basic Rate) channel can be configured as two 64 Kbps or one 128 Kbps channels. The

recommended practice for configuring ISDN for RAS is to assign two B channels as incoming ports to allow maximum access to remote users. Clients have the option to request channel aggregation after a connection is established.

X.25 connectivity can be accomplished through direct access to an X.25 public data network, dial-up access to a remote PAD or RS-232 access to an external PAD. For direct connect, the RAS server or client will use an X.25 adapter card incorporating the *Packet Assembler-Dissassembler* (PAD) circuitry on board. Physical connection is then made to an appropriate dedicated circuit to join the X.25 network. Alternatively, the client connection can be made through dial-up to an external PAD. In this case, the client only needs a standard modem and telephone line. Servers cannot access X.25 through dial-up PADs. Both clients and servers can use an external PAD connected by RS-232 cable. Figure 13.19 compares the different X.25 configurations.

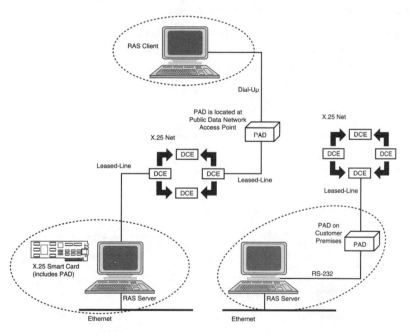

Figure 13.19
Windows NT Remote Access Service using X.25 connectivity.

Configuration of ports and networks is relatively straightforward. Ports have typical asynchronous communications parameters such as modem type, line speed, inactivity timeout, and whether incoming or outgoing calls are allowed. Non-standard modems can be defined by line speed, data bit pattern, parity, and whether the modem is error-correcting or capable of automatic baud-rate adjustment. Commands for modem initialization, hang-up, busy, no-answer and connection reliability can also be specified. X.25 and ISDN parameters are also specified for their respective ports.

Basic security for RAS works well with the Windows NT security model. Users with Remote Access permission are authenticated by the RAS server before being allowed basic access to the LAN. For greater security, a user account may also be required to use a call-back number. RAS supports the use of security hosts between the modem and itself. A security host—a third-party authentication device—controls access to the RAS server. Once successfully logged in to the RAS, a remote user may have the following restrictions:

✔ Access can be limited to the server only

✔ Access can be limited to specific network segments by disabling bindings between transport protocol stacks and associated adapter cards

✔ Access to network resources can be limited by the user account database as if the remote user were logged in to the network locally

Figure 13.20 shows the security protocol sequence when a client attempts to log in to a RAS server. The RAS administrator can monitor certain security-related audit events such as successful logins or one of several failure events.

Figure 13.20
Windows NT RAS security protocol.

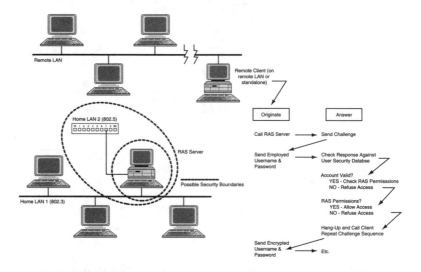

As a Windows NT service, RAS is controlled by the standard service commands START, STOP, PAUSE, and CONTINUE. During a PAUSE period, existing connections are maintained but no new connections are allowed. Network dynamic management is also not allowed during a PAUSE interval. If the STOP command is issued, all connections are broken, and the RAS service is terminated.

IBM LAN Asynchronous Services

IBM provides asynchronous server support through its *LAN Asynchronous Connection Server* (LANACS) Program. LANACS is compatible with DOS-based servers and the *Realtime Interface Co-Processor* (RTIC) Multiport (IBM PC/AT hardware bus) and Multiport/2 (IBM PS/2 hardware bus) adapters. LANACS provides both dial-out and dial-in asynchronous communications through a dedicated server. The server can be connected to Token Ring, PC Network Baseband, or PC Network Broadband LAN topologies. Depending on the server host hardware used and the number of RTIC adapters installed, LANACS can support from 4 to 32 asynchronous ports per server.

An RTIC Multiport or Multiport/2 adapter uses the Intel 80186 processor and up to 512 KB of RAM for on-board communications protocol support. An RTIC Mulitport can have three possible configurations:

✔ Four RS-232C ports

✔ Eight RS-232C ports

✔ Four RS-232C and four RS-422A ports

The RS-422A ports support asynchronous devices (terminals, printers, and so forth) over longer distances and at higher data rates than possible with RS-232C protocol.

SNA and RJE Gateways

Because of the many IBM mainframes used in organizations and businesses, gateways to SNA and RJE hosts are among the most common gateways in LAN installations. Such gateways can be direct-wired to a local mainframe or connected through synchronous modems and a leased landline (or other suitable transport system) to a remote mainframe. As with the asynchronous gateways, SNA and RJE gateways are most often implemented as servers, allowing multiple LAN users to access local or remote mainframe facilities.

Such gateways are composed of two basic parts: the *software terminal emulators* that allow connected PCs to act like IBM remote terminals of various types, and the *data link protocol* that provides basic compatibility with IBM front-end processors. Typical protocols supported include SDLC and Bisynchronous. These are discussed in more detail in Chapters 2, "Communication Channels" and 7, "Wide Area Networks." Supported terminals include 3274/76 cluster controllers (typically emulated by the gateway), 3278 remote terminals, 3279 remote graphics terminals, 3286/3287 printers, and various 3770 RJE equipment. The protocols are implemented on communications adapter cards which connect directly to the appropriate line devices (modems). Emulation software runs on the gateway and may run on workstations.

Gateway Communications' G/SNA and G/BSC

Gateway Communications provides typical SNA and RJE support through its G/SNA line of hardware and software. Non-SNA support is also provided through the G/BSC 3270, which emulates a 3274/3278 combination on a bisynchronous link. The G/SNA PCcom, another unusual subset of this product line, provides a high speed SDLC link between remotely-connected PCs. This type of link supports up to 19,200 bits/sec and has superior file transfer capabilities compared to an asynchronous link. Adapter cards for these products can be either IBM SDLC/Bisync cards or Gateway's enhanced WNIM-186 communications card. The latter offers speeds up to 800 Kbps and two ports, which can be configured as RS-232, RS-422, or V.35. Figure 13.21 depicts a multiple-option layout for the Gateway SNA systems.

Figure 13.21
SNA Gateway configurations.

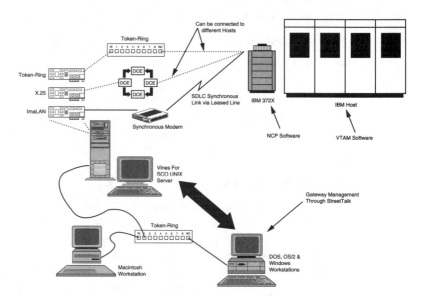

VINES 3270/SNA and 3270/BSC Service

VINES supports IBM 3274/3276 cluster controller and 3278/3279 display/3287 printer *Logical Unit* (LU) emulation. In the SNA system, an LU can be a terminal or printer session. A cluster controller is designed to provide linkage between the SNA network and a number of individual terminals and printers. In the Banyan system, the server acts as the cluster controller and workstations with their attached printers emulate 3270/SNA terminals and printers. Workstations can be either DOS, Windows, or Macintosh clients. The following communications capabilities are available with this service:

✔ Up to 128 concurrent users (96 DOS/Windows users + 32 Macintosh users, or 128 Mac users) allowed per terminal service

✔ Two or more gateways can be active on a single VINES network

✔ Support for DCA's Intelligent Synchronous Communications Adapter (ISCA) and DCA's IRMAtrac Token Ring Adapter to use either SDLC or 802.2 data link protocol

✔ Gateway monitoring to generate statistics showing gateway usage and configuration

✔ Hot Back Up to use multiple gateways on the network for alternate connection paths to the host

SNA terminal support incorporates reconfigurable 3270 keyboard emulation and various status displays covering on-line, connection, keyboard, printer, mode, Logical Unit, and message information. These status displays provide complete information about the current mainframe session.

Novell's SNA Gateway

Novell also offers SNA support with its SNA Gateway. This gateway offers support for up to 32 concurrent logical sessions with mainframe equipment. IBM mainframe environments supported include the following:

✔ IBM 370, 303X, 208X, 43XX mainframe hosts

✔ IBM 3705, 3720, 3725 front-end processors

✔ IBM VTAM and TCAM access methods

✔ IBM CICS, CMS, DSPRINT, ISPF, JES, TSO/SPF applications

The Gateway functions as a 3274 Cluster Controller and workstations function as 3278 or 3279 display Logical Units. Network printers can be assigned as 3287 printer LUs. The Novell SNA Gateway does not require a dedicated server nor does it require special software in those workstations that run SNA sessions as emulating 3278/3279 terminals. The Gateway supports dial-up and leased lines and works with point-to-point and multi-drop circuits. More than one Gateway can exist on a LAN. Three versions are provided that support either 8, 16, or 32 logical SNA sessions.

Software features include Session Hold, Hot Key, and Disk Logging capabilities. Session Hold allows the host session to remain active while the workstation executes a DOS command. Hot Key is a rapid method of shifting between a host session and DOS applications. Disk Logging downloads a screen of host data to a disk file. Figure 13.22 illustrates a typical SNA Gateway setup.

III

Local Area Networking

Figure 13.22
NetWare SNA
Gateway.

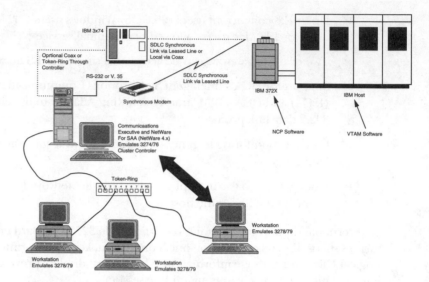

X.25 and Other Gateways

Gateways outside the domain of proprietary and asynchronous networks are most commonly found in X.25 packet-switched network, PSTN or private T-1 network and international Telex applications. X.25—a CCITT-sponsored international standard—functions much the same for public and *private data networks* (PDN) as RS-232-C does for the public switched telephone network. In other words, X.25 is a standard to connect *Data Terminal Equipment* (DTE) with *Data Communications Equipment* (DCE). In this case, the DCE is connected directly to a packet-switched network, just as a V.32 modem (DCE) is connected directly to the PSTN. Some X.25 gateway products allow the server to be configured as either DTE or DCE, depending on the specific application. Figure 13.23 shows some examples of X.25 gateway usage. X.25 gateways for IBM PC and compatible LANs are available from Gateway Communications, 3Com, Novell, and Banyan.

LANs are connected directly by T-1 gateways to high capacity public or private T-1 links. A T-1 link is a standard digital transport methodology, capable of handling up to 24 voice channels, each channel being rated at 64 Kbps. The total data rate of a T-1 link is 1.544 Mbps. T-1 links can be transported by inexpensive microwave systems, *Very Small Aperture Terminal* (VSAT) satellite systems, fiber optics, copper cable, or infrared light-wave links.

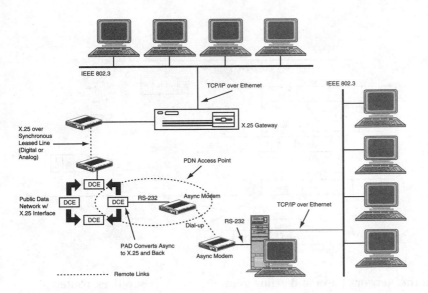

Figure 13.23
X.25 Gateway configuration for LAN-to-LAN connectivity.

Telex gateways are designed to connect LANs to the international Telex network. Such gateways are capable of connecting to the older but more prevalent Telex I or Telex II (also known as TWX) systems, or to the newer but less common Teletex system. Telex gateways may or may not include actual Telex machines. Telex software can be integrated with a LAN's e-mail system so that sending or receiving Telex is the same as sending or receiving any other type of e-mail. A good Telex gateway should have an international directory included as well as the capability to support store and forward operations. The latter is important because many international Telex sessions are not interactive due to time-zone differences.

A fax gateway is closely related to Telex. PC facsimile cards are widely available and require nothing more than an ordinary telephone connection. Some fax cards allow multiple workstation access through fax server software, in effect becoming a fax gateway for LAN users.

Routers

Routers are devices that route LAN traffic between logically separate networks. *Logically separate* means that the connected networks have different Layer 3 network numbers. Network numbers are transparent to Layer 2 protocols because they are contained within the data area of a Media Access Layer packet as shown in figure 13.24.

Local Area Networking

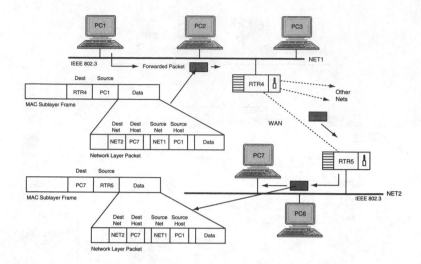

Figure 13.24
Basic router operation using an Ethernet-to-Ethernet example.

Working at the Network Layer and acting as internetwork post offices, router nodes forward packets specifically addressed to them and destined for external networks. Higher layer software determines that data is to be externally routed and ensures that the router address is correct. Thus, the router's external communications configuration must be known to the network operating system. Routers can be connected to more than two networks.

Networks connected by routers have the same transport protocol because the network and transport layer protocols are usually linked. This is the case with XNS, TCP/IP, OSI, and Novell's SPX/IPX. Because they can be connected to more than two networks, routers support multi-path routing. Routers frequently are capable of advanced routing features such as least-cost routing.

Bridges

Bridges connect two physically separate LANs with possibly different higher layer protocol stacks. Bridges work at the Media Access Layer and use only the destination and source addresses contained in the Layer 2 packet format. A *bridge* inspects all packets to determine if the destination address is on the same physical LAN as the source address. Two outcomes are possible: the packet is destined for a node on the same LAN as the source node, or it is destined for a node on the connected LAN. In the first case, the packet is filtered, or discarded, since the destination node recognizes its own traffic. In the second case, the packet is forwarded to the connected LAN. Figure 13.25 illustrates this basic bridge operation.

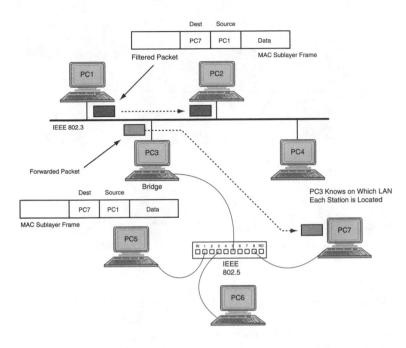

Figure 13.25
A basic bridge operation using an Ethernet-to-Token Ring example.

Bridges can be *local*—directly connecting networks—or *remote*—connecting networks through a wide-area subnetwork (see fig. 13.26). Bridges can also connect more than two LANs in multiple bridge installations (see fig. 13.27).

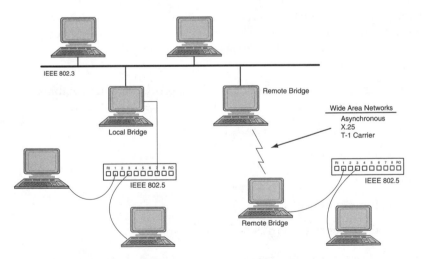

Figure 13.26
Comparison of local and remote bridge configurations.

III

Local Area Networking

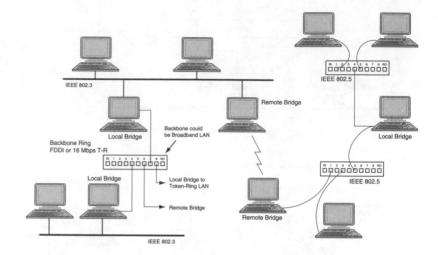

Figure 13.27
Multiple local
and remote
bridge
configuration.

LANs are commonly connected through remote bridges using the public switched telephone network, public or private data networks, and private T-1 links. PSTN bridges use asynchronous hardware and bridge software for dial-up connections to a similarly-equipped remote LAN. X.25 remote bridges use either point-to-point or multi-point configurations with data rates up to 64 Kbps. In the former case, two LAN remote bridges are linked by a direct connection (leased line) or a dial-up line using the X.25 protocol. Multi-point bridges connect to a Public Data Network and can connect to multiple LANs using the PDN. Some bridges support the X.75 PDN interconnect protocol which allows connected LAN users to access overseas packet-switched networks. T-1 bridges typically use the facilities of a private voice/ data network to connect two LANs. T-1 bridges require connection to a T-1 multiplexer similar to T-1 gateways.

The proper use of bridges in a well-designed LAN can provide varying combinations of the following benefits:

✔ Logical extension of a single network

✔ Increased throughput

✔ Traffic filtering

✔ Protocol independence

✔ Higher performance than routers and gateways

Bridges commonly work in learning mode: they automatically determine which network nodes are on each connected segment. These lists of network nodes are called *routing tables*, although the term is somewhat of a misnomer. For purposes of discussion, the network containing the source node will be called the first network, and the forwarded network will be called the second network. Pure bridges know nothing about routing—they only pass the packet to the second network if the destination address is not on the first network's routing table.

Novell's NetWare supports two type of bridges: an *internal* bridge, designed to run in file servers, and an *external* bridge, designed to run in workstations. Internal bridges support up to four dissimilar network adapter cards per file server and are supported by the basic network operating system. External bridges can be either dedicated or non-dedicated and are supported by standalone software compatible with the network operating system. External bridges also handle up to four dissimilar LAN adapter cards.

Why pay extra for external bridge software when the internal bridge is included in the basic LAN software price? The answer is, you pay for increased flexibility. For example, the external bridge could be used to do the following:

✔ Provide a more flexible topology than a server-centric bridge configuration

✔ Provide a repeater function to extend the effective length of a LAN

✔ Add more networks beyond the 4 supported by the file server

To properly configure a Novell bridge, three rules must be followed: each server to be bridged must have a unique name; each network to be bridged must have a unique number; and each bridge software installation must be provided with the unique network numbers of all LANs to be bridged.

Banyan's VINES also uses bridges to switch between up to four LANs and multiple external service gateways. From a hardware standpoint, the Banyan approach differs from Novell in that the bridge node is also a file server and provides one or more gateways to external services. The Banyan network server may be generically described as a network data switch.

IBM uses bridges extensively for internetworking Token Rings. IBM bridges can connect any combination of the following:

✔ 4 Mbps Token Ring

✔ 16 Mbps Token Ring

✔ PC network baseband

✔ PC network broadband

Token Ring bridges are either local or remote. Remote bridges are linked with subnetwork data rates from 9.6 Kbps to 1.344 Mbps. Up to 15 bridges can be paralleled between rings, allowing redundant path routing.

III

Local Area Networking

Repeaters

Repeaters are usually not associated with internetworking per se, but because they often are confused with gateways, routers, and bridges, they are reviewed here. A *repeater* works at the Physical Layer and extends the physical length of a LAN. Repeaters are commonly used in distributed bus networks such as Ethernet and in Token Ring networks. Specifically, repeaters allow two segments of an Ethernet or Token Ring LAN to be connected as one logical LAN. An IBM Token Ring repeater is illustrated in figure 13.28. Because of physical connectivity rules, a limited number of repeaters are allowed on a logical LAN.

Figure 13.28
IBM Token Ring
8218 copper
repeater usage.

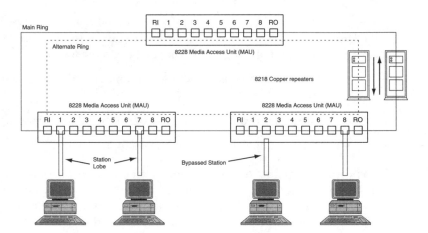

Internetworking Applications

Part I reviewed the basic features of e-mail software and compared e-mail applications to Electronic Bulletin Board Systems and Remote Access software. In this chapter, e-mail is surveyed in relation to its use as a communications network application. E-mail's increased acceptance has been helped along by more powerful hardware, availability of software specifically designed to facilitate the use of e-mail, and an increase in the linkage between dissimilar e-mail systems. This last factor has been evidenced in both wide area or public e-mail systems and in the LAN industry.

Gateways such as those between MCI Mail and the international Telex service, and between MCI Mail and Novell's MHS are the key to achieving critical mass in e-mail systems. *Critical mass* in this context is having enough subscribers to an e-mail service to encourage large numbers of additional individuals and organizations to sign up for service. With its various gateways to international services and to LANs, MCI Mail has probably achieved this plateau. The ultimate goal would be for the dissimilar e-mail services to conform to a common standard so that users could reach more potential correspondents.

Electronic Mail

Major software vendors Novell, Lotus, and Microsoft are evolving new open messaging architectures that are layered into four generic components:

✔ User interface

✔ Internal message handling including mail box services

✔ Directory services

✔ Transport services

NetWare *Message Handling Service* (MHS), Lotus' *Vendor Independent Messaging* (VIM), and Microsoft's *Messaging Applications Programming Interface* (MAPI) represent these vendors' strategies for defining an open messaging architecture. On the international standards side, X.400 represents the effort to consolidate e-mail functions.

X.400

The common standard—CCITT X.400 series protocols on e-mail systems—is composed of 8 parts:

✔ X.400-Message Handling Systems: System Model and Service Elements

✔ X.401-Message Handling Systems: Basic Service Elements and Optional User Facilities

✔ X.408-Message Handling Systems: Encoded Information Type Conversion Rules

✔ X.409-Message Handling Systems: Presentation Transfer Syntax and Notation

✔ X.410-Message Handling Systems: Remote Operations and Reliable Transfer Server

✔ X.413-Message Handling Systems: Message Transfer Layer

✔ X.420-Message Handling Systems: Interpersonal Messaging User Agent Layer

✔ X.430-Message Handling Systems: Access Protocol For Teletex Terminals

Using the preceding terminology, *Message Handling Systems* (MHS) are synonymous with e-mail systems. The X.400 MHS should not be confused with Novell's MHS e-mail system. The X.400 series of protocols belong to OSI model Layer 7, although the X.400 protocol is itself layered for ease of development and implementation. The X.400 series is quite comprehensive and defines basic entities such as *User*

III

Local Area Networking

Agents and *Message Transfer Agents*, several types of services, ranging from essential to optional, and connection standards to other services such as Telex, Teletex, and Group 3 facsimile. Each element in the X.400 standards can be likened to some counterpart in the standard postal service. *User Agents* are correspondents, *Message Transfer Agents* perform post office type service, *addressing schemes* have a purpose and design similar to Zip Codes, certain aspects of the standard are analogous to envelopes, and there is even an analogy for mail bags. Services run the gamut from required to desired (examples are shown in table 13.1).

Table 13.1
Correspondent and Post Office Services in X.400

TYPE OF SERVICE AGENT	BASIC	ESSENTIAL	ADDITIONAL
Correspondent	Message ID	Originator ID	Blind Copy
	Type of Body	Subject	Encryption Status
		Primary Recipient	Importance Indication
		Grade of Delivery	Expiration Date
Post Office	Message ID	Deferred Delivery	Hold For Delivery
	Date/Time of Submission	Delivery Notification	Return of Contents
	Date/Time of Delivery	Probe (trace)	Encoded Data Conversion

In table 13.1, the terms *correspondent* and *post office* have been loosely interpreted from their much more rigorous definitions within the X.400 standards. A *basic service* is inherent in the mail service; an *essential service* is required but only invoked at the user's request; and an *additional service* is optional. Widespread acceptance of this series of standards will have a far-reaching effect on the future of world-wide electronic communications.

Novell's Message Handling Service (MHS)

In the context of this discussion, MHS refers to the Novell implementation of a store-and-forward e-mail system. Within the LAN industry, MHS has become a de facto standard for linking applications with internetwork transport systems. From Novell's perspective, MHS is a general distributed computing architecture that can be used in a variety of applications including e-mail. NetWare MHS handles the communications processing required for this architecture, including file transfer protocols, modem control, routing tables, transport protocols, and error checking. In other words, MHS handles all the issues associated with getting the information from the sending workstation to the destination workstation, error-free, regardless of the differences in LAN and WAN topologies.

MHS is invoked through a relatively simple application program interface called a *Message Control Block* (MCB). MCB is an 18-line ASCII file. An optional text message (*cover letter*) and application file(s) (*enclosure*) represent the mail to be transferred by the MHS process. Any application that can create the 18-line ASCII file can interface to the MCB and the MHS transport system. The ASCII file, the text message, and the attached applications file(s) are packaged by a utility program SEAL.EXE and transmitted to the destination node. At the destination node, a utility program UNSEAL.EXE unpackages the files and transfers the text message and application file(s) to the appropriate directory(s) (see fig. 13.29).

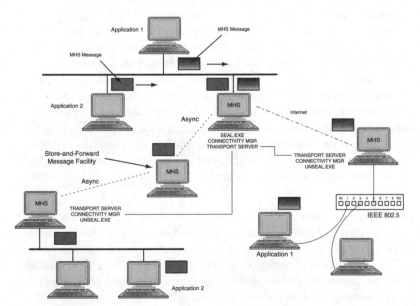

Figure 13.29
Message Handling System (MHS) software operation.

On the sending end, MHS is responsible for queuing the outbound messages and checking the appropriate connectivity path for availability. This might involve an asynchronous modem circuit, a remote bridge, or a local bridge. The 18-line ASCII file functions as an envelope and contains information such as sender identification, destination address, subject line, and identification of the attached file(s). SEAL.EXE adds additional identifying information prior to actually transmitting the message.

Installing MHS on a LAN has internetworking implications. Before looking at these in detail, a few definitions are in order. An *MHS message* contains a header, an optional text file, and an optional attachment. An *MHS application* is any end-user program that submits data to, or receives data from, the MHS transport system. *MHS users* are people who run the applications that use MHS or processes that use MHS to exchange information. Each MHS installation has at least one administrative user who maintains a *routing directory* of addresses and connectivity paths within the *MHS network.* The *MHS Directory Manager* is a process that establishes and maintains the routing directory. An *MHS host* is a single workstation or LAN that runs MHS software. An *MHS hub* is a host that stores and forwards MHS messages for other hosts. An *MHS workgroup* is all users encompassed by a unique workgroup name in the MHS address form:

    Username @ Workgroupname

A *multihost workgroup* is a workgroup that includes two or more hosts. (An entire LAN may be considered a host.) A multihost workgroup could be two directly connected LANs, LANs connected by a wide area network, or a combination of multiple LANs and standalone remote workstations. A multihost workgroup is typically an entire company or a major operating component of a company. One host in a workgroup is designated as a *workgroup-wide router* and maintains a routing directory for every user in the workgroup. A workgroup can contain *internets*, or multiple LANs connected by a local or remote bridge or by a router. One host in an Internet is designated the *internet routing host.* Single LAN or standalone hosts must be routing hosts if connections to other hosts are required. An *MHS network* consists of one or more workgroups and comprises hosts that exchange messages among themselves.

The *MHS Connectivity Manager* is a process that runs in a routing host or a hub to transfer messages to the appropriate destination. The Connectivity Manager uses *Asynchronous Connection Transport servers, Internet Message servers,* and *Gateway servers* to provide the actual transport of messages within an MHS network. Asynchronous and Internet servers handle telephone and bridge connections respectively. Gateway servers provide the link between MHS networks and external e-mail services or other computing environments. The Connectivity Manager and the servers handle the MHS network functions usually associated with OSI Model

Layers 3 and above. Appropriate lower-level LAN or wide area data link and physical protocols are used to establish links among hosts, or between hosts and external services. Figure 13.30 depicts the architecture of an MHS network and shows the relationship between an MHS network, workgroups, internets, hubs, and hosts.

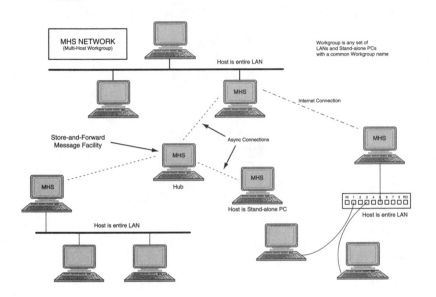

Figure 13.30
MHS network components.

MHS maps well into the X.400 standard. The Connectivity Manager conforms to the functions required in the X.400 *Message Transfer Agent* (MTA). X.400 addressing is accommodated within the extended form of an MHS address, allowing the relatively easy establishment of gateways between MHS and X.400 e-mail systems. The extended MHS address uses the following form:

```
Username.Applicationname@ Workgroupname.Enterprisename
(comment field) <X.400 address extension>
{other non-MHS address extension}
```

NetWare MHS for NetWare 3.*x* supports a variety of e-mail transport systems, including MHS, IBM's *SNA Distribution Services* (SNADS), X.400, and the *Unix Simple Mail Transport Protocol* (SMTP). Each of these resides in a NetWare server as *NetWare Loadable Modules* (NLMs), and the server can switch between the appropriate protocols for routing as required.

The real significance of a capability such as MHS is twofold: the universal interface it offers to a wide variety of applications software, and its interface to the external e-mail world. The latter is accomplished through gateways that allow the use of commercial e-mail services for transport and connection to a much larger body of correspondents. The potential applications for MHS include *electronic data*

III

Local Area Networking

interchange (EDI), remote job entry, daily reports from mobile sales and engineering staffs, project management from remote job sites, mobile data terminals in law enforcement, and structured telecommuting systems. The combination of MHS and internetworking technology provides the foundation upon which distributed applications can be built for business, education, and government. The following e-mail gateways are supported by MHS:

- ✔ cc:Mail
- ✔ IBM CICS
- ✔ DEC VMSMail
- ✔ IBM PROFS
- ✔ MCI Mail
- ✔ CompuServe
- ✔ Banyan
- ✔ Voice mail
- ✔ IBM DISOSS
- ✔ Facsimile
- ✔ IBM SNADS

Vendor Independent Messaging (VIM) Interface

Lotus's *Vendor Independent Messaging* API (VIM) is based on the Open Messaging Interface originally developed by cc:Mail, the market-leading e-mail service purchased by Lotus in February 1991. User applications or third-party software packages call the VIM API for access to any of the supported directory, message handling, or transport services compatible with the VIM specification. Lotus Notes, cc:Mail, IBM's OfficeVision/2, MCI Mail, WordPerfect Office, and Apple all support VIM.

Messaging Applications Programming Interface

Microsoft's Messaging API's (MAPI) structure is similar to VIM except that the user interface is based on the Windows GUI. MS Office applications have been written to exploit MAPI through the use of the Send and Add Routing Slip options in the File menus. Microsoft Mail is also integrated in the MS Office suite. Schedule+, a group application in Windows for Workgroups and Windows NT, makes use of MAPI. There is a Software Development Kit for MAPI that enables the use of Visual Basic and Visual C++ to develop mail-enabled applications such as group expense

reporting and other office workflow products. A subset of the full MAPI calls, known as Simple MAPI, are listed in table 13.2. These API are accessible through high level languages such as Visual Basic and applications with Macro languages such as Microsoft's Excel and Word For Windows.

Table 13.2
Microsoft Mail Applications Programming Interface (Simple)

MAPI FUNCTION	DESCRIPTION
MapiAddress()	Addresses a mail message
MapiDeleteMail()	Deletes a message
MapiDetails()	Displays a recipient details dialog box
MapiFindNext()	Returns the ID of the next (or first) Mail message of a specified type
MapiFreeBuffer()	Frees memory allocated by the messaging system
MapiLogoff()	Ends a session with the messaging system
MapiLogon()	Begins a session with the messaging system
MapiReadMail()	Reads a Mail message
MapiResolveName()	Displays a dialog box to resolve an ambiguous recipient name
MapiSaveMail()	Saves a Mail message
MapiSendDocuments()	Sends a standard Mail message with application documents
MapiSendMail()	Sends a Mail message

Implementation

When implementing e-mail services, organizations have three basic choices as to how to proceed: public e-mail services, usually accessed through specialized providers or as a feature of an online database service; a private service; or a combination of the two. Private services are typically combinations of LANs, stand-alone PCs, and wide area transport services. The wide area services may be privately owned or common carrier facilities. Private e-mail services may incorporate a hierarchical structure of WANs and LANs. The choice of which approach to take in the implementation of e-mail is based both on economics and the affiliation of anticipated correspondents. If a large portion of correspondents are outside the organization, public e-mail or a combination of private and public services is appropriate. Conversely, if most correspondence is within the organization, a private system makes more sense.

The economics of e-mail implementation are based on the anticipated traffic volume between correspondents. Public e-mail services have widely varying rate structures which must be carefully compared to the traffic needs of the potential customer. Charges may be based on any combination of the size of message transmitted, transmission time used for messaging, or standard online charges. Special service options are generally at extra cost. A special service option might be the telephonic notification of the arrival of a message in the recipient's mailbox. Most database services that have e-mail, such as CompuServe, only charge standard online fees. Specialized e-mail providers such as MCI Mail charge by time and size of message. Some e-mail services which cater to larger businesses have minimum monthly charges which offer substantial savings if traffic levels are high enough. Private e-mail costs are dependent on the transport system used to connect sites. Costs can range from standard long-distance telephone rates to monthly charges for leased lines or packet-switched network fees. Cost factors are based on combinations of link distance and time of transmission for dial-up telephone systems, link distance, and monthly fee for leased lines (with or without signal conditioning) or the amount of data transmitted for packet-switched networks.

Lotus Notes

Lotus Notes is a groupware program that is an e-mail system, but it goes far beyond traditional e-mail systems because it integrates multimedia into a shared database paradigm. The database can contain text, graphics, spreadsheets, and images. More importantly, Notes is a multi-application productivity tool that supports electronic conferencing including threaded discussions, electronic meeting support, workflow automation, document storage and retrieval, database replication and synchronization, applications development, and deployment and hypertext authoring. This list is not exhaustive—the extensibility of Notes is such that new applications undoubtedly will evolve from increased product exposure and usage. Third-party applications for Notes have spawned an entirely new subindustry. Several applications exist that use Notes as an intelligent news retrieval engine, for example. Certain limitations within the native Notes product have already resulted in third-party programs that increase its ability to analyze both database and numerical information and display analysis results in a variety of graphic formats.

Notes is a network within a network. Apart from its capability to develop strategic applications within corporations, Notes has a security system and a shared architecture distinct from the underlying LAN and WAN technology that supports it. Notes servers are not LAN servers (not that they couldn't be, but the practice is strongly discouraged), and access to Notes resources is governed separately from access to other LAN resources. A Notes server should be separate from the LAN server and should have almost as substantial resources as the LAN server, if not more. Current Notes server operating system support includes OS/2, NetWare, UNIX, and DOS/Windows. Support for the Windows NT operating system on the Notes server is forthcoming. The Notes server operating system does not have to be the same as the LAN server operating system.

The internetworking capabilities of Notes include server-to-server exchange and support for laptop users. Database replication and mail transfer are the processes most used in the internetwork. Replication allows common databases to become synchronized regardless of when and where updates are made. Users connected to a server only see that server's databases, but servers can see databases on any other server to which they connect. The company address book—present on every server in the organization—contains the following features:

✔ A list of user names, including "forwarding addresses" for those users not directly connected to your LAN

✔ A list of servers in the organization showing whether servers are accessible through LAN connection(s) in the case of local servers, or an asynchronous communications port for remote servers

✔ A list of connections for each server-to-server path showing the communications port (LAN or asynchronous), time of day for start and stop of calling, calling interval, and the server task (mail transfer or database replication)

Additional information in the connection view includes days of week on which calls can be made, conditions under which call-up and routing should occur immediately, routing path cost for use in least-cost route options, and priority for databases to be replicated.

Laptop connectivity is a part of the Notes architecture. Laptop portability precludes keeping company address books or mail routers with the mobile user. Laptop users call the remote server on which their home mail database is kept, resulting in the following sequence of events:

1. Outgoing mail is transferred to the remote server.

2. Databases on the server are replicated to the laptop, including your personal mail database (this results in you receiving your latest mail from the home office).

3. Databases on the laptop are replicated to the server.

Remote laptop users can be either PC- or Macintosh-based as long as the user has the appropriate Notes client software. Figure 13.31 shows the Notes network architecture for server-to-server and mobile user connectivity.

Figure 13.31
Lotus Notes LAN and WAN architecture.

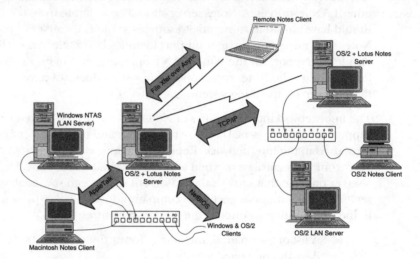

Summary

This chapter reviewed the concepts, hardware, and software that combine to extend the scope of the LAN beyond its immediate boundaries. Traditionally, almost 80 percent of an organization's communications occurs in the immediate vicinity of a typical work group—the availability of an increasing array of on-line databases and the growing sophistication of e-mail may realign this traditional view of office automation communications. Clearly an organization that wants to take advantage of data communications in its daily activities must consider the integration of LANs and WANs. For this reason internetworking is becoming an important element of the design and use of data communications facilities. Because of the diversity of vendors and standards in the data communications marketplace, interoperability has become a central issue in the design of internetworks. The configuration possibilities and options available to the network manager require a sound understanding of the underlying principles and their effect on the marketplace.

Chapter Snapshot

Network operating systems are the heartbeat of local area networking. They directly control or influence performance, administration, interoperability, connectivity, security, and group-enabled applications—in short—every vital function of a network. The history of LANs derives from the history and family tree of network operating systems. This chapter takes an overview perspective of this crucial software, focusing on the principal system used by industry and government today. In this chapter, you will learn about:

✔ The VINES operating system

✔ StreetTalk Directory Service

✔ The NetWare family of operating systems: NetWare 2.*x*, 3.*x*, and 4.*x*

✔ NetWare Directory Services

✔ IBM's OS/2 LAN Server, Communications Manager/2, NetWare Requester for OS/2, OS/2 NetWare interoperability, and TCP/IP for OS/2

✔ LAN Manager 2.*x*

✔ Windows NT Advanced Server

✔ Generic network operating system features, viewed from a comparative basis

14
CHAPTER

Network Operating System Implementation

The preceding three chapters discussed fundamental concepts of LANs: applications support software in the LAN environment, LAN communications architectures, and internetworking. To put these concepts into focus in the context of today's state-of-the-art, this chapter covers the most significant LAN system software products available for PCs. Network operating systems are the focus of this chapter because they represent the most significant area of development and have the largest influence on network performance and standardization.

Every product discussed in this chapter has been field-proven with serious business applications, and has successfully evolved from earlier generations as the LAN industry matured. Each of the major LAN operating system vendors, Banyan, Novell, IBM, and Microsoft, has a strategy for pre-eminence as the LAN marketplace continues to mature. In the long run, the competition is healthy for the growing ranks of network users. The following threads are common to each operating system:

- ✔ A strategy to connect dissimilar computer architectures, including MS-DOS, Windows, Windows NT, OS/2, NetWare, UNIX, and Macintosh

- ✔ The capability to support robust internetworking

- ✔ The capability to accommodate a variety of transport layer protocols

- ✔ Support for a wide variety of network adapter cards through standard interfaces

Some systems reviewed in this chapter would be considered obsolete if today's criteria for robustness and functionality were applied, but nevertheless are still found in significant numbers in all types of organizations. NetWare has evolved from 2.*x* to 4.*x*, and LAN Manager has given way to Windows NT Advanced Server; the newest versions, however, recognize and support their predecessors in mixed environment networks.

Because LAN implementations are constantly changing, this chapter focuses on trends in design and functionality rather than on specific details. This chapter, therefore, provides representative implementations of the concepts discussed in earlier chapters. Internetworking capabilities in these systems were described in detail in Chapter 13, "Internetworking and Interoperability," because of their specialized nature. The products discussed in the following pages include Banyan's *Virtual Networking System* (VINES), Novell's NetWare 2.*x*, 3.*x*, and 4.*x*, IBM's OS/2 LAN Server, and Microsoft's Windows NT Advanced Server.

Some of these are mature systems; some are still evolving, but each is capable of fulfilling a wide variety of demanding LAN requirements. You can compare each system against specific performance requirements by means of the general criteria summarized at the end of the chapter. Note that each comparison should be ranked in the context of your organization's specific needs rather than against some absolute measure. In other words, the best network operating system is the one that most closely fits your organizational objectives.

Perhaps the most confusing situation in the network operating system world is the relationship between Windows NT Advanced Server and OS/2 LAN Server. Both are derivatives of the former LAN Manager NOS. From a networking perspective, Windows NTAS combines a set of LAN Manager APIs with the core APIs of 32-bit Windows. OS/2 LAN Server is a specific implementation of LAN Manager and combines with other communications-related Extended Services to provide a LAN/WAN networking architecture. Because they share a common heritage, interoperability between the two systems is not generally a major problem. How long this situation will last as each product matures is an open question. Both systems are built on the *Server Message Block* (SMB) and NETBIOS as core protocol. They differ in their implementation of other transport protocol stacks and the manner in which they achieve wide area network support. Windows NTAS is clearly aimed at the large installed base of corporate Windows platforms. OS/2 LAN Server and CM/2 are targeted for the IBM applications market, including the S/370 mainframe and AS/400 minicomputer strategic platforms.

VINES Network Operating System

VINES, as the name suggests, is a hardware-independent network operating system based on the UNIX operating system. Versions are available that run on 80386 and 80486 PCs. Both single processors and symmetric multiprocessors are supported. The VINES network supports a variety of LAN hardware types and both asynchronous and synchronous wide area networks. Multiple file servers are supported by several methods of interconnectivity. VINES software enables the establishment of large networks, combining LANs and wide area interconnections, with the capability for users to share information without knowledge of the network routing details.

Figure 14.1 illustrates Banyan's server software architecture. The front end of the VINES Server provides the link to attached PC resources—whether they are located on LANs or act as independent asynchronous terminals. The back end of the server supplies interconnect services to a variety of network types external to the local PC environment. The Services segment of the VINES Server contains the appropriate software to enable information sharing, e-mail, and internetwork connectivity. These software services run under the VINES version of the UNIX operating system.

III

Local Area Networking

Figure 14.1
VINES file server
architecture.

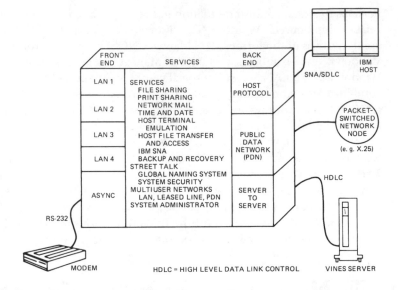

Major Features

Banyan's VINES software includes a number of features, presented in the following list, which together provide users and administrator(s) with a network system that focuses on the needs of enterprise-wide networks.

✔ StreetTalk—A global naming database located throughout the network that identifies and automatically locates various classes of resources

✔ File Service—Server software and workstation shell that enables a workstation's host operating system (MS-DOS, OS/2, or Macintosh) to send remote file requests to a server running a multitasking network operating system (UNIX)

✔ Support for file and record locking conventions of OS/2 and MS-DOS

✔ Security service

✔ Print service

✔ Backup and system recovery

✔ E-mail—A distributed mail system supported throughout all logically connected networks

✔ VINES Network Management—A network management software application that provides a variety of statistics on network operations

✔ Third-party developer support—*Applications Programming Interfaces* (APIs)

✔ Asynchronous Communications—Terminal emulation, modem server capability, file transfer protocol, and multiserver connectivity (See Chapter 13)

✔ IBM 3270 Communications—Complete support for IBM mainframe communications, including emulation of standard terminals and printers (See Chapter 13)

StreetTalk

StreetTalk is the system for naming resources on a VINES network and a fundamental design feature of VINES. "Resources" in VINES parlance can be file volumes, print queues, users, lists, nicknames, connections to other computers, or any other device attached to the network. StreetTalk has three levels of definition: item, group, and organization. A typical StreetTalk name has the following format:

```
Doug@Marketing@XYZ Company,
```

Doug is the item (a user in this case); *Marketing* is the group; and *XYZ Company* is the organization. Although items are limited to certain allowable entities, groups and organizations are limited only by imagination and common sense. Note that the order of StreetTalk names is reversed from the X.500 directory services standard. An important feature of StreetTalk is that assignment of a StreetTalk name is mandatory before a shared resource can be used by anyone on the network. All StreetTalk names are stored in a central database called the *StreetTalk catalog*. This catalog is maintained on each VINES server connected to a logical network. StreetTalk names can be used in "lists" that are in turn given StreetTalk names. A typical item in this category is a distribution list for e-mail. The StreetTalk catalog can be reviewed by anyone on the network but only system administrators can add, delete, or change names in the catalog.

Multiserver StreetTalk installations are possible with VINES. From the user's perspective, the number of servers on the network is transparent. Multiserver installations will become increasingly commonplace as average network sizes in organizations begin to climb. A multiserver situation can arise in several ways, including the following:

✔ Multiple servers on a single LAN

✔ Multiple servers on interconnected LANs

✔ Multiple servers on dispersed LANs connected by some form of long-distance communications (wide area network)

III

Local Area Networking

Figures 14.2 through 14.4 illustrate these situations. On a multiserver network, the StreetTalk catalog is distributed among the servers according to the resources assigned to a particular server. For example, in figure 14.5, two servers are shown, each with its own catalog of names. The total network catalog is the combination of the individual server catalogs. The important feature here is that all network users see the combined catalog, not just the catalog of the server on which they are logged in.

Figure 14.2
Multiple VINES servers on a single LAN.

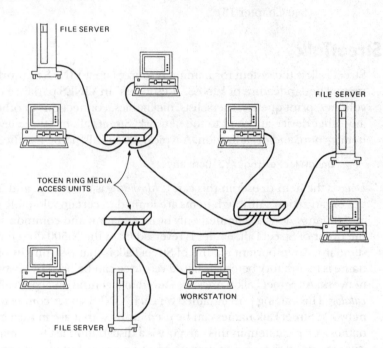

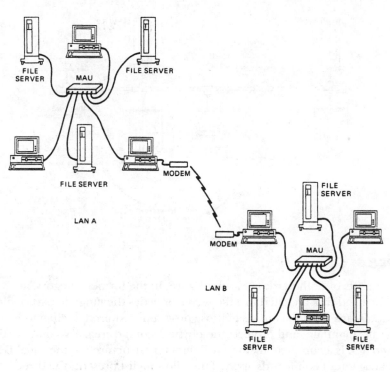

Figure 14.3
Multiple VINES servers in interconnected LANs.

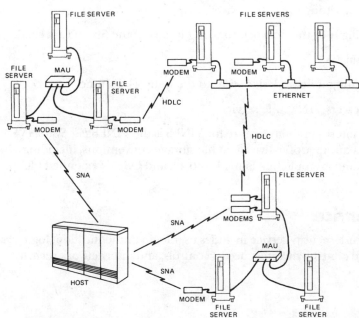

Figure 14.4
Multiple VINES servers with multiple LANs and WAN connections.

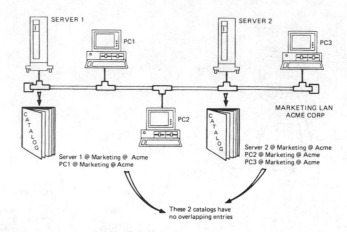

Figure 14.5
StreetTalk catalogs with multiple VINES servers.

File Service

File service consists of both hardware and software. In the former category, a volume on the fixed disk attached to a file server provides the tangible part of file service. The software portion consists of those programs required to effectively manage (create, maintain, and protect) the physical storage area. A volume on the network fixed disk is a complete hierarchical directory structure. All the usual DOS directory management commands apply. The following list presents the three basic steps involved in setting up a file service:

1. Adding it to the network (making it part of the StreetTalk catalog)

2. Starting it

3. Assigning a drive designation to the network volume.

Figure 14.6 depicts VINES file service.

An important interoperability feature for VINES is the VINES *File System* (VFS). VFS supports a number of native client file storage conventions, including MS-DOS, Macintosh AppleTalk Filing Protocol, and OS/2's extended file specifications.

Security Service

Banyan's network security service includes user login authentication, login restrictions, password control, directory access controls, and internetwork security.

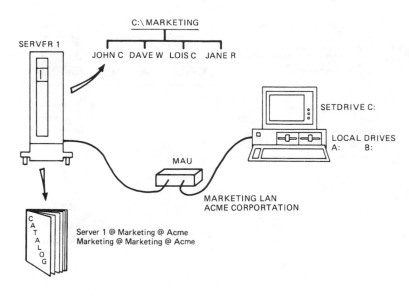

Figure 14.6
VINES file service.

Part of the security mechanism for access control is the association of user passwords with StreetTalk catalog entries. The login authentication process requires a person signing on the network to use the correct password associated with that person's user name (recall that a user name is a StreetTalk item). The login process itself can be restricted by location, time of day, and expiration date of the user name. Location restrictions are specified by server, link (individual LAN or serial port), or specific workstation, as shown in figure 14.7. Passwords can be controlled by restricting users from changing their own passwords, setting a password minimum length, forcing password changes on each login, or assigning a password expiration date.

As in most network operating systems currently on the market, VINES access control to network volumes involves *who* has access to files and *what* an individual can do with the file after access is granted. Each subdirectory in the network file volume has an independently assigned *Access Rights List* (ARL). ARLs specify who can access that particular subdirectory. Each ARL entry can designate one of four levels of access, listed in table 14.1 in descending order of priority:

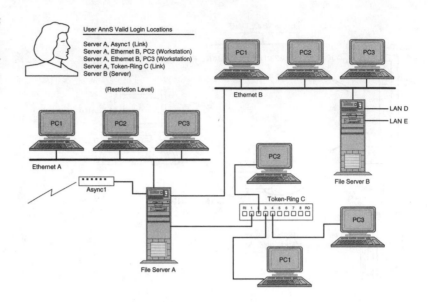

Figure 14.7
VINES login
security by
location
restriction level.

Table 14.1
VINES Subdirectory Access Levels

Control	Set access rights on the parent directory
	Set access rights on the child subdirectory
	Create/delete files and subdirectories
	Modify files and subdirectories
	Read files and subdirectories
	Delete the directory
Modify	Items 2-5 under Control level
Read	Item 5 under Control
Null	No access rights

The login process links users to their assigned resources and access rights (see fig. 14.8). Because ARLs are themselves StreetTalk catalog items, they can be addressed by linkage to groups and organizations as follows:

```
ARL@group@organization
```

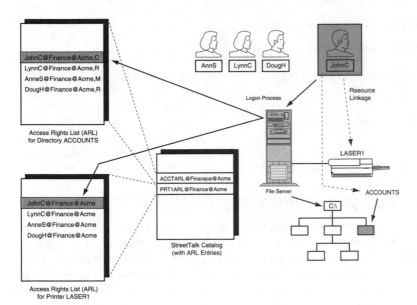

Figure 14.8
VINES login
process and user
resource linkage.

Print Services

VINES print service consists of the following parts:

✔ A printer attached to a server or a PC. Up to 20 printers can be attached to a server. ICA adapters can be used for printer attachment.

✔ Configuration information for the network printer.

✔ Standard network software on workstations to redirect print jobs to the network printer.

✔ A print job queue on the print server hard disk.

✔ Management functions including printer assignments, redirection of print queues, print job scheduling, and review of job status on multiple printers.

Print service on VINES is a standard redirected operation in which print jobs originated at a workstation are redirected to a specified network printer. Network printers can be attached to servers or to any workstation that runs the print service software. The network print server supports spooling of the print job to its hard disk and the associated queue management functions. Logical ports LPT1:, LPT2:, and LPT3: are supported at the user's workstation. Each port has attributes for the following:

✔ Service name (StreetTalk)

✔ Redirection switch

✔ Delay time in seconds prior to commencement of spooling

✔ Form type

✔ Banner page switch

Multiple ports can be redirected to the same printer, each with a different form type such as stationery, draft, or multipart.

Backup and System Recovery (VINES SMP)

Banyan provides certain automatic fault tolerant features in the VINES SMP system. For example, the file server has a battery backup option that causes a "graceful" shutdown process to start if normal power is lost or interrupted. Servers reboot automatically after power restoration regardless of whether battery backup is installed. The server also is designed to continually check for the proper operation of both service functions and installed LAN adapter cards. Certain other failures cause server automatic reboots, including memory parity errors or system "hangs" (a loss of network communications). Backup and recovery procedures on individual workstations are similar to those available in a single-user environment. Any reboot of a workstation of course requires a restart of network login procedures.

VINES SMP also supports disk mirroring and data guarding, described generically in Chapter 11, "Local Area Networks: From the Top Down."

Backup and system recovery operations for VINES SMP rely upon the existence of a full system backup on cartridge tape. As with any computer system that processes critical data, file backups are a must to prevent disaster. Tape operations are controlled from the server console and typically are done by the network administrator. Tape backups are performed on file volumes on the server. Backups can be full system, file-by-file, or individual service. Individual user local backups are the user's responsibility and are accomplished using normal DOS or other workstation operating environment functions.

E-mail Service

E-mail has become more than just a luxury item for LAN systems; it now is considered virtually mandatory in order for LAN software to be competitive. E-mail must also address the internetworking environment to be considered acceptable for most medium to large-scale businesses. Mail service on a VINES network is an optional feature that is designed to operate on network servers. When any server is

started up, mail service is automatically initiated on that server. A user's profile specifies the mail service (that is, server) to which he or she is attached. The mail service capability also supports multiserver installations, in part to provide alternate mail services for network users. This capability provides one element of redundancy in the VINES network system and is a direct benefit of StreetTalk design.

Internetwork, multiple-server connectivity in the mail service is handled through serial connections or by direct, high-speed server-to-server links. VINES monitors all unsent mail and automatically attempts to deliver the appropriate correspondence when a particular serial connection is established. High-speed links are invoked when a remote server is explicitly named in the message address.

Optional gateways to external mail systems are available and include links to MCI Mail and CompuServe's e-mail services. These gateways are effective in tying together VINES correspondents with users on the more popular commercial e-mail services. Users outside the VINES internetwork can access specific VINES users by reference to the StreetTalk name after logging in to the appropriate commercial service. Other mail service gateways can be developed using the third-party development toolkits described later.

Mailing address lists can be maintained within the StreetTalk system or separately. Addressing features include *carbon copy* (CC) and *blind carbon copy* (BCC). A text editor is included with the e-mail system, and standard applications files of any type can be enclosed as a letter attachment. Message folders can be maintained by mail subject content. Mail management features enable the moving of mailboxes between existing servers and other mail services. Although third-party e-mail systems with expanded functions can be used on VINES, such use bypasses the StreetTalk naming convention and much of StreetTalk's internetworking advantage unless the e-mail system is specifically designed for the StreetTalk environment.

Network Management Option

The VINES Network Management Option is one of the more complete analytical tools provided with a PC LAN product. This option presents a real-time picture of server performance and the way network hardware and software are configured. The information displayed is basically raw statistical data and as such must be carefully interpreted. Network Management provides no guidance on actions to take as a result of network activity analysis, some of which follow:

✔ Replacing a network adapter card that has excessive error rates

✔ Relocating high-usage services to more lightly-loaded servers

✔ Adding more RAM to a server

✔ Changing the physical configuration of a LAN

✔ Increasing the performance of shared mass storage devices

✔ Adding additional servers to a LAN

To take appropriate corrective actions as a result of Network Management analysis, the network administrator must have a solid understanding of the strengths and weaknesses of existing systems. The System Administrator manual thoroughly explains the meaning and interpretation of each statistic on the various display screens. Network Management provides a number of displays, each designed to focus upon some aspect of network performance. Among these are the following:

✔ **VINES Network Summary.** Displays a list of all servers with loading statistics. A server can be highlighted for more data in other screens.

✔ **I/O Statistics.** Displays an overview of LAN hardware statistics (by LAN type, including internetwork links) for the selected server.

✔ **LAN Interface Statistics.** Displays more detailed data on a selected LAN hardware type within a server. The following network types are included:

  ✔ 3Com Ethernet

  ✔ SMC ARCnet

  ✔ IBM PC Network

  ✔ IBM Token Ring

  ✔ Proteon ProNet

  ✔ AT&T Starlan

  ✔ Northern Telecom LANStar

✔ **WAN Interface Statistics:**

  ✔ HDLC

  ✔ Asynchronous

  ✔ X.25

✔ **Disk Usage.** Displays data concerning the disk(s) on the selected server.

✔ **Service Statistics.** Displays loading information for each service located on the selected server.

✔ **Network topology.** Displays information concerning all active network devices connected to the selected server.

✔ **File service.** Displays information concerning cache performance, record locking, and open files.

✔ **Communications statistics.** Displays data on communications buffers, transport protocol connections, and sockets (local applications using network services).

Statistics are either raw counts or averaged data. The latter form uses a method known as *Exponential Decaying Averages*, which simply means that the most recent data has the highest weighting.

Network Management can be run from either the server console or any PC on the network. A server without Network Management installed appears on the Network Summary screen but does not have statistics displayed. Network Management can retrieve statistics from anywhere on the network including remote servers in an internetwork. Network Management is itself a service (although not defined as such on the server), and displays statistics about itself on the Service Statistics screen. An enhanced network management package called *VINES Assistant* is available that provides additional functions for the network manager. VINES also supports IBM's NetView, the host-based network management system, and the *Simple Network Management Protocol* (SNMP).

Third-Party Development Support

Banyan provides a set of calls and commands designed to access the basic services of UNIX System V, as well as specific VINES features such as StreetTalk, *StreetTalk Directory Assistant* (STDA), e-mail gateways, and communications services. NetRPC is Banyan's *remote procedure call* (RPC) protocol that supports the development of linkages between client and service processes. NetRPC has a broad functional resemblance to OS/2's Named Pipes. Communications services supported include X.25 and TCP/UDP (the TCP/IP User Datagram Protocol). The objective of these calls and commands is to enable developers to build integrated applications using the distributed processing facilities of VINES. Another objective is to enable the development of additional services that can be added to basic VINES capabilities.

Banyan File Server Support

Banyan no longer distributes dedicated server hardware with the operating system installed. This follows a trend in the NOS industry to decouple operating system software products from dedicated server platforms. The increasing performance levels of server hardware has proven this to be a wise decision, both technically and from a marketing perspective. The architecture of all file servers running VINES server software includes front-end LAN support, back-end communications support, and applications software. Figure 14.1 illustrates the relationship of these components. VINES SMP supports symmetric multiprocessors, such as the Compaq SystemPro.

III

Local Area Networking

NetWare 2.x

NetWare 2.*x* would be considered obsolete by today's standards, but substantial numbers of these systems are still operating in the field. The basic features described in the following sections are core features of NetWare that have only been improved upon with the later generation 3.*x* and 4.*x* versions of NetWare. The 3.*x* and 4.*x* versions are described later in the chapter in the context of the improved capabilities each offers relative to its respective previous version.

Major Features

NetWare 2.*x* is the 80286-based product from Novell that continues a tradition of innovative design and support for demanding corporate network applications. NetWare 2.*x* is upward-compatible with 80386 and 80486 processors, but does not take advantage of the processors' extended performance features. NetWare 2.*x* has the following major elements:

- ✔ **File Service.** File server multitasking software (proprietary) and a user shell for MS-DOS that functions as a redirector for network resource file requests.

- ✔ **File and Record Locking.** Upwardly compatible with MS-DOS 3.1 with significant extensions for transaction (read-modify-write cycle) support.

- ✔ **Print Service.** Transparent network printing from within applications running on the network, including full print queue management.

- ✔ **System Fault Tolerance (SFT).** A multilevel system, featuring redundant directory management, mirrored and duplexed disk drives, an *Uninterrupted Power Supply* (UPS) monitoring function, and a *Transaction Tracking System* (TTS).

- ✔ **Security and Access Control.** Independent user, group, and directory access controls, with eight types of access rights assignable to each.

- ✔ **Virtual File Server Console.** Enabling remote file server management.

- ✔ **Value-Added Processes (VAP) and Value-Added Disk Drivers (VADD).**

- ✔ **Network accounting functions.**

- ✔ **Internal and External Bridges.** Advanced NetWare support for internetworking with a unique feature of being able to configure a bridge

to improve server throughput. (See Chapter 13.)

✔ **Asynchronous Communications.** Terminal emulation, modem server capability (with dedicated PC), file transfers with protocol and support for up to 12 external circuits per modem server. (See Chapter 13.)

✔ **IBM SNA Communications.** 3270 support (3274 Controller, 3287 Printer, and 3278/79 terminals) for up to 32 sessions on a non-dedicated gateway server. (See Chapter 13.)

✔ **Message Handling Service (MHS).** Store-and-forward communications. (See Chapter 13.)

File Service

NetWare 2.*x* file service is a significant extension of the support provided by MS-DOS. The file service portion of NetWare resides on the file server and uses a directory structure that parallels that of MS-DOS. However, the file server directory is managed by NetWare commands rather than MS-DOS commands. Table 14.2 shows the correspondence between DOS and NetWare commands. A NetWare shell resides on each workstation on the network—this shell communicates with the NetWare operating system on the file server. Both the file server operating system and the application-level protocol—*NetWare Core Protocol* (NCP)—between the workstations and file server are proprietary.

Table 14.2
NetWare 2.x/MS DOS Command Correspondence

NetWare Command	MS-DOS Command
MAP	ASSIGN
	PATH
	SUBST
CHKVOL	CHKDSK
VOLINFO	CHKDSK
COMPSURF	FORMAT
NCOPY	COPY

continues

Table 14.2, Continued
NetWare 2.x/MS DOS Command Correspondence

NetWare Command	MS-DOS Command
NDIR	DIR
NPRINT	PRINT
CAPTURE	PRINT
PCONSOLE	PRINT
LISTDIR	TREE
SYSTIME	TIME/DATE
LARCHIVE	BACKUP
NARCHIVE	BACKUP
LRESTORE	RESTORE
NRESTORE	RESTORE

NetWare uses the concept of "network drives." A network drive is one or more of the drive letters A: through Z: mapped to a directory or path on the file server. Thus on workstation 1 in figure 14.9, drive E: is mapped (logically linked) to the following path on the file server:

```
Server1/sys:bwcfiles/lotusdat
```

NetWare supports user attachments to a maximum of eight servers at a time. In this case, mapping must preface the server path with a server name as in the following example:

```
Server1/sys:wordpro/word
```

The user is not required to know the physical location of the servers. This task is managed transparently by the NetWare operating system.

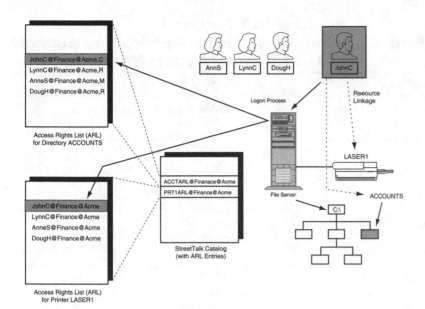

Figure 14.9
NetWare
network drives.

Multiuser File Sharing Service

NetWare uses an extensive array of file-sharing calls in its file server operating system. These go beyond the basic support provided by MS-DOS. MS-DOS uses a scheme of "physical" locks, which means that an actual sector or group of sectors on the shared disk is protected. NetWare supports this scheme and also the older "logical" locking scheme that relies upon cooperation from the application program(s). NetWare also supports a transaction locking system that protects records during a continuous cycle of read-modify-write. This is particularly valuable for database updates and provides the hooks for the Transaction Tracking System used by *System Fault Tolerance* (SFT) versions of the NOS. Semaphores are supported to provide general process or device synchronization. Table 14.3 lists extended locking function calls.

Local Area Networking

Table 14.3
NetWare 2.x Extended Multiuser Applications Support
Interrupt 21h Extended by NetWare 2.x

Physical Locks	Logical Locks
Lock Physical Record	Lock Record String
Release Physical Record	Lock Record String Set

continues

Table 14.3, Continued
NetWare 2.x Extended Multiuser Applications Support
Interrupt 21h Extended by NetWare 2.x

Physical Locks	Logical Locks
Release Physical Record Set	Release Record String
Clear Physical Record	Release Record String Set
Clear Physical Record Set	Clear Record String
Lock File Set	Clear Record String Set
Release File	
Release File Set	*Semaphores*
Clear File	
Clear File Set	Open a Semaphore
	Examine a Semaphore
	Wait Semaphore
Transactions	Signal a Semaphore
	Close a Semaphore
Begin Transaction	
Begin Transaction Update	
End Transaction Update	
Transaction Backout Available	
End Transaction	

NetWare 2.x Print Service

NetWare 2.*x* print service runs on the file server and controls the operation of up to five printers: three parallel and two serial. These printers must be attached to the file server. This version of NetWare does not support network printers distrib-

uted on LAN workstations; however, network printing is supported across all file servers logically attached to the network. In other words, any print job can be sent to any network printer attached to a file server even if the user is not logged in or attached to that file server.

Several commands affect execution of NetWare's print service. These are as follows:

✔ **CAPTURE.** Redirects subsequent printer output to a designated print queue

✔ **ENDCAP.** Terminates redirection

✔ **NPRINT.** Sends printer output directly to a designated printer on a designated file server

Print queues are established, named, and managed by ten file server console commands. These commands enable the creation and destruction of queues and the assignment or detachment of named queues to specific printers on specific file servers. Queued jobs, all queues, and queues assigned to a given printer can be listed. Individual print jobs can be removed from queues or given higher priority within a queue. The console commands include three forms control commands and one printer status command.

PCONSOLE enables the control of print queues from any workstation on the network. PRINTDEF defines printer characteristics and form types. PRINTCON enables users to define custom job characteristics such as number of copies, form type to be used, use of print banners, and file contents (ASCII or BYTE STREAM). Figure 14.10 summarizes the architecture of NetWare 2.x print service.

System Fault Tolerance (SFT)

NetWare 2.x provides a diverse range of fault-tolerant processing for applications critical enough to justify the higher costs. Fault-tolerant processing includes the protection of data against the following:

✔ Hard disk surface defects

✔ Directory and file allocation table (FAT) corruption

✔ Hard disk mechanical failures

✔ Hard disk controller failures

✔ Power surges and failures

✔ System failures during database operations

Figure 14.10
NetWare 2.*x*
print service
operation.

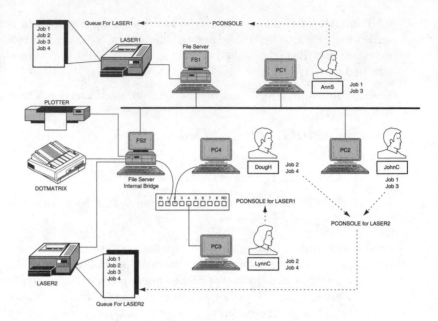

The most basic NetWare SFT feature is surface defect protection. Surface defects on a hard disk platter cause certain data blocks to become unreliable. SFT employs a read-after-write verification and a real-time data redirection process called *Hot-fix*. This process continuously checks data written to disk against the data image still in memory buffers; any errors cause the operating system to mark bad areas on the disk and move the data to a good area. Up to 11 data bits can be detected and corrected per sector.

Redundant directory entries and *file allocation tables* (FATs) are maintained on separate disk cylinders (tracks). These redundant directories and FATs are verified during the power-up sequence and corrective action is taken if the data is bad. This action includes switching to the redundant directory or FAT, marking bad sectors, and moving the data to a safe area.

SFT provides additional protection against failure of a single hard disk or a hard disk transfer channel (controller card failure). Protection against a single hard disk failure is provided by a redundant disk drive on the same disk channel. This feature is called *disk mirroring*. Disk mirroring causes data to be simultaneously written to both disk drives. Should a failure occur in one of the drives, the operator is notified, and the operating disk drive assumes the I/O load. Protection against a disk controller or disk channel failure is achieved by *disk duplexing*, or writing data

through two separate disk channels (controller cards) simultaneously. Another benefit of disk duplexing is faster I/O performance because file read operations can be conducted in parallel through two controller cards. NetWare is specifically designed to support this capability. Mirrored disk and duplexed disk configurations were illustrated in figures 11.17 and 11.18.

UPS monitoring is supported through NetWare file servers and disk subsystems. A UPS provides constant power and battery charging when the commercial power source is operating normally. If the commercial power source fails, the UPS takes over for a predetermined interval depending on the battery size. UPS monitoring enables the server to detect activation of the UPS power source and send a warning message to all active workstations on the network. Prior to shutting itself down, the monitored server writes all data in its memory to disk and closes all files.

The Transaction Tracking System is a feature that operates transparently to an application. The application is usually based on a database management system. A database read-modify-write cycle is considered a transaction. The transaction update to disk is considered either completed, or not started. Any transaction not completed when the client workstation, LAN media, or server fails is backed out of the database at the first available opportunity. In other words, the database is returned, or rolled back to its state just prior to the system failure. This protection is called *automatic rollback recovery*. Rollback recovery was illustrated in figure 11.20. TTS must be active on the file server and database files must be flagged as transactional for TTS to operate. Transaction flagging is the responsibility of the application.

If the NetWare Btrieve record manager is used to create a value-added process for a server-based database management application, a procedure called *roll-forward recovery* or *pre-imaging* is available to protect database files not flagged as transactional. Figure 14.11 depicts the pre-imaging process. Images of database files are stored under separate file names at the time of the first file modifications to build an audit trail of transactions. In case of system failure, archived database images and the audit trail are used to reconstruct all valid files. Pre-imaging is complementary to, but not a part of TTS.

Access Control and Security

NetWare 2.x provides a high degree of network security through the use of login and password protection, user or *trustee* privilege levels, directory privilege levels, and file/directory attributes.

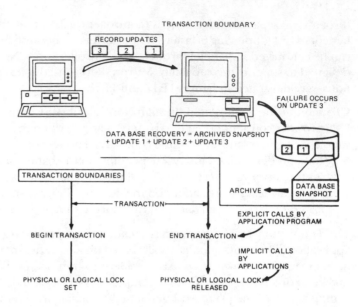

Figure 14.11
Transaction roll-
forward
recovery.

Login is controlled through the use of a user name and associated password. Each network user must have a user name and each user name can optionally be forced to have an associated password. Logins can be controlled by time of day, workstation location, and the number of concurrent logins allowed. User accounts can be assigned an expiration date. The network supervisor can disable a user's account or can lock out a user by activating the Intruder Detection/Lockout option. This option locks out a user who attempts a preset number of logins with the wrong password. Passwords can be managed by specifying a minimum length and by requiring users to periodically change their passwords. Passwords are encrypted and cannot be seen by anyone, including the supervisor level. NetWare keeps an audit trail of all logins and logouts and of accounts that have been locked out.

If a user logs in to more than one file server with the ATTACH command, each subsequent file server must be given a unique user name, but the password from the default file server is valid. Each server independently controls its own access security although passwords are synchronized between file servers. Network security characteristics cannot be modified through physical access to a server, unless the server is non-dedicated. A dedicated server enables only limited access to the NetWare operating system through a control console, and no access to network directories and files.

NetWare 2.*x* security includes logged-in account checks every 30 minutes to determine the following about a particular user:

✔ Whether the user can be logged in during that time period

✔ Whether the user's account has expired or been disabled by the supervisor

✔ Whether the user's account has reached its credit limit

Each logged-in network user carries assigned rights to access various directory levels. These rights are called *trustee rights* in Novell terminology, and they determine what a user can do after access is granted. User rights also can be assigned to *groups,* which are typically organizational collections of users. The eight defined rights are as follows:

✔ **R.** Read from open files

✔ **W.** Write to open files

✔ **O.** Open existing files

✔ **C.** Create and simultaneously open new files

✔ **D.** Delete existing files

✔ **P.** Parental rights; control over the directory and its subdirectories

✔ **S.** Search the directory

✔ **M.** Modify file attributes as defined in table 14.4

These rights can be granted explicitly to a user, or the user can inherit them through security equivalences. *Security equivalences* pass one user's or group's rights to another user or group, thus simplifying the assignment of rights. Each directory and subdirectory level is assigned a *Maximum Rights Mask.* The Maximum Rights Mask has a default value of no restrictions, or the following:

    [RWOCDPSM]

If restrictions are applied, for example the deletion of the right of any user to write in that directory, the mask becomes the following:

    [R_OCDPSM]

The Maximum Rights Mask is designed to provide a maximum allowable level of security for a directory level and applies to all users. Thus if the directory mask does not allow a Write access as in the preceding example, then no user or group can modify files in that directory, regardless of what user or group rights they have assigned. User or group rights automatically extend down to all subdirectory levels unless overridden at a lower level; a directory Maximum Rights Mask applies only to that directory level. The Maximum Rights Mask is combined with trustee rights to form *effective rights* at that directory level. Effective rights are simply the most restrictive of the two levels. Figure 14.12 shows the overall trustee and directory level security implementation.

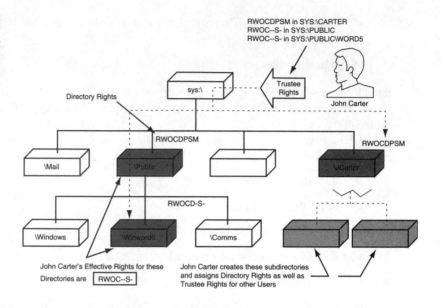

Table 14.4
NetWare 2.x File Attributes

Attribute	Abbreviation
Executable Only	EO
Hidden	H
Indexed	I
Modified	M
Read Only	RO
Read/Write	RW
Shareable	SHA
System	SY
Transactional	T

File attribute security is designed to protect the integrity of programs and data on the file server. Of the file attributes listed in table 14.4, RO, RW, and SHA directly affect security. File attribute security takes precedence over effective rights within the file's directory. Thus a file with an RO restriction cannot be modified even if a user's effective rights otherwise allow that privilege. An RO file cannot be modified, renamed, or deleted. A non-shareable file (a file without the SHA attribute) cannot be accessed by more than one user at a time.

Directories also have attributes, including Normal, Hidden, System, and Private. Normal directories have no attributes set. Hidden directories cannot be seen by users, but a user can change to a hidden directory. System directories do not appear in directory searches. Private directories can be seen by users, but their contents are hidden. If a user has effective Search rights, Private directory contents are visible.

NetWare 2.x Application Programming Interfaces

The value-added process application programming interfaces make certain NetWare features are independently available to third-party application developers. VAPs are Novell's term for third-party services to enhance NetWare. The Btrieve record management system is an example of a VAP and is provided with current versions of NetWare. Btrieve is used for physical record management and can be combined with other VAP data management tools such as NetWare SQL, NetWare XQL, and Xtrieve, as shown in figure 14.13. The combination of these tools with the added fault-tolerant features of TTS and pre-imaging can be used to create sophisticated server-based SQL and conventional database applications. VAPs can be developed as LAN services or used alone or with conventional program code in C, BASIC, Pascal, or COBOL to build higher-level applications.

Value-added disk drivers (VADD) are developed by third-party disk drive manufacturers to make their mass storage devices compatible with NetWare formatting requirements. NetWare offers its own disk subsystems, but encourages maximum participation in the VADD program to provide NetWare users with the broadest base possible of hard disk capability. As the breadth and depth of available mass storage devices continues to increase, the capability to link third-party hardware into the NetWare operating system becomes more significant.

The increased management functions available in current versions of NetWare provide an opportunity to make these functional programming interfaces available to third-party developers. These functions include network accounting, queue management, network diagnostics, the virtual file server console, and network security. An example of a possible third-party application using network diagnostics is an expert system that retrieves network statistics. The expert system uses the statistics and certain configuration rules to provide recommendations on network hardware changes. Figure 14.14 shows the conceptual view of such a system.

III

Local Area Networking

Figure 14.13
NetWare SQL value-added process architecture.

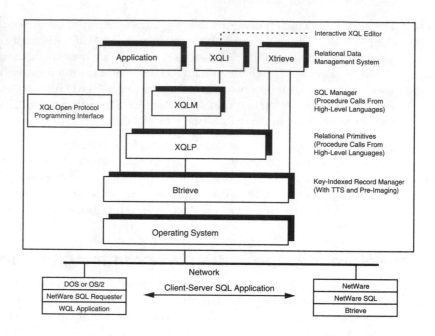

Figure 14.14
Expert System example using a NetWare value-added process and NetWare APIs.

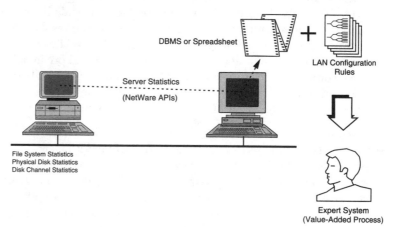

Virtual File Server Console

The *Virtual File Server Console*, or FCONSOLE, is a NetWare 2.*x* utility designed to enable remote execution of file server console commands from any workstation on the network. The remote user must have the security equivalence of a supervisor to use FCONSOLE commands. These commands are listed in table 14.5. The table shows that the supervisor can execute a wide variety of system-monitoring and control functions through the console commands.

Table 14.5
FCONSOLE Remote File Server Monitor and Control

Control the file server	Station's console privileges
Shut down the file server	Restrict management features
File server's status	File system statistics
File locking activity	Disk mapping table
Broadcast console messages	Physical disk statistics
LAN driver information	Disk channel statistics
Purge salvageable files	Connection's open files
Software version	List file connections

Network Accounting

NetWare 2.x supports resource accounting by enabling network supervisors to monitor network usage and bill user accounts. The supervisor can set up a credit limit for each user, monitor the account balance for each user, and create an audit trail for system use. Chargeable elements to each user account include the following:

✔ Connection time to server

✔ Blocks read from disk

✔ Blocks written to disk

✔ Requests received from workstations

✔ Amount of disk storage used

Automatic billing of user accounts is not included in this feature, but can be developed as a value-added process using APIs from NetWare's accounting functions.

NetWare 3.x

NetWare 3.x is the operating system version of choice if enterprise networking is not an organizational requirement. NetWare 3.x is designed specifically to run in an 80386 or 80486 server environment and adds significant features beyond

NetWare 2.*x*. NetWare 3.*x* shares one characteristic of NetWare 2.*x*—it is specifically designed as a server-based operating system. Basic user and management functions remain the same as earlier versions of the operating system, providing a degree of continuity across the product line.

NetWare 3.*x* is designed to take advantage of the 80386 and 80486 32-bit architecture and to provide an open platform on which extended services can be easily added. NetWare 3.*x* also builds on the concept of *Open Protocol Technology* (OPT) to extend NetWare's traditional independence from network media into the transport protocol software world. OPT also provides independence from specific client-server protocols. The latter feature enables the use of different workstation architectures on the same network, including OS/2, Windows NT, MS-DOS-based workstations, UNIX workstations, and the Macintosh.

Major Features

NetWare 3.*x* extends the services provided by NetWare 2.*x*, but retains the "look and feel" of its predecessor. The major enhanced functions (relative to version 2.*x*) implemented for NetWare 3.*x* include the following:

- ✔ Expanded security features
- ✔ Redesigned server architecture emphasizing modular design
- ✔ Open Protocol Technology (OPT)
- ✔ Expanded file service
- ✔ Expanded print service

Expanded Security Features

NetWare 3.*x* implements several security enhancements compared to NetWare 2.*x*. Among these are the Secure Console Option, extended directory and file protection from unauthorized users, creation of a new user category, and increased encryption.

The Secure Console Option limits access to the server to the system supervisor to prevent misuse of the server's open architecture.

Table 14.6 summarizes the differences in capabilities and terminology for extended directory and file security support.

Table 14.6
Access control features
NetWare 2.x versus NetWare 3.x

Right	Meaning	Version
Read	User can read open files in this directory and in subdirectoriess.	2.15
Read	User can open and read files in this directory and subdirectories.	2.2/3.x
Write	User can write to open files in this directory and subdirectories.	2.15
Write	User can open and write to files in this directory and subdirectories.	2.2/3.x
Open	User can open files in this directory and subdirectories.	2.15
Create	User can create files and subdirectories in this directory and all subdirectories.	2.x/3.x
Delete	User can delete files and directories in this directory and all subdirectories.	2.15
Erase	User can delete this directory, the subdirectory and files in this directory, and all child subdirectories and files.	2.2/3.x
Search	User can search the directory.	2.15
Directory Scan	User can see this directory name when scanning the parent directory.	2.2/3.x

continues

Table 14.6, Continued
Access control features
NetWare 2.x versus NetWare 3.x

Right	Meaning	Version
File Scan	User can see the file names of the files in this directory when scanning the directory.	2.2/3.x
Modify	User can change the name and attributes of this directory and child subdirectories.	2.x/3.x
Parental	User can create, rename, and erase subdirectories of this directory and set trustee and directory rights in this directory and its subdirectories.	2.15
Access Control	User can modify the trustee list and Inherited Rights Mask (IRM) of this directory and all child subdirectories and files.	2.2/3.x
Supervisor	User has all rights to this directory and all child subdirectories and files. User can grant supervisor rights for this directory and all child subdirectories and files.	2.2/3.x

In addition to expanded rights definitions, NetWare 3.x extends the rights listed earlier (except for Directory Scan and Create) to individual files as well as to the directory structure. The concept of an Inherited Rights Mask also is new. The IRM specifies rights for directory and file trustees inherited from the parent directory. The Inherited Rights Mask differs from the Maximum Rights Mask in that it applies to all subdirectories of the directory in which it is established. Figure 14.15 shows the difference.

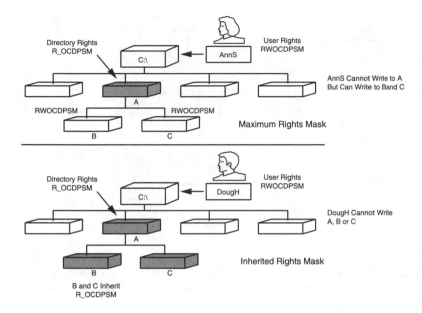

Figure 14.15
Comparison of
NetWare 2.*x*
and 3.*x* directory
rights
implementation.

Previous versions of NetWare support two categories of users: users and a supervisor. NetWare 3.*x* adds a new category: workgroup manager. A *workgroup manager* has supervisor privileges, but the domain is limited to a designated set of users or user groups.

Redesigned Server Architecture Emphasizing Modular Design

The NetWare 3.*x* server software design is a major departure from earlier NetWare versions. This network operating system is designed to provide multitasking and resource management capabilities similar to OS/2, but is not directly related to OS/2. NetWare 3.*x* introduces the concept of *NetWare Loadable Modules* (NLMs). NLMs are used for disk drivers, network adapter drivers, protocol stack drivers, server utilities, and server-based applications. NLMs can be dynamically loaded and linked to the basic operating system. This concept is similar to the Dynamic Link Libraries (DLLs) of OS/2. NLMs are written to a standard interface specification and can access other operating system services (which are also NLMs) through the same specification. Figure 14.16 illustrates this concept. This specification commonality is referred to as a *software bus*. In practice this means that a third-party server-based application could access the *Message Handling System* (MHS) service or file service to provide greater functionality.

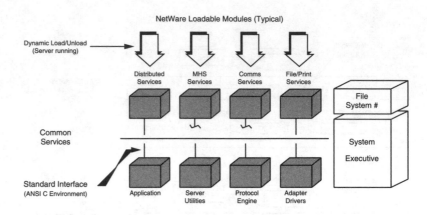

Figure 14.16
NetWare 3.*x*
NetWare
Loadable
Module (NLM)
concept.

Along with NLMs, NetWare 3.*x* design includes dynamic resource reconfiguration, which means improved memory management. This function is provided by the System executive. The following list gives a general idea of the controllable resources, each of which requires its own memory allocation:

✔ Directory cache buffers

✔ FAT tables

✔ File locks

✔ File service processes

✔ Loadable modules (NLMs)

✔ Routing tables

✔ TTS transactions

The bottom line of this capability is to simplify installation by not requiring the network manager to pre-allocate memory for these functions.

Open Protocol Technology (OPT)

Open Protocol Technology might be the most significant improvement in NetWare 3.*x* relative to version 2.*x*. Any network operating system design feature that enhances interoperability would be so judged in today's multivendor networking environment. OPT encompasses media independence, transport protocol independence, and client-server protocol independence. Media independence has long been a part of the NetWare design philosophy. This is reflected in support for a large number of network adapter cards and for bridging between dissimilar network topologies and media. Media independence continues to play an important role in the overall OPT architecture.

Novell's native transport protocol is the *Sequenced Packet Exchange* (SPX) and *Internetwork Packet Exchange* (IPX). These in turn are adaptations from the *Xerox Network System* (XNS) protocol. In NetWare 3.*x*, SPX/IPX have been decoupled from the basic operating system in favor of defining four interface layers: two to invoke transport protocol stacks from applications and NetWare services, and two to support multiple hardware adapters. The upper layer interfaces are NetWare Streams; the lower layer interfaces are the *Open Data Link Interface* (ODI). Streams provides NetWare with a consistent interface to all supported transport stacks and each supported transport stack is given a consistent interface to NetWare. ODI provides hardware adapter drivers a consistent interface to supported transport stacks and each transport stack is given a consistent interface for all supported adapters. Figure 14.17 illustrates these relationships.

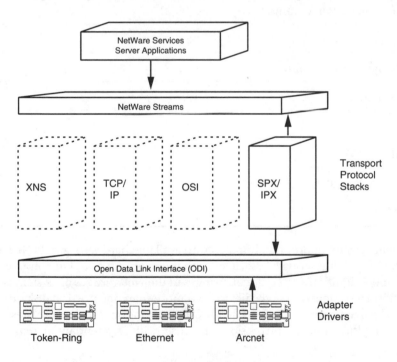

Figure 14.17
NetWare 3.*x* open protocol technology (OPT).

Novell's native client-server protocol is the *NetWare Core Protocol* (NCP). NCP is equivalent to the *Server Message Block* (SMB) protocol used by IBM and Microsoft. Similar protocols are employed by Apple for Macintosh systems and by Sun Microsystems for UNIX environments. These are the *AppleTalk Filing Protocol* (AFP) and *Network File System* (NFS). The stated objective for multiple client-server protocol support is to enable a heterogeneous workstation environment to access the services provided by NetWare 3.*x*.

III

Local Area Networking

Expanded File Service

NetWare 3.*x* provides a major increase in file system capacity relative to its predecessors. Table 14.7 lists the *theoretical* capacities. Keep in mind that many of these
capacities are not realizable without commensurate hardware capability.

Table 14.7
NetWare 3.x Maximum File Service Capacities

Concurrent Open Files Per Server	100,000
Concurrent TTS Transactions	25,000
Directory Entries Per Volume	2,097,152
Volumes Per Server	32
Drives (physical) Per Volume	32
Drives (physical) Per Server	1,024
File Size	4 GB
Adressable RAM	4 GB
Disk Storage Supported	32 TB
Volume Size	32 TB

These capacities, when appropriately mated with available hardware, give PC-based
LANs the I/O capabilities usually associated with minicomputers and mainframes.
One of the more significant operational changes in the NetWare 3.*x* file system is
the capability of a volume or a single file to span more than one physical disk drive.
The practical impact of this capacity is that I/O operations on one or more files
can occur on multiple physical drives simultaneously, with an attendant increase in
throughput.

The increase in file system capacities outlined in table 14.7 supports a greater
number of users on a single server, specifically 250 per server versus the earlier 100
users. Again, this increased operational limit must be tempered with factors
external to the NetWare File System. For example, a particular application may not
satisfactorily run with 250 users if not specifically written to do so. In most practical
systems, the need to support 250 users would lead to a multiserver architecture to
achieve workable performance levels.

Expanded file service also includes support for multiple name spaces. Support for multiple name spaces enables the use of file conventions other than those used by MS-DOS and OS/2. File conventions include items such as file name length, extension format, legal characters, case sensitivity, and other attributes. NetWare's implementation of this feature initially incorporates MS-DOS and Macintosh file types. Extensions to UNIX are planned. Under this scheme, a single file can have more than one file name, each corresponding to a legal file name of, and accessible by a different workstation operating system (see fig. 14.18).

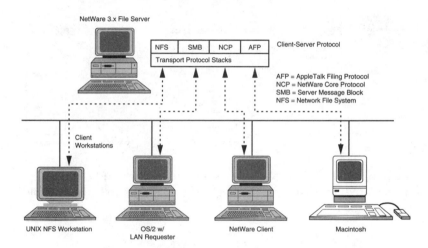

Figure 14.18
NetWare 3.x support for multiple file service protocols.

Expanded Print Service

NetWare 3.x increases the number of network-supported printers to a maximum of 16. Furthermore, the 16 printers are not restricted to physical attachment to file servers, as illustrated by figure 14.19. Print service is provided by a NetWare Loadable Module. Printers attached to the file server are managed by the print service NLM. Printers attached to workstations are managed by terminate-and-stay-resident software on the appropriate workstation.

NetWare 3.x supports Print Service Modes. These modes enable network managers to configure print service queues in one of the following four ways:

✔ Queue only

✔ Forms only

✔ Queue-before-form

✔ Form-before-queue

III

Local Area Networking

Figure 14.19
NetWare 3.*x*
print service
concept.

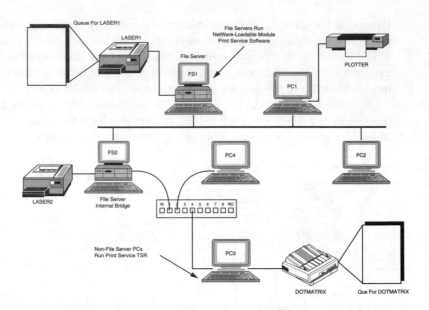

Print jobs are prioritized and completed based on the number and priority of queues and associated print forms. Figure 14.20 shows an example of a multiple queue configuration.

Figure 14.20
Print queue
management in
NetWare 3.*x*.

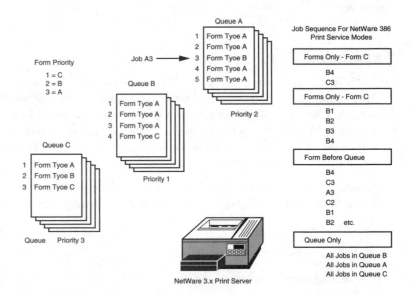

Print service support also includes alert notification, restricted access, and the NetWare PCONSOLE utility. Alert notification notifies users of events such as completed jobs, out of paper, cartridges needing replaced, or other printer errors. Restricted access makes printer queues a resource similar to directories and files with the commensurate control over user access. The PCONSOLE utility enables network managers to perform certain printer management jobs for any network printer, regardless of location. The PCONSOLE utility runs on the designated print server.

NetWare 4.x

NetWare 4.x is a major upgrade from previous versions because it fundamentally restructures security, management, and internetworking capabilities through the introduction of *NetWare Directory Services* (NDS). NDS puts NetWare in the same league with Banyan's VINES for internetworking capability, leaving OS/2 LAN Server and Windows NT Advanced Server as the two remaining network operating systems without a comprehensive internetwork naming system. Many other improvements were made to this NOS, but NDS is clearly the hallmark improvement in version 4.x. Whether to upgrade from NetWare 3.x to 4.x might be a more difficult decision than you think. Although the increased functionality of NetWare 4.x is tempting, the extra training required to incorporate NDS for single-site organizations may not be cost-effective. Clearly arguments can be made for either strategy, but as in all such decisions, the organization's future needs and business outlook should govern the decision-making process.

Major Features

Relative to NetWare 2.x and 3.x, the major features of NetWare 4.x include the following:

✔ NetWare Directory Services (NDS)

✔ Enhanced network security (being evaluated for United States government C-2 level certification)

✔ Least-used file compression and data migration

✔ The use of Virtual Loadable Modules for the NetWare DOS Requester to parallel the use of NLMs on the NetWare server

✔ Advanced media management including support for CD-ROMs

✔ Comprehensive file system and NDS security auditing (AUDITCON)

✔ GUI-based network management tools (NWADMIN)

NetWare Directory Services (NDS)

The biggest single improvement to NetWare in version 4.*x* is the introduction of a hierarchical, object-oriented naming service modeled after the X.500 standard. NDS is viewed as an inverted tree. The most fundamental unit in the directory tree is an object node. The root of the directory tree is an *organization,* as opposed to X.500, which starts with a country name at the root. The next levels are referred to as *organizational units* and there are as many of these levels as are appropriate to the organization. Not surprisingly, the directory tree may very well mirror an organizational chart of the company down to the level of organizational units. The lowest level on the tree is network resources, such as servers, printers, and users. Legal NDS object classes in NetWare 4.*x* are as follows:

- ✔ AppleTalk Filing Protocol Server
- ✔ Alias
- ✔ Bindery object
- ✔ Bindery queue
- ✔ Computer
- ✔ Device
- ✔ Directory map
- ✔ Group
- ✔ Locality
- ✔ NetWare server
- ✔ Organization
- ✔ Organizational person
- ✔ Organizational role
- ✔ Organizational unit
- ✔ Partition
- ✔ Person
- ✔ Printer
- ✔ Print server
- ✔ Profile

- ✔ Queue
- ✔ Resource
- ✔ Server
- ✔ Top
- ✔ Unknown
- ✔ User
- ✔ Volume

Any object in the directory tree containing subordinate objects is called a *container object*. An object with no subordinate objects is called a *leaf object*. Leaf objects include network resources. Objects have properties, or attributes in X.500 parlance. Each object class has properties defined according to a defined object schema. Part of NDS (and X.500) is the concept of object names. Organization names, organizational unit names, and common names are used at the corresponding levels of the tree, where common names are used to define leaf objects. These names are abbreviated O, OU, and CN respectively. Names are referred to in shorthand notation with dot separators as in the following four-level example:

```
CN.OU.OU.O, or BruceC.Admin.San_Diego.RMSL_Traffic_Systems
```

Note the correspondence to VINES StreetTalk names except for the separator character (StreetTalk uses "@").

The NDS tree also is a special-purpose database, with objects as records and properties as fields. This database can be searched according to preselected criteria. This capability provides a useful tool for quickly locating or aggregating related NDS objects. It is important to remember that although the NDS tree looks like a hierarchical file system, it bears no direct relationship to the underlying file system in NetWare. This fact is further underscored by the separation of access rights to NDS objects and properties from access rights to files and directories in the NetWare file structure. The general characteristics of inherited rights in NetWare 3.*x* file trees also applies to objects within NDS trees. Other concepts that apply to NDS trees include partitioning, replication, and time synchronization.

An NDS tree can be partitioned at any node, as shown in figure 14.21. Partitioning has the effect of distributing the NDS tree database according to criteria established by an organization. This action has practical value to preclude any one server in the organization from being saddled with managing the entire organization's tree.

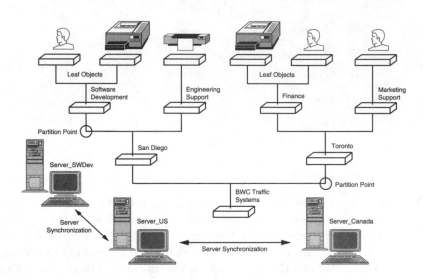

Figure 14.21

Partitioning of a NetWare Directory Services tree.

Replication works with partitioning to provide a degree of fault tolerance for each partition. Replication is similar to the equivalent concept in Windows NTAS, and OS/2 LAN Server's Replication Service. Replication allows NDS directory trees from remote servers to display on a local server. Replication only applies to NDS objects and does not extend to the NetWare file system. As far as NDS is concerned, replication also provides a degree of fault tolerance by maintaining mirrored images of one server's NDS tree on a physically separate server.

Time synchronization also is hierarchical through the use of reference time servers, primary time servers, and secondary time servers. A *reference time server* is one whose time is based on GPS or NIST time reference. Primary time servers can negotiate an acceptable time in the absence of a reference time server. Secondary time servers are those whose time is based on a primary time server. Time synchronization also includes information about time zones and the existence of Summer Time in a particular locale.

File Compression and Data Migration

File compression in NetWare 4.*x* works similarly to Stacker and DoubleSpace except that compression is not done in real time during reads and writes. The objective is to offload least-used files on to a backup media to free up disk space and to prevent accumulation of outdated files on hard disk drives. After a file is compressed, it is still visible to the user in its parent directory. An attempt to access a compressed file results in automatic decompression during the read operation. Several parameters can be set to optimally manage this service, including the following:

✔ Criteria for compression based on time of last access

✔ Time of compression

✔ Free space required for uncompressing

✔ Directory and file masking to prevent compression

Data migration is closely related to file compression because it is a tool to manage on-line disk space. *Migration* is the automatic move of selected files to an off-line storage device such as a Digital Audio Tape or similar. After a file is migrated, it is still listed in the directory, but is physically removed from on-line storage. If the user requests the file, a message appears asking the user to mount the off-line volume. When mounting is completed, the file(s) are moved back to on-line storage. File compression and data migration result in the following six new file attributes:

✔ Compressed

✔ Can't Compress

✔ Do Not Compress

✔ Immediate Compress

✔ Migrated

✔ Do Not Migrate

Virtual Loadable Modules for the NetWare DOS Requester

Virtual Loadable Modules are the NetWare 4.*x* client replacement for the NetWare workstation shells used in NetWare 2.*x* and 3.*x*. Perhaps the major significance of VLM is that it is built on top of the standard MS-DOS Redirector and is more compatible with the Microsoft Redirector architecture than were the earlier shell programs. In theory, at least, this bodes well for interoperability between NetWare 4.*x*, Windows NT, and OS/2. VLM provides a software bus architecture for the client workstation similar to what NLM does for the NetWare server. Figure 14.22 shows this bus and the VLM modules.

Figure 14.22
NetWare 4.*x*
Virtual Loadable
Module (VLM)
concept.

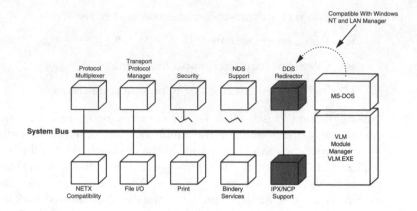

Security Auditing

AUDITCON is the NetWare 4.*x* audit module. Security auditing can be applied to either an NDS container object or to the NetWare filing system. Access to the audit feature is through assigned passwords. File audits include file events, queue management events, server events, and user events. NDS audits include events such as creating, removing, and merging partitions; creating and removing replications; changes in object Access Control Lists; adding, removing, or moving objects; changes in object passwords, replica types, and security equivalences; and user logins and logouts. A variety of customized audit reports can be created.

GUI-based Network Management

NWADMIN is a Windows-based network management user interface that provides a facility to manage the NetWare Directory Service objects. NWTOOLS is a Windows-based network management module that provides users a means to accomplish drive mapping, printer assignments, and network messaging. NetWare 4.*x* includes a DOS version of the Saber Menu System for menu management.

LAN Manager 2.x

LAN Manager 2.*x* is Microsoft's previous-generation network operating system. LAN Manager is an OS/2-based network operating system and relies extensively on OS/2 features such as multitasking, interprocess communications, and the *High Performance File System* (HPFS), described in Chapter 11. As with NetWare 2.*x*, LAN Manager is no longer a current distribution product, having been replaced by Windows NT Advanced Server. However, a substantial number of installations are still operational, and Windows NTAS addresses interoperability considerations with LAN Manager.

LAN Manager is an OS/2-based application on a server, but does not require workstations to be OS/2-based. Workstations running MS-DOS versions of LAN Manager interoperate with the OS/2 LAN Manager server, but with limited function compared to an OS/2 workstation. Other client platforms supported include Macintosh and Windows. LAN Manager provides a set of services based on the advanced capabilities of OS/2—over 125 *Application Program Interfaces* (APIs) are included for network support. These services can be run over UNIX and VAX VMS operating systems to provide server platform flexibility. LAN Manager also runs in a NetWare server environment.

LAN Manager uses resource sharing, redirection, and resource sharenaming conventions based on the original Microsoft Networks (MS-Net). LAN Manager uses the original MS-Net server-workstation file protocol, known as the Server Message Block, although the LAN Manager version is a superset of the MS-Net version. Because of OS/2's inherent features discussed in Chapter 11, the LAN Manager server has a robust set of LAN support services, including expanded LAN management and auditing, expanded security features, improved user interface, and support for multiple transport protocol sets. In its current implementation, LAN Manager does not internally bridge or route between these protocol stacks on the server.

LAN Manager Features

LAN Manager is a family of core services provided to network users. These services include resource sharing and network management. Resources include directories, printers, serial devices, IPC$ (remote execution of programs on a server), and ADMIN$ (remote network administration on a server). Network management services include network security, Alerter, Messenger, Netpopup, and Netlogon. LAN Manager uses the concept of server domains and the associated Replicator service.

General Resource Sharing Concepts

Shared resources (server directories, printers, communications devices, remote execution, administration) are controlled by the NET SHARE command. Resources are assigned sharenames during the network administration process. A sharename is mapped to a resource as follows:

✔ Shared File/Directory—server directory path name

   sharename = c:\netapps\dosapps\word5

✔ Shared Printer—print device name attached to server

   sharename = LPT1 (or LPT2, LPT3)

✔ Shared Comm Device—serial device name or pool of device names attached to server

sharename = COM1
sharename = COM1;COM2

Remote execution and administration are shared with the special sharenames, IPC$ and ADMIN$, respectively. Network Administrators use IPC$ and ADMIN$ to remotely control network security and management from any workstation on the LAN. This feature is not available to Macintosh clients, however.

Network Security Management

LAN Manager uses two types of security systems: network security and resource security. Network security is controlled by a login process and user accounts. The login process checks each user during login for a valid user-name password, set before enabling the user to gain access to the network. Once on the network, users are logged in to one or more servers containing shared resources. Each server invokes resource security by one of two methods: user-level or share-level. Each server on the network uses only one of these systems. Figure 14.23 compares the two security systems. The security type for each server is determined during network configuration. User accounts consist of a user name, password (optional, but highly desirable), group membership, and privilege level. Privilege levels are User, Guest, and Admin. Good security practice dictates that the Admin privilege be limited to the absolute minimum number of people, perhaps a primary administrator and one alternate.

Figure 14.23
Comparison of LAN Manager share-level and user-level file server security.

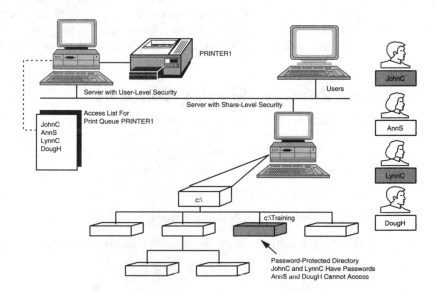

Login security only applies to OS/2-based workstations. MS-DOS workstations running LAN Manager do not support the user account concept. Login security can be either centralized or distributed. Under centralized login security, one server is designated as a central validator of all user login attempts. In a distributed login system, a login request is sent to multiple designated servers—at least one server containing that user's account validates the login request and admits the user to the network.

User-level and share-level resource security use the same means of controlling what a user can do when the resource is accessed. Control is exercised by means of resource permissions, as shown in table 14.8. The difference between the two types of resource security is in how the security is assigned. User-level permissions are assigned through access lists associated with each shared resource. The access lists contain the names of authorized users. Access lists are permanent until changed. Share-level permissions are assigned at the time the resource is shared and persist only as long as the resource is shared. Share-level permissions for a particular resource apply to all users of that resource who have the correct resource password. Passwords are optional for each shared resource in a share-level system and are not used in user-level systems.

Table 14.8
LAN Manager Resource Permission Levels

Resource Type	Permission
Disk C	Create
D	Delete
R	Read
W	Write
X	Execute
A	Change Attributes
P	Change Permissions[1]
Y	Yes (=RWCDA)
N	No

[1]P = Administrators Only for share-level security

continues

Local Area Networking

III

Table 14.8, Continued
LAN Manager Resource Permission Levels

Resource Type	Permission
Spooled Print Queue	Y Yes (=C)
N	No
Comm Device Queue	Y Yes (=RWC)
N	No
IPC (Remote Execution)	Y Yes (=RWC)
N	No

Shared Printing

Shared printing is managed by the use of printer queues. Queues are named with sharenames and assigned to printer ports on the server as described earlier. A single queue can be assigned to a single printer or to a pool of printers. Multiple queues can be assigned to a single printer. Queues have attributes such as authorized users, maximum number of users allowed, priority levels, authorized usage times, print job preprocessing, and separator pages. On share-level servers, queues can be given passwords. Multiple printers attached to the file server provide a choice of the type and quality of printed output. A manager could assign different queue profiles to single-printer servers to set up variations in service for separate entities in a company. One or more queues can be linked to different printers on a multiprinter server to provide a variation in output quality or to even the workload on printers.

Entire print queues and their individual job requests can be directly controlled through the NET PRINT command. Jobs can be held, restarted, deleted, or changed in priority. All existing jobs in a queue can be deleted while keeping the queue itself active. The NET DEVICE command controls the restarting and deletion of jobs on a particular printer.

Support is provided for Postscript printer queues. PostScript printers have resident software that interprets PostScript print definition files transmitted from compatible applications such as Word for Windows or Lotus Freelance for Windows. In LAN Manager, PostScript printer queues are separately defined and managed. The directory path(s) of PostScript dictionaries and downloadable fonts must be specified during the installation of print service. When setup is complete, PostScript queues are managed like any other print queue.

Shared Communications Devices

LAN Manager allows the sharing of non-spooled devices through the use of *communications device queues*. Non-spooled devices typically include some serial printers, plotters, image scanners, and modems. As with printer queues, multiple queues can be established for a single device. Single or multiple queues can be linked to multiple devices. Figure 14.24 illustrates some configuration examples. For communications queues, the NET DEVICE command provides status only, either for a specific device or for all communications devices on the network. Queue linking to devices is controlled through the NET COMM command. The NET SHARE command controls communications queues in the same manner as printer queues.

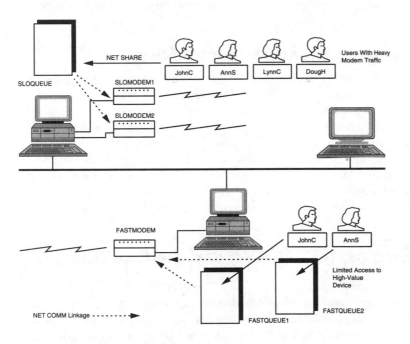

Figure 14.24
Examples of communications queue management in LAN Manager.

Remote Execution of Shared Programs

Server-based applications can be shared on LAN Manager networks. The NET RUN command invokes the remote execution service on the file server. The manner in which this service is shared depends on the type of security used on the file server: user-level security allows specification of R and X privileges for each user, whereas share-level security has no effect on remote execution. Special server paths, called the *runpaths*, must be set up in the LAN Manager initialization file **LANMAN.INI** to contain remotely executable programs. A limit can be set on the number of simultaneously running shared programs. This limit has a significant effect on server performance and must be set with care. In fact, the entire concept of shared programs must be analyzed carefully in the context of a particular network's performance objectives because file server throughput can be significantly degraded by remote execution.

Remote Network Administration

Using the IPC$ and ADMIN$ shared resources, a network Administrator can log in to one or more servers from any workstation and conduct certain administrative tasks, including the establishment and maintenance of automatic alerts, server statistics, server error logs, server audit trails, and user sessions with servers. Both DOS and OS/2 workstations can accomplish remote administrative functions, but Macintosh workstations cannot.

Alerter, Messenger, and Netpopup Services

The Alerter, Messenger, and Netpopup services work together to provide server-to-workstation and workstation-to-workstation messaging. The Alerter service establishes the events and conditions under which alerts are sent from a server to the appropriate workstation. Alerts can be generated by audit, error, or shared resource status events. The Messenger service supports the sending of messages between workstations. Messaging is compatible with the IBM PC LAN Program including the use of Alias names and the forwarding of messages to alternative workstations. Messages or files up to 64 KB can be sent. The Netpopup service provides popup windows on user workstations for the display of alerts and messages.

Server Domains, NETLOGON, and the Replicator Service

LAN Manager server domains provide both a name service and a security service. When a server domain is established, any user logging in to that domain has access to any shared resource in that domain according to his or her access rights. The location of the shared resource is transparent to the user, who needs only to know the name of the resource. The domain system also checks user security access privileges throughout the entire domain, not just the server to which he or she logs in. Each domain has a primary domain controller and one or more backup domain controllers. Other servers can be part of a domain, but not function as a primary or backup controller. The domain system contains the following components:

✔ User accounts database

✔ Resource definition database

✔ Login script database

Figure 14.25 illustrates the architecture of a domain system. The figure shows what databases are maintained on what servers and how the databases are maintained. All types of servers in the domain can verify user logins, but only primary and backup domain controllers can execute login scripts. Only the primary domain controller can make changes to domain databases. A domain must be carefully designed because careless design can cause excessive inter-server traffic on the network. Besides which servers are included in a single domain and what functions those servers perform, the NETLOGON service has tunable parameters which can influence network performance. These parameters are the interval at which the primary controller broadcasts database updates to other servers (pulse interval); when the other servers request the updated database (randomized delay time); and whether a backup or member server requests an update to the user account database when the NETLOGON service starts on that server. Figure 14.26 illustrates these parameters.

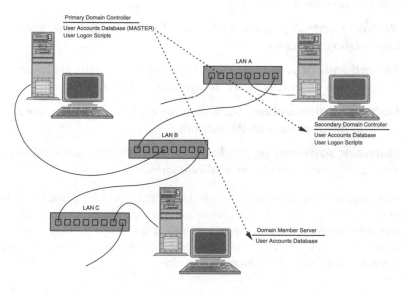

Figure 14.25
LAN Manager server domains.

Figure 14.26
Operation of
LAN Manager
NETLOGON
parameters.

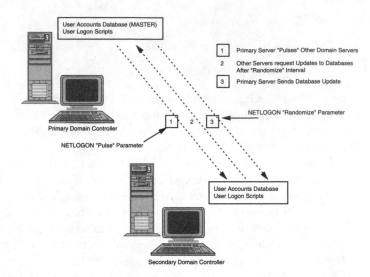

The Replicator Service enables the simultaneous broadcasting of directory and file updates from a source server to one or more destination servers. Some uses of the Replicator Service include the following:

- ✔ **Version Control.** Ensures that file and directory updates are sent to all listed destination servers

- ✔ **File redundancy.** Sends multiple copies of mission-critical files and directories to redundant server storage locations on the network

- ✔ **Document distribution.** Sends multiple copies of important documents to different users on the network

- ✔ **Network software upgrades.** Ensures that system and applications software upgrades are sent to all affected network servers

The Replicator Service applies to servers only. Up to 32 servers or domains can be targeted to receive file updates. The originating server's directory is called the *export directory*; the receiving server's directory is called the *import directory*. The domain system within LAN Manager uses the Replicator Service, as you may have deduced from the preceding discussion on domains.

OS/2 LAN Server and OS/2 Extended Services

OS/2 LAN Server is the server component of IBM's OS/2-based LAN architecture. OS/2 LAN Server is supported by five integrated systems for client-server and internetworking applications development. These are Database 2 OS/2, or DB2/2; Communications Manager OS/2, or CM/2; Network Transport Services/2, or NTS/2; NetWare requester for OS/2; and TCP/IP for OS/2. DB2/2 in turn is supported by Distributed Database Connection Services/2 for remote client-server applications running in a heterogeneous server environment. CM/2 provides connectivity to host mainframes and the IBM SNA architecture. NTS/2 provides NDIS and streamlined NetBIOS transport protocol support. NetWare Requester for OS/2 enables OS/2 clients to access NetWare servers. TCP/IP for OS/2 is the product line that supports the UNIX and Internet network environment. The following paragraphs review each of these components except for DB2/2, which is beyond the scope of this chapter. Figure 14.27 shows the relationship between these communications components.

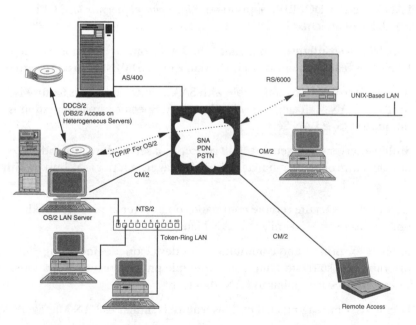

Figure 14.27
OS/2 Communications Services.

Major Features

The OS/2 LAN Server includes services for the sharing of files, printers, and serial devices and for the definition and management of access to resources on the server. A particular network environment can support multiple servers as a single logical entity, referred to as a *domain*. The domain includes the servers and services provided by the servers. One server in the domain is known as the *domain controller,* which is responsible for management of all shared resources within the server domain. In context of the supported workstations, a multiserver domain is referred to as a *single system image.*

OS/2 LAN Server provides a number of features equivalent to those in LAN Manager, as well as some unique features. Similarity to LAN Manager is to be expected because OS/2 LAN Server and LAN Manager are both based on the same OS/2 kernel. These features include the following:

✔ Support for a variety of services including Workstation, Server, Messenger, Popup, Alerter, Netrun, and PCDOSRIPL. These services are similar to those in LAN Manager except PCDOSRIPL, which is unique to OS/2 LAN Server. PCDOSRIPL supports the *independent program load* (IPL) capability of attached PC-DOS workstations.

✔ Capability to configure and manage the LAN from any location on the LAN. This feature is similar to LAN Manager's ADMIN$ shared resource.

✔ Access control system compatible with SAA architecture. This feature is similar to LAN Manager's User-level security. Specific implementation is unique to OS/2 LAN Server.

✔ Multiple server management. The concepts of server domains and domain controllers are similar to LAN Manager, but not as robust as with Windows NT.

✔ Capability to execute remote commands on a server at prescheduled times. This feature is similar to LAN Manager.

✔ Support for printer and communications device queues including prioritization, start/stop times, and multiple physical print destinations. These features are similar to LAN Manager.

✔ User-to-user messaging facility. This feature is similar to LAN Manager.

Communications Manager/2

CM/2 includes several APIs that provide protocol support and services for the following:

✔ APPC LU 6.2 with *Common Programming Interface for Communications* (CPI-C)

✔ 3270 *Server-Requester Programming Interface* (SRPI)

✔ *Asynchronous Communications Device Interface* (ACDI)

✔ Asynchronous Emulation (IBM 3101, DEC VT100)

✔ 3270/5250 Workstation Feature for AS/400

✔ X.25

✔ SNA gateway service

✔ Support for ISDN 2B + D interface

NetWare Requester For OS/2

NetWare Requester for OS/2 provides access to NetWare file servers for OS/2 clients and supports all major NetWare features such as file, print, and communications services; network security; NetWare Directory Services; and fault tolerance. LAN Requester supports all versions of NetWare from 2.*x* to 4.*x*. An OS/2-based client workstation can simultaneously access LAN Server and a NetWare file server with both OS/2 LAN Requester and NetWare LAN Requester installed. Novell and IBM both provide translation software to allow interoperability between the ODI and NDIS multiprotocol interfaces. Through appropriate API, OS/2 and Macintosh workstations can share files through the NetWare file server. Table 14.9 lists APIs available for NetWare Requester for OS/2. Figure 14.28 depicts OS/2 and NetWare interoperability.

TCP/IP For OS/2

TCP/IP for OS/2 is a very complete implementation of the popular internetworking protocol and includes support for the following TCP/IP components:

✔ Async and X.25 internetwork connectivity as well as support for Ethernet, Token Ring, and IBM PC Network

✔ Berkeley Sockets

✔ NetBIOS over TCP/IP

✔ IP, ICMP, RIP, and ARP at layer 3

✔ TCP and UDP at layer 4

✔ X-Windows protocol

✔ Network File System (NFS)

✔ Many applications layer services such as Domain Name System, Simple Mail Transfer Protocol (SMTP), File Transfer Protocol (FTP), Telnet and SNMP among others

✔ SunOS Remote Procedure Calls (currently the most popular RPC implementation)

✔ The MIT Kerberos Authentication Services

Figure 14.28
OS/2 LAN Server and NetWare interoperability.

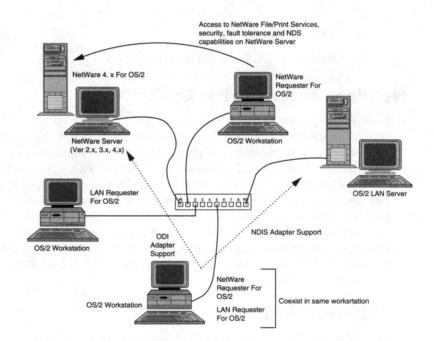

Table 14.9
APIs Supported by NetWare Requester for OS/2

Peer-to-Peer	IPX
	SPX
	NetBIOS
Network Named Pipes	Named Pipes
NetWare Services	Accounting services

Apple File services
Auditing services
Bindery services
Connection services
Data migration services
Deleted file services
Directory services
Extended attributes
File server
File systems services
Message services
Name space services
Path and drive services
Print server
Print services
Queue management services
Synchronization services
TTS
Volume services

Windows NT Advanced Server

Windows NT Advanced Server (NTAS) is the latest in NOS products from Microsoft and is a direct descendant of LAN Manager. NTAS builds on the considerable capabilities of Windows NT as a multitasking, advanced security architecture operating system; just as OS/2 LAN Server builds on the OS/2 operating system.

With Windows NT, each of the four major LAN vendors has a native multitasking operating system foundation—alone among these, NetWare is not yet an independently bootable operating system but relies on MS-DOS, OS/2, or UNIX as a supporting OS. Because Windows NTAS is a descendant of LAN Manager, functionality is very similar to LAN Manager and OS/2 LAN Server, including the use of multiple domain server management. Because of the NTFS file system and enhanced security architecture, NTAS offers a more robust networking environment than LAN Manager, and is the system of choice for those organizations who might be considering a LAN Manager-based network system.

Major Features

As this book goes to press, Windows NTAS is approaching its first anniversary on the market. Stability and functionality in the LAN operating system market is not usually meteoric, therefore, you can expect to see major improvements to this NOS with the second and subsequent releases. The architecture and foundations are strong, but some specific implementations are weak or nonexistent. For example, the server implementation of Mail does not provide any external connectivity options, nor is there support for any type of modem pooling for outbound calls. TCP/IP implementation does not support the universal NFS file system. An X.500 compatible directory naming system is not available. Relative to LAN Manager, Windows NTAS has some differences in features. These differences will widen with future releases and currently include the following:

✔ An open architecture is provided for the integration of third-party client redirectors and for accessing other LAN vendors' servers. For example, Windows NTAS servers can run as applications servers on a NetWare network without disturbing the functions of the NetWare file server.

✔ Remote access server has up to 64 incoming ports (discussed in Chapter 13).

✔ Modem queues are not supported as a resource.

✔ Built-in file-sharing and printing support is provided for Macintosh workstations through the NTFS file system and AppleTalk protocol stack. (Macintosh printers must be connected to the NTAS server, and Mac/PC Mail interoperability is not yet supported.)

✔ Domains can share user account information through Trust relationships, as indicated in figure 14.29.

✔ Discretionary access control for NTFS files is available.

✔ Built-in transaction tracking system support for NTFS files is available.

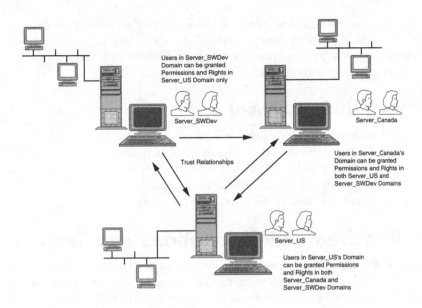

Figure 14.29
Trusted Domain relationships in Windows NT Advanced Server

System Comparisons

Now that VINES, NetWare 2.*x* through 4.*x*, LAN Manager, OS/2 LAN Server, and Windows NT Advanced Server all have been described in some detail, a generic methodology for evaluating these and similar products is provided to aid in the LAN system selection process. A typical use for questions such as those that follow is during the formulation of a *Request For Proposals* (RFP) for a LAN installation or for the evaluation of vendor proposals in response to an RFP.

Note that no attempt is made here to pass quantitative or qualitative judgment on the systems reviewed earlier because product lines in the LAN industry undergo frequent revisions. What may be a major drawback or performance limitation today can disappear tomorrow with a major (or even minor) system redesign. Many real-world performance limitations may not be due to software flaws, but instead can be linked to a lack of adequate hardware to support a particular feature or system capacity.

File Server Hardware Support

No major network operating system vendor currently offers a proprietary file server. All NOS vendors have opted to focus on operating system software and leave hardware design to companies better optimized for that engineering effort. What performance enhancements from the following list are supported as standard items on generic file servers? Which are optional items? The list includes, but is not limited to the following: cache memory, 16-bit or 32-bit memory transfer paths, use of 16- or 32-bit network adapter cards, disk coprocessor support, multiple disk I/O channels, high-speed processors (80486/66 Mhz or better), and multiple media for backup and archival.

Support for Multiprocessors

Does the network operating system support either or both symmetric or asymmetric multiprocessors down to the thread execution level? In a *symmetric multiprocessor*, each processor can be assigned to execute any thread in a process. *Asymmetric multiprocessors* assign operating system functions to one processor and all the remaining functions are allocated to the remaining processes.

Memory Required on Workstations and Servers

With the advent of new operating systems, a wide variety of extended memory managers, and larger applications, memory requirements for network operating systems have become much more critical. By the time you load OS/2, LAN Manager, and one or two major applications, the memory requirements on workstations can easily exceed 6–8 MB. What are the minimum memory requirements of the network operating system on both workstations and servers, and are configuration options available to reduce RAM requirements? To what extent are memory restrictions lifted by the new generation of integrated OS/NOS systems typified by Windows NT?

Network Mass Storage Options

How many total megabytes of disk storage are supported? What is the maximum file size supported by the network operating system? What is the maximum partition size? Can hard drives be daisy-chained? If so, how many? List all the possible hard drive combinations with the resulting mass storage capacities.

Shared Printer Support

How many printers can be connected to a file server? What is the number of serial printers? Parallel printers? Do printers require a dedicated PC-based server or can they be located anywhere on the LAN, including user PCs and dedicated non-PC server hardware? Can applications software print requests be immediately run without leaving the application? Can printers be set up to handle different form sizes and formatting options? How are network printers set up by the network administrator? Are print-spooling queues controllable by the network administrator? What print-spooling features are supported by the print service?

Other Shared Device Support

What other shared devices are supported by the network operating system? Modems? Fax machines? Telex? Plotters? High resolution and color laser printers? Scanners and imagers? CD-ROMs and other image storage devices? Hardware and software support requirements for specific brands and model numbers should be ascertained.

Support for Multiple File Types

What file systems do the network operating system support? Candidates include Macintosh, HPFS (OS/2 and Windows NT), NTFS (Windows NT), FAT (MS-DOS), NetWare, and UNIX. Through what protocol are the file systems accessed? Does the system support the NFS standard? Does the system support POSIX file system requirements?

Support for Multiple Client Workstation Types

Which workstation clients do the operating system server support? Typical candidates are MS-DOS, OS/2, Windows, Windows for Workgroups, Windows NT, and UNIX. Are the client redirectors (or requesters, as they may be called) supported by the NOS vendor or a third-party vendor, including other NOS vendors?

Support for Multiple Transport and LAN Access Protocol

Does the network operating system support transparent binding between application layer protocols and different transport protocol stacks? What stacks are supported among TCP/IP, NetBIOS and NetBEUI, SPX/IPX, OSI, or DLC? Can the transport protocol be bound to multiple physical and data link layer implementations, including multiple hardware adapters within each implementation?

Protocol Options and Interoperability

What *Interprocess Communications* (IPC) APIs does the network operating system support? Can protocols be run in parallel or are they singularly selectable? What client-server protocol facilities are supported? What workstation/file server protocols are supported? What workstation host operating system, network operating system, and transport protocol combinations are interoperable on a single network? What file server combinations support these workstation combinations? List all the interoperable workstation/file server combinations with required hardware and software configurations.

Distributed Naming Support

Does the network support a distributed naming service? Is the naming service permanent or does it log out with the user or when the network node shuts down (for example, NETBIOS)? Does the naming service support password-protected logins by users? What network entities does the naming service recognize? Does the naming service support internetworking through X.500 or an equivalent directory naming system? Does the naming service recognize and map NETBIOS-compatible names?

Internetworking and LAN/WAN Connectivity

What other networks can be attached to this one using either bridges or gateways? Does the file server support internal bridges? Are external (to the file server) bridges supported? If so, must the bridge workstation be dedicated to communications? What communications gateways are available? APPC/LU6.2? IBM 3270/SNA? 3270/Bisynchronous? Remote Job Entry (RJE)? X.25 packet-switching? High-capacity T-1 links? Frame Relay and ATM? Asynchronous? Is stand-alone, remote PC dial-in supported? What protocol do servers use for internetworking connections?

Host System Access Capabilities

Does the network support access to popular host-based systems? What mainframe or minicomputer operating systems, telecommunications access methods, control systems, and front-end processors are supported? What mainframe or minicomputer applications can be executed through network gateway processors? Does the network support IBM's *Advanced Program-to-Program Communications Protocol* (APPC)? How many mainframe sessions can be active on the network at one time?

File Locking Standards Supported

Does the network operating system support physical byte-range locking? Logical byte-range locking? Transaction activity? File locking? Is file locking automatic for single-user applications? Check what file and byte-range locking function calls are implemented, including those that extend MS-DOS or OS/2 lock service.

Access Control and Security

What safeguards prevent unauthorized users from entering the network and logging in to the file server(s)? What access control method is used to protect directories, files, and other shared resources? What resources are protected by the security system? Does the network support encryption systems? Is some type of user

authentication procedure used? Is the security kernel in the process of being certified to a United States government standard as defined by the Department of Defense Orange Book? Is auditing supported for users and resources?

Fault Tolerant Design

Does the file server have a hot standby feature (mirrored servers)? Is it backed up by a battery or other uninterruptible power supply? Is the UPS connected to a logical port on the file server for automatic shut-down features? Are disk directories and file allocation tables mirrored on alternate disk surfaces? Are individual disk drives mirrored? Is disk drive duplexing supported? Does the network operating system have built-in support for transaction fault-tolerance, such as transaction logging and transaction roll-forward and roll-back recovery?

E-Mail

What type of e-mail system, if any, does the network software package support? Is it capable of internetworking? Does it gateway to commercial store-and-forward e-mail services, such as MCI Mail and CompuServe's InfoPLex? Are editor capabilities built in? Can external editors be used? What network server configuration is required to run e-mail applications? Is Message Handling Service supported? VIM? MAPI? Does it currently or is it scheduled to support international X.400 and X.500 e-mail standards?

Backup and Archiving Capability

What streaming tape devices does the network operating system recognize? What other types of storage devices are supported for backing up the primary mass storage device? How many megabytes of tape storage are supported? What are capacities of other backup media? Can backups be made while the network is up and running? Are backup devices centralized on servers or distributed on the network? What logical directory units does the backup system handle? Can backups be set for time intervals, clock times, or both?

Network Performance Monitoring

What system, if any, is used to monitor network performance? Are statistics kept in real-time and used to present graphic analysis of network performance? Can the monitoring system be used in a reasonable fashion to predict performance bottlenecks? Can an experienced network administrator use the network monitoring system to plan hardware and software upgrades, such as the need to add more servers? Will the monitoring system help in determination of server and other shared resource load balancing?

Network Utilities

What other types of general software support are provided to the users and to the network administrator by the network operating system? Are utilities supported by a graphical user interface such as Windows or OS/2's Workplace Shell? Is some type of batch-processing facility or other customization technique available? Do dedicated file servers use a remote console for control? If so, what types are supported? What network management facilities are included? Is Simple Network Management Protocol supported?

Summary

Notice that none of the preceding questions are related to the clock speed of network media systems, network topology considerations, the type of media employed, nor the hardware efficiency of network adapter cards. This is consistent with the treatment of hardware-independent network software architectures in this chapter. Every major network hardware implementation is supported by at least one of the systems reviewed in this chapter, and many are supported by more than one operating system.

This book does not attach relative importance weights to the preceding factors because importance can only be related to the desired application and the needs of the organization. One commonly accepted method to arrive at a semi-objective ranking during an RFP evaluation process is to attach a criterion weighting and a scoring range to each factor being evaluated. The final score is then a weighted average of the factor scores.

This chapter reviewed the leading network operating systems for PC-based LANs. With each of these systems, some clear trends are discernible: greater support for interoperability within networks and between networks and increased standardization of core services. As LANs continue to proliferate and network software becomes even more sophisticated than the current generation, some of the more likely trends are as follows:

✔ Support for the newer multiprocessor-based servers primarily focusing on symmetric configurations.

✔ Increased reliance on multitasking operating systems, providing standardization and higher performance for server-based operating systems and making proprietary DOS extensions unnecessary. Major competition for server-based operating systems will come from OS/2, Windows NT, UNIX, and NetWare.

✔ Improved network operating system support for host-based connectivity solutions including application level interoperability and the use of host-based systems as network resource servers (for example, IBM's AS/400).

✔ Increased acceptance of standard internetworking protocols, evolving from the need to build more sophisticated distributed applications that span multiple LANs and WANs. TCP/IP has become a dominant standard for this purpose, but the OSI protocol will make increased inroads. Operating systems such as OS/2, VINES, NetWare, and Windows NT now support concurrent use of multiple logical transport protocol stacks.

✔ Increased development of distributed applications using the client-server model. This trend will lead to a new generation of LAN sophistication and to virtual parity with the minicomputer world. Distributed applications will in turn drive the implementation of more sophisticated security and fault-tolerant features in LANs. NetWare 4.*x* and Windows NT are nearing United States government C-2 level certification.

✔ Expanded development and automation of network management facilities, including the integrated management of local and wide area networks; and increased support for industry standards, such as SNMP.

✔ Increased emphasis on applications designed to exploit the capability to connect workgroups locally and remotely to accomplish a variety of collaborative tasks such as electronic meetings, desktop videoconferencing, electronic conferencing, and e-mail.

III

Local Area Networking

Chapter Snapshot

The decreasing size and increasing power of laptops and the appearance of the first generation Personal Digital Assistants have fueled a significant interest in wireless communications within the PC industry. The number and variety of wireless data products being introduced almost daily is staggering. The communications industry in general, and the wireless industry specifically, are even more fluid than the PC industry. For those more familiar with the wired world of Ma Bell, wireless networking may seem like entering the world of the unknown. In this chapter, you will learn about:

- ✔ The nature of the wireless data networking market

- ✔ Wireless technology basics and terminology

- ✔ Cellular radio networks including the new digital networks and the emerging satellite and Cellular Data Packet Distribution services.

- ✔ The mobile data networks such as ARDIS, RAM Mobile Data and Nextel

- ✔ The future of geosynchronous and low-earth-orbiting satellite data services

- ✔ The Personal Communications Service

- ✔ Wireless LANs, including both radio and light-based systems

- ✔ A case study showing how traditional wired networks can be integrated with a variety of wireless data services

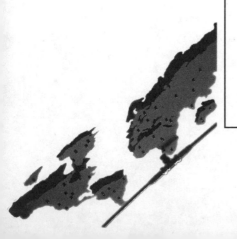

Wireless Networking

So far this book has focused on wire-based wide area and local area networks. Wiring is inherently restrictive because data must be confined to a prescribed path that can be both expensive to install and difficult to access. The latter restriction is particularly noticeable with the significant increase in the popularity and use of notebook computers. Chapter 12, "Local Area Networks: The Communications Perspective," briefly mentioned the concept of wireless LANs. This chapter explores the entire concept of wireless networking and its significance to the emerging world of mobile computing. The data transmission perspective of wireless networking is emphasized because a major move is underway to expand wireless access to the voice telephone network.

Wide area networks rely heavily upon the capability to access a switched or leased local access line (wire-based, of course). Of the three major components of the *public-switched telephone networks* (PSTN)—*switching, transmission,* and *local access*—the local access portion has had the least technical innovation Switches are now largely digital and provide a host of value-added network features. Transmission systems have become largely high-capacity microwave, satellite, and fiber-optic paths. Only local access still relies upon the existence of the same twisted-pair copper wiring used since the inception of the telephone. Local access is increasingly expensive to install and expand, especially in the more remote areas. Many leased lines used today are marginal in quality, and their long-term financial and technical viability are becoming increasingly suspect. One solution is to bring fiber access to customer premises, which is relatively expensive and for some areas may be a long time in coming. Another solution is wireless access.

This chapter discusses the potential market for wireless networking, with emphasis on mobile applications. Some background material on the nature of the radio frequency spectrum as a media for networking is presented, and the concepts of the existing cellular radio network and its relationship to the PSTN are explored. The shortcomings of current cellular technology and the steps being undertaken to increase its usefulness for data applications are discussed. Other wireless wide area data network systems including satellite systems and their applications are examined, as well as the evolving *Personal Communications Service* and its relationship to data networking. The emerging world of wireless LANs and the way they fit into the larger enterprise networking strategy is explored. Finally, a case study on the integration of wireless and wired network technologies to solve a transportation-related problem is presented.

The Wireless Networking Market

A recent study completed by Ram Mobile Data, a leading mobile data network provider in the United States, United Kingdom, and Canada, estimates the size of the wireless networking market at 10 million users. These users cover almost every facet of the American private and public sectors: field service, public transit, public safety agencies, freight and package delivery, sales, white collar professionals, rental agencies, utilities, point-of-sale systems, inventory control—the list seems limited only by the imagination. Often mobile computing is considered the exclusive realm of white collar professionals with hosts of notebook computers in hotels, conferences, airports, and the like, but in reality many aspects of our daily workplace rely on moving data from a remote site to a central fixed computing system. This fixed system can be a mainframe, LAN, single PC, or gateway to a third-party network. Remote site equipment can be notebook and pen-based PCs, palmtop PCs, *Personal Digital Assistants* (PDAs), specially designed mobile terminals for vehicles, or handheld data terminals such as those used by rental car agencies to record vehicle check-in data at the point of return.

In general, applications fall into the following six principal categories:

✔ Computer-aided dispatch

✔ Internal database access

✔ Public network access (third-party networks)

✔ Fleet monitoring

✔ Remote data collection

✔ Messaging (one-way e-mail)

The matrix in table 15.1 summarizes the major applications by market segment across these principal categories. As the mobile computing market matures with the introduction of new products and services, additional categories and market segments will emerge.

Table 15.1
Mobile Data Benefits and Uses by Market Segment.

	Computer-Aided Dispatch	Internal Database Access	Public Network Access	Fleet Monitoring	Remote Data Collection (Telemetry)	Messaging and Electronic Mail
Field Service Office		Inventory Management				Efficient, Time-Saving Commun-ications
Field Service - Home & Utilities	Real-Time Routing & Scheduling				Remote Meter Reading	Field Status Customer Status
Personal Transport - Taxi & Limo	Efficient Resource Allocation			Automatic Vehicle Location & Sales		
Public Transport				Fleet Monitoring & Routing		Efficient, Time-Saving Commun-ications
Local Trucking	Efficient Resource Allocation	Customer Records Update				Efficient, Time-Saving Commun-ications
Long-haul Trucking		Customer Records Update		Fleet Monitoring & Routing		Next Assignment Scheduling
Courier Services	Efficient Resource Allocation	Package Delivery & tracking		Fleet Monitoring & Routing		
Field Sales - Financial & Real Estate		Price Quotes Property Listings	Stock Prices Financial News			2-Way Messaging & Paging - Email
Field Professionals		Field Reports	Stock Prices Newsletters			2-Way Messaging & Paging - Email
Public Safety/Emergency Services	Efficient Resource Allocation	Vehicle/Person Wants/Warrants		Automatic Vehicle Location & Sales	Motorist Aid Systems - EMS Medical Data	Resource Coordination

Wireless Technology Background

The *ether* was one of the first media used for experimental local area networking with the *Aloha Net packet radio* system. This network was used in Hawaii to connect remote terminals to a central processing facility. Amateur radio operators are increasingly using packet radio systems and the technology appears to have promise for specialized LAN applications. Packet radio systems can extend networking to ranges beyond cable-based radio frequency systems through the use of

Local Area Networking

III

repeater stations and line-of-sight transmission. Radio-based LANs are subject to *Federal Communications Commission* (FCC) regulatory action because they depend on radio frequency (RF) broadcast transport systems. The FCC has responsibility for spectrum allocation, licensing, and basic technical standards for civilian uses of the radio frequency spectrum in the United States. The *National Telecommunications and Information Agency* (NTIA) has equivalent responsibility for government uses of RF spectrum.

The major parameters of interest in radio frequency systems are *frequency, wavelength* (derived from frequency), *power, modulation, channel access,* and *channel width* (bandwidth). The frequency of a radio wave is expressed by the number of cycles per second (*Hertz,* or *Hz* in current usage). One KHz (Kilohertz) equals 1,000 Hz (Megahertz); one MHz equals 1,000 KHz; and one GHz (Gigahertz) equals 1,000 MHz. Audio frequencies span the range of human hearing and cover the electro-magnetic spectrum from 20 Hz to 20 KHz. Radio frequencies range from 3 KHz to above 30 GHz according to the spectrum allocation shown in table 15.2. The primary usage shown is only a general overview of that spectrum—many services overlap into other than their primary allocations. Certain characteristics of radio transmission are critically dependent on frequency. These include absorption, attenuation, transmission range (also depends on transmitter power), and bandwidth. The frequency at which a transmitting station operates is called its *carrier frequency.*

Table 15.2
Audio and Radio Frequency Spectrum Allocation

Frequency Range	Spectrum Designation	Abbreviation	Primary Usage
20 Hz to 20 KHz	Audio Frequency	AF	Hearing range
3 KHz to 30 KHz	Very Low Frequency	VLF	Submarine broadcast
30 KHz to 300 KHz	Low Frequency	LF	Commercial broadcasting
300 KHz to 3 MHz	Medium Frequency	MF	Commercial AM broadcasting
3 MHz to 30 MHz	High Frequency	HF	Long range communications

Frequency Range	Spectrum Designation	Abbreviation	Primary Usage
30 MHz to 300 MHz	Very High Frequency	VHF	Mobile communictions; TV; commercial FM broadcasting
300 MHz to 3 GHz	Ultra High Frequency	UHF	Mobile communictions; microwave point-to-point
3 GHz to 30 GHz	Super High Frequency	SHF	Microwave point-to-point; satellite communications
30 GHz and Above	Extremely High Frequency	EHF	Satellite communications

Wavelength is derived from frequency according to the following relationship:

```
                    300
Wavelength(Meters) = — — — — — — —
                  frequency (MHz)
```

Wavelength becomes a significant indicator of potential absorption problems because radio waves can be absorbed by material approximately equal to their wavelength. For example, the wavelength of a 10 GHz microwave system is about 1.2 inches, or about the length of some varieties of pine needles. It is reasonable to expect that a 10 GHz microwave signal would have great difficulty penetrating an area containing these types of pine trees.

Power is expressed in *watts* and is a rough indicator of range to be expected from a radio system. *Output power* is measured at the antenna lead of a transmitter. Output power can be concentrated by use of a *directional gain antenna*—in this case, *Effective Radiated Power* (ERP) is measured at a distance of three meters from the antenna. Directional gain antennas put the maximum ERP in a specific direction determined by antenna design and placement. This principal is used extensively in the location and design of microwave point-to-point radio links, which use highly directional drum-type antennas like those utilized by the telephone company and TV stations. Power levels are also critical determinants of whether FCC licensing is

III

Local Area Networking

required for a wireless system. *Spread spectrum wireless transmission* (described later) does not require licensing as long as the output power does not exceed 1 watt. This power can be increased up to 4 watts ERP by use of high gain antennas.

Modulation refers to the method by which the carrier frequency of the transmitter is varied to convey intelligence. The two most common methods are *Amplitude Modulation* (AM), used by broadcast stations operating in the medium frequency band (540 to 1,620 KHz); and *Frequency Modulation* (FM), used by broadcast stations in the very high frequency band (88 to 108 MHz). In AM, intelligence (music, voice, data) is conveyed by varying the amplitude (strength) of the carrier wave, commonly called the *carrier*. In FM, intelligence is transmitted by varying the frequency of the carrier. The simplest type of modulation is *Carrier Wave* (CW), in which the carrier is turned on and off according to the *Morse Code* convention. The notion of modulation also is used in modem technology; common modulation types include *frequency shift keying* (FSK) and *quadrature phase amplitude modulation* (QPAM).

The concept of channel access by multiple stations is as important in wireless systems as it is in copper and fiber-optic systems. AM and FM broadcast stations, as well as several other two-way radio services in the RF spectrum, operate on an exclusive channel assignment basis. These channels are assigned through a *frequency coordination process*, usually done within a local geographic area, and subsequent licensing by the FCC. Shared spectrum systems include cellular, trunked radio, packet radio, and spread spectrum systems. Each of these is described at greater length later in the chapter.

Channel width, or *bandwidth*, describes the width of a frequency range that is used to modulate a carrier signal. Bandwidth is measured from the lowest to the highest frequency used in a radio channel. For example, the bandwidth for FM broadcast stations is 200 Khz—police and public safety two-way, narrowband FM radios use 25 or 30 KHz bandwidths, depending on how a particular service has been defined by the FCC. AM broadcast stations use a 10 KHz bandwidth. For a data transmission system, supported data rates are dependent on the bandwidth used for the network—the higher the bandwidth, the higher the maximum possible data rate.

Wireless LANs are becoming a viable alternative to the more traditional wired systems. A *wireless LAN* can use either *infrared* or *microwave radio* frequencies as the carrier medium; LAN products exist for both technologies. The major operational differences between infrared and microwave are *directionality* and *susceptibility* to interference—infrared requires a fixed line-of-sight path between transmitter and receiver, whereas microwave can use either directional or omnidirectional broadcast patterns. An infrared system is subject to blockage by solid objects, whereas microwave systems are subject to interference from other microwave emitters. Wireless LANs are inherently short range (typically operating within an office complex at distances up to 500–1,000 feet).

Microwave systems can use a single carrier frequency, such as the Motorola Altair Plus *wireless in-building network* (WIN), or spread spectrum, such as Telxon's Arlan, Proxim's RangeLAN, and NCR's WaveLAN. Spread spectrum systems operate on one of three bands allocated by the FCC: 902–928 MHz, 2400–2483.5 MHz, and 5725–5850 MHz. Single frequency systems operate on the *Digital Termination Service* (DTS) band of 18–19 GHz. Spread spectrum systems operate at data rates of up to 250 Kbps, whereas DTS systems can operate up to 15 Mbps.

Spread spectrum systems operate using one of two *code division multiple access* (CDMA) technologies: frequency-hopping, or direct sequence coding. The ultimate objective is the same—to spread the radio energy over a wide spectrum of frequencies. These frequencies fall into one of the three following bands:

✔ 902–928 MHz

✔ 2.4–2.4835 GHz

✔ 5.725–5.825 GHz

Operation in these bands does not require FCC licensing as long as power output does not exceed 1 watt. *Frequency-hopping* spread spectrum is a relatively easy concept; the frequency band allocated is divided into discrete frequency slots. The transmitter changes frequency in a random pattern during each time slot division, as shown in figure 15.1. Each user (transmitter) follows a different frequency-hopping sequence, thus attaining a CDMA capability. *Direct sequence* spread spectrum is somewhat more difficult. Each bit in the data stream is broken into very small signal durations, called *chips*. Each chip is then logically combined with a pseudo-randomly chosen noise pattern with a signaling rate equal to the chip rate. The chip rate is much higher than the data rate and is transmitted over the entire available bandwidth, achieving a spreading of the signal—hence the term *spread spectrum*. The data signal is extracted at the receiver according to the known pseudo-random code. Each transmitter in the spread spectrum band operates with a different pseudo-random noise code, thereby achieving a code division multiple access capability. Figure 15.2 outlines direct sequence spread spectrum.

Wireless systems have been used in metropolitan area networks for some time, particularly in point-to-point applications using 23 GHz microwave systems. These microwave systems use antennas with very narrow beam-widths, requiring precise path alignments and a clear line-of-sight. These microwave systems are popularly used as backbones for carrying high-speed voice, data, and video information, and are typically found on building tops in urban and suburban areas. One common high-speed standard is known as *T-1,* which is a methodology developed by the telephone industry to replace long distance copper transmission systems. T-1 consists of 24 64-Kbps data rate channels, nominally used for 24 digital voice transmissions. The same T-1 system can be configured to carry 24, 56-Kbps data circuits. *Fractional T-1* enables use of subsets of T-1 to provide smaller bandwidth channels for reducing cost when the full T-1 data rate is not required.

Figure 15.1
Frequency-hopping spread spectrum.

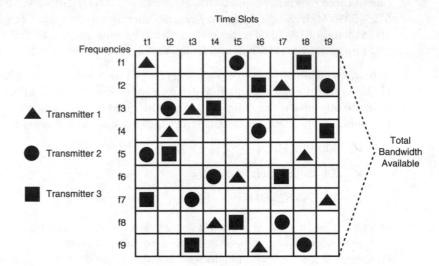

Spread spectrum radio systems are increasingly being used in medium range outdoor applications, formerly the province of microwave systems. With highly directional antennas and appropriate antenna heights, these systems can reach up to three to five miles, with data rates of 128 Kbps and beyond. No licensing is required, making this technology even more popular. These radio systems are cost-effective alternatives to using leased lines and short-haul microwave systems as LAN-to-LAN backbones. These applications are discussed later in this chapter.

Cellular Radio Network

The cellular radio system is currently an analog radio system that in many markets is rapidly approaching its capacity. As this occurs, the cellular industry is gearing up for a conversion to digital radio techniques, which will realize from a three- to twenty-fold increase in channel capacity depending on the digital access scheme used for the conversion. This section focuses on both the current analog system design and its limited data transmission capability, and the industry plans for expansion and increased functionality through digital technology.

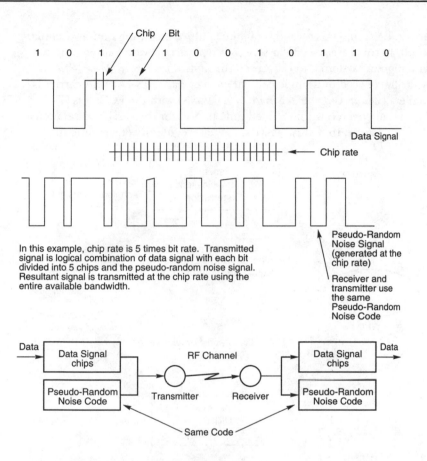

In this example, chip rate is 5 times bit rate. Transmitted signal is logical combination of data signal with each bit divided into 5 chips and the pseudo-random noise signal. Resultant signal is transmitted at the chip rate using the entire available bandwidth.

Figure 15.2
Direct sequence spread spectrum.

Current Analog System

The cellular radio network has been in existence since 1983 when the first system was established in Chicago. Cellular coverage is expanding rapidly from urbanized areas into suburban and rural regions. Each FCC-designated metropolitan area, known as a *Metropolitan Statistical Area* (MSA), has two cellular carriers: a wireline carrier and a non-wireline carrier. The *wireline carrier* is associated with the regulated *Local Exchange Carrier* (LEC) providing primary telephone service for that area; the *non-wireline carrier* can be any other non-regulated entity. For example, in Los Angeles, AirTouch Communications (formerly known as PacTel Cellular) is the wireline carrier. PacTel Cellular was a non-regulated entity of Pacific Telesis who also owns Pacific Bell, the regulated provider of PSTN service in some areas of Los Angeles. Los Angeles Cellular Telephone Company (LA Cellular) is the non-wireline carrier. LA Cellular is owned by a joint venture including McCaw Cellular and Bell South. In rural areas, cellular service is typically provided along or near the Interstate highway system and is licensed through *Rural Service Areas* (RSAs). RSAs are typically covered by a single cellular carrier. Each MSA or RSA carrier is required to file a *Cellular Geographic Service Area* (CGSA) with the FCC; this CGSA must be 75-percent covered within a fixed time period for the carrier to retain its operating license. Figure 15.3 illustrates the cellular regulatory environment.

Figure 15.3
Cellular radio regulatory environment.

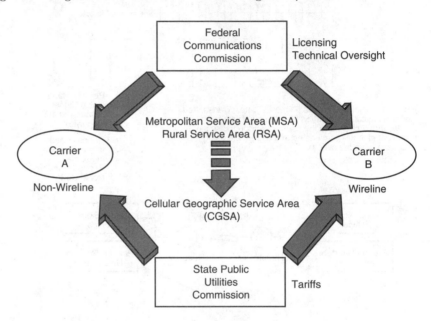

The current cellular system is an analog system, which means that the voice transmissions are not digitized. However, network control is accomplished through the use of high-speed (10 Kbps) digital channels. The cellular system has 832 full-duplex voice and control channels allocated in the 800 MHz radio spectrum. This discussion refers to the cellular system as a cellular *radio* system rather than a cellular *telephone* system. Cellular system characteristics are more influenced by the nature of radio propagation than by the characteristics of the PSTN with which it connects. Cellular radio networks are controlled by a *Mobile Telephone Switching Office* (MTSO) connected to a PSTN Central Office through high-capacity trunk lines. The MTSO in turn is linked to a network of remote cell sites through microwave, fiber-optic, or leased telephone lines. Each cell site is designed to cover a limited area (typically three to five miles in diameter) and has a certain number of voice and control channels assigned. In assigning the cellular radio spectrum, the FCC allocates 416 channels to each of the wireline and non-wireline carriers.

Of these 416 channels, a few are set aside for system control; the remainder are used for two-way voice or data. Figure 15.4 describes the current cellular architecture.

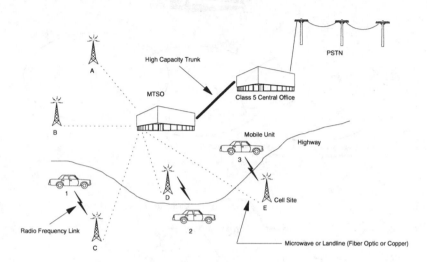

Figure 15.4
Basic cellular radio-telephone operation.

As mobile users drive through an area serviced by a cellular radio network, their vehicles are handed off from cell to cell, as shown in figure 15.5. This handoff procedure introduces some unique challenges for data transmission because of the characteristic signal drop during the handoff. This signal drop is audibly noticeable, but not adverse to successful voice communications. As a result, special modems were developed for data transmission on cellular networks. Even in fixed cellular data applications, the statistical nature of radio propagation dictates robust modem protocol. Special mobile applications rely upon constant real-time data updates while a vehicle is moving, providing a great challenge to cellular data engineering. Several wireless developments are under way that address mobile computing requirements. These are discussed in the remainder of this chapter.

Two of the major enabling technologies used in today's cellular systems are *trunking* and *frequency reuse*—methods used at cell sites to maximize spectrum efficiency. Each cell site has a set number of transceivers, typically varying from 8 to 40. Each transceiver represents one frequency pair, or channel. Cell site controllers take each incoming call request and assign it to the next available transceiver. A full-duplex circuit is then established between the mobile unit and the called party. This constitutes the trunking methodology. Frequency reuse is accomplished by a frequency spatial allocation plan similar to that shown in figure 15.6. The capability to reuse frequencies depends upon the use of low power at the cell sites and a generally low altitude antenna. Unlike conventional radio repeater sites, cell sites are not usually located on high points in a metropolitan area.

III

Local Area Networking

Figure 15.5
Cellular radio
handoff process.

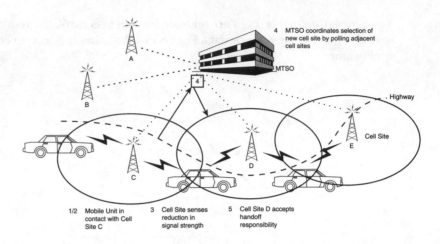

4   MTSO coordinates selection of
    new cell site by polling adjacent
    cell sites

MTSO

Highway

Cell Site

1/2 Mobile Unit in   3 Cell Site senses   5 Cell Site D accepts
     contact with Cell   reduction in   handoff
     Site C   signal strength   responsibility

Figure 15.6
Cellular radio
frequency reuse
pattern.

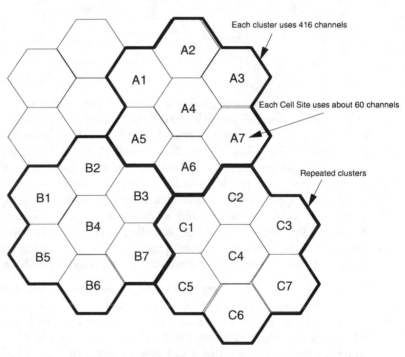

Each cluster uses 416 channels

Each Cell Site uses about 60 channels

Repeated clusters

One of the major issues in the practical use of cellular networks is the coverage
that they offer in a given area. Because cellular radio is an RF system, propagation
can never be predicted with certainty. Fringe areas therefore exist in most coverage
areas. These fringe areas provide low signal margins, making voice and data

transmissions subject to dropouts and fades. To alleviate this problem, cellular carriers use low-cost cellular repeaters designed to fill in coverage in marginal signal areas. A common repeater configuration is to extend the nearest cell site linearly down a freeway or highway (see fig. 15.7). The repeater merely repeats existing channels from a cell site that it can see—no increase in capacity is provided. Another technique found in current systems is the use of microcells. *Microcells* are a further subdivision of cell sites into smaller coverage areas. Microcells are commonly placed in, or near buildings to provide enhanced in-building coverage in certain high-priority coverage areas.

Figure 15.7
Cellular repeater operation—linear highway scenario.

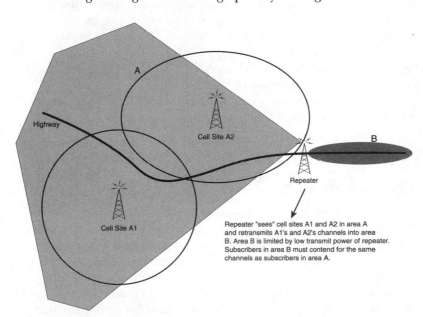

Repeater "sees" cell sites A1 and A2 in area A and retransmits A1's and A2's channels into area B. Area B is limited by low transmit power of repeater. Subscribers in area B must contend for the same channels as subscribers in area A.

The Evolution of Digital Cellular

Because of declining capacity in the larger markets and the paucity of advanced digital services available, the cellular industry has seen the need to convert the cellular radio system from analog to digital. The difficulties in this conversion process are acceptance of a digital standard and determining a marketing strategy to support transition. At least three digital standards are vying for market acceptance (in this case the "market" is the cellular common carriers): *Time Division Multiple Access* (TDMA), *Extended TDMA* (E-TDMA), and *Code Division Multiple Access* (CDMA). TDMA was developed by AT&T; E-TDMA by Hughes Network Systems; and CDMA by Qualcomm. Each of these standards describes a method whereby multiple subscribers can access a single radio channel at the cell site. The FCC has seen fit to allow the marketplace to determine the acceptance of these competing technologies. This stands in stark contrast to the tight standardization imposed upon the current analog cellular industry in the early days of cellular radio.

During the introduction of digital cellular, analog systems will continue to function for a considerable length of time. This has created the need to develop a dual analog/digital mobile transceiver. Current analog transceivers have become a virtual commodity item because the primary revenue generator for the industry is ongoing access and usage fees. The introduction of dual-mode transceivers temporarily changes the economics of system expansion. In market areas such as Los Angeles, New York, Chicago, and Washington DC, digital conversion is anxiously awaited, especially at cell sites that carry the burden of the highest traffic volumes. General consumer acceptance may very well lag behind the technical need, however, because of the almost certain increase in cost. Digital cellular will have to offer significant value-added enhancements in service to overcome traditional market inertia at the outset. These enhancements are likely to be based on an improved data transmission architecture.

Cellular Digital Packet Data (CDPD) Service

The cellular industry has begun to see the need to develop new technology solutions to fuel its high growth rate and to maintain a competitive position in the mobile data market. Some industry observers predict that data will become the predominant mode of mobile communications well before the end of the century. CDPD is a packet-switched technique using the existing RF infrastructure that contrasts with the circuit-switched mode of data transmission currently employed in analog cellular systems. Some significant differences exist between traditional cellular architecture and CDPD (see fig. 15.8). Note that *Mobile Data Base Stations* (MDBSs) will generally be the same cell sites serving current cellular subscribers. The major difference is in the networking between the MDBS and *Mobile Data Intermediate Systems* (MDISs). The latter is generally located within an MTSO facility. The MDBS uses a protocol known as *Digital Sense Multiple Access* (DSMA) to referee access to a single data channel within an MDBS sector. The major difference between classical Ethernet CSMA and DSMA lies in who carries out the referee function. In CSMA, each individual subscriber (adapter card) self-determines access. In DSMA, the MDBS is responsible for this function for all mobile subscribers within its sectors. In this context, a sector equates to a single RF channel.

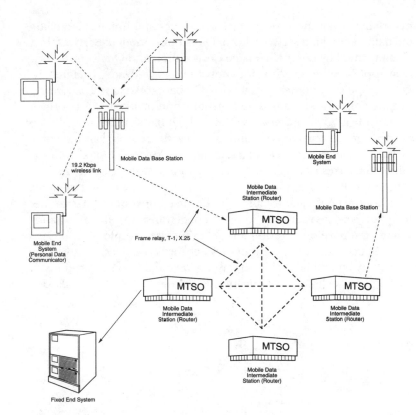

Figure 15.8
Cellular digital packet data (CDPD) architecture.

Satellite-Based Networks

Satellite communications systems have been operational for many years, but the prohibitive cost of building, launching, and supporting such systems keeps their application confined to military and high-volume commercial use. This situation is beginning to change. New satellite component and launching technologies, as well as a growing market for high-volume, wide-area data applications, is driving the emergence of lower-cost systems that eventually will compete favorably with terrestrial networks. The major advantage of satellite systems is their capability to cover areas that cannot be economically covered by terrestrial networks. How quickly critical mass can be achieved to reduce access and subscriber equipment costs to levels competitive with cellular and other existing wireless data networks is yet to be seen.

Several vendors are in the advanced planning stages for establishment of satellite-based voice and data networking services. Loral Qualcomm Satellite Services, Inc., a new corporation formed by Loral Aerospace Corporation and Qualcomm, Inc., has submitted an application to the FCC for Globalstar, a worldwide, satellite-delivered voice and data communications service. Globalstar uses the *Low-Earth Orbit* (LEO) satellite concept, with a planned constellation of 48 satellites worldwide. The orbit altitude is 750 *nautical miles* (NM), which has significantly different characteristics than a geosynchronous satellite system with an orbital altitude of 22,500 NM. Globalstar uses the concept of a satellite as a "super cell-site," with direct connectivity to a terrestrial MTSO. Thus, the MTSO "sees" the satellite system as just another cell site, but with greatly expanded traffic-carrying capability. Figure 15.9 describes the Globalstar architecture in the context of cellular connectivity. Globalstar plans services spanning voice and data transmission, paging and one-way messaging, and position determination. Mobile users would have handheld devices that contain a single number accessing all services, regardless of location. Compatibility is planned for the emerging Personal Communications Service, US CDMA digital cellular, and European GSM digital cellular standards.

Figure 15.9
Globalstar Low Earth Orbiting (LEO) satellite architecture.

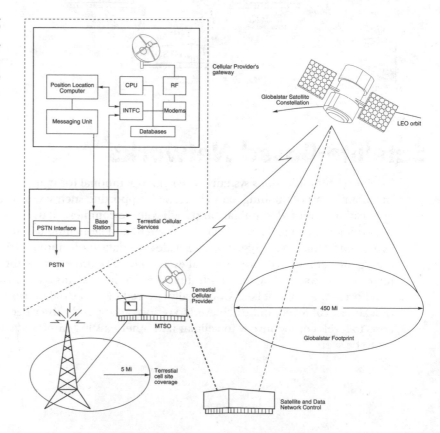

Another provider, Orbital Communications Corporation, is set to launch the first of 26 Orbcomm LEO satellites in 1994, with the remainder scheduled for deployment in late 1995. Unlike Globalstar, the Orbcomm constellation will operate at 425 NM orbital altitude and will offer a more limited form of data-only service. Orbcomm applications will typically be in the area of remote data acquisition, fleet tracking, personal "Mayday" type services, and other applications that use small message sizes. Orbcomm will not be an economical solution for file transfer type applications. The Orbcomm system design is depicted by figure 15.10.

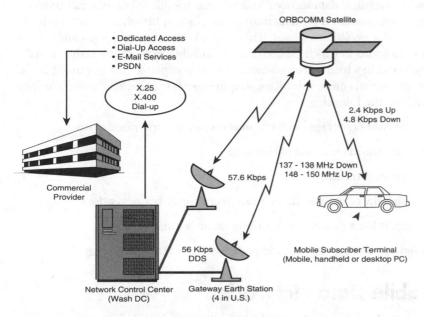

Figure 15.10
Orbcomm Low Earth Orbiting (LEO) satellite architecture.

One obvious advantage of a satellite-based network system is its capability to cover almost all the United States, including thousands of square miles of rural areas not now covered by terrestrial systems. This capability, coupled with the inevitable lower prices resulting from a greatly increased subscriber base, should result in many new mobile applications for wireless networks that are not now feasible. The key to this expansion is the extent and effectiveness of new services provided by cellular carriers and the overall capacity of the satellite-based services. Another key is the economics of producing affordable user terminals that can reliably access the services provided by the satellite segment. The Department of Defense *Global Positioning System* (GPS) provides an excellent example of how these economics work. Early portable GPS systems developed for commercial applications were somewhat bulky and cost upwards of $5,000. In a period of about two years, these systems were routinely priced in the $500-$1,000 range and are now available as

PCMCIA cards for integration into notebook and palmtop computers. It is not at all unlikely that mobile satellite data terminals will also be available in PCMCIA form in the same, or even lower price range, within two years of service availability.

Mobile Data Networks

Because of the perceived inadequacy of the cellular radio network to provide reliable and economical data services, and because traditional mobile radio voice technology is not optimized for data transmission, a new breed of carrier service is emerging, called a *mobile data network*. This network is optimized for packetized data communications in which messages are relatively short (on the order of 512 bytes or less), and in which store-and-forward is an acceptable delivery mode in the absence of interactive communications. Requirements for an effective mobile data network include the following:

✔ Nationwide coverage, with emphasis on major urbanized areas

✔ Pricing based on actual packet usage

✔ Open architecture

✔ Availability of suitable RF modems from a number of vendors

✔ Support for a variety of computing architectures

✔ High-traffic capacity with adequate expansion margin

RAM Mobile Data Network

One such system found in the United States is the Ram Mobile Data network. Ram Mobile Data also is an international system with coverage in the United States, United Kingdom, and Canada; further coverage throughout Europe is planned. Ram Mobile Data uses the Swedish Telecom-developed MOBITEX system, a worldwide standard for mobile data networking.

System Architecture

MOBITEX is a hierarchical system, as shown in figure 15.11. The *Network Control Center* (NCC) is the nationwide hub that provides system-wide control functions and centralized subscription and billing services. The next layer in the hierarchy is the *Main Exchange* (MHX). Main exchanges are regional in scope and provide the connectivity between *Area Exchanges* (MOX) and the NCC. Area Exchanges are generally associated with urban areas and are the connection point for a network

of remote base station sites. Area Exchanges also are used for the direct connection of fixed terminals, as shown in figure 15.11. Base stations provide the basic mobile radio coverage for the area controlled by the Area Exchange.

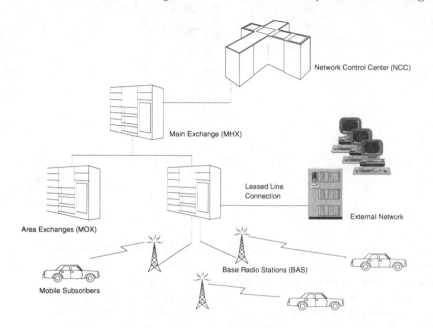

Figure 15.11
MOBITEX hierarchical structure used by RAM Mobile Data.

Base stations are trunked radio systems operating in the 896–901 MHz band for mobile transmission and 935–940 MHz band for mobile receiving. *Trunked radio systems* are a common way to increase the efficiency of spectrum usage. Trunking is used by the cellular radio industry at individual cell sites and by various mobile radio users in the 800 MHz band. Figure 15.12 illustrates the operation of a trunked radio system. In one popular configuration, a central controller at the radio site is connected to several repeaters. A *repeater* is an RF device that receives an incoming transmission on one frequency and transmits (repeats) it on a second frequency. These two frequencies are usually referred to as a *channel pair*. A channel pair is required to support full duplex voice and data operation between mobiles and fixed stations. Each incoming radio transmission causes the controller to search for the next available repeater. In this manner, the frequency spectrum is most efficiently used.

A common analogy for trunking is to consider the advantage of having a single queue that is serviced by many bank tellers, instead of having each teller service his or her own queue. The "controller" in a bank queue is the next individual in line, who determines when the next teller is available and where that teller's window is located.

Figure 15.12
Typical five-
channel trunking
system.

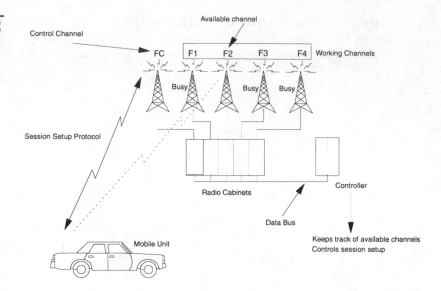

The base station network is similar in many respects to the cellular radio paradigm. The stations are relatively low-powered and employ a frequency reuse scheme. Handoffs are not used, however, because the messages are so short that even a mobile customer would not exit a single coverage area during a transmission. Another major difference between the cellular network and MOBITEX is that cellular uses circuit switching, and MOBITEX uses packet switching. This is a reflection of the voice orientation of cellular radio and the data orientation of MOBITEX.

System Operations

Subscribers gain access to the network through radio connectivity to the nearest base station or by wireline access to the Area Exchange as described earlier. When a subscriber activates a connection to the network through one of these means, they are registered on the system. Datagram packets with maximum information of 512 bytes are the fundamental unit of data packaging. Longer messages with multiple 512-byte packets are possible, but the user is responsible for transport layer implementation to ensure end-to-end reliability and sequencing. The basic message packet structure contains sender, addressee, packet type, distribution list, and timestamp headers.

All messages are routed to the destination using the lowest possible layer of the network. If the source and destination are registered on the same base station, a message between them goes no higher than the base station. Base stations communicate their registered users to a common Area Exchange; Area Exchanges communicate their consolidated users to a common Main Exchange; and the NCC

maintains an active list of all users registered on the system through communications with all connected Main Exchanges.

The types of subscribers include the following:

- ✔ Mobile terminals
- ✔ Fixed terminals
- ✔ Individuals
- ✔ Groups

The following services are provided by the MOBITEX system:

- ✔ ASCII text messages
- ✔ User-defined data messages
- ✔ Higher-protocol (HP) messages
- ✔ One-byte status messages (256 predefined messages)
- ✔ Group messages
- ✔ Closed user groups
- ✔ Password protection for individual subscribers (required)
- ✔ Store-and-forward messaging

Messages can be sent to a specific destination, to several specific destinations, or to a group of destinations identified by a group number. Fixed and mobile terminals can have up to seven individual subscribers logged in simultaneously. A single individual subscriber can only log in to a single terminal, however. A single fixed or mobile terminal can belong to a maximum of 15 groups. Group messages are restricted to the area served by a single Area Exchange. The search area within that exchange cannot exceed eight base stations and/or fixed terminals. Subscribers can belong to a maximum of eight closed user groups. A closed group is used for enhanced security and precludes its members from communicating outside the group.

The system allows for store-and-forward operations, which may be necessitated by the destination not being registered or by loss of radio contact between the mobile subscriber and a base station. Subscribers have mail boxes that can store up to ten messages for periods from 12 to 24 hours depending on how the system is set up. The message format provides for timestamps that enable the network to indicate the time of receipt. This time is used in the store-and-forward mode to indicate message storage duration. The network also updates all active subscribers with current network time.

Terminal Protocol

Fixed terminals communicate with the Area Exchange at layers 1 and 2 of the OSI model. The allowed protocols include the following:

✔ HDLC (CCITT X.21bis at layer 1, HDLC at layer 2); maximum data rate of 64 Kbps

✔ X.25 (X.21bis at layer 1, X.25 at layer 2); maximum data rate of 64 Kbps

✔ IBM Binary Synchronous Communication (X.21bis at layer 1, BSC at layer 2); maximum data rate of 2,400 bps

✔ MOBITEX Asynchronous Communication (CCITT V.24 at layer 1, MASC at layer 2); maximum data rate of 2,400 bps

✔ Other protocols, such as IBM's SNA 3270, are supported through X.25 gateways.

Fixed terminals can be connected to more than one Area Exchange if the user's application requires extra redundancy or connectivity. The system also accommodates external network connections to the Area Exchange. These connections are accommodated through gateways at the Area Exchange and include other X.25 networks, SNA networks, and similar types of WAN architecture.

Mobile terminals include vehicular, portable, and handheld devices connected to an 8-Kbps radio modem. Mobile terminals communicate at the data link layer using a method based on the slotted ALOHA protocol. Mobile terminals continuously monitor a system channel for network operating parameters and permission to transmit. The mobile terminal is responsible for monitoring signal quality at the base station. When the mobile terminal desires to switch base stations, it transmits a <ROAM> signal to the new base station to inform the network of its change in connectivity.

Ardis

Ardis is the evolutionary outgrowth of the radio data network that Motorola installed for the IBM field service force in the early 1980s. This network was designed for field service engineers to enhance their connectivity with home offices for crucial functions such as inventory control, service call tracking, and e-mail. This network grew into a commercial venture called the *Data Radio Network* operating in New York, Los Angeles, and Chicago, primarily serving local governments and other field service organizations. In April 1990, IBM and Motorola agreed to form a new corporation called Ardis to be 50-percent-owned by each party. Ardis is designed to serve field service and repair personnel; transportation companies such as courier and overnight shipping services; public safety agencies

such as police, fire, and emergency medical services; insurance claims representatives; and field sales forces.

Ardis Network Design

The Ardis network differs somewhat from its competitor, RAM Mobile Data, in that it is built on a standard Motorola data radio architecture that includes over 1,200 radio base stations in over 400 metropolitan areas, and 31 Radio Frequency/ Network Control Processors (RF/NCPs) strategically located around the country. The RF/NCPs are connected in turn to four message switches located in Lincolnshire, IL, Lexington, KY, Glenrock, NJ, and Los Angeles. User equipment consists of mobile subscriber terminals that contain three functional components: an RF modem, an intelligent terminal device, and applications software. The system also supports connectivity between the message switch and a customer's host computer system. The customer's host can be a single PC, a LAN gateway, or a mainframe.

The base stations use the 800 MHz frequency spectrum, in the general vicinity of, but not overlapping or interfering with cellular radio systems. The radio network supports a full-duplex data channel that transmits data in both directions at 4,800 Bps. The data transmission protocol is a proprietary Motorola protocol called *MDC-4800.* The base stations are designed with overlapping coverage to provide a robust in-building coverage pattern over the areas served. A somewhat greater coverage area exists for standard mobile operation. A major difference from the MOBITEX-based RAM Mobile Data Network is the use of a single RF frequency in a particular metropolitan area. RAM uses trunked multiple frequencies in a particular coverage area. All base stations are connected to RF/NCPs through a leased line telephone network.

The RF/NCP performs several functions, including the following:

✔ Maintenance of subscriber registration information

✔ Maintenance of last-known position information of mobile subscribers

✔ Transmission of ACK/NAK protocol messages to the message switch to facilitate flow and error control of message packets

✔ Performance of diagnostic routines on the network and transmission of alarm messages to the network management system

An extensive communications network connects base stations to RF/NCPs; RF/ NCPs to message switches; message switches to each other; and customer host equipment to message switches. This network consists of high-speed leased lines, intelligent multiplexers, Data Service Units (DSUs), and modems. Modems are primarily leased line equipment but have a dial-up (switched line) capability in the event of leased line failures.

Customer Equipment

Customer equipment can consist of a variety of configurations. Motorola sells a mobile radio modem, the MRM-420. This modem connects to any standard computing device with an RS-232C data port such as a laptop PC. The modem has an integrated 800 MHz full-duplex radio, operating in the Ardis standard frequency band. The radio portion also supports transmission and reception on the 450–470 MHz UHF band for special applications. Motorola also provides the Envoy handheld communicator. This device is designed as a *Personal Digital Assistant* (PDA) and contains an integrated radio modem, the Magic Cap operating system, and the Telescript communications language. The radio modem is the same as that used in the MRM-420. These modems use the Motorola 4800 Bps air interface standard.

Magic Cap, from General Magic Corporation, is an operating system/utility environment especially designed for PDA equipment. General Magic's Telescript communications language ushers in the concept of using "agents" to perform remote tasks. An *agent* is an interpreted program transmitted to a remote machine that can, in effect, execute the user's desired action on that machine. The results are then returned to the user through the wireless network. This paradigm is a superior means of accomplishing remote tasks in comparison to a standard client-server dialog of request/response, particularly in the limited data rate environment characteristic of wireless networks. Telescript and the Envoy also work on RAM mobile data and SkyTel wide-area-paging networks.

Perhaps the most versatile Ardis customer equipment is the IBM 9075 PCradio. This device is a full-capability, Thinkpad notebook PC with a data radio modem (4,800 to 19,200 bps), landline FAX (2,400 bps), and cellular FAX (9,600 bps) capability built in. Applications software includes the PCradio Radio Frequency Communications Manager and IBM Personal Communications/3270. The latter enables 3270 connectivity through wireless data networks, such as Ardis. A similar, but much smaller device is the *Poquet Communicating Computer* (PCC). The PCC has a built-in 9,600 bps modem designed for transmission over landlines or cellular radio and a 4,800 bps mobile radio modem compatible with the Ardis network.

Customer equipment can be connected to the message switches through direct leased lines or *Value Added Networks* (VANs). Regardless of the type of connection, the following protocols are supported:

- ✔ LU 6.2
- ✔ X.25
- ✔ SNA 3270
- ✔ Bisync 3270

✔ Bisync Point-to-Point

✔ Asynchronous

System Expansion

Ardis system expansion includes a 70- percent increase in the number of base stations to improve radio coverage reliability in major market areas, and an increase in data transmission rates up to 19,200 bps in the 30 largest markets. The system also implements automatic roaming capability to enable users' terminals to be recognized in any of the 400 metropolitan areas served by Ardis.

Nextel

The *Specialized Mobile Radio* (SMR) industry has long been dominated by many small operators offering private dispatch and telephone interconnect services to a wide variety of business customers. SMR systems are typically operated as trunked systems in the 800 and 900 MHz bands. Mountaintop antenna sites have always been a premium asset in the SMR industry, because SMR base station and repeater sites operate best with high altitude sites and high power to cover wide areas. Frequency allocations in a geographic area typically are spread among several operators. In high volume markets, SMR licenses are a valuable commodity.

Nextel is an outgrowth of the SMR industry and, through a series of acquisitions of SMR operators and their licenses, now is the dominant player in the new *Enhanced SMR* (ESMR) industry. Nextel was originally known as Fleet Call and began by acquiring SMR licenses in New York, Los Angeles, Chicago, Dallas, Houston, and San Francisco. The acquisition of Dispatch Communications added new markets in the Northeast, Midwest, and Southwest. Motorola then sold Nextel 2,500 frequencies in 21 states. Additional acquisitions added coverage in San Diego, Las Vegas, and Midwest markets. Nextel also owns a major interest in other large ESMR operations such as CenCall, with extensive Rocky Mountain coverage; and Dial Page, which covers nine Southeastern states. The first Nextel network operation began in Southern California in August 1993, with coverage in Los Angeles and points north to Santa Barbara, east to Palm Springs, and south to northern San Diego County.

Nextel's rapid rise to prominence in the ESMR market is based on its successful effort to change fundamental FCC rules regarding the offering of SMR service. The FCC allowed Nextel to build wide-area digital SMR systems with cellular-like characteristics. This required a change in the old FCC rule that prohibited reuse of SMR frequencies within 110 miles of a tower site. Enhanced SMR systems use multiple low-power sites and employ frequency reuse just as is done in cellular systems. ESMR offers a greater variety of services, however, and unlike cellular systems, has features that appeal to the several million private dispatch users in the

United States. These dispatch users encompass both the private and public sectors, from businesses and utilities to local government public safety services.

The technology base for Nextel is the *Motorola Integrated Radio System* (MIRS). MIRS is closely related to the European GSM digital cellular standard. MIRS uses 4.2 Kbps to digitally encode speech, compared to the current TDMA digital voice standard of 7.9 Kbps. Therefore, six voice channels can fit into one 25 KHz SMR channel. In fact, the air interface standard (affecting linkage between mobile subscribers and base stations) compresses 64 Kbps of bandwidth into a 25 KHz radio channel. MIRS technology offers ESMR operators the capability to offer the following services:

✔ Digital voice

✔ Dispatch service with automatic roaming

✔ Packet-switched data (not yet available, but planned in 1995)

✔ Circuit-switched data (4.8 Kbps per user)

✔ Message mail (up to 140 alphanumeric characters—similar to RAM, Ardis, and Orbcomm systems)

Nextel's ESMR service initially looks very much like the forerunner of PCS, with a variety of services that can be offered through a single, multifunction handset. The handset family from Nextel can function as a normal mobile telephone, an alphanumeric pager and messaging device, and a dispatch terminal. The MIRS technology will compete with CDMA in the PCS marketplace. The only component lacking to provide common nationwide coverage is a means to offer service in more remote rural areas. For this, satellite coverage is currently the only feasible option.

Mobile Data Networks Versus Cellular Radio

An inevitable comparison must be made between the capability of dedicated data networks and the cellular radio service to handle the data transmission needs of business users (see table 15.3). Note, however, that with the entrance of Nextel and CDPD into the mobile data market, these distinctions may become somewhat blurred.

Personal Communications Service (PCS)

You probably are familiar with the standard cordless telephones used in many homes for wireless access to the PSTN. These phones provide a degree of freedom from the length of a telephone wire, but they still tie the caller to a specific, location-dependent telephone number. Extending this technology so that it provides voice and data regardless of where a person is—at home, traveling, or at work—and works with a single phone number that goes where the person goes defines the commonly-held vision of the *Personal Communications Service* (PCS).

The earliest realization of the PCS concept was in the United Kingdom with a service called *Cordless Telephone-Second Generation* (CT-2). CT-2 uses the Telepoint concept, which can be thought of as a short-range, wireless telephone booth system. Major limitations to the CT-2 concept include the following:

✔ Inability to hand off calls from one telepoint terminal to another

✔ Range limitation

✔ Inability to accommodate incoming calls

The first two limitations mean that CT-2 calls must be made from relatively fixed locations, which clearly delineates CT-2 and the mobile cellular services. Another standard is emerging in Europe known as CT-3, which is targeted to the wireless PBX market. CT-3 supports handoffs as well as two-way calling. CT-3 also supports integration with ISDN, thus making low-speed data services available.

Table 15.3
Comparison of Mobile Data Network to Cellular Radio

Mobile Data Networks	Cellular
Multi-function network	Primarily designed for voice communications
Digital technology	Currently analog technology (conversion to digital in future)
Nationwide coverage in urban and suburban areas Seamless networking	Nationwide coverage including many rural areas Some carriers have seamless networking
High data rates supported	Relatively low data rates
Multiple host connections	Limited host connections
Standard interface to Ardis, RAM, and Nextel networks	No single standard for modem to telephone interface

continues

Table 15.3, Continued
Comparison of Mobile Data Network to Cellular Radio

Mobile Data Networks	Cellular
Error-free transmission inherent in architecture	Architecture not designed for error-free data transmission
Store-and-forward operations	No store-and-forward capability
Optimized for in-building and portable coverage	Some providers not optimized for in-building and portable coverage
Software applications available	No software applications available
Billed on actual bytes sent	Billed on connect time basis
No long distance charges	Long distance and roaming charges incurred on some calls
Efficient for short, bursty data transfers	Better suited for longer data packets
Coverage expansion limited to radio infrastructure	With satellite expansion, terrestrial coverage could be common nationwide

The FCC began hearings on PCS in July 1989. In October 1990, the FCC received over 100 responses from the Notice of Inquiry into the establishment of new Personal Communications Services. Clearly significant interest exists in how these services are to be defined and regulated by virtually every segment of the telecommunications industry. The major regulatory issues involve spectrum allocation and access technology.

The FCC has allocated 360 MHz of spectrum to provide adequate PCS in general conformance with the domestic telecommunications policy of having multiple licensees within defined service areas. This PCS band will be located between 1,850 and 2,210 MHz (1.85–2.21 GHz). This same spectrum range encompasses much of the long-haul microwave services, which will be encouraged to move elsewhere. Not surprisingly, many microwave system licensees are unhappy over the cost and effort required to switch to new microwave spectrum. This spectrum will be allocated in an auction process scheduled to begin as this book goes to press. PCS licenses will be granted for *Basic Trading Areas* (BTAs) and *Major Trading Areas* (MTAs). The difference in the two types of licenses is in the area and population

base covered. PCS auction rules will allow multiple bids to provide the opportunity for potential service providers to acquire regional and nationwide licenses. Three preferential "pioneer" licenses were awarded in early 1994 for MTAs in Southern California, the New York metropolitan area, and the Washington-Baltimore metropolitan area to three companies that invested heavily in development of PCS technology—Cox Cable, Omnipoint, and American Personal Communications. Each of these companies provided a major contribution to PCS technology.

One of the major goals of PCS is to provide personal telephone numbers that can be used by an individual regardless of location. The current system of assigning telephone numbers links these numbers to instruments at fixed locations. The major challenge for this new scheme is one of database management. For the personal phone number system to work, the number must be recognizable and billable independent of the caller's location.

In a sense, PCS will compete with the new digital cellular technology, not for spectrum allocation, but for the capability to provide common low cost wireless access for voice and data services. Many cellular common carriers dispute this assertion, saying that instead, PCS is a natural extension of the services provided by the cellular industry. They point to the fact that many carriers are now using microcell technology, including the capability to provide reliable cellular service within buildings. Likewise, the PSTN industry correctly asserts that PCS must ultimately rely on the existing wireline system, as does the cellular network.

Wireless LANs

Wireless local area networks, or as they are sometimes called, *local area wireless networks* (LAWNs), have achieved a certain degree of maturity in the LAN marketplace, despite their relative newness to the LANscape. Several products and at least two major technology options are available: radio-based and infrared-based systems. An established market for such LANs exists, and they represent one of few existing forms of wireless networking. In 1990, the IEEE 802 Project formed the 802.11 Working Group to establish standards for wireless LANs.

Two compelling reasons for installing a wireless LAN are the need for rapid, but temporary deployment of a LAN, and the growing presence of laptops in the office environment. Although excellent products are available that enable laptops to connect to existing LANs, the need to connect to a fixed point is anathema to the idea of portable computing. The potentially high cost of wiring in certain building environments is another reason to investigate wireless technology. This reason requires a much more thorough analysis of the economic and operational trade-offs. A realistic scenario includes the combination of wired and wireless LANs in an office environment.

III

Local Area Networking

Radio-Based LANs

Radio-based LANs can be designed to operate on fixed frequencies or by using a technique called *spread spectrum*. Fixed- frequency systems require FCC licensing. Motorola, long accustomed to seeking spectrum allocations from the FCC, has received licenses for a minimum of one two-frequency channel in the 18.825 to 19.205 GHz band for all metropolitan areas in the United States with a population greater than 30,000. These licenses entitle Motorola to operate exclusively in this band within a 17.5 mile radius in all the approved areas.

Motorola is the primary supplier of systems using fixed frequencies. The Motorola Altair Plus *Wireless In-Building Network* (WIN) system operates in the 18.820 to 18.870 and 19.160 to 19.210 GHz bands using low-power radios (25 milliwatts). The Altair system requires licensing by the FCC—a process that Motorola handles for its customers. Figure 15.13 shows the Altair architecture in the context of a typical cubicle type office space. The primary components are a single Control Module and a number of User Modules. The Control Module acts as the central transmitter for a microcell. Each microcell can contain up to 50 Ethernet devices. The User Modules can be connected to as many as eight workstations or other Ethernet devices. The Control Module can be connected to a wired Ethernet segment or to a file server with an Ethernet adapter using standard BNC (ThinNet), AUI (ThickNet), or UTP connections. The User Modules are connected to their devices through BNC or UTP wired connections. An Altair Plus network typically supports an area of 5,000 to 50,000 ft^2 depending on building construction.

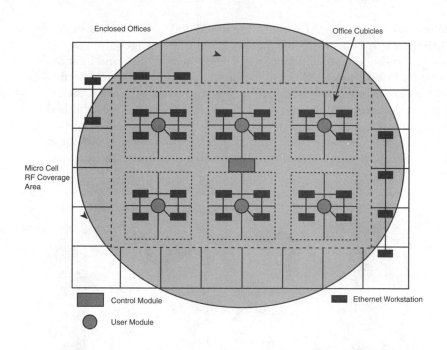

Figure 15.13
Motorola's Altair Plus II Wireless In-building Network (WIN) topology.

A major problem with RF transmissions in the 18 GHz spectrum is multipath propagation. *Multipath propagation* results when radio waves bounce off solid objects in different directions and recombine out of phase at the receiver to cause distortion and fading. Motorola solved this problem through the use of six-sector electronically-scanned antenna beams. Each RF unit (Control Module or User Module) has six 60-degree antenna sectors, providing up to 36 different signal paths between any two RF units. High-speed electronic logic determines the optimum sector for signal reception and switches antenna sectors appropriately.

The capability to support full 10 Mbps Ethernet in an RF environment is made possible by custom chip design within the RF units. The primary elements of an RF unit consist of a high-performance RF *Digital Signal Processor* (DSP), a Gallium Arsenide-based miniaturized radio transceiver, and a high speed packet switch on a single *Complementary Metal Oxide Semiconductor* (CMOS)- based chip. The electronics package in an RF unit uses *Very Large Scale Integration* (VLSI) and *Application Specific Integrated Circuit* (ASIC) technology. These technologies have enabled what would not have been considered feasible just five years ago. At a signaling rate of 7.5 MHz and a modulation scheme that supports 2 bits/Hz, a gross data rate of 15 Mbps is possible. This gross data rate supports a net data rate of 10 Mbps after taking overhead into account. The maximum effective throughput on the RF link is 3.3 Mbps.

III

Local Area Networking

Motorola uses the same technology to provide the Altair VistaPoint inter-building wireless Ethernet link. Four additional pieces of equipment are required to establish a wireless building-to-building link: A *Main Module* (MM) and its antenna assembly, and a *Remote Module* (RM) and its antenna assembly. Antenna assemblies can be located inside or outside a building as long as they are pointed at each other. A green light on the MM or on the RM indicates that a link is established. The modules attach to a wired Ethernet segment. A VistaPoint installation is illustrated in figure 15.14. Filter tables on each module hold up to 1,000 Ethernet addresses and function to isolate traffic as desired on either side of the wireless link.

Figure 15.14

Motorola Altair VistaPoint inter-building architecture.

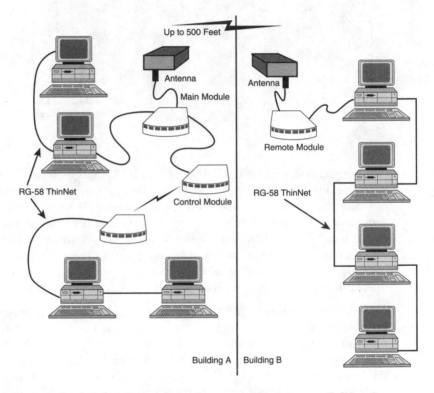

Some of the initial vendors offering spread spectrum systems are California Microwave, Proxim, Inc., O'Neill Communications, Windata, Inc., NCR, and Telesystems, SLW Inc. California Microwave has a system called Radiolink, which is a frequency-hopping system. The data rate for this LAN is 250 Kbps, and the maximum range is 1,000 feet. Performance figures for the Proxim and O'Neill systems are similar. NCR's WaveLAN and Telesystems SLW's Advanced Radio LAN (ARLAN) use the direct sequence methodology and feature higher data rates on the order of 1–2 Mbps.

A WaveLAN network is a peer-to-peer architecture, in contrast to Motorola's centralized Altair system. WaveLAN operates in the 902–928 MHz band. The WaveLAN network adapter card is a typical expansion card—the external antenna connects to the adapter by a five-foot cable. Ranges from 100 to 400 feet are possible within a typical office environment. WaveLAN uses a CSMA/CA access protocol at the physical and data link layers. Bridging between wired LANs and WaveLAN in a Novell LAN is accomplished with two or more adapter cards in a Novell server with the appropriate bridge software. Third-party vendors offer bridging and hub functionality for WaveLAN. A remote bridge is available that links two wired Ethernets at distances of up to three miles. Figure 15.5 shows a WaveLAN configuration.

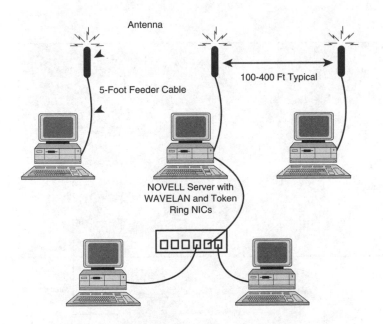

Figure 15.15
WAVELAN architecture showing bridging to a wire Token Ring network.

ARLAN also operates in the 902–928 MHz band and is a peer-to-peer network. ARLAN offers a Wireless Ethernet Hub that connects to a wired Ethernet segment and a wireless Ethernet bridge. The bridge can provide a wireless link between two wired Ethernet segments because it operates at the MAC layer level. An ARLAN Ethernet Hub acts similarly to an Altair Control Module because it can establish a small microcell by linking to other ARLAN adapters. Figure 15.16 depicts a typical ARLAN installation.

Infrared-Based Wireless LANs

A major supplier for IBM-compatible infrared LANs is InfraLAN. Unlike WaveLAN, ARLAN, or Altair, InfraLAN is based on the 802.5 Token Ring access protocol. An InfraLAN base unit looks like a Token Ring MAU, except that it only has six ports rather than the usual eight. These six ports accommodate up to six attached PCs using standard IBM Type 1 cable. Two optical nodes attach to the base unit. These nodes provide the standard ring-in, ring-out function with adjacent base units. A wired Token Ring can be connected to a base unit by configuring ports 1 or 6 as a ring-in or ring-out, respectively. A typical multi-LAN InfraLAN installation is depicted in figure 15.17. Base units can be separated by up to 80 feet in a typical office environment. Because infrared is a strict line-of-sight system, installation of optical nodes as high as feasible in the office is recommended. Otherwise, people moving around in the office would cause light beam blockage and a resulting loss of data. InfraLAN operates with either 4 Mbps or 16 Mbps Token Ring LANs.

Figure 15.16
ARLAN architecture showing configuration of Ethernet hubs.

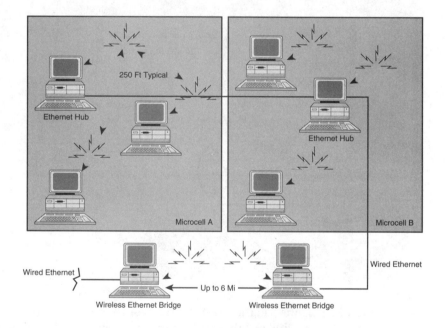

The Wireless Vision—A Case Study

Most people who live in urban areas are all-too-familiar with the adverse effects of increasing traffic congestion. Lost time in traffic jams reduces overall productivity. Congestion breeds lower air quality, increased accident rates, and loss of mobility. The Minnesota Guidestar program is an innovative public-private partnership designed to attack these problems in the Minneapolis-St. Paul metropolitan area. Several elements of the Guidestar program have become field operational tests sponsored by the Federal Highway Administration. One of these is the Genesis

Project. Genesis is designed to provide traveler information through a variety of wired and wireless accessible databases. These databases are maintained by public agencies who have access to a variety of traffic sensors that can determine areas of congestion. The databases also contain data on availability of alternative modes of transportation such as transit and ridesharing systems and various hazardous weather phenomena.

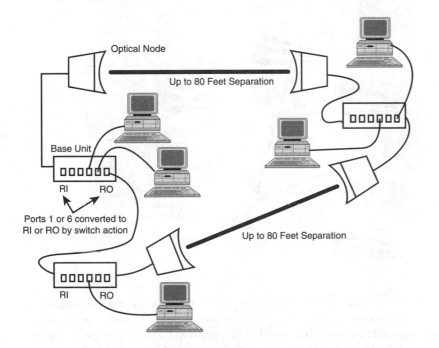

Figure 15.17
Architecture for InfraLAN infrared LAN.

Wired access is through standard modem ports that can be dialed into from any available PC. Wireless access is through laptops, notebooks, alphanumeric pagers, and Personal Digital Assistants. Wireless dissemination also can be through one-way paging systems. Satellite connectivity is possible in the future, particularly if the need arises to reach more remote areas of the state. Figure 15.18 shows the Genesis architecture. The Fixed End portion of the system consists of a standard wired LAN with external gateways to various data suppliers. Other gateways connect the Fixed End LAN to communications services providers such as cellular, paging, and e-mail carriers. The communications carriers collectively provide the Mobile End of the Genesis system.

Mobile End users have access to a variety of functions, the availability of which depends on whether they have access to PDAs, notebooks, or pagers. Users can enter profiles such as pre- and post-trip durations, trip routes, trip frequency, and scheduled times for trips. Based on user profiles, the Fixed End system then

III

Local Area Networking

provides trip status, travel duration advisory, real-time incident advisories, planned event advisories, alternate mass transit routes available, and can even forecast route delays. Users also can request detailed transit route, schedule, and fare information.

Figure 15.18

Genesis project Fixed End and Mobile End architecture.

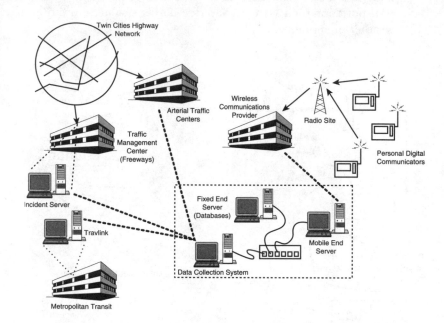

The Fixed End system will be connected to a variety of data sources including the Minneapolis and Golden Valley traffic systems (arterial traffic status), the Minnesota Department of Transportation Traffic Management Center (freeway incident data), and another Minnesota Guidestar system called Travlink (transit data). Travlink derives its real-time transit status information from *automatic vehicle location* (AVL) systems on transit vehicles. The Traffic Management Center derives its data from a network of ramp meter devices, surveillance cameras, and traffic lane detectors. Systems such as this also can use "probe" vehicles equipped with AVL to determine current travel times between key points in the highway network. The probe vehicles typically communicate real-time position data to the TMC through a packet data network such as RAM or Ardis.

In operation, the Genesis system works as depicted in the following scenario. Mr. Campbell, a sales manager working in downtown Minneapolis, lives several miles away from Center City. On certain days, his commute downtown is slowed by adverse weather conditions and non-recurring incidents, as well as normal freeway congestion. When his personal auto is not required at work, Mr. Campbell takes an available transit route in preference to driving himself. As part of each day's user profile, Mr. Campbell enters his travel destination, desired time of arrival, and

preferred mode of travel. His *personal communications device* (PCD) has alternate routes and modes of travel stored, based on his entered preferences. In the morning, his PCD provides a wake-up alarm in sufficient time to enable him to get to work based on the current travel conditions.

When Mr. Campbell begins his commute trip, the PCD alerts him to any occurring incidents and recommends alternate routes depending on his stored preferences. If he needs to travel to the airport or around town on business trips, local travel conditions for that time of day are provided, along with estimated travel times and alternative routing as necessary. Likewise, on the return commute from work to home, Mr. Campbell receives an alarm to leave work based on any evening engagements and the evening rush hour traffic conditions.

Summary

This chapter describes the salient features of wireless networking and its impact on networking in general. Several wireless systems were discussed including cellular, wireless data networks, the Personal Communications Service, and wireless LANs. Clearly wireless technology is here to stay and its ultimate impact is limited more by regulation and economics than by technology. Today's society is increasingly mobile; an established need exists to move computing power to the "scene of action." This phenomenon drives the expansion of wireless services that can seamlessly connect portable computing devices to a variety of existing wireless and wireline networks. Dragging along acoustic couplers for a portable computer and looking for the nearest telephone booth will become events of the past. Whether wireless networking can fulfill what appears to be a limitless potential depends largely on a number of challenging regulatory, economic, and institutional issues.

The wireless industry is currently undergoing rapid growth and is constantly changing direction. What seems clear, however, is that consumer choices for mobile data transmission will increase greatly in the next five years, and that the cost for wireless access will decrease as the number of mobile users grows. PCMCIA cards will become the preferred packaging for a wide variety of mobile products including one-way paging and messaging, two-way data transfer, position determination using the Global Positioning System (GPS) navigational satellite constellation, and voice communications. Remote accessibility will become more common as the new, lower cost Low-Earth-Orbiting satellite systems become a reality. The decade of the 1990s will see a significant expansion of our capability to compute and network from virtually any location. The wireless world that is rapidly taking shape promises a quantum leap in personal connectivity that you only could dream about five years ago.

III

Local Area Networking

Part IV

Appendixes

APPENDIX

ASCII Character Set

What Morse Code was to the telegraph operator, computer communication codes and controls are to the PC. They are a standard sequence of signals that can be translated into meaningful information by recipients. Without standardization of these signals, however, significant incompatibilities between equipment made by different vendors would have developed. Fortunately for the PC user, there are standards for character codes and communication controls that have kept many of these potential problems from developing.

There are two predominant character codes currently in use in the United States. The *American Standard Code for Information Interchange*, or ASCII (pronounced askey), is by far the most widely used character code throughout the world. The IBM-developed *Extended Binary Coded Decimal Interchange Code*, or EBCDIC (pronounced ebb-see-dick), is the other major code and is used for communication between and with all IBM mini- and mainframe computer equipment. There is also a third code, called the *Baudot code*, in use on older communications equipment. The characteristics and applications of each of these codes are discussed in this appendix and in Appendixes B, C and D. Because of the predominant use of the ASCII code in communications, that code is explored in detail in this appendix and in Appendix B, "Communication Controls."

The ASCII character set is the most universally used convention for the encoding of alphanumeric characters and is a new twist for IBM equipment. Before the introduction of the IBM line of personal computers, all IBM equipment except the System/34 minicomputer used the IBM-developed EBCDIC character set as a standard interchange code.

IBM and Microsoft originally selected ASCII for the IBM PC because of its international acceptance. The first 128 characters of the IBM PC ASCII character set are defined by the ANSI *X3.4-1977 (Revised 1983), Code for Information Interchange.* Two other world standards organizations have published almost identical character codes, further ensuring ASCII as an international standard for communications between computers from different vendors. The other two standards are: *Alphabet Number 5* of the *International Consultive Committee for Telephone and Telegraph* (CCITT); and *Standard Number 646, 7-Bit Coded Character Set for Information Processing* of the *International Standards Organization* (ISO).

Almost all American computer hardware companies and many foreign hardware producers support the ASCII code, which places the PC in an excellent community of standardized communications hardware and software. Participation in communication networks using commercially available hardware and software is assured because of this standardized code usage.

A translation table showing the binary coding of the standard 7-bit ASCII character set is shown in figure A.1. The characters included in this set are 26 uppercase letters, 26 lowercase letters, 10 numbers, and other special text characters found on most typewriter keyboards. A set of standard communication control codes is also provided and is discussed in detail in Appendix B.

Figure A.1
Standard ASCII character set.

								0	0	0	0	1	1	1	1
								0	0	1	1	0	0	1	1
								0	1	0	1	0	1	0	1
7	6	5	4	3	2	1									
x	x	x	0	0	0	0		NUL	DLE	SP	0	@	P	'	p
x	x	x	0	0	0	1		SOH	DC1	!	1	A	Q	a	q
x	x	x	0	0	1	0		STX	DC2	"	2	B	R	b	r
x	x	x	0	0	1	1		ETX	DC3	#	3	C	S	c	s
x	x	x	0	1	0	0		EOT	DC4	$	4	D	T	d	t
x	x	x	0	1	0	1		ENQ	NAK	%	5	E	U	e	u
x	x	x	0	1	1	0		ACK	SYN	&	6	F	V	f	v
x	x	x	0	1	1	1		BEL	ETB	'	7	G	W	g	w
x	x	x	1	0	0	0		BS	CAN	(	8	H	X	h	x
x	x	x	1	0	0	1		HT	EM	)	9	I	Y	i	y
x	x	x	1	0	1	0		LF	SUB	*	:	J	Z	j	z
x	x	x	1	0	1	1		VT	ESC	+	;	K	[	k	{
x	x	x	1	1	0	0		FF	FS	,	<	L	\	l	|
x	x	x	1	1	0	1		CR	GS	–	=	M	]	m	}
x	x	x	1	1	1	0		SO	RS	.	>	N	^	n	~
x	x	x	1	1	1	1		SI	US	/	?	O	_	o	DEL

The standard ASCII characters shown in figure A.1 can be represented by seven data bits, but the special ASCII extension characters developed by IBM and Microsoft for the IBM PC require eight data bits. Seven data bits give you the ability to combine two things (either a 1 or a 0) seven at a time, resulting in a number of possible unique combinations equal to 2 to the 7th power. If you perform that computation, you find that the result is 128. This value equals the number of standard ASCII characters (0–127). If you do the same computation by taking two things eight at a time, you will find that the result is 256, which equals the total number of ASCII characters shown at the end of this appendix. This simply means that IBM and Microsoft ASCII characters with values greater than 127 can only be represented with eight data bits. This is the case whether the character is being stored in an ASCII file or transmitted long distance to another microcomputer.

The ANSI standard for ASCII characters divides them into two major categories according to their function. Characters used to generate readable text are labeled *graphic characters* and characters used to achieve action are labeled *control characters*. The former of these categories is somewhat misleading because the standard ASCII graphic characters are actually normal text characters. The term *graphic* would better apply to the *special extension characters* provided by IBM and Microsoft in the PC character set. The special characters and symbols with values of 176 through 223 are useful in the creation of graphic images while in the text display mode. Figure A.2 shows the hierarchy of ASCII characters based on the ANSI standard, and includes the special extension characters.

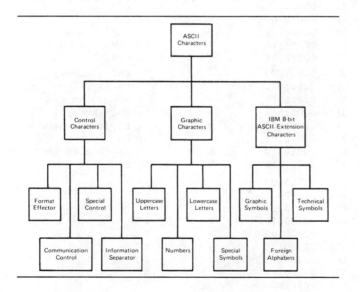

Figure A.2
Hierarchy of ASCII characters.

Table A.1 contains the standard 7-bit ASCII character set (decimal values 0–127) and the IBM/Microsoft special 8-bit ASCII character set (decimal values 128–255). The control character designations for ASCII decimal values 0–31 are also shown.

The ASCII Character Set

Decimal	Hex	Octal	Binary	Graphic Character	ASCII Meaning
0	0	0	00000000		^@ NUL (null)
1	1	1	00000001	☺	^A SOH (start-of-header)
2	2	2	00000010	●	^B STX (start-of-transmission)
3	3	3	00000011	♥	^C ETX (end-of-transmission)
4	4	4	00000100	♦	^D EOT (end-of-text)
5	5	5	00000101	♠	^E ENQ (enquiry)
6	6	6	00000110	♠	^F ACK (acknowledge)
7	7	7	00000111	·	^G BEL (bell)
8	8	10	00001000	■	^H BS (backspace)
9	9	11	00001001	○	^I HT (horizontal tab)
10	A	12	00001010	■	^J LF (line feed – also ^Enter)
11	B	13	00001011	σ	^K VT (vertical tab)
12	C	14	00001100	♀	^L FF (form feed)
13	D	15	00001101	♪	^M CR (carriage return)
14	E	16	00001110	♫	^N SO
15	F	17	00001111	☼	^O SI
16	10	20	00010000	►	^P DLE
17	11	21	00010001	◄	^Q DC1
18	12	22	00010010	↕	^R DC2
19	13	23	00010011	‼	^S DC3
20	14	24	00010100	¶	^T DC4
21	15	25	00010101	§	^U NAK
22	16	26	00010110	▬	^V SYN
23	17	27	00010111	↨	^W ETB
24	18	30	00011000	↑	^X CAN (cancel)
25	19	31	00011001	↓	^Y EM
26	1A	32	00011010	→	^Z SUB (also end-
27	1B	33	00011011	←	^[ESC (Escape)
28	1C	34	00011100	∟	^\ FS (field sep↲
29	1D	35	00011101	↔	^] GS
30	1E	36	00011110	▲	^^ RS (record se
31	1F	37	00011111	▼	^_ US
32	20	40	00100000		Space
33	21	41	00100001	!	!
34	22	42	00100010	"	"
35	23	43	00100011	#	#
36	24	44	00100100	$	$
37	25	45	00100101	%	%
38	26	46	00100110	&	&
39	27	47	00100111	'	'
40	28	50	00101000	(	(
41	29	51	00101001	)	)
42	2A	52	00101010	*	*

Decimal	Hex	Octal	Binary	Graphic Character	ASCII Meaning
43	2B	53	00101011	+	+
44	2C	54	00101100	,	,
45	2D	55	00101101	-	-
46	2E	56	00101110	.	.
47	2F	57	00101111	/	/
48	30	60	00110000	0	0
49	31	61	00110001	1	1
50	32	62	00110010	2	2
51	33	63	00110011	3	3
52	34	64	00110100	4	4
53	35	65	00110101	5	5
54	36	66	00110110	6	6
55	37	67	00110111	7	7
56	38	70	00111000	8	8
57	39	71	00111001	9	9
58	3A	72	00111010	:	:
59	3B	73	00111011	;	;
60	3C	74	00111100	<	<
61	3D	75	00111101	=	=
62	3E	76	00111110	>	>
63	3F	77	00111111	?	?
64	40	100	01000000	@	@
65	41	101	01000001	A	A
66	42	102	01000010	B	B
67	43	103	01000011	C	C
68	44	104	01000100	D	D
69	45	105	01000101	E	E
70	46	106	01000110	F	F
71	47	107	01000111	G	G
72	48	110	01001000	H	H
73	49	111	01001001	I	I
74	4A	112	01001010	J	J
75	4B	113	01001011	K	K
76	4C	114	01001100	L	L
77	4D	115	01001101	M	M
78	4E	116	01001110	N	N
79	4F	117	01001111	O	O
80	50	120	01010000	P	P
81	51	121	01010001	Q	Q
82	52	122	01010010	R	R
83	53	123	01010011	S	S
84	54	124	01010100	T	T
85	55	125	01010101	U	U
86	56	126	01010110	V	V
87	57	127	01010111	W	W
88	58	130	01011000	X	X
89	59	131	01011001	Y	Y
90	5A	132	01011010	Z	Z

continues

The ASCII Character Set, Continued

Decimal	Hex	Octal	Binary	Graphic Character	ASCII Meaning
91	5B	133	01011011	[	[
92	5C	134	01011100	\	\
93	5D	135	01011101	]	]
94	5E	136	01011110	^	^
95	5F	137	01011111	_	_
96	60	140	01100000	`	`
97	61	141	01100001	a	a
98	62	142	01100010	b	b
99	63	143	01100011	c	c
100	64	144	01100100	d	d
101	65	145	01100101	e	e
102	66	146	01100110	f	f
103	67	147	01100111	g	g
104	68	150	01101000	h	h
105	69	151	01101001	i	i
106	6A	152	01101010	j	j
107	6B	153	01101011	k	k
108	6C	154	01101100	l	l
109	6D	155	01101101	m	m
110	6E	156	01101110	n	n
111	6F	157	01101111	o	o
112	70	160	01110000	p	p
113	71	161	01110001	q	q
114	72	162	01110010	r	r
115	73	163	01110011	s	s
116	74	164	01110100	t	t
117	75	165	01110101	u	u
118	76	166	01110110	v	v
119	77	167	01110111	w	w
120	78	170	01111000	x	x
121	79	171	01111001	y	y
122	7A	172	01111010	z	z
123	7B	173	01111011	{	{
124	7C	174	01111100				
125	7D	175	01111101	}	}
126	7E	176	01111110	~	~
127	7F	177	01111111	Δ	Del
128	80	200	10000000	Ç	
129	81	201	10000001	ü	
130	82	202	10000010	é	
131	83	203	10000011	â	
132	84	204	10000100	ä	
133	85	205	10000101	à	
134	86	206	10000110	å	
135	87	207	10000111	ç	
136	88	210	10001000	ê	
137	89	211	10001001	ë	

Decimal	Hex	Octal	Binary	Graphic Character	ASCII Meaning
138	8A	212	10001010	è	
139	8B	213	10001011	ï	
140	8C	214	10001100	î	
141	8D	215	10001101	ì	
142	8E	216	10001110	Ä	
143	8F	217	10001111	Å	
144	90	220	10010000	É	
145	91	221	10010001	æ	
146	92	222	10010010	Æ	
147	93	223	10010011	ô	
148	94	224	10010100	ö	
149	95	225	10010101	ò	
150	96	226	10010110	û	
151	97	227	10010111	ù	
152	98	230	10011000	ÿ	
153	99	231	10011001	Ö	
154	9A	232	10011010	Ü	
155	9B	233	10011011	¢	
156	9C	234	10011100	£	
157	9D	235	10011101	¥	
158	9E	236	10011110	₨	
159	9F	237	10011111	ƒ	
160	A0	240	10100000	á	
161	A1	241	10100001	í	
162	A2	242	10100010	ó	
163	A3	243	10100011	ú	
164	A4	244	10100100	ñ	
165	A5	245	10100101	Ñ	
166	A6	246	10100110	ª	
167	A7	247	10100111	º	
168	A8	250	10101000	¿	
169	A9	251	10101001	⌐	
170	AA	252	10101010	¬	
171	AB	253	10101011	½	
172	AC	254	10101100	¼	
173	AD	255	10101101	¡	
174	AE	256	10101110	«	
175	AF	257	10101111	»	
176	B0	260	10110000	▓	
177	B1	261	10110001	▒	
178	B2	262	10110010	▓	
179	B3	263	10110011	│	
180	B4	264	10110100	┤	
181	B5	265	10110101	╡	
182	B6	266	10110110	╢	
183	B7	267	10110111	╖	
184	B8	270	10111000	╕	

continues

The ASCII Character Set, Continued

Decimal	Hex	Octal	Binary	Graphic Character	ASCII Meaning
185	B9	271	10111001	╣	
186	BA	272	10111010	║	
187	BB	273	10111011	╗	
188	BC	274	10111100	╝	
189	BD	275	10111101	╜	
190	BE	276	10111110	╛	
191	BF	277	10111111	┐	
192	C0	300	11000000	└	
193	C1	301	11000001	┴	
194	C2	302	11000010	┬	
195	C3	303	11000011	├	
196	C4	304	11000100	─	
197	C5	305	11000101	┼	
198	C6	306	11000110	╞	
199	C7	307	11000111	╟	
200	C8	310	11001000	╚	
201	C9	311	11001001	╔	
202	CA	312	11001010	╩	
203	CB	313	11001011	╦	
204	CC	314	11001100	╠	
205	CD	315	11001101	═	
206	CE	316	11001110	╬	
207	CF	317	11001111	╧	
208	D0	320	11010000	╨	
209	D1	321	11010001	╤	
210	D2	322	11010010	╥	
211	D3	323	11010011	╙	
212	D4	324	11010100	╘	
213	D5	325	11010101	╒	
214	D6	326	11010110	╓	
215	D7	327	11010111	╫	
216	D8	330	11011000	╪	
217	D9	331	11011001	┘	
218	DA	332	11011010	┌	
219	DB	333	11011011	█	
220	DC	334	11011100	▄	
221	DD	335	11011101	▌	
222	DE	336	11011110	▐	
223	DF	337	11011111	▀	
224	E0	340	11100000	∝	
225	E1	341	11100001	β	
226	E2	342	11100010	Γ	
227	E3	343	11100011	π	
228	E4	344	11100100	Σ	
229	E5	345	11100101	σ	
230	E6	346	11100110	µ	
231	E7	347	11100111	τ	

Decimal	Hex	Octal	Binary	Graphic Character	ASCII Meaning
232	E8	350	11101000	◊	
233	E9	351	11101001	θ	
234	EA	352	11101010	Ω	
235	EB	353	11101011	δ	
236	EC	354	11101100	∞	
237	ED	355	11101101	φ	
238	EE	356	11101110	∈	
239	EF	357	11101111	∩	
240	F0	360	11110000	≡	
241	F1	361	11110001	±	
242	F2	362	11110010	≥	
243	F3	363	11110011	≤	
244	F4	364	11110100	⌠	
245	F5	365	11110101	⌡	
246	F6	366	11110110	÷	
247	F7	367	11110111	≈	
248	F8	370	11111000	°	
249	F9	371	11111001	·	
250	FA	372	11111010	·	
251	FB	373	11111011	√	
252	FC	374	11111100	ⁿ	
253	FD	375	11111101	²	
254	FE	376	11111110	∎	
255	FF	377	11111111		

APPENDIX

Communications Controls

As noted in Appendix A, the first 128 characters of the IBM PC character set are defined by the *American National Standards Institute* (ANSI) in the *American Standard Code for Information Interchange* (ASCII). This ASCII code (pronounced as-key) is used in almost all computers made in America with the notable exception of IBM mini- and mainframe computers. Such standardization has contributed significantly to the development of computer technology and the standardization of computer communications.

The ANSI-standard character set, along with the extended IBM PC ASCII character set, are discussed in general in Appendix A. This appendix provides a detailed description of a subset of the ANSI-standard characters that were originally designed to provide communications and printer controls. These *control characters*, the first 33 ASCII characters, are shown in figure B.1. This table also provides a brief description of each control character and the control group that it falls within. Refer to the diagram of the hierarchy of ASCII characters shown in Appendix A, figure A.2 to get a better feel for the relationship between these control characters and other ASCII characters.

Figure B.1
ASCII control
characters.

ASCII Value	Mnemonic Character	ASCII Character	IBM Function	Group	Communication Usage
000	^@	NUL	null	CC	Null character—filler
001	^A	SOH		CC	Start of heading
002	^B	STX		CC	Start of text
003	^C	ETX		CC	End of text
004	^D	EOT		CC	End of transmission
005	^E	ENQ		CC	Enquiry
006	^F	ACK		CC	Acknowledge affirmative
007	^G	BEL	beep	SC	Audible alarm
008	^H	BS	backspace	FE	Backspace one position
009	^I	HT	tab	FE	Physical horizonal tab
010	^J	LF	line feed	FE	Line feed
011	^K	VT	home	FE	Physical vertical tab
012	^L	FF	form feed	FE	Form feed
013	^M	CR	carriage return	FE	Carriage return
014	^N	SO		SC	Shift out
015	^O	SI		SC	Shift in
016	^P	DLE		CC	Data link escape
017	^Q	DC1		SC	XON or resume
018	^R	DC2		SC	Device control 2
019	^S	DC3		SC	XOFF or pause
020	^T	DC4		SC	Device control 4
021	^U	NAK		CC	Negative acknowledgement
022	^V	SYN		CC	Synchronous idle
023	^W	ETB		CC	End of transmission block
024	^X	CAN		SC	Cancel
025	^Y	EM		SC	End of medium
026	^Z	SUB		SC	Substitute
027	^[	ESC		SC	Escape
028	^\	FS	cursor right	IS	File separator
029	^]	GS	cursor left	IS	Group separator
030	^^	RS	cursor up	IS	Record separator
031	^_	US	cursor down	IS	Unit separator
127		DEL		SC	Delete

Although the control characters are represented by 7 digital bits, just as the other ANSI-defined characters, they produce more than printable results when received by certain devices. These "characters" act as signals to control specific operations of printing, display, and communications devices. The entire group of ASCII control characters is sometimes called *non-printing control characters,* but the label does not apply to personal computers that operate under PC- or MS-DOS. All but one of these characters have been assigned a graphic representation by IBM and Microsoft, as you can see in Appendix A, table A.1. Unfortunately, this dual role of control and graphic character depiction does cause some confusion for PC users who wish to display or print these images.

Most of the first 33 IBM PC characters can be displayed on the PC screen but getting them onto the screen may take some imagination. Using DOS commands such as TYPE to send a file containing these characters to the screen may produce different results than sending them to the screen from within a software application such as a communications software package. DOS, and the BASIC language that uses DOS services to display characters, will react to the control aspects of these characters, whereas software written in other languages such as C or assembly can send these images directly to the display buffer in memory, thereby bypassing their control side effects.

Another aspect of control characters that may cause confusion is the way they are listed in tables or in text. The 33 control characters are often depicted as a caret followed by a letter or symbol which implies that they can be formed by the combination of two non-control ASCII characters. The confusion comes from the use of the caret to represent the Ctrl key on the PC keyboard that can be used in combination with a letter or symbol to create a control character. When the Ctrl key is held down and a letter or symbol key is pressed, a control character is generated, but DOS displays the results for many of these characters as the caret followed by the letter or symbol. For example, the Ctrl-C keystroke combination used to abnormally terminate a DOS task also produces a ^C on the display.

The caret-symbol depiction of control characters should be viewed as a convention that allows authors to show or discuss control characters in text without using lengthy titles for them. This convention has evolved over many years and is not likely to change with the PC even though these characters are now assigned special graphics symbols. One reason the graphics symbols are not likely to become an accepted method of depicting control characters is that word processors and text editors normally translate these characters into the caret-symbol format automatically so they can be printed on standard printers. If the actual control characters were to be sent to the printer, they would not print as graphics symbols—they would produce the results discussed in the following paragraphs.

Control Character Groups

The ANSI standard breaks the ASCII control-character group down into three functional subgroups. These groups are *communication controls, format effectors,* and *information separators.* There is a fourth group not categorized by the ANSI standard that performs special functions; these characters are labelled *special control characters,* for later reference. Figure B.1 shows the control group associated with each of the 33 control characters.

To eliminate ambiguity and establish specific guidelines for the use of communication control characters, ANSI has given each character a unique definition. These definitions and the specific use the PC makes of these characters are discussed next. References to applications of these characters as printer controls are generalized and may not apply to all printers used with the PC. Refer to the manual that comes with a printer to determine its specific use of control characters.

Logical Communication Control

The ANSI definition of a *communication control* (CC) character is a character that controls or facilitates data transmission over a communications network. Several of these characters are illustrated in the discussion of bisync protocol in Chapter 2 and file transfer protocols in Chapter 6. These logical communication control characters are typically used in both asynchronous and synchronous serial protocols for data transfer handshaking. They tell the receiving device what to expect as data; they indicate a transition in type of data being transmitted; or they are used to verify proper transmission and receipt.

SOH

The *Start of Heading* (SOH) is used in bisync data streams to denote the start of a message heading datablock. Stations in a network check the data that follow this character to determine whether they are to be recipients of the data that will follow the heading. In essence, it is a "listen to see if your name is called" signal for stations in a network.

The SOH character is sometimes used in asynchronous communications to transfer a series of files without handling each file as a separate communication. The SOH character is used during the transfer of multiple files to signal the beginning of the filename of each file before transfer of the file begins. In asynchronous communications, there is only one receiver monitoring the communication line, so there is no need for a destination device address to follow the SOH character; only the filename of each file is needed. This type of file transfer is often limited to communications between microcomputers using the same communications software, because it is not a standardized file-transfer protocol.

The SOH is also used with the Xmodem file-transfer protocol to signal the start of a 128-byte data-block transfer. This character is followed by two block number bytes used to ensure that blocks are transferred properly.

STX

The *Start of Text* (STX) control character is also used in the bisync protocol. It signals the end of heading data and the beginning of information data.

ETX

The *End of Text* (ETX) control character is a bisync protocol signal that tells a receiver that all information data have been transmitted. This character can also be used to signal the beginning of block check characters used to detect communication errors.

EOT

The *End of Transmission* (EOT) control character is used to indicate the end of transmission of all data associated with a message sent to a particular device. This character also tells other devices in a network to check further transmissions for the presence of messages directed to them. The EOT character is the end frame for a message that is initiated by an SOH character. It is also used in the Xmodem protocol to indicate the end of a file transfer.

ETB

The *End of Transmission Block* (ETB) control character indicates the end of a particular block of transmitted data. The bisync protocol uses this character instead of an ETX character when data are transmitted in two or more blocks instead of a single continuous block.

ENQ

The *Enquiry* (ENQ) control character is used to request a response from a communication receiving station. It may be used to obtain the identification of a device or to determine the status of transmitted data. Some PC asynchronous communication packages use this character in protocol file transfers. In response to the receipt of the ENQ character, a receiving device may be required to respond with the number of the last block successfully received. This nonstandard application of ENQ facilitates the retransmission of data blocks that were not properly received by the destination device.

ACK

The *Acknowledge* (ACK) control character is used to verify proper communication between a transmitter and receiver. One application of ACK is in detecting errors in transmitted data. After receiving a block of data, a receiver may be required to send the transmitter an ACK character indicating that the error-check character or characters show no transmission error. The transmitter may be required to receive the ACK before more data can be transmitted.

DLE

The *Data Link Escape* (DLE) control character is used to modify the meaning of a limited number of subsequent characters. It is used in the bisync protocol along with other control characters to signal the start and end of data field transmission in the transparent mode.

NAK

The *Negative Acknowledge* (NAK) control character is used to indicate improper communication between a transmitter and a receiver. This character is generally transmitted by a receiver to initiate a retransmission of data when an error-check indicates the presence of data transmission errors. The ENQ, ACK, and NAK characters are often used together for protocol data transmission that does not involve user interaction. These signals take place between two communication software packages and, when they are being properly executed, are transparent to the user. The NAK is also used in the Xmodem protocol to tell the transmitting computer that the receiving computer is ready to start a file transfer.

SYN

The *Synchronous Idle* (SYN) control character is used in the bisync protocol to initiate or maintain communication synchronization when no data are being transmitted. This character performs a function similar to the stop bit in asynchronous communication—it maintains a known signal on the data line when no data are being transferred. The interruption of a series of SYN characters is an indication of heading or data information to follow.

Physical Communication Control

This group of communication controls are used with physical devices such as printers, displays, and other computers.

NUL

The *NUL character* is, as its name implies, a *null entity*. It is often used as a non-printing *time delay* or *filler character* and is especially useful for communicating with printing devices that need a finite amount of time for positioning the print head. Communication terminals that print hard copy often require at least two NUL characters following each carriage return to give the print head sufficient time to return to the left margin before receiving the next character. Some host system software packages allow you to specify a certain number of nulls to be transmitted to your computer after each carriage return.

DEL

The *Delete* (DEL) character is not actually a character but is used to erase or obliterate characters. The PC BASIC editor uses this signal to remove characters positioned above the cursor. The character also causes the IBM Graphics Printer and Proprinter to delete the last received character. Other applications of the DEL character are comparable to the time delay application of the NUL character. The DEL can affect information layout or equipment control, however, which necessitates careful placement of the character.

CAN

Cancel (CAN) has many different applications, depending on the vendor, but it is generally used to denote an error in data transfer. The character is an indication that the data received should be disregarded.

EM

The *End of Medium* (EM) control character is used to indicate either the physical end of a data medium (data storage, representation of communication material) or the end of a portion of data medium containing desired data.

SUB

The *Substitute* (SUB) control character is used for controlling the accuracy of data communication. It replaces a character that is determined to be in error, invalid, or impossible for the receiving device to display or print.

Format Effectors

The *format effector* (FE) characters are used to control the position of characters being printed or displayed. Sending these characters to the IBM printer either directly or as a BASIC CHR$(n) string allows you to produce text formatting. Word-processing packages use these control characters in the control of text layout.

BS

The *Backspace* (BS) control character is used to control the active print position for both the visual display monitor and the printer. This character moves the PC cursor to the left one position, assuming the cursor is not in column one when the character is executed and removes any character displayed in the position vacated. The key that produces this character is sometimes called the backspace delete key because of the action it produces. This character can be transmitted as data just as any other character is transmitted, but it is normally used only when data are transmitted in the conversation mode. Properly designed communication software performs a backspace when the character is received instead of printing a new character.

HT

The *Horizontal Tabulation* (HT) control character causes the active printing device to move to the next predetermined position before printing the next character. The HT character is executed on the PC keyboard by using special tab stop keys and can be executed on IBM printers by performing a BASIC LPRINT CHR$(9).

LF

The *Line Feed* (LF) control character causes the active printing position to advance to the same column position in the next line. The results produced by this character are often confused with that of the carriage return (CR) discussed next. The line feed does not advance the cursor or print head to the first column of the next line unless it is preceded by a CR. Most business-oriented communications packages do not send line feeds with CRs unless specifically instructed to do so, and a file received without line feeds cannot be properly listed on a PC monitor until they are added. Using the DOS TYPE command to display such a file results in a stream of text that moves rapidly across the screen in a single line.

VT

The *Vertical Tabulation* (VT) control character causes the active printing or display position to advance to the same column a predetermined number of lines down from the present line being printed or displayed. Some conventions use the VT to move the cursor or print head to the first column of the new line. Transmitting a VT character to an IBM printer produces the same result as a single line feed—the print head moves down one line, but the column position remains the same.

FF

The *Form Feed* (FF) control character clears the PC display and places the cursor at the upper left-hand corner of the screen. This is often used by bulletin board and host systems to clear the display before starting a new function. If the communication session is being captured to a printer as it is displayed on the PC monitor, the FF character used to clear the display can result in a lot of wasted paper. As the FF clears the screen, it is also received at the printer where it will advance the printer head to the next logical top of form or to a predetermined line on the next form or page.

If the print head is at the top of a page when the printer is turned on, transmitting an FF character to an IBM printer while in the "On Line" mode will cause the printer to advance the print form to the top of a new page, regardless of the number of lines already printed on the page. If the print head is not at the top of a page when it is turned on, an FF will cause the paper to advance but not to the top of a new page. The logical top of form that will be advanced to on receipt of an FF is the line position on a new page that matches the line position of the print head when the printer was powered up.

CR

The *Carriage Return* (CR) control character advances the active print or display position to the first column of the same line. Unless the carriage return is followed by a line feed, the characters that follow the carriage return will overstrike characters already printed on the line. This will often be the case when printing or displaying files that were received electronically from host or bulletin board systems because those systems normally do not send line feeds after each carriage return. The carriage return is also used to initiate the printing of a line when used with a PC printer. The printer captures all characters it receives in an area of its memory called a print buffer, then sends those characters to the print head when it receives a carriage return or an LF, or when the print buffer has received enough for one full print line.

Information Separators

Information separator (IS) characters are used to control the separation of logical divisions of information as the information is transmitted over communication channels. These characters are not generally used in communications and will not be reviewed in detail in this text.

FS

The *File Separator* (FS) control character is used to mark a logical boundary between files being transferred.

GS

The *Group Separator* (GS) control character is used to mark logical boundaries between groups of transmitted data.

RS

The *Record Separator* (RS) control character is used to mark the boundaries between records in data transmission.

US

The *Unit Separator* (US) is the final information-separator control character, and it is used to mark the logical boundaries between distinct units of data.

Special Control

The *special control* (SC) characters are used for printer control, data transmission speed-matching, or special data transmission error signaling. Some of these characters, such as ESC, perform communication control functions, but they are not included in that category by the ANSI standard.

BEL

The *Bell* (BEL) is a special ASCII control character that performs a function in keeping with its name. This character may be included in a text file or it may be transmitted between devices to signal the need for human attention. When transmitted in the conversation mode, which can be done by pressing the CTRL and G keys simultaneously, the character will cause a speaker connected to the PC to emit an attention-getting beep.

SO

The *Shift Out* (SO) is a special ASCII control character that serves to extend the standard graphics character set. The receipt of this character turns on the double-width printing mode of the IBM printer for the remainder of the line of text or until a DC4 control character is received. This same character is used by other printers to extend the character set to special graphic symbols used in math and engineering.

SI

The *Shift In* (SI) control character may be used to reset the receiving device to the Standard ASCII character set. It is also used by some printers to reset the print mode initialized by the Shift Out character. IBM printers do not use this convention, however. They use the DC4 character to frame or terminate the printing of double-width characters and use the SI character to initiate compressed mode printing. The compressed mode is retained until the printer receives a DC2 character.

DC1

The *Device Control 1* (DC1) control character is an electronic toggle switch. Its function may be different for different vendor-supplied equipment, but it is generally used to control communications data flow. For local display of files, this character (a Ctrl-Q) will re-initiate the listing of a file that was temporarily halted by a DC3 character (a Ctrl-S). In data communications, this character is often designated as XON and is used to re-initiate the transfer of data that was temporarily halted by the transmission of an XOFF character. The PC may or may not use this handshake convention, depending on the communication software being used. Many communication programs written in the BASIC language are capable of transmitting the XON to a host but are incapable of recognizing the receipt of either XON or XOFF characters because of the limited data-handling speed of the BASIC interpreter.

DC2

The *Device Control 2* (DC2) control character is also a toggle switch control character, and its role varies with vendor applications. The DC2 character is used with the IBM Graphics Printer and Proprinter to turn off the compressed printing mode and empty the print buffer.

DC3

The *Device Control 3* (DC3) control character is another ASCII toggle switch, and it is often used with the DC1 character for data transfer speed-matching. The DC3 character is an XOFF, and it is used to temporarily halt the transmission of data. When a receiving device has received all the data it can handle, it may send the host an XOFF to stop the flow of data. When the device has printed or saved all the data received before the XOFF was transmitted, it will send an XON character to the host to re-initiate data transmission.

As indicated with the DC1 character, many BASIC communication programs are capable of sending XOFFs but cannot recognize XOFFs received from other microcomputer or host systems. To recognize and act on received XOFF characters, a BASIC program would have to compare every character bit pattern received to the XOFF bit pattern as other characters are being received and displayed, printed, or saved. This comparison technique would slow down data handling and result in longer file transfers. Assembly-language communication programs, on the other hand, often use an interrupt design that reacts quickly to XOFF characters, thereby making them excellent programs for transferring large files. This character is also used to temporarily halt the local listing of a file. It can be invoked by holding down the Ctrl key then pressing either the S key or Num Lock key.

DC4

The *Device Control 4* (DC4) control character is the fourth and last electronic toggle switch used in the ASCII character code, and like the other four toggle characters, its role often varies depending on the vendor. This character turns off the IBM printer double-width print mode that is initiated by the Shift Out character.

ESC

The *Escape* (ESC) control character is used extensively for communications with printers and to produce color and graphics on a PC monitor. It is normally transmitted just before the transmission of other characters or numbers to provide character code extensions or control code extensions. The sets of characters used to control printers vary from one printer design to another. The IBM printers are capable of accepting escape code sequences to perform such functions as underlining and predetermining the values for horizontal and vertical tabs. Other dot-matrix printers are designed to accept over 30 escape codes to perform these same functions, plus many other advanced features such as dot-addressable graphics control. The key to proper use of this character is the compatibility of software and hardware combinations.

EBCDIC Character Set

ASCII Binary Code	EBCDIC Binary Code	Character
1000000	01111100	@
1000001	11000001	A
1000010	11000010	B
1000011	11000011	C
1000100	11000100	D
1000101	11000101	E
1000110	11000110	F
1000111	11000111	G
1001000	11001000	H
1001001	11001001	I

continues

ASCII Binary Code	EBCDIC Binary Code	Character
1001010	11010001	J
1001011	11010010	K
1001100	11010011	L
1001101	11010100	M
1001110	11010101	N
1001111	11010110	O
1010000	11011000	P
1010001	11011000	Q
1010010	11011001	R
1100101	11100010	S
1010100	11100011	T
1010101	11100100	U
1010110	11100101	V
1010111	11100110	W
1011000	11100111	X
1011001	11011000	Y
1011010	11011001	Z
1011011		[
1011100		\
1011101		]
1011110		^
1011111	01101101	_

ASCII Binary Code	EBCDIC Binary Code	Character
1100000	01111101	
1100001	10000001	a
1100010	10000010	b
1100011	10000011	c
1100100	10000100	d
1100101	10000101	e
1100110	10000110	f
1100111	10000111	g
1101000	10001000	h
1101001	10001001	i
1101010	10010001	j
1101011	10010010	k
1101100	10010011	l
1101101	10010100	m
1101110	10010101	n
1101111	10010110	o
1110000	10010111	p
1110001	10011000	q
1110011	10011001	r
1110011	10100010	s
1110100	10100011	t
1110101	10100100	u

continues

ASCII Binary Code	EBCDIC Binary Code	Character
1110110	10100101	v
1110111	10100110	w
1111000	10100111	x
1111001	10101000	y
1111010	10101001	z
1111011		{
1111100	01101010		
1111101		}
1111110		~
1111111		DEL
0000000	00000000	NUL
0000001	00000001	SOH
0000010	00000010	STX
0000011	00000011	ETX
0000100		EOT
0000101	00101101	ENQ
0000110		ACK
0000111		BEL
0001000		BS
0001001		HT
0001010		LF
0001011		VT

ASCII Binary Code	EBCDIC Binary Code	Character
0001100	00001100	FF
0001101		CR
0001110		SO
0001111		SI
0010000		DLE
0010001		DC1
0010010		DC2
0010011		DC3
0010100		DC4
0010101		NAK
0010110	00110010	SYN
0010111	00100110	ETB
0011000		CAN
0011001	00011001	EM
0011001	00111111	SUB
0011011	00010111	ESC
0011100		FS
0011101		GS
0011110		RS
0011111		US
0100000	01000000	SP
0100001	01011010	!

continues

ASCII Binary Code	EBCDIC Binary Code	Character
0100010	01111111	"
0100011		#
0100100	01011011	$
0100101	01101100	%
0100110	01010000	&
0100111	01111101	'
0101000	01001101	(
0101001	01011101	)
0101010		*
0101011	01001110	+
0101100	01101011	'
0101101	01100000	—
0101110	00100100	.
0101111	01100001	/
0110000	11110000	0
0110001	11110001	1
0110010	11110010	2
0111100	11110011	3
0110100	11110100	4
0110101	11110101	5
0110110	11110110	6
0110111	11110111	7

ASCII Binary Code	EBCDIC Binary Code	Character
0111000	11111000	8
0111001	11111001	9
0111010	01111010	:
0111011	01011110	;
0111100	01001100	<
0111101	01111011	=
0111110	01101110	>
0111111	01101111	?

Baudot Character Set

Baudot Code	Lowercase	Uppercase
11000	A	-
10011	B	?
01110	C	:
10010	D	$
10000	E	3
10110	F	'
01011	G	&
00101	H	British Pound
01100	I	8
11010	J	'

continues

Baudot Code	Lowercase	Uppercase
11110	K	(
01001	L	)
00111	M	
00110	N	.
00011	O	9
01101	P	0
11101	Q	1
01010	R	
10100	S	Bell
00001	T	5
11100	U	7
01111	V	;
11001	W	2
10111	X	/
10101	Y	6
10001	Z	"
11111	Letters (Shift to lowercase)	
11011	Figures (Shift to uppercase)	
00100	Space	
00010	Carriage return	
01000	Line feed	
00000	Blank	

I

INDEX

INDEX

INDEX

INDEX

INDEX

INDEX

INDEX

INDEX

INDEX

INDEX

N

INDEX

INDEX

INDEX

INDEX

INDEX

X–Y–Z

INDEX

Communications and Networking for the PC Fifth Edition

REGISTRATION CARD

NRP

Fill out this card to receive information about future Communications and Networking books and other New Riders titles!

Name _____ Title _____

Company _____

Address _____

City/State/ZIP _____

I bought this book because: _____

_____

I purchased this book from:
☐ A bookstore (Name _____)
☐ A software or electronics store (Name _____)
☐ A mail order (Name of Catalog _____)

I purchase this many computer books each year:
☐ 1–5   ☐ 6 or more

I currently use these applications: _____

_____

_____

_____

I found these chapters to be the most informative: _____

_____

I found these chapters to be the least informative: _____

_____

Additional comments: _____

_____

☐ I would like to see my name in print! You may use my name and quote me in future New Riders products and promotions. My daytime phone number is: _____

New Riders Publishing 201 West 103rd Street • Indianapolis, Indiana 46290 USA

Fold Here

PLACE
STAMP
HERE

New Riders Publishing
201 West 103rd Street
Indianapolis, Indiana 46290
USA

WANT MORE INFORMATION?

CHECK OUT THESE RELATED TITLES:

	QTY	PRICE	TOTAL

Inside Novell NetWare, Special Edition. This #1 selling tutorial/reference is perfect for beginning system administrators. Each network management task is thoroughly explained and potential trouble spots are noted. The book also includes a disk with an extremely easy-to-use workstation menu program, an MHS capable E-Mail program, and workgroup management tools. ISBN: 1-56205-096-6.   ____ $34.95   _____

NetWare 4: Planning and Implementation. The ultimate guide to planning, installing, and managing a NetWare 4.0 network. This book explains how best to implement the new features of NetWare 4.0 and how to upgrade to NetWare 4.0 as easily and efficiently as possible. ISBN: 1-56205-159-8.   ____ $27.95   _____

Downsizing to NetWare. Get the real story on downsizing with *Downsizing to NetWare.* This book identifies applications that are suitable for use on LANs and shows how to implement downsizing projects. This book lists the strengths and weaknesses of NetWare—making it perfect for managers and system administrators. ISBN: 1-56205-071-0.   ____ $39.95   _____

LAN Operating Systems. Learn how to connect the most popular LAN operating systems. All major LAN operating systems are covered, including: NetWare 3.11, Appleshare 3.0, Banyan VINES 5.0, UNIX, LAN Manager 2.1, and popular peer-to-peer networks. The following client operating systems are covered as well: MS-DOS, Windows, OS/2, Macintosh System 7, and UNIX. This book clears up the confusion associated with managing large networks with diverse client workstations and multiple LAN operating systems. ISBN: 1-56205-054-0.   ____ $39.95   _____

Name _____

Company _____

Address _____

City _____ State ____ ZIP _____

Phone _____ Fax _____

☐ Check Enclosed   ☐ VISA   ☐ MasterCard

Card #_____Exp. Date _____

Signature _____

Prices are subject to change. Call for availability and pricing information on latest editions.

Subtotal   _____

Shipping   _____

$4.00 for the first book and $1.75 for each additional book.

Total   _____
Indiana residents add 5% sales tax.

New Riders Publishing 201 West 103rd Street • Indianapolis, Indiana 46290 USA

Orders/Customer Service: 1-800-428-5331
Fax: 1-800-448-3804

Fold Here

New Riders Publishing
201 West 103rd Street
Indianapolis, Indiana 46290
USA

PLACE
STAMP
HERE

GO AHEAD. PLUG YOURSELF INTO MACMILLAN COMPUTER PUBLISHING.

Introducing the Macmillan Computer Publishing Forum on CompuServe®

Yes, it's true. Now, you can have CompuServe access to the same professional, friendly folks who have made computers easier for years. On the Macmillan Computer Publishing Forum, you'll find additional information on the topics covered by every Macmillan Computer Publishing imprint—including Que, Sams Publishing, New Riders Publishing, Alpha Books, Brady Books, Hayden Books, and Adobe Press. In addition, you'll be able to receive technical support and disk updates for the software produced by Que Software and Paramount Interactive, a division of the Paramount Technology Group. It's a great way to supplement the best information in the business.

WHAT CAN YOU DO ON THE *MACMILLAN COMPUTER PUBLISHING* FORUM?

Play an important role in the publishing process—and make our books better while you make your work easier:

- Leave messages and ask questions about Macmillan Computer Publishing books and software—you're guaranteed a response within 24 hours
- Download helpful tips and software to help you get the most out of your computer
- Contact authors of your favorite Macmillan Computer Publishing books through electronic mail
- Present your own book ideas
- Keep up to date on all the latest books available from each of Macmillan Computer Publishing's exciting imprints

JOIN NOW AND GET A FREE COMPUSERVE STARTER KIT!

To receive your free CompuServe Introductory Membership, call toll-free, **1-800-848-8199** and ask for representative **#597**. The Starter Kit Includes:

- Personal ID number and password
- $15 credit on the system
- Subscription to CompuServe Magazine

HERE'S HOW TO PLUG INTO MACMILLAN COMPUTER PUBLISHING:

Once on the CompuServe System, type any of these phrases to access the Macmillan Computer Publishing Forum:

GO MACMILLAN   **GO BRADY**
GO QUEBOOKS   **GO HAYDEN**
GO SAMS   **GO QUESOFT**
GO NEWRIDERS   **GO ALPHA**

Once you're on the CompuServe Information Service, be sure to take advantage of all of CompuServe's resources. CompuServe is home to more than 1,700 products and services—plus it has over 1.5 million members worldwide. You'll find valuable online reference materials, travel and investor services, electronic mail, weather updates, leisure-time games and hassle-free shopping (no jam-packed parking lots or crowded stores).

Seek out the hundreds of other forums that populate CompuServe. Covering diverse topics such as pet care, rock music, cooking, and political issues, you're sure to find others with the same concerns as you—and expand your knowledge at the same time.

Become a CNE with Help from a Pro!

The NetWare Training Guides are specifically designed and authored to help you prepare for the **Certified NetWare Engineer** exam.

NetWare Training Guide: Managing NetWare Systems

This book clarifies the CNE testing process and provides hints on the best ways to prepare for the CNE examinations. *NetWare Training Guide: Managing NetWare Systems* covers the following sections of the CNE exams:

- NetWare 2.2 System Manager

- NetWare 2.2 Advanced System Manager

- NetWare 3.*x* System Manager

- NetWare 3.*x* Advanced System Manager

ISBN: 1-56205-069-9, **$69.95 USA**

NetWare Training Guide: Networking Technology

This book covers more advanced topics and prepares you for the tough hardware and service/support exams. The following course materials are covered:

- MS-DOS

- Microcomputer Concepts

- Service and Support

- Networking Technologies

ISBN: 1-56205-145-8, **$69.95 USA**

OPERATING SYSTEMS

INSIDE MS-DOS 6.2, 2E

NEW RIDERS PUBLISHING

A complete tutorial and reference!

MS-DOS 6.2

ISBN: 1-56205-289-6

$34.95 USA

DOS FOR NON-NERDS

MICHAEL GROH

Understanding this popular operating system is easy with this humorous, step-by-step tutorial.

Through DOS 6.0

ISBN: 1-56205-151-2

$18.95 USA

INSIDE SCO UNIX

STEVE GLINES, PETER SPICER, BEN HUNSBERGER, & KAREN WHITE

Everything users need to know to use the UNIX operating system for everyday tasks.

SCO Xenix 286, SCO Xenix 386, SCO UNIX/System V 386

ISBN: 1-56205-028-1

$29.95 USA

INSIDE SOLARIS SunOS

KARLA SAARI KITALONG, STEVEN R. LEE, & PAUL MARZIN

Comprehensive tutorial and reference to SunOS!

SunOS, Sun's version of UNIX for the SPARC workstation, version 2.0

ISBN: 1-56205-032-X

$29.95 USA

To Order, Call 1-800-428-5331

WINDOWS TITLES

ULTIMATE WINDOWS 3.1

FORREST HOULETTE, JIM BOYCE,
RICH WAGNER, & THE BSU
RESEARCH STAFF

The most up-to-date reference for
Windows available!

Covers 3.1 and related products

ISBN: 1-56205-125-3

$39.95 USA

WINDOWS FOR NON-NERDS

JIM BOYCE & ROB TIDROW

This helpful tutorial for Windows
provides novice users with what they
need to know to gain computer
proficiency...and confidence!

Windows 3.1

ISBN: 1-56205-152-0

$18.95 USA

INSIDE WINDOWS NT

FORREST HOULETTE, RICHARD WAGNER,
GEORGE ECKEL, & JOHN STODDARD

A complete tutorial and reference to
organize and manage multiple tasks and
multiple programs in Windows NT.

Windows NT

ISBN: 1-56205-124-5

$34.95 USA

INTEGRATING WINDOWS APPLICATIONS

ELLEN DANA NAGLER, FORREST HOULETTE,
MICHAEL GROH, RICHARD WAGNER, &
VALDA HILLEY

This book is a no-nonsense, practical
approach for intermediate- and
advanced-level Windows users!

Windows 3.1

ISBN: 1-56205-083-4

$34.95 USA

GRAPHICS TITLES

INSIDE CORELDRAW! 4.0, SPECIAL EDITION

DANIEL GRAY

An updated version of the #1 best-selling tutorial on CorelDRAW!

CorelDRAW! 4.0
ISBN: 1-56205-164-4
$34.95 USA

CORELDRAW! SPECIAL EFFECTS

NEW RIDERS PUBLISHING

An inside look at award-winning techniques from professional CorelDRAW! designers!

CorelDRAW! 4.0
ISBN: 1-56205-123-7
$39.95 USA

CORELDRAW! NOW!

RICHARD FELDMAN

The hands-on tutorial for users who want practical information now!

CorelDRAW! 4.0
ISBN: 1-56205-131-8
$21.95 USA

INSIDE CORELDRAW! FOURTH EDITION

DANIEL GRAY

The popular tutorial approach to learning CorelDRAW!...with complete coverage of version 3.0!

CorelDRAW! 3.0
ISBN: 1-56205-106-7
$24.95 USA